CHANGING DIRECTION

British Military Planning for Post-war Strategic Defence, 1942–1947

'It is easy to criticise peaceful democracies for their habitual lack of preparedness when a war breaks out, but it is only fair to recognise that the dice are loaded against them. Dictators, bent on aggression, . . . are masters of their own time-table. They are free to decide when to strike, where to strike, and how to strike, and to arrange their armament programmes accordingly. Their potential victims, the democracies, with their inherent hatred of war, . . . do not know when or where the blow will fall, or what manner of blow it will be.'

Lord Ismay,
Memoirs, p. 81

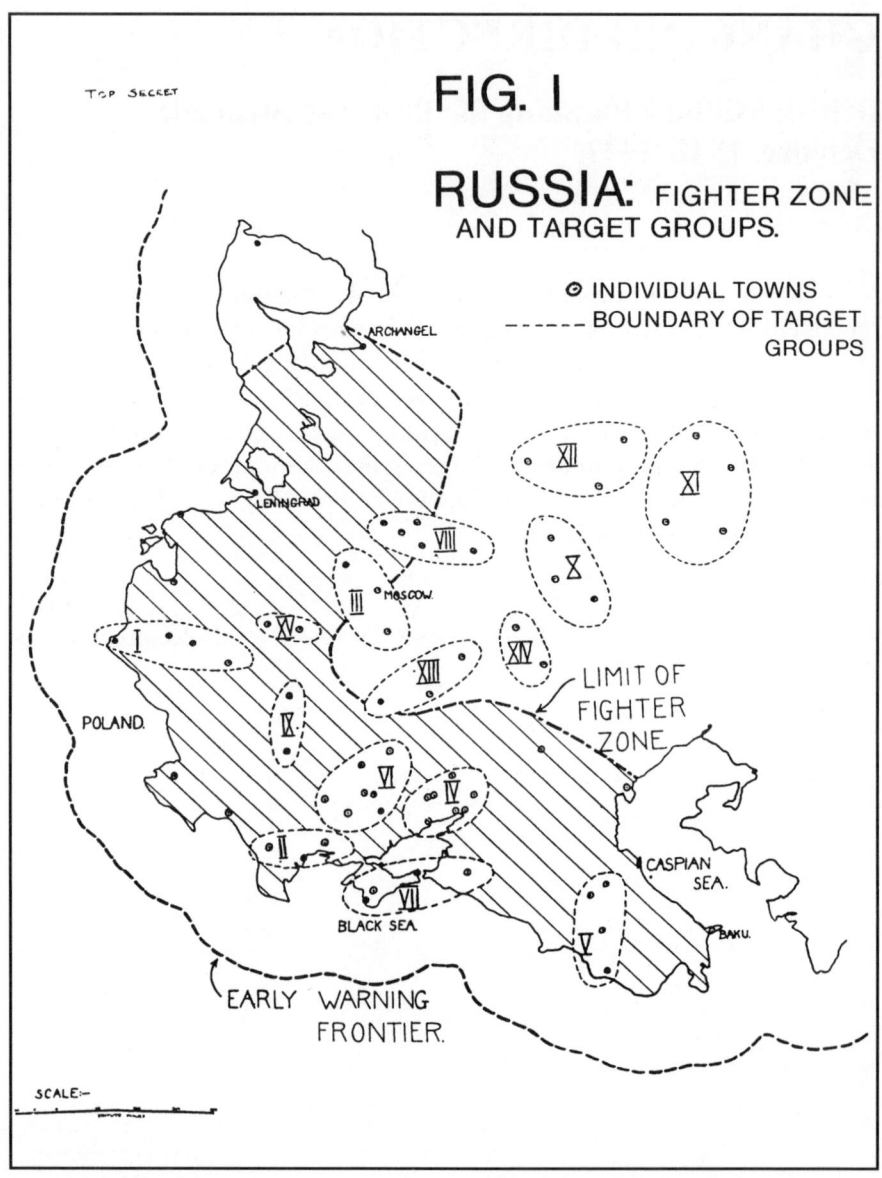

First hypothetical grouping of Soviet cities for an atomic attack, drawn up in April 1946. (See Chapter 5, pp. 228–30, DEFE 2/1252: TWC(46)14, 13 April 1946)

CHANGING DIRECTION

British Military Planning for Post-war Strategic Defence, 1942–1947

Second edition

Julian Lewis

FRANK CASS
LONDON • PORTLAND, OR

First published by The Sherwood Press, 1988
This edition published in 2003 in Great Britain by
FRANK CASS PUBLISHERS
Crown House, 47 Chase Side, Southgate
London N14 5BP

and in the United States of America by
FRANK CASS PUBLISHERS
c/o ISBS, 5824 N.E. Hassalo Street
Portland, Oregon, 97213-3644

Website: www.frankcass.com

Copyright © 1988, 2003 Julian Lewis

British Library Cataloguing in Publication Data

Lewis, Julian, 1951–
    Changing direction: British military planning for post-war
    strategic defence, 1942–1947. – 2nd ed.
    1. World War, 1939–1945 – Equipment and supplies 2. Nuclear
    weapons – History 3. Great Britain – Military policy
    I. Title
    355′.033541′09044

ISBN 0-7146-5399-3

Library of Congress Cataloging-in-Publication Data

Lewis, Julian, 1951–
    Changing direction: British military planning for post-war strategic defence,
        1942–1947/
Julian Lewis. – 2nd ed.
        p. cm.
    Includes bibliographical references and index.
    ISBN 0-7146-5399-3
        1. Great Britain – Military policy – History – 20th century. 2. Great
    Britain – Defenses – History – 20th century. 3. Great Britain – History, Military – 20th
    century. 4. World War, 1939–1945 – Great Britain. 5. World War, 1939–1945 –
    Influence.
    1. Title

    DA69 .L49 2002
    355.′033541′09044 – dc21

                                                                        2002041144

Printed in Great Britain by Biddles Ltd, Guildford and King's Lynn

To Pamela, Nina,
Jenny and Françoise

CONTENTS

NOTE ON FORMERLY WITHHELD DOCUMENTS

Listed below are the principal files in which were contained copies of almost all the previously 'closed' or 'retained' documents cited in footnotes to Chapters 5 and 6, and in the Appendices of the first edition of *Changing Direction*.

Chapter 5: The Joint Technical Warfare Committee and the Future Nature of Warfare 1945–46

AIR 8/1004	Footnote 64
DEFE 2/1251	Footnotes 9–11, 18, 34, 36–8, 40–2, 49, 51, 62, 76, 79, 80, 84, 86
DEFE 2/1252	Footnotes 63, 77–8, 82, 93–5, 97, 99–101, 103 (also Frontispiece & Map on p. 231), 104, 110, 112, 114
DEFE 2/1348	Footnote 87

Chapter 6: The Joint Planning Staff and an Approved Defence Strategy 1945–47

AIR 8/1446	Footnotes 108, 110, 111
AIR 20/2740	Footnotes 112–5
CAB 21/2086	Footnotes 35, 36, 80, 81, 83, 85
CAB 21/2096	Footnotes 60–2, 147, 149, 150, 155–7, 159
FO 371/57315	Footnote 120 (in folio U2930/2930/70)

Appendices

CAB 21/2096	Source for Appendix 7
DEFE 2/1252	Source for Appendices 4 & 5
FO 371/57315	Source for Appendix 6 (ii) (in folio U2930/2930/70)

LIST OF PLATES

Between pp. 206–7

Nigel Ronald [*NPG*]; Sir Alexander Cadogan [*NPG*]; Sir Orme Sargent [*NPG*]; Christopher Warner [*GA*]

Colonel Oliver Stanley [*NPG*]; Brigadier Guy Stewart [*NPG*]; H. M. Gladwyn Jebb [*Lord Gladwyn*]; William Cavendish-Bentinck [*Duke of Portland*]

Members of the War Office General Staff on V.E.-Day [*Brigadier F. C. Curtis*]; Colonel Arthur Cornwall-Jones [*NPG*]

Sir Henry Tizard [*GA*]; Professor Sir George Thomson [*GA*]; Professor Patrick Blackett [*GA*]; Professor Desmond Bernal [*PL*]

Major-General Gordon MacMillan [*NPG*]; Rear-Admiral Robert Oliver [*NPG*]; Dr Henry Hulme [*H. R. Hulme*]; Dr Paul Fildes [*NPG*]

Churchill and the Chiefs of Staff in 1945 [*IWM*]; Admiral Sir John Cunningham [*NPG*]; Marshal of the R.A.F. Sir Arthur Tedder [*NPG*]

Field-Marshal Viscount Montgomery [*NPG*]; Vice-Admiral Sir Rhoderick McGrigor [*NPG*]; Air Marshal Sir William Dickson [*IWM*]

Brigadier Charles Richardson [*IWM*]; Acting Rear-Admiral Charles Lambe [*NPG*]; Group Captain Edmund Hudleston with Sir Arthur Tedder [*IWM*]

Assistance in picture research and permission to reproduce copyright photographs is gratefully acknowledged in respect of: The Duke of Portland; Lord Gladwyn; General Sir Charles Richardson; Brigadier and Mrs Francis Curtis; Dr H.R. Hulme; Mr Sebastian Best of Godfrey Argent Photographers [*GA*]; Mr David Chandler of the National Portrait Gallery, London [*NPG*]; Imperial War Museum [*IWM*]; Peter Lofts Photography [*PL*]; and the librarian of the Royal Society.

(*Note:* Military ranks ascribed to serving officers in picture captions are those held at the time of events referred to in the text, and thus do not always exactly correspond to the ranks indicated on the uniforms in individual photographs.)

LIST OF MAPS

FOREWORD

The late Professor R. V. Jones FRS, Head of Scientific Intelligence, Air Ministry, 1939–1946

The desperate situation of Britain in 1940 demanded every effort, both national and individual, if we were to survive: and those of us who were most involved became conditioned to thinking of almost nothing but the war until it was won. We did not regard too kindly those who were less involved and who turned their energies, prematurely we thought, to post-war planning. 'Every time the fortunes of war turn in our favour,' I wrote after Alamein, 'up springs a crop of post-war planners', although also suggesting that as soon as we could confidently foresee the defeat of Germany some of the best of our colleagues should be released to think about post-war policy.

Dr Lewis has written a scrupulous and lucid account of strategic planning for the defence of British interests at the highest level—that of the Chiefs of Staff. There the same factors were at work as those that I encountered at my lower level, and even earlier: the first proposals for post-war strategic planning came from the Foreign Office, a body less immediately involved than the Chiefs with military operations. We can sympathise with the Chiefs who, while agreeing in principle, stated on 26 February 1942 that 'such problems must of necessity take a relatively low priority in the work of the Joint Planning Staff'. Since Benghazi had fallen only a month before, the *Scharnhorst* and *Gneisenau* had sailed up the Channel in the past fortnight, and Singapore had surrendered only nine days ago, the Chiefs could hardly be expected to enthuse. Churchill pungently shared their distrust: 'I hope that these speculative studies will be entrusted mainly to those on whose hands time hangs heavy.'

Although some progress was made in the following months it was difficult for the preoccupied Chiefs to contemplate a world in which they might have to co-operate in a Combined Chiefs organisation including Russia and China, or even a military staff based on a United

Nations. As the Chief of the Air Staff, Portal, whimsically commented in February 1944, 'the sensible thing to do would be to appoint our successors now and tell them to go on winning the peace while we go on winning the war'.

On the political side the planners had much to argue about; Germany and Japan must be neutralised as military powers, warm and close relations with the United States—essential as these were—should not push us too much into a back seat, the Commonwealth should be safeguarded and developed, a balance in the Middle East struck and Russian expansionism opposed. It was clear that relations with the Soviets were not going to be easy: it was only the flagrant attack of Germany on Russia that had brought us into an alliance that, from the start, had been difficult. Although, to my own knowledge, we had refrained from any attempt at espionage against the Russians, once they were formally our allies, they did not observe a reciprocal code. While we knew nothing about the activities of Philby and his associates, at least one case came to light of a communist exploitation of a sexual relationship to procure the theft of documents from an Air Staff office: the incident was suppressed in the interest of good relations, but it indicated that the Soviet attitude had hardly mellowed.

Such indications need to be borne in mind if the reader is not to be unduly shocked by the chilling list in Dr Lewis's Appendix 5 of Russian cities which might be subject to nuclear attack in a future war, even though this is balanced by a corresponding list of British cities. Both lists came from the 1946 revision studies of the report of Sir Henry Tizard, who in November 1944 had accepted the invitation of the Chiefs of Staff to chair a sub-committee of the Joint Technical Warfare Committee. The aim was to forecast the developments in weapons and methods of warfare over the next ten years. Not untypically, the Tizard sub-committee was hampered by being specifically excluded from the atomic developments then being pursued jointly with America, (although the embargo had inevitably to be lifted after Hiroshima in August 1945, when the revising committee became an early exponent of the doctrine of nuclear deterrence). It correctly foresaw the paramount roles of radar and electronic warfare, along with the appearance of supersonic fighters, the guided-missile ship and nuclear submarines so fast that they could outdistance convoys and their escorts. It also called—in vain, as it turned out—for a reduction in the time between the design and the production of new weapons.

All these matters and many others are brought to light by Dr Lewis in his fifth chapter, which I for one have found of outstanding interest. This is partly because of personal involvement in some of the aspects; but it also provides admirable material for any student who wishes to investigate in the light of actual post-war developments the degree to which new weapons and techniques can be forecast by men of high qualifications in defence science. Along with Appendix 8, the chapter also shows that a sensational allegation that Churchill was roaring to drench the Ruhr with anthrax in 1944 was falsely based on a slapdash treatment of documentary evidence. Dr Lewis's patient unravelling of the documentary tangle in that episode is exemplary: at the same time the truth which it presents, though unsensational, is none the less interesting for the future concerning biological and chemical warfare. And once again we find the doctrine of deterrence: 'We have concluded,' advised the Deputy Chief of the Air Staff regarding biological warfare, 'that any one form of defence may prove impracticable. We feel therefore that we should ensure that we are ready to counter this form of warfare on a heavy scale at short notice.'

In his sixth and last chapter Dr Lewis covers the years 1945 to 1947, when the post-war world was taking shape and optimistic illusions were being dispelled. Greatest among these had been the idea that the Russians had been misjudged by the Chiefs of Staff, and that there was little reason to fear their post-war attitude if they were encouragingly nurtured as friends. By 1946 the Foreign Office had to acknowledge that the actions of the Soviet Union in Eastern Europe after Yalta had shown that the Chiefs of Staff had been right. As Dr Lewis recounts, the Foreign Office had to some extent become 'a victim of its own propaganda and a dupe of its own wishful thinking'—much as the Admirals had been in resisting the introduction of convoys in 1917. Overall, the Chiefs of Staff emerge with much credit from the account, as do their scientific advisers.

While it is a commonplace to warn of the danger of preparing 'to fight the last war all over again', it is well to recall the precept of Thucydides that history is philosophy teaching through examples. We in World War II, for instance, would have been better prepared if Lord Tiverton's work on operational research in 1917 (or perhaps Alfred Ewing's 1927 lecture on the running of an intercept and cryptographic organisation in World War I) had not in the meantime been forgotten. Fortunately this need not be so regarding the lessons of World War II, where many have now been drawn for posterity; and in this book Dr

Lewis has enhanced them by distilling from an immense amount of intricate labour such a discerning and objective account of British post-war strategic planning.

R. V. Jones.

ACKNOWLEDGEMENTS

I wish to record my gratitude to the Duke of Portland, Lord Gladwyn and Brigadier A. T. Cornwall-Jones, each of whom granted me lengthy interviews as well as reading sections of my manuscript. Brigadier Cornwall-Jones in particular took considerable trouble to convey to me some idea of the atmosphere in which the military planners operated, and I am very sad that his death prevented me from showing him the results of his help. Lord Zuckerman, Professor R. V. Jones, Dr H. R. Hulme and Group Captain W. P. Harvey kindly corresponded with me on individual points. None of the above, of course, should be held responsible for the opinions expressed and the interpretations made in this book, which are mine alone.

Messrs J. Robertson and J. W. Cheatle of the Cabinet Office dealt patiently with many enquiries and granted 'Special Access' to documents whenever this proved possible. In the Ministry of Defence, Mr J. F. Smith checked and cleared sensitive references, and Miss S. K. B. Glover and Mr D. E. R. Breeze supplied career details for the first three sections of Appendix 1. Dr Uri Bialer, Miss Louise Davis, Mrs Moira Elegant, Mr Norris McWhirter, Miss Frances Rand and Miss Areila Samuel gave advice or assistance on questions of presentation or content.

Miss P. Methven of the Liddell Hart Centre for Military Archives, King's College, London, granted access to the Alanbrooke Papers. I also received help from library staff at the Royal United Services Institute for Defence Studies; Christ Church, Oxford; and—especially—the Public Record Office, Kew. The supervisor of my doctoral thesis, on which this book is based, was Mr Wilfrid Knapp of Oxford University. I am deeply indebted to him for his constant encouragement, support and friendship.

Finally, I am grateful to the Controller of Her Majesty's Stationery Office for permission to reproduce extracts from, and transcripts of, Crown-copyright records in this volume.

J. L.

ABBREVIATIONS

ACA	Ministerial Committee on Armistice Terms and Civil Administration
ACAE	Advisory Committee on Atomic Energy
ACAS(P)	Assistant Chief of the Air Staff (Policy)
ACAS(TR)	Assistant Chief of the Air Staff (Technical Requirements)
ACIGS(O)	Assistant Chief of the Imperial General Staff (Operations)
ACIGS(W)	Assistant Chief of the Imperial General Staff (Weapons)
ACNS(W)	Assistant Chief of the Naval Staff (Weapons)
ADGB	Air Defence of Great Britain
APW	Armistice and Post-War Committee
AWC	Atomic Weapons Sub-Committee
CAS	Chief of the Air Staff
CCGP	Co-ordinating Committee on Guided and Propelled Missiles and Projectiles
CCO	Chief of Combined Operations
CIGS	Chief of the Imperial General Staff
CNS	First Sea Lord and Chief of the Naval Staff
COHQ	Combined Operations Headquarters
COS	Chiefs of Staff
DCAS	Deputy Chief of the Air Staff
DCOS	Deputy Chiefs of Staff
DMO	Director of Military Operations
DNOR	Director of Naval Operational Research
D of P	Director of Plans
DRP	Defence Research Policy Committee

FO	Foreign Office
F(O)PS	Future (Operational) Planning Section
FORD	Foreign Office Research Department
FRPS	Foreign Research and Press Service
ISCCW	Inter-Service Committee on Chemical Warfare
ISSBW	Inter-Service Sub-Committee on Biological Warfare
JIC	Joint Intelligence Sub-Committee
JPS	Joint Planning Staff
JSM	Joint Staff Mission
JTWC	Joint Technical Warfare Committee
JWPS	Joint War Production Staff
LCS	London Controlling Section
MO 11	Directorate of Military Operations, Section 11 (*later:* Directorate of Civil Affairs, War Office)
MSC	Military Sub-Committee of the Ministerial Committee on Reconstruction Problems
PHP	Post-Hostilities Planning Sub-Committee
PHPS	Post-Hostilities Planning Staff
RCM	Radio Counter-measures
STRATS	Strategical Planning Section
VCAS	Vice-Chief of the Air Staff
VCIGS	Vice-Chief of the Imperial General Staff
VCNS	Vice-Chief of the Naval Staff
VCOS	Vice-Chiefs of Staff

PREFACE TO THE FIRST EDITION

Contrary to appearances, the sub-title of this study is not a tautology. Whereas the word 'Strategic' refers to the nature of the plans with which it is concerned, the word 'Military' refers to the status of the planners who conceived them. Both terms are employed a little loosely. The latter is used in its broad, inter-Service sense to indicate that the planners to be considered are the British Chiefs of Staff and their subordinates, and no-one else. The former is used in a relative way to indicate that the plans to be examined are the most comprehensive schemes for post-war defence which were being produced at any given time. Thus, some rather limited topics are dealt with in depth in the first three chapters, because they comprised the greater part of post-war defence planning between 1942 and mid-1944; but they are virtually disregarded thereafter, because the wider issues upon which they had a bearing were by then themselves systematically being tackled. Lesser matters consequently ceased to be pointers to an unformulated wider strategy and became, instead, mere derivatives of more comprehensive plans. As such, they are no longer of interest to this examination—which traces the evolution of planning from the first Foreign Office approach to the military authorities in February 1942 to Prime Ministerial endorsement of an overall strategic defence plan in June 1947.

It is essential to stress that contributions from politicians, diplomats and other officials enter the picture only in so far as they directly influenced the work of the military planners—by calling it forth, by affecting its contents, or by determining its finality through endorsement or rejection. The book takes its structure from the unfolding progression of that work, and the activities of non-Service bodies are rigorously excluded in those cases when they did not impinge upon it. This explains the marginal coverage of politicians prior to the end of the war and of diplomats thereafter, though members of both groupings undoubtedly held and expressed opinions about post-war defence requirements throughout the period encompassed by this study. The same strict standard of relevance is applied to such military problems as the retention of conscription, the course of demobilisation, and the preparation of Estimates for the Services in peacetime: where they did not affect the choice of a strategy, there is no justification for their being considered. This explains, for example, why the setting up of the Ministry of Defence in 1947 (which barely touched the structure of the C.O.S. planning organisation) is hardly mentioned, whereas the establishment and reorganisation of the specialised post-war planning bodies is most carefully examined. Nor is any attempt considered justifiable to link the contents of particular plans to extraneous contemporary developments unless a connection can be shown to have existed. Not only would that be sheer speculation, it is perfectly clear on the evidence available that military planning derived much of its continuity from *the determination of the Chiefs of Staff to formulate a long-term strategy covering all reasonable possibilities*, and not one founded on unreliable predictions of what was likely to occur.

The aim of this book is to reconstruct the events which led to the production of an approved defence strategy. In doing so, it shows how and when answers came to be provided by the Service planners to the following questions: (1) Against whom would a post-war strategy be necessary, and why? (2) What would be the nature of a future war, if one occurred? (3) What measures should be taken in such a war against such an enemy? It also illustrates the way in which official machinery operated in dealing with such matters; and it sheds incidental light on the character of British foreign policy during an important period in international history.

The material here assembled falls into three main divisions. The background and strategic planning role of the Military Sub-Committee have not previously been recounted, possibly because central M.S.C. records were not preserved; this story therefore had to be pieced together from the files of the Foreign Office and the Joint Planning Staff secretariat. P.H.P. and P.H.P.S. material was readily available; but, although accounts of the work of these bodies in connection with the future of Germany have previously been compiled, this is the first full examination of their role in post-war strategic defence planning. Nearly all the principal papers for 1946–47, upon which the bulk of Chapters 5 and 6 is based, were not intended for public scrutiny despite the expiry of the normal thirty-year closure period. Having nevertheless managed to discover copies of these, the author was able to reach amicable agreement with the responsible authorities in the Ministry of Defence over which items should not be published in the interest of national security.

INTRODUCTION TO THE
SECOND EDITION

Changing Direction was published in 1988 on the basis of research completed in 1981. In the seven years before publication, little or no new primary material had been released. Documents closed for 50 years remained closed. Retained material remained retained. In one notable case—Operation 'UNTHINKABLE'—lost material remained lost. In more than a decade since publication, however, it has become possible to fill several small, but significant gaps in the story of the origins of post-war defence planning. In this period, too, occasional references to *Changing Direction* in a variety of studies—by Peter Hennessy (*Never Again*, 1992), Correlli Barnett (*The Lost Victory*, 1995), David Cesarani (*Justice Delayed*, 1992), Tom Bower (*The Red Web*, 1989), the late R.V. Jones (*Reflections on Intelligence*, 1989) and Norman Friedman (*The Fifty-Year War*, 2000)—indicated that it might be worth updating the work. Most recently, two excellent volumes on post-war British intelligence—Richard Aldrich's *The Hidden Hand* (2001) and Sir Percy Cradock's *Know Your Enemy* (2002)—have explicitly drawn on *Changing Direction* as a specialist source. All this has encouraged me to expand it and bring it before a wider audience. I am grateful to Frank Cass and Mick Read for making this possible.

When the first edition was published, the United Kingdom was still locked into the closing stages of the Cold War. Since its end, there has been an acceleration of releases of formerly withheld material. Most of those references on pages 411–42 listed as 'closed' or 'retained' (and all those to which 'special access' was given, as they were overdue for release in the early 1980s) are now freely available at the Public Record Office. It had been possible to write the book by finding individual copies of withheld documents buried in Departmental subject-files, most notably the closed Joint Technical Warfare Committee papers in DEFE 2/1251–2 and the retained Overall Strategic Plan papers in CAB 21/2096. Yet, it had to be accepted that in a few areas—the J.I.C., the post-war L.C.S., the missing J.P.S. papers on 'UNTHINKABLE'—a small part of the jigsaw would remain unfilled. The passage of time and the easing of restrictions now enable it to be completed.

The task has been made much easier by the invaluable assistance of Mrs Tessa Stirling, Mr Richard Ponman and Miss Debbie Neal at the Cabinet Office Historical Section in Westminster. Professor Richard Aldrich of Nottingham University generously applied his expertise to several loose ends. My Parliamentary assistants, Colin Smith and Diana Brooks, as always gave their unfailing help, and the staff of the Public Record Office, Kew, displayed all the courtesy and efficiency which I learned to appreciate over twenty years ago. I am also grateful to the Codrington Library, All Souls College, which accepted my earlier source material for the use of future researchers in Oxford.

The newly available material is set out in the seven sections which follow. To avoid undue repetition, some foreknowledge of the contents of the original book is presupposed, but hopefully not too much. Readers familiar with the original text should find the concentration of new research into this introductory chapter a help rather than a hindrance; those new to the story should find the extensive cross-referencing from new text to old adequate to guide them through the labyrinth.

1. The Biological Warfare Programme, 1944

One ancillary topic was covered in Appendix 8[1] of *Changing Direction*. This consisted of my February 1982 *Encounter* article challenging a televised claim that Churchill urged the use of biological warfare against Germany during the V-weapon crisis of July 1944. The initiator of the story, BBC *Newsnight* reporter Robert Harris,[2] alleged that it was 'arguably the last great Allied secret of the war'. More prosaically, the late Professor R.V. Jones and I maintained that the British biological warfare programme was intended only for retaliation against the use of biological warfare (B.W.) by others. We regarded the 'plans' to attack six German cities with 'N' (anthrax) as not only impractical but simply hypothetical—given both the non-availability of 'N-bombs' and the documentary evidence that Churchill proposed using gas, not germs,

---

1. See pp. 388–405 below
2. Mr Harris has subsequently become a deservedly successful novelist—specialising in fiction about the Second World War.

against the V.2 rocket threat.[3]

Though our interpretation was generally accepted,[4] some doubts might have remained while the files of the C.O.S. Inter-Service Sub-Committee on Biological Warfare were unavailable. Now they are open, and the following typical extracts speak for themselves:

> The Porton Experiments Sub-Committee [of the Bacteriological Warfare Committee of the War Cabinet[5]] was therefore set up in September 1940, to organise experiments at Porton under conditions outlined in a letter from Lord Hankey to Air Marshal Peck, the Chairman of the Sub-Committee, dated 24th September 1940. Inter alia, it was laid down that 'it is only by a full examination of methods of attack that we can develop effective means of defence', and the Committee was 'so to frame the programme of the Porton experiments that if these methods were employed against us by the enemy, we should be in a position to retaliate effectively at fairly short notice.' . . . Work started at Porton in November 1940, and has necessarily been directed almost entirely to the exploration of offensive possibilities, in order to supply evidence on which defensive action can be taken and on which a means of retaliation could be based if authorised.[6]

* * * *

> The Prime Minister has approved a proposal that a preliminary order should be placed by this country for half a million of these [anthrax] bombs . . . There can of course be *no* question of either country [Britain or the United States] using this form of warfare except by way of retaliation for

---

3. See R.V. Jones and J.M. Lewis: 'Churchill's Anthrax Bombs: a Debate' in *Bulletin of the Atomic Scientists*, November 1987
4. Martin Gilbert: *Road to Victory—Winston S. Churchill, 1941–1945* (London, Heinemann, 1986), pp. 775–6, 839–42 & 864–5; Gerhard L. Weinberg: *A World at Arms* (Cambridge, C.U.P., 1994), pp. 559–60 & 1068, note 111
5. The Bacteriological Warfare Committee of the War Cabinet was the predecessor of the Inter-Service Sub-Committee on Biological Warfare set up under the Chiefs of Staff in June 1944. See pp. 211–3 below
6. CAB 81/53: BW(42)2, 2 April 1942 Annex II: 'Bacteriological Warfare: General Review—Memorandum by Dr P. Fildes', 31 March 1942. That the Porton team was set up under Paul Fildes in September 1940 is apparently confirmed in CAB 81/53: BW(40)35, 23 September 1940 & CAB 81/58: BW(44)20, 29 September 1944, though August was implied in the biographical memoir of Fildes by Dr G.P. Gladstone, and other former colleagues, cited on p. 211 below.

its adoption by the enemy, and then only after consultation with one another.[7]

* * * *

Thank you for your minute of 9 May. I am glad to note that satisfactory progress is being made and trust you will press on with [B.W.] research, especially into countermeasures. I approve the highest priority for all that is required for the *latter*.[8]

* * * *

On 7.1.44, the B.W. Operational Panel accepted Dr Fildes' estimate that [a] half-million of the 4-lb [anthrax] bomb would be required for retaliatory attack on Germany . . . [9]

* * * *

The possibility cannot be excluded that Hitler, faced with imminent military disaster, might order the use of biological warfare. While we think that the German General Staff would be at least as reluctant to employ biological as gas warfare unless they believed that it would decisively avert the defeat of Germany, we recognise that the temptation to use biological warfare would, in a supreme crisis, be very much greater than the temptation to use chemical warfare, as its effect would be very much greater than would be the effect of gas. On the other hand we have no evidence that even in their mass murder organisations the Germans have ever used biological agents to kill human beings.[10]

* * * *

7. Having proved that one [B.W.] agent at least could be used against us, it became a question of what action should be taken. It is sometimes

7. CAB 122/1599: Ismay to Field Marshal Sir John Dill (head of the British Joint Staff Mission, Washington), 1 April 1944 (original emphasis by Ismay)
8. CAB 136/13: Prime Minister's Personal Min No M.585/4, Churchill to Brown, 21 May 1944 (original emphasis by Churchill). Ernest Brown, a successor to Hankey as Chancellor of the Duchy of Lancaster, had just suggested handing over his responsibility for the B.W. programme to the C.O.S.
9. CAB 136/13: 'Status of negotiations regarding the production of the 4-lb Chem. F. Bomb in U.S.A.', 8 July 1944
10. CAB 81/124: JIC(44)310(0)(Final), 18 July 1944 This paper, drafted at the height of Churchill's exchanges with the Service chiefs about the V-weapons, thus indicates knowledge by the Joint Intelligence Sub-Committee of the use of gas to exterminate victims of the Nazis.

thought that it is possible to inoculate against bacterial attack, but this of course is impossible . . . Obviously the enemy will not select a bacterium against which there is a protection by inoculation; he will select one, such as N, against which we cannot yet protect man.

The policy was then adopted to set up a defence by threat of retaliation, and this policy demanded that any use of bacteria proved by experiment to be adequate should be developed and produced ready for use in retaliation at short notice.

8.   Having proved N to be practicable, we had to consider the production of finished weapons as soon as possible as our only specific defence against a bacterial attack . . .

9.   Our reason for selecting N as our first study was that technically it was the most obvious choice. The Germans were alleged to be experimenting with this agent before the war, and, if this is true, they may also have developed a practicable weapon. For this reason, when we became satisfied that N was a potential danger, we started work on a specific defence against it. This is a problem which has been worked on sporadically for many years, and, although cattle can be successfully inoculated, man cannot. By intensive work we hope without much assurance to succeed, and indeed have made some little progress. It has been alleged by Mr Ernest Brown [Chancellor of the Duchy of Lancaster] that the Prime Minister wishes this work to be driven with highest priority.

10.   The primary object of our work at this late stage of the war is therefore to try to develop a specific defence against N, and not to prove the practicability of other offensive weapons.

11.   Nevertheless, as a secondary matter, we are continuing work on the offensive side . . . without, however, supposing that results will be available during this war. Our reason for this is to keep in touch with offensive developments.[11]

* * * *

I had the intention of asking for the release of myself and my personal staff immediately it could be agreed that the danger of a German [B.W.] attack

---

11.   CAB 81/58: BW(44)9, 21 July 1944 This assessment by Dr Fildes, which concluded that 'It seems probable that the possible Service applications of our work have been exaggerated', was drawn up at precisely the time when—according to commentators such as Harris and Barton J. Bernstein—'Perhaps British leaders were . . . also considering the advantages of ultimately initiating bacteriological warfare'. (Barton J. Bernstein: 'Churchill's Secret Biological Weapons', *Bulletin of the Atomic Scientists*, January/February 1987)

had passed, even before the 'end' of the European War. I doubt whether anyone could suggest that the danger is very great even now, and I question whether it would be to the national advantage to keep us on this sort of work very much longer.[12]

* * * *

I think I should emphasise that our interest in the whole [B.W.] project is purely defensive; by that I mean that we have no intention of indulging in this form of warfare except as a retaliation for its institution by the enemy. From this point of view the less effective it is proved to be in any respect, the better we are pleased![13]

Far from the previously closed files proving the existence of a British plot to launch an anthrax attack, they show conclusively that the B.W. programme was designed for retaliation—in the absence of inoculation—against biological warfare if begun by others. Let us now turn from 'The Plan that Never Was' to the problems of the post-war world, which the Service chiefs knew they would eventually confront.

2. The J.I.C. and the Russians, 1944

In September 1943, the Chiefs of Staff had approved making the first military attempt to assess 'the probable long-term impact of Russian policy on British strategic interests' after the war.[14] Although the idea had originated with the Joint Planning Staff, it was—as with so many other post-war problems—promptly reallocated to another component of the C.O.S. organisation. This was the Post-Hostilities Planning Sub-Committee, then chaired by a Foreign Office nominee. On 12 October,

---

12. CAB 136/12: Dr Paul Fildes (head of B.W. research) to Captain G.H. Oswald (Secretary of the Inter-Service Sub-Committee on Biological Warfare), 3 November 1944 In the event, Fildes was still in place at the end of the Japanese war, when the I.S.S.B.W. successfully urged the Chiefs of Staff to secure 'a satisfactory organisation for the continuing control' of biological warfare research (CAB 81/58: BW(45)17(Final), 7 August 1945). The Service chiefs agreed on 13 September and Defence Committee approval was secured the following month (CAB 81/58: BW(45)22, 14 September 1945 & BW(45)23, 8 October 1945). See pp. 213–5 below
13. CAB 136/12: Captain G.H. Oswald (Secretary, I.S.S.B.W.) to Colonel H. Paget, British Army Staff, Washington, 11 November 1944
14. See p. 59 below

the P.H.P. resolved to seek guidance from the Joint Intelligence Sub-Committee but, a fortnight later, the J.I.C. decided merely to comment on a draft appreciation to be prepared instead by the Foreign Office.[15]

When the Foreign Office paper appeared on 10 February 1944, it painted an optimistic picture of post-war Soviet priorities: a 'search for security', fear of Germany, recovery from the ravages of war, internal development, and a willingness to experiment with a policy of co-operation with America and the United Kingdom in a post-war international security system.[16] This message was largely carried forward by the Post-Hostilities Planners in the Russian appreciation they finally produced on 1 May 1944, which notably omitted consideration of 'the possibility that Soviet Russia might attempt to extend her influence over Western Europe' after the war.[17]

How far the P.H.P. appreciation had been influenced by the views of the Service Directors of Intelligence can now be seen from the declassified J.I.C. commentary which was completed on 20 March 1944. In response to the Foreign Office analysis, the J.I.C. agreed that after two world wars the Russians would do their utmost 'to ensure that Germany can never again be a military menace', and that they would insist upon very severe peace terms in the immediate post-war period. However, Russian fear of Germany should steadily diminish as the Soviet Union became conscious of her own increasing power. As well as a population advantage over the Germans approaching three-to-one, the Russians could expect to outstrip Germany in industrial development:

> The Soviet Union's military efficiency has been one of the surprises of this war; we see no reason to suppose that Germany over a long period is likely to hold the margin of superiority that she still had in 1941. Unless Germany's military recovery is actively supported by Great Britain and America, it is likely to be a matter of twenty or thirty years before she is again in a position to be a menace to European peace. By that time the Soviet Union will probably be so powerful, if no internal upheavals occur, as to have little or no need to fear Germany alone.

Only if it seemed that a combination of other powers was seeking to use German strength against the Soviet Union, might she be tempted to form

---

15. See pp. 58–60 below & CAB 81/91: JIC(43)53rd Mtg (0)(5), 26 October 1943
16. CAB 81/120: JIC(44)60(0), 11 February 1944 See also pp. 90–1 below & footnote 107 to p. 92 below
17. CAB 81/45: PHP(43)1(0)(Final), 1 May 1944 See pp. 91–6 below

an alliance with Germany herself.

As well as forecasting post-war superpower status for the Soviet Union, the J.I.C. anticipated trouble from Moscow's links with communist organisations in other countries:

> Such organisations are potential and willing instruments of Soviet policy and feel a loyalty to the Soviet Government which often overrides that owed to their own country. This dangerous tendency was clearly demonstrated by the communist parties in Great Britain and France in the early stages of this war.

There was no reason to suppose that Stalin's dissolution of the Communist International[18] had destroyed the links between the Soviet authorities and foreign communist parties:

> The question is what use the Soviet Government will make of this political weapon in the post-war world. We believe that Soviet underground activity in foreign countries will not be guided by purely ideological considerations in pursuit of world revolution as an end desirable in itself. It is more probable that the Soviet will use this weapon as one of the means of supporting the foreign policy it favours at the moment.

The Directors of Intelligence thus saw potential Soviet post-war subversion as opportunistic. If co-operation with the United Kingdom seemed satisfactory, the risk of arousing antagonism by 'provocative interference in British internal politics' would be small. By contrast, if dissatisfied with Anglo-Soviet relations, the Soviet Union would undoubtedly exploit to the full her link with the Communist Party of Great Britain.

Possibly bearing in mind some of the left-wingers recruited to assist the British war effort, the J.I.C. felt it necessary to add a disclaimer:

> It cannot, however, be assumed in the post-war world that every person who has at one time or another been labelled 'communist' belongs to a world movement controlled by the Soviet Union. Nor would it be right to assume that left-wing parties to which the Soviet Union is favourable would necessarily be anti-British or subversive merely because the Soviet Union favours them.

---

18. See footnote 101 to p. 141 below

The Soviet Government would no doubt tend to support the 'proletariat' everywhere; but they would be equally prepared to back 'even right-wing dictators' if in any particular case it happened to suit their policy.

The J.I.C. disagreed with a suggestion in the Foreign Office paper that, despite British post-war vulnerability to the Soviet Union in the Middle East, there would be 'no reason to anticipate that a dearth of oil will impel Russia to supply her own needs from the Middle East'. Future Soviet oil requirements would greatly increase with industrial development and—like the Americans—the Russians might think it strategically desirable to conserve their own domestic sources. This could lead to a clash with the United Kingdom and the United States over Middle Eastern supplies. Finally, although it was true that at least five years would be needed to rehabilitate those areas occupied by and recaptured from the Nazis, 'the development and expansion of industry in other parts of the Soviet Union will have been going on all the time'. To overestimate the need for Soviet rehabilitation might cause post-war Soviet military potential to be underestimated.[19]

The J.I.C. was to return to these issues in the autumn of 1944—during a prolonged period of open disagreement between the Chiefs of Staff and the Foreign Office over post-war planning and the Soviet Union.[20] In May, the Post-Hostilities Planning Sub-Committee had been replaced by the Post-Hostilities Planning Staff, whose three Service Directors soon emerged as strong advocates of the need for precautionary planning against possible Soviet hostility. The RAF's Director of Post-Hostilities Plans, Air Commodore Peter Warburton, proposed at the end of July that the J.I.C. should be asked to estimate Soviet strengths and weaknesses in relation to post-war British strategic interests, and this was duly carried out in a paper produced on 22 August.[21]

Once again, the Foreign Office paper of 10 February on future Soviet foreign policy was taken as the political starting point; once again, the J.I.C. saw no reason significantly to dissent from it; yet, once again, there was a subtle difference of emphasis. If the Soviet Union's intentions were peaceful, the mere maintenance of conscription in a country of that size would yield armed forces

> on a scale considerably larger than the strict needs of her own security
> would justify. And if she were planning to embark on war with a first-class

---

19. CAB 81/121: JIC(44)105(0)(Final), 20 March 1944
20. See pp. 119–43 below
21. See pp. 135–6 below & footnote 85 to p. 136 below

military power or powers, she would have the capacity to build up land and air forces on a gigantic scale, and would have the economic, and particularly industrial, resources to maintain them in action.

There was even some evidence of an intention substantially to expand her navy, though not in respect of capital ships or aircraft carriers.

Overall, it was clear that the Soviet Union would have the capability to attack the British Commonwealth at any time—certainly within the next ten years—if she saw sufficient advantage in doing so. Disputes might most probably arise in the Middle East. The Soviet Union would want defence in depth for her Caucasian oilfields and this could encroach on British sources of oil in Persia and Iraq, and on British lines of communication via the Mediterranean to India and the Far East. Any Soviet expansion in the Far East might also lead to a clash with the United States, into which the British Commonwealth would probably be drawn. Much would depend, however, on the general state of Anglo-Soviet relations 'and particularly how far Russia is satisfied with the sincerity of our desire to collaborate with her'.

Soviet potential strengths and weaknesses were then examined for her war economy and for each of her armed forces in turn. Even before the war, the country had little dependence upon imports, on account of the scale and distribution of natural resources and the size and growth of the labour force. During the war, new industrial areas had been developed in geographically remote areas such as the Urals. These now constituted the main source of Soviet armaments supply:

> The events of the past three years have conclusively shown that Russia has with some help from abroad been able to maintain a war effort comprising large-scale and prolonged military operations in spite of the loss of the Ukraine—once her chief industrial base—and of the industrial centre of Leningrad.

Oil production, however, was heavily concentrated in the Caucasus—which would remain the source for at least three-quarters of all Soviet oil supplies for several years to come. Refineries and pipelines such as those at Baku would be targets vulnerable to aerial attack. Some current shortages could be deduced from the pattern of imports from the Allies: 'foodstuffs, raw materials, mechanised transport and certain specialised types of war equipment', but such shortages would probably be overcome as recovery proceeded and as strategic stores were built up. Nor were there many obvious industrial or communications bottlenecks, except possibly the Volga waterway and canal system.

Despite attempts to do so, no battleship had been completed since the Revolution and the Soviet Union would probably remain unable to construct aircraft carriers unaided for several years. Still, she had proved her capacity for building light cruisers, destroyers and submarines—the types of vessels needed for the sort of war she might wish to wage. Her military manpower would not be a limiting factor, as it was expected to be greater in five to ten years than it had been at the outbreak of war in 1941. Motor transport was the weakest element of Soviet land forces, but the quality of most fighting equipment was high and almost on a par with that of the Germans. This particularly applied to small arms, guns and tanks:

> The finish is not up to British standards but workmanship on all essential parts and instruments is very good . . . [Russia,] in spite of her enormous losses, has continued to develop her numerical superiority in weapons and equipment until, according to the Germans,[22] it has reached a crushing superiority . . . The Russians are very keen on new ideas and develop and apply new technique very rapidly . . . Some Russian ideas and equipment have been so good that the Germans have copied them. For instance, the general design of the T.34 tank formed the basis for the German Panther tank . . . Russia has made swift strides in technical development and has shown amazing capacity to master technical problems and make good early shortages and handicaps.

If the Soviet Union chose to make the effort, her post-war production of aircraft could rival that of any major power. After four years of war with Germany, the first-line strength of the Soviet air force had risen from about 8,000 to about 11,000. Though 'a rough and ready affair' by British or American standards, where operational efficiency, technical equipment and organisation were concerned, it had great capacity for improvisation and 'in spite of many defects it works'. Often at considerable cost, it did the job it was designed to do—to give 'violent, heavy and effective support to the army'. So far as was known, its ground support organisation had never failed to ensure that the Soviet air force kept up with the advancing armies.

---

22. This information was presumably derived from signals intelligence and/or prisoner-of-war interrogations.

Although no large strategic bomber force had been created in the Soviet Union, this would be quite feasible given time to design appropriate aircraft and equipment. The development of airborne rockets had proved what the Russians could do:

> The Russians were pioneers of the rocket fired from aircraft and are evincing profound interest in the 'flying bomb'. We should not assume that Russia will lag behind in the development of air warfare along the unorthodox lines upon which Germany is now working.

Russian plans for the creation of a strategic bomber force, and for the defence of the Soviet Union against aerial attack, would probably depend upon the extent to which such new methods of air warfare could be developed.[23]

It can therefore be seen that, at the very time when the Chiefs of Staff were confronting the Foreign Office over its reluctance to consider potential Soviet post-war hostility, their Directors of Intelligence clearly saw the risks of any Anglo-Soviet rift. Though determined to prepare for a failure of the proposed world security organisation so relied upon by the Foreign Office, the Service Chiefs were well aware that military conflict with the Soviet Union would be a most hazardous undertaking.

3. Planning the 'UNTHINKABLE', 1945

In May 1945 the Joint Planning Staff prepared a paper on a Continental war between the Soviet Union and the Western Allies. That much had been in the public domain since 1959, when the diaries of the wartime C.I.G.S., Sir Alan Brooke, were published. Over twenty years later, however, the Cabinet Office Historical Section believed that no finalised papers had been prepared or preserved.[24] Indeed, no apparent gaps existed in the series of Chiefs of Staff or J.P.S. memoranda. There matters rested until October 1998, when a national newspaper reported the discovery of the elusive material in a newly released Cabinet Office file innocuously entitled 'Russia: Anglo-US Discussions on Post-war Defence Organisation'.[25]

---

23. CAB 81/124: JIC(44)366(0)(Final), 22 August 1944
24. See p. 242 below & footnote 2 thereon
25. Ben Fenton: 'Churchill's Plan for Third World War against Stalin', *Daily Telegraph*, 1 October 1998 & Julian Lewis: 'Churchill's "Unthinkable" War', *Daily Telegraph*, Letters, 5 October 1998

The significance of Brooke's repeated references to the 'unthinkable' war against Russia, in his diary entry of 31 May,[26] could now be fully appreciated—for that had been the precautionary name given to the J.P.S. study. Although the file began only with the 29-page paper finalised by the Joint Planners on 22 May 1945, it is easy to see why Churchill had requested it. As early as 28 February, the Prime Minister's Private Secretary, John Colville, had described his anger at Soviet betrayal of the Yalta Declaration on Liberated Europe:[27]

> In the evening came sinister telegrams from Roumania showing that the Russians are intimidating the King and Government and setting about the establishment of a Communist minority government with all the technique familiar to students of the Comintern. The P.M. was dining at Buckingham Palace, but Eden rang me up and said he viewed these events with great concern because [Deputy Foreign Minister] Vyshinsky, who was their executor, had come fresh from the understanding and undertakings of Yalta. When the P.M. came back, I spoke to him of the position and he said he feared he could do nothing. Russia had let us go our way in Greece; she would insist on imposing her will in Roumania and Bulgaria. But as regards Poland we would have our say. As he went to bed, after 2.00 a.m., the P.M. said to me, 'I have not the slightest intention of being cheated over Poland, not even if we go to the verge of war with Russia'.[28]

Throughout March and April, the Prime Minister's forebodings increased with the relentless tightening of the Soviet grip on Poland.[29] At the end of March, the leader of the Polish Underground Army, the leader of the Polish Socialists, and key representatives of the other democratic Polish political parties were lured to a meeting with the Soviet authorities in Pruszkow, near Warsaw. Despite a promise of safe conduct, all fifteen of them were seized by the Russians. Churchill was appalled. Unsure if they were dead or alive, he telegraphed to Eden in San Francisco:

> The case about the fifteen Poles, as admitted by Molotov to the Americans is one on which we must soon tell Stalin quite plainly what the consequences

---

26. See p. 243 below & footnote 4 thereon
27. See p. 261 below
28. Sir John Colville: *The Fringes of Power—Downing Street Diaries, 1939–1945* (London, Hodder & Stoughton, 1985), pp. 565–6
29. Martin Gilbert: *Road to Victory—Winston S. Churchill, 1941–1945* (London, Heinemann, 1986), Chapters 64–8 *passim*

will be. The perfidy by which these Poles were enticed into a Russian conference and then held fast in the Russian grip is one which will emerge in
great detail . . . and there is no doubt that the publication in detail of this event
. . . would produce a primary change in the entire structure of world forces.

Nothing could prevent 'a great catastrophe', he added, 'but a meeting and
a showdown as early as possible at some point in Germany which is under
American and British control'.[30]

The importance of the Polish dimension was clear from the 22 May
J.P.S. report on Operation 'UNTHINKABLE'. The overall object was
defined as 'to impose upon Russia the will of the United States and
British Empire'. Even if that were restricted to 'no more than a square
deal for Poland', the military commitment involved might be unlimited:

> A quick success might induce the Russians to submit to our will, at least
> for the time being; but it might not. That is for the Russians to decide. If
> they want total war, they are in a position to have it.

The task should therefore be examined first on the basis that only total
war would achieve the stated aim, and then on the basis that 'a quick
success would suffice to gain our political object and that the continuing
commitment need not concern us'.

As a hypothetical starting date for hostilities, the Joint Planners had
been told to select 1 July 1945. They were to take for granted the 'full
support' of Anglo-American public opinion, so that the current high
morale of British and United States forces would continue. They were
also to assume 'full assistance from the Polish armed forces and . . . the
use of German manpower and what remains of German industrial
capacity', but no help from any of the other Western Powers apart from
the use of their bases and military facilities. The Russians and Japanese
would be expected to form an alliance.

The total war scenario would require the Soviet Union either to be
occupied to such an extent that further resistance became impossible, or
to be defeated in the field so decisively that she would have to abandon
the fight. If the Russians withdrew without being decisively beaten, they
would probably exploit the immensity of their territory and use those

---

30. P.M.'s Personal Telegram No T.771/5, 5 May 1945, quoted in Gilbert, *op. cit.*, pp.
    1333–4. Churchill was to learn on 21 June that twelve of the fifteen seized Poles had
    been given long prison sentences. (Their arrest at the end of March had been
    confirmed by the Russians only on 4 May.)

tactics which had worked against the Germans:

> There is virtually no limit to the distance to which it would be necessary
> for the Allies to penetrate into Russia in order to render further resistance
> impossible. It is hardly conceivable that the Allies could penetrate even as
> far as, or as quickly as, the Germans in 1942 and this penetration produced
> no decisive result.

Nor was the alternative of a climactic battle more likely, given the
existing three-to-one superiority of Soviet over Western strength in
Central Europe:

> Although Allied organisation is better, equipment slightly better and
> morale higher, the Russians have proved themselves formidable opponents
> of the Germans. They have competent commanders, adequate equipment
> and an organisation which, though possibly inferior by our standards, has
> stood the test.

Despite the fact that only a third of the Soviet divisions were thought to
be of high quality, there would be no prospect of the West winning a total
war without a very long-term mobilisation and deployment in Europe of
the vast resources of the United States. The re-equipment and
reorganisation of German manpower and of that of all the West European
allies would also be essential.

The J.P.S. omitted to consider 'the chances of revolution in the
U.S.S.R.—on which we are not competent to express an opinion', and the
prospect of an atomic bomb was never mentioned.[31] All that remained,
therefore, was the possibility that 'a quick and limited military success
would result in Russia accepting our terms'. This was a matter for
political judgement; but, before any such judgement were made, the Joint
Planners warned, three risks must be considered. First, if the attainment
of a limited goal did not cause Soviet compliance, the result would be an
unintended total war. Secondly, even a limited campaign could not dictate
where hostilities took place. Battles might have to be fought in locations
world-wide. Finally, even if all went according to plan, no lasting result
was likely to be achieved: 'The military power of Russia will not be
broken and it will be open to her to recommence the conflict at any time
she sees fit.'

---

31. The first test explosion of an atomic device—at Alamogordo, New Mexico—was
    not to occur until mid-July.

Nevertheless, the J.P.S. dutifully examined what action could be taken to try to inflict such a blow on the Russians as would cause them to accept Anglo-American terms, 'even though they would not have been decisively defeated and, from the military point of view, would still be capable of continuing the struggle'. One annex examined the strength of the Soviet armed forces. The Soviet navy was dismissed as small, out of date, ignorant and inefficient. The Soviet air force was stated to have a total first-line strength of 16,500 machines, compared with almost 9,200 Allied aircraft. 'Their pilots are always reasonably competent, sometimes brilliant, and they have vast experience in short-range tactical operations in support of the Army', though not being nearly as well-trained or disciplined as their British and American counterparts.

It was the Red Army which posed by far the greatest threat. Despite sustaining an estimated ten or eleven million permanent casualties, it would still consist of just over seven million men by July, plus 600,000 NKVD (Special Security) troops. The vast majority of these forces were in the European theatre:

The Russian Army has developed a capable and experienced High Command. The Army is exceedingly tough, lives and moves on a lighter scale of maintenance than any Western Army and employs bold tactics based largely on disregard for losses in attaining a set objective. Security and deception are of a high quality at all levels. Equipment has improved rapidly throughout the war and is now good . . . On the other hand, the Russian Army is now suffering from heavy casualties and war-weariness. The standard of tactics and training is, on the whole, lower than that of the German Army . . . There is a marked shortage of well-educated and trained Staff Officers and intermediate commanders, which inevitably results in over-centralisation. There is widespread evidence that the Russian Command is finding considerable difficulty in maintaining discipline in the Russian Army abroad. Looting and drunkenness are prevalent and are symptoms of a war-weary army in contact with higher material standards than obtain at home. Any renewal of war in Europe would prove a severe strain on the Red Army.

Taking into account the internal security commitments of the Russians—notably in Poland—and the different size and shape of Red Army formations, the J.P.S. calculated that there would be the equivalent of 140 infantry divisions, 30 armoured divisions and 24 tank brigades facing any Allied land offensive into North-East Europe. By contrast, the

United Kingdom, its Dominions, the United States and the Poles would be able to muster 50 infantry divisions, 20 armoured divisions, 5 airborne divisions, 9 armoured or tank brigades and 15 infantry brigades in North-West Europe.

As for potential German help, it might be possible to put into the field a maximum of 10 divisions in the early stages of any campaign against the Soviet Union, though not by 1 July. The German General Staff and officer corps would probably choose to side with the Western Allies, as would the civil population on account of 'ingrained fear of the Bolshevik menace and of reprisals by the Russians'. Yet, many veterans would be relieved that the war was over, even though it had been lost. Some would be soured by defeat; some fearful of a return to the Eastern Front; some undermined by war-weariness and Soviet propaganda; some uneasy about changing sides, and some content to see the Western Allies and the Russians at each other's throats.

How would the outbreak of hostilities affect the various theatres? In Europe, the Russians might occupy much of Norway and exploit their predominance in the South East to cut off British access to the area, including Greece. In the Far East, the planned final offensive against Japan would have to be postponed, leading to a stalemate in the Japanese war. In India and most of the Middle East, attempts to stir up trouble could probably be contained—except in Persia and Iraq, where an extremely dangerous situation would arise:

> It appears almost certain that Russia would take the offensive in this area in view of the valuable oil resources to be gained and the extreme importance of these areas to us.

With only three Indian brigade groups to defend the region against an estimated eleven Soviet divisions, its loss would be unavoidable.

If a land campaign were unleashed into North-East Europe, naval superiority could be used in the Baltic to secure the left flank of the Allies and harry the right flank of the Russians. For the same reason, it would be wise to aim for the early capture of Stettin:

> This would appear to indicate that one of the main thrusts should be along the north German coast, assisted by amphibious hooks which would allow us to exploit our superiority in amphibious warfare.

The other main thrust would be on the axis Leipzig-Cottbus-Poznan-Breslau:

The main armoured fighting would probably develop east of the Oder-Neisse line and upon its outcome the result of the campaign would probably depend. If the result was favourable, we might reach the general line Danzig-Breslau. Any advance beyond this, however, would increase the danger resulting from the salient formed by Bohemia and Moravia, from which the Russians would be under no necessity to withdraw. Unless, therefore, we have won the victory we require west of the line Danzig-Breslau, it appears likely that we shall, in fact, be committed to a total war.

Facing odds of two-to-one against in armour and between three and four-to-one against in infantry, any such offensive would clearly be 'a hazardous undertaking'. With adequate warning—such as would follow from any realignment of Western public opinion prior to hostilities—the Russians might well be able to prevent any advance by Allied forces. They would probably hold the bulk of their armoured divisions well to the rear, as a strategic reserve ready to counter-attack east of the Oder and Neisse rivers if a breakthrough were achieved. All in all, the Joint Planners concluded that:

> There is no strength in our strategic position . . . we should be staking everything upon one great battle, in which we should be facing very heavy odds.

If a war were begun, it was likely to become total war, both long and costly:

> Our numerical inferiority on land renders it extremely doubtful whether we could achieve a limited and quick success, even if the political appreciation considered that this would suffice to gain our political object.[32]

According to Brooke's diary,[33] the Chiefs of Staff discussed the J.P.S. report on 24 May and 31 May; but it was not until 8 June that the outcome was communicated to the Prime Minister. The report had stated that, owing to 'the special need for secrecy', the normal staffs in the Service Departments had not been consulted. The Service chiefs were similarly cautious, keeping the full J.P.S. study to themselves and sending Churchill what Ismay described, in his covering minute, as just 'the bare

---

32. CAB 120/691: [No JPS reference] (Final), 22 May 1945—Operation 'UNTHINKABLE'
33. See pp. 242–3 below

facts, which they can elaborate in discussion with you, if you so desire. They felt,' Ismay added, 'that the less was put on paper on this subject the better'.

In four short paragraphs, they set out the latest estimate of Soviet and Allied land and air forces in Europe on 1 July. These were now summarised as: 64 United States divisions, 35 British and Dominion divisions, and 4 Polish divisions, with 23 of this total of 103 being armoured ones. Against these, the Russians would have 264 (equivalently calculated) divisions, including 36 armoured ones. There would be 6,048 tactical and 2,750 strategical Allied aircraft, the totals for the Russians being 11,802 and 960 respectively—a reduction in the estimate in the J.P.S. report. Though the Allies could achieve 'dominating superiority' at sea, it was 'clear from the relative strength of the respective land forces that we are not in a position to take the offensive with a view to achieving a rapid success'. The Chiefs of Staff concluded:

> Our view is, therefore, that once hostilities began, it would be beyond our power to win a quick but limited success and we should be committed to a protracted war against heavy odds. These odds, moreover, would become fanciful if the Americans grew weary and indifferent and began to be drawn away by the magnet of the Pacific war.[34]

Far from contesting these conclusions, Churchill immediately changed his approach. Instead of contemplating a Western attack, he directed the Service chiefs on 10 June to investigate how a *Soviet* assault could be resisted. His minute stated:

> I have read the Chiefs of Staff note on 'UNTHINKABLE' dated 8th June, which shows Russian preponderance of 2–1 on land.
> 2. If the Americans withdraw to their zone and move the bulk of their forces back to the United States and to the Pacific, the Russians have the power to advance to the North Sea and the Atlantic. Pray have a study made of how then we could defend our Island, assuming that France and the Low Countries were powerless to resist the Russian advance to the sea. What Naval forces should we need and where would they be based? What would be the strength of the Army required, and how should it be disposed? How much Air Force would be needed and where would the main airfields be located? Possession of airfields in Denmark would give us great advantage and keep open the sea passage to the Baltic where the Navy could operate.

---

34. CAB 120/691: Unnumbered Ismay minute, covering unnumbered COS report, 8 June 1945

The possession of bridgeheads in the Low Countries or France should also be considered.

3. By retaining the codeword 'UNTHINKABLE', the Staffs will realise that this remains a precautionary study of what, I hope, is still a purely hypothetical contingency.[35]

It was not until 11 July that the J.P.S. completed their comprehensive reply and it is, therefore, almost certain that Churchill never saw it. The 1945 General Election took place on 5 July, although the results could not be known until 26 July once the servicemen's votes had been counted. Churchill flew to France on 7 July, for his first significant rest since becoming Prime Minister five years earlier. On 15 July he flew from Bordeaux to Berlin for the Potsdam Conference, returning to London on 25 July to discover the following day that his Government had been heavily defeated.[36] Consequently, the second 'UNTHINKABLE' report—though preserved in the Secretariat file—seems not to have drawn comment from the Chiefs of Staff.

Nevertheless, it embodied the first J.P.S. attempt after the defeat of Germany to cater for potential military aggression by the Soviet Union against the United Kingdom. Although, once again, the normal staffs in the Service Departments could not be consulted because of 'the special need for secrecy', it gave a foretaste of the approach which the C.O.S. machine would adopt as the Soviet threat developed. Unlike the first 'UNTHINKABLE' report, it was in the form of a draft minute intended to be sent directly to the Prime Minister. No longer did the Joint Planners have to cast the United Kingdom in the unwelcome role of initiator. They were now facing the scenario with which they and the rest of the C.O.S. organisation were traditionally familiar: how to defend the country against aggression begun by others.

Four main methods of possible Soviet attack were examined. *Cutting British sea communications*, by air or submarine attack, was ruled out at least for several years. It would also take years for the Russians 'to build up the necessary amphibious forces and Merchant Navy to give them even a slight chance' of *invading the British Isles:*

---

35. CAB 120/691: P.M.'s Personal Min to Ismay for C.O.S. Committee, 10 June 1945
   The last three words, 'purely hypothetical contingency', were in Churchill's own handwriting and replaced 'highly improbable event' in the draft of this minute.

36. Martin Gilbert: *Never Despair—Winston S. Churchill, 1945–1965* (London, Heinemann, 1988), pp. 57, 59 & 105

We rule out the practicability of decisive invasion by airborne operations alone. In mounting a large-scale seaborne operation, the Russians would be faced with the considerable task of constructing a large amphibious fleet and training their personnel in a new method of warfare.

Though currently designed for close tactical operations in support of the Red Army, *Soviet air power* was great enough to pose a threat; but the Joint Planners were confident that Allied air forces would adequately be able to counter it. It would be possible to do this with existing squadrons initially. However, in order to go onto the offensive, there would need to be a return to levels of Anglo-American strength as they had been when Germany surrendered—230 fighter squadrons, 100 tactical bomber squadrons and 100 heavy bomber squadrons.

The real danger lay in the use of *rockets and pilotless aircraft*, with which the Soviet Union was entirely conversant:

> The Russians are, therefore, likely to begin large-scale production of these weapons at an early date. We must expect a far heavier scale of attack than the Germans were able to develop, and we do not at present see any method of effectively reducing this. This would be the main threat over the considerable period which must elapse before the Russians can contemplate any attempt at invasion.

Churchill had raised the question of retaining bridgeheads on the Continent. If practicable, this could reduce the danger of attack by long-range rocket and other new weapons. Yet, Soviet numerical superiority meant that no lengthy front could be maintained in Western Europe—and, unless such a front were held deep into France and the Low Countries, the scale of rocket attack would not be seriously reduced. Any bridgeheads selected would have to be in areas like Denmark, Western Holland, Le Havre, Brittany or the Cherbourg Peninsula, where a comparatively large area might be defensible by a relatively small force:

> Such bridgeheads would, however, offer the enemy a well-defined, compact target. Their defence would, therefore, impose a heavy and continuous drain on our resources . . . If used as bases for a return to the continent, we should be sacrificing surprise and would enable the enemy to build up against us at leisure.

Although naval and air power would mainly be relied upon to prevent invasion of the British Isles after the Russians overran Western Europe, garrisons would be needed for towns as well as mobile land forces to defeat any enemy troops who managed to reach the United Kingdom. Some 20 divisions would be required, most being deployed south of the line from the Wash to the Severn, with the highest concentration in the South East. Given that much equipment would be lost—as at Dunkirk— if the Allies were forced to withdraw from Western Europe, it would be necessary to remove from the Continent 'as much heavy equipment as possible as soon as war with Russia appears imminent'.

As its main conclusion, the second 'UNTHINKABLE' report stated:

> It is only by use of rockets and other new weapons that the Russians could develop any serious threat to the security of this country in the initial stages. Invasion or a serious attack upon our communications could only be undertaken after a period of preparation which must last some years.[37]

Given the way in which Western European defence was to develop during the Cold War, the second 'UNTHINKABLE' paper was revealing: it demonstrated how British military planners regarded Continental Europe as indefensible against Soviet land attack, even when Anglo-American forces were still close to their maximum wartime levels. Many of these ideas were to resurface in the Overall Strategic Plan[38] finalised in May 1947, despite the fact that in the meantime the atomic age had begun.

4. The J.I.C. and the Russians, 1946

Although the sustained Foreign Office attempt to 'infiltrate' the C.O.S. post-war planning machinery from 1942 had ended in failure in August 1944,[39] the model on which it had been based—the Joint Intelligence Sub-Committee—had continued to function with successive Foreign Office chairmen. *Changing Direction* is a history of British military planning for post-war defence, not British military intelligence about it. Yet, the J.I.C.'s findings (like the diplomats' opinions) had some bearing on what the Service chiefs decided, and merit some attention for that reason.

---

37. CAB 120/691: [No JPS reference] (Final), 11 July 1945—Operation 'UNTHINKABLE'
38. See CAB 21/2096: DO(47)44, 22 May 1947, reproduced in full as Appendix 7, pp. 370–87 below
39. See pp. 50–4, 68–74, 88–9, 103–7, 118–9 & 122–5 below

As has been seen, during 1944 the J.I.C. was involved on two occasions in assessing probable Soviet intentions and capabilities after the war. This was specifically to assist the work of the Post-Hostilities Planners.[40] On 18 December 1944, the J.I.C. had finalised a third paper, supposedly setting out its estimate of 'Russia's Strategic Interests and Intentions from the Point of View of her Security'. It shared the sympathetic and optimistic outlook of the Foreign Office at that time—which was hardly surprising given that a member of the F.O. Services Liaison Department had actually been its principal author.[41]

Just over a year later, on 2 January 1946, the Joint Intelligence Staff were issued with terms of reference by the J.I.C. to review the December 1944 paper

> in view of subsequent developments (which may have been contrary to Russia's expectations at the time) especially the strength of Russia's position relative to her Allies at the end of the European and Far Eastern wars, and in view of the use of the atomic bomb.[42]

However, a first attempt at the task did not entirely satisfy the Chiefs of Staff. On 28 February, the J.I.C. was instructed to amend it to include some estimate of the Soviet Union's internal problems and how these might affect her intentions and foreign policy. Furthermore, whilst the Chiefs of Staff generally agreed with the report's conclusion that

> Russia would pursue every means to seek her ends short of a major war, it was felt that a warning should be included in the paper of the dangers inherent in the pursuit of such a policy, in that it might not prove possible for a nation to avoid becoming involved in a war.[43]

The amended final report was produced the following day. As in the case of its predecessors, it could only be speculative—relying largely on 'deductions', 'reasonable conjecture' and very limited information:

> we have little evidence to show what view Russia herself takes of her strategic interests, or what policy she intends to pursue. We have practically no direct intelligence, of a detailed factual or statistical nature, on

---

40. See Section 2 above
41. See p. 136 below & footnote 87 thereon
42. CAB 81/132: JIC(46)1(0)(T.R.), 2 January 1946
43. CAB 81/132: JIC(46)1(0)(Supplementary T.R.), 28 February 1946

conditions in the different parts of the Soviet Union, and none at all on the intentions, immediate or ultimate, of the Russian leaders. For example, we have no intelligence whatever on two such crucial questions as whether Russia intends to continue her demobilisation during 1946 and whether Russian industry is to any substantial extent being reconverted from wartime requirements for the needs of peace.

Given the firm control exercised by the Soviet regime, intelligence was difficult to obtain:

> Decisions are taken by a small group of men, the strictest security precautions are observed and far less than in the case in the Western Democracies are the opinions of the masses taken into account.

During 1945, four factors would have newly influenced the Soviet leadership. From March onwards, when the Rhine had been crossed, the speed of the Western Allies' advance might have made the Russians fear that they would reach Berlin first and then tear up their previous agreement on zones of occupation. The Russians would also have seen the advent of the atomic bomb as 'a new threat to that security for which they have been striving ever since 1917'. British and American attitudes were appearing to harden against Soviet aspirations in South-East Europe and other areas; but it was also clear that both countries were 'incomparably weaker' than in the summer of 1945:

> Great Britain is faced with great man-power and financial problems leading to rapid demobilisation, while the United States has let her military forces disintegrate, and since the death of President Roosevelt has an executive which lacks decision.

On the other hand, the Soviet Union faced a 'gigantic' task of reconstruction. The J.I.C. saw no reason to doubt Molotov's statement that over 17,000 towns and 70,000 villages had been destroyed during the war, together with nearly 32,000 industrial enterprises and 98,000 collective farms. Despite all this, alone of the 'Big Three', the Soviet Union was engaged in a large-scale re-equipment of her land forces. Rebuilding the Soviet Navy would be even harder, given the loss of major shipbuilding centres to the Germans and their subsequent destruction:

> It is evident, however, from the energy displayed by the Soviet naval

representatives outside the U.S.S.R. in ferreting out naval information from shipbuilding to naval tactics, and embracing much technical matter including the construction of 16-inch guns, that the U.S.S.R. intends to pursue her policy of building a large navy . . . Russia now possesses about 210 submarines, including 10 ex-German. She takes a great interest in submarine warfare and in this particular arm of the Naval Service she has shown herself to be more proficient than in any other. She is, however, still inexperienced in attack tactics.

It appeared that some 4,500,000 men had been demobilised by 1 January 1946, leaving some 4,640,000 remaining in the Red Army, with a normal monthly intake of about 120,000. The gross loss of Soviet manpower due to the war was estimated at just below 14 million, including 11,200,000 permanent military casualties. Of the latter figure, some 6,200,000 were fatalities. At the present rate, it would take until 1952 for war casualties to be replaced.

Although it was the declared objective of Soviet policy to raise living-standards for the Russian people, Stalin had indicated that this—and the task of reconstruction—would take fifty years. Nor did the J.I.C. view it as anything other than a secondary Soviet aim. It would not be allowed to interfere with the goal of raising the industrial potential for defence purposes: 'If there is to be any conflict between them, the Soviet Government would let the additional increase in the standard of living go by the board.' The Soviet Union presented a phenomenon new in modern European history:

a vast land empire containing within its frontiers a large, youthful and rapidly expanding population, nearly all the raw materials essential for an adequate war economy, and an industry capable of supporting in the field armies substantially larger than those of any other Power in Europe.

During the war she had managed to mobilise some 22 million men, in comparison with about 14 million American and 12 million British Empire servicemen. It was tentatively estimated that she would not acquire atomic weapons before the early 1950s, and not in significant numbers until the period 1955–60. Some American economic experts had recently predicted that the burdens of the new Soviet Five-Year Plan would make it impracticable to construct an atomic bomb production plant. The J.I.C. was less complacent:

it would be dangerous to assume that the Soviet Union cannot develop the economic resources necessary for the building up of atomic bomb production plant and at the same time carry through their planned programme of reconstruction and long-term development. The Soviet rulers are not likely to be diverted from their fundamental aims by lack of outside assistance. Russia is prepared to do without economic assistance, if it does not suit her, and she has probably based her long-term economic plans on the assumption that she will not receive any.

The J.I.C. was insistent that the Soviet leaders anticipated reaching a predominant position eventually, without having to resort to war. This would not prevent them trying to secure objectives by bluff, but they 'must also realise that America would be unlikely to stand aloof' from any major conflict. The Soviet Union was therefore 'likely to be deterred by the existence of the atomic bomb'.

In the United Nations Organisation the Soviet Government was keen to play a leading part:

> Unlike the policy of some other countries, there is no element of altruism in the Russian attitude to U.N.O. Russia intends to participate for purely selfish reasons and ends. Russia will seek to emphasise that she is a progressively-minded Power, concerned with the welfare of the downtrodden; nevertheless, her only intention will be to derive the maximum benefit for her own policy.

Involvement in the U.N.O. would enable the Soviet Union to concern herself in all world affairs, to appeal to peoples over the heads of their governments, and to use the veto to prevent the organisation from endangering her interests. She favoured the predominance of the Security Council and the 'Big Three' as additional insurance against U.N.O. interference. Yet, there were two points of reservation to be made about any Soviet wish for co-operation with the Americans and British in this context:

> Firstly, that Soviet vital interests will never be sacrificed for the sake of such co-operation; and secondly, that the Soviet Union will rely on its own strength, and not on international agreement, as the ultimate basis of its defence. The first of these reservations limits the field of Big Three co-operation to subjects where there is a coincidence of interests—chiefly in preventing the resurgence as military powers of the States defeated in the 1939–45 war.

There were already signs of the Russians 'concentrating their aggressive tactics' on issues where they might drive a wedge between the British and American Governments, and encouraging left-wing parties and 'anti-imperialist' movements wherever possible. Although the Comintern had been formally dissolved in 1943, it was certain that much of its machinery had survived and was currently 'under the exclusive control of the Soviet Government':[44]

> Although this control was considerably weakened during the war, it is now being tightened again, and in countries where Russian influence is predominant Russia gives direct support to the local Communist Party and exercises direct control. We believe that, in more distant countries, such as France, Italy, Holland, Belgium and Norway, the control exercised by Russia is less peremptory and detailed . . . All the devices of publicity and propaganda are used to ensure that foreign Communist Parties follow the official Russian line, and there is evidence that Dimitrov and other foreign Communists in Moscow, who had previously formed the praesidium of the Comintern, continued during the war period to work in the closest collaboration with the People's Commissariat of State Security.[45] This Commissariat is the lineal descendant of the O.G.P.U. . . . There is no evidence of direct political instruction to the Communist Party in Great Britain since the dissolution of the Comintern, but in America the dismissal of the Communist leader Earl Browder, who interpreted the Tehran agreement as calling for the dissolution of the Communist Party in the United States, shows that Russia can still exact obedience by indirect methods.

In the long run, it was unlikely that the Russians would be satisfied with the degree of control which they could exercise over the working-class movements throughout the world by means of Communist parties alone:

> They will therefore infiltrate into democratic international organisations until Communist influence is predominant. Russia is concentrating at

---

44. See footnote 101 to p. 141 below
45. Georgi Dimitrov (1882–1949), Bulgarian revolutionary, was Executive Secretary of the Comintern in Moscow from 1934 until its ostensible dissolution in 1943. Thereafter he directed the section of the CPSU Central Committee which continued to control the foreign (i.e. non-Russian) Communist Parties, until becoming the post-war dictator of Bulgaria in 1945. The People's Commissariat of State Security—the N.K.G.B.—existed in parallel with Beria's N.K.V.D. from February to July 1941, and again from April 1943 to March 1946. It specialised in activities comparable to those of the N.K.V.D. in conquered or reconquered countries. When not directing the N.K.G.B., its head—Vsevolod Merkulov—worked directly for Beria. Both were executed in the power struggle after Stalin's death in 1953.

present on the World Federation of Trade Unions as the most suitable and effective organisation, and she is also backing up international movements, such as the World Youth Congress and the International Women's Organisation, in which Communist influence already predominates.[46]

In spite of the changes to international Communist policy caused by the war, three main points of 'the old Comintern programme' were once again to the fore in Soviet propaganda:

> First, reformist Socialists in other countries are attacked and it is asserted that Social Democrats are supporters of imperialist wars and that they have betrayed Marxism by their collaboration with the capitalist régimes. They are represented in propaganda as being 'the agents of capitalism within the working class'. Secondly, the Communist Parties are ordered to conduct anti-imperialist campaigns in colonies and semi-colonial territories. Thirdly, the first strategic aim of the Communist Parties in each country is still to bring under their influence the majority of the members of the working class, especially the younger generation, and the mass organisations of the proletariat, *e.g.*, trades unions, factory committees, co-operative societies, sports clubs and cultural organisations.[47]

Turning to the geographical situation in which the post-war Soviet Union found herself, the J.I.C. clearly identified the main strengths and weaknesses. Only from the west could a major strategic land threat be mounted against the Russians; but they now enjoyed frontiers corresponding to those established by Peter the Great and lost as a result of the First World War. In addition, Eastern Galicia and the port of Königsberg had been gained, together with defensive depth equivalent to the width of Poland—'the maintenance of whose Government under

---

46.   See p. 362 below. As well as infiltrating existing international organisations, such as the W.F.T.U., and turning them into front bodies, the Soviet Union founded a propaganda network of such international groups in the 1940s and 1950s headed by the World Peace Council. All of the principal ones were still in existence at the end of the Cold War. See also: footnote 89 to p. 224 below; Sir Clive Rose: *The Soviet Propaganda Network—A Directory of Organisations Serving Soviet Foreign Policy* (London, Pinter Publishers/New York, St Martin's Press, 1988); Paul Mercer: *'Peace' of the Dead—The Truth behind the Nuclear Disarmers* (London, Policy Research Publications, 1986)

47.   Given the similarities of the themes and analysis in this section of the J.I.C. report and Christopher Warner's soon-to-be-written memorandum on 'The Soviet Campaign against this Country and Our Response to It' (see pp. 262 & 359–63 below), it seems highly probable that the Foreign Office had—once again—substantially influenced the J.I.C.'s consideration of post-war Soviet problems.

Russian influence is a major interest of Russian policy'—plus the width of the Soviet Zone of Germany.

Soviet occupation of Romania, Bulgaria and Hungary—'whose Governments she is also determined to keep in a position of subservience to Russian policy'—conferred similar advantages in Central and South-East Europe. In the Far East, the Soviet Union had restored her losses from the 1904–5 war with Japan, enhancing her strategic position still further by the acquisition of the Kurile Islands. Yet, in the south, there was no similar 'belt' of 'satellite States'. Her frontier with Turkey was slightly less favourable than prior to 1914 and she no longer retained the zone of influence in Persia agreed with the British in 1907:

> In this area, therefore, the aim of Russian policy is to include Turkey and North Persia in the belt of border States where her influence will be paramount, in order to improve her strategic position so as to ensure that these countries shall never be used as a base of attack against her. She will use her claims for a new régime of control in the Straits and the establishment of a Russian base there, for the cession of Kars, Ardahan and Artvin by Turkey, for oil concessions in North Persia, and for the 'democratic' reconstruction of the Government at Tehran as methods for this end. She will use every means, short of becoming involved in a major conflict with the Great Powers, to attain it.

There was recognition that defensive objectives could spill over into expansionism. Thus, given the Soviet Union's interests in preventing Scandinavia being used as a 'jumping-off' base for offensive operations against her, the J.I.C. concluded that she would probably 'seek to extend her influence over the whole of Scandinavia by whatever means she can'. Her western frontier could be seriously threatened only by Germany, acting alone or in combination with other powers. This would encourage a policy of keeping Germany weak and isolated from potential allies:

> The intense Russian pressure which has recently been directed towards the fusion of the Communist and Social Democratic Parties, and the continuous propaganda carried out by the Communist Party in favour of a unified and centralised Germany, suggest that Russia may also have more positive aims . . . In order to prepare the ground for Communism, it is to be expected that she will seek to break down what remains of the social structure by fostering prolonged economic depression. By such means, Russia may hope, in time, to create a unified Communist Germany under her own control.

As it would be a major Soviet strategic interest to ensure that Poland could never again be used as a base for hostile operations, the Soviet Union would be 'reluctant to withdraw the major part of her troops' from that country 'until she is satisfied that her influence in Poland is assured'.

In Western Europe and the Mediterranean, intrigues could be expected to involve the Franco regime in Spain, the government of Portugal, Tripolitania and—via Tito—Venezia Giulia. The Soviet Union's principal interest, however, remained the denial to the Western Powers of territory and resources which could be used for hostile action against her:

> The Soviet Government's relations with the Western Powers are governed by the fear that sooner or later there will be formed a Western European bloc hostile to the Soviet Union, and their policy to each of the countries of Western Europe is primarily directed towards preventing this.

Powerful Communist parties would be used to increase Soviet influence in Italy and France, at the expense of the United Kingdom, which was regarded as 'the natural leader' of any Western European group of states. In South-Eastern Europe, by contrast, Soviet-backed minority Governments were already in place in Romania and Bulgaria. Soviet policy would thus be one of consolidation rather than expansion. Only if the Russians were prepared to sacrifice good relations with the United Kingdom, would attempts be made to bring Greece and the Aegean Islands under their control. Yet, pressure on Turkey would continue, in order to gain control of the Black Sea Straits and

> in order to detach her from British influence, to cause her to terminate the Anglo-Turkish Alliance, and to make her part of the Russian zone of influence with a Turkish Government subservient to Moscow . . . We have no intelligence enabling us to predict whether, if she succeeds in her aim in Turkey, Russia will use her newly-gained position there to put forward further claims and seek to expand her area of predominant influence still further into the Eastern Mediterranean . . . and the Middle East.

Nevertheless, her approach would be cautious, given the risk of generating sufficient opposition to constitute the threat of a major war with the United Kingdom alone or in combination with the United States.

A similar strategy could be expected presently in Northern Persia, as it was from there that aerial attacks against Soviet oilfields in the Caucasus could most reliably be launched. Subsequently, attempts might be made to stir up trouble in the Arab world by fanning the flames of Kurdish nationalism and Armenian discontent. No action had yet been taken against Afghanistan or India. In the Far East, the main Soviet concern would clearly be the future of Japan. When Allied troops withdrew from Japan and from their zone in Korea, five years hence, trouble might well ensue. There was also the potential for clashes with China over the future control of Manchuria.

As a general conclusion, the J.I.C. stated that:

> The long-term aim of the Russian leaders is to build up the Soviet Union into a position of strength and greatness fully commensurate with her vast size and resources. They estimate the time needed to attain it to be of the order of 50 years. They are convinced that an ultimate position of predominance in the world will inevitably result from the strength of Russia's national resources and potential, and from the superiority of the Soviet system.

Despite the incentives towards expansionism in strategically important regions, it was not thought likely that the Soviet Union would feel tempted to resort to a major war to obtain her ends:

> We remain . . . convinced that she will make every effort to avoid war in the period [of military and industrial reconstruction] . . . We have insufficient evidence to enable us to estimate firmly how long this period is likely to last. It is, however, unlikely that her oil output will have been restored to pre-war level before 1950, or that she will have significant quantities of atomic weapons before about 1955–60, though she may develop biological warfare agents a good deal earlier.

By 1955–60, Soviet industry would have made the country self-sufficient in time of war. Manpower losses should have been made good by about 1952, and the first post-war Five-Year Plan was due for completion in January 1951. At that time the situation would need to be reviewed, but at least until then 'it should be safe to conclude that Russia will do her best to avoid a major conflict'. As the Chiefs of Staff had instructed the J.I.C. to point out, this state of affairs could still lead to disaster. The main Soviet aims seemed to be security, reconstruction and—in the short term, at any rate—the avoidance of actions likely to provoke a war with the United States and/or the British Commonwealth:

But we have also concluded that, in seeking a maximum degree of security, Russian policy will be aggressive by all means short of war. In brief, although the intention may be defensive, the tactics will be offensive, and the danger always exists that Russian leaders may misjudge how far they can go without provoking war with America or ourselves. It is not for us to recommend policy, but it is clear that the situation will require constant watching.[48]

One more J.I.C. paper is worthy of note, because it was initiated at precisely the time when the long divergence of Foreign Office and C.O.S. views about post-war planning and the Soviet Union came to an end. It also coincided with the combined efforts of Bevin and Alanbrooke to counter Attlee's opposition to Britain's role in the Middle East.[49] On 2 April 1946, Christopher Warner, head of the Foreign Office's Northern Department, had circulated his watershed memorandum on 'The Soviet Campaign against this Country and Our Response to It'.[50] The following day, at the instigation of the Foreign Office, the J.I.C. decided to commission an appreciation of 'Russia's Strategic Interests and Intentions in the Middle East'.[51] The Joint Intelligence Staff were promptly instructed to prepare an examination of 'the kind of material which the Russians might exploit, i.e. among the Kurds, Armenians, etc., in the Middle East area, generally'. That such considerations had been put aside since the ending of the 1939–41 Nazi-Soviet pact was clear:

there is information available in the form of previous reports of the [Joint Intelligence] Sub-Committee prepared in 1940 and 1941 on the Russian threat to Kurdistan and probably also appreciations in the War Office on Middle East problems dating from the same period.[52]

On 6 June, exactly two years after the Western invasion of Nazi-occupied Europe, the J.I.C. issued its assessment of the strategic regional threat posed by its former Soviet ally. Although based on the wider report of 1 March, there was a distinct toughening of language:

---

48. CAB 81/132: JIC(46)1(0)(Final)(Revise), 1 March 1946
49. See pp. 252–64 below
50. See pp. 262 & 359–63 below
51. CAB 81/94: JIC(46)16th Mtg (0)(2), 3 April 1946
52. CAB 81/132: JIC(46)38(0)(T.R.), 4 April 1946

The Soviet Government have . . . resumed the traditional Russian policy of southern expansion, which was temporarily suspended between the fall of the Czarist régime and the war of 1939. The Soviet Government will implement this historic policy by every means short of war. Their ultimate goal is clear, but the intermediate moves will be opportunist and their order of priority flexible.

Given the vital importance to the Soviet Union of her Caucasian oilfields and the displacement eastwards of her industrial centre of gravity, the Middle East was adjacent to her most vulnerable flank:

The Soviet Union regards it as essential to eliminate any strong Power or combination of Powers from areas in which she is vulnerable. She has appreciated that the British Commonwealth constitutes a potential threat to her security in the Middle East, and it is, therefore, part of her policy to weaken the British position in that area.

Furthermore, she could expect to find 'a less solidly united Anglo-United States front' in the Middle East than in other parts of the world, and she had a strategic interest in being able to deny Middle Eastern oil resources to the British, even if unable to exploit them fully herself owing to transport difficulties.

In pursuing these aims, the Soviet Union would 'continue to make the greatest possible use of the unrest and economic want' which existed in the Middle East, and would 'neglect no opportunity of exploiting nationalist feeling in order to weaken the British position'. She would try to exploit her status as a Moslem Power, whilst—irrespective of inconsistencies—also 'championing the causes of Christian minorities when it suits her book to do so'. There were already signs that the Soviet Union was using the Orthodox Church as a means of reverting to Russia's pre-revolutionary role as the protector of Christendom and the heir of the Orthodox Byzantine Empire. However, her main effort in respect of Middle Eastern minorities would be directed at the Kurds, stimulating their nationalist feelings whilst carefully concealing the goal of communisation.

Arab nationalism would also offer opportunities to the Russians, especially in Egypt, Iraq and Palestine:

to the Arab world as a whole, Great Britain looms large as the Great Power most closely interested in the area; this inevitably entails points of friction, and means that Great Britain is the Power most likely to be blamed by dissatisfied nationalists. By the same process Soviet Russia, as Great Britain's potential opponent in the Middle East, comes naturally to be regarded, by short-sighted Arab patriots, as a useful ally in their struggle to rid themselves of apparent restrictions on their full independence.

Nor should the attractiveness of Communism be ignored, so far as 'certain elements among the student and labouring classes' of Middle Eastern peoples were concerned. For the most part, however, 'although the [Middle Eastern Communist Parties'] leaders are thoroughly indoctrinated, the majority of sympathisers are not interested in Marxism, and do not understand it'. Economic aspirations, rather than doctrinal convictions, explained their propensity to be influenced by the Russians.

The J.I.C. listed its estimate of Soviet strategic intentions in four component areas of the Middle East. In Turkey the aims would be the establishment of a government subservient to Russian interests, a revision of the status of the Black Sea Straits, and the siting there of a Soviet base. Pressure on Persia would continue, with attempts to undermine British interests in the south and to dominate the whole country. In the Arab world, anti-British feeling would be fuelled with the intention of weakening and ultimately supplanting British influence; for example, the difficult situation in Palestine would be exploited to the full. Only in Afghanistan and India was the J.I.C. prepared to concede that the Russians might 'play a waiting game'.

Lack of reliable information from within the Soviet Union was fully acknowledged:

> Russia's military preparations within her own frontiers, if known to us, might provide important pointers to her future intentions. We have, however, insufficient intelligence concerning both the Order of Battle and the locations of Red Army formations and Air Forces to enable us to form any picture of their main areas of deployment.

The 'Russian search for security' was seen as 'a constantly expanding process without fixed limits'. Soviet Middle Eastern policy would probably be one of 'gradual penetration'; but, although Soviet aims would disrupt the international and internal arrangements of the countries in the region, 'they do not at present include any intention to collide head-on with Britain'. The Soviet Union's tactics would be more flexible and less predictable than her aims. Sudden opportunities would be seized, and there would be no need for one set of objectives to be secured before another came under attack:

> Furthermore, the Soviet Union would not be deterred by any moral considerations from advancing as rapidly as possible, if she thought she could do so without a major war. In carrying out Russia's historic policy the Soviet Government may be expected to make full use of all modern methods short of war (such as the war of nerves, the fifth column and the puppet government).[53]

On 7 June 1946, the Chiefs of Staff approved this J.I.C. report for circulation to the Prime Minister, Foreign Secretary and American Service chiefs, among others.[54] They could have been forgiven, as they did so, for reflecting on the extent to which their warnings, two years earlier, about the nature of the post-war world had been borne out by events.

5. The Secret Alliance: Anglo-American Links, 1946–47

C.O.S. opinion had always been sceptical about the notion of entrusting post-war security to a 'world organisation'. Foreign Office emphasis on that approach had led to repeated clashes with the Service chiefs in 1944.[55] They viewed the key to future security as the continuation of the Combined Chiefs of Staff[56] after the war. It is clear that, by February 1946 at the latest, their American counterparts agreed with them. The question was: should Anglo-American machinery for military collaboration continue to function openly, or would it 'have to go underground' for political reasons? On 16 March 1946, the British Joint Staff Mission in Washington—who represented the C.O.S. on the Combined Chiefs of Staff Committee—reported that both sides were 'completely of one mind'. They knew that it was not a question of producing arguments to persuade one another that the C.C.S. should continue to operate:

> The problem is a far more difficult one in as much as we must produce

---

53. CAB 81/132: JIC(46)38(0)(Final)(Revise), 6 June 1946 See also p. 272 below
54. CAB 21/2086: COS(46)90th Mtg (3), 7 June 1946 See also p. 272 below
55. See pp. 68–70 & 119–43 below
56. See footnote 42 to p. 68 below

arguments which will persuade our Heads of State that we have a good case which they in turn can explain to the world.

While international tension remained high, the American Chiefs of Staff were confident that the C.C.S. would safely carry on 'at least for six months and perhaps for a year or even more'; but they did not think that the U.S. State Department would support the raising of the issue of permanent military collaboration, given the current level of international friction.[57]

It was decided, therefore, to prepare a draft report to the President and Prime Minister, which the Combined Chiefs of Staff would hold in readiness 'to be produced if an unforseen challenge should be directed against [Anglo-American] collaboration'. The draft bluntly set out the limitations of the new United Nations Organisation:

So long as the power of the veto remains in the Charter of the United Nations, there can be no co-ordinated military planning in that organisation to meet a situation in which there is disagreement among the great powers. This leaves a serious gap in the individual security systems of the United States and Great Britain which from the military point of view it is highly desirable to fill.

Commenting on this, the Joint Planning Staff pointed out that the head of the British Joint Staff Mission, Field Marshal Wilson, felt that it might be difficult to persuade the U.S. Chiefs of Staff 'to put forward the chief military argument, namely the weakness inherent in the United Nations Charter owing to the effect of the veto, since there are political objections to using this argument to the American public'. The Joint Planners endorsed Wilson's view that any attempt to delete this argument must be resisted 'since it is the crucial issue'.[58]

At their meeting on 22 May, the Chiefs of Staff endorsed this approach. In an attempt to square the circle, Ismay stated that it should be stressed that 'the Combined Chiefs of Staff organisation, far from being rendered redundant by the institution of the [U.N.] Military Staff Committee, would in fact be a valuable complement to it'. The

---

57. CAB 121/349: JSM 204 (SOCNOC), J.S.M. to C.O.S., 16 March 1946 The telegram indicating the U.S. Chiefs' preference for an 'underground' arrangement (JSM 182, 9 February 1946) is still retained under section 3(4) of the Public Records Act. However, it is cited in CAB 121/349: JP(46)39(Final), 20 May 1946.
58. CAB 121/349: JP(46)39(Final), 20 May 1946

V.C.I.G.S., Lieutenant-General Simpson, added that any tendency by the Americans to advocate that the C.C.S. should continue covertly rather than openly 'should be strongly resisted'. This was agreed.[59]

As the British had largely anticipated, the draft statement for the President and Prime Minister was 'pigeon-holed at the request of the U.S. Chiefs of Staff'. It was not until the end of January 1947 that the British Joint Staff Mission in Washington re-opened the issue with the British Service chiefs. The J.S.M. pointed out that 'most of the work done by the C.C.S. and its principal sub-committees relates to problems in Italy'. These would largely disappear with the signing of the Italian Peace Treaty, so there was a risk that the continuation of the Combined Chiefs of Staff 'might shortly become the object of adverse criticism in certain sections of Congress and the press'. The J.S.M. had reviewed the draft paper prepared the previous May and now felt that the case for collaboration

> should not rest upon the immaturity of U.N.O., nor upon the lack of security inherent in the Veto. We should prefer to stress the fact that, as it is unthinkable for our two nations to be opposed in any war, we must be ready to make our combined effort against any aggressor both as effective and as economical as possible. Economy by avoidance of duplication is not only a practical ideal but one which should commend itself politically to both countries.

The Joint Staff Mission had, in fact, come to realise that by far the greatest part of Anglo-American military collaboration could be—and, indeed, was being—maintained by the individual British Service Missions directly with their corresponding American Service Departments. Seldom was it necessary for collaborative matters to be handled at C.C.S. level:

> We are of the opinion, therefore, that this collaboration could be effectively continued after the dissolution of the Combined Chiefs of Staff *provided* we were allowed to maintain Joint Missions on the present lines and on an appropriate scale . . . The departure of Field Marshal Wilson at the end of March, which is likely to coincide with the ratification of the Italian Peace Treaty, provides a possible opportunity of dissolving the Combined Chiefs of Staff Committee with a flourish of trumpets, under cover of which a

---

59. CAB 121/349: COS(46)81st Mtg (6), 22 May 1946

statement that British Joint Service Missions would continue in Washington for good reason (which could be given) might in fact be welcomed here by a considerable majority.

The J.S.M. recognised that the American Chiefs of Staff might prefer to leave well alone, if the President was prepared to see the C.C.S. Committee continue for at least another year. That would, of course, be welcome.[60] The important point was that, as events had developed, the continuation of the unprecedented level of Anglo-American military collaboration, begun with the creation of the C.C.S. in February 1942, would be assured for the future—whether the formal structure of the Combined Chiefs of Staff remained in existence or not.[61]

One major development in the meantime had been an American approach to the Prime Minister about the common military use of ports and air bases by the U.S. and United Kingdom. Attlee had requested the views of the Chiefs of Staff on 27 August 1946, and the matter was discussed in depth three days later. Predictably, the Service chiefs seized their opportunity. The Chief of the Naval Staff, Sir John Cunningham, thought that the initiative had arisen from the wish of the U.S. Navy for unrestricted access to Malta and Gibraltar:

> The U.S. State Department's approach was a most important advance and one that should receive our strongest support. In his opinion we should accept it and every effort should be made to obtain complete reciprocity throughout the world between the British Empire and the United States.[62]

The matter was taken up with the Americans by the Foreign Secretary, Ernest Bevin, in September, and the Chiefs of Staff continued to press for equivalent arrangements to apply to military aircraft and airfields as well as to warships and ports.[63] On 11 December, the Foreign Office duly received confirmation from Washington that the continuation of reciprocal wartime arrangements for naval visits (and existing more

---

60. CAB 121/350: FMW 287, J.S.M. to C.O.S., 30 January 1947
61. In the event, the C.C.S. was wound up only in 1949, after the creation of N.A.T.O. See Richard A. Best Jr.: *Co-operation with Like-minded Peoples—British Influences on American Security Policy, 1945–1949* (Greenwood Press, Westport, Connecticut, 1986), p. 36
62. CAB 121/349: COS(46)133rd Mtg (5)(Confidential Annex), 30 August 1946
63. CAB 121/349: COS Sec Min 1071/6, Ismay to Addis, 4 September 1946; COS(46) 136th Mtg (7)(Confidential Annex), 6 September 1946

limited arrangements for the mutual use of air facilities) had been agreed by the State Department.[64]

Also at the end of August 1946 had occurred a dramatic development leading to the reactivation of the 'UNTHINKABLE' file, which had lain dormant since the completion of the second J.P.S. report a year earlier. On 30 August, Field Marshal Wilson sent Ismay a 'Private and Eyes Only' telegram from the Joint Staff Mission in Washington:

> 1. We had lunch with the United States Chiefs of Staff today and a very frank and informal discussion afterwards.
>
> 2. The United States Chiefs of Staff felt strongly that the state of affairs in Europe had reached a stage when the uncontrollable developments of events arising from some local incident might grow into a major conflict, however unwilling Russia or ourselves might be to become involved, and that it would be reprehensible if we did not start immediately to prepare an appreciation of the broad European situation as opposed to the local situation regarding Venezia Giulia.[65] This appreciation would be with the object of uncovering the many diverse problems which would inevitably lead to the production of an inter-Allied plan to be used in the event of aggression by Russia.
>
> 3. Their thinking agrees with ours in that any reinforcements despatched to stabilise an attack in the Venezia Giulia area would no doubt arrive in that area too late to be of use in the preliminary stages, as at that time the conflagration would have ceased to be local and would probably have spread to central Europe. Therefore, any reinforcement plans would have to be based on the possibility of their being utilised in any area to support operations which might grow out of a local act of aggression.
>
> 4. Assuming that an attack in the Venezia Giulia area would rapidly develop into a general conflict in Europe, with Russia as main aggressor, it was apparent that planning should cover two phases (A) stabilisation of the situation and formation of a bridgehead (B) offensive operations to readjust the situation.

Wilson reported the American Service chiefs' view that the opening phase must involve withdrawing from the respective Anglo-American

---

64. CAB 121/350: Telegram No 7057, Inverchapel to F.O., 11 December 1946
65. At the end of the war, Tito had laid claim to the whole of the Italian province of Venezia Giulia, including the major port of Trieste. The dispute reached crisis proportions, with serious prospects of an attack on the occupying Allied forces by Yugoslav partisans. With the British and Americans determined not to give way, the threat eventually failed to materialise.

occupation zones into a bridgehead. The U.S. Army Chief of Staff, General Eisenhower, seemed to favour this being in the Low Countries rather than in Italy or elsewhere. Choosing the Low Countries would bring Allied forces under the protection of air cover from forces based in the United Kingdom, would involve only short lines of communication with bases in the United Kingdom, and would help to protect the British Isles from long-range weapons launched from the Continent:

> Whether the Low Countries were decided upon or not, it was essential to agree between us in the first instance where a bridgehead was to be held and to coordinate an overall plan for a strategic withdrawal to that area.

Turning to the second phase—that of counter-offensive operations—Eisenhower felt that a self-contained plan would be essential, so that it would not be thwarted by the 'considerable disorganisation' which would undoubtedly follow a Soviet attack. His air force counterpart, General Carl Spaatz, referred to the restrictiveness of British airstrips from which to operate American B-29 squadrons, as an example of the type of problem which would be exposed in the course of detailed planning. The American Service chiefs told the Joint Staff Mission that:

> the United States planners would be instructed to commence preparing an overall appreciation immediately. They [the U.S. Service chiefs] proposed all future discussion to be restricted to a Chiefs of Staff and Planners level, with the possible exception of the incorporation of a Ministry of Transport Planner. On no account at this stage should discussions be permitted outside this level on either side of the Atlantic and the absolute minimum should be committed to paper. When an outline plan of action had crystallised from the overall appreciation, our respective Commanders-in-Chief designate in Europe and their Chiefs of Staff should then be brought in. The Americans are anxious to agree on the command organisation to be set up for the various fronts which operations might cover and that their composition should be considered at an early date.[66]

The Chiefs of Staff responded to this bombshell on 3 September. As in the Joint Planners' second 'UNTHINKABLE' report in July 1945, the scenario was one of possible Soviet aggression, rather than a campaign to be initiated by the British and Americans. The British Service chiefs told

---

66. CAB 120/691: Telegram FMW 271, Wilson to Ismay, 30 August 1946

Field Marshal Wilson in Washington that they were 'in broad agreement' with the U.S. Chiefs of Staff, and that C.O.S. planners would be ready to *'exchange information'* with U.S. planners who were expected to be in Paris in mid-September:

> We have underlined the words 'exchange information' because it is on this basis and on this basis alone that we have felt able to accede to the wishes of the U.S. Chiefs of Staff for talks on the Staff level. If the matter were to develop into anything more than an exchange of information and it was thought necessary to extend the study circle, we should immediately have to seek Ministerial authority for proceeding.

The message to Wilson confirmed that the most rigid security precautions were being taken, with copies of the telegrams between Ismay and Wilson being issued 'for the personal information of each of the Chiefs of Staff and to *nobody else'*. In view of this there could be no question of a Ministry of Transport planner being brought into the picture.[67]

Within a fortnight, this careful approach was in tatters: the C.I.G.S., Field Marshal Montgomery, was on a 'private visit' to Canada and the United States. He decided unilaterally that

> the time had come for Britain, Canada, and the U.S.A. to co-operate closely in all defence matters; discussions should deal not only with standardisation [of weapons] but should cover the whole field of co-operation and combined action in the event of war. Obviously it would save time, and help me when I got to Washington, if I could get the agreement of the Canadian Prime Minister before I left Canada. I therefore asked if I could stop for a couple of hours at Ottawa on my journey to the U.S.A. and see Mr Mackenzie King, and this was arranged. He agreed in all respects with my suggestions and authorised me to inform the President of the United States accordingly. I reported the result of this meeting to the Chiefs of Staff in London, and wondered how my activities would be viewed in Whitehall circles.[68]

---

67. CAB 120/691: Telegram 2984, C.O.S. to Wilson, 3 September 1946 (emphasis in original)
68. Viscount Montgomery, *The Memoirs of Field-Marshal Montgomery* (London, Collins, 1958), p. 438 In their accounts, Montgomery and his later biographer Nigel Hamilton (*Monty: The Field-Marshal, 1944–1976* (London, Hamish Hamilton, 1986) pp. 656–9) claim too much credit for him in securing agreement by the Canadians and Americans for unified strategic defence planning *'before* another war was thrust upon them'. The process was already under way. The question was: at what stage should the Combined Chiefs of Staff involve the Heads of Government? Montgomery successfully did so, but at the cost of bypassing his own political masters and alienating his fellow Service chiefs.

With the cat out of the bag, the Prime Minister now had to be informed. Attlee telegraphed to the C.I.G.S. in Washington on 14 September, warning him that

> The issues now raised are of the utmost importance and potential value, and any leakage would have the gravest consequences . . . I note that you are meeting the United States Chiefs of Staff on Monday. While there is no objection to further exchanges of information or even discussion of methods of procedure, you should be careful to avoid entering into any specific commitments.[69]

The level of distrust between the C.I.G.S. and his fellow Service chiefs created by these manoeuvres can be gauged from the request by General Hollis—telegraphed to the J.S.M. Secretary on 16 September—for a separate report on Montgomery's meeting with the U.S. Chiefs of Staff scheduled for later that day. Clearly, the other Chiefs of Staff lacked confidence in any account which the C.I.G.S. himself might give:

> We assume that Field Marshal Wilson will be present at today's meeting with U.S. Chiefs of Staff. If so, I think Chiefs here would appreciate a personal report from Field Marshal Wilson giving his account of how things go.

Montgomery had claimed that Eisenhower had been keen for him to raise the question of combined strategic defence planning with President Truman. Eisenhower had also told him of other U.S. politicians already aware of the moves being made. Hollis's telegram continued:

> We are a little puzzled this end at one aspect of these developments which otherwise seem most promising if this *carte blanche* attitude of Americans is a reality. We understood all along that U.S. Chiefs of Staff laid great emphasis on keeping all this business clear of their Ministers. We conformed but felt that we were walking rather a tight rope. Now we learn from C.I.G.S. that 'The Secretaries of War and Navy were already fully in the picture as to what had already been going on in this matter below the surface'. Frankly, Prime Minister was a bit disturbed at possibility of State Department getting in on this with all that that might entail, and Chiefs of

---

69. CAB 120/691: Telegram No 3080, P.M. to Wilson for Montgomery, 14 September 1946 The text was almost certainly drafted within the Chiefs of Staff organisation.

Staff here share his anxiety. I do not yet know how our Foreign Secretary has reacted.[70]

On 18 September, Field Marshal Wilson sought to reassure Whitehall:

Although I have not been present at discussions with Eisenhower and American Chiefs of Staff, C.I.G.S. has kept me fully in the picture . . . He seems to have been at pains to make it clear to Americans that he was not speaking as a representative of the C.O.S. Committee but would of course report American views to his colleagues together with recommendations for certain action. My presence at meetings might have conveyed opposite impression . . . No action on any of the subjects discussed will be taken here until we get instructions from C.O.S. in London after return of C.I.G.S. . . . C.I.G.S. visit here has gone very well and many high ranking U.S. officers have remarked on it and on change of attitude in the Press towards him.

Yet, Wilson also expressed 'surprise' that the American Secretaries of State for the Navy and the Army had been let into the picture:

My understanding is that in all three countries knowledge of what is going on is to be strictly confined to heads of Governments and the Service Chiefs and their intimate Service Advisers. Can only hope [that the] circle in Washington will not be further widened. American Chiefs of Staff are, I think, as 'security-conscious' as we are.[71]

Meanwhile, the anticipated trip to Paris by the U.S. Directors of Plans had materialised, and by 27 September they were holding talks with the C.O.S. organisation in London. It was agreed to send the Future Planning Section of the J.P.S. to Washington in November. This special senior team had been set up in the summer and issued with terms of reference—'to provide a reasoned background against which H.M. Government can formulate Commonwealth Defence Policy in its widest aspects'—on 20 August.[72] In anticipation of the F.P.S. visit, three copies of the revised report on Future Development in Weapons and Methods of War, finalised by the C.O.S. Joint Technical Warfare Committee on 25 April and

---

70. CAB 120/691: Telegram No DOTEL 545, Hollis to Price, 16 September 1946
71. CAB 120/691: Telegram No FMW 274,Wilson to Ismay, 18 September 1946
72. See pp. 268–70 &, for its ultimate report, pp. 293–315 below

approved by the Defence Committee of the Cabinet on 22 July,[73] were now sent to Washington for the personal use of the U.S. Directors of Plans. At the same time, the British Joint Staff Mission was asked to create a suitable cover plan to explain the presence of the F.P.S. in Washington.[74]

Despite the episode of Montgomery's visit, strict security was still being applied and, on 11 October, the J.S.M. provided a detailed response which read, in part:

> 3. We are in favour of a comprehensive cover plan to embrace activities of all members of the team, who are probably known to be planners. We suggest that they say they are engaged in the preparation of a report on the strategical lessons of the recent war and that they are over here to discuss the question with U.S. authorities.
>
> 4. American planners agree with above suggestion but fear it will not hold water in certain circles in the Pentagon and Navy Department. It is doubtful whether any overall cover plan will in fact fool everybody. They suggest that there should be a second Top Secret cover plan for use when the first plan is obviously unconvincing and that this would be that the real object of the visit is to discuss military standardisation. This would cover Canadian participation but cannot be used as the open cover plan since the subject of standardisation is also Top Secret.[75]

While the details of the Future Planners' mission were being resolved, another journey had been undertaken: General Eisenhower had come to London and met the Chiefs of Staff informally over lunch at the American Embassy on 10 October. In preparation for this, Hollis had briefed Ismay at the beginning of the month:

> I take it that the all-important subject is that which we have had under Most Secret consideration during the last few weeks. As to this, the Joint Planners are producing a paper setting out the main points in their discussions with our friends.

---

73. CAB 131/3: DO(46)89, 8 July 1946 (covering TWC(46)15(Revise), 1 July 1946) & CAB 131/1: DO(46)23rd Mtg (3), 22 July 1946 See also pp. 232–41 below
74. CAB 120/691: Telegrams Nos DOTEL 550 & 551, Hollis to Price, 27 September 1946
75. This supplementary cover plan had been sufficient to mislead the present author into believing, wrongly, that future strategic policy had not been discussed in Washington (see footnote 122 to p. 290 below). The cover story worked because Anglo-American-Canadian standardisation really had been discussed in addition to future strategic collaboration (see CAB 84/86: JP(46)224(Final), 13 December 1946).

It was also proposed to discuss Anglo-American co-ordination of military radio frequencies: a brief for the meeting explained that, without the continuation of this, any combined future military activity would be seriously jeopardised and might be completely prevented. Vitally important, too, would be an agreement that 'the armed forces of the United States and the Commonwealth should use identical cypher equipment and that a fully qualified Combined Technical Committee should be established'. This matter had been raised with the Chiefs of Staff by the Director-General of the Secret Intelligence Service, who was proposing to visit the United States presently. Finally, it would also be worth mentioning the discussions already under way about the possible reciprocal use of ports and air bases by U.S. and British Commonwealth armed forces.[76] Other subjects added to the list were the need to keep the Combined Chiefs of Staff in being, the design of aero-engines and the availability in a future war of different types of oil fuel, unhelpful statements by President Truman about the Palestine situation, and Soviet subversion in the Middle East: a topic viewed gravely in the United Kingdom which was 'examining the possibility of taking some positive action to counter these activities in the Middle East and elsewhere'.[77]

An account of the private discussion at the Embassy on 10 October was immediately prepared and sent to Washington for Eisenhower to confirm or amend. He and the British Service chiefs had agreed that it seemed certain that the United States and the British Commonwealth would be Allies in any future global war:

> It was therefore incumbent upon them to concert plans together in so far as this was possible, having regard to political susceptibilities.

As 'our potential opponent' would have the initial advantage of being able to prepare for war in secret and to launch a surprise attack:

> Our first aims should therefore be to hold (a) places vital to our war-making capacity and (b) those places from which we could hit back.

Three areas fell into these categories—the British Isles, the Eastern Mediterranean, and the Continent. For the United Kingdom base the main

---

76. CAB 121/350: Unnumbered Minute, Hollis to Ismay, 1 October 1946 & undated Aide-Mémoire
77. CAB 120/350: COS Sec Min 1236/6, probably Hollis to Chiefs of Staff, 8 October 1946

threat remained long-range rockets and guided missiles. The building up of defensive measures against these would be essential. For the Eastern Mediterranean commitment it would be vital to control the Straits of Gibraltar, the Sicilian Narrows (including Sicily and Crete), Cyprus, Cyrenaica and, as always, Malta. The decision to fight to remain on the Continent, however, marked a major shift from the position taken by the Joint Planning Staff in the second 'UNTHINKABLE' report in July 1945 and by the Chiefs of Staff themselves—other than Montgomery[78]—up until the present:

> it was agreed that the recent joint American/British exchanges of information on the Planning level had produced an answer which was unduly pessimistic. The instructions to the American and British Planners should now be to the effect that we should plan for holding a bridgehead on the Continent, probably in Holland. This bridgehead would be organised with two alternative objects: first, if the enemy attack developed in overwhelming strength and with the high speed forecast by the Planners, we should at least be able to evacuate the American and British forces now on the Continent, and the bulk of their equipment, in an orderly manner. Alternatively, if the enemy strength did not prove so great, or he did not push his advance, it might be right for us to hold on.

This had, of course, been reported to the Chiefs of Staff as Eisenhower's view in Field Marshal Wilson's telegram of 30 August. Its acceptance also marked a victory for the C.I.G.S. in his argument with his colleagues on this vital issue.

It was felt that American forces in Italy should withdraw southwards in the event of a major threat in the Central Mediterranean rather than trying to join American forces in Germany. Any Soviet naval threat was discounted except possibly from captured German U-boats. As 'the development of an air offensive in the shortest possible time was essential', it was agreed that U.S. Mustangs and Thunderbolts would be very valuable in the early stages. There would be benefit if some could be kept on a care-and-maintenance basis in the United Kingdom. Apart from discussing the list of specific remaining topics—including Japanese prisoners in the Far East, as well as radio frequencies, cryptographic collaboration, oil fuels and Palestine—Eisenhower and the Chiefs of Staff agreed to instruct their respective Planning Staffs to re-examine the

---

78. See pp. 275–6 below

whole problem of strategy in the event of sudden Soviet aggression.[79]

Within a week, Colonel George Mallaby of the Joint Planners' Secretariat was informing their American counterparts of the action put in hand. The War Office Director of Plans would be visiting Germany forthwith to discuss the new scenario with the Chief of Staff of British land forces and with representatives of the other Services in Germany. They, in turn, would liaise with the staff of General MacNarney, who had succeeded Eisenhower in command of United States forces in Germany. After a suitable period of reflection, the British and American officers concerned would then come to London for discussions with the Joint Planners.[80]

Under their cover description as the 'Strategical Research Team', the Future Planning Section duly arrived at New York in the liner *Queen Elizabeth* on 11 November. Their tripartite talks with the Canadian and United States planning teams began 'in a most favourable atmosphere' two days later.[81] During their stay, Brigadier-General Lincoln, Mallaby's American contact, supplied the Joint Staff Mission with the text of the interim directives which had been issued to the U.S. land and naval commanders in Europe, following the meeting in London between the British and American planners in September. Both the Commanding General, U.S. Forces European Theatre (USFET) and the Commander, Naval Forces, Europe had been instructed to make 'plans and preparations for . . . meeting a major emergency'.[82]

The discussions continued until 25 November and were felt to have gone 'remarkably well'.[83] The Future Planning Section returned to Southampton on 4 December, with an agreed plan for holding a bridgehead on the Continent after a Soviet offensive. As Hollis later telegraphed to Wilson, this was

> put before the Chiefs of Staff in December, who approved its general conclusion that the best course in the event of Russian aggression in

---

79. CAB 121/350: Unnumbered Letter, Ismay to Eisenhower, covering Aide-Mémoire of Private Discussion with C.O.S., 10 October 1946 The Cabinet Office Historical Section has obtained a copy from U.S. archives (ref. NND 770012) of a slightly amended version of this aide-mémoire, sent by Ismay to Eisenhower on 17 October 1946, and has inserted it into CAB 121/350. It shows that the 10 October discussion had considered the possibility of hostile Russian U-boats being manned by Germans.
80. CAB 120/691: Telegram No DOTEL 563, Mallaby to Price for Lincoln, 16 October 1946
81. CAB 120/691: Telegram No LETOD 772, Price to Hollis, 13 November 1946
82. CAB 120/691: Telegram No LETOD 775, Price to Mallaby, 18 November 1946
83. CAB 120/691: Telegram No LETOD 779, Price to Mallaby, 22 November 1946

present circumstances would be to withdraw British and U.S. forces into the Zeebrugge-Dunkirk area.

It would also be necessary for British forces in Germany to have an alternative withdrawal route into the Rotterdam area, 'in case enemy action made it impossible for them to withdraw further south'.

The British and the Americans recognised that the plan, as drafted, was far from complete. It would be impossible to turn it into a practical scheme, capable of implementation at short notice, without involving a much wider circle of staff officers:

> Although the American Planners were in general in favour of taking the plan further, the Chiefs of Staff felt that, provided [a] sufficient warning period of say six weeks were given, it would be possible to make a complete plan upon the outline conception already agreed.[84]

On 19 December, Lieutenant-General Hollis—who had recently succeeded Ismay as Chief Staff Officer to the Minister of Defence— minuted to the Prime Minister:

> You will remember that some little time ago the Chiefs of Staff met you in very secret session to report the progress which had been made in the exchanges of information between our and the American Staffs on certain matters of common interest.
> 2. These exchanges of information have continued, and the Chiefs of Staff feel that the time has now come for you to be informed of the present position. Perhaps the best way would be if you would permit me to give you a general statement orally.
> 3. On one point the Chiefs of Staff ask for your instructions. We have gone about as far as we can in the preparation of an *outline* plan to meet certain eventualities. The Americans are now pressing us to get down to the preparation of a *detailed* plan. This would involve bringing in a good many people who are so far unaware that any exchanges of information have been taking place, with the consequential risk of a leakage. The Chiefs of Staff consider that it would take somewhere around six weeks to complete the plan in detail and possibly a further six weeks before the contemplated plan could be put into operation. Their view is that this time-lag should, in present circumstances, be accepted but subject, of course, to constant review.

---

84. CAB 120/691: Telegram No DEF 96, Hollis to Wilson, 16 January 1947

4. If you share their view that we should go no further at present in the preparation of joint plans, it will help the Chiefs of Staff if they can inform their American colleagues that they are under instructions from their Government not to proceed further with the detailed plan at the present time.[85]

By 16 January 1947, Attlee's consent enabled the Chiefs of Staff to ask the military commander of the British zone in Germany—Montgomery's successor, Air Marshal Sir Sholto Douglas—to instruct his staff officers 'that no further work should be done'. At the same time, Field Marshal Wilson in Washington was informed of developments, including the Service chiefs' view that 'it would be better for political and security reasons to discontinue all combined work on the problem'. He was requested to seek 'an early opportunity to explain this position verbally to General Eisenhower' and, if he agreed, to ask him to give the appropriate instructions to his Commanders and his staff.[86]

Given the close collaboration between the Americans and the British Joint Planners, Colonel Mallaby wrote to his U.S. counterpart— Brigadier-General 'Abe' Lincoln—on 15 January to explain in detail what the Chiefs of Staff had done:

> Directors of Plans have asked me to write to you to explain a little more fully what has happened on the question of the Bridgehead in North-West Europe. By the time you get this letter you will have been told by General Eisenhower that our Prime Minister has decided that we shall not do any further work on this project.

Mallaby reviewed the preliminary planning carried out, the keenness of the USFET representatives to go much further, and the British Service chiefs' concern about 'avoiding any leakage and the danger of provoking the very thing we wished to avoid'. His letter continued:

> Directors of Plans feel that you may be disappointed with this result, and obviously it would be desirable, if we could, to have a complete plan on which we were all agreed and ready to act. At the same time, they feel that a very considerable point has been gained in getting agreement on the destination and line of withdrawal. They are extremely grateful to you and

---

85. CAB 120/691: Unnumbered Minute, Hollis to Attlee, 19 December 1946 (emphasis in original)
86. CAB 120/691: Telegram No DEF 95, Hollis to Douglas, 16 January 1947 & Telegram No DEF 96, Hollis to Wilson, 16 January 1947

your colleagues for coming to London for the initial discussions with USFET. They believe that with the contacts thus established it should be possible if this grisly emergency arose to produce a complete combined plan with the minimum of delay.[87]

Although the Chiefs of Staff were more cautious than the Americans in respect of combined Anglo-American anti-Soviet planning at this stage, the foundations had been laid for future defence collaboration. The Combined Chiefs of Staff, the Joint Staff Mission and the individual Service missions were still in being. The principle of post-war military collaboration had been confirmed, its practice strengthened in several important respects, and a basic plan to meet sudden Soviet aggression had been agreed. Exchange visits by key personnel had generated contacts and opened lines of communication.

One example of the opportunities created could be seen immediately after Eisenhower's meeting with the Chiefs of Staff in London on 10 October 1946. Although the subject of deception had not been mentioned at the meeting, Ismay had felt able to attach a minute on the subject to his aide-mémoire sent to Eisenhower as soon as it had been held. It related how, until the end of the war:

> both American and British deception staffs in the European theatres were basing all their work on principles which had emerged largely from earlier British experiences in the Mediterranean Theatre. Viewed now in retrospect we still believe these to be sound, and intend to work on the same lines in future.

There were obviously many advantages in British and American deception staffs continuing to work in parallel. Currently, this was ensured by personal continuity through 'the U.S. Army officers at present assigned to these duties in the Joint Security Control Organisation, both Colonel Harris and Lieut-Colonel Sweeney having been formerly the senior American officers of the deception staffs respectively in the N.W. Europe and Mediterranean theatres'. However, there was divergence where naval

---

87. Mallaby to Lincoln, 15 January 1947 A copy of the original letter, declassified from the U.S. archives (ref. NND 770076), has been obtained by the Cabinet Office Historical Section and inserted in CAB 121/350 together with an American file note—probably by Lincoln—indicating Eisenhower's reaction: 'The Chief of Staff thinks we might burn this letter from George Mallaby. . . . It has too much information in one letter. Do not distribute any copies.'

deception was concerned, as American experience in the Pacific had been cut off from the lessons learned in Europe. Thus, Ismay suggested, the head of the Allied deception organisation in the Mediterranean from 1940 to 1945—Brigadier Dudley Clarke—might usefully 'pay a liaison visit to Washington' in order to discuss 'the lessons which we believe here to have emerged from the experiences of Deception during the war'.[88] They were lessons which the C.O.S. organisation did not intend to forget.

6. Strategic Deception Planning, 1945–47

While still C.O.S. Secretary, Hollis had consulted Dudley Clarke before drawing up a paper, on 8 September 1945, entitled 'Deception Organisation in Peace'. It viewed 'preparation for war' as 'the first requirement in peace'. This meant that

> measures will be needed to ensure that effective organisations for practising both strategic and tactical deception are ready to operate at the very shortest notice in the event of a national emergency.

A small permanent Deception Staff should be formed under an Army staff officer, aided by a Royal Navy Commander and Royal Air Force Wing Commander. Housed in the Cabinet Office, alongside the Joint Planning and Intelligence Staffs as at present, the unit would

> Maintain the closest liaison with the Secret Organisations to ensure that machinery for implementing Deception by Secret Intelligence methods will be available as required.

Similar links with the Foreign Office would enable military deception to be accomplished through diplomatic channels, whenever necessary; whilst contacts with the individual Services would secure the machinery to carry out tactical deception 'by physical means (visual, aural, mechanical, etc.)'. Strategic deception would probably not be employed regularly or on any large scale in peacetime, but might on occasion be deemed necessary by the Service chiefs or the Foreign Office.[89]

---

88.   CAB 121/350: Ismay Note for Eisenhower, attached to Aide-Mémoire of Private Discussion with C.O.S., 10 October 1946
89.   CAB 80/97: COS(45)564(0), 8 September 1945 See also footnote 109 to p. 239 below

Ministerial approval for such proposals, however, was neither sought nor secured for the greater part of a year.

In April 1946, the revision of the Tizard report on Future Development in Weapons and Methods of War specifically recommended the continuation in peacetime of the London Controlling Section—the deception body within the C.O.S. machine.[90] When the Defence Committee of the Cabinet endorsed the revised report on 22 July, it agreed that

> the Chiefs of Staff should maintain and make use of the Deception Organisation which should be conversant with the latest developments in weapons and methods of war.[91]

The L.C.S. now had a mandate to re-emerge and reconstitute itself. It drew up proposals in March 1947 which recognised that key changes were required. In war, strategic deception had focused primarily on military operations, but in peacetime it would be 'concerned as much with foreign policy as with imperial strategy'. No longer could the L.C.S. report solely to the Chiefs of Staff. Decisions on deception policy henceforth 'must be made only on the highest level by those responsible for the conduct of the country's political and military affairs'.[92]

It was therefore suggested that the Minister of Defence needed to create a special executive committee to oversee and direct the work of the L.C.S. and its Controlling Officer. The Controlling Officer should be a member of the new body, together with the three Directors of Plans (representing the Service chiefs), the heads of the Foreign Office and of the Civil Service, and their counterparts in M.I.6 and M.I.5—'since their services are likely to be required in the implementation of future plans'. Finally, the chairman should be the Chief Staff Officer to the Minister of Defence, Lieutenant-General Hollis, after whom the committee should be named.[93]

A heavy burden of responsibility lay on the L.C.S. whose three

---

90. CAB 131/3: DO(46)89, 8 July 1946 (covering TWC(46)15(Revise), 1 July 1946) For the wartime Official History of the L.C.S. and related bodies—completed in 1980 and published a decade later—see Michael Howard: *British Intelligence in the Second World War, Volume 5—Strategic Deception* (London, HMSO, 1990)

91. CAB 131/1: DO(46)23rd Mtg (3), 22 July 1946 The meeting was chaired by Attlee, who described the Joint Technical Warfare Committee's revised paper as 'a Report of great importance with very wide implications'. Among those present were Bevin (Foreign Secretary), Dalton (Chancellor of the Exchequer), Chuter Ede (Home Secretary) and Alexander (First Lord of the Admiralty), as well as the Chiefs of Staff.

92. CAB 81/80: LCS(47)1, 31 March 1947

93. CAB 81/80: LCS(47)1(Revised), 5 June 1947

members were the Controlling Officer, a second general staff officer and a civilian representative of the Security and Intelligence Services. On behalf of the Hollis Committee, they were to 'control and co-ordinate all deception policy in peace', to formulate cover and deception schemes 'for all major war plans', to ensure the provision of trained specialist staffs as required, and to lay the foundations for credible 'intelligence channels' to convey stories to their intended target audiences. In addition, their plans had to be prepared in close consultation with the Joint Planning Staff of the Chiefs of Staff, prior to submission to the Hollis Committee.[94]

The wartime deception planners had been able to operate with the benefit of strict censorship and a high degree of security. Without these advantages, physical deception—such as the creation of phantom, or 'notional', armies—could no longer be practised effectively. The work of the L.C.S. would thus be directed 'mostly towards influencing a potentially hostile government on matters concerned with policy of the highest national importance'. In war, deception plans were prepared for the short or medium term; in peace, quick results were not to be expected and long-term schemes would require a variety of sub-plots to cater for fluctuating worldwide conditions over time.

At the outset, the L.C.S. realised that deception need not necessarily mislead; it could be used to 'assist political and military policy by conveying the truth through intelligence channels to a potential enemy, who is reluctant to believe it when received through normal diplomatic channels'. This certainly applied when dealing with 'a difficult and suspicious nation such as the Russians', who possessed 'a highly developed espionage system' and might be more prone to believe information derived from it rather than conveyed openly.

By early May 1947, committees had been set up in Germany, Austria and Egypt to devise methods of carrying out deception schemes drawn up in London. The question was: where to begin conceptually? As the 'three pillars' of current strategic planning, the defence of the United Kingdom, the maintenance of its sea communications and the protection of its strategic interests in the Middle East, were prime candidates for consideration. Since all would be affected 'in some way or another by the threat of atomic and biological warfare', however, it was decided to concentrate on mass destruction weapons.[95]

---

94. CAB 81/80: LCS(47)11(Final), 21 November 1947 & HC(47)1, 8 December 1947
95. CAB 81/80: LCS(47)2, 6 May 1947 According to Dennis Wheatley, a member of the wartime L.C.S., he had suggested the use of 'scientific deception' against post-war potential enemies as early as December 1944. (See pp. 238–9 below; see also pp. 291–3, 328–34 & 379–84 below, for the 'three pillars').

A key factor in this choice was the emphasis placed on such weapons in the revised Tizard report on Future Development in Weapons and Methods of War, completed by the C.O.S. Joint Technical Warfare Committee in mid-1946.[96] By 9 June 1947, when the L.C.S. drew up a draft deception policy for 'Atomic Scientific Research and Production', it had also seen an early version of the C.O.S. Overall Strategic Plan entitled 'Future Defence Policy'. That report clearly identified the Soviet Union as posing 'the most formidable threat to our interests . . . especially from 1956 onwards'—when she would probably be able to use some atomic and biological weapons. It spelt out the importance of showing an ability and intention to take immediate offensive action if attacked. This would be most effective in deterring war. If conflict nevertheless began, any prospect of survival and victory would partly depend on having increased and exploited 'our present scientific and technical lead, especially in the development of weapons of mass destruction'.[97]

Consequently, the deception planners framed their approach to 'deter aggression by the Russians by exploiting our present lead in research and production' of atomic bombs. They also realised that pure deception would be 'open to immediate detection with grave consequences', if it were attempted without adequate knowledge of the extent of Soviet intelligence about the British atomic programme:

> It is already well known that Communist activities have penetrated many of our industrial concerns, and there is every reason to presume that the conduct of our atomic research has also been penetrated. Until the extent of this is known to us, it would be unwise to exploit our knowledge, except where we are certain this is unique.

Instead, the L.C.S. preferred the use of devious means to underline Britain's *genuine* scientific progress and total preparedness to use atomic weapons from the outset if attacked. Deception was to be the handmaid of deterrence.

One drawback was recognised to be the delicate issue of Anglo-American exchanges of atomic research information. This had become 'almost non-existent' while talks continued at the United Nations Organisation about the international control of atomic energy:

---

96. See pp. 232–9 below
97. COS(47)102(0)(Draft) quoted in CAB 81/80: LCS(47)3(Preliminary Draft), 9 June 1947 The Overall Strategic Plan had been finalised as DO(47)44 on 22 May 1947, and is reproduced in full as Appendix 7, pp. 370–87 below

Should discussions with the U.S.S.R. prove to be abortive, then it is likely that British co-operation with American scientists will reach the same standard as that pertaining during the war . . . In exploiting any aspect of research or production [by revealing it] to the Russians, care must be taken that we do not use information gained from the Americans for this purpose. We are anxious to regain liaison with America and any use of their knowledge without their sanction would prejudice our chances.

Four aspects of the British lead in research and production were therefore identified 'as being suitable for treatment' by the L.C.S.: progress in manned aircraft designed to carry atomic weapons, advances in anti-aircraft defence, a change from water to air cooling in the design of British atomic piles, and experiments towards obtaining atomic energy without using uranium.[98]

This preliminary draft paper seems never to have been finalised, but some of its ideas were carried forward into a more authoritative study issued on 17 September 1947.[99] This aimed to 'reduce the strategic effectiveness of attack on the United Kingdom by the Russians using weapons of mass destruction'. It recognised that the introduction of atomic warfare had 'rendered the United Kingdom more vulnerable to attack than at any time in our history'. War in the next five years seemed unlikely as the Soviet Union had not yet developed the atomic bomb, but there seemed to be

no technical reason why Russia should not have developed atomic energy, and be in possession of approximately 50 atomic bombs by 1956. She may have biological weapons before this date.

There is therefore sufficient time at our disposal for a deception plan to be effective, but as results will take longer to achieve in peace than they did in war, in order to attain the aim in the time at our disposal the plan should be put into effect as early as possible.[100]

The L.C.S. acknowledged that the United Kingdom lacked any detailed intelligence of Soviet progress in atomic and biological weapons

---

98. CAB 81/80: LCS(47)3(Preliminary Draft), 9 June 1947
99. CAB 81/80: LCS(47)7, 17 September 1947—'A Deception Policy for Peace calculated to Assist the Future Defence of the United Kingdom against Aggression by a Potential Enemy using Weapons of Mass Destruction'
100. The first Soviet atomic test actually took place only two years later, on 29 August 1949.

research. It was safe to assume that the United States and United Kingdom held a lead, and it was known that the Russians were making strenuous efforts to reduce this: 'It is therefore of the highest importance that every opportunity should be taken of misleading their researches.' Clearly, the key position of the United Kingdom within the Commonwealth made it 'a main target for Russian aggression' in the event of hostilities. Would it be sensible to deceive the Soviet Union by exaggerating the efficiency of British air defences? Only, the L.C.S. now believed, during the period *before* Soviet acquisition of the atomic bomb:

> The nature of the mass destruction weapon is such that the efficiency of our defence, to be of any use as a deterrent from attack, must be of the order of one hundred per cent. Any plan to exaggerate our defences, unless the exaggeration implied this efficiency, would, we believe, serve merely to encourage the enemy to increase the scale of his attack, in order to make sure that the number of missiles necessary to eliminate the United Kingdom were dropped at the outset.

Exaggerating British ability to stop incoming bombers could help deter an aggressor—but only if he were armed with conventional weapons alone. Then there would be no question of him destroying the United Kingdom with just a few successful sorties, and every aircraft destroyed really would reduce the impact of each raid.

Since the best deterrent to atomic or biological attack would be fear of immediate and effective retaliation, it was important to encourage a Soviet belief that this could be launched 'from areas other than the United Kingdom'. The home islands should be made to appear less central than they really were, in terms of concentrated industry and population as well as the means of retaliatory attack:

> Existing emigration schemes and industrial development throughout the empire can form the basis for a deception plan for the world-wide dispersal of white population and heavy industry, and thereby detract from the vulnerability of the United Kingdom, simultaneously adding to our Imperial strength.

The success of such a deception plan would depend on a plausible story being put over to the potential enemy in line with, and seemingly confirmed by, contemporary evidence. Owing to the long time-scales involved, the plan would have to be flexible. Otherwise it could be falsified by unpredictable events. What was needed was 'a fundamental story upon which all subsequent action will be based and future plans developed'. That basic story was duly set out.

It centred on a 'notional' review, by the Defence Committee of the Cabinet, of how the United Kingdom could be safeguarded from attack by a European aggressor armed with mass destruction weapons. This review had supposedly decided that the British Isles were now so vulnerable that four key measures, 'which will take time to become effective', should be begun at once:

(a) To arrange for the dispersal of our retaliatory forces throughout the Commonwealth so that, despite [the] success of an initial attack on the United Kingdom, we should still retain adequate strength to hit back with equal or greater effect.

(b) To start a re-distribution of industry and population throughout the Commonwealth.

(c) To plan and prepare the emergency dispersal of war industry within Great Britain, and the evacuation of all personnel not actively engaged in the war effort to camps throughout the country.

(d) To plan for the higher direction of the war from alternative sites outside the United Kingdom.

Initially, the first and last of these themes would be developed by reference to 'notional' committees; but advantage could also be taken of 'all topical events which lend themselves to deceptive treatment', such as the visits of various VIPs to different parts of the Commonwealth.

Belief in British retaliatory capability was the key to the country's security:

We envisage that the threat of retaliation will prove a decisive and flexible weapon, as a future deterrent to aggression. Once the Russians are convinced of our intention to retaliate, by a careful build-up over a period of years, the latent threat can be increased to a peak at will by the movement of a comparatively small number of aircraft and notional weapons of mass destruction. It can, of course, be played down equally easily.

The theme that industry and people were being redistributed throughout the Commonwealth would be promoted by 'large scale misrepresentation'. For example, existing emigration schemes could be passed off as part of a 'higher Commonwealth strategy'. Similarly, if a light engineering works were set up in South Africa by a British firm, this would be 'fed' to the Soviet Union as a 'shadow' factory to which the parent company in the United Kingdom would transfer its military work and skilled personnel on the outbreak of war:

> Over a period of time, we consider that, owing to the uniform development of industries by areas, an impression will be created of an organised development of potential war industrial areas throughout the Commonwealth.

As for the emergency dispersal and evacuation of industry and people within the United Kingdom, this notion would initially be promoted by systematic exaggeration, with the ultimate possibility of creating dummy camps as potential targets in the event of a conflict.[101]

Side by side with the development of a theory of long-term deception, the L.C.S. had been marshalling its thoughts about an 'overall deception policy for the immediate future'. Even an interim policy would enable a start to be made on building up the channels through which detailed deception measures must eventually be fed. The object of future deception was stated to be: 'To deter, and if possible prevent the Russians from waging war against the Western Democracies.' This could best be served for the time being by the following technique:

> To emphasise, and if necessary exaggerate, our potential war strength in order to convince the Russians that we are prepared and will use this strength immediately if transgressed [against] in any way.

In their May 1947 report to the Defence Committee on 'Future Defence Policy',[102] the Chiefs of Staff had listed five principal tasks of the armed forces. The deception planners considered these in turn. With regard to *Technical Research and Development*, not only the British lead in atomic warfare but also in areas affecting any of the three Services might be exploited. For example, an attempt could be made 'to influence the design of sea mines by exaggerating the importance of a particular type'. The development of an air *Offensive Force*, to enhance deterrence, gave opportunities to convey veiled threats by referring to the future design of nuclear-capable strategic aircraft. The *Defence of the United*

---

101. CAB 81/80: LCS(47)7, 17 September 1947
102. See CAB 21/2096 & CAB 131/4: DO(47)44, 22 May 1947, reproduced in full as Appendix 7, pp. 370–87 below

Kingdom against aerial and seaborne threats required a deception policy to be started soon 'to minimise the scale of any likely attack'. *Control of Sea Communications* could probably best be assisted by misleading an enemy on relevant technical developments.

The fifth defence task—*Defence of the Middle East*—was considered vital, but too closely linked with American policy for serious deception measures to be attempted before British and American co-operation in deception became completely integrated once again. Nevertheless, the L.C.S. saw it as a suitable subject for a long-term study. The United Kingdom's weakening position in the Middle East must be disguised and, to this end,

> true information of a minor character concerning, for example, British military aid to the Turks should continue to be passed to the Russians with the object of demonstrating our firm intentions in this area. This will also assist in establishing [deception] channels.[103]

The Hollis Committee considered all this at what seems to have been its first meeting, on 10 October 1947. It formally decided that:

> (a) *The object of deception policy* should be to deter and if possible prevent the Russians and their satellites from armed aggression in Europe, Middle East (including Afghanistan), India and Pakistan.
>
> (b) *The overall deception policy* to attain this object should be to emphasise and if necessary exaggerate our potential war strength in order to convince the Russians that we are prepared, and will use this strength immediately if attacked in any way. The strong likelihood of United States intervention if we were attacked should be borne in mind.

To implement this overall policy, the L.C.S. was asked to examine the possible role of deception as applied to the five defence tasks in the following order of priority: first, *Technical Research and Development,* including applications to the development of *Offensive Force* and the *Control of Sea Communications;* next, *Defence of the Middle East;* and, finally, *Defence of the United Kingdom* itself. As well as the defence tasks, however, the deception planners were also to consider any steps which could be taken 'to counter or discredit Russian activities in the spread of Communism and overthrow of non-communist regimes'.[104]

---

103. CAB 81/80: LCS(47)4(Final), 29 July 1947
104. CAB 81/80: LCS(47)10, 3 November 1947

In October 1947, the Hollis Committee had also approved the planned deception concerning future dispersal of British retaliatory forces throughout the Commonwealth. This was one of four themes the L.C.S. wanted the Director of Military Intelligence to include when briefing the C.I.G.S. for his tour of Africa in November and December. They urged that, 'at his discretion, in public utterances', Montgomery should stress the United Kingdom's high priority for scientific research and the intention to create balanced British forces 'capable of achieving an effective concentration at the decisive time and place anywhere in the world'. To this end, he could claim, great flexibility would be required— a flexibility made possible by the 'tremendous advantages' of the vast area of the Commonwealth. It was natural, he might add, that the dispersal of British Commonwealth forces in time of peace was 'in itself a symbol of strength in any war of the future'.[105]

During 1947, the L.C.S. had also become involved in Middle Eastern issues, but only on terms of its own choosing. On 8 July, it had firmly rejected proposals for using false sailing orders to divert away from the Mediterranean vessels carrying illegal immigrants to Palestine. The hazards were clearly spelt out. As a maritime power, the United Kingdom had much to lose 'by initiating a policy entailing irregular conduct towards ships on the high seas'. There was no guarantee that an innocent ship might not be targeted; indeed, a guilty ship-owner might realise what was happening and deliberately run 'a completely innocent and legally documented ship with the intention of embarrassing us if she is detained or interfered with'. To avoid detection, it would be necessary for an Arab group or a dissident Jewish faction to be blamed; yet, it was 'unlikely that any foreign powers will believe any of these parties well enough equipped and organised technically to indulge in intervention of this kind'.

Above all, any passing of false messages by wireless telegraphy 'will almost certainly cause the Jewish organisations to change their frequencies and codes, with a consequent loss of signals intelligence to ourselves'. Nor should repercussions at the United Nations be overlooked:

> As the case for Palestine is under review by the United Nations Organisation at the present time, it is a singularly inappropriate moment for any underhand or illegal conduct on our part to be disclosed. The disclosure of any actions on our part on a par with those contemplated above may well prejudice our cause at this exceedingly tricky juncture.[106]

---

105. CAB 81/80: LCS(47)9, 6 November 1947
106. CAB 81/80: LCS(47)5, 9 July 1947

Rather than be rushed into reckless short-term initiatives, the deception planners were determined steadily to evolve their peacetime schemes in accordance with the Overall Strategic Plan for 'Future Defence Policy'. An outline plan to undermine the spread of Communism in the Middle East illustrates their preferred technique. The L.C.S. believed that

a weak link in world Communism as it is practised today, is the fact that, while purporting to support nationalism, it is in reality interested only in the exploitation of that nationalism for the furtherance of Russian interests.

Thus, if the policy of a Communist Party in a strongly nationalistic country were shown to be against that country's best interests and in favour of the interests only of the Soviet Union, this would generate strong anti-communist feeling. The strategic importance of one vital area suggested a plan:

Our aim is . . . to discredit Communism in the Arab States of the Middle East by exposing the Communist policy in this area, as being one designed to prevent the alliance of the Arab states into a defensive union, and to play up all points of difference between them, in order to keep the Middle East weak militarily.

If this could be done by means of planted material—and 'the Security Service have agreed that the idea is practicable'—three consequences would follow: the value of deception in discrediting Communism would be proven; the Arab states would be alerted to the potential threat of Russian aggression; and some nationalistic feeling might be diverted away from the British. The operation would be carried out in Egypt, a leading Arab state with strong nationalist sentiment and with a Communist Party which 'is in active existence . . . and is known to us'. Even if the 'plant' were denounced, Communist denials of responsibility would still generate some plausibility for it. Provided that it was carried out skilfully, 'the chances of its being traced back to British authorities are negligible'.[107]

There is no evidence that the L.C.S. ever received the approval they sought to send one of their members to Egypt 'in order to decide further details on the spot', and no sign that a detailed plan was ever drawn up for final approval as they had suggested. The file of L.C.S. and Hollis

---

107. CAB 81/80: LCS(47)6, 17 September 1947

Committee memoranda indicates a relatively low level of activity over the two-year period from March 1947, focusing on arrangements, analysis and technique rather than actual operations.[108] One critical problem was the contrast between the flow of intelligence about wartime Germany and the lack of it about peacetime Russia. As a later L.C.S. review clearly acknowledged, on probably the most important topic of all:

> With regard to Atomic Research . . . we possess insufficient intelligence at the present time as to the precise lines of Russian effort to undertake a major policy of misdirection.[109]

Nevertheless, if nuclear deception would have to remain on hold for the time being, nuclear deterrence was being viewed by the Chiefs of Staff as absolutely central to the future security of the United Kingdom.

7. The Atomic Bomb and Deterrence, 1946–47

The release of the C.O.S. Secretary's Standard File for 1946–47,[110] containing Confidential Annexes to the minutes of C.O.S. meetings, shows in more detail how the Service chiefs assessed and embraced the notion of deterrence at a relatively early stage. On 13 November 1946, two months before Attlee and five of his senior ministers took the decision to produce British atomic weapons,[111] Viscount Portal—who had stepped down as Chief of the Air Staff at the end of 1945—met the C.O.S.

---

108. It was not until 1950 that the L.C.S. was revived 'on an operational basis, renamed the Directorate of Forward Plans . . . and deployed in a Cold War context'. It had, however, maintained 'a reservoir of the specialist skills and knowledge learned during the war' in the interim. See Richard Aldrich (ed.): *Espionage, Security and Intelligence in Britain, 1945–1970* (Manchester, M.U.P., 1998), pp. 229–30

109. CAB 81/80: LCS(49)1 (Annex A), 7 January 1949 Nevertheless, in November 1949, the Controlling Officer, John Drew, recommended that Soviet intelligence should be fed 'an exaggerated estimate of the power of our weapons and the efficiency and numerical strength of our armed forces' in the hope of helping to avert war 'until of course the aggressive intentions of the Communist leaders have atrophied, and it becomes possible for Russia to be a trustworthy member of the Committee [?comity] of Nations'. Drew also outlined a deception plan for linking 'various prominent Soviet Communists with various opposition movements', to provoke purges, to 'wreck the whole Stalinist structure', and thus to 'weaken the capacity of the Soviet Union to wage war'. (DEFE 28/43: 'Future Deception Policy', 24 November 1949)

110. DEFE 32/1

111. See footnote 129 to p. 295 below

Committee in his capacity as Controller of Production, Atomic Energy, in the Ministry of Supply. He explained that no responsibility had yet been allocated for the manufacture of an atom bomb and that two years' research would be needed on its technical construction before any fissile material would be required. While the project was under way, it would be important to maintain secrecy in relation both to technical information and to political affairs at home and abroad. However, even greater secrecy would be 'necessary to ensure or even initiate Anglo/American exchange of information on the technical manufacture of atomic bombs'.

> In this last respect, he [Portal] was reasonably confident that the Americans would be disposed to release some information to himself, which might not otherwise be available.[112] Nevertheless, the extent to which they would release this information would depend on their assessment on how well we could guard their secrets.

As for allocating responsibility for building the British bomb, there were three possible routes: either by an official mandate from the Prime Minister; or by an unofficial mandate 'whereby, after explaining the position to the Prime Minister, nothing would be recorded, but authority would be given [to Portal] to proceed with the manufacture under his responsibility'; or by allowing the details of manufacture to be discussed by the normal departmental machinery for weapon development. The Chiefs of Staff agreed with Portal's preference for the 'unofficial mandate' formula and invited him to notify Attlee accordingly. They also promised to try to prevent any reference to details of the project from being raised in the Service Departments. Apart from the Minister of Defence, A.V. Alexander, who was shown the sole copy of the record of the meeting, only Sir Henry Tizard, as Chairman-designate of the new Defence Research Policy Committee,[113] was scheduled to be briefed on the situation.[114] Not surprisingly, such separated and secretive arrangements would cause problems later.

At the end of March 1947, the Future Planning Section of the J.P.S. presented its voluminous 'Review of Defence Problems'.[115] The process of drafting and discussion leading to the production of the Overall

---

112. This might well have contravened the McMahon Act, signed by President Truman on 1 August 1946, which obstructed the exchange of American nuclear information even with close allies.
113. See p. 191 & footnote 141 to p. 318 below
114. DEFE 32/1: COS(46)167th Mtg (3)(Confidential Annex), 13 November 1946
115. See pp. 268–70 & 293–315 below

Strategic Plan on 22 May[116] moved into higher gear. In the course of this, a Staff Conference was held on 17 April at which the Service chiefs were joined by Tizard and by the Minister of Defence.[117] The account of that meeting, now available, clearly shows the thinking of Tedder, Cunningham and Tizard in response to the Minister's questions—though barely that of Montgomery whose sole recorded contribution was, sensibly enough, to doubt if the transfer of large portions of the arms industry from the United Kingdom to the Commonwealth was feasible.

Alexander quickly drew attention to the principles governing the future build-up of the Services. The three basic ones remained defence of the United Kingdom, security of sea communications, and defence of the Middle East. Yet, two more had been added by the Chiefs of Staff: research and development, and counter-offensive forces. Of these, he realised the role of the former but asked how the latter fitted into the general framework. In reply,

> SIR JOHN CUNNINGHAM said that the need for counter-offensive forces was to enable us to counter-attack in the event of being attacked. Through the development of modern weapons and the increased vulnerability of the U.K., the adage that attack was the best means of defence had increased in emphasis since counter-offensive forces had become an essential means of defence. The force, therefore, had two main roles—first, as one of the principal means of defence, and secondly, as a deterrent in peace to the outbreak of a further war. He thought the country would accept the arguments for these essentials of defence.

The C.N.S. added that the location of these counter-offensive forces would depend on the state of international relations and 'to some extent' on decisions from the United Nations Organisation. Tedder also pointed out that, as the British contribution to the U.N.O. would be provided from this source, the counter-offensive forces 'would have to be mobile and at instant readiness either to defend ourselves or to fulfil U.N.O. directions'.

Turning to scientific research and development, Tizard stated that the vital requirements for organising such work were not being fulfilled. Universities were without modern equipment and there was 'a lack of certain classes of scientists, particularly for biological warfare'. Alexander accepted that research and development were 'of the first importance' and promised to help. In the meantime, he wondered if the

---

116. See pp. 317–31 below
117. See p. 318 below

Services would need re-equipment with current weapons or whether this could wait until new weapons were developed and available— 'particularly those of mass destruction'. Cunningham replied that large expenditure on improving current weapons was not needed, though orders placed at the end of the war would be required to bridge the gap until the arrival of entirely new ones.

When the Minister explained that 'one of the criticisms he had to meet in Parliament was that under attack from weapons of mass destruction the United Kingdom would become untenable as a base', Tedder responded that

> these arguments assumed that at the outbreak of hostilities the enemy would immediately use atomic bombs; secondly, that we would have no effective measures with which to meet such an attack. The first assumption was dangerous and probably even erroneous. The second assumption could not at present be confirmed or denied since there was much research to be done on the methods of defending ourselves, and assessments made on the effectiveness of our counter-offensive in limiting the attack from the enemy.

Tizard added that 60 per cent of the British Commonwealth's industrial potential and manpower were concentrated in the United Kingdom. It would be well worthwhile to study the practicability of dispersing industry, exporting manpower and siting certain types of arms factories in particularly secure locations.

In answer to one question about the possibility of accidental war with the Soviet Union in the next few years, Tedder said that the chances of this were 'very slight', as in the opinion of the Chiefs of Staff 'Russia wished at all costs to avoid a war before she had achieved the manufacture of atomic weapons'—or at least much greater industrial parity with the United States. In response to another,

> he agreed that it could be argued that the existence of armaments had never stopped war, but the converse was also true in that disarmament had never prevented war. None of these policies had been effectively applied in peace and the difficulty was lack of an international authority which would enforce either one of the policies. The Chiefs of Staff regarded the period from 1956 onwards as comparable to 1933 and thereafter. On the latter occasion we were extremely weak and war had followed. This should never happen again. The need was at all times to show our preparedness to defend what we considered to be our rights.

Endorsing this view, Tizard stressed the role of technical and scientific superiority in industry and the Services as the only way to counteract our inability to compete with others in terms of manpower. It followed that any so-called 'qualitative disarmament' would always react to the disadvantage of the United Kingdom. This was the concept of seeking progressive arms reductions aimed at giving approximate technical parity to each competing country. Tizard explained that such a move would destroy the United Kingdom's 'brain-power' lead over other nations and force her to compete on the basis of manpower alone. By contrast,

> It should not worry us, for example, if on a quantitative basis it was agreed that the British army should be limited to 200,000 and the Russians to 1,000,000 so long as we retained the freedom of applying our scientific developments to our arms equipment.

The problem, according to Alexander, was the political difficulty of finding firm ground on which to fight proposals for reducing the armed forces 'almost to nothing' while awaiting the development of entirely new weapons with which to equip them. He had also been advised that, 'from the scientific and army point of view . . . war was most unlikely for the next 15 years'. If this became 'widely known to the public', he felt that

> His Majesty's Government would be subject to considerable pressure for not having given sufficient priority to industrial recovery as the first line of defence. There might be a revival of arguments to re-institute the '10 year rule'.[118]

---

118. The Cabinet Office file on the 'Ten Year Rule', CAB 21/2093, contains a prescient memorandum by Sir Maurice Hankey, dated 9 January 1931, when he was Secretary to the Committee of Imperial Defence. After warning of German 'irredentism', Soviet 'imponderabilia' and 'universal economic depression', he observed: 'As a nation we have been prone in the past to assume that the international outlook is in accordance with our desires rather than with the facts of the situation . . . We are also apt to forget how suddenly war breaks out. In 1870, a fortnight before the event, we were not in the least expecting the outbreak of the Franco-Prussian War. The same was true in 1914. A fortnight after the murder of the Austrian Archduke, a debate took place in the House of Commons on foreign affairs. The European situation was hardly referred to at all. More attention was given to the preparations for the next Peace Conference! . . . There was no statement made on the subject of the European crisis in Parliament until July 27, and the Austro-Serbian question did not become the principal news and the subject of the first leading article in "The Times" until July 27. We really had, at the outside, not more than ten days' warning. The League of Nations procedure ought to give us more warning than that—but nothing like ten years! How foolish a Government would have looked that had reaffirmed an assumption of ten years of peace during the early part of 1914! And yet there was less talk of war on the Continent then than now, and the outstanding problems were less acute . . . We are disarmed morally and to a great extent materially.' In May 1944, Hankey's son would strongly oppose any reversion to the 'Ten Year Rule' (see pp. 101–2 below).

On the threat of large-scale disarmament and its effect on deterrence, Tedder replied that

> if the armed forces were reduced to this position, their ability to expand and reorganise would be sufficiently crippled to mean a very long period before they became comparable in efficiency to those of a potential enemy, let alone superior to them. The reason gas warfare had not been employed during the last war, was that each contestant knew the other was in a position to retaliate. This knowledge prevented its use by either side.

As for the 'Ten Year No-War Rule', all were in agreement. Cunningham predicted that the reintroduction of the rule would cause a rapid rundown of the Services, which would take a decade or more to reverse from the moment a threat was identified. Tizard stated that the only safe planning basis was to proceed on a 'likelihood of war' assumption:

> The probability of war in the next five years would be small, would then rise gradually in the following five years, and increase more steeply after ten years.

Indeed, the Minister's own memorandum[119] to the Chiefs of Staff, drawn up in February but currently before the Committee, had spelt out his own view of the need to resist

> any tendency to embark upon the kind of policy which was pursued with such detriment to our fortunes between World War I and World War II, namely the 'Ten Year No-War Rule'. The evils of this policy did not lie so much in the prophecy that no major war would occur for a period of ten years from the time the rule was instituted, but in its cumulative detrimental effect on our defence preparations as a whole by reason of its annual renewal. This is a mistake which we must not make again.

Both Tedder and Tizard emphasised that 'the best deterrent to war in peacetime' was the knowledge that the United Kingdom would be 'prepared to use weapons of mass destruction immediately'. Cunningham pointed out that there might be circumstances when the United Kingdom alone became involved in war with the Soviet Union, but even if this happened British policy in peace was to secure American assurances

---

119. CAB 21/2096 & DEFE 5/3: COS(47)33(0), 18 February 1947

of 'material help at the earliest possible moment following the outbreak of war'. There would also be a need for 'an immediate supply of atomic bombs'.

Alexander expressed surprise at the Service chiefs' opinion that no reliance could be placed on receiving substantial support from any European Allies. Could not France recover enough strength and prosperity to give leadership to Western Europe? Would not a Franco-Belgian-Dutch partnership offer the British defence in depth? Should not the United Kingdom do everything possible to help reconstruct West European states, reorganise their armed forces and build 'a strong Western European region of defence'? Tedder's reaction was revealing. He said that

> the Chiefs of Staff agreed that this should be their aim in peacetime, but they had emphasized the word substantial. They estimated that up to 1956–60 there could be little effective contribution from these countries even though their armed forces had been reorganised on a reasonably efficient basis. What was lacking was not so much the material aspects as the strength of character and will to fight for their rights.

When the Minister asked if it was 'necessary that forces should exist today' to combat a future wartime threat to sea communications from submarines, shore-based aircraft and mine-laying, Cunningham explained that it was essential to preserve nucleus forces which could be expanded to meet such threats as they developed. The 'whole German technique' was available to the Russians 'whom we knew already possessed 240 submarines'. Moreover, if it were conceded that Soviet forces had the power to march through Europe, this would provide them with all the necessary bases from which to threaten our sea communications in the Atlantic and Mediterranean.

Given the long-running disagreement between the Chiefs of Staff and the Prime Minister on the strategic importance and defensibility of the Middle East,[120] it was only to be expected that Alexander would advise them to set out 'full supporting arguments' for maintaining the United Kingdom's presence there in all circumstances. What if British negotiations failed in Palestine and Egypt, and American support were withdrawn from Greece and Turkey? Even then, said Tedder, it would remain a major objective to hold on to the British position in the Middle

---

120. See pp. 253–60, 270–1 & 292 below

East. Its physical evacuation in peacetime would simply mean 'our having to re-occupy bases there in war to prevent the enemy from doing so'. Concurring, Cunningham summed up the region's central role in C.O.S. strategic thinking:

> a cardinal principle of our foreign policy must be to prevent the Middle East from falling into Russian hands. If our defences were to be shorn of the Middle East areas, we should lack defence in depth and begin the next war by fighting to defend direct attacks on our territories and support areas. The military disadvantages of evacuating the Middle East included impairing our ability to withstand the initial critical period before we could launch our counter-offensive.

If there were to be a Mediterranean dimension, Alexander wanted to know, what would be the implications for the Malta and Gibraltar bases? Tedder acknowledged that Malta would be vulnerable to atomic attack, but said that the Chiefs of Staff viewed as unlikely the use of a potential enemy's limited supply of atomic bombs on territories such as Malta, rather than on 'far more profitable targets' such as the United Kingdom itself. On Gibraltar, Cunningham observed that

> the only possible alternative was Ceuta. The proposal for an exchange of Ceuta for Gibraltar had been examined before[121] but the Chiefs of Staff had agreed that since the modern developments of war and the geographical position of Gibraltar had further limited its defensive and transit value, the alternatives to Gibraltar should be examined again.

The 17 April Staff Conference then concluded with agreement on a series of steps leading to the production of the report on 'Future Defence

---

121. See pp. 75–7 & footnote 66 to p. 76 below That footnote refers to a September 1943 paper by Lieutenant-General Sir Noel Mason-Macfarlane, Gibraltar's Governor and Commander-in-Chief, which has now become available with the lapsing of its 50-year closure period. As anticipated, it considered the option of exchanging Gibraltar—though only as a last resort. It might be traded for 'a suitable locality' in Spanish Morocco, southern Portugal or Tangier. Mason-Macfarlane favoured the Tangier option, particularly in preference to Ceuta, but he added: 'As regards Gibraltar, I am myself most strongly opposed to bartering it. It is now so strong and of such tremendous value to us that we ought definitely to keep it even at the risk that a hostile Spain would neutralise its value as a base. On the other hand, if there should be no other possibility of acquiring Tangier, and if Tangier could be made to meet our Naval and Air requirements, I think we ought at least to consider the question.' (CAB 84/56: JP(43)338(Final), 27 September 1943)

Policy'. It would need to be completed and approved by the Cabinet 'within the next eight months'.[122] In fact, it was printed on 22 May, endorsed by Attlee, Bevin and Alexander at a further C.O.S. Staff Conference on 11 June, and circulated thereafter only to the Chancellor of the Exchequer and the three Service Ministers.[123]

The adoption of the Overall Strategic Plan confirmed the realignment of post-war defence planning to meet a potential Soviet threat. Although it was thus the appropriate point at which to conclude *Changing Direction*, one later document from the Secretary's Standard File for 1947 deserves to be put on the record—if only for the insight it gives into the strategic thinking of the Vice-Chief of the Air Staff, Sir William Dickson. Dickson—who had signed the overall plan, on Tedder's behalf, with Cunningham and Montgomery—was successively to become the United Kingdom's first formal Chairman of the C.O.S. Committee and first Chief of the Defence Staff in the 1950s. A former Director of Plans in 1942 at the start of British post-war military planning, he would continue to influence defence policy from within the C.O.S. organisation for much longer than most of his wartime contemporaries.

It was on 29 October 1947 that Lord Portal again attended a C.O.S. meeting to discuss the development of the British atomic bomb. The compartmentalised arrangements, agreed at the 13 November meeting the previous year, were now creating difficulties. Atomic research priorities were not properly being matched with those in other fields supervised by Tizard's Defence Research Policy Committee. There was doubt, too, if sufficient strategic guidance had been taken from the Chiefs of Staff when the proposed scale of atomic weapons production had been decided. Portal readily acknowledged that the C.O.S. 'bore the responsibility for providing strategic guidance', and stated that he was willing to co-operate with them fully. He reminded them that their views on the scale of production had been sought[124] and had been submitted to Attlee at the beginning of 1946:

After due consideration, the Prime Minister approved the present production programme which involved construction of one large pile, since

---

122. DEFE 32/1: COS(47)54th Mtg (Confidential Annex), 17 April 1947
123. See pp. 324–34 below & CAB 21/2278: Prime Minister's Personal Mins Nos M.274/47, M.275/47 & M.276/47, 8 July 1947
124. See footnote 129 to p. 295 below. The C.O.S. had argued unsuccessfully for the construction of two 'graphite piles' for the production of plutonium, rather than only one.

modified to two smaller ones, each of half the capacity, and work on the first of them was proceeding with the utmost urgency. He [Portal] thought it was true to say that this scale had not been related to our strategic policy, although it was in fact known at that time what the general effect of the use of such weapons was likely to be, and the number of weapons which their capacity would provide.

Portal knew very well the sensitivity of the Air Staff about exclusion from involvement with scientific military matters. The Air Staff had been the sternest critics of the original Tizard report between July and September 1945, when Portal was C.A.S. and his A.C.A.S. (Policy)—Dickson—was briefing him on this very issue.[125] Now, as V.C.A.S. himself, Dickson took the lead in spelling out the concerns of the Service chiefs:

he had no doubt that, whatever the past or present, it was the constitutional responsibility of the Chiefs of Staff to decide and to recommend to His Majesty's Government on the strategic implications of atomic warfare. The Air Staff were studying this matter . . . Provisionally it was thought that it might take some 50/60 atomic bombs to destroy the war potential of the United Kingdom, and it was estimated that Russia by 1960 could be in a position to deliver that number of bombs over the United Kingdom . . . he thought it must be an inescapable assumption that attacks on the heaviest scale could be made over the shortest possible time in an endeavour to throw us off our balance and to destroy the United Kingdom as a war base. Our intention, therefore, would be to prevent these attacks and the only method of prevention, he thought, was to provide sufficient deterrent. This deterrent could only take the form of a force of heavy bombers held available to deliver a similar heavy and concentrated attack against the aggressor.

It would not be possible to estimate precisely the number of aircraft and atomic bombs which the Soviet Union would regard as enough to deter her from attacking the United Kingdom:

At the present time the most that could be said was that it would take 600 atomic bombs to destroy the 60 Russian towns of a population of over 100,000 situated within a range of 1,500 miles of our air bases in the United Kingdom and the Middle East.

---

125. See pp. 188–91 below

Alternatively, some 300 bombs would be needed to destroy those towns of a population of over 500,000 within a similar range:

> The provisional estimate of the number of bombs required would, therefore, be in the nature of at least 300, and preferably nearer 500.

What help might be received from the Americans? Dickson viewed the availability of atomic bombs held in the United States as being 'of little deterrent value' to the United Kingdom:

> The only effective deterrent was the Russian knowledge that we were in possession of adequate stocks of bombs and had the ability to use them at a few hours' notice. From this it could be deduced that Russian action would be greatly influenced by their knowledge of the number of piles that we possessed.

Although some might criticise—on grounds of vulnerability—the idea of holding large stocks of atomic bombs in the United Kingdom, the V.C.A.S. believed that, if the retaliatory force were efficiently dispersed,

> it would not be possible to prevent our taking immediate counter-offensive action on a very heavy scale. He emphasized that it seemed that however strong our war potential was, only our immediate ability to take rapid offensive action on a heavy scale would prove a sufficient deterrent.

Portal did not disagree, but advised the Chiefs of Staff of the need to consult him about the practicability of manufacturing a given number of atomic weapons by any given date. He warned that, if they stated as a minimum requirement more bombs than could be produced or financed at the time in question, then it might be argued that none should be constructed at all—'since the minimum thought necessary was beyond our means'.

As in 1945, Tizard felt excluded from atomic weapons issues.[126] His Defence Research Policy Committee had no mandate to discuss research priorities for their production and, although he was a member of the Advisory Committee on Atomic Energy,[127] he could not recall any occasion when it had discussed the impact of the atomic bomb on future strategy:

---

126. See pp. 181–2 & 191 below
127. See pp. 190–1 below

He felt, therefore, that there was a serious gap in the co-relation of scientific effort as between atomic and other weapons. He had reason to believe that developments in atomic weapons would, in fact, greatly affect developments in other types of weapons and war material and unless these effects could be studied as a whole and in relation to each other, there was a danger that our scientific effort might not proceed on the right lines.

One example was the relatively low priority which had been given to anti-submarine warfare, owing to the ignorance which existed about possible uses for atomic devices in this role. Tizard recommended the setting up of a committee—either under the D.R.P. Committee or in the Ministry of Defence—to bridge the vital gap which had been identified, and on which both the Services and the scientists would be properly represented. This was approved in principle.

Portal also drew attention to the impact of United States law which forbade any exchange of atomic information, including with the United Kingdom. He still hoped to reach agreement on 'a defence research programme which fitted with ours so that neither country was wasting effort by duplication'. The lack of information from the Americans was forcing the British, with their limited scientific resources, to devote more time and work to the production of atomic energy and less to other research projects. Whilst a new committee could deal with policy recommendations, he stressed that implementation of the programme would have to remain the responsibility of the Ministry of Supply.

All agreed that there was little prospect of dispersing atomic research and production throughout the Commonwealth and little point in trying to do so:

> the ability to produce atomic weapons in the Commonwealth would not seem to be of any great value in providing an adequate deterrent to likely aggressors, as this deterrent depended on the actual location of bombs in this country and our ability to deliver them at very short notice.[128]

In terms of the strategic concepts, the political constraints and the vocabulary of deterrence, the discussions at the 17 April Staff Conference and the 29 October C.O.S. meeting would have been easily recognisable by students of defence in 1967 and 1987, not just in 1947. They were, in fact, a microcosm of the debates replayed time and again throughout the

---

128. DEFE 32/1: COS(47)133rd Mtg (1)(Confidential Annex), 29 October 1947

Cold War until the collapse of the Soviet Union. The thesis of *Changing Direction* was, and remains, that British military planners adjusted to the looming breakdown in Anglo-Soviet relations with foresight, prudence and exceptional rapidity. The fundamental strategy—which stood the test of time for four decades in the context of N.A.T.O.—was fully developed and approved by the summer of 1947. It was a very different outcome from that envisaged by the Foreign Office, when first raising the subject of post-war defence planning with the Chiefs of Staff early in 1942.

1

THE FOREIGN OFFICE ORIGINS OF POST-WAR STRATEGIC PLANNING 1942

1. The Diplomatic Background and the Chiefs of Staff Machine

On 20 February 1942 General Sir Hastings Ismay, Chief Staff Officer to the Minister of Defence, circulated a letter from the Foreign Office with the following wry comment: 'I am afraid that it means more work for the Joint Planners, but I do not see how we can get out of it.'[1] What it contained was the first formal request to the British Chiefs of Staff for post-war strategic guidance. The issue which underlay this request was, however, by no means a recent one.

As far back as November 1940, shortly before his appointment as Acting Foreign Minister in the Norwegian government-in-exile, Trygve Lie had raised the question of a future Atlantic security system.[2] By January 1941 his ideas had crystallised into a scheme for post-war British and American bases to be set up in Norway, with all three countries administering supplementary outposts in Greenland, Iceland and the Faroes.[3] These proposals had received a certain amount of attention, including a vague and cautious welcome from the Admiralty, which really regarded post-war matters of this kind as far too speculative for practical evaluation.[4] However, their impact had been largely stultified by the failure of the Ministerial Committee on Reconstruction Problems[5] to devote time to their consideration on referral in March 1941, and by the sudden transformation three months

---

1. CAB 119/64   2. N7471/213/30   3. N214/87/30   4. N693/87/30
5. *Ibid.* Set up under the Minister without Portfolio in February 1941, this committee was charged with the preparation of 'practical schemes of reconstruction, to which effect can be given in a period of, say, three years after the war' and 'a scheme for a post-war European and world system'. It had no Service representatives and its orientation was primarily economic. (RP(41)1)

later of the Soviet Union into an ally behind whose back no such scheme dare be considered.[6]

Subsequent revival of the bases plan was due partly to Lie's persistence, notably in enlisting the support of his Dutch and Belgian counterparts;[7] partly to American entry into the war, which made the notion of her future participation in post-war security arrangements seem less utopian; and partly to a suggestion by the Soviet leader that:

> We should have no objection to Great Britain having naval bases in Norway or Denmark, but we would like a guarantee by certain Powers as to the entrance to the Baltic Sea,[8]

which cleared the way at least for exploratory talks with Norway on the subject.

At a high-level meeting in the Foreign Office on 14 January 1942 it was suggested that the bases plan was one of only a few ideas for post-war arrangements with both practical value and a possibility of general acceptance. Consequently, just over a year after its initial formulation, a decision was taken to approach the Chiefs of Staff for strategic guidance on the scheme.[9] The question was, how could they reasonably be expected to furnish it in the middle of a war? It was obvious that the Service chiefs themselves would have little or no time to devote to the preparation of post-war strategic appreciations for the Foreign Office. What they could be expected to do, however, was to arrange for such matters to be dealt with by an appropriate inter-Service body:

> As such a body will certainly be required for the consideration of other similar post-war strategic problems as and when they arise, a decision to set it up might usefully be taken in connection with this particular question.

In the view of the permanent head of the Foreign Office, Sir Alexander Cadogan, 'if some special committee could set out the case succinctly, it ought not to give the Chiefs of Staff much trouble to pronounce on the desirability or otherwise of the scheme in one form or another'.[10] Yet, instead of openly suggesting the creation of such a committee, the

---

6. N6510/87/30   7. N7205/87/30   8. N518/463/30   9. N463/463/30
10. N518/463/30

eventual approach by the Foreign Office was to be couched in rather more cautious terms.

The Cabinet Office tradition of informal civil–military liaison on organisational matters had for some time been reflected in important links between the Foreign Office and the Chiefs of Staff machine. The latter had come into being on an integrated basis in 1924, as a result of the recommendation of the Salisbury Committee on National and Imperial Defence that

> In addition to the functions of the Chiefs of Staff as advisers on questions of sea, land or air policy respectively, to their own Board or Council, each of the three Chiefs of Staff will have an individual and collective responsibility for advising on defence policy as a whole, the three constituting as it were a Super-Chief of a War Staff in Commission.[11]

From April 1940 onwards the workload of the main body had been shared with a Vice-Chiefs of Staff Committee which acted as its *alter ego*, the other principal branches of the organisation being its Joint Planning Staff, set up as a sub-committee in 1927, and its Joint Intelligence Sub-Committee, dating from 1936.

The key figure concerned in any approach on post-war planning arrangements would clearly be General Ismay, who had retained his position of Deputy Secretary (Military) to the War Cabinet on joining the Chiefs of Staff Committee as an additional member in May 1940; but the Foreign Office also had the advantage of a direct involvement at two levels in the C.O.S. machine. The J.I.C. and J.P.S. were, respectively, composed of the Directors of Intelligence and Directors of Plans of the three Service Departments, coming together in committee—on the model of the Chiefs of Staff—to initiate and pronounce upon the reports produced by their subordinate inter-Service staffs. It was the Foreign Office which supplied the chairman of the J.I.C.—William Cavendish-Bentinck, who was one of two full members of the sub-committee from Civil Departments. There was also liaison with the J.P.S. at the staff-officer level, the Foreign Office representative being Clifford Norton, through whom, on this occasion, the opening moves were made.

On 12 February 1942 Norton met Ismay informally for advice on

---

11. Quoted in: S.S. Wilson, *The Cabinet Office to 1945* (London, H.M.S.O., 1975), pp. 70–1

how best to frame the request for considered inter-Service views on long-term strategic questions. Ismay agreed that 'it was undesirable at this stage of the war to put in official minutes the fact that this sort of work was in our minds, necessary though it may be,' and it was at his suggestion that Cadogan's formal approach to the Chiefs of Staff a week later was rather more delicately phrased.[12] Instead of requesting the establishment of a special committee to consider the 'long-term problems of a mixed political and strategic nature' beginning to confront it, the Foreign Office merely asked for permission to approach the Joint Planning Staff directly for such advice. 'I should add,' wrote Cadogan, 'that we could regard their work as purely exploratory until the time came when it was necessary for one reason or another to ask the Chiefs of Staff, and probably ultimately the Cabinet, to give the matter their attention.'[13]

Ismay saw to it that copies of this letter were circulated privately to the Chiefs of Staff, instead of being given normal distribution as an incoming paper to the committee. On 26 February authority was duly given for the Foreign Office to 'hold discussions' with the Joint Planners on what the minutes of the C.O.S. meeting described as 'long-term foreign policy'.[14] In notifying Cadogan of this decision, however, Brigadier Leslie Hollis—the principal secretary to the committee—advised him that, though very ready to agree to his request, the Chiefs of Staff hoped he 'would understand that such problems must of necessity take a relatively low priority in the work of the Joint Planning Staff'.[15]

The subdivision of the J.P.S earmarked by Ismay to handle post-war planning was the Future (Operational) Planning Section. It had come into existence some eighteen months previously as a direct result of the Prime Minister's strengthening of the Joint Planning Staff. It was founded to prepare long-term plans for the defeat of the Axis well in advance of their becoming practical possibilities. In December 1940 Churchill had installed the then Major Oliver Stanley, M.P., as its chairman in order that 'by virtue of a broad outlook and background and detachment from current day to day problems' he might assist its members to plan for the future on profitable lines.[16] By the beginning of

---

12. N978/463/30　13.　CAB 119/64 & N978/463/30
14. COS(42)65th Mtg (8)　15.　N1150/463/30
16. AIR 8/1354 Stanley had been Secretary of State for War in the Chamberlain government, but some felt that Churchill had erred in his choice in appointing him to spur on the C.O.S. machine towards more offensive planning. According to one

1942, however, as the Directors of Plans pointed out in a note to the Chiefs of Staff, conditions had changed significantly 'since 1940 when almost any operation was beyond our resources'.[17] The original task given to the F.O.P.S. was well-nigh complete. The plans it had drawn up were no longer distant dreams but medium- and short-term possibilities. As such, they were passing into the province of current planners in the Strategical and Executive Planning Sections of the J.P.S. on the one hand, and of commanders in the field on the other. Conversely, pressure of work on the 'S' and 'E' sections was steadily increasing, and the Directors of Plans felt that these sections would benefit considerably from the winding-up of the F.O.P.S. and the distribution of its personnel between them. Whilst declining to permit this, at their meeting on 10 February the Chiefs of Staff sought to integrate the work of the F.O.P.S. more closely with that of the strategic planners by broadening its functions and transferring its personnel from Richmond Terrace to the main office at Storey's Gate.[18] Thus, at the very time that Norton was broaching the Foreign Office request for strategic guidance on a longer-term basis than any yet attempted, Colonel Stanley and his colleagues were shifting their emphasis in the opposite direction. Nevertheless, the diplomats had succeeded in getting a foot in the door and the way was now clear for post-war planning to begin.

2. First Steps in Strategic Planning: the F.O.P.S. and the Bases Plan

Although a strategic questionnaire on the bases proposal had been approved by the Foreign Secretary for submission to the Chiefs of Staff on 18 February, and their permission for J.P.S. involvement obtained just over a week later, its transmission to the Joint Planners did not occur until 13 March.[19] The reason for this delay was an internal Foreign Office debate as to whether the military planners should be asked to examine the Norwegian proposals in isolation, or whether the possibility of bases in Belgium and the Netherlands should also be

---

member of his section, Stanley 'had a brilliant mind and . . . could argue a case with great ability. But he was a destructive critic, and I never knew him to put up an original idea', (D. Wheatley, *The Time Has Come* (London, Hutchinson, 1979), iii. 222–3). Late in November 1942 Stanley became Colonial Secretary and was not replaced as F.O.P.S. 'Director'.

17. JP(42)94   18. COS(42)45th Mtg (10)   19. JP(42)279(0)(T.R.)

considered.[20] Even before this, Anthony Eden had warned his officials that Churchill and Attlee had deprecated the general idea of post-war bases in Cabinet, and he had suggested that it would be 'wiser to leave this task until we see our Russian way a little clearer'. This objection had been overcome by Cadogan only on the basis of the need to prepare a reply in view of the Norwegian approach.[21] Nevertheless, when the Foreign Office memorandum was eventually despatched, the covering letter by the head of the Northern Department, Christopher Warner, advised the J.P.S. to keep it in mind that the particular question of international bases in Norway, Iceland, Greenland and the Faroes was part of a larger question:

> *viz.* whether it might not be desirable that a wider scheme of international bases should form an important part of the post-war security system in Europe. Thus conceivably bases might be established in Denmark, Belgium and Holland as part of the system for controlling the North Atlantic approaches and the North Sea, . . . and the same system might perhaps be applied in Greece for instance in connexion with the control of the Eastern Mediterranean.[22]

As might have been anticipated, the immediate result of this advice was for the F.O.P.S. to be issued with terms of reference by the Joint Planners' secretariat, requiring it first to examine the strategic desirability of a general scheme of international bases for post-war European security, and only then to assess the specific Norwegian proposals.[23] Given the need for a speedy response to the latter, this caused some dismay at the Foreign Office, and representations were made via Norton.[24] Under the circumstances, the F.O.P.S. had little option but to reverse its procedure, and a draft was produced for approval by the Directors of Plans on 3 April.[25] The following day, the first tentative inter-Service views on post-war British defence strategy were forwarded to the Foreign Office.

These rested on the assumption that the potential future threat to Europe would come from a revived Germany alone, and against this prospect the bases plan was coolly received. Whilst accepting that to use Norwegian bases would be one way of keeping open the highway of the Atlantic, the planners' preference was to achieve this by ensuring 'that the potential enemy is never in a position to start an attack upon

---

20. N1150/463/30   21. N518/463/30   22. N1150/463/30
23. JP(42)279(0)(T.R.)   24. N1441/463/30   25. JP(42)63rd Mtg (7)

it'. The post-war control of Germany should not depend on defensive bases from which to ensure her defeat once again, but on

> the maintenance of a sufficient striking force and the will to use it, so that any military revival in Germany can be immediately and decisively checked.

It would take some two generations to re-educate the Germans and, in the interim, they should be kept in a state of sufficient defencelessness for the British to be able 'ruthlessly to use our air striking force against targets necessarily civilian in character'. The Joint Planning Staff recognised that it was for others to decide if political conditions would permit the adoption of such a strategy. Assuming that they would, however, offensive air bases in France or the Low Countries would be needed for its implementation, not defensive ones as suggested by Lie, which would create major new commitments in competition with the main strategic aim.

If, on the other hand, the preferred military policy proved politically unacceptable as a long-term solution, then it followed that the British would have to be prepared 'to meet at some time or other a new German attack comparable in scale to that of 1939'. Yet, even though access to bases controlling the North Atlantic approaches and the North Sea would be strategically desirable in these circumstances, the extra burden of defending them required careful consideration. To defend a base in Norway would involve accepting a commitment to protect the whole country. This would be intolerably heavy without American participation and an active Norwegian contribution, guaranteed by tripartite treaty. In return for the former, Britain should be willing to reciprocate the offer of bases, given the importance of having 'the U.S.A. over here, so as to ensure their full collaboration in the defence of Great Britain in any future war.[26]

The planners' caution in basing their examination on a threat from Germany alone was remarked upon by Warner, who felt it 'rather unsatisfactory that they should not have taken other potential threats into consideration at all'. After analysing the report on 7 April, his colleague, John Somers Cocks, had summarised Foreign Office attitudes to the Soviet Union in the early days of the Grand Alliance thus:

---

26. JP(42)354

Everyone, I think, is agreed that Russia will be a very powerful state both economically and militarily when she has recovered from the devastation of the present war, and the only uncertainty is the length of time it will take her to recover. It would be a bold prophet who would predict that the present Anglo-Russian alliance will survive indefinitely . . . we cannot foretell whether Russia might not at some time in the future decide that Narvik and the Swedish iron mines were an essential part of her *lebensraum*.[27]

At his suggestion and with Warner's concurrence, the J.P.S. was requested on 14 April to re-examine the strategic aspects of the bases proposal 'on the assumption that (a) Russia, or (b) Russia and Germany, are the potential enemies'.[28]

In the event, this modification did little to strengthen the strategic case for Norwegian bases in the view of the Service planners. The F.O.P.S. produced a draft paper pointing out that, whilst they had previously selected Trondheim and Stavanger as suitable locations for defensive bases against a resurgent Germany, it was

doubtful whether, in a war against Russia, or against Russia and Germany combined, these bases could be held long enough to make them worth the additional defence commitment they would undoubtedly entail;

and it was likely that any base in northern Norway would be rendered unusable by air action, even if not captured by a *coup de main* on the outbreak of a war with the Soviet Union.[29] The final version of this paper as approved by the Directors of Plans was somewhat more moderate in tone, and regarded Stavanger as necessary for control of the sea passage from the Baltic to the Atlantic in the event of war with Russia alone. But it confirmed the impracticability of protecting more northerly bases, whose reconnaissance functions could more securely be carried out by the British being 'prepared to seize bases in the Faroes and Iceland (C) on the outbreak of war, if these had not been obtained by negotiations in peace'.[30]

The Joint Planners' scepticism received reinforcement in a memorandum drawn up by the Foreign Office figure in closest touch with them—Oswald Scott, who had recently replaced Norton as liaison

---

27. N1806/463/30
28. JP(42)401(0)(T.R.)   29. JP(42)432(0)(Draft)   30. JP(42)497

officer. With the general approval of Oliver Stanley, he challenged the whole basis on which the Foreign Office was proceeding:

> In attempting to furnish answers to these questions at this stage of hostilities there is, I believe, real danger that our solutions for long-term problems may be influenced more by the circumstances in which we live than by those which are likely to prevail during the period ten to fifty years after the war.

There could, he asserted, be no continuing guarantee that the voluntary abrogation of sovereignty by governments-in-exile under the stress of war would be persisted in by their successors for years to come. The millions of pounds it would cost to establish post-war Continental bases would be better invested in 'time-gaining elements' of naval and air defence for Great Britain, assuming that she would lack the will required for early offensive action against potential threats.

These remarks were received unsympathetically in the Foreign Office, where the main concern was the value of the bases plan as a vehicle against post-war isolationism—'an expression of a wish on the part of the Norwegian and other Governments that England and the United States should participate in a mutual defence system after the war,' as the head of the Central Department described it.[31] In fact, matters were now reaching a stage when Cabinet permission would have to be sought for an exchange of views with the Americans to take place. For this purpose, it was expected that a comprehensive J.P.S. report would need to be prepared, embodying inter-Service views on the various aspects of the bases proposal in a single document.[32] However, in the course of the F.O.P.S. re-examination of the original bases paper of 4 April, a number of parallel developments had been taking place which were to alter the entire question of how post-war strategic planning was to be undertaken.

3. The Shift towards a Separate Sub-Committee

As soon as the principle of direct diplomatic access to the Joint Planning Staff had been established in consequence of Lie's initiative, action had been begun to co-ordinate future Foreign Office requests for strategic advice on all subjects with a long-term military aspect. The

---

31. N2550/463/30   32. N2551/463/30

prime mover in this respect was Nigel Ronald of the General
Department.

In view of the low priority which the Chiefs of Staff intended the
J.P.S. to assign to such work, Ronald stressed the need for his
colleagues 'to make up their minds which of their questions they regard
as most urgent'. He suggested advising the Service planners that, set in
order of importance, these were: (1) disarmament and control of ex-
enemy countries; (2) proposals for naval and air bases; (3) Middle
Eastern questions; and (4) the preparation of Foreign Office handbooks.

Whilst it was agreed at a meeting of departmental heads on 12 March
that the first of these was clearly the central issue to which the 'other
matters on which the Foreign Office would be likely to desire guidance
were all really complementary', there was considered to be insufficient
data available to tackle so vast a problem for the time being:

> It would, for the present, be more satisfactory if politico-strategic
> questions were addressed to the Joint Planning Staff as they became
> actual. Such a piecemeal approach . . . was less satisfying in theory than
> the formulation of a carefully planned programme, but there were
> insurmountable difficulties in the way of achieving anything like this at
> present.

In the words of the Minister of State, Richard Law, it was felt that 'if we
flung the whole problem at the heads of the military we should not get
any answers until the war was finished'. Just as the Northern
Department was in process of submitting its memorandum on the bases
proposal, other departments should do the same as and when issues
became ripe for consideration.[33]

The first of these issues to do so was the scheme to produce a series of
Foreign Office handbooks, cited by Ronald as the fourth priority and
stemming from instructions given by Eden in 1941 to the Foreign
Research and Press Service.[34] This semi-official body of academics
based on the Royal Institute of International Affairs had been set up at
Balliol College, Oxford, in 1939 under Professor Arnold Toynbee.
Funded jointly by Chatham House, Oxford University and the
government, it was charged with the preparation of memoranda giving
political and historical backgrounds to situations on which government

---

33. C3562/685/62   34. W343/81/49

bodies had requested information.[35] By late December 1941 the F.R.P.S. had drawn up a provisional scheme for the production of twenty volumes[36] designed for the use of ministers and senior officials in connection with the eventual peace settlement. They were to provide concise factual descriptions and objective analyses of probable post-war problems against which senior decision-makers would be able to judge departmental recommendations as they arose.[37]

Early in January 1942 Ronald had written individually to the intelligence directorates of the Service Departments for strategic guidance on the handbooks, only to be redirected by two of them towards the Directors of Plans or the F.O.P.S.[38] With access to the Joint Planners secured in February and a piecemeal approach decided upon the following month, it had not been long before Clifford Norton was authorised to write to them for assistance. This he did on 21 March. The F.O.P.S. was asked to advise on the extent to which matters of strategic interest should be included, and on how responsibility for writing about them should be divided between Service professionals and the F.R.P.S. academics.[39] The Joint Planners' approved reply of 21 April was uncompromising:

> We feel very strongly that as far as purely strategic questions are concerned . . . the inclusion of suggested solutions for separate countries is definitely wrong. Any appreciation of our post-war strategic requirements intended for the use of Ministers should be prepared to cover the whole world picture and must receive the prior authority of the Chiefs of Staff. Piecemeal production by separate Service Departments or individual 'professors' might prove dangerously misleading.

Not even purely factual surveys of the strategic problems of an area covered by a given handbook should be undertaken for inclusion in advance of the overall appreciation. They would more properly form a part of that appreciation, as a background to its conlusions. Only after it had been drawn up might relevant extracts be considered for inclusion in the appropriate volumes.[40]

---

35. W1375/1375/50 In April 1943, in circumstances of some acrimony, the F.R.P.S. was to be completely absorbed by the Foreign Office and merged with its Political Intelligence Department to become the Foreign Office Research Department. (U1898/26/72, U2587 & U2725/2278/750)
36. CAB 119/64   37. W343/81/49   38. W343 & W821/81/49
39. W821/81/49   40. JP(42)427

This was, of course, the antithesis of the approach chosen by the Foreign Office at its meeting of 12 March; but it was fully consistent with the preferred approach of the J.P.S. to its examination of the bases plan, which had had to be reversed because of the need for a prompt answer to the Norwegians. What was more, despite issuing terms of reference to the F.O.P.S. to report on the desirability of the wider question of international bases[41] and to supply the Foreign Office with a list of principal post-war strategic requirements,[42] the Joint Planners were clearly beginning to doubt the extent to which their future planners could continue to be imposed upon. Referring to the overall strategic survey that it had focused on as the first step, their reply to the handbooks enquiry concluded that

> It is clear that the preparation of this appreciation will be a big job, necessitating, if it is to be done properly, the creation of a whole-time body, drawn from all three Services and working under the general guidance of the Directors of Plans.

If the Foreign Office wished such work to be begun, it should contact the Chiefs of Staff forthwith to suggest the creation of such a body.[43]

Considering that this had been the very idea behind the original Foreign Office approach to the Chiefs of Staff in February, Ronald was far from discouraged by the lack of a constructive response from the Joint Planners on the handbooks scheme. He was thinking in terms of the creation of two new bodies, both of which would operate on the basis of data assembled by research centres such as the Foreign Research and Press Service.[44] One should be composed—as the J.P.S. was now suggesting—of inter-Service post-war planners, outlining strategic requirements; the other should be a 'military section' located in the Paymaster-General's office at Richmond Terrace to co-ordinate these strategic plans with post-war reconstruction schemes emanating from the Reconstruction Problems Committee.[45] In the event, as will be seen, both these functions were to be combined in a single sub-committee with less than satisfactory results, but for the time being the

---

41.   JP(42)362(0)(T.R.)   42.   JP(42)309(0)(T.R.), covering C2943/685/62
43.   JP(42)427   44.   W5996/81/49
45.   *Ibid.* The Paymaster-General, Sir William Jowitt, had succeeded to the chairmanship of this committee upon the resignation of Arthur Greenwood as Minister without Portfolio late in February 1942. Unlike his predecessor, Jowitt did not have a seat in the War Cabinet.

catalogue of Foreign Office requests to the Joint Planning Staff continued to expand.

Work on the revised bases appreciation citing the Soviet Union as a potential enemy was by now well under way.[46] A draft reply had been prepared by 22 April and was scheduled for consideration by the Directors of Plans on 1 May,[47] when two more approaches followed in quick succession—the Eastern Department submitting a request for 'a study of our post-war strategic requirements in the Arab States as soon as possible'[48] and the Northern Department re-submitting its bases questionnaire yet again, this time on the assumption that Belgium and the Netherlands would shortly associate themselves with the Norwegian proposals.[49] Though neither of these departments had been involved in Ronald's handbooks enquiry, to the hard-pressed Director of the F.O.P.S. their requests were the final straw. In a strongly worded note on 4 May Stanley reminded the Directors of Plans of their decision that it was 'wrong and dangerous to deal with our post-war strategic requirements piece-meal country by country', of their recommendation that the first step should be an overall world strategic survey, and of their advice to the Foreign Office to request the formation of a special inter-Service committee if it wanted this work to be done. Turning to the latest approaches, he commented:

We have already dealt with Norway and if we now deal with the Low Countries and the Middle East it is clear that we are well on the way to doing exactly what the Directors condemned, *viz*: dealing piece-meal with the strategic problem instead of tackling it first as a whole, and then relating the answers to specific questions to the agreed principles.

Stanley concluded that the question of creating an '*ad hoc* body' to deal with post-war strategy should be taken up again, but this time 'in a more definite way'.[50] As far as the F.O.P.S. was concerned, Foreign Office arrangements for consultation with the Joint Planning Staff had come

---

46. See pp. 7–8 above
47. JP(42)432(0)(Draft) & JP(42)87th Mtg (6)   48.   E2583/49/65
49. N2081/463/30—missing, but obtainable in JP(42)461(0)(T.R.) On 17 April, the Netherlands Foreign Minister, van Kleffens, had confidentially informed Eden of the agreement of his government with those of Belgium and Norway on the principle of Atlantic security as a 'formula that would tempt the United States to take some part in a security system', and of a forthcoming joint approach to the British and Americans on this basis. (C4681/685/62)
50. JPS Sec Min 42/483 in CAB 119/64

to a dead end just over two months after the Chiefs of Staff had sanctioned it.

Stanley's paper was not, however, the only one submitted to the Directors' meeting on 8 May. Ronald, informed of his initiative, stepped in with a copy of a draft paper he had prepared for Eden to submit to the Cabinet on the creation of a military section in the Paymaster-General's office—

> not to define future military policy but to collect such facts as are known and to act as liaison between the various departments concerned with these problems and to assist and direct research on the most profitable lines.[51]

Reaffirming their opposition to any piecemeal consideration of post-war strategy, the Directors of Plans went on to draw attention to a vicious circle that would still confront their preferred approach: an overall strategic background could be prepared only if a framework of political hypotheses were to be agreed by the Foreign Office as a working basis, but to a certain extent these would in turn be dependent on post-war strategic requirements.[52] Ronald, however, was not to be diverted, and sidestepped the Joint Planners' request that consideration of his memorandum on the military section be postponed by promising them complete liberty 'to suggest what form the new body should take'.[53]

On 17 May Ismay was told of these developments and immediately stressed the need to ensure that any such body would work under the direction of the Chiefs of Staff organisation, even if attached to the office of the Paymaster-General, as Ronald had suggested.[54] The Directors of Plans accordingly resolved that it should be given the status of 'a small additional sub-section of the Joint Planning Staff on permanent "loan" to the Paymaster-General'.[55] Simultaneously, they began to divest their existing organisation of outstanding commitments to the Foreign Office: they agreed that there would be 'little useful purpose' in the F.O.P.S. making preliminary examination of the Middle Eastern or Belgian–Dutch bases issues,[56] and an attempt by Ronald to have five F.R.P.S. papers vetted for the handbooks series

---

51. JPS Sec Min 42/497 in CAB 119/64   52. JP(42)90th Mtg (7)
53. JPS Sec Min 42/504 in CAB 119/64
54. JPS Sec Min 42/540 in CAB 119/64
55. JP(42)99th Mtg (Revise)(3)   56. JP(42)101st Mtg (3)

progressed no further than the J.P.S. secretary—though the Future Planners had previously agreed to consider such items of mere 'secondary strategic interest'.[57] Everything was to await the coming of the new body which, its Foreign Office advocates intended, should break the circle of interdependent strategic and political hypotheses by first of all considering 'those purely military requirements without which no German army would be able to launch an offensive', and then, in the light of the experience gained, tackling 'the broader question of strategic requirements when the main lines of future policy have been traced'.[58]

On the face of it, all this was compatible with the Joint Planners' insistence that there could be no general strategic survey until post-war foreign policy had to some extent been formulated and that there should be no piecemeal regional appreciations in advance of the general survey. In other words, for the time being, there should be no strategic planning on matters of primary importance at all. It was, however, a departure from Ronald's original scheme of a military section to *co-ordinate* reconstruction plans with post-war strategic plans produced by a new J.P.S. sub-section. The latter was not now to be created as a separate entity, though its status was to be nominally conferred on the former, which was also to be entrusted with the consideration of immediate post-war problems of secondary strategic significance.

The justification for siting the military section amongst the 'reconstructionists' had been because of its originally proposed role as a civil-military co-ordinator. Provided that it confined its strategic planning activities to immediate military problems arising on the cessation of hostilities, as it was supposed to do, its separation from the central C.O.S. machine need not be harmful. The Directors of Plans had made a special effort to ensure the implementation of Ismay's recommendation that the military section should be under the authority of the Chiefs of Staff.[59] Theoretically, this meant that no strategic advice would be tendered without the Joint Planners' approval. Nevertheless, isolation from the main planning organisation would increasingly become anomalous if the duties of the military section eventually expanded to include the giving of 'advice on the preparation of strategic post-war plans'—as was now being envisaged by the Joint

---

57. W5996/81/49 & JPS Sec Min 42/545 in CAB 119/64
58. JPS Sec Min 42/553, circulating note by Scott, in CAB 119/64
59. JP(42)99th Mtg (Revise)(3); 101st Mtg (3); 102nd Mtg (3); 103rd Mtg (Revise)(1)

Planning Staff.[60] What was more, although the mere fact of being isolated would in no way justify departing from the Joint Planners' decision against piecemeal appreciations, it made it more likely that such departures could occur. That the J.P.S. secretariat promptly transferred the outstanding Foreign Office enquiries to the new section on its establishment, made it practically certain that they would occur.[61]

---

60. JPS Sec Min 42/558 in CAB 119/64
61. JPS Sec Min 42/653 in CAB 119/64

2
THE MILITARY SUB-COMMITTEE 1942–43

1. Birth Pangs of the New Organisation

The oblique manner in which the proposed creation of a post-war military planning body was presented to the War Cabinet in the summer of 1942 closely resembled the way in which the Chiefs of Staff had been persuaded to allow the J.P.S. to be approached at the end of February. The cause of this, however, was not so much a need for discretion about the type of work being contemplated, as a genuine vagueness about the boundaries within which the new organisation would function. No draft directive covering proposed terms of reference had been prepared for the War Cabinet, which was merely requested to give the Paymaster-General *carte blanche*

> in concert with the Service Ministers and the Chiefs of Staff, to make such arrangements as they see fit to ensure that the mass of factual information which already exists should be properly sifted and presented in such a form as to assist those responsible for deciding policy, Ministers and Service Chiefs alike, when the time for so doing arrives.[1]

The memorandum embodying this request was the direct descendant of that which Ronald had submitted to the Joint Planners' meeting on 8 May, when Stanley's protest note had been considered and the problem of interdependent post-war strategic and political desiderata had been first spelt out.[2] As such it remained orientated towards Ronald's concept of a co-ordinating body rather than a planning organisation. Indeed, it had not been until 19 May, five days after this Cabinet paper had been finalised, that the suggestion was made to tackle 'the simpler

---

1. WP(42)205(Revise)   2.   JP(42)90th Mtg (7)

military problems' as a ' "running-in" task', prior to eventual consideration of broader questions of post-war strategy.[3]

The main point requiring governmental approval was, in fact, a constitutional one stemming from the fact that Jowitt's Reconstruction Problems Committee lacked military representation, though its terms of reference were broadly drawn, and Jowitt himself lacked 'any express authority to direct research in the fields in which Service Ministers were primarily responsible for policy'. It was principally the need to extend the scope of his functions to enable such work to be done without 'adding to the existing burden of those engaged in the conduct of the war', that had brought the creation of the new body to the attention of the War Cabinet.[4] There was thus no question of government pressure in favour of post-war strategic planning at this stage, nor any certainty that the organisation to be established would play a part in the development of such planning. The nearest indication of this possibility at the War Cabinet meeting of 1 June, which conferred the authority requested, was hardly specific—Sir James Grigg, the Secretary for War, remarking that the topics to be considered would include:

> such matters as armistice terms, measures of control to prevent clandestine rearmament, and other military issues which would affect our policy after the war.[5]

Grigg's emphasis on the armistice and control aspects of the new body's work reflected the fact that the War Office was the only Service Department to have taken a positive interest in Ronald's planning initiatives. This interest arose from a War Cabinet decision in February 1941 that 'responsibility for the administration of enemy territories to be occupied . . . must in the first instance lie upon the War Office'.[6] A branch to handle these duties—M.O.11—had been duly set up under Lieutenant-Colonel Frederick French[7] within the Directorate of Military Operations at the end of the following month. For the first year of its existence, M.O.11 had mainly been concerned with

---

3. JPS Sec Min 42/553 in CAB 119/64   4.   WP(42)205(Revise)
5. WM(42)70th Concls (5)
6. F.S.V. Donnison, *Civil Affairs and Military Government: Central Organisation and Planning* (London, H.M.S.O., 1966), pp. 23–4
7. Subsequently, Deputy Director of Civil Affairs (Military Government), War Office

organising the administration of occupied areas in Africa. By March 1942, however, it was pressing for the establishment of a special committee in anticipation of the day when British forces would return to the Continent. A few weeks later, French had produced an assessment of 'The Conditions that will Obtain when Allied Forces Enter Western Europe', pointing out that:

> In this dangerous turmoil of confusion and distress . . . the presence of an effective authority to solve immediate economic needs, to provide and drive administrative machinery, to 'hold the ring' in the political field so that popular mandates may emerge and to maintain order while Western Europe recovers her balance, will be recognised by all concerned as not merely desirable but imperative . . . The importance of the earliest stages is manifest.[8]

It was against this background of increasing War Office concern with immediate post-war problems that the Director of Military Operations, Major-General John Kennedy, had written to Ronald on 10 March noting that, whereas the definition of post-war strategic requirements and estimates of the forces needed to secure them could probably be handled by the F.O.P.S.,

> the wider aspects of economic and industrial control, propaganda, moral disarmament and so on . . . would to a great extent fall out of the purview of the Joint Planning Staffs.

Sooner or later a strong inter-departmental committee, possibly under a Foreign Office chairman, would almost certainly become necessary to tackle these wider issues, and in this connection Kennedy suggested that Ronald might utilise the services of Brigadier William van Cutsem.[9]

Van Cutsem had served as a Deputy Director of Military Intelligence earlier in the war,[10] but had been 'on loan' from the War Office to the Foreign Office for work involving the clandestine Special Operations Executive. During this period he had drawn up a series of memoranda commenting in depth upon a subject of which he had had first-hand experience in post-1918 Germany—the protracted military control of a defeated enemy country and the measures required to

---

8.   C4173 & C4174/241/18   9.   C3562/685/62
10.   JPS Sec Min 42/1116 in CAB 119/64

prevent its unauthorised rearmament.[11] His papers stressed that, whereas it might seem 'rather a waste of time to think about the possibly distant subject at all just now', a German collapse, when it did come, might do so very suddenly. At the close of the last war, there had been 'not so much lack of planning, but too much uncontrolled, unco-ordinated and unrealistic planning, and the failure of the Allies to agree on post-war policy, especially long-term policy, and to set up efficient machinery'.[12]

These views closely paralleled a preoccupation in the Foreign Office 'to avoid "thinking in watertight compartments" by separate bodies on the same subject'. Ronald, its co-ordinator *par excellence*, noted on 8 April that van Cutsem was being considered for appointment to the secretariat of the Reconstruction Problems Committee where, in his view, 'he would be invaluable . . . as a link with the J.P.S.–F.O.P.S. set up.'[13] A fortnight later, Ronald and Law met Jowitt and one of his senior officials to open discussions on co-ordinating machinery. By 3 May it had been settled that War Cabinet permission should be sought to widen the Paymaster-General's responsibilities to enable him to 'set up a small military section under Brig[adier] van Cutsem at Richmond Terrace'. The Chiefs of Staff were also to be approached 'for their part to set up a section in their organisation which can direct the strategic side of the enquiry'.[14] But before this could be done, there came the F.O.P.S. revolt and consequent decision to bring the proposed military section itself under the aegis of the Chiefs of Staff with the formal status of a J.P.S. sub-section. Quite unexpectedly, therefore, van Cutsem found himself earmarked for service with a body which, it was true, would initially be 'concerned with the collection and sifting of data' as originally intended, but which was also now scheduled to be called upon 'at a later date . . . to give advice on the preparation of strategic post-war plans and to make recommendations on points which might arise under that head'.[15]

With War Cabinet permission to proceed secured on 1 June, the Chiefs of Staff themselves became formally involved with post-war planning developments for the first time since the original Foreign Office approach in February. However, they had been sounded informally on the Foreign Office proposals at the suggestion of the War

11. See W3465/81/49, C2657, C3740, C3778, C3967 & C4167/241/18
12. C2657/241/18 covering two lectures in W.O. Politico-Military Course at Cambridge   13. C2926/241/18   14. C4450/241/18
15. JPS Sec Min 42/558 in CAB 119/64

Cabinet Secretary, Sir Edward Bridges, during their meeting on 18 May when—

although there was no discussion, the Chiefs of Staff expressed themselves favourably inclined towards the suggestions put forward.[16]

On 10 June, they approved Ismay's recommendations that a new military section be set up in Jowitt's office, on permanent 'loan' to the Paymaster-General until its task was completed.[17] Whilst accepting that the new body would 'comprise a new separate section of the Joint Planning Staff', the Service chiefs nevertheless immediately agreed to a step which made future comparability with other J.P.S. sub-sections unlikely in the extreme. The Chief of the Air Staff, Sir Charles Portal, claimed that the person 'best qualified in the Air Ministry to serve in this post-war planning section was a civilian'—which really reflected R.A.F. reluctance to spare a Grade I General Staff Officer for such duties.[18] The individual whom the Air Staff had in mind[19] was Dr James Spaight, Principal Assistant Secretary at the Air Ministry from 1934 to 1937 and the author of numerous publications on such topics as *Air Power and Cities* (1930), *An International Air Force* (1932) and *Air Power in the Next War* (1938). Though an eminent and respected figure, as a retired civil servant he could in no way be described as closely in contact with current strategic thought in the Service planning divisions. Futhermore, the irregularity of his appointment paved the way for the Admiralty to nominate a retired Rear-Admiral, Roger Bellairs, as its representative, thereby securing the chairmanship of the new body by outranking van Cutsem, whom Ronald, Jowitt and the Joint Planners had been expecting to hold this position. Bellairs had served as Director of the Admiralty's Plans Division from 1928 to 1930, but his active naval career had ended two years later. After a period in the League Permanent Advisory Commission, he had returned to the Admiralty on the outbreak of war and had taken part in secret staff talks with the Americans early in 1941.[20] Like Spaight, he was essentially out of touch with the mainstream of departmental planning, and his appointment was made in the context of similar departmental scepticism as to the value of his proposed activities. As one Admiralty minute complained, without contradiction:

---

16. CAB 21/2294 17. COS(42)297 18. COS(42)175th Mtg (8)
19. ACAS(P)/CR/209 in AIR 20/3739 20. Ismay, *Memoirs*, pp. 216–7

it seems impossible adequately to curb the activities of those who in time of war wish to consider post-war problems: the best thing to hope is that their activities will be limited by the staff available, and that the problems to be considered will be reconsidered, as they only properly can be considered, when the conditions prevailing at the end of the war are known.[21]

Despite its lack of enthusiasm for the new body, the Admiralty set about trying to enhance its status, secure in the knowledge of having nominated its most senior member. This involved seeking alterations to the draft directive to what was currently termed the 'Post-War Planning Section'.

The Strategical Planning Section of the J.P.S. had been invited to prepare draft terms of reference for it on 12 June.[22] Its first attempt, the following day, was largely based on a paper[23] drawn up by the War Office Director of Plans, Brigadier Guy Stewart, after consultation with van Cutsem. It listed as subjects for study the armistices of 1918 and 1940, the attempts at disarmament and control of defeated enemies thereafter, and the main problems considered by the Disarmament Conference of 1932–35. On the basis of lessons drawn from these events, the new section would turn its attention to (1) future armistice terms, (2) main principles and likely problems of Allied occupation in Europe, and (3) 'long-term strategic requirements'.[24]

The last of these items had not been suggested in Stewart's memorandum, which had pointed out that any strategic survey required as a background to enable the new section to turn from past lessons to future possibilities, 'would have been drawn up presumably by the STRATS [Strategical Planning Section] or by the post-war planning section in close contact with the STRATS'. This point appeared to be covered in a later draft[25] of 15 June, which specified that the section 'will obtain strategic guidance from the Strategic Section of the Joint Planning Staff' (though even then van Cutsem confessed himself 'a little apprehensive' that the work of the two sections might overlap in this area).[26] By the time a final version was approved by the Directors of Plans for consideration by other departments, however, this provision had been toned down:

---

21. ADM 1/12072
22. JP(42)595(S)(T.R.)   23. JPS Sec Min 42/634 in CAB 119/64
24. JP(42)597(S)(Prel. Draft)—missing, but obtainable in CAB 119/64
25. JP(42)597(S)(Draft)—as above
26. Letter to Howkins of 18 June in CAB 119/64

The Post-War Planning Section will refer matters *on which they require strategic guidance* to the Strategic Section of the Joint Planning Staff . . . .[27]

When the paper was duly circulated to the Service Ministries for their concurrence, as required by the War Cabinet's decision of 1 June, this weaker provision was allowed to stand. Although the Air Ministry secured the deletion of specific reference to future study of 'our long-term strategic requirements',[28] the directive which was eventually accepted by the Chiefs of Staff[29] still contained provision for the three new section members to be

collectively responsible for representing the joint Service viewpoint in regard to strategic questions and matters of interest to the Services generally.[30]

In addition to this, the appointment of a Rear-Admiral as chairman, albeit one reactivated from the Retired List, effectively ruled out the setting up of the new body as a fourth sub-section of the Joint Planning Staff, even were the nomination of a civilian as one of its Service members to be overlooked. It had now to be accorded a 'somewhat higher' status. The solution chosen by the Admiralty and incorporated in the final directive was to constitute it instead as a 'Military Sub-Committee' *of* the Ministerial Committee on Reconstruction Problems.[31] This made nonsense of the second paragraph of the same directive, which read:

The Sub-Committee will be under the general direction of the Chiefs of Staff Committee through the Directors of Plans, and will be on permanent loan to the Paymaster-General, being accommodated in his office.

Instead of being a sub-section of the Chiefs of Staff machine on permanent loan to the Paymaster-General—as intended when this paragraph had originally been drafted—the M.S.C. was now to be a sub-committee of the very organisation to which it was supposedly being loaned, and not even formally a part of the organisation which

---

27. JP(42)637 (Author's emphasis)   28. A/POL/ALL/13 in ADM 1/12072
29. COS(42)247th Mtg (3)   30. COS(42)380
31. Admiralty minute to Hollis of 9 July 1942, in ADM 1/12072

was supposedly lending it. The incoherence of this provision could only foster still further the degree to which the members of the new body would feel themselves set apart from the Joint Planning machine.

Not without justification did Ronald comment on 9 July that it had taken 'a distressingly long time' to get the military section under way.[32] It was nearly three months since the Foreign Office had requested an appreciation of the strategic value of international bases in Belgium, the Netherlands and Norway. Notwithstanding the negative attitude of the F.O.P.S. and the Directors of Plans, it still hoped to obtain one. The anxiety of the Joint Planning organisation to shed its post-war planning responsibilities, coupled with the vague status and ambiguous programme of the new 'Sub-Committee', meant that the diplomats might just succeed in this aim.

2. The Demise of the Bases Plan

Although the procedures and terms of reference of the Military Sub-Committee were not to be finalised until the second half of August 1942,[33] the Foreign Office wasted no time in approaching its personnel as soon as their identity became known. On 9 July, a preliminary meeting was held at Richmond Terrace between the three Service representatives, Nigel Ronald and H.M. Gladwyn Jebb who, as head of the Foreign Office Economic and Reconstruction Department which was just being established, 'would be the medium for requests and enquiries on the part of the Military Sub-Committee'. Not all the questions considered were procedural ones. In particular, it had always been Ronald's intention for any new body to work in close co-operation with the F.R.P.S., which would provide it with background material to co-ordinate and detailed studies to assess. Consequently, it was decided that:

> in connection with the Peace Handbooks under preparation, the Military Sub-Committee should consider to what extent the relevant strategic problems could be dealt with in them.[34]

There was little room for manoeuvre on this question in reality, as all were quite aware. Both the F.O.P.S. and the Directors of Plans had specifically ruled out consideration of all but secondary strategic issues

---

32. N3121/463/30
33. JP(42)145th Mtg (2) & COS(42)247th Mtg (3)   34. U120/120/70

for the handbooks, and a copy of their decision had been included in the material transferred to van Cutsem by the Joint Planners' secretary on 17 June.[35] For the time being, it remained only for the M.S.C. to dispose of the five Foreign Research and Press Service papers on war potential and arms control, held over since 18 May pending its own creation.[36] This it did by setting aside the first four as 'too general for useful comment at present', and suggesting with reference to the fifth that:

> the possibility of the total abolition of armaments (other than individual small arms for police purposes) should be considered as a means of breaking once and for all the military spirit of Germany and preventing the maintenance of her military tradition.[37]

Whilst consideration of such problems of control with strategic implications clearly fell within the orbit of immediate M.S.C. activities, the preparation of piecemeal post-war strategic appreciations assuredly did not. It was true that the draft directives still being circulated included long-term strategic planning among M.S.C. responsibilities, and that the J.P.S. papers passed over to van Cutsem included Foreign Office enquiries on security in the North Atlantic and in the Middle East. Yet, as has been seen, the Directors of Plans were totally against regional surveys prior to a global one, which, they believed, would have to await a clearer view of future foreign policy. By the time Jebb wrote to Bellairs at the end of July, however, urgently requesting M.S.C. views on the bases proposal before an approach was made to the War Cabinet, a draft appreciation on the subject was already well under way.[38] Though modelled to some extent on the previous F.O.P.S. bases papers, its production disregarded the whole basis of Stanley's revolt, which had been that the J.P.S. should travel no further along that path. Still, the Joint Planners' secretariat raised no objection on this point of principle when Bellairs requested a meeting with the Strategic Section to discuss the M.S.C. draft, but merely circulated the documentation for its preliminary consideration.[39]

The Military Sub-Committee's first major strategic draft was completed on 4 August 1942. This was some three months after the

35. U396/61/72 & JPS Sec Min 42/653 in CAB 119/64
36. JPS Sec Min 42/545 in CAB 119/64   37. MSC/30/2 in U606/61/72
38. N3121/463/30 & Bellairs, letter to Howkins of 5 August, in CAB 119/65
39. JP(42)727(S)(T.R.)

Future Planners had sent their last one on post-war security—reassessing Lie's plan in the event of Soviet hostility—to the Foreign Office. In the interim, on 26 May, a twenty-year treaty of alliance had been concluded between Britain and the U.S.S.R. This was deemed sufficient by the M.S.C. for the significance of the wider bases scheme to be considered 'from the point of view of an attack by Germany alone'. To this the Foreign Office was to raise no objection. As in the earlier Joint Planners' replies, the emphasis was on preventing the Germans from launching a *blitzkrieg* in the first place. This meant that Germany 'must not only be disarmed by the terms of the armistice but must be kept effectively disarmed for a very considerable period' under the supervision and control of occupation forces. To maintain these forces—were they developed—only administrative supply bases in Germany and the Low Countries would be necessary. On the other hand—were they not deployed—the alternative of a system of bases in Norway, Belgium, the Netherlands and Denmark would entail commitments to defend the host countries and to garrison the bases to a level probably in excess of any contribution that Britain would otherwise have made to a German occupation force. Noting that

> The present war abounds in instances of failures to hold restricted areas
> in the event of concentrated attack,

the M.S.C. nevertheless went on to express itself in favour of such bases as part of the general peace settlement. They would be needed as a precaution against failure to ensure the continued subjection of the Germans and as a sign to them that 'the United Nations mean to stay and work together'. Given the resultant obligations to Norway, Belgium and the Netherlands, and the dependence of the last two on the safeguarding of France's eastern frontier, it was

> evident that the defence of all these territories would be an impossible
> commitment for His Majesty's Government to undertake unless these
> nations themselves bore their full share and unless the United States also
> participated.[40]

The Sub-Committee's decision in favour of the scheme, despite its *caveat* on the negative aspects, caused a degree of puzzlement in the Foreign Office, which received a copy of the draft prior to its

---

40. *Ibid.*, Annex II

consideration by the Strategic Section of the J.P.S. As Jebb noted succinctly:

> What they really seem to say is 'If you keep Germany down bases are unnecessary; if you don't, then they will be ineffective!' But they then proceed to argue in favour of bases, presumably on the grounds that they could constitute a sort of reinsurance.

Frank Roberts of the Central Department felt that the value of such a reinsurance would lie in the mixing together of British and Continental interests, which would encourage the lesser allies to take practical steps for their own security. His view that

> we should not make these arrangements dependent upon American participation, however desirable this might be. Without it they may be even more necessary to us![41]

was endorsed by Cadogan's Deputy Under-Secretary, Sir Orme Sargent, though in complete contradiction to the M.S.C.'s thrice-stated opinion in the paper that the full collaboration of the United States would be essential in any bases scheme for Atlantic security. The Foreign Office was really less concerned with the actual strategic views of the Service advisers than with the mere fact of their having produced conclusions generally favourable to the bases scheme. These would enable a claim to be made in any approach to the War Cabinet that the Services approved of the proposal for post-war Continental bases; but no sooner had the Strategic Section turned its attention to the Sub-Committee's draft than Jebb learned from van Cutsem that it had run into trouble:

> It seems that the [Strategic Planners] do not take very kindly to the Military Sub-Committee's draft paper and want to make their replies much more vague and conditional.[42]

In view of the consistent J.P.S. hostility to the preparation of separate regional appreciations, this development should have caused little surprise. That strategic guidance for the M.S.C. should be provided by the Strategic Section rather than by the F.O.P.S. could be justified only because the strategic problems with which the M.S.C. was supposed to

---

41. N4245/3271/30 42. N4586/463/30

deal—initially, at least—were assumed to be *immediate* post-hostilities ones. It was only the fact that the STRATS had been earmarked for this role that prevented the draft on the bases plan being considered by Colonel Stanley's section as of long-term strategic significance. Had it been referred to the F.O.P.S., it would almost certainly have been totally extinguished as incompatible with declared J.P.S. policy on post-war planning. As it was, after a meeting with the Strategic Planners on 10 August, the M.S.C. did manage to produce a 'revised' paper, but it was one bearing very little resemblance to the original draft.[43] Instead it reverted to the Joint Planners' consistent view that present acceptance of the bases plan would be premature and might place the government in

> a difficult position if it amounted to undertaking a particular commitment before the general post-war strategic requirements had been settled.

This problem could be tackled only after the Military Sub-Committee had investigated the best methods for maintaining disarmament and control of defeated enemy states; after decisions about future world organisation and tasks of the respective Allied nations had been made; and after the trend of future developments in warfare had become clearer. In order to keep the offers open, they should be welcomed in principle, but any future acceptance of them should be deferred, 'pending further study of the general problem of which they form only a part'.[44]

The question now arose of what to do with the first full M.S.C. paper based on advice from the Strategic Section: should it be treated like a normal J.P. draft and put up to the Directors of Plans for approval? In the opinion of Major le Mesurier, the J.P.S. secretary currently most concerned, this would tend to create so great a burden for them as to defeat the object of setting up the M.S.C. on loan in the first place. On the other hand, as he wrote to van Cutsem, it would not be satisfactory to send out important papers over the signatures of the Directors unless they had actually studied the questions themselves.[45] Accordingly, a precedure was adopted whereby copies of all papers produced by the

---

43.   MSC/51 in CAB 119/65
44.   PWP(42)1 in CAB 119/65 (Regardless of its formal title, the M.S.C. continued to be described, within the J.P.S. secretariat, as the 'Post-War Planning Section' for the greater part of its existence; hence the 'PWP' reference given to some of its papers.)   45.   JPS Sec Min 42/870 in CAB 119/64

M.S.C. would be circulated to the Joint Planners for information before normally being forwarded to their destinations. As Jebb explained to his colleagues, in future

> whenever we ask the Military Sub-Committee for an opinion they will give it off their own bat and will circulate copies to the Directors of Plans. Only in the event of one of the Directors disagreeing violently with anything in the draft will it be necessary for the matter to be taken up any higher.[46]

The finalised paper on the bases plan was sent to the Foreign Office on 15 August under cover of a note clearly stating that neither the full J.P.S. nor the Chiefs of Staff had considered it.[47] Subsequently, le Mesurier confirmed that—provided that this point continued to be made—there would be no objection to the paper being annexed to a Foreign Office memorandum to the War Cabinet. What the Foreign Office wished to do, however, was to annex the earlier M.S.C. draft, which had been much more to its liking; but Sargent abandoned the idea once Bellairs pointed out that 'the final paper . . . of the 15th August should be considered the official version for submission to the War Cabinet, whereas the [earlier] paper . . . can be used as background in the Foreign Office'.

Though disappointed at the 'extreme caution' of the official inter-Service appreciation, most Foreign Office members involved persisted in the view outlined by Richard Law that the existence of international bases would go far to provide 'that element of confidence which was so conspicuously lacking between the two wars . . . even if . . . their actual value *during* a war would be negligible'.[48] However, an attempt to persuade Eden to allow the adoption of a positive political line with the Americans without prior reference to the War Cabinet was unsuccessful. He declared it 'very difficult to share the general enthusiasm for this scheme', and vetoed the taking of further action without political clearance at the highest level.[49] The Foreign Office memorandum that was eventually considered by the War Cabinet on 3 November conceded that the M.S.C. had felt unable to express a definite view on the military aspects for the time being, though recommending 'that we should take grateful note of the generous offer'.[50] Not only did the War

---

46. N4586/463/30   47. *Ibid.*, JPS Sec Min 42/885
48. N4594/463/30   49. N5554/463/30   50. WP(42)480

Cabinet decline to commit itself to informing the Americans that the bases plan had its political support, it adopted, *mutatis mutandis*, the Joint Planners' approach to post-war planning by deciding

> that before our representatives entered into any detailed examinations of this suggestion, the War Cabinet should reach certain general conclusions as to the broad lines on which we hoped to see international security re-established after the war.[51]

Ironically, this postponement of any definite verdict on the bases proposal stemmed from a recent initiative by Jebb, who had drawn up a 'Four Power Plan' in an 'attempt to formulate general [foreign] policy in the light of such indications as we have of American and Soviet intentions during and after the war'.[52] It was with reference to this development that the War Cabinet opted for delay, inviting instead the submission of a further memorandum dealing with the wider issues of post-war international security.

This time the Foreign Office advocates of the bases plan had to admit defeat and concede that 'it would certainly be preferable for the Cabinet to decide on general principles of security before considering details'. [53] It was felt that it would have to be left to the Americans to provide incentives to the minor Powers to keep their invitations alive. In the event, although the issue did not die, it was for a time displaced from the centre of the post-war strategic stage. At the end of 1943, Warner was to note 'the position about "Atlantic Security" still to be that H.M.G. and the U.S. Government do not wish to go ahead on this matter until the wider scheme of international security has been worked out'.[54] It would not be until July 1944 that he and Jebb would feel able to take an active interest in the bases plan once more—this time in the context of a Western European regional association within a global scheme for international security to which successive versions of the 'Four Power Plan' had by then given rise.[55]

3. Friction with the J.P.S., Concord with the Foreign Office: the Middle Eastern Papers and the 'Four Power Plan'

Of the four major issues originally held over until the creation of the Military Sub-Committee, by the end of August 1942 there remained

---

only two. These were the requests for 'rough provisional indications of what the Service advisers anticipate are likely to be our principal post-war strategic requirements', and for a detailed assessment of such requirements in the Middle East.[56] As in the case of the bases proposal, the absence of a general strategic survey did nothing to prevent the production of a regional one: by 9 September, a draft Middle Eastern appreciation had been completed for consideration by the Strategic Section of the J.P.S.[57]

It defined Britain's main strategic interests in the area as the protection of 'Imperial communications on the security of which our world strategy must be built' and the safeguarding of Middle Eastern oil supplies, which, with the probable growth of American and Soviet consumption of local deposits, would become increasingly important. The former comprised routes through the Mediterranean and Red Seas and along the Nile Valley and Persian Gulf; links between Egypt, the Levant and Iraq, and Persia; and communications between the Persian Gulf and Russia 'to maintain contact with our Ally as an alternative to the Mediterranean and Black Sea route should this . . . be closed'. The latter consisted of extensive deposits in Iraq, South Persia, the Arabian shore of the Gulf, and Egypt. Though envisaging a complex network of garrisons, bases and treaty rights to secure all these interests, the M.S.C. was reluctant to speculate about the nature of potential threats to them. Whilst a few remarks were made about possible Soviet encroachments upon Persia, that was mainly in response to specific Foreign Office queries. As in the case of its original bases appreciation, the sub-committee tended to take the continuation of the wartime alliance for granted, assuming, for example, that eventual defeat of Japan would restore the British Commonwealth to its pre-war position in the Far East, though 'its ties with the United States, Russia, China and the Dutch East Indies will be closer'.[58]

On 21 September, le Mesurier discussed the handling of this paper with the Directors of Plans. Their objections to the production of isolated regional surveys such as this had apparently declined with the relieving of their own organisation of the task of undertaking them. Bellairs was given the alternatives either of submitting the draft to the full J.P.S., if the matter could be allowed to 'stand over for a few weeks',

---

56.   JP(42)309(O)(T.R.) covering C2943/685/62 & JP(42)456(O)(T.R.) covering E2583/49/65   57.   MSC/55 in CAB 119/65
58.   PHJP/MSC/3 in CAB 119/65

or of having it considered by the Strategic Section as initially suggested.[59] In the event, even the latter failed to discuss it with the M.S.C. until 30 October.[60] On 9 November, the sub-committee resubmitted its paper to the J.P.S. in the hope that this—its third revised version—would be agreed 'on further consideration' by the Strategic Planners. The Eastern Department had been patiently awaiting the appreciation since the end of April and the Foreign Office was now pressing for it urgently.

Considerable changes had already been secured by the Strategic Planners. All coyness about prediction had disappeared. The paper was now based on the assumption that a minimum number of states would be friendly: namely, Greece and Turkey, and a United States whose co-operation could be counted upon as a deterrent to aggressors.

> As regards other members of the United Nations, whilst every effort is made to improve our relations with Russia and it is a cardinal principle in our post-war policy to prevent Russia from joining Germany in a bloc hostile to the United States and the British Commonwealth, Russia remains a doubtful quantity. The other United Nations are weak and absorbed in internal problems for several years, so that they will be unable to afford us much assistance in the military sphere, even should they all wish to do so.

To the primary strategic interests of oil and Middle Eastern communications identified by the M.S.C., a third had been added—the use of the area as an important base from which Britain could 'exercise pressure against Southern Europe in the event of developments hostile to Anglo-American interests'. The sub-committee had also incorporated stronger references to preventive measures against the Soviet Union, such as the securing of rights of occupation in Eritrea and Italian Somaliland to meet the air threat caused to communications if Russia established herself near the Gulf. On the protection of the Persian oilfields from Soviet encroachment, however, it baulked at the Strategic Planners' insistence on maintaining ground and air forces ready to move northwards to a strong natural line running through the Elburz Mountains and across Persian Azerbaijan. Apart from the logistical problem, the M.S.C. maintained that the preparation of such forces would inevitably be regarded by Russia as a major threat,

---

59. JPS Sec Min 42/1059 in CAB 119/65   60.   MSC/55 in E7171/49/65

particularly to her vital Caucasian oil supplies; that it would be inconsistent with the promise of future collaboration contained in the Anglo-Soviet Treaty; and that it would work against the aim of preventing Russian alignment with Germany against the West, which had been spelt out as a cardinal principle of post-war policy in the paper's opening paragraph.[61]

For its part, the Strategic Section was not prepared to fall in with Bellairs's suggestion that it should reconsider its attitude on points of divergence and let the paper stand. On 4 December, it replied with a counter-blast against the entire approach of the Military Sub-Committee:

> The Post-War Planning Committee [*sic*] consider that we should start off by assuming that certain countries—and in particular Russia—will be friendly, subsequently mentioning some modifications which would have to be made to our requirements in the event of Russia turning out to be hostile . . . . We, on the other hand, consider that at this stage of the discussions on post-war reconstruction, the only sound basis is to start off by assuming that we may be threatened by *any* country, except the U.S.A., state what areas we or our Allies require to be able to occupy to meet such threats, and then make it clear to the Foreign Office that if they can take political action which will rule out all possibility of this or that threat arising, then our requirements to occupy the relevant areas will, of course, disappear.[62]

That very day, Charles Baxter of the Eastern Department wrote to van Cutsem querying the fate of the Foreign Office's long-outstanding Middle Eastern enquiries, and reiterating that in the absence of 'any authoritative statement of British strategic needs, it is not always easy to avoid commitments which may later prove embarrassing and events beyond our control may make it impossible to go on hedging indefinitely'.[63] Van Cutsem's reply, in recounting the reasons for the delay, pointed out that in any case the final version would not constitute an 'authoritative statement of British strategic needs' as it would not have been seen by the Chiefs of Staff.[64] Still, Baxter's letter gave the Brigadier an opportunity to advise le Mesurier that if the Directors of Plans could not adjudicate between the M.S.C. and the Strategic

---

61. JP(42)986(S)(T.R.) covering MSC(42)3(3rd Revise)
62. JP(42)991(S)—missing, but obtainable in CAB 119/65
63. E2583/49/65   64. E7171/49/65

Planners within the next few days, the draft would have to be despatched as it stood.[65]

As in the case of the sub-committee's directive, the greatest interest was taken by the War Office Director of Plans, who chaired the J.P.S. meeting at which the paper was considered on 10 December.[66] The result was full endorsement, on all main issues, of the Strategic Section's position. From the purely military point of view, the Joint Planners stated, the only safe assumption was that all countries other than the United States—and probably Greece and Turkey also—were potential enemies. The Foreign Office might provide 'diplomatic security' against some, leaving 'military security' as a prerequisite for the remainder. As for any suggestion involving Soviet control of Persian Azerbaijan, this would be 'fraught with danger and must be avoided at all costs'.[67] Van Cutsem, the sole M.S.C. representative at the meeting, undertook to recast the appropriate parts of the appreciation, inserting in particular a new section elaborating upon the role of the Middle East as an offensive base housing reinforcements and a strategic reserve. All in all it was anticipated that, under one set of circumstances or another, rights of transit or of garrisoning for British forces would be needed in Egypt, Palestine, Transjordan, Cyrenaica, Iraq, the Lebanon, Syria, Persia, Aden and the Gulf shiekhdoms, Cyprus and the Dodecanese, British and Italian Somaliland, Eritrea, and the Sudan. On 14 December, the final version was forwarded to Baxter via Jebb—though, even at the last, the J.P.S. secretary still felt its assumptions about the post-war orientations of some states to go 'a good way beyond what was considered safe by Directors of Plans'.[68]

The troubled history of the Middle Eastern paper merely served to strengthen le Mesurier's view, which he had 'reason to believe is shared by a number of more important people', that the sub-committee was unlikely to be able to achieve much beyond the discussion of armistice terms, though tending to stray far more widely in its activities. Whilst its members were 'obviously highly intelligent people',

> ... All three are of a certain age, and they strike me as being exceptionally out of touch with current thought, and from such

65.   JPS Sec Min 42/1383 in CAB 119/65
66.   This was Stewart's last such contribution: at the end of January 1943, he was killed in an air accident returning from the Casablanca Conference.
67.   JP(42)197th Mtg   68.   U1821/1179/70 & JP(42)1025

conversations as I have had with them I have the impression that the post-war world will be so very different from anything they can conceive that their military plans are likely to be based on false premises.[69]

Whatever the Service planners thought of the M.S.C.'s assumptions, no such divergence existed between them and those of the Foreign Office. With the bulk of the Middle Eastern study completed in September 1942, Bellairs had turned his attention to the remaining request for a general strategic survey. On 27 October, he had written to Jebb enclosing a skeleton plan and asking for information on which to base political assumptions for the survey. This would forecast the political and military situation in 'about 1947'; incorporate seven regional examinations of military needs; 'aim at [the] minimum strategic requirements of the United Nations'; and be 'drafted from the point of view of the combined staff of the principal United Nations'. Bellairs's justification for addressing the task from the standpoint of this non-existent body was that 'it would be impracticable to attempt to consider a problem of this magnitude from the point of view of Great Britain alone'. Far from being disconcerted by this visionary proposal, Lord Hood, one of Jebb's assistants in the Economic and Reconstruction Department, minuted:

> The political background which the M.S.C. require should emerge from our discussions on the 4 Power Plan.[70]

This referred to the equally visionary proposals of his departmental head, which, as has been seen in connection with the bases plan, were to be considered by the War Cabinet prior to any further consideration of particular post-war security schemes. Jebb's long memorandum, well received at the highest Foreign Office levels, had examined what was understood to be current American thinking on a future global system:

> In theory, the world after the war should be run by the United Nations as a whole, but in practice major decisions should be taken by a small 'policy committee' of the four Great Powers. . . . The whole rather loose system would, in fact, be based on immense American sea and air power and (in a slightly secondary degree) on the British navy and air force and the Russian army.

69. JPS Sec Min 42/1116 in CAB 119/64
70. U1179/1179/70 covering MSC/50/1 & MSC(42)5(3rd Draft)

Such a scheme, Jebb believed, would depend upon two assumptions:
(1) that the United States, United Kingdom and Soviet Union would,
after the war, 'be both able and willing to enter into . . . world-wide
commitments in order to prevent any other nation from again troubling
the peace'; and (2) that the object of and incentive to such continuing
Great Power co-operation would be to hold down Germany and Japan
for as long a period as possible. The picture he painted embraced the
long-cherished Foreign Office scheme for confederations of the smaller
Powers in Eastern Europe.[71] These would 'collaborate with the Soviet
Union for defence purposes' and 'constitute a real buttress against
German penetration'. Primary responsibility for Europe would fall on
Britain and the U.S.S.R for geographical reasons and 'by virtue of the
Anglo-Soviet Treaty, which . . . however, need not preclude arrangements being made by Great Britain in Western Europe and by the
Soviet Government in Eastern Europe in order to control the foreign
policies of the local Powers'. In this context, the British and possibly
the Americans might negotiate special arrangements for naval and air
bases bordering on the North Sea. It was essential to allay Soviet
suspicions that the Western Allies aimed to use Russia to win a victory
presaging Anglo-American domination of the post-war world. Jebb
concluded that, whilst unlikely to commit themselves fully until the war
was over, the Russians were likely to be willing to adhere to the plan 'if
reassured as to the sincerity and good intentions of Great Britain and
the United States' in making 'a genuine offer of co-operation on a basis
of absolute equality'. If they rejected such co-operation,

> we should inevitably be driven into forming some kind of anti-Soviet
> front, and in doing so we should have eventually to accept the
> collaboration of Germany.[72]

These ideas were received with great enthusiasm by the members of
the M.S.C. at a meeting with Hood and Ronald (who, as Jebb's
superior, retained overall authority in his department's affairs). On 3
December, in a note to the latter covering suggested minor amendments,
Bellairs described the plan as 'excellent and just what is required for

---

71.　Throughout 1942, the F.R.P.S. in particular had studied this question in great
　　　detail: see especially C2167/241/18 and U420/61/72—a lengthy paper by
　　　J.D. Mabbott and extensive minutes thereon.
72.　U742/742/70 For a full account of the Four Power Plan as an aspect of foreign
　　　policy at this time, see: Sir Ll. Woodward, *British Foreign Policy in the Second
　　　World War* (London, H.M.S.O., 1976), v. 1–21.

guidance'.[73] This was just one week before the Directors of Plans met on the Middle East appreciation and declared the only safe military planning assumption to be the potential enmity of everyone after the war, except the Americans. The only comfort the M.S.C. could take from that J.P.S. meeting was the conceding of the principle that regional strategic surveys might, after all, be acceptable: despite the difficulty of making satisfactory evaluations 'until we knew more precisely what our general policy was going to be and what territories we should require to defend . . . , it was necessary to attack the problem somewhere, and it might be that the present appreciation would assist the Foreign Office in studying the wider world picture'.[74]

If the Joint Planners knew that on 27 November the War Cabinet had given 'general approval'[75] to Eden's suggestion that

> we should regard the conception of the Four Powers, working within the framework of the United Nations, as the present basis of our foreign policy,[76]

they chose to make no mention of the fact. Nor did the M.S.C., either then or later, while quietly pressing on with its own ideas in the more congenial Foreign Office mould. In January 1943, the members of the War Cabinet were issued with a revised version of Jebb's scheme, which had by then become known as the 'United Nations Plan'.[77] The M.S.C.'s appreciation of this paper was supplied to the Foreign Office in draft form via Jowitt on 12 March, without prior reference to the Joint Planning Staff.[78] Regardless of the caution which the latter had previously injected into its Atlantic and Middle Eastern surveys, the sub-committee reverted to a sanguine view of probable post-war Soviet intentions, citing the twenty-year treaty of alliance and adding that

> Russian interests in south-eastern Europe, the Middle East and the Pacific would seem to involve her in concern for the future peace of these regions in which the British Commonwealth also has direct interests.

There would be 'everything to gain' if the plan could be made to succeed. Continued co-operation by the three main Powers would ensure the safety of the British Isles and imperial communications, as well as the security of the Middle East and essential oil supplies. Since

73. U1797/742/70   74. JP(42)197th Mtg   75. WM(42)161st Concls (2)
76. WP(42)516   77. WP(43)31   78. MSC draft memo in U1158/402/70

there was danger that the Americans might favour at first a policy of partial isolation from Europe, and that the Soviet Union—bent on internal recovery—might not wish to take part in any world organisation, it was necessary

> that whilst keeping the ideal of a world organisation in mind and framing long-term plans accordingly, our policy should aim at attaining agreement on regional plans of a less ambitious nature which particularly concern the security of the British Empire.

Such plans should cover the Atlantic, North-West European, Middle East and Mediterranean, and Pacific and Indian Ocean areas. In the first of these regions, there was every prospect of full American co-operation. In the second, countries such as Norway, Denmark, Belgium, France and the Netherlands would probably 'in their own interests wish to enter into a western European pact which would include the United Kingdom'. Their occupation by an aggressor would pose a severe threat to the security of the United Kingdom. Consequently, the British should consider providing, with others, a strategic reserve to serve as an international police force operating from Continental bases defended by the host nations. For the Eastern Mediterranean and Middle East a regional agreement was desirable with Egypt, Persia, Turkey, Greece, Iraq and the Soviet Union; another, with France and Spain, should cater for the Western Mediterranean; and the Indian and Pacific Ocean regions should be divided into four zones under the responsibility of various permutations of the 'Four Powers', France and the Netherlands. Whilst pointing out that these proposals were not antagonistic to the United Nations Plan and might form a stable foundation for it, the Military Sub-Committee viewed such 'lesser schemes of regional security' as a more modest alternative should the ideal of quadripartite control not be agreed. How a lesser scheme of this type would have to be adapted in the face of open hostility between the Great Powers was not, however, considered.

Despite a good reception for the draft in the Economic and Reconstruction Department, Ronald felt it premature to take matters further before Dominion views on the central plan had been obtained. Nevertheless, it enabled Jebb to represent the next version of his scheme[79] as a 'consensus', embodying the ideas, *inter alia*, of the

---

79.   WP(43)300

Military Sub-Committee—although at no stage had the remainder of the Chiefs of Staff organisation been consulted at any level.[80]

Nor was this the only unilateral excursion into strategic planning by the members of the M.S.C. In October 1942, the Foreign Research and Press Service had produced its own assessment of the original bases plan.[81] Entitled 'The Question of an Atlantic Security System', it recommended a regional arrangement integrated with similar ones under a world system run by the Great Powers, but did not suggest Soviet participation in the Atlantic area. This naturally caused concern in the Foreign Office, which forwarded a copy of the paper to Bellairs. On 6 February 1943, the Military Sub-Committee supplied its comments, framing them in accordance with the memorandum on the United Nations Plan, which it had also been allowed to examine:

> It is considered that the U.S.S.R. should certainly be included, as part of the proposed system in the F.O. paper W.P.(43)31 of 16.1.43. She can assist in the control of the area between the Atlantic and the North Sea, which is as much in her interests as in our own.[82]

Once again, at no stage were the Strategic Planners or Directors of Plans consulted about the tendering of this opinion. Neither had they sanctioned the adoption of the Four Power Plan as the basis for post-war *military* planning in the first place. Their view would almost certainly have been that the fact that it was War Cabinet policy to work for continued Great Power co-operation after the war neither entailed nor justified failing to plan on the hypothesis that it might in reality break down. The Military Sub-Committee had been directed to assume a minimum of friendly states in the preparation of strategic plans, although this was against the inclinations of its members. It had inherited terms of reference to produce a global survey, which dated from the short F.O.P.S. period of post-war planning responsibility when the Directors of Plans had clearly condemned any positive commitment to the bases idea which it was now freely advocating. That the M.S.C. could behave in this way was partly because of its ambiguous status, which allowed its opinions to be channelled through Jowitt rather than the C.O.S. organisation; partly because of its isolated position and vague directive which, though giving it the option of consulting the J.P.S. on strategic matters, did not specifically require

---

80. U2889/402/70   81. U1047/61/72   82. U641/58/72

it to do so; partly because of its originally intended role as a mere collator and co-ordinator, which gave it direct access to the Foreign Office and F.R.P.S.; partly because of the development and political endorsement of theories of world organisation, which matched its own predilections; but principally because the Chiefs of Staff and Directors of Plans had lacked both time and inclination to turn sufficient attention away from prosecution of the war to monitor the M.S.C. efficiently and keep it under control.

Examination of the final strategic paper it completed makes it hard to avoid the conclusion that the sub-committee tended to tailor its approach to post-war planning according to the particular body with which it was dealing. Out of the Middle Eastern survey had emerged a need, conceded by the Joint Planners themselves, to examine strategic requirements after the war in the Mediterranean area as a whole. Given this link, it was to be expected that the new paper would be based upon the same assumptions as those underlying the survey which had given rise to it. As has been seen, the Directors of Plans had ruled that those should be cautious in the extreme. On this occasion, however, no formal list of assumptions for planning was spelt out and, although it took from 10 January to 25 June 1943 to pilot the M.S.C. draft through the J.P.S. machine, none was attached to the final version. Once again, the M.S.C. came into conflict with the Strategic Section for placing more emphasis on the security of communications than on protection of oil supplies, and once again its emphasis was reversed; but at least the overall conclusions of the paper required little alteration.

As amended, the Mediterranean survey justified the post-war maintenance of British strength in the area on the following grounds: (1) primarily to protect the Middle East by the exercise of air and sea power in the Eastern Mediterranean; (2) similarly to prevent a European aggressor coming south through the Balkans from crossing the sea and eventually threatening communications in the Indian Ocean by seizing a position in East Africa; (3) to preclude a corresponding southward thrust—in the Western Mediterranean— aimed at the North African Atlantic shores and enabling British communications in that ocean likewise to be threatened; (4) to secure the Mediterranean as an important mercantile highway; and (5) to serve as a power base from which influence could be exerted upon Southern Europe and Turkey. Possibilities of Soviet, French and Italian hostility were all considered. In the Eastern Mediterranean, the main requirements would be the maintenance of existing bases at Haifa and Alexandria, and in Cyprus, Cyrenaica and the Suez Canal area. Access to Crete and possibly to other Greek islands would be important in the event of a hostile U.S.S.R., but,

> until the probability of such action by Russia can be foreseen, it would be premature to exert any pressure on Greece for the right to establish bases in her other islands in order to meet a threat which appears remote.

The right to move forces to and through a number of Arab countries should a threat of war develop would also be desirable, especially in defence of oil supplies to Haifa, given a hostile Russia or France. In the latter case, it would be necessary to invade Syria and the Lebanon to remove the threat to Palestine. In the Western and Central Mediterranean, defence would depend on Gibraltar, Malta and Crete, augmented by access to bases in Algeria, Tunisia and areas to the south of the Straits of Gibraltar. On the basis of this outline, it was recommended that post-war policy should aim at continued friendly relations with France, Greece, Turkey and the Soviet Union, whilst keeping Spain at least neutral and Italy disarmed and unable to join in hostile combination with France against the United Kingdom.[83]

In January 1943, the Foreign Office had held a preliminary meeting on the Middle Eastern appreciation which had been the cause of such friction between the Military Sub-Committee and the Strategic Section of the Joint Planning Staff. Prospects of retaining even existing military facilities in Egypt had been viewed as doubtful, and, given the importance of denying the Russians any pretext for refusing to withdraw from Northern Persia after the war, it had been concluded that the long-term defence of the Suez Canal and of Abadan would probably have to be undertaken from external bases.[84] As Hood had remarked when that M.S.C. paper was received, to defend all the interests it described would require 'greater military facilities in the various countries than we have hitherto possessed. Politically this may be impractical.' It had seemed to him that the solution might be a regional defence scheme under the hoped-for world organisation, with Britain as senior partner supplying a strategic reserve enjoying rights of access and transit in local member states.[85] However, all further speculation had been postponed pending receipt of the wider Mediterranean study.

---

83.   MSC/53(4th Draft) & MSC/53(Final) in CAB 119/65
84.   U516/516/70   85.   U1821/1179/70

The Military Sub-Committee met in conference with the Foreign Office on 23 June, when the new paper was all but complete. The Strategic Section's amendments had been incorporated and the Directors of Plans were about to approve it on an individual departmental basis instead of giving it full consideration at a J.P.S. meeting.[86] Jebb, as chairman of the meeting, outlined the Foreign Office belief that

> the maintenance of Britain's position in the Middle East and Mediterranean would depend to an increasing extent on the judicious blending of force and consent. Military safeguards, however complete in themselves, would not suffice unless they were accompanied by the political goodwill of the countries situated in the area.

The attitude of the Soviet Union would be crucial, a friendly Russia having to be included—if only nominally—in any Middle Eastern security system set up. Warner added that Britain's

> policy was certainly to go all out for Russian co-operation, and the Russian response so far was encouraging . . . therefore we should take a co-operative and friendly Russia as the present working hypothesis for our plans,

though having in reserve alternative plans should such hopes fail to be realised. The M.S.C. undertook to adopt this line of approach in revising its appreciations, ignoring the fact that it did not accord with J.P.S. instructions for the consideration of post-war strategic problems. Furthermore, when asked by Jebb if Britain would be likely to have enough forces to meet all the commitments set out,

> M.S.C. said that their plans were based on the premise of some general security system and that, assuming effective disarmament of the Axis powers and Russian co-operation, they were confident that the United Kingdom would be able to discharge all the defence obligations mentioned.[87]

Although the latter assumptions might be excused as an *ad hoc* response to a question which had not yet been considered within the C.O.S. organisation, the former 'premise' had specifically been

---

86.   JPS Sec Min 43/530 in CAB 119/65   87.   U2937/516/70

rejected as the basis for the Middle Eastern paper by the Directors of Plans. It was true that the assumptions of the Mediterranean study had not been listed in the paper, but those of the Middle Eastern one giving rise to it had—and they provided for the anticipation of little more than American co-operation. Thus, Group Captain Roland Vintras, the Air Force member of the Strategic Section, in writing to his Deputy Director of Plans on 30 April, had expressed the view that the Mediterranean study had been

> written on the same assumptions as the Sub-Committee's paper on Post-war Middle East Strategic Requirements . . . These assumptions look at the problem from the British point of view. In the absence of any Foreign Office policy as to what the post-war international set-up is likely to be, this is presumably the only way of looking at it.[88]

Not only was the M.S.C. now claiming not to have written it on those assumptions, it had manifestly failed to bring to the attention of the Joint Planners its enthusiastic involvement with diplomatic thinking on 'Four Power' lines. This failure was particularly ironic in the light of Ronald's original conception of the Military Sub-Committee as a co-ordinating body. In its state of limbo between the Foreign Office and the Chiefs of Staff machine, dabbling in strategic matters as never really intended, the sub-committee was effectively contributing to a line of approach by the one of which, it had reason to believe, the other did not approve. The prospect of a world security scheme based upon the Atlantic Charter had been mentioned only twice in the entire Mediterranean appreciation. It did not feature in the Middle Eastern paper at all. If the M.S.C. really considered that it was 'basing' its strategic plans on the assumption of a general security scheme, its failure to spell this out in the Mediterranean paper reflected, at best, muddled thinking or, at worst, a desire to avoid being overruled yet again by the harder line of the J.P.S.

The sub-committee's days as a semi-independent agent were, however, rapidly drawing to their close. Towards the end of May 1943, Bellairs had learned with some bewilderment of moves to reform his organisation.[89] What he did not know was that these had been afoot since early in April, and that the Foreign Office—so enthusiastically

---

88. Vintras letter in CAB 119/65
89. E. Bridges, confidential note of 31 May 1943, in CAB 21/2294

served by the M.S.C.—had been deeply involved in them right from the outset.

4. Radical Surgery at Richmond Terrace

In the twelve months of its existence, the members of the Military Sub-Committee were employed in the examination of a wide range of subjects of which their controversial strategic appreciations formed only a fraction. At the beginning of 1943, they produced the first British project for the zonal occupation of Germany.[90] By March, they were proposing measures for the total disarmament and eventual deindustrialisation of that country, and considering armistice terms for Italy, Romania and Finland.[91] Detailed examinations of German and Italian methods of occupation and control in France and North Africa were carried out on the basis of captured enemy documents;[92] a rough estimate of post-armistice troop requirements was undertaken for the War Office; and a review of possible future disturbed areas in Europe was also drawn up.[93] Although studies of this sort to resolve immediate post-hostilities military problems did not fall into the category of strategic planning as such, their proposals would sometimes clearly have had a bearing upon it if eventually implemented. This particularly applied to a paper which the M.S.C. finalised towards the end of June as a plan for the future Polish-German frontier. It recommended the cession to Poland of territories including Danzig, East Prussia, Upper Silesia and parts of Pomerania, and the compulsory westward transfer of some 4¼ million Germans. This would yield the military advantages of reducing the length of the frontier, lessening the threat of German offensives to the south or east, and making Allied control of the Baltic more practicable by increasing Polish access to the sea. It would also yield the political advantage of nullifying 'any efforts the Germans might subsequently make to use these districts as they did the Sudetenland up to 1938'.[94] Despite these strategic implications, it does not appear that the sub-committee felt it necessary to consult the Joint Planning Staff about the paper before the question of its own future came up for consideration.

90. T. Sharp, *The Wartime Alliance and the Zonal Division of Germany* (Oxford, Clarendon Press, 1975), p. 36
91. JP(43)20th Mtg (4) & Donnison, *op. cit.*, pp. 83–6
92. See MSC/14/4, MSC/14/4/1 & MSC/40/4 in WO 106/2759
93. MSC(43)6/6—Progress Report No. 10 in CAB 21/2294
94. MSC/54 in ADM 116/5118

Apart from its periodic *contretemps* with the Strategic Planners, the main liaison between the M.S.C. and the Chiefs of Staff organisation had been by monthly report. By early February 1943, Bellairs had received indications that something more might be required by the Chiefs of Staff to ensure that M.S.C. papers, 'particularly those of a strategic nature', had their general approval. His anxious enquiry whether they were

> satisfied with the present procedure under which we make sure that in the strategic sphere we do not put forward anything contrary to the ideas of the Directors of Plans[95]

was followed up on 3 March with a direct approach to Ismay, who assured him that, unless there was a direct conflict with the Joint Planners, the Service chiefs would wish neither to intervene themselves nor to sanction his alternative suggestion of approaches being made to the Vice-Chiefs. Ismay pointed out that the sub-committee's work was mainly 'exploratory' and did not commit the Chiefs of Staff to any definite decisions; but, if Bellairs thought that he had succeeded in forestalling criticism on this score, he was much mistaken. The following week, the Directors of Plans approved a suggestion from their secretariat that they should meet the M.S.C. for a general discussion of its activities, since the Joint Planning Staff might presently 'at short notice, be instructed to report on the type of problem with which the Post-War Planning Section [*sic*] deal'.[96] When this meeting was duly held on 19 March, Bellairs took the opportunity to add to his résumé of work then in hand a statement of the main strategic problem:

> the Military Sub-Committee found itself in the position of having to make various assumptions from time to time which in the absence of a central policy approved by His Majesty's Government might prove unsound.

Once again, no mention was made of the progress of the United Nations/Four Power Plan at War Cabinet level, though barely a week had elapsed since the sending of the M.S.C.'s draft comments upon it to the Foreign Office.[97] This was a curious omission and must have been prompted either by sheer muddle-headedness on the part of the M.S.C. or by awareness of having overstepped the mark in favouring a scheme

---

95. MSC/9 in CAB 119/64
96. JPS Sec Min 43/318 in CAB 119/64   97. See p. 37 above

it knew to be generally at variance with J.P.S. ideas. On the whole, the
latter is the more likely explanation—the M.S.C.'s responsiveness to
the post-war assumptions of the Foreign Office belying its professed
caution with the Joint Planners. Although Ismay had turned down
Bellairs's attempt to go over the heads of the Joint Planners to obtain
strategic guidance, Bellairs renewed it by suggesting that the Chiefs of
Staff should make recommendations to the War Cabinet on post-war
military requirements in Europe. He was, perhaps, banking on eventual
endorsement of M.S.C. ideas higher in the C.O.S. machine or
subsequently by the politicians whom he knew to have adopted the
'Four Power' thesis as the basis for post-war foreign policy. All he
secured, however, was an invitation to formulate 'the broad principles
which should be adopted as a background against which . . . post-war
problems could be considered'. These would simply be assessed by the
J.P.S. in the normal way and forwarded to the War Cabinet via Jowitt
once approved by the Directors of Plans.[98]

In the end, the event which sealed the fate of the M.S.C. came from
an unexpected quarter: van Cutsem had failed to attend the 19 March
meeting with the Joint Planners, and, shortly afterwards, Ronald felt it
necessary to inform his Foreign Office colleague, William Cavendish-
Bentinck, that the Brigadier was suffering from a breakdown in health
and might be unable to continue as a member of the sub-committee. To
Cavendish-Bentinck's responsibilities as chairman of the Joint Intelligence Sub-Committee had been added, the previous year, those of
Foreign Office adviser to the Directors of Plans. In this second
capacity, he responded with alacrity to Ronald's suggestion that
'advantage might be taken of this accident . . . to get someone put in
who had the confidence of the Army Council'. In Cavendish-
Bentinck's view, more radical steps were essential:

> If the Military Sub-Committee is allowed to continue indefinitely with its
> present composition and method of work there will be trouble sooner or
> later. The only way in which this trouble can be avoided is by appointing
> a Führer for this body with drive . . . who would have the confidence of
> the Chiefs of Staff.

A reformed committee would tender periodical reports to the Service
chiefs who might well dislike being forced to deal with it fairly
frequently,

---

98.   JP(43)20th Mtg (4)

but it is no use having this body dealing with military questions working under a civilian Minister and only receiving rather vague guidance from the Directors of Plans, who have not got the time to pay attention to them.

The recent meeting between the Joint Planners and the M.S.C. had been 'rather futile' and its conclusion 'merely intended to fob off the Military Sub-Committee'.[99] Cavendish-Bentinck arranged to take up the whole question with the Directors of Plans on 9 April and pointed out to them that

as in fact the Chiefs of Staff had—as is usual with anything tiresome— passed the direction of the Military Sub-Committee to the Directors of Plans, they ... [were] liable to be held responsible for the work—or failure in the work—of this Sub-Committee.[100]

It was generally agreed that the present position was unsatisfactory, that the directive to the M.S.C. was too obscurely worded to indicate how far the Joint Planners were responsible for it, that a high-level chairman and a change of personnel might be necessary, and that a reconstituted committee might report directly to the Vice-Chiefs of Staff. According to the Joint Planners' confidential record of this meeting, they decided that, before taking any further action, they should 'ascertain exactly what progress the Military Sub-Committee had made in the study of an Italian armistice'. On the basis of their findings, it noted laconically,

it would be possible for Directors to decide whether the existing machinery could be adapted to provide the service needed, or whether it would be necessary for them to approach the Chiefs of Staff with a view to substituting some alternative organisation.[101]

Cavendish-Bentinck explained matters to Ronald and Jebb somewhat more bluntly:

As a first step it was decided to ask the Military Sub-Committee to inform the Directors of Plans as soon as possible what military commitment would be involved in ensuring the execution of the armistice

---

99.   U2231/2231/70   100.   U2232/2231/70
101.   JP(43)30th Mtg (Confidential Annex)—missing, but obtainable in CAB 119/64

terms proposed for Italy. It is believed that the Military Sub-Committee will have some difficulty in answering this question. They have not yet prepared the draft memorandum (as requested on March 19th) setting out the broad principles which should be adopted as a background against which our post-war problems could be examined.

Their reply would provide an occasion for the Joint Planners to raise the whole question of the M.S.C. with General Ismay, but Cavendish-Bentinck was unimpressed with this ploy:

> I expect that Admiral Bellairs will find some reply dodging the ball which has been bowled him in regard to the commitment involved . . . and will suspect that we are out to do down his Sub-Committee and take away his job. I told my colleagues so, but they complained that as usual I am too suspicious.[102]

Jebb responded by suggesting a direct approach to Ismay by the Foreign Office unless the J.P.S. put forward a serious scheme promptly, but on 21 April their secretariat complied with a draft minute to Brigadier Hollis, stating plainly that there was

> no inter-Service body in existence at the present time which is properly constituted to examine . . . the shape which the end of the war in Europe is likely to take and the proper measures for the Allies to meet the situation likely then to arise.

It cited the M.S.C.'s tenuous contact with the Service Departments, its isolated position under the Reconstruction Problems Committee, and its tendency to 'refrain from troubling either level of the Chiefs of Staff organisation', given their more urgent concerns. For the first time, attention was drawn to the original War Cabinet decision to set up a sifting and collating body—which was all that the M.S.C. should have been—though no mention was made of the Joint Planners' responsibility for letting it become embroiled in strategic matters. A fresh sub-committee was required, composed of officers currently employed in the Service Departments and a Foreign Office representative. Though served by a permanent staff, they should meet only as and when necessary to consider draft papers drawn up for their approval for

---

102.   U2232/2231/70

submission to the Chiefs of Staff directly or to the War Cabinet via the Foreign Secretary:

> The general conception would be that the new Sub-Committee would form, with the J.P. and the J.I.C., a third sub-committee of the Chiefs of Staff, the whole forming the Joint Staff.[103]

Well pleased with these proposals, Cavendish-Bentinck urged Hollis to act upon them speedily, and on 11 May they were endorsed at a meeting convened by the Secretary to the War Cabinet, Sir Edward Bridges. It was agreed to seek a general blessing for the new scheme informally from the Vice-Chiefs, the head of the Foreign Office, and the Service Ministers, before approaching Jowitt on the impending loss of a part of his organisation. The following day Jebb duly minuted Cadogan, pointing out that for some time it had been evident that the M.S.C. was 'hardly . . . up to its job'. The situation had changed since the spring of 1942 when 'Armistice and related problems' had seemed very remote from realities, but although the Chiefs of Staff were now ready to take such matters seriously, neither they nor the Joint Planners could be expected

> to confide their hopes and fears to a Committee sitting in the midst of a group which seems to them (rightly or wrongly) to be composed of long-haired, woolly-minded, starry-eyed Reconstructionists.

An integrated organisation under the Chiefs of Staff, and with regular Foreign Office representation, strongly appealed to both Cadogan and Eden, who backed the proposals at once.[104] Simultaneously, Hollis broached the subject with the Vice-Chiefs of Staff, adding that

> we did not wish to put anything on paper for the moment, since the Military Sub-Committee would be unaware that any reorganisation was on foot.[105]

Initial reluctance on their part gave way in the face of support for reform from the Director of Military Operations, General Kennedy, and by the end of the month Bridges felt that the way was clear to write to the

---

103. JPS Sec Min 43/501 in CAB 119/64
104. U2234 & U2235/2231/70
105. COS Sec Min 329/3, in CAB 21/2294

Ministers concerned. A reluctance openly to attack the competence of the existing M.S.C. personnel led him, however, to stress the 'greatly enhanced . . . importance of the work now being done' by the sub-committee as the main reason for reconstituting it. Yet, as Jowitt pointed out to him at a tense and unhappy meeting on 31 May, the examples of new ground to be examined cited in his letter 'were all in fact covered by the existing terms of reference . . . . What really were the proposals all about? . . . Admiral Bellairs, who had now heard of these proposals from the Admiralty, did not understand what they were all about.'[106] Indeed, on receipt of Bridges's letter, the Permanent Secretary to the Admiralty Board—Sir Henry Markham—had thought it 'peculiar' that nearly all the proposed subjects for study were 'already comprehended in the directive issued to the Committee'.[107] It was to take considerable tactful manoeuvring on the part of the War Cabinet Secretary to mollify the parties concerned, as well as a personal approach to Markham on 21 June—'I am under constant pressure to get a move on with this matter but am handicapped by the absence of any reply'—to secure the agreement of the Admiralty.[108]

Whether such agreement would ever have been forthcoming had the question of personalities been openly discussed may well be doubted. Cavendish-Bentinck had consistently advocated a clean sweep of M.S.C. personnel. He suspected that Bellairs owed his position to 'a long-standing friendship with the First Sea Lord' and predicted that his departure 'would probably be no loss from the work point of view'. He endorsed Jebb's assessments of van Cutsem ('excellent as an accumulator of facts . . . [but] quite hopeless in other respects') and Spaight ('a charming but rather deaf old gentleman . . . who is . . . entirely out of touch with his Department'), and concluded:

> that Admiral Bellairs should press strongly for the retention of Mr. Spaight is to my mind a further indication that Admiral Bellairs himself had better be got rid of . . . we want to get together the strongest body that we can, and the sternest voice, and certainly the guiding hand, should be that of the representative of the Foreign Office, who should be Chairman.[109]

106.   Bridges's confidential note of 31 May 1943, in CAB 21/2294
107.   ADM 1/12853
108.   Bridges to Markham & A.V. Alexander to Bridges, in CAB 21/2294
109.   U2235 & U2471/2231/70

As Jebb later reported, such views were not confined to the Foreign Office staff. On 23 June, Bridges told him

> in great confidence that a member of his Secretariat had suggested to him that no real progress could be made unless 'the whole existing M.S.C. was blown up'. I asked him what was meant by this and he said it meant getting rid of Admiral Bellairs, Brigadier van Cutsem and Mr. Spaight and replacing them by more dynamic characters.[110]

Although Jebb and Bridges felt that the loss of Bellairs should be avoided, it was agreed that, if his two colleagues were retained, more senior figures should be installed above them. Cavendish-Bentinck was also somewhat disappointed to see that the draft War Cabinet paper which Bridges produced at the end of June did not specifically lay down Foreign Office assumption of the chairmanship. He considered that even if Jebb, as his department's nominee, were to become chairman by mutual consent, this would 'not be as satisfactory as a Cabinet ruling that the Foreign Office representive is to be the Chairman'; but the prospect of further delays led Ronald to suggest that the original War Cabinet conclusion setting up the M.S.C. had been sufficiently vaguely worded to cover what was now proposed and to obviate the need for further governmental approval.[111] Though professing himself 'rather fed-up with the Foreign Office' and insisting upon eventual ratification at least by the Ministers concerned, Bridges agreed to this change of direction.[112] As he must have realised, the paper he produced for Hollis to submit to the Vice-Chiefs of Staff on reconstituting the M.S.C. as an 'International Security Committee' clearly overstepped the provisions of the War Cabinet's decision of June 1942. The paper then approved had provided for Jowitt's

> setting up a military section in his office whose function it would be not to define future military policy, but to collect such facts as are known, to act as liaison between the various departments concerned with these [armistice and control] problems and to assist and direct research on the most profitable lines.[113]

What was now proposed was a new sub-committee specifically empowered to

---

110. U3033/2231/70   111. ·U3498/2231/70
112. Bridges, minute to Hollis of 6 July 1943, in CAB 21/2294
113. WP(42)205(Revise)

put forward solutions for problems likely to arise in connection with the occupation of enemy territory in so far as such problems are connected with those presented by the administration of any instruments of surrender or with questions of general politico-strategic importance . . . [and] to advise the Foreign Office on the military and strategic aspects of these political and administrative questions.[114]

In evaluating these proposals, the V.C.I.G.S., Lieutenant-General Archibald Nye, generally welcomed the notion of a post-war politico-strategic planning body modelled on the Joint Intelligence Sub-Committee, headed by part-time Directors from relevant departments, and served by existing full-time personnel augmented by 'the introduction of younger blood'.[115] On 15 July, the Vice-Chiefs approved the suggested reconstitution, but—possibly in an attempt to outbid the opposition—the V.C.N.S. indicated that the Admiralty representative would be its Director of Plans.[116] This immediately gave the other Vice-Chiefs 'some idea of following the Admiralty's suit and appointing all three Directors of Plans to the new Sub-Committee', as Hollis reported to Bridges, which 'would indeed have made us all look foolish, since one of the objects of the reorganisation was to relieve the Directors of Plans of as much responsibility as possible for the Military Sub-Committee's work'.[117] By the V.C.O.S. meeting of 22 July, however, the notion of drafting the Joint Planners had fallen by the wayside. It was decided to give the Service Departments discretion to send up to two representatives each, provided that they arranged to keep any employed full time on post-war planning closely in touch with departmental policy. Nye's suggestion that the Foreign Office supply a chairman was approved, and a new directive based on Bridges's proposals was finally agreed.[118]

As well as emphasising their primary tasks relating to armistice and control problems, the directive charged the members of the 'Post-Hostilities Planning Sub-Committee' (as Nye had renamed it) with collective responsibility for 'representing the Joint Service viewpoint in regard to post-hostilities strategic questions', and acting 'as a channel through which the Service Departments can exchange views with the Foreign Office and with other interested Departments of State'.[119] Reports would be tendered, as appropriate, to the Chiefs of Staff

---

114.   COS(43)193   115.   COS(43)198   116.   COS(43)114th Mtg (2)
117.   Hollis, note of 16 July 1943, in CAB 21/2294
118.   COS(43)117th Mtg (1)   119.   COS(43)199(Final)

Committee or to the Ministerial Committee on Armistice Terms and Civil Administration,[120] which was about to be set up under Clement Attlee to advise the War Cabinet on the subjects embraced by its title. These proposals were accepted by Jowitt and the Service Ministers by the end of July, freeing a relieved Bridges from further intrigues to create a post-war planning apparatus.[121] The first that the War Cabinet knew of this development was on 31 July, when the Vice-Chiefs' final paper covering the directive to the new organisation was circulated to them for information only.[122]

As to personnel, all the members of the M.S.C. survived its reform, but van Cutsem and Spaight were respectively subordinated to a Major-General, Maurice Grove-White, and a retired Air Vice-Marshal, Sir Arthur Longmore, who had been in command of the R.A.F. in the Middle East from 1940 to 1941. Bellairs was augmented by Humphrey Waldock, an academic and legal expert who had joined the Admiralty on a temporary basis in 1940 and risen to the level of Assistant Secretary. Jebb duly attained the chairmanship, from where he could attempt not only 'to point out at a very early stage the F.O. interest in whatever matter may be under discussion' by the Post-Hostilities Planners, but also to 'exercise some real influence over the purely military side of their work' in a process he candidly described as one of 'infiltration'.[123]

Cavendish-Bentinck had predicted that

> with a few more applications of the knife the Military Sub-Committee, which has hitherto been a figure of fun, can be made into a body which will inspire confidence and start off on the right leg our brave new world ... from the moment when our enemies surrender.[124]

His efforts had certainly resulted in a closing of the gap separating the activities of the 'Four Power Planners' in the Foreign Office from those of the Servicemen in the C.O.S. organisation, who viewed post-war contingency planning in a much more cautious and sceptical light—

---

120.   WP(43)350 & ACA(43)1 The A.C.A. Committee came into existence on 4 August 1943, to 'consider and where necessary advise the War Cabinet' on terms of surrender and the administration of occupied and liberated territory. From 26 November 1943, it was served by an Official ('A.C.A.O.') Committee of permanent representatives from the Service Ministries, Foreign Office and Ministry of Production. (See ACA(43)19)   121.   CAB 21/2294
122.   WP(43)351 covering COS(43)199(Final)   123.   U2471/2231/70
124.   *Ibid.*

when they could be persuaded to consider it at all. Post-war planning was now officially on the Chiefs of Staff agenda, though not the P.H.P.'s main priority; but it still remained to be seen if the greater Foreign Office interest in the subject would enable it to influence the military in its preferred, optimistic direction.

3
THE POST-HOSTILITIES PLANNING SUB-COMMITTEE 1943–44

1. The Straits Appreciation and the Palestine Papers

The new sub-committee was to complete more than sixty assorted studies during the ten months of its existence. As in the case of the M.S.C., however, only a small proportion of its output would fall squarely into the category of long-term strategic planning. By far the greater part would deal with such problems as the surrender, occupation, zonal division, military rule and future frontiers of defeated enemy states. Though clearly bearing upon post-war military requirements, these studies seldom involved fundamental consideration of the principles according to which such requirements would have to be determined. Nor, indeed, were first principles always spelt out in the main strategic papers that were drawn up—though it was characteristic of the Directors of Plans to ensure that the first piecemeal appreciation which the P.H.P. produced for them should promptly lead to a wider examination of the field in which it lay. The point of departure was Russia's post-war position in the Dardanelles; the study to which it led was of the likely effects of her post-war policy on Britain's overall strategic interests.

As early as January 1943, the Joint Planners had given some thought to possible Soviet claims for unrestricted use of ice-free ports after the war, and had predicted that a demand to control the Straits between the Eastern Mediterranean and Black Sea might be made before the close of hostilities.[1] The Foreign Office response had been to dismiss the question of what Britain's attitude should be in the face of any such demand as too hypothetical to be considered in advance of particular circumstances becoming known. All that could be said for the time

---

1. Scott, minute to Northern and Southern Departments, in CAB 119/65

being was that, apart from a brief period during the First World War, it had been

> an axiom of British foreign policy that the Soviet Union should not have physical control of the Straits nor unrestricted use of this exit from the Black Sea.

Under the twenty-year Montreux Convention of 1936,[2] Turkey had been appointed 'sole guardian of the Straits', and further reaffirmation of the fact would only encourage the Turks to persist in refusing to enter the war on the Allied side. Such a move would constitute 'conclusive evidence' that continued Turkish control of the Dardanelles was so important to the British that they would be obliged to support it at the peace settlement whether or not Turkey abandoned neutrality.[3]

Six months later, however, the Foreign Office had begun to have second thoughts. A letter from the Southern Department to the Chiefs of Staff on 5 July asked firstly whether a Turkish declaration of belligerency would still be more of an asset than a liability in the context of current military intentions, and secondly whether it would still be essential to Britain's post-war position in the Mediterranean that Russia should not control the Dardanelles—

> either because under conditions of modern warfare the free passage of a belligerent Russian fleet through the Dardanelles would not constitute the same dislocation of strength in the Mediterranean as would formerly have been the case, or because our Treaty of Alliance with Russia or the strengthening of our strategical position in the Mediterranean would entitle us to run the risk of such dislocation if political considerations required it?

This change of approach stemmed from a paradoxical increase in Turkish determination to remain neutral in the aftermath of British victories in Tunisia: 'in [Turkish] eyes the danger of Russian aggression *after the war* increases in exact proportion as the danger of German aggression *during the war* grows less'.[4] Clearly, if the Chiefs of Staff still wanted Turkey to join the Allies and if Soviet control of the Straits

---

2. *Convention regarding the Regime of the Straits* of 20 July 1936 (Cmd. 5551) An account of the background to this treaty is contained in JP(43)294(Final) Annex.
3. JPS Sec Min 43/137, covering F.O. reply to Scott, in CAB 119/65
4. COS(43)364(0)

need no longer give rise to concern, real pressure could be brought to bear on the Turks by threatening to abandon them to any Russian encroachment from the north.[5]

On 23 July, the Chiefs of Staff approved a peremptory reply by the Joint Planners that the Foreign Office be informed that no decisions on Mediterranean strategy after the elimination of Italy had yet been taken, and that policy towards Turkey could not be reconsidered until the larger question had been settled.[6] Since the primary issue of Turkish belligerence could not be resolved, the secondary one of post-war Russia and the Straits was ignored until a further request was received that it be dealt with in its own right. This task clearly came within the province of the Post-Hostilities Planners, to whom the J.P.S. referred it on 11 August.[7] They took the view that

> it was most desirable that action from the strategic point of view should not be taken which would antagonise either Russia or Turkey,[8]

and produced their appreciation of long-term strategic needs in the area before a week had passed. It considered the greater danger by far lay in the offensive potential of any zone ceded to the Russians as a means of controlling the Straits rather than in the actual passage through the waterways of Soviet naval units. Not only could such territory be used to house an air force capable of attacking the Suez Canal and coast of North Africa, it would also enable deployment of striking forces against the eastern frontier of Greece and along a second frontier with Turkey. Whilst the naval threat could probably be countered from the bases envisaged in the M.S.C.'s Mediterranean survey, the creation of a Russian land and air threat from the Straits region was highly undesirable. Nor was there any justification, in the view of the sub-committee, for abandoning traditional support for Turkish control of the Dardanelles and the Bosporus. The most that could be contemplated as an alternative to Soviet control was that Russia be granted free rights of passage for surface ships through the Straits unless at war with Turkey. Physical control of the waterways should remain in the hands of the latter.[9]

The P.H.P. report formed the basis of a draft reply to the Foreign

---

5. U3765/2231/70   6.   JP(43)240(Final) & COS(43)170th Mtg (0)(8)
7. PHP(43)5(T.R.) in U3763/516/70   8.   PHP(43)4th Mtg (1)
9. PHP(43)5(Final)

Office prepared by the Joint Planning Staff on 24 August. Terse in the extreme, this accepted the analysis of the relative air, land and naval threats which would result from the creation of a Soviet enclave bordering on the Straits. It added that the granting of such control would greatly simplify any attempt to operate Russian submarines in the Eastern Mediterranean, but also pointed out that an air threat comparable to that from the area of the Straits would come into existence if Soviet airfields were established in Bulgaria. No mention was made of the P.H.P.'s suggestion that the alternative of allowing their surface vessels unrestricted rights of passage might placate the Russians. Nor indeed was there any reference to possible changes in the Montreux Convention short of giving full physical control to the Soviet Union.[10] This omission was unsatisfactory, in the view of the V.C.I.G.S. According to Nye, such a slackening of restrictions might have a different impact on British strategic interests than would a radical change in control. 'Upon the advice which the Chiefs of Staff gave to the Foreign Office on this matter, might depend most important issues of policy,' so it was necessary to expand the paper and consider all eventualities.[11]

On 20 September, the Joint Planners produced their revised report: the existing convention was felt to constitute satisfactory protection for British interests at no greater cost than the provision of diplomatic support to the Turks and the maintenance at a reasonable strength of the Mediterranean fleet and Middle Eastern garrisons. Neither physical control of the Straits nor unrestricted rights of passage through them should be accorded to the Russians. The one would increase their effectiveness in any attack on Turkey, the Balkans, or Mediterranean sea communications; even the other would leave them 'well placed to make as their opening moves against Turkey or Greece the seizure of vital ports and airfields in the Northern Aegean'. Nevertheless, if total intransigence on either of these aspects would lead to more dangerous claims in other directions, some revision of the Straits convention might prove to be the more advantageous course. The prospect of an increased Soviet threat to Persia and the Gulf by way of the Caucasus was particularly to be avoided. The Directors of Plans concluded that, were the Russians to raise the question of revising the convention, it would be premature to return a negative answer without having first assessed Britain's entire post-war position *vis-à-vis* the Soviet Union.

---

10. JP(43)283(Final)   11.   COS(43)197th Mtg (0)(9)

This assessment they now proposed to undertake in conjunction with the Post-Hostilities Planners.[12]

When the Chiefs of Staff approved the report for the Foreign Office on 22 September, they endorsed this suggestion of a wider examination;[13] but when the subject came up for detailed consideration the following day, the Joint Planners promptly secured their agreement to the entire burden being passed across to the P.H.P. It was agreed to state, as the political basis for this study, that it was government policy to remain on terms of close friendship with the U.S.S.R. The 'importance of keeping secret the fact that such a study was being made' was especially stressed, lest it be 'subject to misinterpretation with possibly unfortunate effects upon Anglo-Russian relations'. Finally, it was decided that the Foreign Office should be asked to approve terms of reference for:

> an appreciation of the probable long-term impact of Russian policy on British strategic interests. The object of the appreciation is to formulate the basic principles on which the Chiefs of Staff should found their military advice when called upon to express an opinion on questions of policy affecting Russia,

and the Northern Department was duly contacted.[14]

Although Warner was pleased with the Service chiefs' decision to undertake the study, he realised that it would be a difficult paper to produce in the absence of 'any real evidence as to what is Russian policy as regards the future'. The forthcoming Three Power Conference in Moscow might provide some indication of it, but it was doubtful if Soviet intentions had crystallised:

> The Russians are in fact likely to have two alternative policies and not to make up their minds finally until they can assess the results of co-operation with us during the war.

It would be on the basis of these two alternative policies, concluded Warner, that the P.H.P. paper would probably have to be drafted.[15]

The Post-Hostilities Planners met to discuss how best to proceed on 12 October. The agenda of the meeting reflected the exceptional care being taken to keep the proposed study a secret, referring to it only as 'a

---

12.   JP(43)294(Final)   13.   COS(43)223rd Mtg (0)(1)
14.   COS(43)224th Mtg (0)(1) & Annex I   15.   N6007/499/38

certain appreciation',[16] and the minutes were circulated out of series under a special designation. In the event, the principal conclusion was that before the main task could be tackled it would be necessary to ask the Joint Intelligence Sub-Committee to indicate

> the lines on which Russian policy might be expected to develop in the post-war years, and the questions in relation to which that policy would be likely to impact upon vital British interests.[17]

Given the almost total lack of genuine intelligence about Soviet intentions, however, the method actually adopted was for the J.I.C. to confine itself to commenting on points of detail in a Foreign Office 'background' assessment of the probable post-war situation. Although this meant that the greater part of the P.H.P.'s 'formidable task'—as Jebb had described it—was, in effect, being carried out in the Foreign Office, he and his colleagues on the sub-committee continued to be engaged in a second regional appreciation. This would serve to show to some extent how the Chiefs of Staff viewed post-war strategic requirements in the Middle Eastern theatre.

At its inaugural meeting on 4 August, the Ministerial Committee on Palestine had decided to seek an assessment of long-term military needs in that country from the Post-Hostilities Planners. Three weeks later, they had responded with a concise appreciation of the Middle East as a whole, of which Palestine was considered to be 'strategically part of the hub'. That paper had reverted to the old M.S.C. preferences of listing the security of communications above the protection of oil supplies, of omitting to mention the possibility of using the region for offensive purposes as a third vital interest, and of specifying no planning assumptions about future potential enemies. The nature of the measures required to safeguard the two listed interests would depend upon such unforeseeable factors as: the character of any international security body which emerged 'to safeguard the general peace of the world'; whether or not America relapsed into isolationism; future Anglo-Soviet and Anglo-Turkish relations; a decision about siting a substantial strategic reserve in the Middle East; the availability or otherwise of military facilities in Arab states and former Italian colonies; and the attitude of the Arab governments to whatever regime

---

16. PHP(43)18th Mtg (inserted in lieu of minutes)
17. PHP(43)1st Mtg (0)(1)

that might be established in Palestine. Notwithstanding all this uncertainty, however, it remained

> clear that we shall need to draw the greater part of the oil supplies of the British Commonwealth both in peace and in war from Iraq, South Persia and the Persian Gulf.

Consequently, the oil pipelines and lines of communication with oil-producing states passing through Palestine were of major concern to the United Kingdom. The peace and security of the country would, therefore, be of the 'utmost importance', and its continued occupation by British forces after the war would be essential.[18]

By November 1943, the Palestine Committee had decided that partition was 'the most likely policy to provide a solution to the Palestine problem' and the Chiefs of Staff were asked for their comments on a plan to create four distinct states in the Levant.[19] The first attempt to estimate the military implications of this plan was made by the P.H.P. in a paper which appeared over the signature of Bellairs on 13 December. It took a relatively strong line with the assumption that

> any world security organization which may be set up after the war will not initially be of a character to relieve the British Empire and Commonwealth of responsibility for ensuring their strategic position in the Levant.

It reinserted the use of the Middle East as an offensive base in its list of strategic requirements; pointed to the record of the Iraqi and Egyptian governments since independence as 'a warning against placing too much reliance upon the three proposed independent Levant States as pillars of our security in time of crisis'; and concluded that British rights to land, sea and air base facilities in all four post-war Levant countries would have to be secured by means of broadly framed treaties binding each state.[20]

On this occasion the P.H.P. paper had to be cleared at the highest

---

18.   PHP(43)6(Final)
19.   COS(43)299 The four states were to be: Greater Syria, comprising Syria, the Arab parts of Palestine, and Transjordan; the Lebanon; a Jewish state; and a Jerusalem state. All would be independent, except the fourth, which would be under British administration.   20.   PHP(43)41(Final)

level, as the Ministerial Committee had specifically requested the opinion of the Chiefs of Staff on the partition proposals. Since the C.I.G.S., Sir Alan Brooke, was visiting British and American force commanders in Italy and subsequently went on leave,[21] it fell to Nye to represent the War Office viewpoint at C.O.S. meetings on 16 and 22 November. At the first of these, he cast doubt on the degree of precision with which Britain's post-war strategic requirements had been stated in the report and suggested a brief postponement of further consideration of it.[22] As in the case of the Straits appreciation, Nye stressed the 'great military importance' of the questions involved, and he took the trouble of having the P.H.P. paper re-written in the War Office and circulated as an alternative to the original. It was on the basis of this re-draft that the Post-Hostilities Planners were instructed by the Service Chiefs to revise their report.[23] Although the general arrangements recommended for the area remained unchanged, the definition of strategic requirements underwent considerable modification. Control of the Suez Canal now headed the list—as a means of denying 'to any enemy European state access to the Indian Ocean and Far East through the Middle East', of imposing an economic blockade, and of mounting offensive operations from the region.

Next came the safeguarding of oil resources and their lines of supply—entailing 'freedom of movement for our armed forces in each State, and absolute priority of passage over all means of communication in time of emergency or war'. The third vital requirement was the safe use of airfields in the Levant—of great economic value in peace, this would become a strategic necessity in war. Finally, secure British control in the Middle East would serve another two essential purposes—the protection of the main sea route to the East, and the convenient location of strategic reserve forces at a nodal point in imperial communications.[24]

The revised study was approved by the Chiefs of Staff on 5 January 1944, though not without reservations by Brooke, who remarked that it still required 'strengthening'[25] and who subsequently insisted on representations being made to the War Cabinet to point out that

---

21. Sir A. Bryant, *The Alanbrooke Diaries: Triumph in the West, 1943–1946* (London, Collins, 1959), pp. 122–3, & Brooke, *Diary* (Alanbrooke Papers), 5/8, p. 58   22. COS(43)306th Mtg (0)(6)   23. COS(43)312th Mtg (0)(7)
24. PHP(43)3(0)(Final)   25. COS(44)3rd Mtg (0)(12)

the [partition] proposals themselves, if implemented, would seriously increase the difficulty of ensuring that . . . strategic requirements were secured.[26]

This aptitude for opposing post-war proposals viewed as militarily unrealistic was to be exercised to the full in the months ahead.[27]

2. The 'Four Power' Thesis and the Clash with the Chiefs of Staff

It was not until over six months after the establishment of the Post-Hostilities Planning Sub-Committee that the fundamental question of post-war world security came to a head. This was due partly to the much greater concentration of effort on the 'control' rather than the 'strategic' dimension of the P.H.P.'s brief, and partly to the protracted process of re-drafting, which delayed production of a paper on the subject. The issue had, however, very nearly been joined at a relatively early stage of P.H.P. activity in 1943.

On 24 August, the Vice-Chiefs of Staff had approved a suggestion by Nye that the sub-committee should examine the post-war size of the forces of Britain's European allies and the sources from which they should be equipped.[28] When the P.H.P. considered these questions on 8 September, it resolved that

what was required in the first instance was a paper based on the general scheme of the United Nations Plan showing the danger areas of the world, the security forces which would be required for these areas, and the composition and organisation of the forces needed.[29]

As a first step, an interim report was prepared for the Chiefs of Staff which distinguished between the forces required immediately after the end of the fighting and those needed subsequently for long-term security. Before the latter could be estimated, it was deemed 'essential to obtain approval for certain definite assumptions' upon which planners could base their calculations and without which any such

---

26. COS(44)15th Mtg (0)(11)
27. For revealing insights into the personalities of Brooke, Ismay, Nye and Kennedy, and an evocation of the atmosphere in which they worked, see: G. Mallaby, *From My Level* (London, Hutchinson, 1965), Ch. 2.
28. COS(43)237 & COS(43)134th Mtg (4)   29. PHP(43)10th Mtg (2)

estimate would be 'useless and misleading'. Five political assumptions were accordingly proposed:

(a) That some kind of world organisation on the general lines suggested by the Foreign Secretary in his paper entitled 'The United Nations Plan' (W.P.(43)300) will come into existence, if only in a provisional form, at some stage after the termination of hostilities with Germany, and possibly before the end of the war with Japan.
(b) That the United States are prepared to play an important part in organising the security of Europe.
(c) That the Soviet Union continues to follow a policy of close collaboration with Great Britain and with the United States.
(d) That France and the minor European Allies join in the scheme for a World Organisation.
(e) That the phrase 'A scheme for international policing' used in the Chiefs of Staff's instructions[30] implies some system whereby, when so directed, each State concerned places all or part of its forces at the disposal of a World Authority, acting through a Supreme Commander in any given area.

Upon this basis, if approved, the sub-committee proposed to divide up the world into a system of military zones, and to study the military organisation required to provide security in those covering Europe and the Atlantic, and the Mediterranean area.[31]

That the Chiefs of Staff were not altogether in tune with internationalist assumptions of this kind was, to some extent, already becoming apparent. On 17 September, they dismissed as unnecessary and undesirable P.H.P. plans for a Supreme Allied Commander for the whole of Germany and for the inclusion of 'contingents from the forces of the other two great powers and of the smaller powers interested' within each occupational subdivision of the country.[32] Yet, when the sub-committee's suggested list of assumptions came before the Chiefs of Staff less than a fortnight later, the C.I.G.S. adopted a relatively mild attitude towards them. Remarking that they 'seemed to him reasonable', Brooke confined himself to deprecating estimates of post-war force requirements in Europe as 'a waste of time' in advance of War Cabinet

---

30. These had actually referred to nothing more far-reaching than 'the provision of contingents for any scheme of international policing which may be decided upon'. 31. PHP(43)17(Final)
32. COS(43)219th Mtg (0)(13) & PHP(43)7(a)(Final)

guidance as to how Germany was to be occupied.[33] Consideration of the P.H.P. paper was consequently deferred for the time being. It did eventually resurface briefly—in the course of sub-committee business on 20 December[34]—only to be promptly put to one side and presently overtaken by events when the Chiefs of Staff pronounced upon Jebb's strategic *pièce de résistance*: the military counterpart to the Four Power Plan.

It was one of the newcomers to post-war planning, Sir Arthur Longmore, who had made the opening moves to propose specific military arrangements for an international security scheme. Having prepared a rough draft on the subject in the autumn of 1943 and discussed it at a low level in the Air Ministry,[35] he had submitted it to his P.H.P. colleagues on 18 October. At this meeting it was claimed to be no more than a tentative approach, designed to elicit the reactions of the Chiefs of Staff and incorporating 'examples of what *might* be rather that what *should* be'. Hood attended as the Foreign Office representative on this occasion, and it was his 'guiding hand' which could be detected in the ensuing discussion. It was pointed out that a world security system would have few attractions for the Russians unless initially directed against the defeated Axis. Nevertheless, it was also suggested that such a scheme offered the only possibility of Britain being able to obtain access to various post-war bases. Those desired in Iraq and Saudi Arabia, for example, would almost certainly not be made available on a bilateral basis. This was the line that Hood had taken in response to the M.S.C.'s list of Middle Eastern requirements in December 1942, and it provoked a warning from Professor Charles Webster—the F.O.R.D. representative at the meeting—that

> No scheme which was clearly designed to further British interests under
> a cloak of internationalism would have any prospect of success.[36]

Of more immediate concern to the Post-Hostilities Planners, however, were their own prospects of success in persuading the Chiefs of Staff to endorse the general conception of a world security system. In this endeavour, arguments such as Hood's would clearly be of value.

Successive draft papers were examined at seven further meetings of

---

33. COS(43)230th Mtg (0)(11)   34. PHP(43)33rd Mtg (2)
35. PHP(43)1st Mtg(0)(2)(Re-designated 18th Meeting of the sub-committee: see pp. 59–60 above)   36. PHP(43)19th Mtg (1)

the sub-committee between 29 October 1943 and 27 January 1944. In mid-November, one was actually finalised on the principle of forming

> on a regional basis, in advance of any emergency . . . combined forces composed of contingents drawn from the various nations in the 'region' which would at intervals exercise together under the control of some duly appointed supreme commander.[37]

Given the scepticism which had greeted similar P.H.P. proposals concerning Germany alone, the chances of this paper proving acceptable to the Chiefs of Staff were limited—notwithstanding their seeming acquiescence in the five political assumptions previously formulated. In the event, it had still not been considered by them when the sub-committee's main effort, entitled 'The Military Aspect of any Post-War Security Organisation', appeared in its final format on 3 February 1944. Jebb's lengthy cover note, which the P.H.P. adopted[38] as a preamble to the finished version, made it perfectly clear that the sub-committee harboured no illusions about likely reaction to the contents. It sought to justify production of the paper by reference to the 'Declaration of the Four Nations on General Security', signed on 1 November 1943 after the Moscow Conference of Foreign Ministers. Its fourth article had committed the Soviet Union, the United States, Britain and China to recognition of:

> the necessity of establishing at the earliest practicable date a general international organization, based on the principle of the sovereign equality of all peace-loving states and open to membership by all such states, large and small, for the maintenance of international peace and security.[39]

In reality, as has been seen, drafting of the paper had begun prior to this conference; but the making of the Declaration, and the prospect of imminent tripartite talks to implement its provisions, enabled it to be passed off 'as a military brief [for use] by the British representatives in the forthcoming discussions'. As such, it would commit neither the United Kingdom government nor the Chiefs of Staff to all or any of the

---

37. PHP(43)24(Final)   38. PHP(44)3rd Mtg (1)
39. Quoted in: W. Knapp, *A History of War and Peace, 1939–1965* (London, R.I.I.A. & O.U.P., 1967), p. 47

proposals it embodied. Approval in principle by the latter would simply imply that the Service chiefs regarded nothing within it as 'actually repugnant', and that they considered nothing omitted from it to be vitally important. The scheme outlined was intended to chart a middle course between impractical notions of fully internationalised policing forces, dependent on the creation of a world government, and existing systems of 'nuclear alliances'—i.e. ones negotiated bilaterally between individual Powers. Jebb concluded with an argument of calculated pragmatic force:

> Whatever doubts may be felt as to the possibility of establishing any really effective world security organisation, the fact remains that only by co-operating with the American administration in their attempts to do so are we likely to induce them and their people to play that part in the post-war world which will be almost essential if a revival of some new aggressive Axis is to be avoided . . . It remains true in our view that in the absence of something like nuclear alliances, world peace cannot be preserved for very long; but it is also true that in the absence of some scheme which can at least be represented as a step towards the creation of an international society, we are not in practice likely to get our nuclear alliances.

Every effort had been made to adopt a similarly businesslike approach in the layout of the substantive paper: any world security scheme would be bound to fail unless the governments of the Four Powers continued to co-operate wholeheartedly in its support, and unless they and their peoples retained the will to act to enforce peace. The organisation must be kept simple, with clear-cut objectives and familiar types of administrative machinery. It would be designed to disarm Germany and Japan, to keep them disarmed, and to prevent them or any other aggressor from upsetting international security. Mere economic sanctions were unlikely to deter a regime that was ready to resort to force. On the other hand, total integration of different national forces could not be achieved in the absence of a world state. Instead, co-ordination of strategic plans and military contingents should be carried out by a Military Staff Committee of representatives of the Four Powers. These representatives would be under the supervision and control of the Service authorities of their respective countries, so that members of the 'World Council' would not receive different military advice from different sources:

On an emergency arising, it would be for the World Council, on the advice of the Military Staff Committee, to decide what proportion of the forces at its disposal would be needed to deal with the situation.

In order to be capable of functioning smoothly when required, the various contingents would have to have co-operated extensively in peacetime by exercising together and jointly occupying key areas such as the Kiel Canal. The existence of an effective Military Staff Committee and the provision of facilities for joint garrisoning and training would constitute the principal modifications to pre-war attempts at organising international security.[40]

The Chiefs of Staff considered all this at their meeting on 17 February and resolved to instruct the members of the sub-committee 'to re-write their paper on a broader basis and to put forward proposals of a more general nature'. Although—according to the official record—they accepted that 'some form of international organisation for maintaining world security would eventually be set up', it was generally agreed to be currently 'too early to attempt to forecast the probable composition of such an organisation'.[41] As Jebb, who had been invited to attend the relevant part of the meeting, later reported to Cadogan, this hardly did justice to what had occurred:

> I was kept waiting for about ¾ hour while the Chiefs of Staff argued the paper as between themselves. After about ½ hour an agitated secretary (who is a friend of mine) came out and told me that the paper had "all gone wrong". . . . When I went in I was consequently not surprised when the C.I.G.S. said that they did not like the paper at all . . . How could the World Council or whatever it was 'dispose' of the national forces concerned? It was a most unrealistic conception and bore no relation to reality.

With regard to the Military Staff Committee, Brooke stated quite bluntly that 'he and his colleagues were opposed to the whole idea . . . which in their opinion could never be made to work'. The key to future security was to continue the Combined Chiefs of Staff[42] after the war: it would be 'almost inconceivable' to have even Russia associated with

---

40. PHP(43)24a(Final)   41. COS(44)50th Mtg (0)(3)
42. Set up in February 1942 to co-ordinate British and American strategy, the C.C.S. comprised the Service chiefs of both countries, with the British Chiefs of Staff Committee represented—between conferences—by members of its Joint Staff Mission in Washington.

this, and the addition of other nations, such as the Chinese, would make it 'quite unworkable'. In any case, what was the point of such a body as the P.H.P. proposed? Jebb replied that its role would be defined as keeping Germany and Japan in order. The whole conception rested on the post-war co-operation of the three Great Powers and China.[43] If this were accepted, some such scheme was inevitable; otherwise, the entire question clearly lapsed. His report continued:

> It was pretty clear that the Chiefs of Staff for their part did *not* accept the Four Power thesis. They argued that what in practice was likely to happen was that the Combined Chiefs of Staff would continue in being; that the Russians would have a very large sphere of their own in which they would have their own 'security' organisation; and that China was anyhow rather a joke.

In their view, though there might be some kind of 'World Council', it would meet only at intervals. The national representatives upon it would be accompanied by their own Service advisers, to whom they would turn whenever in need of military guidance. There would be no requirement for a standing military organisation: in practice,

> any 'incident' which occurred in the Soviet sphere would be dealt with by the Soviets and in the rest of the world it would be dealt with by the Combined Chiefs of Staff. Why should the Chinese be dragged into the Kiel Canal? And might not our scheme result in bringing the Russians into that area when if we did nothing they might stay out?

Although Anglo-American and Soviet military power was currently very great and might be overwhelming at the end of hostilities, conceded Jebb in reply, 'it would, relatively speaking, undoubtedly decline in the post-war years'. Other major Powers, such as a restored France, would at least have to be associated with the Combined Chiefs of Staff in some way. As for the Chinese and the Kiel Canal,

> we had never contemplated their participation in this 'regional' scheme; while for their part the Russians would be bound to be in the neighbourhood. The only question was whether we should be there too.

---

43. 'As any plan must', minuted Cadogan at this point.

When Brooke concluded that the paper should be re-written to lead up solely to those of its conclusions ruling out a completely internationalised 'Police Force', pointing out the need for any world organisation to be initially directed against Germany and Japan, and stating the *sine qua non* of whole-hearted Great Power co-operation for its success, Jebb felt bound to remark that he 'did not think that would altogether do as a brief for our unfortunate representatives' at the forthcoming Washington talks on post-war international security. It was this which prompted the Chief of the Air Staff to suggest, somewhat whimsically, a way out of the impasse: consideration of such questions—which were possibly of more importance even than the war—was really not a task for the present Chiefs of Staff but rather one for their successors. Since he and his colleagues did not have the time to consider them properly, Portal continued,

> the sensible thing to do would be to appoint our successors here and now and tell them to go on winning the peace while we go on winning the war.[44]

Brooke also took the view that

> so long as many major strategical problems affecting the conduct of the war still confronted the Chiefs of Staff, they could not devote the necessary time and attention to complex post-war problems,

and it was agreed that Ismay and Bridges should review the existing organisation for dealing with post-hostilities problems and submit recommendations for its adjustment.[45]

With this conclusion at least, Jebb was prepared to concur. The whole incident had convinced him that the present machinery was unsatisfactory—an opinion shared by Cadogan, who angrily observed:

> Unfortunately, the P.H.P. are an emanation of the C[hief]s of S[taff], so that their papers have to be submitted to these pundits ... it is ridiculous that a paper of this kind should, at this stage, go to the C[hief]s of S[taff], and ridiculous that they sh[oul]d kill or maim it.

Although he concluded that it was for the government to try to outline the scheme for post-war security and to direct the Service chiefs

---

44.   U1751/748/70   45.   COS(44)50th Mtg (0)(4)

accordingly,[46] the fact of the matter was that diplomatic 'infiltration' of the C.O.S. machine had turned out to be a double-edged weapon. When Jebb succeeded in injecting Foreign Office ideas into military planning from his internal vantage-point, formal inter-departmental approaches drawing attention to possible points of contention could be avoided; but the converse was now seen to be that, when confronted with P.H.P. suggestions deemed to be undesirable, the Chiefs of Staff could reject them out of hand with much less compunction than if they had openly been presented as Foreign Office policy.

It appeared, for a time, that head-on confrontation would be inevitable. Jebb drafted a long letter from Eden to the C.I.G.S., praising the rejected paper as an 'excellent effort', reiterating the need for substantive proposals to be tabled at Washington, and suggesting that ministers be invited to resolve any specific military objections. This letter was never despatched. As a result of urgent consultations between Bridges and Ismay, it was agreed that the best way of relieving the Chiefs of Staff of their irksome responsibility for post-war questions was by persuading the Vice-Chiefs to shoulder the entire burden. Not only did the latter most closely approximate to Portal's notion of a 'shadow' C.O.S. Committee, they had—over four months previously—made a point of insisting that any future major changes in the P.H.P. should be submitted for their approval before implementation.[47] On 7 March, Jebb was able to report that, following the application of considerable persuasive pressure, they would probably be considering the world security paper afresh in the near future 'without reference to views previously expressed by the Chiefs of Staff'. It also seemed probable that the Vice-Chiefs would be taking some decision about the structure of the sub-committee itself, since it had been

> felt for some time that P.H.P. would function better if its principal members were not 'whole time' but were doing a job of work in their own Departments.[48]

Given the fact that the whole question of reorganisation had arisen solely as a result of Jebb's *contretemps* with the Chiefs of Staff, he might have been expected to regard this prospect with a certain amount of suspicion. That he viewed it instead with equanimity and even enthusiasm may be explained by the Vice-Chiefs' apparent willingness

---

46. U1751/748/70   47. COS(43)147th Mtg (9)   48. U1751/748/70

to take United Nations matters seriously. On 16 March, they conceded in principle that it was 'necessary to "take the plunge" and put forward some proposals as a basis for discussion'.[49] Tentative approval of the contentious paper, and of a supplementary document on United Nations bases, followed seven days later—subject only to minor amendments.[50] Yet this reversal of the very C.O.S. decision which had brought the future of the P.H.P. under scrutiny did not imply Service satisfaction with its overall performance. Whether Jebb knew it or not, there was

> a general feeling that the Organisation was not working as efficiently or smoothly as the other Inter-Service bodies, and that re-organisation . . . was necessary.[51]

An estimate[52] of P.H.P. defects had been drawn up by Ismay, but it was Kennedy who undertook the task of suggesting remedial measures. In his capacity as Assistant C.I.G.S. (Operations) since October 1943, Kennedy had retained his concern with post-war planning in the War Office. On 23 March, he submitted his recommendations[53] to the same V.C.O.S. meeting that finally approved the paper on post-war world security. The most important of these was a proposal to replace the six Service members of the existing sub-committee by three P.H.P. 'Directors', working from their own ministries and meeting as required on the model of the Joint Planning Staff. This was accepted in principle by the Vice-Chiefs, though the Admiralty and Air Ministry representatives felt some qualms at the loss of continuity and experience entailed. The decision taken, it was generally agreed that

> The main difficulty would be in finding the right men to fill the new appointments of the Directors of P.H.P., and it was recognised that unless men of the right calibre could be found, the whole proposal would fall to the ground.

---

49. COS(44)88th Mtg (0)(1)
50. COS(44)98th Mtg (0)(1) & (2); PHP(44)8(Final)
51. COS(44)98th Mtg (0)(7) (Confidential Annex), in COS Sec's Standard File (CAB 79/89)
52. Ismay memorandum circulated to V.C.O.S. on 2 March 1944—copy obtainable in AIR 20/2681
53. Kennedy memorandum—not circulated in the C.O.S. series, but copy obtainable in AIR 20/2681

Kennedy's aim was not to alter the functions of the P.H.P., but to change its composition and bring it—at last—into the mainstream of departmental activity. Jebb's position as chairman was never called into question. He had been sounded on the proposed reorganisation and was believed to be 'in full agreement' with it.[54] A strict paralleling of the J.P.S. structure would have reduced his role merely to that of a Foreign Office 'adviser' to the Directors; but, although the new 'Post-Hostilities Planning Staff' was designed to be a 'duplicate' of that body, its continuing armistice and control responsibilities gave it a wider political dimension. This factor, the precedent of diplomatic chairmanship of the Joint Intelligence Sub-Committee, and Jebb's advantage of incumbency, together ensured that he would still be at the helm as post-war strategic planning grew in scale and importance.

It was to take another two months to bring the P.H.P.S. into being, though the detailed arrangements for its mode of operation were settled quite quickly. A directive for the new organisation was approved by the Vice-Chiefs on 30 March.[55] This no longer stressed the primacy of armistice and control problems over post-war military planning. With regard to the former, a Deputy Director of Civil Affairs would serve as a fifth full member providing a close link with War Office preparations for military government and administration. In respect of the latter, specific instructions were laid down for the Directors:

> you will consult the Joint Planning Staff and ensure that the views you
> put forward to the Chiefs of Staff are in line with current military policy.
> If you wish yourselves to initiate the study of a problem in this category
> you will first obtain the approval of the Chiefs of Staff.

On appointment, the Service members of the P.H.P.S. would be required to set up small departmental staffs to help them evolve post-war military policy within their respective ministries, and to attempt to create 'properly balanced inter-service teams' to operate in the office of the new organisation.[56] Whether intentionally or not, the effect of such measures was bound to be a reduction in diplomatic room to manoeuvre within the military machine. No longer would an unsolicited and unauthorised study like the post-war world security paper be able to find its way on to the C.O.S. agenda. Nor would the development of an idiosyncratic P.H.P.S. line be likely to prosper—in such studies as

---

54.   COS(44)98th Mtg (0)(7) (Confidential Annex)
55.   COS(44)105th Mtg (0)(1)   56.   COS(44)59

were permitted—given increasing integration with the Service
Departments. As for the creation of properly balanced drafting teams,
this could only enhance the attention paid to strategic planning, which
had hitherto devolved upon only one of the P.H.P.'s four sub-
sections.[57] Its inability to cope with the demands being made upon it
had been reported to Kennedy back in January, when many of its
papers were already 'long outstanding which the Chiefs of Staff decided
should be treated as a matter of urgency'.[58] The sub-committee had,
indeed, made so much more progress with its armistice and control
work that its senior secretary even suggested transferring the other
three sub-sections elsewhere to finish their task, 'leaving the new Post-
Hostilities Planning Staff to deal only with the strategical aspects of
World and Imperial Security'.[59] Though nothing came of this idea for
the present, it was to be revived at a later stage.

Only on 20 April were the Vice-Chiefs able to confirm the identity of
the incoming Directors, and a further period of over three weeks was
then laid down for the transition.[60] Apart from Brigadier French from
the Civil Affairs Directorate, the War Office supplied Brigadier
Francis Curtis—one of Kennedy's Deputy Directors of Military
Operations. From the Admiralty came Captain C.C.A. Allen—a
former secretary to the Committee of Imperial Defence, the pre-war
Cabinet body served by the Chiefs of Staff. For the Air Ministry,
another former member of the Cabinet Office, Air Commodore Peter
Warburton, joined the P.H.P.S. from the British Joint Staff Mission in
Washington. Of his three main new colleagues, Jebb had met Curtis
and Warburton by the beginning of May and had 'formed a very good
impression of them'. They were, he reported, 'highly intelligent' men
who would be likely to make 'a first class team' on settling into their new
roles.[61]

3. The Final Phase of Piecemeal Planning

The P.H.P. had pressed on with the preparation of a variety of strategic
papers while its plans for a world organisation slowly took shape and
the consequences of its clash with the Chiefs of Staff gradually
unfolded. Towards the end of August 1943, Nye had told the Vice-

---

57. See: PHP(43)31(Final)
58. Grove-White to A.C.I.G.S. (O.) in WO 32/10358
59. PHP(44)27(Draft)
60. COS(44)130th Mtg (0)(2)   61.   U3498/573/70

Chiefs that the 'War Office were experiencing a growing need for a definition of post-war military policy' for the first two or three years after the war,[62] but his projected paper on the subject had not materialised by the beginning of 1944. In the meantime, the sub-committee had produced a study on the prevention of German military resurgence by means of aerial bombardment. By concluding that

> Though air power can achieve some measure of control by itself, it can only do so at the risk of having to use a degree of force which is not likely to be sanctioned by the British Government,[63]

this appreciation contradicted the Joint Planners' previous declarations in favour of ruthless employment of the air weapon. Brooke viewed air power as a method of reducing the number of ground troops to be deployed to a greater extent than the P.H.P. thought possible, and Portal claimed that 'bombing or machine gunning with extreme accuracy' would be possible once Germany had been totally disarmed. He added that

> The use of air power would be no more brutal or indiscriminate than the use of ground forces for the same purpose, and he saw no reason why His Majesty's Government should be more reluctant to use the one arm than the other.

The paper was therefore rejected by the Chiefs of Staff on 5 January.[64] On the following day, Kennedy began to press for the P.H.P. to be given 'some fresh direction' from Brooke and his colleagues for the systematic examination of post-war defence problems.[65] Once again, no C.O.S. memoranda appeared to set this process officially in train, but it was probably an informal approach from the War Office which led the sub-committee to begin a study of post-war security in South-East Asia and the Pacific, and to develop an assessment of the long-term value of Gibraltar—on which it was already working—into a parallel regional survey of the Western Mediterranean and North-Eastern Atlantic.

The question of Gibraltar had been raised the previous September by its Governor and Commander-in-Chief in a paper which the Joint Planners had referred to the P.H.P. This spelt out a number of post-war

62. COS(43)197th Mtg (0)(3)   63. PHP(43)25(Final)
64. COS(44)3rd Mtg (0)(14)   65. WO 106/5184

problems which would affect the future of the fortress, and it is probable that it aired the possibility of trading it with Spain for alternative base facilities on the other side of the Straits.[66] Such a deal had certainly been recommended by at least one of the Directors of Plans, Air Commodore William Elliot, when the M.S.C. was preparing its Mediterranean survey three months earlier,[67] but it was not explicitly dealt with in the preliminary draft report completed by the strategic sub-section of the P.H.P. on 25 February. A secure position in the area was considered essential for post-war British strategic needs, which would be fourfold: to control sea routes through the Western Mediterranean; to give additional flexibility to similar control in the North Atlantic, by means of which such tasks as any blockade of Western Europe would be undertaken; to prevent military penetration of West Africa (either via Italy or via Spain) through North-West Africa; and to provide a staging-post for airborne supplies and reinforcements to the Middle East, India, the Far East and Southern Africa. No list of political assumptions was included, but there was one implied reference to the possibility of post-war Soviet hostility. Wartime defence of the Middle East had proved possible despite the virtual closure of the Mediterranean route as the German North African campaign had itself been dependent upon vulnerable seaborne supplies. In a future war, however, the draft suggested

> that to maintain the land and air forces required to hold the Middle East against an attack through Turkey or Persia by a major European power,

it might well be essential to keep open Britain's Mediterranean communications.

The analysis which followed fully acknowledged the value of Gibraltar as a first-class naval base, a fortress of great natural strength,

---

66. This paper, JP(43)338, is being withheld from public inspection until at least 1994. Of the relevant Foreign Office file, Central Dept. No. 3433 of 1944, there is currently no trace at the Public Record Office. The idea appears to have dated from October 1940, when included in one of a series of papers written by the novelist Dennis Wheatley in a private capacity for the J.P.S. (See: D.Wheatley, *Stranger Than Fiction*, (London, Hutchinson, 1959), pp. 219–21)

67. JPS Sec Min 43/734 in CAB 119/65 (It was to the Air Ministry that Wheatley submitted most of his papers.)

an airfield and convoy anchorage. Yet its physical limitations, its liability to future air attack from as far afield as Central Europe, and its total dependence on Spanish goodwill—or, at least, neutrality—would be grave disadvantages after the war. Any attempt at holding a perimeter inside Spain itself in a crisis could be expected to succeed only if the enemy's main forces were fully engaged elsewhere:

> Otherwise, it would only be a question of time before the enemy could build up superior strength against us and eject us.

On account of this vulnerability, it was considered that a base area in North-West Africa would be more likely to fulfil Britain's strategic requirements. For the control of North Atlantic communications, it should be supplemented by improved facilities in the Azores—which could also be used to furnish better air cover to Gibraltar. The desirability of a presence on both sides of the Straits and the lack of comparable port facilities to the south were cited as reasons for retaining Gibraltar in addition to the new base area. At the very least, the latter should comprise Tangier and the north-west portion of Spanish Morocco, covering some forty square miles and affording considerable scope for construction and development. Ideally, the whole of Spanish Morocco should be acquired, since this would not only further augment the air-base facilities but also provide a common land frontier with the French. Their friendship was 'in any event necessary to [British] interests in the Mediterranean area'. Indeed, apart from a friendly or at least neutral Spain, a firm alliance with France giving access to air and naval bases from French Morocco to Tunisia would be the main safeguard for Britain in the Western Mediterranean.[68]

The sub-section's paper came before the full sub-committee on 2 March. Less than a fortnight had passed since the Chiefs of Staff had rejected its world security paper, and the whole future of the P.H.P.'s approach to that question was still in the balance. Jebb and his colleagues had nevertheless been pressing ahead with their sequel categorising the various kinds of 'United Nations bases' which might function within a general security scheme. This espoused the principle that

---

68.   PHP(43)45(Preliminary Draft)—missing, but obtainable in U1762/748/70

in any arrangements which may be made we should endeavour to secure that United Nations bases available for our use, are established in such places as will further our strategic interests.[69]

With this in mind, Jebb immediately sought to tie in the Western Mediterranean draft with the P.H.P.'s international security conceptions, by insisting that

in order to bring the paper within the realm of practical politics, the political difficulties should be set out in more detail, together with the fact that a system of United Nations bases might obtain for Great Britain facilities unobtainable by any other means.[70]

Few changes of any importance were, in fact, incorporated before the diplomats intervened with their comments. One fairly early draft did mention the possibility of bartering Gibraltar—but only in the context of ruling that completely out of the question.[71] Hood reiterated his belief in British requirements being fulfilled, if at all, under the aegis of an international scheme,[72] and went on to expose a striking inconsistency in the argument of the planners: if Gibraltar were retained as suggested, it would meet most British needs unless Spain came under hostile control. Yet the need for facilities in French territory had been cited in consequence of the vulnerability of the *southern* shore to enemy action from Spain. A base in Spanish Morocco thus appeared to be either unnecessary or untenable. Frank Roberts, whose Central Department was primarily concerned, concurred and pointed out the impossibility of obtaining one in addition to an alliance with France and concord with Spain. The only way to mollify the latter in the event of a move into Spanish Morocco would be to satisfy some of her demands against the French; but that would hardly be compatible with the development of the Anglo-French co-operation rightly deemed to be essential. If designs on Spanish Morocco were abandoned, however, there would be some prospect of erecting a scheme based upon Gibraltar, French North Africa, Tangier and the Azores.[73]

The final paper appeared on 26 April. It had been drastically abridged by Grove-White after War Office complaints at the inordinate length of the drafts.[74] It had also been amended to emphasise

---

69. PHP(44)8(Final)
70. PHP(44)23rd(Private) Mtg—missing, but obtainable in U1950/573/70
71. PHP(43)45(2nd Draft)—missing, but obtainable in U2268/748/70
72. U2079/748/70   73. U2268/748/70   74. PHP(44)19th Mtg

that Britain's entire position in the area would depend upon French facilities, should Gibraltar become untenable; that overland communications circumventing the Straits should urgently be developed between the Atlantic and Mediterranean coasts of North-West Africa; that air cover from French Morocco and Algeria would be essential to protect British shipping, whether or not the Straits remained open; and that, so far as Spanish Morocco was concerned, permission should be sought for the right to use airfields to cover the Straits—but only under conditions of emergency, and possibly in the context of United Nations arrangements. The Azores barely rated a mention, as air support for naval forces in the Eastern Atlantic should now also be mounted from anticipated bases in French North African territory.[75]

With the study thus brought to a satisfactory conclusion from the point of view of his department, Roberts was alarmed to be told that the Chiefs of Staff were unlikely to do more than take note of it, pending the question becoming 'actual' at the end of the war. The Central Department had been monitoring its progress 'with a view to having a solid foundation on which . . . [to] think out policy in consultation with H.M. representatives concerned' on such increasingly imminent questions as the future of Tangier. In Roberts's view, there could be no question of the Service chiefs 'simply pigeonholing this paper and leaving it as it stands'.[76] What had happened was that the final P.H.P. meeting on the paper—to which the Foreign Office had sent no representative—had agreed it to be 'unreasonable to expect that the Chiefs of Staff would be prepared to commit themselves at the present time to a definite decision as to . . . future [British] requirements in the area of the Straits'. In accurate anticipation of C.O.S. attitudes, the sub-committee felt them to be more likely merely to 'express general agreement' with its conclusions and to circulate them appropriately as a 'background' for long-term planning.[77]

Another month elapsed before the paper was taken and approved by the Vice-Chiefs of Staff. When Jebb explained Foreign Office anxiety to have the paper so that discussions on regional security could be begun, they were at pains to point out that

> it would be essential to make it clear that this study was purely exploratory in character, carried no governmental approval and called for no executive action.

75. PHP(43)45(Final) 76. U3554/748/70
77. PHP(44)36th(Private) Mtg (1)—missing, but obtainable in U3707/748/70

If the Foreign Office needed a copy, it was agreed that Jebb should write officially to request one.[78] This he did on 27 May, stressing diplomatic cognizance of its 'tentative' and 'preliminary' nature; but, although it no longer made even implicit reference to possible Soviet hostility, the Vice-Chiefs remained unwilling to incur the degree of 'risk in sending a Staff study of this nature overseas' except in summarized form.[79]

Although the Gibraltar study had been on the P.H.P. agenda since the previous autumn, terms of reference for a survey of post-war security in South-East Asia and the South-West Pacific had been issued only on 7 February 1944.[80] This region was, therefore, the first to be considered purely in response to the pressure for a more systematic approach to post-war imperial defence planning. It had been selected for examination right at the outset, since its defence would affect the security not only of British Imperial possessions in the Far East but also of Australia, New Zealand and India.[81] Given the successful domination by Japanese militarism in the present conflict, the question was how to prevent recurrence of a similar situation 'as the result either of a resurgence of Japan or of aggression by some other Eastern Power'.[82]

The preliminary draft of this paper, circulated on 28 April, rested upon an assumption of post-war co-operation by the United Kingdom, the United States, France, Portugal and the Netherlands in defence of their mutual interests in the area. Although these interests were left undefined, three possible aggressors were identified: the Japanese—'a progressive and ambitious people [who] are likely to seize any opportunity to avenge their defeat'; the Russians—who, though showing no sign at present of a desire to move eastwards, 'might one day become as great a threat in this region as has been Japan'; and the Chinese—whose growing manpower and nationalism were unlikely to prove a serious menace unless first brought under the control of one of the other two Powers. Nor would Russia or Japan be able to pose a direct threat to British interests in advance of an interim programme of major territorial expansion.

Unless backed by force, no proposals for economic sanctions would be sufficient to prevent a revival of Japanese power. At the first signs of

78. COS(44)172nd Mtg (θ)(3) (See also pp. 98–9 below)
79. COS(44)477(0) & COS(44)179th Mtg (0)(4)
80. PHP(44)3(T.R.)—missing, but obtainable in U1383/748/70
81. PHP(44)38(Final)   82. PHP(44)3(T.R.)—*loc. cit.*

attempted military resurgence, rapid and effective enforcement action would be essential:

> Experience had, however, shown the difficulty of recognising the first signs of aggressive expansion as such, and of reaching agreement as to the necessity of taking forcible steps even when the danger has been recognised.

Arrangements for security had, therefore, to cater for potential failures in the policy of prevention. The main aim should be to confine Japan to her own islands, for without access to the resources of North China and Manchuria at the very least there would be no way in which she could start to mount a serious threat. After the end of occupation, this process of confinement would consist of naval and air control of the surrounding seas backed by a strategic air corps poised to attack the mainland and a mobile army reserve ready for instant deployment. To implement such a plan,

> the United Nations would require bases in N[orth] China and Korea at least, and possibly in the Vladivostock area as well. The whole-hearted co-operation of China and Russia would obviously be essential.

Should all this come to nought, however, and Japanese expansionism get under way, an additional network of bases would be needed from which to impede communications from Japan to her forces moving south. Running from the Marshall Islands, through the Carolines, Philippines and Formosa, to the coast of China, these bases would anyway have to be occupied in war to pre-empt their use by Japan as a springboard for further advances. With full American and Chinese co-operation, it would be possible in the immediate aftermath of victory to preserve such existing equipment and facilities as might be required after the war, and thus to avoid having to build up the base organisation from scratch:

> if this opportunity is not taken, it appears . . . to be very doubtful whether the base facilities will in fact be provided in advance of an emergency.

Even more precautions would be needed to meet the possibility of China becoming hostile or falling under the control of a hostile Russia or Japan. From the south of the country, British interests in India,

Burma, Malaya and Borneo would be vulnerable to direct attack. The western flank of the bases chain might well be turned—Formosa (or, failing that, Indo-China) then becoming of crucial importance. China's poor internal communications made it likely that any build-up of assault forces in the south would have to be attempted by sea. Control of the sea routes concerned would therefore go far to eliminate all varieties of threat from this quarter. Further insurance against overland attack could be gained by securing the China-Burma border and the northern frontier of Indo-China. As French weakness in the last-named country might be long-lasting, it was also recommended that the United Kingdom should be willing to lend assistance in its defence. Finally, any hostile moves by the Soviet Union would call for counter-measures already subsumed in the preparations to deal with China or a revived Japan. Consequently, Russian hostility did not require separate consideration and the possibility of it developing would not have to be brought in to complicate discussions with Britain's potential associates in the area.[83]

The principal modifications to this preliminary scheme which greeted the incoming P.H.P. Directors in May were greater emphasis on the risk of relying 'on an untried World Security Organisation', clearer acknowledgement of dependence upon American participation, and recognition of the fact that

> the working of the U.S. political machine may result in some delay before their assistance becomes effective in the event of a sudden attack.

Under such circumstances, the United Kingdom should be prepared to act alone in the early stages to try to prevent any serious breach in Australian, New Zealand and Malayan defences; but this could be regarded only as

> a very temporary expedient, and . . . in the absence of full U.S. co-operation all we could hope to do would be to prevent a *coup de main* by a comparatively small force.

Most significantly, so far as the Russians were concerned, it was pointed out that Soviet ability simultaneously to threaten British

---

83. PHP(44)3(Prel. Draft), redesignated as PHP(44)6(0) (Prel. Draft)—missing, but obtainable in U4150/748/70

interests in Europe and the Middle East meant that the provision of adequate forces for the Far East would become 'difficult if not impossible' in the event of a breakdown in Anglo-Soviet relations.[84] However, the drawing of general conclusions for the study was a task for the drafting stage to come, and in the intervening months the impact of the new Post-Hostilities Planners and of the Service chiefs themselves would decisively be felt.

Although the more diplomatic attitude of the V.C.O.S. Committee had enabled Jebb to salvage his United Nations paper after its mauling by the Chiefs of Staff in February, there developed a limited but perceptible reduction in the emphasis on internationalism in subsequent P.H.P. studies. On a few occasions, it is true, the sub-committee had been prepared to consider strategic matters independently of any influence which might be brought to bear by a world organisation, albeit reluctantly. Thus, on 2 February, it had advocated post-war British control of the Italian islands of Pantellaria and Lampedusa in the Sicilian Channel, though recognising that their strategic value would be slight—if not wholly non-existent—in the event of continued United Nations collaboration. It was 'only on the assumption that a powerful aggressor once more threatens the security of our Mediterranean communications' that the islands would have military significance. The appearance of such an aggressor had therefore been assumed, but the question of his identity had not been considered.[85] This sort of reticence was only a little less in evidence by the beginning of April, when the P.H.P. prepared a brief for use in Anglo-American conversations about post-war Middle Eastern oil. This stressed the relative insecurity of the United Kingdom's Persian and Iraqi sources given their 'proximity . . . to possible aggression'. From a deterrence point of view, it recommended acceptance of any American claims to a strategic interest in the region's oil deposits; but, though concerned with what was described as 'the only potential external menace to our Middle East oil interests that exists', the paper still steered clear of actually naming the Soviet Union. It concluded with a warning to the British delegation not to suppose that this menace was considered real at the moment—'on the contrary, it is quite possible that it will never materialize'. In any case, it would be 'highly dangerous' to give to the Americans any hint that such a threat was even being considered, let alone taken

---

84. PHP(44)6(0)(2nd Prel. Draft)—missing, but obtainable in U4150/748/70
85. PHP(43)32(Final)

seriously.[86] The Directors of Plans, in commenting favourably upon the brief, expressed themselves with a style in stark contrast to that of the P.H.P.:

> Russia is a potential future danger to the Middle East area. Even if she could meet her total oil requirements from her own resources, she might still be tempted to look with envy upon the outlet to the Indian Ocean afforded by the warm water ports of the Persian Gulf.

They concluded that to be able to count upon American assistance against this danger would be an overriding advantage,[87] and this forthright assessment of the situation was adopted by the Vice-Chiefs in their covering note to the Ministerial recipients of the sub-committee's brief.[88] The Joint Planners also set the tone for a P.H.P. paper on whether to offer the Americans unrestricted use of British bases after the war. This concluded that

> while we do not wish to arouse the suspicions of Russia or any other State . . . it is essential that we should ensure, to the greatest extent possible, the prompt military co-operation of the United States in any future major war in which we may be engaged, whether this co-operation is secured under a world security organisation or not;

but, while not disputing this to be the 'overriding consideration', the Vice-Chiefs insisted on 2 May that 'it would be impossible to run the risk of antagonising the Russians by an announcement . . . before the success of "OVERLORD" was fully assured'.[89] By this time, too, reference had been made to possible Soviet hostility in the preliminary draft of the Far Eastern survey, but it was the need to examine the air defence of Great Britain in the decade following Germany's defeat which led the P.H.P. openly to consider an exclusively Russian threat for the first time since the Black Sea Straits appreciation of August 1943. That was the investigation which had prompted a call to assess the impact on British strategic interests of post-war Soviet policy—a project which was only just coming to fruition.[90] Throughout the life of the Military Sub-Committee, the Directors of Plans had agitated for individual strategic problems to be considered only in relation to

---

86.   PHP(44)3(0)(Final)   87.   JP(44)95(Final)   88.   COS(44)322(0)
89.   PHP(44)4(0)(Final) & COS(44)142nd Mtg (0)(8)
90.   See Section (4), pp. 90–7 below

comprehensive background assessments of this sort. Now that its successor organisation—the P.H.P.—was itself about to be extinguished over two years after that agitation had begun, movements were just starting to be made in the direction urged by Oliver Stanley and the J.P.S. so long before.

Attention had first been drawn to the future of Anti-Aircraft Command by the V.C.I.G.S. in February 1944. Nye saw its potential as one of the most lucrative sources of manpower for demobilisation when the war in Europe was over but the anticipated struggle against Japan remained. He realised, however, that a post-war policy for air defence would have to be formulated before any such releases could be planned. On 17 February the Vice-Chiefs of Staff had therefore instructed the Post-Hostilities Planners to undertake this initial task.[91] Since the global Russian appreciation was still a long way from completion, no estimate of the likelihood of aerial attack by the Soviet Union could immediately be prepared. The first draft report on the air defence question did not, in fact, appear until the end of April[92]—when the strategic sub-section of the P.H.P. was found to have wasted considerable time and effort in drawing up detailed technical recommendations which the full sub-committee deemed to exceed its terms of reference.[93] This led to another round of redrafting and delayed completion of the paper until the middle of May.

In considering the danger of air attack against the United Kingdom, the P.H.P. discounted any prospect of bombardment by the Germans. Unless the Allies failed to carry out their intention 'completely to destroy her ability to make war again', Germany was unlikely to be permitted any military aircraft during the ten-year period concerned. Nor was it probable that the French could develop an appreciable air threat by the mid-1950s. The only significant risk arose from possible Soviet opportunism in the event of 'weakness and indecision on our part'. Though Russia's immediate post-war aims were expected to be security and internal development, there could be no guarantee of their not becoming more threatening before another ten years had elapsed. An international security system might fail to materialise, and it would in any event 'be unwise to rely on such a system alone for the defence of Great Britain'. Nor should the possibilities of Germany being allowed to rearm, of other countries being deterred from collaborating in

91. COS(44)25 & COS(44)51st Mtg (0)(3)
92. PHP(44)20(Prel. Draft)—missing, but obtainable in U3978/3978/70
93. PHP(44)26th Mtg

defence by British unpreparedness, or of 'a sudden attack by a treacherous enemy', be entirely overlooked. The solution would be to adopt an air defence system designed for expansion to full war strength within a two-year period, 'on the assumption that two years' warning will be received before the outbreak of a major war . . . [though] not losing sight of the possibility of sudden and unexpected attack at lesser notice'. Technical superiority—especially in the field of radar—should be maintained by intensive research and development; but, in most of its other aspects, air defence would have to depend upon the preservation of skills and upon the degree of organisational flexibility achieved. Thus, a small section of coastline should be maintained at full development for training purposes as 'a complete working model of A.D.G.B.', whilst skeletal civil defence services and factories producing relevant equipment should be structured on lines permitting rapid increases in the scale of their operations.[94]

The Air Staff had been closely involved throughout the development of this paper and were happy to endorse its recommendations.[95] When it came before the Vice-Chiefs, however, an amendment was agreed in connection with the danger of sudden attack, which the P.H.P. had rather vaguely mentioned merely keeping in view. This made it clear that the new system should be 'capable of affording on mobilisation at the outbreak of war an immediately effective defence', quite apart from the requirement of providing for full expansion over a two-year period. Having made their point, the Vice-Chiefs approved the report as a policy basis for detailed planning by a specialist sub-committee, but they did so only tentatively. Their caution in adopting it was prompted by the impact which technical advances might have on future problems of air defence; but, as Jebb later told his Foreign Office colleagues, their decision to limit its eventual circulation was prompted by the 'delicate nature' of the comments about the Soviet Union.[96]

Jebb's first intimation of the real significance of P.H.P. reform came with the sub-committee's completion of its second report on future Anglo-French relations, which coincided with the advent of the new organisation on 19 May. Its first report had been drawn up in January in response to a Foreign Office request for inter-Service views on the value of American involvement in the post-war defence of Indo-China. Whilst acknowledging the importance of such help in the course of the

94. PHP(44)20(Final)
95. AIR 20/2738—A.C.A.S.(P.) brief of 24 May 1944
96. COS(44)172nd Mtg (0)(2), COS(44)484(0)(PHP), & U4584/3978/70

present Far Eastern conflict, the P.H.P. had stressed the need to secure post-war French co-operation in Europe where

> a rearmed Germany would constitute a more immediate menace to the Heart of the Empire than a rearmed Japan to the security of the British Commonwealth and Empire in the Far East.

So long as there was any threat of aggression by a European Power, it would remain strategically essential that

> our policy should aim at maintaining a strong and friendly France, or that even if she remains weak she should at least be friendly.

Neither purpose would be served by infringing her sovereignty in Indo-China, and it would therefore be preferable to secure the necessary American participation by establishing United Nations bases in the country rather than depriving the French of their possessions.[97] These comments, drawn up prior to the Service chiefs' attack on the Four Power Plan, had been forwarded to the War Cabinet by the Foreign Office without being submitted to the C.O.S. Committee: on 24 February, it had become Government policy to support the continuation of French sovereignty over Indo-China if agreement to site international bases at strategic points could be reached.[98]

The importance of good Anglo-French relations had subsequently been re-emphasised in such papers as the Western Mediterranean and draft Far Eastern strategic surveys. The sub-committee therefore decided to prepare an appreciation of the subject as a whole, bringing such references together, buttressing them by identifying possible further benefits in Madagascar and the Levant, and concluding that:

> (a) if France is in a weak or chaotic state after this war, our own strategical position may be adversely affected;
> (b) if France in addition is ill-disposed, our strategical position may be compromised;
> (c) if France recovers a measure of her strength and is still ill-disposed, it may even be seriously endangered.

---

97.   PHP(44)2(0)(Final)
98.   WP(44)111 Annex 2 & WM(44)25th Concls (4)

It followed that, on military grounds alone, the British should do their best to restore stable conditions in France and to ensure close collaboration with her for purposes of defence.[99]

The Post-Hostilities Planning Sub-Committee met for the last time on 19 May, in a joint session with two of the new Directors. The minutes recorded approval of the draft A.D.G.B. and Anglo-French papers, as well as a closing exchange of compliments between the incoming and outgoing members.[100] Curtis and Warburton remarked that they would

> always be in debt to the old Committees |—the M.S.C. and the P.H.P.—| for the work they had done in breaking new and very difficult ground and for the progress that had been made in spite of the fact that everybody's attention was riveted on the more urgent problems of the war.

Jebb, in particular, was singled out for praise by all concerned for having 'conducted the business of the Committee with the utmost skill, patience and tact'; but, as he later minuted to his Foreign Office associates, on Anglo-French relations all had not run smoothly:

> With great difficulty I succeeded in persuading my new Air Ministry representative to swallow the conclusions in this paper (which I dictated myself).

It had then been agreed that the Service Directors should take soundings of the likely reactions of their respective Chiefs of Staff, before placing the matter on their agenda. By 23 May, this had been done and the results were disquieting. As far as Jebb could tell, the Admiralty was in favour, though its representative on the V.C.O.S. Committee, Vice-Admiral Sir Neville Syfret, was understood to have a jaundiced view of the French as a result of his wartime experiences. The C.I.G.S. and V.C.I.G.S. were believed to favour the paper, but Brooke, in particular, was 'very difficult of access and nobody ever seems to know what line he will take at any given moment'. As for the Air Ministry, Warburton's scepticism appeared to have accurately reflected high-level conviction that France would permanently be a third-rate Power whose goodwill no great effort should be made to enlist. Jebb concluded with the hope that Cavendish-Bentinck would be

---

99.   PHP(44)32(Final)   100.   PHP(44)29th Mtg (1), (2), & (4)

able 'to do some lobbying behind the scenes'.[101] In the event, the Vice-Chiefs approved the paper on 1 June, subject to two amendments. One was the insertion of a recommendation by the V.C.A.S., Air Marshal Sir Douglas Evill, that

> it can and should be plainly demonstrated to the French that . . . [close] collaboration is in the military interest of France if she wishes to maintain her independence.

The other was the deletion of the P.H.P.'s suggestion that the report be sent to the Armistice and Post-War Committee[102] of the War Cabinet—because it was decided to include it in a series of tentative 'Staff studies' stated to be lacking in any form of governmental authority.[103] As the Vice-Chiefs did not propose to send the report to the Foreign Secretary unless he chose to request one, Jebb

> took the Secretary of State's name in vain and wrote a letter saying Mr. Eden would be very grateful to be supplied with a copy.

On receipt, he duly directed it to the Foreign Secretary so that it might 'in some slight degree strengthen his hand in any discussions . . . with those who are not altogether convinced that a strong and friendly France is a major British interest'.[104]

Superficially, this episode was the clearest case yet of what could be accomplished by energetic 'infiltration' of the military planning machine. The Foreign Office had received back from it the very ideas it had fed into it—but these now appeared over the signatures of the Vice-Chiefs of Staff. Obtaining their approval had, however, been a decidedly uphill struggle, and it was clear that, in future, any feelings of Service scepticism would find more accurate reflection at meetings of the Post-Hostilities Planners.

The French appreciation was not, strictly speaking, the last strategic paper largely drafted by diplomats to be fathered on the military in this

---

101.   U5780/4404/70
102.   The A.P.W. Committee had replaced the A.C.A. Committee in April 1944. Also chaired by Attlee, it had terms of reference widened to include consideration of 'general political and military questions in the post-war period'. In this field, Jebb was the official link between its secretariat and the Foreign Office. (See: WP(44)222 & APW(44)1)
103.   COS(44)485(0)(PHP) & COS(44)179th Mtg (0)(3) (See also pp. 98–9 below)   104.   U4582/4404/70 & U5911/748/70

way. There remained the long-delayed global examination of probable Soviet policy and post-war British strategic interests, which was not to be finally adopted by the Vice-Chiefs until 15 June. In reality, though, this had been in a virtually completed state since the beginning of May, and thus amounted to a *fait accompli* as far as the new Directors were concerned.

4. The Russian Appreciation

It had been to the Foreign Office Research Department—successor to the F.R.P.S.—that Jebb had addressed his request for a paper to serve as the political background to the P.H.P.'s Russian appreciation. This had taken some three months to produce, and, on its appearance in the first week of 1944, it had been found to be lacking in any general forecast of the course of post-war Soviet policy. By the time that Warner had remedied this deficiency and cleared the revised paper with Sargent and Cadogan, another month had gone by, and it had not been until 10 February that the Foreign Office version was settled.

It predicted that the 'fixed point' of Russia's foreign policy after the war would remain what it had supposedly been since Stalin's victory over Trotsky: namely,

> the search for security against any Power or combination of Powers which might threaten her while she was organising and developing her own domain.

In particular, her experiences at the hands of the Nazis would make the treatment of Germany the single most important factor governing her attitude to the Western Powers. At least five years would be needed for the Soviet Union to recover from the ravages of the war, and many years more to realise a programme of internal development. She would therefore be unlikely to risk the disruption which a major conflict would involve, unless she came to

> suspect us of having designs hostile to her security, and that largely depends on whether she is satisfied with the measures taken to render Germany (and Japan) innocuous.

In American and British eyes, Soviet methods and demands in relation to Germany might appear to be 'very drastic', but unless they were dealt with adequately, Russia would 'always be in fear of an eventual combination with Germany against her, . . . be more preoccupied with her own security and . . . take her own measures to provide it'. Whilst stopping short of an attempt to ally herself with the Germans, except as a last resort,

> she would be constantly manoeuvring to increase the strength of her own position in Europe by establishing her influence in European countries through Left-wing Governments and by interfering in their internal affairs both through intrigue and through power politics. Outside Europe, too, she would no doubt follow a similar aim.[105]

For the five-year rehabilitation period, Warner concluded, the Soviet Union would constitute no menace to British strategic interests and would almost certainly experiment with a policy of co-operating with the United States and United Kingdom in a post-war security system. The continuation of such co-operation in the following phase of internal development would depend upon the results of the first five years—'and in particular if she is satisfied that we have no intention of allowing Germany's power to be restored'. A successful outcome might cause the experiment to become an established feature of Soviet foreign policy and prolong the period indefinitely in which it posed no threat to major British interests. Were the world organisation to fail, this need not necessarily spell the end of co-operation with the United Kingdom. Even if it did, however, outright expansionism might still not ensue: the Russians then confining their efforts to undermining Anglo-American influence, exploiting their pre-eminence in the Eastern hemisphere, maintaining their strength in the air and on land, but possibly developing their potential to threaten Britain's position in the Middle East.[106]

With the political background paper available at last, work on the substantive appreciation was rapidly put in hand by the P.H.P. Curiously, an early draft of 8 March entirely omitted consideration of Continental Europe from its region-by-region survey of likely Soviet aims and claims, though remarking—in connection with the potential weight of a Soviet air attack upon the United Kingdom—that

---

105. 'Is she not doing this now?' queried Eden when he saw a printed copy of the paper in May. Characteristically, this did not prevent him from endorsing it, though striking at the heart of its central thesis. (See: N2832/183/38)
106. N1008/183/38

Russia's overwhelming superiority in land forces in Europe will give her the power, should she wish to use it, to advance rapidly westward.[107]

Though this gap in presentation had been filled by the time that the finalised paper emerged on 1 May, the conceptual limitations of the overall study were clearly spelt out in its preamble:

> our conclusions . . . have been prepared in close consultation with the Foreign Office, and have taken account of all available evidence of Russia's post-war intentions. It should be noted, however, that no attempt has been made to deal with the possibility that Soviet Russia might attempt to extend her influence over Western Europe . . . [or] to dominate the continent of Asia.

Either of these developments would seriously threaten British interests, but the evidence currently available did not 'in any way suggest that the desire for wholesale domination of this sort [was] in the mind of the Soviet leaders or their people'. The furthest that the P.H.P. would go in considering a possible Continental threat from Russia was to point out that, even without any clash between her present aims and those of the United Kingdom, the actual or potential domination of Europe by any one Power or group had always been regarded as a menace to Britain's vital interests. At the end of the war, the Soviet Union would almost certainly emerge as the principal land Power in Europe:

> Unless therefore our security is once again to be entrusted to what are euphemistically described as 'diplomatic resources', this situation, however Soviet policy turns out, clearly calls, if only as a precautionary measure, for the maintenance of a high level of armaments by ourselves, together with France and our other natural associates in Western Europe . . . if any vacuum in Western Europe appears, it is asking too much of human nature not to suppose that the Soviets would attempt to make use of it for their own purposes.

Apart from any such temptation to opportunism, Russia's post-war objectives were taken to comprise: security against aggression,

---

107.   PHP(43)1(0)(2nd Prel. Draft)—missing, but obtainable in ADM 116/5118 It is not possible to say whether it was the observations of the Joint Intelligence Sub-Committee on the Foreign Office paper which led to P.H.P. reluctance to pronounce on possible Soviet expansionism in Europe. At the time of writing, the relevant document—believed to be JIC(44)105(0)(Final)—was still under review for de-classification, together with other wartime intelligence material.

development of internal resources, and the maintenance of adequate military power. For the first of these, neighbouring states—notably those to her west—would need to be brought 'under her influence', so as to prevent their participation in groupings hostile to the Soviet Union. This, at least, would be her general aim. Since no-one would be likely to attack her, a policy of isolationism might seem most sensible in the long term, allowing, as it would, concentration upon the tasks of rehabilitation and development. 'For the purposes of this paper', however, the P.H.P. chose to assume that Russia would adhere to the Moscow Declaration of 1943,[108] and thus 'play her part' in some post-war security scheme based on quadripartite co-operation. That such involvement would not preclude the posing of potential threats to various British interests, was made clear in the regional assessments which followed.

In the Arctic, Russia might develop a western fleet based on Murmansk which could affect the United Kingdom's strategic position; but her territorial claims against Finland, the Baltic States and Eastern Poland were thought to be directed against any future German moves in these areas. It was similarly to be anticipated that her desire 'to prevent any risk of a revival of the German menace in Central and South-Eastern Europe' would lead to the exertion of 'powerful influence' upon Poland, Czechoslovakia, Hungary, Romania, Bulgaria and Yugoslavia. Only in the last of these countries might geography prevent such influence amounting to domination. As for Germany herself, whilst specific Soviet intentions for her eventual fate had yet to be made known, the

enormous power of the Russian land forces in Europe after Germany is defeated ... [would] give the Soviet Government the ability, if they wish[ed], to dominate Germany for an indefinite period.

In the Mediterranean, Soviet feelers for military facilities in Yugoslavia and air bases in Italy should be resisted by diplomatic means, if possible; but, now that Stalin had shown an interest in removing the limitations on Soviet rights of passage through the Black Sea Straits, the British attitude to revision of the Montreux Convention might be taken by the Russians as a test case for the area. This was because there would be 'little potential danger to British strategic interests in such a

---

108.   See p. 66 above

revision', given a powerful air force in the Middle East and projected post-war bases in the Eastern Mediterranean.

Special mention had been made of the security of Middle Eastern oil supplies early in the paper as one of Britain's strategic interests, all the remainder being subsumed under the general requirement of safeguarding the components and communications of the British Commonwealth and Empire. With Northern Iraq only three hundred miles from Caucasian airfields, the main potential threat both to communications and to oil supplies was felt to lie in the Middle East. In Persia, fear of Russia would make Soviet influence predominant in the northern provinces, though there was no evidence that the Russians were seeking control of the central government. In Afghanistan, formerly a troublesome buffer state, the British and the Russians were currently co-operating 'to the embarrassment of the local trouble-makers', but the country would 'always continue to be a potential source of friction to Anglo-Soviet relations'. Finally, in the Far East, there were no known nor probable Russian aims which could threaten British strategic interests; not until there existed a strong Soviet navy and air force in the area, operating from bases further south than any yet available, would any such threat be able to arise.

The aspects of Soviet internal development and likely force levels after the war were dealt with in short order. As to the former, Stalin's 'internal policy' and the achievements of the Red Army had succeeded in ensuring the survival of the Soviet system. Repatriation, reconstruction, modernisation and the full exploitation of resources might take up to a total of twenty years to carry out:

> If it is safe to prophesy in any way as to the probable policy of the U.S.S.R., it may be said that she is more likely to expend her energy and resources upon achieving these aims towards a higher standard of comfort, liberty, culture and contentment of her people, than to follow a policy of external aggrandisement at the expense of other States, which might involve her in another war, with all the consequent setbacks to her peaceful economic development.

As to the latter, with the defeat of the Germans and the present condition of France, Russia would undoubtedly remain the greatest land Power in post-war Europe. This 'overwhelming superiority' would give her the ability to move westwards rapidly, overrunning air bases in the process from which the United Kingdom would be within effective bombing range. Aerial parity at least should be the British requirement. Only Russia's navy might prove to be a weakness—if it remained limited in size and hemmed in by the narrow waters of the Black Sea Straits and the Skagerrak. A revived intention to build a fleet for operation from an ice-free Arctic base could lead to the creation of a significant threat in the North Atlantic area.

Given its self-imposed restriction on considering aggression in Europe, the P.H.P. appreciation summed up British strategic interests which might be endangered by Soviet hostility as: (1) Iraqi and Persian oil supplies—though the United States would become involved 'automatically', by virtue of American interests in the Middle East; (2) Mediterranean communications (also affecting oil supplies)—were the Russians to move against Turkey; and (3) vital sea communications generally—were the Soviet navy to be upgraded.

It was concluded that, failing the realisation of a world security system, friendly relations with the Soviet Union should be encouraged on a bilateral basis, and that, to this end,

> we should not oppose any reasonable demands of the U.S.S.R. where they do not conflict with our vital strategic interests. . . . In exchange, we should expect support by the U.S.S.R. of such strategic interests.

The United Kingdom's limited post-war forces should be organised for rapid concentration and mobility, with a strategic reserve probably stationed in the Middle East. In that area, too, British policy should aim at American involvement in meeting any Soviet threat which might develop. Adequate naval superiority and at least parity in the air would be necessary, as well as the close collaboration with Western European countries, which would, in any case, be required to forestall German resurgence. [109] Yet, whilst conceding that such collaboration 'could not entirely prevent' the Russians from filling the expected Continental power vacuum if they so desired, the P.H.P. made no reference to any possibility of United States assistance in Europe. It seemed prepared, after all, to make recommendations in connection with the very Soviet threat to Europe which the appreciation was supposedly not considering. The criterion for inclusion was not, apparently, their likely efficacy, but merely their ability to be justified by reference to some threat other than a Soviet one. To the extent that such multi-purpose solutions were unavailable, it could always be claimed that the problem concerned had

---

109. PHP(43)1(0)(Final)

not been covered by the appreciation anyway, rather than embarking on contingency plans to meet unpleasant possibilities which the diplomats deemed unlikely.

Despite a closing caveat about the need for 'continual modification in the light of further information regarding the policy of the U.S.S.R.', a speculative report based on negligible data, and omitting consideration in any depth of the most serious potential Soviet threat, was hardly likely to arouse great enthusiasm amongst the members of the Joint Planning Staff. Thus, in a brief for the V.C.N.S., the Admiralty Director of Plans—Captain Guy Grantham—criticised it as over-optimistic and largely conjectural:

> There is a lack of any real evidence concerning Soviet long-term policy; we do not even seem to be able to forecast Russian short-term policy.

In view of this uncertainty, he recommended that the Vice-Chiefs do no more than note the paper and concur merely in the suggestion that it be subjected to a process of perpetual review.[110] With a significant number of strategic post-war papers now coming up for consideration, however, steps were about to be taken[111] to confer on them all, once approved, a special status analogous to that afforded to Jebb's world security proposals after eventual endorsement by the V.C.O.S. Committee. As in that earlier case, this was to enable the Vice-Chiefs to require changes to be made on points of detail, whilst neither formally committing the Services to Foreign Office attitudes embodied in such reports, nor provoking another confrontation with the diplomats by rejecting them out of hand. When the Russian appreciation was considered on 25 May, its over-optimism or otherwise did not feature as a subject of debate. Neither did the all-important omission to consider a Soviet threat to Western Europe—an issue which could hardly, in fact, have been squarely faced up to by the Service chiefs without running into further trouble with the Foreign Office. Having inherited the paper from their predecessors on the sub-committee, the members of the Post-Hostilities Planning Staff were instructed by the Vice-Chiefs merely to make a few limited revisions. These mainly concerned the likely growth of a Soviet air threat, given that future

---

110.   Grantham brief of 25 May 1944 in ADM 116/5118
111.   See pp. 98–9 below

strategic bombers would probably have an operational radius of 2,000 miles and that

> The United Kingdom, which was a concentrated and vulnerable base, was only 1,000 miles from the Curzon Line, and there was no depth to our defence.

Greater emphasis was to be placed on the magnitude of this threat, but it was decided in the interests of flexibility not to make specific reference to a desire for aerial parity.[112]

The final P.H.P.S. version, appropriately amended, was produced on 6 June—as the Western Allies were landing on the Normandy coast and the battle for France was beginning.[113] Though the Vice-Chiefs approved it without demur as an exploratory study, and had it circulated over their signatures on 15 June,[114] this in no way implied a continuation of Foreign Office ascendancy in post-war military planning. In the first place, Jebb's co-operative colleagues on the P.H.P. had been swept away. It was soon to become clear that their internationalist orientations had gone with them. Their replacements were far more closely integrated with their own departments, and almost immediately came to view themselves as post-war counterparts to the Directors of Plans—whom they were rapidly to outdo in scepticism where Foreign Office aspirations were concerned. They had had no real say in the compilation of the Russian appreciation, though being required formally to put the finishing touches to it during their first few days in office. In any case, the tentative nature of its endorsement and the fact of its evasion of the main issue—possible Soviet aggression in Europe—meant that the new Directors effectively had a free hand to deal with the major question of tripartite disharmony as they saw fit. That they intended to make full use of it had already become perfectly obvious by the time that the Russian appreciation was finally circulated.

---

112. COS(44)172nd Mtg (0)(4) The Curzon Line was the 1919 Russo-Polish frontier, and marked the minimum territorial claim upon which the Soviet Union could be expected to insist successfully—whatever the fate of the Central European states.
113. PHP(44)13(0)(Final)
114. COS(44)195th Mtg (0)(1) & COS(44)527(0)(PHP)

4

THE POST-HOSTILITIES PLANNING STAFF 1944–45

1. The 'Basic Assumptions' Controversy

The V.C.O.S. meeting of 25 May which gave general approval to the Western Mediterranean and A.D.G.B. studies and first considered the Russian appreciation also set events in train which polarised relations between the Foreign Office and the P.H.P. Directors within a few weeks of their appointment. Now that post-war strategic studies were beginning to appear on a regular basis, it was felt that special measures would be needed to ensure that

> no misunderstandings should arise over the status of these post-war papers . . . which were being made now so that the Chiefs of Staff would be in a position to give military advice at reasonably short notice when called upon to do so.

They in no way suggested what final policy should be and

> inevitably included political assumptions and other factors not strictly military in character which were essential to a proper consideration of the military problem but which might at any time require revision. Though appearing over the Chiefs of Staff's signatures they were in fact nothing but Higher Staff studies possessing in their present form no governmental authority and unsuitable for anything but selective circulation.[1]

Hollis consequently produced a memorandum on 27 May restricting the normal circulation of long-term strategic appreciations to within the Chiefs of Staff organisation. Exceptions would be made only in

---

1.   COS(44)172nd Mtg (0)(1)

response to specific requests for copies, and these requests would have to be referred to the Vice-Chiefs in cases of doubt. Papers in this restricted category were to be given a special designation in the C.O.S. series and were to be prefaced with a prominent notice proclaiming their 'purely exploratory' nature, their lack of ministerial authority, and the absence of any intention to use them as a basis for executive action.[2]

All this had a rather familiar ring. Two years earlier, Cadogan's original approach for guidance from the Joint Planning Staff had stressed its 'exploratory' nature, but that had not prevented papers by the M.S.C. from being utilised in their own right by the Foreign Office and even being referred to at War Cabinet level. 'Executive action' on long-term strategy was obviously a somewhat limited option prior to the end of the war in Europe, as the papers in question would relate to a subsequent period. Nor could it be doubted that, when that future became the present, hypothetical plans might well need drastic alteration in the light of unforeseen circumstances. Nevertheless, the fact remained that they were *not* to be just pigeon-holed in the interim at the level of the Post-Hostilities Planners. Before being put to one side, they were first to be submitted to the Chiefs or Vice-Chiefs of Staff for general approval and sent back for revision or re-writing if regarded as unsatisfactory. The main justification for treating their circulation with great care lay less in their provisional nature than in the delicacy of their contents: for there was every prospect that long-term strategic appreciations would have at least to consider the possibility of post-war Soviet hostility. Any revelation that such considerations were currently in mind could clearly prove politically embarrassing in the short-term, irrespective of any effect on continued collaboration with the Russians after victory.

Having dealt with the question of how to handle such reports, the Vice-Chiefs turned to the question of their future production. Echoing complaints by the Directors of Plans and others since 1942, Nye remarked that post-war strategic problems 'had perhaps so far been tackled in a rather piecemeal fashion', and the P.H.P.S. was instructed to put forward proposals for dealing with them in an orderly manner.[3]

This formal instruction was closely in accord with the wishes of the

---

2.   COS(44)470(0)   3.   COS(44)172nd Mtg (0)(5)

incoming P.H.P. Directors, and was almost certainly given in the knowledge that systematic planning was precisely what they wanted to undertake. Already, on 13 May, there had been an informal discussion between Foreign Office and P.H.P. representatives on the formulation of 'basic assumptions' for post-war strategic appreciations, and the preliminary paper to which this had given rise was under active consideration by the P.H.P.S. at the time of the Vice-Chiefs' meeting. It listed four alternative hypotheses which might underlie future strategic papers, and it pointed out that hitherto it had never been clear upon which of them past reports had been based. The first—that British defence problems should be considered *in vacuo*—it dismissed as impracticable. The United Kingdom would clearly be 'unable to support a war against the Soviet Union' without American or European allies; nor, for that matter, could armed opposition to the United States be effective unless mounted in concert with Soviet forces at least. Although the second assumption—that defence would depend upon post-war co-operation with the United States alone—certainly had to be taken seriously, the preparation of papers on this basis was described as unrealistic in advance of its adoption as government policy; for its use would amount to an admission that 'all future planning must be on the basis of some Anglo-American anti-Soviet coalition'. It was the third possibility which was 'now commonly made in all political planning'—that Three Power military collaboration could reasonably be expected to continue after the war. If this were accepted, the presence of a world security organisation—the final hypothesis considered—would be largely immaterial from the planning point of view:

> A Great Power Alliance . . . implies by itself the sort of military co-operation contemplated in the Chiefs of Staff proposal for a Military Staff Committee under some World Council.

The possibility of Russia breaking away from the alliance should not be disregarded and might be made more likely in the long term if the British were seen to be militarily unprepared. Accordingly it was suggested that future strategic appreciations should be written on the double basis, not only of continuing tripartite co-operation over the next ten years, with the primary aim of preventing renewed German or Japanese aggression, but also of the maintenance of British forces sufficient

(a) to form in association with the U.S.A. the nucleus, in Western Europe, of successful resistance to any Russian attempt to dominate the Continent, and
(b) to cause the Russians at least to think twice before attempting any policy of expansionism in the Middle East or Eastern Mediterranean.

Although drafted by one of the diplomatic representatives at the meeting which had led to its being prepared, this preliminary paper was attacked by every Foreign Office Department to which it was referred. The head of the North American Department, Nevile Butler, thought it unsafe to assume that

if the Soviet Union broke away and became our actual or potential enemy, she would also become an enemy of the U.S.A. . . . [making America] associate herself in helping us form a nucleus in Western Europe of resistance to a Russian attempt to dominate the Continent.

Despite powerful forces of antipathy towards Russia in some sections of American society, there were also elements of attraction, which, in combination with traditional isolationism, would 'almost certainly make it impossible for a U.S. Administration to entangle itself in anything like the Crimean War'. For the Northern Department, Christopher Warner deplored the issuing of any standing directive to the Post-Hostilities Planners 'on the lines of (a) or (b) which would give all their papers an anti-Soviet approach and spread the "fear of Bolshevism" among the rabidly anti-Soviet Services'. He particularly deprecated any body under Foreign Office chairmanship asking the Chiefs of Staff for such a directive. In the Central Department, however, Frank Roberts took the view that

Russian military planning is done entirely on the basis of the military security of Russia and is not made dependent upon the continuance of friendship with this or any other country.

Both he and Robert Hankey of the Eastern Department were strongly opposed to any reversion to 'the now notorious ten years rule', adopted in August 1919 and effectively cancelled only in November 1933, which had laid it down as axiomatic that the British Empire would not be engaged in a war with another major Power for a decade at least.[4] They believed that the effect of this rule on rearmament had been one of the main reasons for British unpreparedness before the Second World War, and that the United Kingdom must

> at all costs avoid ... any rigid assumption which we shall be embarrassed later on to say is officially out of date at any given moment.

Whereas Warner objected to that part of the preliminary paper qualifying the recommended assumption of Three Power co-operation, Roberts and Hankey therefore disapproved of the making of any such assumption at all. Together with Cavendish-Bentinck, they suggested that future strategic appreciations, whilst giving full weight to the Foreign Office objective of maintaining close tripartite collaboration, should be based on an expectation of British Commonwealth possession of

> armed forces sufficient to retain the respect of both her powerful allies and to discourage any temptation on the part of either of them or of any other Power to encroach upon the vital interests of the Commonwealth.

The latter should be defined as the security of the sea and air approaches to the United Kingdom, the prevention of Europe from being dominated by any one Power, and the protection of British overseas territories, bases and imperial communications.[5]

Yet, even as this was being worked out, members of the P.H.P.S. were busily incorporating the contents of the preliminary paper into a draft note for the consideration of their Directors. Drawing heavily on the original, it appeared on 26 May and forthrightly argued that

> Soviet policy cannot at this stage be predicted with any certainty and we cannot jeopardise the security of the British Commonwealth by failing to take account of a Soviet break away in our planning.

---

4.   For a detailed account of· the origin and development of this planning assumption, see: S. Roskill, 'The Ten Year Rule—The Historical Facts', *Journal of the Royal United Services Institute for Defence Studies* (March 1972), pp. 69–71.   5.   U4379/748/70

The assumption of continued tripartite co-operation remained un-changed, but that of the maintenance of forces to deal with possible Russian hostility was stated more generally in terms of a capability

> in association with the United States of America, successfully to deter the U.S.S.R. from advancing their own interests to the detriment of either the British Empire or the United States.[6]

In the face of this frontal attack on a rather undesirable topic, the Foreign Office chairman of the Post-Hostilities Planners found himself in a difficult situation. Jebb's hand could be traced in the insertion, in a revised draft dated 7 June, of cautionary phrases about possible United States domestic strife and resurgent isolationism. Despite a reference to the finding of the Russian appreciation that 'there is at present no evidence of any Soviet desire to dominate the World', the burden of the paper and the nature of the proposed assumptions remained essentially the same.[7] In attempting to obtain Foreign Office permission for him to put his signature to such a paper for the Vice-Chiefs to consider, Jebb unwittingly drew attention to the anomaly of his position within the strategic planning apparatus:

> May I emphasise . . . that it would be highly undesirable for me either to hold up the present paper or to allow it to go in without my signature. I should of course like to get the approval of the authorities here to the formula (whatever it may be) before the paper goes in; but I suggest that it is not essential that I should do so. For the Foreign Secretary will be in a position to state his official view when he is formally consulted by the Chiefs of Staff.

The Foreign Office chairmanship was, in fact, a relic from the previous planning organisation as it had tortuously evolved. Strictly, it should have been reduced to mere advisory representation when the decision to reform the P.H.P. Sub-Committee on the lines of the Joint Planning Staff was taken. While there was a general convergence of diplomatic and inter-Service views—as on most questions of armistices, occupation and control—full Foreign Office participation worked well enough; but once latent divisions on strategic planning began to emerge, they could be resolved only on an inter-departmental basis. The diplomats'

---

6.   PHP(44)12(0)(Draft)—missing, but obtainable in U4978/748/70
7.   PHP(44)12(0)(2nd Revised Draft)

avowed intention to 'infiltrate' the C.O.S. machine and influence its planning in directions favoured by the Foreign Office could not hope to succeed on major issues where the Chiefs of Staff or their subordinates held strongly opposing opinions and their P.H.P.S. representatives accurately represented these in committee. All it could do was to secure concessions of a marginal nature, whilst leaving the Foreign Office chairman out on a limb.

Jebb knew perfectly well that there was 'an undoubted tendency in the Service Departments to regard the Soviet Union as a *potential* enemy'. This was 'naturally reflected to some extent' in his own committee, convinced though he felt its members to be 'both of the necessity of working for a tripartite solution of our difficulties and of the probability that it may be attained'. Although it could be argued that the P.H.P.S. should adopt only the more optimistic of the two suggested assumptions in preparing its plans, he recognised that it would

in practice be impossible to get the Service Departments willingly to agree that the type of papers which they have in mind should never make the faintest allusion to, or contemplate the possibility of Russia making the slightest effort to push her interests at our expense.

He therefore felt it best for the Foreign Office to accept the proposed formula and to rely upon him to see that the resultant appreciations were not distorted by 'silly anti-Soviet prejudice' or by attempts to single out Russia as the only potential enemy.

All this was anathema to Jebb's superiors. Ronald, his Under Secretary, wished to defer the committing of any assumptions to paper in advance of imminent Three Power talks in Washington—which, he calculated, 'should provide some of the essential data for any really useful set of assumptions'—and he regarded American 'defection' from the maintenance of post-war security as more of a probability than a Soviet threat to it. Sargent, in turn, considered the whole paper to be

tendentious and out of focus and in contradiction with the policy of H.M. Government as conducted by the Foreign Office . . . [which] is not based upon the assumption that in the foreseeable future we may have to deter the Soviet Government by force of arms from advancing their own interests at our expense.

Not only should the Vice-Chiefs look to the Foreign Secretary for political assumptions, the latter would be unable to offer any that could hope to be valid for longer than two years in advance. In his opinion, a return to the inter-war system of estimating the date of future British involvement in a major conflict would be a development to be welcomed. Apparently, the notion of preparing for possibilities before they became probabilities did not enter into his deliberations. Finally, Cadogan himself sought to evade the whole question:

> If P.H.P. enquire of us now about assumptions, we can only answer that they must, in present circumstances, assume almost anything. I imagine they assume total German and Japanese defeat and disarmament. But we haven't got these yet.

To proceed now would be a waste of time and manpower. The Chiefs of Staff should be told that the problem was insoluble at present, and advised to turn their attention instead to planning Service requirements for the Japanese war after the defeat of Germany.[8]

On 15 June, with no agreed paper in sight, the issue was brought before the Vice-Chiefs of Staff—though the official record of the meeting made no mention of the fact.[9] As Jebb later reported to Sargent and Cadogan, somewhat defensively, it would have been impossible to prevent discussion of the subject even had he been so inclined: Allen and Warburton were determined to thrash out the question of basic assumptions. Whilst conceding that future strategic papers would have to include 'allusions to what (if anything) might be done to guard against the risk that the relations of the Great Powers between themselves might not be all that we hoped', Jebb made it clear that the Foreign Office felt that the formula proposed went too far. Even if the alliance did break down, threats might vary from region to region and there was no guarantee that Russia would be the sole potential enemy. If there had to be assumptions of this sort at all, they should either be on the lines proposed by Roberts and Hankey or just general alternative hypotheses of the continuance or breakdown of tripartite collaboration. Allen and Warburton retorted that it was unrealistic not to contemplate what steps could be taken against potential Russian encroachment upon British strategic interests, and argued that 'purely strategic

8. U6253/748/70
9. COS(44)195th Mtg(0) See also AIR 20/2681: COS Sec Min 1011/4, 13 June 1944; Warburton & Colyer minutes, 14 June 1944

planning ought not to be unduly influenced by political considerations'. For the moment, however, Jebb had his way—the Vice-Chiefs agreeing after an hour's debate that formal assumptions need not at present be worked out; but they added that future papers must be so constructed as not to ignore any potential risks in the area being considered. The 'off-the-record' discussion also showed Jebb 'no disposition to want to plan operations against the Soviet Union' on the part of the Vice-Chiefs of Staff, but rather a concern lest post-war economies and popular reaction would prevent the maintenance of sufficient forces to protect British interests generally. This assessment was endorsed by Cavendish-Bentinck, whose years of involvement with the C.O.S. organisation best qualified him to judge:

> I have seen it said in minutes that the Service Departments are violently anti-Russian. I do not think that this is quite correct. They are peeved with the Russians because the latter have been on the whole unco-operative. Moreover there is an unbridgeable gulf between the mentality of our own soldiers and sailors and that of the Russians. However the Service Departments are not confident that we shall be indefinitely on good terms with the Russians and that our interests will not clash both in Europe and in the Middle East. Consequently they consider that we should be in a position to hold our own, though war with Russia would be even more distasteful to the Service Departments than war with Germany was to Sir Horace Wilson.

Sargent's response was merely to return to the theme of six-monthly statements of the general lines of foreign policy, to be produced to serve as the political basis for strategic plans appertaining to each succeeding two-year period. Although Cadogan approved of the idea of continually reviewing the situation, he claimed that if the present enquiry was for just the general approach to foreign affairs which it was hoped to pursue during the next two years, this could be stated

> quite easily: 'We hope to maintain co-operation with the U.S. & the U.S.S.R. for the defeat and holding down of Germany & Japan, with the assistance, as we hope, of a World Organisation.'

The whole point was how to plan if this co-operation broke down and the world security organisation failed to materialise or to function:

The wretched P.H.P. are asked to plan on the 'assumption' of either or both these failures. I maintain that they *can't*, and that you can't even formulate the assumptions.

To plan in a practical way now was impossible. First, tripartite collaboration might be assumed; then, no effective world organisation; then, American isolationism; then, alternatively or concurrently, a break with Russia; and so on, 'through every permutation and combination'. 'That way,' he concluded, 'lies Bedlam.'[10]

Whether the Foreign Office liked it or not, however, largely as a result of its own professed anxiety to plan 'in a practical way' as far back as 1942, there had come into being an inter-Service apparatus for the exploratory consideration of post-war strategic questions. Its personnel were neither bound by, nor inclined to the view that the provision of post-war forces should be governed by short- or medium-term diplomatic predictions of what conflicts *would* occur. They looked instead to the physical potential of other Powers, and sought to estimate and prepare for such conflicts as *could* occur. Had there been a multiplicity of potential post-war enemies amongst the Great Powers, their approach might indeed have been as impracticable as Cadogan claimed: there would simply have been too many contingencies against which to guard. In the planners' eyes in mid-1944, however, the options were straightforward. After the defeat of the Axis, only two other Great Powers would remain; war with one of them was unthinkable, but with the other a conflict could not be ruled out. Whilst it was the aim of the diplomats to prevent such an outcome, it was the duty of the Services to make such plans as were possible to survive it if it transpired nevertheless. From the discharge of that duty the military planners had no intention of being diverted.

2. Two Views of a Western Bloc

Although the 'Basic Assumptions' paper had effectively been stifled, the Foreign Office victory was one of form rather than substance. In response to their instructions of 25 May, the P.H.P.S. had submitted an ordered programme of work to the Vice-Chiefs at the 15 June meeting. So far as strategy was concerned, this envisaged the completion of a full

10. U6254/748/70 Sir Horace Wilson, a senior Treasury civil servant seconded to 10 Downing Street from 1937 to 1940, had been the *éminence grise* of Neville Chamberlain's 'inner Cabinet' of Appeasers.

series of regional surveys on the model of the Western Mediterranean paper which had already been approved. First would be considered the security of the North Atlantic and Western Europe, and that of the Far East—these two papers being 'largely concerned with the problems of preventing a resurgence of Germany and Japan', according to the programme. After production of parallel studies covering the Eastern Mediterranean and Middle East, and India and the Indian Ocean, the cumulative findings of the regional surveys would be embodied in an overall summary of the British Empire's world-wide strategic requirements.[11] The Vice-Chiefs approved these proposals, though rejecting a further request for permission to make observations upon such highly controversial inter-Service questions as the relative importance of sea and air power in a future major war.[12]

Jebb had appreciated that there was no possibility of preventing the proposed planning schedule, however distastefully the Foreign Office might regard it. His own suggestion that each paper be based upon more general premises went considerably beyond Cadogan's wholly negative approach, as it left open the door for the examination of possible Soviet hostility whenever deemed appropriate in the course of each survey. This the Vice-Chiefs must surely have realised when ordering all potential risks in a given area to be considered, though declining to specify particular ones in the form of 'Basic Assumptions'. Had it not been for later intervention by the Service chiefs themselves, however, the evidence suggests that Jebb might have succeeded after all in bridging the gap between his P.H.P.S. associates and his Foreign Office colleagues.

The initiative in getting the North Atlantic study under way now devolved upon the Post Hostilities Planners' secretariat. This had been strengthened in the spring of 1944 by the accession of Colonel Arthur Cornwall-Jones, who had been serving in major secretarial positions since the outbreak of war.[13] At the beginning of May, he had prepared draft terms of reference for a North Atlantic survey on the basis of assumptions agreed by the P.H.P. Sub-Committee. These anticipated a friendly United States—which might, however, be subject to delay before coming to Europe's aid—and the use of bases in the territory of similarly friendly, but enfeebled, European allies.[14] By 16 May, the

---

11.   PHP(44)11(0)(Final)   12.   COS(44)195th Mtg (0)(2)
13.   When Hollis succeeded Ismay as Chief Staff Officer to the Minister of Defence at the end of 1946, it was to be Cornwall-Jones who replaced him as Senior Assistant Secretary (Military) of the Cabinet.   14.   PHP(44)8(0)(T.R.)

whole question of such assumptions was—as has been seen—already under consideration with the Foreign Office, and a joint meeting of incoming and outgoing P.H.P. members declined to endorse the draft terms 'in view of the pending reorganisation' of the Sub-Committee.[15] With the intervention of the Vice-Chiefs on the handling of such topics, even as he sought to keep the project moving ahead, Cornwall-Jones frankly confessed his doubts to his counterpart in the British section of the Combined Chiefs of Staff:

> I do not know how you chaps are finding this P.H.P. business, but I find it much more difficult than ordinary straightforward war planning. In the latter, you can and, indeed, must produce an answer to a problem on which somebody has got to act in the reasonably near future . . . . In this, one already feels the strains and stresses of interests which so long as the war lasts are at least working towards the same end.[16]

The immediate problem was eased by the airing of the 'Basic Assumptions' controversy at the V.C.O.S. Committee meeting on 15 June. Two days later, he therefore reminded the Post-Hostilities Planners that they all appeared to agree at least on two broad possibilities:

(a) That the tripartite alliance is an effective organisation.
(b) That it may break down.[17]

On 19 June, the chairman and Directors accepted these alternatives as the basis on which to assess the measures required to secure British strategic interests in the North Atlantic and Western Europe after the war.[18] This project was accorded top priority—Cornwall-Jones later describing it as 'quite the biggest thing we have tackled in P.H.P. yet'[19]—largely on account of a further intervention by the Foreign Office.

Although the *contretemps* with the Chiefs of Staff in February 1944 had brought about the P.H.P. reorganisation which was now causing further friction with the diplomats, the controversial paper on the

---

15. PHP(44)14th (0) Mtg (1)—missing, but obtainable in U4424/748/70
16. CJ/44/163 in CAB 122/1566—a file of covering letters from the records of the J.S.M. in Washington, to which copies of various P.H.P. papers were sent
17. CJ/44/172 in U5910/748/70
18. PHP(44)17(0)(T.R.)—missing, but obtainable in U5909/748/70 & CAB 21/1614   19. CJ/44/215 in CAB 122/1566

military aspects of any post-war world security organisation (which had started these developments) had been tentatively endorsed as a V.C.O.S. memorandum in March.[20] This had been submitted to the Armistice and Post-War Committee on 22 April as one of a series of papers for eventual use by the British delegation at forthcoming tripartite talks on the subject in Washington.[21] Jebb's proposals of 1942 were thus on the verge of attempted translation into practice, and, since they had always envisaged a role for regional defensive groupings— including one in Western Europe—under a world system, urgent attention now began to be paid to this dimension. On 11 May, copies of a provisional Foreign Office memorandum on Western Europe had been distributed to the Post-Hostilities Planners, under cover of a note by Cornwall-Jones warning them that the Chiefs of Staff would probably be required to comment prior to its further circulation to the Prime Ministers of the Dominions. Such a commentary, he felt, could serve as a useful background to future strategic studies by the P.H.P.S.[22] It was therefore decided to use the forthcoming North Atlantic security paper as the vehicle by means of which the Foreign Office need for Service views on post-war Western Europe could be met.[23] Apart from adding urgency to the production of the survey, this was to have far-reaching consequences.

The final version of the Foreign Office memorandum was not despatched to the Chiefs of Staff until 22 June, but the Post-Hostilities Planners had, in the meantime, little cause for apprehension about any proposal for a Western European defence system—even if welcoming one for reasons rather different from those of the diplomats. As Cornwall-Jones observed on 31 May, in a minute drafted to ensure that a full C.O.S. examination could be carried out before Ministerial approval for Foreign Office suggestions was sought,

> When it comes to examining the proposition I personally do not feel that it will be necessary to put forward any arguments against it. If, as the Foreign Office seems to think, it will be possible to persuade the Russians to think that it is not directed against them, then I cannot see how we should lose . . . if, in spite of our efforts, the worst happened and our relations with the Soviet Union deteriorated we should at least have some line of defence in Western Europe on which to fall back and we should not be confronted either by a Sovietised Europe or by a Europe dominated by Germany.[24]

---

20.   COS(44)282(0) based on PHP(43)24a(Final) (See p. 72 above)
21.   APW(44)1st Mtg (1) & APW(44)4   22.   CJ/44/74 in WO 193/303
23.   PHP(44)17(0)(T.R.), *loc. cit.*   24.   CJ/44/132 in CAB 21/1614

The Foreign Office view, as set out in the memorandum which was eventually submitted, was that British participation would be essential in any arrangements for closer European co-operation if an end were to be put to internecine conflicts on the Continent. Not only might non-participation enable another German attempt at domination to be made, but with the existence of a political vacuum in Europe 'the mere course of events, as distinct from any particular ambitions on their part', might impel the Russians to try to organise Europe on their own lines. The fact that Western Europeans were actively taking steps to organise their own defence would be welcomed by those Americans who were coming to regard the United Kingdom as an 'advanced defence outpost' of the United States, though it had to be admitted that American isolationists might see this as an excuse to opt out. Stalin's 1941 remark[25] about the British assuming a Western European defence role was again resurrected, and the whole scheme was presented as a regional tier, possibly linked with a 'United Nations Commission for Europe', but, in any case, 'clearly subordinated to the World Organisation (when constituted)'. The Soviet Union would be represented at the latter two levels, whilst the regional group would be held together, probably by a multilateral defence treaty between the United Kingdom, France, Holland, Belgium, Norway, Denmark and Iceland, with further accessions perhaps occurring later. The memor-andum projected onto the Russians the British Foreign Office propensity for shaping policy by reference to apparent intentions rather than actual capabilities: thus, whilst the United Kingdom had 'above all' to avoid creating the impression of seeking a Continental bloc intended to exclude the Soviet Union, the effect on post-war Anglo-Soviet relations of the adoption of such a scheme was genuinely expected to be beneficial. According to the Foreign Office paper, the twenty-year Treaty of Alliance concluded with the Russians in May 1942 lay

> at the base of our whole European policy and we should try to reinforce it by all means in our power. The formation of some Western European security system would, however, reinforce rather than detract from the Anglo-Soviet Treaty, more especially if the Russians, with our approval, constructed some similar security system in Eastern Europe—and they will almost certainly do so whether we approve it or not.

A Continental commitment would add depth to the defences of the United Kingdom and lead to the building-up of France as an ally in the

---

25.   See p. 2 above

control of Germany. Any increased risk of British involvement in the defence of Western Europe would primarily arise if the world security organisation proved to be a failure.[26]

As the Foreign Office had specified the need for urgent guidance, with its delegation leaving for Washington within a month, strenuous efforts by the strategic sub-section of the P.H.P.S. led to the production of a comprehensive draft report on 7 July. This aimed to determine the measures required to safeguard British strategic interests in the North Atlantic and Western Europe after the withdrawal of Allied occupation forces from Germany. Those interests were defined as the security of the United Kingdom—the heart of the Empire, its base of operations, and the main source of British manpower and industrial strength—and as that of its sea and air communications with the Commonwealth and Empire and with the United States. The problem was then considered in two long annexes corresponding to the two basic assumptions which Cornwall-Jones had managed to extract from the controversy between Jebb and the Directors of Post-Hostilities Plans.

On the assumption of continued Three Power co-operation under-pinning a world organisation, there could be no threat to British strategic interests in the area. The problem would be limited to deciding how best to take part in enforcing Peace Treaty provisions upon Germany once she had been disarmed and the forces of occupation had been withdrawn. Echoing appreciations by both the M.S.C. and J.P.S. in 1942, the draft stressed that timely and decisive offensive action would render this task neither difficult nor unduly onerous:

> The restrictions imposed on Germany by the Peace Treaty must be simple and clear-cut, so that the necessity for them will be fully appreciated by the public and any infringement of them will be readily discernible . . . if a single breach is allowed to pass unpunished, a policy of appeasement tends to set in, and once begun quickly leads to total collapse of all restrictions.

Air action would be the most potent method of deterrence and retribution—economical, speedy and psychologically effective. Unlike in 1942, however, offensive air bases in France and the Low Countries were no longer seen as essential. A modern air force would be able to operate efficiently from the United Kingdom directly; but, should

---

26.   COS(44)113

public opinion preclude this, or particular circumstances in Germany render unsupported air action inappropriate, re-occupation by land forces would become necessary. In this situation, an eastern group of states focused on the Soviet Union and a western one focused on the United Kingdom and a revived France and backed by Canada and the United States, would have to be mobilised. Great Britain's world-wide commitments and limited manpower resources would force her to look to her allies to provide the bulk of the Western European group's ground forces. However, the Foreign Office believed such collaboration almost certainly to depend upon the stationing of token British contingents on the Continent as an earnest of political determination. The draft therefore concluded that

> From our point of view, it would be a fatal mistake to refuse such undertakings if they are the only means which will secure the wholehearted co-operation of France, Belgium, Holland, Denmark and Norway and thus ensure the success of preventive action against Germany.

American contributions to air striking forces based in the United Kingdom, and preferably also to land forces on the Continent, would imply a welcome recognition of the involvement of United States strategic interests with the security of Western Europe; but such participation would not be essential in circumstances of continued tripartite harmony, active Soviet co-operation, and material support from across the Atlantic.

The possibility of tripartite discord was considered in the remainder of the paper—but principally in respect of the threat from a rearming Germany. Whilst the United States might at best be actively involved in helping the British, or might at worst remain neutral, it was assumed that Soviet behaviour could range from continued assistance to outright hostility. Cadogan had predicted that attempts to consider 'every permutation and combination' of possible factors would lead to 'Bedlam', but the P.H.P.S. argued that, from whichever angle the problem was viewed, a Western European defence system would still be required. With America isolationist but Russia still co-operating, Germany would be dealt with by a European system of alliances, with the United Kingdom and Soviet Union organising their respective halves. With Russia unco-operative, the British would take the lead in Western Europe—with or without American help—and the role of her

Continental allies would be enhanced accordingly. Failing either Soviet or United States support, this allied assistance would become absolutely essential, whilst

> If, in addition, Russia were hostile we should have to try to augment the Western European Group and in the last resort this might even entail coming to some arrangement with our ex-enemies.

Any type of tripartite rift would give the Germans an opportunity to revive militarily, if only because of reluctance to admit failure of the world organisation upon which so many hopes had been based. In this event, an offensive Continental strategy would be indispensible:

> The rapidity with which a modern attack can develop and the need for the quickest possible action to suppress the first signs of aggression both indicate clearly that the best way of safeguarding our interests is to take the initiative at the outset. The cost of this insurance may be considerable, but in the long run we are convinced it will be the cheaper policy.

Thus, a very large effort to maintain a base in the Denmark-Schleswig area (with additional facilities in Norway) would be well worth making, to stifle at birth any naval threat from the German North Sea and Baltic ports. Failing this, a whole network of naval and air bases would have to be brought into play to meet threats to North Sea and North Atlantic communications. Similar reasoning was applied to the prospect of aerial attack. A belt of air defence from Norway, through Denmark and the Low Countries to south-east France and possibly Spain, should be set up to serve the unified air forces of the Western European allies, but a determined enemy would always be able to break through to attack British cities and communications:

> The only sure way to stop him is to prevent him building bomber aircraft. We must, therefore, have bomber forces based on this island and be prepared to use them to destroy German factories at the first sign that they are manufacturing aircraft, flying bombs, or any similar weapon.

As for land forces, the moral effect of permanently establishing a small British contingent on the Continent would be out of all proportion to its size and could well prove decisive in ensuring Western European co-operation. That the Americans might fail to intervene only accentuated the importance of being ready to attack Germany 'by air, sea and land on the first sign of rearmament', before the situation became completely uncontrollable.

The prospect of Soviet hostility was summarily treated: even with Germany impotent, it was most unlikely that a westward advance by the Russians could effectively be resisted on the Continent, though an attempt to stem it should be made. The United Kingdom would then probably be compelled to fall back on her home islands and Atlantic bases. A long-drawn-out war would be inevitable, with nothing but American intervention being able to restore the situation. Nor would that be probable even with American aid, should Germany actively combine with the Russians in aggression. The British would, indeed, be hard put even to retain control of their own islands in the face of such a formidable combination of manpower and resources. A Soviet alliance with the Germans had therefore to be prevented 'at all costs'.[27]

Foreign Office reaction to this draft paper was, for the most part, enthusiastic. For the Central Department, Roberts endorsed the thesis that, with the requisite willpower and sufficiently close collaboration with Western Europe, the United Kingdom could thwart a fresh German threat regardless of whether or not America and Russia retired into isolation. The North American and French Departments also welcomed the draft, but the question of a hostile Russia was fully considered only in the Northern Department. Warner criticised the conclusions based upon that hypothesis as unnecessary to the arguments of the paper. In his view they merely stated the truism that the Soviet Union would be a formidable adversary, and in combination with Germany a still more dangerous one:

If anything is required instead of this whole passage w[oul]d it not suffice to say that the co-operation of the western powers w[oul]d be equally in our interests if Russia ceased to collaborate with us, and U.S. assistance w[oul]d be even more valuable (or essential)?[28]

Warner was, in fact, assessing the paper primarily in respect of the need for inter-Service views on the value or otherwise of a Western European defence system. Since the P.H.P.S. was in favour of this no matter which of its various assumptions were posited, the passages on

27. PHP(44)17(0)(Draft)—missing, but obtainable in U6283/748/70
28. U6283/748/70

Soviet hostility naturally seemed immaterial so far as the Foreign Office enquiry was concerned. Yet, to the Post-Hostilities Planners, the paper was to be first and foremost a regional strategic survey, the scope of which they had no intention of restricting. Their incorporation of answers for the Foreign Office gave a certain impetus to what had been, in any case, a pre-existing task; but it was also to have the more important consequence of making it more likely that the Chiefs of Staff would examine the survey themselves, instead of leaving it to the V.C.O.S. Committee, since a copy of the finished product was destined for Foreign Office use.

For the present, as successive drafts were forwarded to the Foreign Office, an argument was developing between Warner, as head of the department most concerned with the Soviet Union, Cavendish-Bentinck, as senior diplomat in the Chiefs of Staff machine, and Jebb, as chairman of the body producing the papers. Referring once again to the sections on possible Russian hostility, Warner contended that it would be 'quite improper' for a Foreign Office representative to sign a paper

> which barely conceals that it is thought that Russia is just as likely to be an enemy as Germany, and is quite likely (circumstances unspecified) to join with Germany against us . . . and that even suggests that we may *wish* to combine with Germany against Russia,

without the sanction of higher authority. He reminded his colleagues of the Foreign Office view that

> the most important point in securing Russian collaboration after the war will be to convince Russia of our determination to go with her in holding Germany down and that only in the event of our appearing to play with Germany against Russia is Russia likely to try to get in first with Germany.

The more cynical Cavendish-Bentinck criticised the draft for relying on inspection after the end of occupation as a means of forestalling clandestine rearmament in Germany, and for recommending what might amount to the tying-up of British forces on the Continent for likely annihilation on the outbreak of another war; but he sided with the P.H.P.S. over the Russian question:

I do feel that if we give the impression of persistently refusing to allow any mention that Russia may later on be non-co-operative and even hostile, we shall have in the Service Departments the same reputation vis-a-vis Russia as Sir Horace Wilson had as regards Germany from 1937 to the outbreak of the present war, with the result that they may tend to discount our opinions and regard us as being ostrich-like so far as Russia is concerned.

Jebb, concurring, drew the all-important distinction between a political prediction of what would probably occur and a strategic study of what could possibly occur—the 'Foreign Office view' of means to retain Soviet goodwill was 'entirely irrelevant to the present paper', which fell into the latter category. Even Cadogan conceded that since Russian non-co-operation, though contrary to British wishes, was an 'ominous possibility', the paragraphs in which it was considered should not be removed; but the main argument over military planning and the Soviet Union was only just beginning.[29]

On 20 July, Jebb and the P.H.P. Directors put their signatures to the North Atlantic survey. In its final form, it comprised little more than a summary of the more detailed early drafts. Germany and Russia were cited as the only European countries that could seriously threaten British strategic interests, France being ineffective unless acting in concert with one or other of them. A successful world organisation would require the preparation of military resources in Western, as in Eastern Europe—solely to deal with Germany should trouble occur after the end of the occupation. In this situation, the components of security would be prompt use of air power, including the deployment of air-transportable troops; an intelligence organisation to give the earliest possible warning of any need to strike; political will, backed by public opinion, in favour of clear-cut and decisive action; and recourse, if necessary, to Allied re-occupation of Germany in whole or in part. Similar measures would suffice in the absence of a world organisation, even if Western Europe had to undertake them alone. Only in the face of active Soviet hostility would a Western group probably prove ineffective, in which case it was

an unpleasant fact that ... Germany is the only country whose geographical position, manpower and other resources could provide the aid which might be essential to our preservation ... [though] it would be

---

29.   U6791/748/70

folly to risk prejudicing our relations with the U.S.S.R. by any change in our policy towards Germany,

so long as the Anglo-Soviet Alliance endured. To defend the sea communications of the United Kingdom, a network of air and sea bases in North-West Africa, the Azores, Eire and the Arctic would be required, in addition to several on the Continent. Finally—probably in deference to Cavendish-Bentinck's observations on the point—the P.H.P.S. shied away from the previous strong recommendation that limited land forces should be permanently stationed in Europe:

> In our view the desirability of our accepting any permanent continental commitment is a matter which would more appropriately be considered by the Military Staff Committee of the World Council at a much later stage, and is one on which a decision cannot possibly be taken at present . . . . At a later stage it might be appropriate for members of the [Western European] Group to discuss plans for other eventualities (*e.g.*, the breakdown of the World Organisation), and we could then consider whether it would be practical for us to accept any new commitments.[30]

As soon as he saw the paper, Warner returned to the attack, noting that nothing was said as to when Soviet expansionism might occur and deprecating any Foreign Office endorsement—in a paper for submission to the Chiefs of Staff—of the notion of building up Germany as a safeguard:

> The distance to the next step—"we had better start building up Germany pretty soon and so we had better not knock her down too completely"— is a very short one, particularly for the military mind and for those who suffer from the anti-Bolshevik complex.

Though he appreciated the 'danger of Russia as clearly as anyone', he could see no need at all for the Foreign Office to approve rather loose talk about the Soviet Union overrunning Europe in the unspecified future. Cavendish-Bentinck replied that he had never heard any Service officer expressing those sentiments, nor noticed members of the Service Departments suffering from that syndrome; and Jebb commented testily that

---

30. PHP(44)17(0)(Final)—withdrawn, but obtainable in U6691 & U6792/748/ 70, and in CAB 79/78 (attached to COS(44)248th Mtg (0)(14))

if it is suggested that the Foreign Office representative on the P.H.P. should spend his time restraining his colleagues from even mentioning the possibility of a hostile Russia, it will neither increase the authority of the Foreign Office nor serve any other purpose than that of encouraging the Service Departments to support heresies which they otherwise might be argued out of.[31]

In the normal course of events, the P.H.P.S. paper would probably have come before the Vice-Chiefs of Staff, who had already shown themselves to be more willing than the full C.O.S. Committee to smooth over differences with the diplomats on post-war international security schemes. Since the 'exploratory' regional survey was also to serve as practical guidance for the Foreign Office delegation to Washington,[32] however, on this occasion it fell to the Chiefs of Staff themselves to consider it. This they did on 26 July, and 'shot down' the paper, as one P.H.P.S. secretary later recounted, 'if not in flames at any rate with a distinct smell of burning!'[33] Whilst the formal minutes merely recorded instructions to the C.O.S. secretariat to draft a letter in reply to the Foreign Office and to the Post-Hostilities Planners to re-write their report, 'taking a more realistic view of the situation with which we shall be confronted in the event of a breakdown of world organisation', a full account of the meeting was drawn up for restricted circulation.[34]

According to the Chiefs of Staff, the P.H.P.S. 'had failed to face up to the hard military facts of the problem'. It was quite true that efforts must be made to ensure the success of the proposed world organisation, and that the primary object would be to see that Germany did not rise again; but the 'real military problem' that had to be confronted was the fact that the world organisation might break down. In that eventuality,

the creation of a Western European Group would only be a first step towards a system which, if the security of these Islands were to be secured, must include a part, if not the whole of Germany . . . and, however unpalatable the fact might be, there might well come a time when we should have to rely on her assistance against a hostile Russia.

---

31. U6792/748/70
32. Tripartite conversations on proposals for a future world organisation were to be held at Dumbarton Oaks in Washington from 21 August to 28 September 1944. (See: Knapp, *op. cit.*, pp. 63–5)
33. Davison letter to Redman of 27 July 1944 in CAB 122/1566
34. COS(44)248th Mtg (0)(14)

Consequently, the case for and against dismembering Germany after her defeat would have to be argued with this consideration in mind.[35] In the words of the formal reply sent to the Foreign Office the following day, the position of the Chiefs of Staff was that

> we must on no account antagonise Russia by giving the appearance of building up the Western European block against her . . . for this reason the immediate object of a Western European Group must be the keeping down of Germany; but we feel that the more remote, but more dangerous, possibility of a hostile Russia making use of the resources of Germany must not be lost sight of, and that any measures which we now take should be tested by whether or not they help to prevent that contingency ever arising.[36]

As far as Jebb could discover, the Chiefs of Staff were 'profoundly sceptical', both of a world organisation ever coming into being and of the United States ever coming to the assistance of the United Kingdom quickly enough should serious trouble occur on the Continent. With Germany reduced to impotence—for a time, at least—and war with the Americans unthinkable, this left Russia as the only Power which would be in a position to menace British interests after the war and therefore as the principal *potential* enemy of the United Kingdom. Thus, in their view, the second half of the P.H.P.S. paper needed strengthening, 'as representing both the worst and the most likely contingency'.[37]

This was a line of argument which had most forcefully and most recently been stated by the British Representative with the French National Liberation Committee, Alfred Duff Cooper:

> There will doubtless be some who . . . will argue that if Russia be very powerful it is with Russia that we should make an alliance in order to obtain security[38] . . . . But the alliance of the wolf and the lamb is ever an

---

35. COS(44)248th Mtg (0)(14) (Confidential Annex)—missing, but obtainable under cover of COS Sec Min 1287/4 in U6793/748/70 and in CAB 21/1614 (Full text in Appendix 3(i), pp. 349–50 below)
36. COS(44)249th Mtg (0)(7) & COS Sec Min 1289/4 in U6793/748/70
37. U6793/748/70
38. *Cf.* the comments of Warner's Northern Department subordinate, Geoffrey Wilson, in January 1943 on an isolated memorandum by Thomas Preston of the Cairo Embassy. Preston, a former member of the British Legation in Lithuania, had predicted post-war annexations by the Russians in Europe on the model of those of the Baltic States. Wilson minuted that he seemed 'to assume that movements of social revolution in Europe are mainly created by Soviet

uneasy partnership and the advantages accruing to the lamb are apt to prove temporary. To promote friendly relations and to conclude treaties of non-aggression with the Power most likely to aggress is obviously desirable, but to rely upon the permanence of such agreements or the observation of such treaties is unwise.[39]

Eden's reply to Cooper's despatch had been written the day before C.O.S. rejection of the P.H.P.S. paper. It recognised that Russia was 'clearly aiming at some system in Eastern Europe in which she would take the lead', and it conceded that the possibility of an expansionist policy on her part could not be ruled out. Nevertheless, it maintained that

a Western group organised as a defensive measure against the possibility of Russia embarking at some future date on a policy of aggression and domination would be a most dangerous experiment which might well precipitate the evils against which it was intended to guard.[40]

In his *post-mortem* minute on the Chiefs of Staff meeting, written on 28 July, Jebb felt it hardly necessary to add that they had now read both despatches and were '100% in agreement with Mr. Cooper'. Jebb's own position had now shifted much closer to Warner's. He no longer felt that it was possible to disentangle the strategic and political issues, since the mere fact of preparation for the former would have severe ramifications upon the latter; and he concluded that

the adoption (in advance of any necessity to do so) of a policy of building up our enemies so as to be able to defeat our allies[41] would seem, if it were to be taken literally, to derive from some kind of suicidal mania.

---

propaganda and the example of the U.S.S.R. In fact they are in essence perfectly natural local growths which the Russians may try to use . . . we shall only suppress them (if we want to) at our peril. Our best insurance, far more effective than mere military occupation, is to spot as early as possible which are going to be the emergent social groups in the various countries and to try to make them our friends. If they are friends of the Russians too, so much the better.' (N499/499/38 (1943))

39.   Cooper Despatch to Eden, No. 295 of 30 May 1944, in WP(44)409 One of the strongest opponents of pre-war Appeasement, Cooper had resigned as First Lord of the Admiralty in disgust at the 1938 Munich agreement.
40.   Eden Despatch to Cooper, No. 311 of 25 July 1944, in WP(44)409
41.   That this was no misrepresentation, at least of the C.I.G.S.'s thinking at this time, is confirmed by Brooke's diary entry for 27 July: 'we must from now on regard Germany in a very different light. Germany is no longer the dominating

The only comfort from Jebb's point of view was that, for whatever reasons, Service opinion and Foreign Office policy were at one in favouring the creation of a Western European defensive bloc.

Now that the central issue was out in the open, Warner hoped that the War Cabinet would give a clear decision on policy and planning by which the Chiefs of Staff would have to abide. Roberts remarked that the latter were 'not only crossing their bridge before they come to it but even constructing their bridge in order to cross it', but Cavendish-Bentinck felt it only natural that they should regard the Soviet Union as a potential danger. He stressed that their 'unfortunate discussion' had resulted from lack of time to consider the issue properly; consequently, Brooke's views had been 'taken in raw form'. In his opinion, the Chiefs of Staff might modify their position if Jebb put a separate paper forward explaining the Foreign Office argument when the survey came to be re-written. This would do away with the necessity for ministerial involvement. On 1 August, a meeting chaired by Sargent approved this procedure.[42] Revised terms of reference had been issued to the P.H.P.S. three days earlier, and the first steps towards re-writing the North Atlantic survey were already being taken.[43] Before a new version could be produced, however, the whole question of long-term strategy against a possibly hostile Russia was to come to its climax over proposals for the dismemberment of Germany after defeat—and the Foreign Office was to find itself deprived of its valued position at the head of the post-war military planning machine.

3. From Decapitation to Dismemberment

With the Service chiefs fully roused by the abortive P.H.P.S. survey, events followed one another in rapid succession. At the same meeting which approved the formal C.O.S. statement to the Foreign Office on the Western bloc idea, instructions were issued to the Joint Planning Staff to submit a report on 'certain aspects of the organisation of Post-

---

power in Europe—Russia is. Unfortunately, Russia is not entirely European. She has, however, vast resources and cannot fail to become the main threat in fifteen years from now. Therefore, foster Germany, gradually build her up and bring her into a Federation of Western Europe. Unfortunately, this must all be done under the cloak of a holy alliance between England, Russia and America. Not an easy policy, and one requiring a super Foreign Secretary.' (Bryant, *Triumph in the West*, p. 242)

42. U6793/748/70
43. PHP(44)17(0)(Revised T.R.)—missing, but obtainable in U6793/748/70

Hostilities Planning'.[44] On the basis of the J.P.S. diagnosis, surgical measures were once again deemed necessary—and on 2 August Ismay told Cadogan what they ought to be. Making no direct reference to the present dispute, he pointed out that Foreign Office chairmanship of the Post-Hostilities Planners had been retained in May 'for the sake of continuity'. Now that the reconstituted body had been functioning for some time, the Chiefs of Staff felt that

> it is sufficiently well established to undergo any further changes which the scope of its work may suggest.

This work was to prepare examinations of post-war strategic problems to enable the Chiefs of Staff to submit 'purely military advice' to the government. To this end, close contact with the Foreign Office was particularly valuable, especially in view of the 'ability and address of Mr. Gladwyn Jebb'—for whose work they felt 'nothing but gratitude and appreciation'. Nevertheless, the role of the P.H.P.S., as now defined, could not be 'precisely served with a Foreign Office official as permanent Chairman'. The duty of the Chiefs of Staff was to give military advice based upon military considerations, and the stage for compromise between military and political views was not at staff level but in the War Cabinet itself. Just as the presence of a Foreign Office adviser to the Directors of Plans ensured the giving of due weight to political factors when more immediate military plans were formulated, so should parallel representation be maintained in the post-war planning field. With the J.P.S. and P.H.P.S. likely to merge as their work converged after victory in Europe, it was all the more important to ensure that they corresponded exactly. Therefore, it was proposed that in future

> the Foreign Office representative would serve as an associate member of the Post-Hostilities Planning Staff exactly on the same footing as Mr. Cavendish-Bentinck on the Joint Planning Staff.[45]

Cadogan replied, three days later, expressing 'entire agreement' that henceforth the Foreign Office representative should neither preside

---

44. COS(44)249th Mtg(0)(2) The J.P.S. report—like Kennedy's in March—was not put into circulation, and no copy of it seems to have survived.
45. Ismay letter to Cadogan of 2 August 1944 in U6770/573/70 (also reproduced as COS(44)143 Annex I)

over the P.H.P.S. nor sign its reports to the Chiefs of Staff.[46] His suggestion that the existing arrangement should, however, continue in respect of armistice and control papers prepared for other bodies, merely drew a response from the Service Directors that they should shed this side of the work completely and free the Foreign Office representative from the need to sign any P.H.P.S. reports.[47]

How the diplomats really regarded all this was summed up in an intemperate minute by Jebb's departmental deputy, John Ward, on 18 August—Jebb himself by then being embroiled in the Dumbarton Oaks conversations on post-war world organisation. Ward noted that Cadogan's proposal to reorganise the P.H.P.S. on a ' "Jekyll and Hyde" basis' had failed to go forward to the Vice-Chiefs as intended,

> the reason being (as I already suspected) that the Military Directors of the P.H.P.S. are hatching a counter-project designed to rid themselves of the 'control' work hitherto done by the P.H.P.S.

Allen, Curtis and Warburton were, in his view, 'temperamentally uninterested' in such matters as occupational machinery. In this they differed completely from the original members of the Post-Hostilities Planning Sub-Committee, which had been established primarily to deal with such non-strategic matters and had done useful work in that respect. Furthermore, they seemed to be 'cutting their own throats by trying to shuffle out of control work', since, as soon as the fighting ceased in Europe, the J.P.S. would reclaim the post-war strategic planning tasks with which the P.H.P.S. had temporarily been entrusted. Ward's conclusion that

> In view of the tendencies and recklessness shown by the present Directors of P.H.P., we need not regret these gentlemen committing hara-kiri,

was none the less an admission of the final defeat of diplomatic infiltration of the post-war military planning apparatus which the

---

46. Cadogan letter to Ismay of 5 August 1944 in U6770/573/70 (also reproduced as COS(44)143 Annex II)
47. PHP(44)66 & COS(44)306th Mtg (0)(7)

Foreign Office had been so largely responsible for erecting in the first place.[48]

There can be little doubt that Ward's attitude to his Service colleagues was heartily reciprocated by them:

> P.H.P.S. took care to keep this paper from its F.O. 'associate member'!
> It is the usual story, but this time even more foolishly worded,

he commented the following month, when Cavendish-Bentinck drew attention to a draft study of the 'Procedure for Assessing the Size of Post-War Forces'.[49] This had resulted from a suggestion by the C.I.G.S. on 7 September that the Post-Hostilities Planners should now examine imperial strategy after the period of occupation, 'as a basis on which the ultimate structure of the Services' could be calculated.[50] The P.H.P.S. pointed out that its present series of regional studies would lead to a world-wide strategic review of the situation in 1955—so far as that could be anticipated. To assist in the preparation of this review, it was suggested that

> Since a hostile Russia is one of our basic assumptions and would constitute a most serious threat to our strategic interests . . . a special inter-Service team should undertake a study of the courses of action open to an aggressive Russia.

A high-level body to examine future trends in warfare and in scientific development should also be established as soon as possible. Then, on the basis of these studies, conclusions about the post-war structure of the Services might reasonably be drawn.[51]

When copies of this draft paper were 'suddenly produced' at a J.I.C. meeting on 18 September, as Cavendish-Bentinck later noted, he and his colleagues agreed that an inter-Service team to take the part of the enemy would be 'a dangerous body, as its opinions are based on

---

48. U6770/573/70 In his account of this period, written in 1972, Jebb said of his relationship with the P.H.P.S. that 'towards the end of 1944, I seem to remember that I rather faded out of this strictly strategical picture'. Despite the suddenness of his removal from the chairmanship, this is not an inaccurate description, given that—as will be seen—he continued to co-operate with the organisation during the remaining months of its existence. (Lord Gladwyn, *The Memoirs of Lord Gladwyn* (London, Weidenfeld & Nicolson, 1972), p. 137)   49.   U7619/748/70
50.   COS(44)819(0) & COS(44)304th Mtg (0)(14)
51.   PHP(44)23(0)(Draft)—missing, but obtainable in U7619/748/70

hunches, surmise, guesswork, etc., instead of hard facts and correct intelligence';[52] and they also took the view that it was better not to put the admitted possibility of a hostile Russia down on paper for the present.[53] The latter observation was prompted by the fact that—possibly in view of the tough line taken by the Chiefs of Staff—the Post-Hostilities Planners had sought in the draft to re-phrase their basic assumptions to read:

(i) In the absence or breakdown of a World Security Organisation, Russia is a potential enemy.
(ii) An effective World Security Organisation is in existence.[54]

On 6 October, the Service chiefs considered the final version of the paper, which had dropped the idea of requesting a special team to act in the role of the enemy but retained the reformulated basic assumptions. After the meeting, Hood was able to record that

The bald assumption that the U.S.S.R. will be our enemy in 10–15 years' time seems to have been too much even for the Chiefs of Staff and this paper has been withdrawn.[55]

According to the C.O.S. minute, it had been felt that the report went further than was currently practicable and that some of its assumptions did not accord with Foreign Office policy.[56] However, in writing to tell Cornwall-Jones—now Secretary to the J.S.M.—of its fate, Major Patrick Davison of the P.H.P.S. secretariat explained that the paper had been withdrawn for 'security reasons'. Although the Chiefs of Staff had

shot down the proposals both for a J.I.C. Russian appreciation[57] and also for a high-level Committee to study the lessons of the war,

---

52. Early in the war, the J.I.C. had had problems with a special organisation known as the 'Future Operations (Enemy) Section' ('F.O.E.S.'), set up to try to visualise German moves in advance. (See: Davison/Cornwall-Jones correspondence in CAB 122/1566 & F.H. Hinsley *et al., British Intelligence in the Second World War* (London, H.M.S.O., 1979), i. 296–7)
53. U7619/748/70   54.   PHP(44)23(0)(Draft), *loc. cit.*
55. U7703/748/70   56.   PHP(44)23(0)(Final) & COS(44)330th Mtg (0)(4)
57. The final version of the paper had suggested that the J.I.C., rather than a special separate team, should be asked to examine the options open to a hostile Soviet Union.

it was as a result of a 'show-down' between the Foreign Office and the Chiefs of Staff on the 'old Russian issue' that he and his colleagues had been instructed to

> increase security measures as regards any of our papers across which the 'shadow of the Bear' should chance to fall.[58]

As Hood was well aware, the fact that the regional and world strategic surveys were still to proceed on Cornwall-Jones's original assumptions of the presence or absence of an effective world organisation, still left plenty of scope for the P.H.P.S. to develop its 'anti-Soviet complex'; but at least that formula had

> the merit of not advertising this unfortunate fact and the decency to place the success of a World Organisation above its failure.[59]

Nor, in the event, were detailed investigations into the lessons of the war and into likely progress in technology long to be postponed. Within a month, this project would be taken up by the Chief of the Air Staff, admittedly in connection with an unrelated matter, but very much along the lines suggested by the Directors of the P.H.P.S.[60] Despite what some Foreign Office officials preferred to believe, the views of the Service chiefs now coincided with those of the post-war planners to a much greater extent than at any time since the F.O.P.S. had opted out in 1942.

Ever since the rejection of the first North Atlantic survey on 26 July, it had been only a question of time before matters came to a head between the diplomats and the Chiefs of Staff. The interim C.O.S. reply on Germany and a Western bloc had been the first step in this direction; the removal of Jebb from the P.H.P.S. chairmanship was the second; and the revision of the North Atlantic survey would have been the third but for the prior need to reply to a Foreign Office request for guidance as to the effect on British strategic interests of the permanent partitioning of Germany.[61] This request had been sent on 7 June and covered a departmental memorandum expressing characteristic concern that whatever stance the United Kingdom adopted on this

---

58. Davison letter to Cornwall-Jones of 17 October 1944 in CAB 122/1566
59. U7703/748/70   60. See pp. 178–9 below
61. This topic is fully covered as a major aspect of foreign policy in Woodward, *op. cit.*, v. 203–10.

question of dismemberment, she might fail in the all-important task of convincing the Soviet Union of the sincerity of her intentions. A failure to support dismemberment might lead to the Russians 'suspecting our motives on the major question of Germany', but the opposite course could result in 'the division of Germany into eastern and western spheres of influence, which would destroy any hope of a joint control of European affairs'.[62]

That the Post-Hostilities Planners were less convinced of the degree to which security would depend upon demonstrations of sincerity than upon factors in the post-war balance of power, was made abundantly clear on 25 August in a paper described by Ward as

> by no means the sort of document which I imagine we originally hoped to obtain from the Chiefs of Staff . . . .

It assumed that three states roughly corresponding to the expected zones of occupation might result from a process of dismemberment, and considered the significance of such a development for the strategic interests of the United Kingdom. These comprised the prevention of German rearmament and renewed aggression on the one hand and the need to insure against possible Soviet hostility on the other. With regard to the former, the division of Germany would make it harder for the succession states to plan and execute a concerted rearmament programme and easier for the Allies to apply coercive measures. It might add to the tasks of the occupation forces, and would certainly require that Anglo-American public opinion be

> educated to understand and approve the use of force as the ultimate sanction for keeping the new German States both disarmed and permanently separated.

If the Russians were eventually to become hostile, a complete military reorientation would be essential:

> we should require all the help we can get from any source open to us, including Germany. We must above all prevent Germany combining with the Soviet Union against us.

It was open to question whether a united Germany would be more likely to side with the Soviet Union or with the United Kingdom, but it

---

62.   COS(44)508(0)

was hardly probable that the Russians would permit German rearmament unless they were sure of maintaining their domination over the rearmed country. The British could therefore never expect to secure tangible help from a united Germany against a hostile Soviet Union. Yet, by accepting dismemberment, they could expect instead eventually to bring North-Western and possibly Southern Germany, too, into the orbit of a Western European group. This would increase available military potential and add depth to the defences of the United Kingdom.[63]

This paper was greeted with a chorus of disapproval from the diplomats, headed by Jebb's deputy on the P.H.P.S. Ward's commentaries on the draft and final versions derided it as cursory, childish and dangerous. He attacked 'the almost Fascist assumption' that public opinion could *be brought* to accept the use of force to maintain an artificial dismemberment indefinitely, and denied the practicability of partition:

> To anyone who has any first-hand knowledge of modern Germany and can appreciate the absurdity of rigid international frontiers wandering up German hills and down German valleys, this assumption seems to beg the whole question.

He had, in accordance with Sargent's instructions, held entirely aloof from the paper at P.H.P.S. meetings over the previous fortnight, and had 'not attempted any more to tone down its anti-Russian extravagances'. It was illogical to advocate dismemberment as a means of keeping the Germans weak for an initial period, and then to expect 'to be able suddenly to bring part if not all of Germany into an anti-Russian alliance and to have the advantage of German war potential'. Nor could the Russians fail to realise any such British motivation—thus probably precipitating the very menace it was desired to avert. The 'anti-Russian bias' of the military planners would distract Ministers' attention from the dismemberment problem in its purely German aspect, and the Foreign Secretary should therefore press the Chiefs of Staff to suppress the P.H.P.S. paper for the time being at least.[64]

Unfortunately, from Ward's point of view, it quickly became clear that the issue could not be side-stepped so easily. On 9 September, the Chiefs of Staff approved the report and had it forwarded to the Foreign

---

63. PHP(44)15(0)(Final)—withdrawn, but obtainable in C11955/146/18
64. C11955/146/18

Office in a slightly amended form serving only to strengthen the original line.[65] On 20 September, it was reproduced as one of two appendices to a note prepared for the A.P.W. Committee in which the Foreign Secretary strongly attacked any consideration of the German problem from the angle of reinsurance against possible Soviet hostility. It seemed to Eden that

> any such conception should be avoided like the plague in our consideration of German problems. If we prepare our post-war plans with the idea at the back of our minds that the Germans may serve as part of an anti-Soviet bloc, we shall quickly destroy any hope of preserving the Anglo-Soviet Alliance and soon find ourselves advocating relaxations of the disarmament and other measures which we regard as essential guarantees against future German aggression.

The attached departmental memorandum denounced the attitude of the Chiefs of Staff as 'little less than fantastic' and as 'playing with fire'. It went on to re-state, in the same terms as in the original 7 June memorandum, Foreign Office anxieties about choosing a policy on dismemberment which would not generate Soviet suspiciousness, and it argued that the advantages cited on security grounds for a policy of partition were illusory. In particular, there was claimed to be

> the strongest political objection to basing any of our plans for Germany on the possible need to use Germans one day as allies against an aggressive Russia.[66]

It was the production of this Foreign Office paper which precipitated the 'show-down' which Davison later recounted to Cornwall-Jones.[67] On 2 October, the Chiefs of Staff urgently requested a meeting with the Foreign Secretary on the whole question of post-war strategic planning. They set out their case in a note based upon a draft submitted by Portal.[68] This denounced the Foreign Office approach *in toto*. To write papers on the basis of Russia as a possible enemy was, according to the diplomats, to fly in the face of accepted government policy, which aimed at the maintenance of good Anglo-Soviet relations and at the establishment of an effective world security organisation; but the

---

65.	COS(44)303rd Mtg (0)(5) & COS(44)822(0)
66.	APW(44)90—withdrawn, but obtainable in C13517/146/18
67.	See pp. 126–7 above		68.	COS(44)323rd Mtg (0)(6)

Chiefs of Staff had to maintain an open-minded approach in studying long-term strategic questions:

> No-one will dispute for a moment the value of friendship with Russia or of a successful world organisation. No-one would be better pleased than the Chiefs of Staff if a permanent solution to our military problems could be achieved by this means. We should be very foolish if we advocated measures which would hinder the perpetuation of the present close relations between the three great powers. But it is the duty of the Chiefs of Staff to examine all serious eventualities. We cannot be debarred from taking into account the possibility that for some reason or other the world security organisation may break down, and that Russia may start forth on the path to world domination, as other continental nations have done before her.

A failure to consider this would be a repetition of the disastrous error of the inter-war years, when all planning had been based upon the assumption that the League of Nations would ensure the security of the British Empire:

> The examination of an unpleasant situation which may perhaps arise is in no way incompatible with the pursuit of a policy designed to prevent that situation arising. Yet the Foreign Office seems to recoil from the precaution of considering how to insure against the failure of our policy. They seem in effect to presume that the policy we intend to pursue is bound to be successful provided no thought is taken to meet the possibility of failure.[69]

The Foreign Office response to this—in a minute probably written by Sargent—rested on the belief that Soviet discovery of the existence of such hypothetical planning would precipitate moves to render Western bloc aspirations ineffective, and also to ensure that Germany would be on the side of the Russians rather than of the British. The Soviet Union was 'in an excellent position to achieve both these aims', but was apparently not expected to try to do so unless provoked by the Service Departments thinking in terms of a possible conflict with Russia or committing such thoughts to paper. Quoting Lord Salisbury—'if you believe the soldiers, nothing is safe. Some of them want to occupy the

---

69. COS Sec Min 1659/4—missing, but obtainable in C13518/146/18 (Full text in Appendix 3(ii), pp. 350–3 below)

moon, in fear of an invasion from Mars'—another Foreign Office official summed up the prevailing diplomatic view:

> The Chiefs of Staff make their proposal because they are suspicious of the Russians. The Russians are unlikely to fulfil the Chiefs' of Staff fears unless they become suspicious of us, and they will not justify our suspicions of them. We are threatened by a vicious, suspicious circle. Let us not describe the first arc.[70]

At the meeting between Eden, Sargent and the Chiefs of Staff on 4 October, Portal took the lead by explaining Service concern at Foreign Office opposition to examination of the hypothetical worst case: the United Kingdom confronted by a unitary Germany dominated by, or in collaboration with a hostile Soviet Union. Eden and Sargent stressed, in turn, the risks of focusing upon distant dangers at the expense of more immediate ones, and of encouraging the Russians

> to think that their innate suspicions of us were well-founded and that our talk of collaboration was not sincere.

Portal met these objections directly. He believed that the Soviet attitude towards dismemberment had been changing throughout 1944 and now seemed to favour keeping Germany as a unit:

> Could we not tax the Russians with this, and indicate that we were concerned at this change which we felt might spring from a desire to build up Germany against us? He did not see why we should unduly handicap ourselves for fear of breeding suspicion in the Russian mind. We were just as much entitled to take wise precautions as were the Russians.

In studying this question, the C.A.S. continued, the Chiefs of Staff had taken the keeping down of Germany as their starting-point; but they had felt that the combination of Germany and Russia would be so powerful that steps ought to be taken to prevent it materialising. Nor could there be any threat from the Germans for the next ten or fifteen years, added the V.C.I.G.S., if Germany were thoroughly defeated and disarmed. In viewing a possible resurgence over a longer period, the possibility that Russian policy might by .then have changed had also to be considered.[71]

---

70. C13518/146/18   71. N6177/183/38

If the Foreign Office representatives produced answers to these points, they were not recorded in the minutes. There was not the slightest prospect of the Chiefs of Staff changing their approach in the absence of a government ruling that war with the Soviet Union could be excluded from their calculations. What they were willing to concede was the taking of special measures for the handling of papers containing the contentious hypothesis. Then, as Davison later told Cornwall-Jones, 'honour. . . [was] satisfied by the withdrawal of both the Foreign Office paper and the Chiefs of Staff paper', each of which was to be re-written.[72]

The meeting also resolved to inform the Prime Minister of the existence of disagreement on the future of Germany, and on 6 October the C.O.S. approach was given encouragement when Ismay reported that Churchill's response had been to say that he understood both Roosevelt and Stalin to be even more in favour of dismemberment than he was himself.[73] On 12 October, Allen, Curtis and Warburton were called in by the Chiefs of Staff and instructed to revise their dismemberment paper. This time they should bring out more clearly the 'crucial fact' that a unified Germany would pose a greater threat to security than a divided one, and should emphasise that this held good independently of the need to secure German help against other threats which might arise in the long term.[74] The revised report, which was completed on 15 November, adhered to the original strategic themes concerning both Germany and the Soviet Union. It granted that, as there could be no question of reversing measures to eliminate German war potential unless and until it was clear that a major clash with the Russians was unavoidable, it might well be too late to achieve full rearmament of the Germans to augment Western strength in a conflict. Nevertheless, the added defensive depth and the reduction in German help available to Russia, wrought by partition of the country, would be greatly to the United Kingdom's strategic advantage.[75]

In the event, Eden proved reluctant to reopen the issue or to take it up with the A.P.W. Committee, and by the time it was next considered—in April 1945—the Russians were, indeed, beginning to back-pedal on the issue, as Portal had anticipated. The ministers then agreed that it would be pointless to seek Service views until concrete proposals for the future of Germany emerged—especially as it was rapidly becoming

72. *Ibid.*, & Davison letter to Cornwall-Jones of 17 October 1944 in CAB 122/ 1566   73.   COS(44)330th Mtg (0)(3)   74.   COS(44)336th Mtg (0)(5)
75.   PHP(44)15(0)(Revised Final) & COS(44)1012(0)(PHP)

obvious that separate administration of the Soviet zone would probably amount to a *de facto* state of dismemberment, whether the British liked it or not.[76]

Ironically, the main significance of the revised P.H.P.S. report, which the Chiefs of Staff approved as a tentative 'Staff Study' on 5 December, lay less in its contents than in the manner of their presentation.[77] This was in accordance with the third of three rules promulgated on 24 October as a result of the meeting between Eden, Sargent and the Chiefs of Staff. Henceforth, when it was necessary to refer to the possibility of Soviet hostility:

(1) In the case of papers destined for consideration only by the Chiefs of Staff it is necessary that Russian problems shall be considered frankly and in a normal manner; but such papers both as regards drafts and finals should receive a very restricted circulation.[78] Even in these papers it is desirable that challenging captions should be avoided in prominent headings if possible.

(2) Any strategic appreciation or report which may have to go before the A.P.W. Committee or receive a circulation other than to the Chiefs of Staff should, if possible, be confined to the immediate problems of keeping Germany and Japan down, and any reference to a future threat from Russia should be in polite and circumlocutory terms.

(3) If it should be impossible, in the case of papers referred to in (2) above, to deal adequately with Russian considerations in brief and anodyne phrases, the offending paragraphs should be placed in an Annex to which no reference would be made in the main body of the paper. This annex should receive a very restricted circulation.[79]

The adoption of this code was to have one effect which even those most fearful of the misdirection of sensitive papers had not anticipated. Throughout the second half of 1944, a lively liaison had existed between the P.H.P.S. secretariat and the British Joint Staff Mission in

76.   A report on a French proposal for indefinite international control of 'Rhenania' (the Rheno-Westphalian basin) after the end of the total occupation of Germany, was also prepared by the P.H.P.S. on similar lines to the Dismemberment paper; but, although it was forwarded to the Foreign Office in January 1945, neither it nor the revised Dismemberment report had been circulated to the A.P.W. Committee by April. (PHP(44)22(0)(Final); APW(45)40; PHP(45)14(0)(T.R.); APW(45)10th Mtg (2); Woodward, *op. cit.*, v. 243–4, 335)   77. · COS(44)390th Mtg (0)(11)

78.   Outside the P.H.P.S. itself, this amounted in practice to a total of four copies to each Service Department and a further two to the Foreign Office.

79.   COS(44)346th Mtg (0)(13)(Confidential Annex)

Washington, with the former furnishing copies of current papers to the latter on a weekly basis. On 14 November, Davison regretfully informed Cornwall-Jones that there would be 'no more games of Russian scandal for the J.S.M.', as papers or annexes on possible Soviet hostility were no longer to be supplied. This, in turn, put an end to the parallel practice whereby Cornwall-Jones had circulated copies of such material (including the original, unexpurgated Dismemberment report of 25 August) to the British Embassy in Washington via its principal contact with the J.S.M.—the Soviet spy, Donald Maclean.[80]

4. Western Europe: Agreement to Disagree

After the rejection of the North Atlantic survey by the Chiefs of Staff on 26 July, Air Commodore Warburton quickly established himself as the most forceful and persistent of the Post-Hostilities Planners where the Soviet Union was concerned. On 31 July, he circulated a note in which he argued that the Russian appreciation drawn up by the old P.H.P. Sub-Committee in May suffered from the same defect as the North Atlantic paper—it took too great an account of hopes and fears, instead of concentrating upon 'stark realities'. The fact that he did not himself dissent from its broad conclusions about Soviet intentions did not encourage him to let them colour consideration of the strategic possibilities:

> While Russia may have perfectly satisfactory intentions for the future, I suggest it is fair to assume that she will certainly take advantage of the very strong position she will be in at the peace discussions, to secure for herself such strategic needs as she may feel will stand her in good stead in the more distant future, even though she may have no well-defined intentions at present to exploit her advantage.[81]

Warburton pressed for an attempt to be made to predict what the pattern of Soviet aggression would be if the Russians were to decide to attack, but the idea was eventually vetoed by the Chiefs of Staff in October.[82] Nor did his other main proposal work out quite as expected. This was to ask the J.I.C. to chart the salient strengths and weaknesses of Soviet economic and military power, and also to supplement the

---

80. See: Davison/Cornwall-Jones correspondence and circulation notes thereon, in CAB 122/1566—quoted on p. 427 below

81. Note by D.P.H.P., Air Ministry—copy in U6793/748/70

82. See pp. 125–6 above

previous Russian appreciation by considering the possibility of aggression in Europe or Asia.[83] A paper was duly prepared before the end of August; but, though described as 'explosive' by Sir Andrew Noble, who now handled such matters in Cavendish-Bentinck's Services Liaison Department, it apparently represented 'rather a setback for the would-be drinkers of Russian blood', according to the secretary of the P.H.P.S.[84] Its contents and mode of production can be deduced[85] with a high degree of probability from a J.I.C. study of 'Russia's Strategic Interests and Intentions from the Point of View of her Security', presented to the Chiefs of Staff in December 1944. Then, Cavendish-Bentinck was to note that that paper was 'largely the handiwork of Sir A. Noble'—his own Foreign Office colleague—who had 'kept in close touch' with the Northern Department to Warner's evident satisfaction.[86]

Like the earlier Russian appreciation, the December study was essentially an exercise in speculation. It embodied the Foreign Office view that the Soviet Union would at least experiment with a policy of tripartite collaboration. She would require a period of absolute security in which to recover and to achieve her supposed aim of raising popular living-standards to something approaching Western levels. She would favour the military and economic disarmament of Germany and also, perhaps, her dismemberment. British and French determination to hold 'the other side of the ring' in this connection would be 'the acid tests of the sincerity of their collaboration'. Attempts by the Western Powers to court Germany would be seen as a threat to Soviet security, to be countered by combination with, or a preventative attack upon that country. As for Russia's strategically-important neighbours, the Soviet Union would aspire to 'a position rather similar to that of Great Britain in Egypt': she would allow them their independence so long as she could ensure their pursuit of a policy favouring her security.[87]

---

83. PHP(44)20(0)(Final)
84. U6875/748/70 & Davison letter to Cornwall-Jones of 30 August 1944 in CAB 122/1566
85. The memorandum itself—JIC(44)366(0)(Final)—was still under review for de-classification by the Cabinet Office at the time of writing.
86. N678/20/38 (1945)
87. JIC(44)467(0)(Final)(Retained—Cabt. Off.)—also circulated as COS(44) 1053(0)(PHP) Annex. The pleasure of the Foreign Office at the inclusion of a paper containing these views amongst the Service chiefs' exploratory staff studies, was to be tempered in January 1945 by C.O.S. refusal to circulate it to the War Cabinet. (COS(44)411th Mtg(0)(3), COS(45)29th Mtg(3) & N678/20/38 (1945))

On the assumption, then, that these were also the views furnished to the P.H.P.S. in August as a result of Warburton's initiative, they could have made very little difference to the planning process already in hand. So far as *predictions of Soviet intentions* were concerned, the Post-Hostilities Planners had been faithfully following this line in any case. On 25 August, for example, they had completed a reply to an enquiry from a specialist C.O.S. sub-committee interested in the threat of attack on certain British bases after the war.[88] In full accordance with the original Russian appreciation, they had stated that, during the immediate post-war years,

> the U.S.S.R. is likely to be fully engaged (with the other United Nations) in the occupation and control of Germany, and with her own rehabilitation.

She would be 'most unlikely' to try to further her interests aggressively at British expense. Although a long-term Soviet threat might develop, no circumstances could be foreseen leading to a surprise attack on the United Kingdom in the first two years after victory over Germany, and the threat to bases was considered remote.[89] This report had passed smoothly through a meeting of the Vice-Chiefs of Staff on 31 August, indicating that they, too, had no wish to differ with Foreign Office estimates of what the Russians should be expected to do.[90] A reiteration of these estimates by Noble and/or the Joint Intelligence Sub-Committee—if, indeed, this is what actually happened—was therefore largely superfluous. However, it may be that the August paper was welcomed by the diplomats, not because it anticipated no Soviet aggression, but because it took a pessimistic view of the options open to the United Kingdom if she wished to consider a policy of confrontation with the Russians.

There were other points of convergence to compensate for some of the tension between the military planners and the Foreign Office, even where Europe was concerned. On 30 October, the Foreign Office requested military advice on the setting up of a Western European group (to provide 'security against Germany'), now that the Dumbarton Oaks conversations had cleared the way for regional defence associations to be formed under a world organisation.[91] The reply of the P.H.P.S., as amended by the Vice-Chiefs, stressed the 'paramount

88. COS(44)108   89. PHP(44)18(0)(Final)
90. COS(44)294th Mtg (0)(7)   91. COS(44)934(0)

importance' of including a strong France in any Western group, together with Belgium, the Netherlands, Norway and Denmark as soon as a government was established there. Iceland, Sweden, Spain and Portugal might also be included at a later stage. It was recommended that preliminary talks with the countries concerned should be kept to an informal basis in the ordinary course of business, and that the United States and Soviet Union should be apprised of all developments—the latter so that she

> should have no grounds for thinking that the proposed Group is in any way directed against herself.[92]

As Cornwall-Jones had said at the end of May, when the Western bloc idea was first being mooted, allies were allies—and there was no reason for the Service chiefs to oppose Foreign Office wishes to acquire them against the Germans, however naive it might be to think that the Russians would not object.[93]

Further friction was nevertheless unavoidable as successive drafts of P.H.P.S. regional surveys began to appear. It had always been the intention simply to pigeon-hole them on completion, to await the day when the Chiefs of Staff would be called upon to advise the government on long-term strategy. All Eden's intervention had done was to restrict the extent of their prior circulation. Their contents and presentation basically conformed to the pattern decreed by Brooke when the North Atlantic paper was rejected in July. Indeed, the first attempt at revising that study had been almost as great a factor, on receipt in the Foreign Office, in provoking Eden's attack upon the Chiefs of Staff as had the Dismemberment report. 'This seems to me a terrible paper however it is looked at,' Eden minuted before his meeting with the Service chiefs. More surprisingly, Warner intervened with the remark that

> we ourselves (without any paper-writing) liked the idea of a Western bloc . . . because of its possible value against a hostile Russia as well as against Germany,

---

92. PHP(44)26(0)(Final), COS(44)361st Mtg (0)(3) & COS(44)955(0)
93. It was to be Churchill's strong opposition to any undertaking of a Continental commitment on behalf of indefensible allies after the Americans had returned home which precluded further progress on a Western bloc while his government remained in office. (See: CAB 21/1614 & Woodward, *op. cit.*, v. 192–8)

before reiterating his familiar argument that talking about this aspect would provoke Soviet counter-measures which would not otherwise be taken.[94]

It is, however, very difficult to reconcile this uncharacteristic claim by the head of the Northern Department with the vehemence of the opposition to the Chiefs of Staff approach which he and his colleagues usually employed.[95] Time and again the military planners were attacked and condemned, not simply for lack of tactical discretion, but for alleged 'anti-Soviet bias' *per se*. On 23 September, for example, just two days after Warner wrote this minute, his subordinate, Geoffrey Wilson, commented in some detail on a despatch from the British ambassador to Moscow, Sir Archibald Clark-Kerr. Taking up a reference by Clark-Kerr to Soviet media attacks on ' "nests of Fascist opposition" in the Western democracies', Wilson observed:

If we make the necessary allowance for Soviet terminology, this too, unfortunately, has an element of truth in it. The people who, whether consciously or unconsciously, are doing their best to wreck the Anglo-Soviet Alliance, are by no means confined to 'obscure people without honour in their own country' .... The recent P.H.P. papers on the dismemberment of Germany, the Western European bloc, and the Middle East[96] show that the authors or, more probably, those whom they serve, have not the slightest faith in the Anglo-Soviet Alliance. We have been assured by the Service Departments that these views are confined to Top Secret papers, but the suspicion and even hostility of the Service Departments towards Russia are now becoming a matter of common gossip .... [The ambassador] ought to be warned that there is more in the 'nests of Fascist opposition' business than he might suppose.[97]

Some six weeks later, when a lone memorandum was circulated, unfashionably predicting Soviet domination of Eastern and Central Europe to the exclusion of Russia's allies and anticipating a continuing rift

---

94. U7618/748/70
95. Jebb has confirmed to the author that the feelings of Warner, Ronald and others at this time were genuinely Russophile, and that Foreign Office opposition to anti-Soviet contingency planning was by no means based on mere tactical considerations. (Interview with Lord Gladwyn, 12 November 1980)
96. Two early draft versions of the P.H.P.S. Middle Eastern regional survey had by this time been circulated within the Foreign Office. (See: U7841/748/70)
97. N5598/183/38

so long as so wide a gulf remains between the political, constitutional and economic system of Soviet Russia and that of our own,

Wilson was scornfully to remark that little attention needed to be paid to its author.[98] However, as far as the Service chiefs were concerned, all this ceased to be of importance with the removal of direct diplomatic interference from the strategic planning process. It was the revision of the regional survey of requirements in the North Atlantic and Western Europe after the war which showed this process of separation to be almost, if not entirely, complete.

On resuming his place as P.H.P.S. 'associate member', Jebb was reluctant to continue the policy of standing aloof from strategic papers, as practised by Ward at Sargent's behest. Despite all the recent acrimony, he even went to the lengths of drafting an alternative set of conclusions on Western Europe, embodying the Foreign Office viewpoint.[99] These, though not accepted by the Service Directors,[100] nevertheless influenced the final version which appeared on 9 November. Another restraining factor was probably the J.I.C.'s response to Warburton's questionnaire, in the drafting of which diplomats may well have been involved. For whatever reason, although the section of the report assuming an effective world organisation to exist now mentioned the need not to let the Russians predominate in any preventative reoccupation of Germany which became necessary, it still emphasised that

> Any signs of weakness in our policy towards Germany would arouse the gravest suspicions and would endanger our relations with all the Powers now allied to us.

Similarly, although the focus of the paper shifted from detailed advocacy of a Western bloc to detailed consideration of rearming the Germans, the conclusions with regard to the latter were fairly cautious. Even if the Soviet Union did become aggressive, she would still probably prefer an acquiescent to a strong Germany. Whatever the nature of relations with the Russians, Western European aid against possible German resurgence would be important—and the arrange-

---

98. N7629/183/38 The author of the memorandum was the same individual, Thomas Preston, whose earlier warnings on the same subject had been similarly dismissed in January 1943. (See: footnote 38 to p. 120 above)
99. U7975/748/70   100. U8181/748/70

ments to obtain it would *a fortiori* be of value in countering a Soviet threat. No such threat before 1955 was anticipated, though Russian expansionism before this date would be possible. By then, however, after a decade of recovery and development, the Soviet Union would have a male population in the 15–34 age-group of some 37 million, in comparison with figures of 7, 6 and 11 million for the United Kingdom and Eire, France, and Germany respectively. British strategic interests could be at risk not only in Western Europe and the North Atlantic, but also in the Mediterranean, Middle East, India and the Pacific. There was also the prospect of internal security problems—even in the United Kingdom—arising from resumed activity by the Third International[101] on a greater scale than ever before.

If the Western European states were not to be overwhelmed by a hostile Russia, the prompt employment of American forces would be crucial. Although

> any German promise to fight on our side . . . . would at best be unreliable,

and German industry would be very vulnerable to air attack from the east, measures involving the reoccupation of Germany would add depth to the British defence whilst remaining consistent with declared policy towards that country. It followed that:

> we should in no circumstances agree to evacuate our zone in Germany unless the U.S.S.R. evacuated hers, and in the event of some serious breakdown in our relations with the U.S.S.R., we should have no hesitation in reoccupying our zone.

Nevertheless, the adoption of measures inconsistent with the prevention of renewed German aggression would alienate the Western European allies and antagonise the Soviet Union. None should be resorted to unless and until a major clash with the Russians was clearly unavoidable. The continued enforcement of safeguards against a German military revival would at least serve to minimise any prospect

---

101. Set up in 1919 to foster, co-ordinate and control the activities of communists abroad, the 'Comintern' had been dissolved by Stalin in May 1943—presumably as a gesture of goodwill towards his allies. In reality, many of its functions were presently taken over by other organs of the Soviet Communist Party, most notably by the International Department of the CPSU Central Committee.

of a deadly Russo-German combination being forged against the West.

As well as American and Continental assistance, Canadian and Irish co-operation would be required for the respective provision of resources and bases. Irish bases should form part of a system embracing all the Western European allies, Spain, Portugal, French North Africa, Spanish Morocco, the Azores, Greenland, Iceland and the Faroes. Though attacks on Soviet naval power would remain feasible, the overrunning of the Continent would once again throw the United Kingdom onto the defensive at sea. With the advent of methods of long-range bombardment, a forward air-defence system in Europe would be needed. This should be supported by passive defence measures at home, including re-location as well as protection. The prevention of invasion would depend upon command of the English Channel, with air power playing an even greater part than hitherto. Land forces would be essential to protect British bases from airborne assault. Great importance should also be attached to the application of science to warfare: if the United Kingdom fell behind in this respect, she could be reduced to a state in which she would be quite incapable of offering effective resistance to invasion. For their part, the Russians would not be susceptible to blockade and—apart from their Caucasian oilfields—would be relatively invulnerable to strategic bombing:

> Our best chance of offensive action lies in furthering by all possible means our technical development of all forms of warfare in order to enable us to strike at Soviet bases, industry and communications from a great distance with new weapons and novel forms of warfare.

Armed with this technical superiority, the United Kingdom would thus depend for her overall security on the states of Western Europe remaining free from domination by Germany or by Russia, on their co-operating with one another in a grouping centred on a strong and friendly France, and on the prospect of prompt military aid by the United States in the event of a threat arising.[102]

Considering that the Post-Hostilities Planners had made significant concessions to the Foreign Office view on German assistance, it was hardly surprising that the C.I.G.S. and his colleagues refused to give 'unqualified approval to the paper or its conclusions' for the time being.[103] The well-tried technique of designating it an 'exploratory Staff

---

102.   PHP(44)27(0)(Final)   103.   COS(44)374th Mtg (0)(13)

Study' enabled them to let it stand for the present, whilst not committing themselves to the views it contained. Jebb felt that he had reason to be pleased with the final product and described the section on Germany as 'entirely sensible'; but his Foreign Office superiors were less than happy at having to reconcile themselves to a situation in which military planning to meet possible Soviet hostility had become a fact of life. Resignedly, when acknowledging receipt of a copy of the survey, Cadogan stated that Eden would not be making any comment upon it unless the Chiefs of Staff wanted him to do so. Perhaps not surprisingly, they in turn decided that it would be unnecessary to trouble the Foreign Secretary on this particular occasion. [104]

5. The Balance of the Regional Surveys

Four more regional strategic surveys were to be drawn up by the P.H.P.S. before the long-envisaged global appreciation appeared. Those dealing with the Far East and the Middle East already existed in draft form, even before the Service chiefs' confrontation with Eden and Sargent. [105] Once the fundamental question of anti-Soviet contingency planning was settled, a fairly regular production programme was able to come into effect. The slowly increasing involvement of the Joint Planning Staff in post-war strategic matters was also beginning to be felt, and some of the results of this narrowly pre-empted the presentation of the first of the remaining P.H.P.S. surveys.

On 26 October, the Chiefs of Staff considered a minute[106] by the Prime Minister on future British and Soviet interests in the Far East. Its concern was with the strategic implications of Soviet acquisition of warm-water bases in the Northern Pacific, a question already examined in the Foreign Office, and it was to the Directors of Plans that the task of making an assessment was given. [107] By the time that this was produced, on New Year's Day 1945, the December report on Soviet intentions—drafted by Noble in the name of the J.I.C.[108]—had received preliminary C.O.S. approval as an exploratory paper. The Foreign Office line it embodied coloured the Joint Planners' report,

---

104. U8181/748/70 & COS(44)405th Mtg (0)(11)
105. See: U7658 & U7841/748/70 for copies of the respective P.H.P.S. draft reports
106. This minute, serial no. M.1025/4, was circulated personally to each Chief of Staff and does not seem to have survived. Its contents are deduced from JP(44)278(0)(T.R.) and the resultant paper.
107. COS(44)349th Mtg (0)(1)   108. See p. 136 above

which duly anticipated no post-war aggression by a Soviet Union sure of Anglo-American collaboration, but wishing 'to improve her strategic frontiers and to draw the states lying along her borders into her strategic system'. For greater security in the Far East, she would probably seek to add Manchuria, Korea, Sakhalin and the Kuriles to existing Soviet possessions, thereby creating a self-sufficient bloc and denying essential war resources to the Japanese. Despite evidence of an intention to develop an ocean-going navy, Soviet repossession of Port Arthur and Dairen in Southern Manchuria would probably not signify a desire to station major units in the area. Air power and light naval forces would suffice to protect the approaches to Russian territory, and the resources allocated to this task—and as a safeguard against Japanese resurgence—would be inadequate to penetrate an Anglo-American chain of bases to the north of the strategic sea routes. Consequently, although the maintenance of a large Far Eastern fleet by the Russians would 'constitute a potential threat to British strategic interests in the Pacific', their re-acquisition of the warm-water bases under consideration need not adversely affect those interests, provided that their policy in the area would indeed be 'primarily defensive'.[109] To all this the Chiefs of Staff raised no objection. The paper was approved on 4 January, and a reply to the Prime Minister based upon it was despatched the following day.[110] Its conclusions, as well as those of the J.I.C. appreciation, were thus available before the completion of the corresponding regional paper by the Post-Hostilities Planners at the end of the month.

As has been seen, this survey had originated almost a year earlier and had been passed to the incoming Directors on the demise of the P.H.P. Sub-Committee.[111] But for the urgent revival of the 'Bases Plan' by the Foreign Office in the form of the Western bloc proposals, the Far Eastern paper would have been the first regional survey to be produced on the controversial alternative basic assumptions. By January 1945, however, its appearance gave rise to relatively muted diplomatic opposition.

British strategic interests in South-East Asia and the Pacific were defined as the security of Australia, New Zealand and Western Canada, and the defence of such possessions and dependencies as Hong Kong, Malaya, North Borneo, New Guinea and various small

---

109. JP(44)278(Final)   110.   COS(45)6th Mtg (1) & COS(45)7th Mtg (8)
111.   See pp. 75 & 80–3 above

islands forming part of the imperial defence system. Though the successful protection of this area would also largely safeguard India and Burma from an attack from the east, their post-war security was to be considered in a separate study.

The strategic problems of the Far Eastern theatre were unique in being mainly concerned with wide oceans and great distances where sea and air power would be the dominating factors. They resolved themselves into the establishment and maintenance of a network of bases from which offensive action could be mounted. Yet the scale of British commitments elsewhere would rule out any such operations in the Far East in the event of war between the United Kingdom and a major Power. The United States, by contrast, had greater interests in this area than in any other, and was far better placed geographically to defend them. American co-operation should therefore be taken as the cornerstone of British policy, irrespective of any differences of opinion on political or economic matters. In accordance with the J.I.C. report, it was also assumed that Russia would control Port Arthur and Dairen, resume sovereignty over Southern Sakhalin, and exert some degree of strategic control over Manchuria and Korea—the former being regained by China, the latter becoming an independent state, 'subject to a period of tutelage under the U.S.S.R. on behalf of the United Nations'.

The functioning of an effective world organisation would limit the task of the United Kingdom to sharing in the control of Japan, local security commitments aside. This would be carried out by destroying her empire and strictly regulating her imports of raw materials. Economic control of this sort, though backed by a willingness to use force, could nevertheless revive the very economic and political factors which had largely been the cause of current Japanese aggression—the restriction of an increasing population to a limited area with diminished resources. To cope with these conditions, non-military solutions were essential. The United Nations should supply forces to control communications in the Sea of Japan and in the East China and Yellow Seas; a strategic bombing force for direct action against Japan; and a mobile troop reserve, capable of speedy deployment by air or sea to any centre of unrest in the region. These forces could operate from bases in Korea, Manchuria, China, Formosa and the Pescadores.

In the light of 'J.I.C.' views on her intentions, it was considered improbable that Russia would encourage a revival of Japan, even if East-West relations deteriorated. Nor, according to the Joint Planners' recent assessment, was it likely that she would adopt an aggressive Far Eastern policy, though she could, if she wished, expand her naval and air forces sufficiently to pose a very considerable threat. China would be able to constitute a serious menace by 1955–60 only if infiltrated by a hostile Soviet Union, but the scope of this menace would be limited to the continent of Asia. It thus appeared that

> a major threat to our interests could only arise if the U.S.S.R., contrary to expectations, adopted an aggressive policy in the Far East.

If the Russians did become hostile, they would have to exercise some degree of control over Japan so that that country could not be used as a base for Anglo-American offensive action. Since, however, there was no question of attempting to enlist Japanese support against the Soviet Union in the period under consideration, all measures necessary to deal with such a Soviet threat would be equally applicable against a rearmed Japan:

> It should thus be possible to pursue a policy of co-operation with the U.S.S.R. which would provide for the participation of the United States and ourselves in the control of Japan, and at the same time to take certain measures to insure against the potential threats from a hostile U.S.S.R.

Hence, local counter-offensive action and the protection of sea communications against a hostile Russia would mainly be undertaken from the same bases in Formosa and the Pescadores which were envisaged as operating under Anglo-American control for the containment of Japan on behalf of the United Nations. Similar air and naval forces would be required for each eventuality, and Australian and New Zealand troops might be called upon to assist in defending the bases. As the defection or defeat of China might render Formosa untenable, a reserve chain of bases should be prepared, covering Indo-China, Borneo, Celebes, the Admiralty and Solomon Islands, and Fiji; but this alternative would be less satisfactory and less economical. Subsidiary bases at Shanghai, Hong Kong and Hainan would also be valuable, provided that their indefensibility was fully recognised and that no wasteful commitments in respect of them were entertained. Stable conditions in Indo-China, Siam and Malaya, and the co-operation of the French and the Dutch, would be necessary for the security of the reserve base network to be assured.

It would be impossible to forecast internal security problems until Japanese-occupied territory had been recovered, but the point was stressed that advantage should then be taken of the opportunity that would arise to preserve existing military facilities in the region. With regard to any attack upon the west coast of Canada, the direct threat thus posed to the American continent would clearly result in the bringing into operation of a United States defensive plan. Consequently, although British forces and bases would undoubtedly be involved, the nature of the involvement could not usefully be assessed prior to the holding of staff talks with the Americans.

The conclusions of the survey focused upon the importance of full and early United States support, the desirability of a world organisation, if practicable, the primacy of air and sea power in the region, and the possibility of Soviet hostility as the sole major potential threat to British strategic interests. This threat would depend upon a measure of control over Japan, to secure the Soviet flank against attack, and upon the development of Soviet sea and air power in the Pacific. Neither Russia nor Japan should be allowed to acquire greater influence in China than that of the Western allies, if the danger to British interests were not markedly to be increased. Anglo-American failure to prevent this would greatly enhance the strategic importance of Indo-China. Singapore, Sydney and Auckland would serve to support British bases in the two South Pacific networks, whilst the United States assumed the primary burden further to the north.[112]

Apart from the greater openness with which a possibly hostile Russia was considered, the general line of the Far Eastern survey broadly corresponded to that of the draft prepared by the old sub-committee. This was made possible by the view shared by both bodies that any steps to be taken with the Russians in mind would coincide with those required to cater for the Japanese. The head of the Far Eastern Department of the Foreign Office, John Sterndale Bennett, did not agree. He regarded the proposed measures as

> over-elaborate for the mere purpose of keeping down a truncated and disarmed Japan.

Would it not be obvious that they were really directed against the Russians, thus tending to precipitate the very conflict which, it was wished, might be avoided? Some Foreign Office attitudes were

---

112.   PHP(44)6(0)(Final)

nevertheless beginning to harden—notably those of the ex-chairman of the P.H.P.S.:

> However much we may desire it,

Jebb minuted on 24 February,

> we cannot say for certain that Russia will continue to be friendly, and I cannot imagine that any military establishments which we might set up in, e.g., Formosa, are likely to incline the Soviet Government against us. On the contrary, the stronger we are in general, the more likely the Soviet Government is to work with us . . . if the Soviet Union wishes to muscle in on our bases in Formosa, we had better hurry up and suggest that we should muscle in on their base at Port Arthur.

This time, even Geoffrey Wilson was willing to concede that the 'possibility of a hostile U.S.S.R. . . . cannot be left out of account'. His main criticisms were that the Japanese pretext was lacking in credibility and that, as Cavendish-Bentinck and his colleague Roger Allen maintained,

> the trouble with this paper was a failure to emphasise, or even take into account, the necessity of cutting our coat according to our cloth.

This was, however, a misdirected criticism, given that the purpose of the surveys was to explore strategic desiderata within each area without—at this stage—reference to priorities.

Eventually, despite a generally bad reception by the diplomats, it was the fact that the report would in any case be put aside as a staff study on restricted circulation, which carried the day. Ronald ruled against the reopening of an argument with the Chiefs of Staff whom he did not expect even to read such 'preparatory-schoolboy stuff', and the subject was allowed to lapse.[113] In fact, the survey was considered by the Chiefs of Staff on 21 February, approved with minor amendments, and reprinted over the signatures of Brooke, Portal and Syfret.[114] It was the first full-scale strategic study to run the gauntlet without incident since the V.C.O.S. Committee had approved the P.H.P.S. planning programme in June 1944.

The next regional survey to appear was that covering the Eastern

---

113. U890/36/70   114.   COS(45)48th Mtg (7) & COS(45)120(0)(PHP)

Mediterranean and Middle East. Over six months' work had been put into it by the time it was finalised on 27 March, and it differed from the earlier studies in making no pretence of giving equivalent consideration to the alternative 'basic assumptions'. Virtually the whole paper was devoted to a potential Soviet threat to the area, a successful world organisation receiving very limited attention almost as an afterthought. British strategic interests were listed as oil; the sea route through the Mediterranean; the airfields serving East Africa, India, the Far East and Australia; sites for an administrative base and for the Imperial Strategic Reserve; and security for those states with which defence agreements had been concluded.

Only the Russians could threaten these interests by 1955–60—Germany alone would hardly be capable of doing so. Penetration of Italy, Greece, Turkey or Persia by the Soviet Union, coupled with her existing dominance in Romania and Bulgaria, would significantly heighten the danger:

> The U.S.S.R. is now the greatest land Power in the world. In the post-war period, she is likely to increase her offensive power by the development of her fleet and her strategic air force. There is not at present any indication that she intends to try to dominate the whole of Europe or Asia, nor does there appear to be any economic or strategic reason which might impel her to do so. Nevertheless, an aggressive U.S.S.R., working on interior lines of communication, could attack us in Europe, the North Atlantic, the Middle East, India, the Pacific and, possibly, North-West Canada. We should thus have to take into account the possibility of a simultaneous attack in many parts of the world.

It would be obvious to the Russians that the loss of Middle Eastern oil would seriously impair British ability to resist in other theatres. As the Noble/J.I.C. report had indicated,[115] if war appeared imminent the first Soviet blow might well take the form of denying these resources to the West. The desirability of defending the Persian oilfield was quite plain, but the practicability of the task was open to grave doubt. Not only would a Soviet land attack be feasible, despite the difficulty of Persian and Turkish terrain, but no part of the Middle East would be beyond

---

115. 'In the event of a threat of hostilities with Great Britain and the United States and possibly even if there was a threat of operations in the Middle East by the United States alone, Russia would have a strategic interest in being able to deny them the oil resources of the Middle East.' (COS(44)1053(0)(PHP) covering JIC(44)467(0)(Final)(Retained—Cabt. Off.))

bomber range from Soviet bases by 1955–60. A substantial naval threat could also be mounted from the area of the Black Sea and the Aegean.

Only American aid would be capable of redressing the balance of forces, though French co-operation would be valuable. There was, however, 'little scope for counter-offensive action which might cripple the U.S.S.R. as a whole'. If she were bent upon aggression, it was likely that she would first re-deploy the existing concentration of refineries in the Caucasus; but there would be some scope for attacking her forces as they advanced through Persia, Turkey or Greece. Despite their strategic importance in affording defensive depth, these three countries could be offered help by the Commonwealth on a scale which would 'at best be meagre'. British policy towards them should have three principal aims: to foster the closest links possible without arousing Soviet hostility; to ensure that the stability of their governments gave Russia no excuse for intervention; and to discourage them from developing any roads, railways or airfields which would be more likely to assist a Soviet advance than to strengthen resistance to one.

It would be essential to maintain good relations with Egypt, Iraq, Saudi Arabia and the Levant states, and also to remedy the deficiencies of existing pacts. In particular, a strict interpretation of the 1936 treaty with Egypt would not cater for the recommended siting of the main administrative and naval bases of the United Kingdom—nor for the location of the Imperial Strategic Reserve—in that country in peacetime. To avoid generating Soviet hostility or creating precedents for other Powers to make corresponding demands, it might be necessary to settle for considerably less than the full range of British strategic requirements. The essential prerequisite in the area would be an ability to inspire confidence in the Middle Eastern states:

> We must be prepared to counter any measures of Soviet political warfare or other subversive propaganda designed to undermine our position in these States. If we fail to maintain our prestige, there is a danger that, in the face of a threat of Soviet attack, the Middle East States might throw in their lot with the U.S.S.R.

Highly mobile reserve forces would be needed to make the best of such defensive arrangements as could be agreed. Nor could the Russians reasonably raise objection to the presence of an Imperial Strategic Reserve in a region so central to the British Commonwealth as the Middle East.

If, in the worst case, Soviet forces succeeded in overrunning the oil-fields and reaching the Suez Canal, recourse should be had to alternative bases in safer areas to the south and west of the theatre. To develop such facilities in the Sudan, Eritrea and East Africa might be impracticable, but

> Forces withdrawing westwards . . . would be in a more favourable case. They would be able to use base facilities and communications in Libya and French North Africa, which are nearer to the main sources of supply in the United Kingdom and the United States. Moreover, they would be operating in territory which has to some extent already been developed.

This supplementary network would consist of main repair bases supporting operational bases, which, in turn, would serve: (1) to contain the threat to the Western Mediterranean, Central Africa and East Africa, and to the Indian Ocean, whilst keeping open southerly overland and aerial lines of communication and the Cape sea route to the east; and (2) as centres from which counter-offensive action could be undertaken to recover lost territory in North Africa and the Middle East.

According to an estimate by the Petroleum Division of the Ministry of Fuel and Power, by the period under consideration the oil supplies of the British Commonwealth and Empire and of the Americas,

> without the Middle East production, . . . would fall short of requirements by 40 million tons per annum if the British Empire were engaged in a major war and the U.S.A. were neutral. If the U.S.A. were also at war, the deficit would be increased to 53 million tons per annum.

The P.H.P.S. therefore urged action to be taken, as a matter of the greatest strategic importance, to reduce British dependence on Middle Eastern oil in time of war. Other sources should be located for exploitation, even on a non-commercial basis. Oil storage and synthetic production facilities should be considered for expansion, and the non-military uses of oil for contraction. Alternative types of fuel, more secure locations for refineries, and the subsidising of an enlarged British tanker fleet for longer journeys from east and west, were also possibilities. Even if the Petroleum Division's figures were only approximately correct, they disclosed a situation of such potential danger as to require 'an early and full investigation of the problem in relation to the national economy'.

The aspects of internal security and the role of a world organisation were briefly considered. Limited British resources would be severely strained in fulfilling the commitments entailed by the former. The cardinal rule would be to attempt to create a friendly and contented Arab world by eliminating every possible cause of dispute; but it was most unlikely that this could be achieved in respect of the Palestine problem. As for the United Nations, since the greatest threat to the strategic interests of the United Kingdom in the Middle East lay in possible Soviet hostility, a successful world organisation was eminently desirable—not because it would be able to restrain a Great Power, but because its very existence as a going concern would imply the continuation of tripartite co-operation, would help to cement Anglo-Soviet relations, and would increase the likelihood of American participation in the defence of the region. Retention of Soviet friendship was a vital British interest: it was therefore to be hoped that agreement could be reached with the Russians to establish Persia as an independent state in fact as well as in name, and that the 'very grave potential threat' to Western oil supplies need not inevitably materialise.[116]

The principal Foreign Office commentary on this report was written by Robert Hankey of the Eastern Department on 31 March. Although he—like Frank Roberts of the Central Department—had never participated in the vituperative attacks upon the P.H.P.S. by members of the Northern and Reconstruction Departments and others, the steady hardening of Foreign Office attitudes was shown by a conspicuous lack of dissent from his remarks. Hankey felt that the Middle Eastern survey might 'perhaps be criticised as emphasising overmuch' the potential danger from the Soviet Union. He did not personally believe there to be any fundamental clash of interests between the British Empire and that country, but he held to the view that

> we are very much less likely to have trouble with the Russians if we are strong. Respect seems in practice to be the thing most worth having in dealing with the Soviets.

The report was useful in that it showed the strategic measures necessary to confirm the British hold on the Middle East. Its emphasis upon the equally vital importance to both the United States and the

---

116.   PHP(45)10(0)(Final)

United Kingdom of the oil resources of the Persian Gulf was particularly significant. Hankey was concerned that the Americans and Russians were

> rapidly consolidating their hold on the areas which they consider vital to them. The Caribbean and the Central and North Pacific are likely to become American lakes; the Balkans, East Europe and the Baltic are becoming a Soviet preserve. We should keep pace and dig ourselves in, politically and strategically, in the areas shown to be essential to us.[117]

Each of the three Service chiefs had something to say about the completed paper. The First Sea Lord, Sir Andrew Cunningham, agreed that steps should be taken to reduce dependence upon Middle Eastern oil, but challenged the Petroleum Department's figures as over-pessimistic. Portal returned to the point which he had argued against Eden in October:

> if we decided that it was desirable to take a certain measure for the protection of our strategic interests, he doubted whether we should be deterred therefrom by the possibility of such action being unpalatable to another Power.

In deference to reservations expressed by Brooke about the disadvantages of considering strategic needs on a regional basis, it was agreed merely to note the survey, pending the production of the global appreciation. On the oil question, the Ministry of Fuel and Power was to be asked to re-examine and confirm its estimate of the importance of the Middle Eastern supplies and to report on peacetime measures to reduce dependence upon them.[118] This it duly did—though not until 3 November—adhering on the whole to its original position. As for alternatives, reserve stocks, substitute fuels, steps to reduce military requirements for petroleum, and exploration in areas other than the Middle East, were the only possibilities of improving the situation.[119] This time the Chiefs of Staff felt obliged to accept the Ministry's assessment and to rule that future reviews of strategic requirements would have to take it into account.[120]

It had originally been intended to prepare just one more regional

---

117. U2273/36/70   118.   COS(45)90th Mtg (14)
119. COS(45)644(0)   120.   COS(45)269th Mtg (14)

survey—that covering India and the Indian Ocean area—before production of the global appreciation. Post-war security in the Western Mediterranean and North-Eastern Atlantic had been dealt with in the one regional survey completed by the P.H.P. Sub-Committee, and this had been provisionally approved in the normal way by the Vice-Chiefs of Staff in May 1944.[121] As has been seen, however, Roberts and Jebb had—with some difficulty—succeeded in extracting a copy from the C.O.S. machine for preliminary use in the formulation of foreign policy, and to this there was a sequel. On 7 October 1944, Roberts wrote to the Chiefs of Staff informing them that there was 'no practicable way' in which Spain could be persuaded in advance of an emergency to concede to the United Kingdom alone the desired facilities in Spanish Morocco. Since the need not to antagonise Spain ruled out the contravention of her wishes, the sole prospect now appeared to lie in a 'Western Mediterranean Commission' in which both countries and the United States might participate. Yet this would mean effectively conceding some say in the supervision of Gibraltar to the Spanish as members of the suggested body, and the Foreign Office wanted to know if the military importance of the facilities sought to the south of the Straits justified any such concession.[122]

On 14 November, the Joint Planning Staff was instructed to examine the specific question of the military aspects of Anglo-Spanish relations.[123] It reported, three weeks later, that

> If Spain is friendly or neutral, the threat to our Atlantic communications will be negligible and the threat to Gibraltar and the Straits limited to air attack from distant bases,

but that the situation would in each case be serious were she to be hostile or under hostile control. Free use of the Straits was not so vital as to warrant incurring the enmity of Spain, and provided that radar cover from Spanish territory were available, the risk of shipping losses could be reduced to acceptable proportions.[124] In approving this paper on 14 December, the Chiefs of Staff instructed the P.H.P.S. to supply the answer to Roberts's letter and also to revise the original Western Mediterranean survey.[125] By 8 January, the reply to Roberts was ready. It stated that any loss of exclusive British control of Gibraltar would be

---

121. See pp. 75–80 above
122. COS(44)890(0)   123.   COS(44)369th Mtg (0)(6)
124. JP(44)288(Final)   125.   COS(44)401st Mtg (0)(2)

strategically unacceptable and quite possibly 'the thin end of the wedge leading to the achievement of Spanish aspirations in Gibraltar'. Instead of a Western Mediterranean Commission as a means of gaining control over facilities in Spanish Morocco, it was suggested that arrangements involving no surrender of Spanish control would suffice—provided that agreement could be reached for the required radar facilities to be available in time of war. The Spanish might welcome the status of equal partnership implied by such a scheme, and the inclusion of Portugal, if possible, would further assist the protection of Atlantic communications.[126] With all this the Chiefs of Staff concurred,[127] and the Post-Hostilities Planners turned their attention to revising the regional survey.

The probable explanation for the non-completion of the wider study until 19 May is that great efforts were simultaneously being made to produce the global appreciation. There was also a case for delaying the last two regional surveys until the global one was far advanced, so as to forestall further criticism from the C.I.G.S. about compartmentalised post-war planning. Certainly, attempts were made to link the Western Mediterranean paper with the North Atlantic and Middle Eastern surveys already issued, as well as with the J.P.S. and P.H.P.S. studies prompted by the Roberts enquiry. As in the Middle Eastern survey, there was no *pro forma* attempt to deal with the subject on alternative hypotheses of world organisation success or failure. The revised survey was a straightforward examination of requirements for defence against an enemy in Central Europe. This could only be the Soviet Union and/or a rearmed Germany; but for the purposes of the argument it did not, apparently, matter which.

In 1955–60, the United Kingdom would still need to be able to control sea communications in the Eastern Atlantic, and in the Straits and Western Mediterranean, and also to protect air-transport routes to the Middle East, West and South Africa, India and Australasia. French co-operation was assumed, given the equivalence of British and French interests in the area being considered. The use of French possessions there would, in fact, be essential if Spain or Italy were overrun or became hostile. The United States was continuing to attach increasing importance to the security of the West African coast, with a view to that of the Americas themselves and of their Atlantic communications. Assistance from this quarter, too, in a common

---

126. PHP(44)24(0)(Revise)(Final)   127. COS(45)11th Mtg(13)&COS(45)30(0)

regional policy, should thus 'not be difficult to obtain'. Were Western Europe to be overrun, bases in the Azores would be needed for coverage of the Atlantic sea routes. The Anglo-Portuguese Alliance should therefore be maintained. It was also important that Italy should look to Western Europe rather than to the Russians, for her geographical position might enable her to pose a serious threat in the Mediterranean if hostile or under hostile occupation. Should this occur, it would become necessary to seize Sicily and Sardinia to deny them to the enemy, to head off loss of control in the Sicilian Narrows, and to forestall any invasion of North Africa and Malta. Gibraltar should be retained as a strongly fortified naval and air base. It could be of value in this capacity only while Spain remained at least neutral; otherwise, its role would be to deny the use of the Straits to an enemy as long as it could hold out as a fortress. Hostile control of Spain would gravely jeopardise Atlantic communications, and, for this reason, Spanish enmity should not be incurred by attempts to insist on facilities to guard the less important Mediterranean route. With the loss of the Iberian peninsula, it would be essential to deny the North and West African mainland and the Eastern Atlantic islands to the enemy:

> So long as we could prevent an enemy establishing air supremacy over the Straits and their approaches, the invasion of North-West Africa would be very difficult, if not impossible,

but this would be a considerable commitment which would involve both the occupation of Spanish Morocco and a considerable air effort.

The French should be encouraged to develop their overland African routes which bypassed the Straits, and the capacity of the strategically secure air route over Central Africa via Takoradi should be further increased. Malta should be kept as an operational base controlling the Sicilian Narrows, but its loss—and that of Gibraltar—could be offset so far as air communications were concerned by the preparation of staging-posts in the Azores, French Morocco and Tripolitania. If the Straits themselves were to be adequately defended, the air-defence system proposed in the North Atlantic survey would have to be extended down through the Western Mediterranean to French North Africa. Radar facilities in French Morocco, Spanish Morocco and the Tangier Zone would be needed in time of war, and so would airfields in the first two of these regions, if not in all three. It was in this connection that a world organisation might be of value:

Under [its regional] ... arrangements, we should hope to obtain the facilities which we require in Spanish Morocco and the eastern Atlantic islands.

Provided that exclusive British control of Gibraltar was not compromised, it would be very desirable for Spain, France, Portugal and the United States to join with the British in a regional security system.[128]

Since the paper was essentially just a revision of the earlier survey, it contained no surprises for the Chiefs of Staff and was noted in the normal way on 1 June. Copies were to be sent to the Governor and Commander-in-Chief at Gibraltar, and to his counterpart in Malta, and the Foreign Office was given permission to send a summary of its contents overseas on the same basis as had been agreed for the 1944 survey.[129] Otherwise, it generated negligible military or diplomatic comment.[130]

The same applied to the final regional paper—on India and the Indian Ocean—which had also been completed on 19 May. On this occasion, the Soviet Union was identified as the sole potential enemy to be considered and the question of a world organisation was again relegated to a short concluding section. Attacks might come from the north-west, from the east, and even (by air) from the north to a limited extent.

The first of these possibilities would be by far the most serious, despite the overland communications problem which would face the Russians in Persia and Afghanistan:

Soviet invasion of Persia and Afghanistan would be a necessary prelude to land attack on India. Whereas Persia is unlikely seriously to oppose a Soviet advance, Afghanistan would probably resist invasion to the limit of her resources. Such resistance is, however, unlikely to be of much effect.

For both defensive and offensive reasons, the Soviet Union would probably try to increase her influence over the Afghans in time of peace, with a view to ensuring control of the lines of communication through their country in time of war. As in Persia, British policy should be to foster its independence as a buffer state. The United Kingdom should aim at:

---

128. PHP(45)6(0)(Final)
129. COS(45)142nd Mtg (13)   130.   See: U3923/36/70

(a) Resisting the spread of Soviet influence in these countries and building up our own position in them without forfeiting the goodwill of the U.S.S.R.

(b) Ensuring stable Governments possessed of armed forces at least adequate to enforce internal security, so as to give the U.S.S.R. no excuse to intervene in their internal affairs.

(c) Discouraging, so far as political and commercial considerations permit, the development of any roads, railways or airfields which are clearly more likely to assist a Soviet advance than to strengthen the defence against it.

Invasion of Burma and India from the east was an altogether more indirect danger. It would be dependent upon the extent to which the Russians had advanced into South-East Asia and towards the Western Pacific. An attack from South China would be limited by poor overland links with Burma, but the danger would be substantially increased if the Soviet Union occupied Indo-China and Siam. The willing co-operation of these countries with the Russians would ensure the security of their lines of communications and make substantial manpower resources available to improve them. If the Malay barrier were also to be overcome, the grave threat of a combined seaborne and overland invasion would arise. The capture of Singapore and of airfields in Malaya and Siam would give the Russians control of the South China Sea and at least partial control of the Bay of Bengal. Under these conditions, their deployment of forces and scale of attack against Burma would be restricted only by the quantity of shipping and aircraft available. As to defensive measures, a recent P.H.P.S. paper on the 'Post-War Strategic Importance of Siam'[131] had highlighted its role in both the defence of Indo-China and the security of Malaya should Indo-China fall. The retention of a Western grip on this region would depend upon the effectiveness of the measures for the protection of South-East Asia set out in the Far Eastern survey. The key to the defence of Burma would be a close association between its military command and that of the Indian forces. A joint effort to seal off the passes on the North-East Burmese frontier should be backed by the availability of highly mobile land and air forces to deal with any airborne attack. The provision of good land and air communications between India and Burma would be essential for supply purposes. If a seaborne attack materialised after an

---

131.   PHP(45)3(0)(Revised Final) of 30 March, provisionally approved at COS(45) 87th Mtg (15) of 4 April 1945

enemy advance into Malaya and Sumatra, Trincomalee in Ceylon would become the only main fleet base covering the Indian Ocean—a burden otherwise to be shared with Singapore—and the Cocos Islands would become the only air-staging link between India and Australia.

By 1955–60, virtually the whole of India and the Arabian Sea would be within the range of air attack from Russian Turkestan, and a number of northerly cities on the sub-continent would be within the range of escort fighters and could be subjected to heavy aerial bombardment:

> The larger Indian cities, with their inflammable and congested buildings and their crowded populations, are particularly vulnerable to air attack. Such attacks might well cause general panic and adversely affect morale throughout India, with disastrous repercussions on the country's war effort in general and her industrial effort in particular.

Since a heavy scale of air attack could be anticipated, air defence systems would have to be developed in North-West India and in Burma and Assam. Passive defence measures should be considered, but great difficulties could be expected in making these effective. The main targets for counter-offensive air strikes would be Soviet oilfields in the Caucasus and advancing forces in Persia, Afghanistan, South China or Siam; but there would be 'little scope for counter-offensive action which might cripple the U.S.S.R. as a whole'.

As for allies, neither the United States nor France could be expected to co-operate actively, unless as a result of becoming embroiled with the Soviet Union elsewhere, for their interests in this theatre were small. The best hope for American involvement in peacetime would be under the aegis of the world organisation. The principal political factor to be considered, however, was the future status of India herself. It was assumed that:

(a) India, Burma, and the British mandated and Colonial territories in this area will remain within the British Empire, and that the defence of these territories will continue to be an Imperial responsibility.

(b) The future Government of India will accept liability to provide forces for service in British Empire or United Nations interests, in addition to assuming responsibility for her own local defence against aggression by any State other than a Great Power.

It was considered possible that, if India achieved full Dominion status by 1955–60, her leaders might decline to provide forces for Empire defence or might remain neutral in a future war. Nor could the possibility of secession from the British Empire be entirely ruled out. Neutrality or secession would seriously prejudice British strategic interests, not only in the Indian Ocean area but also in the Middle East and in the Pacific. It was, however, 'considered most unlikely that these eventualities would, in fact, arise'.[132] Every endeavour should be made to obtain the right to station strategic reserves in India after she became a Dominion—a concession which, according to the India Office, there seemed a reasonable chance of securing. Base facilities for strategic air forces would also be required.

Apart from her value as a base from which to reinforce adjacent theatres, India was strategically important geographically in relation to such vital imperial communications as the oil route via the Straits of Hormuz and the Arabian Sea. Her potential contributions of manpower and resources to the British war effort in a future conflict would also be of great value if, as anticipated, she proved willing to participate in operations in the Middle East and South-East Asia as well as locally. A contented and politically stable India should be the aim, reducing the British military commitment needed to maintain her internal security and securing the strategic benefits which her co-operation would confer.[133]

The main Foreign Office comments on this paper were made in late February when the draft version was circulated. Hood conceded that it was 'inevitable' that a study of the defence of India should picture the Soviet Union as the potential enemy, but added that, in his opinion,

> If the Soviet Union wished to conquer India . . . it would set about it by making our position in India untenable by provoking internal unrest.

He thought that any attack upon the frontiers would be only a

---

132. India and Pakistan were to be established as Dominions in August 1947. Burma declined to join the Commonwealth on achieving independence in January 1949, but India remained within it, despite adopting a republican constitution the following year. Some five years later, the former C.I.G.S. was to comment: 'With the loss of India and Burma, the keystone of the arch of our Commonwealth Defence was lost, and our Imperial Defence crashed. Without the central strategic reserve of Indian troops ready to operate either east or west we were left impotent. . . . And yet, I do not see how we could have remained in India, and I think we were right in withdrawing when we did; but few realised what the strategic loss would amount to.' (Bryant, *Triumph in the West*, p. 533)   133.   PHP(45)15(0)(Final)

subsidiary move by comparison, but felt that any lack of emphasis on internal security in the survey was a matter for the India Office. For the Northern Department, Wilson agreed:

> This paper runs very true to P.H.P. form, and as we can do nothing about the main line I doubt if it is worthwhile trying to fiddle with the details.

Some parts of the draft were highly political and much over-simplified, in his view, and he found it 'difficult to take very seriously the Soviet threat to India via Indo-China and Malaya'.[134] When the final version appeared three months later, it was decided to do no more than point out a drafting error to the Post-Hostilities Planners.[135] As Davison remarked in reply, however, like all the regional surveys the paper would soon be superseded by the global appreciation; and it was probably for this reason that at their meeting on 1 June the Chiefs of Staff were prepared to forward copies to the India Office and to the Commander-in-Chief, India, 'as a preliminary indication of their views', despite Cunningham's strong reservations about various P.H.P.S. recommendations concerning naval bases in the area.[136]

With the completion of the up-dated Western Mediterranean and the Indian Ocean area surveys, the programme of work originated by the Post-Hostilities Planning Sub-Committee in February 1944, and modified and confirmed four months later by the Post-Hostilities Planning Staff and V.C.O.S. Committee, was almost complete. Apart from the unexpected flurry over German dismemberment, seven regional strategic papers had been produced. Only two of these—the first Western Mediterranean and the Far Eastern studies—had eventually appeared above the signatures of the Chiefs of Staff or the Vice-Chiefs of Staff. Of the two dealing with the North Atlantic area, one had been rejected outright and the other merely noted—a fate which also befell the last three studies, largely because of the imminence of a more comprehensive report. It was a mixed record for the Post-Hostilities Planners, but one that was overshadowed from the end of 1944 onwards as their energies were increasingly concentrated upon the preparation of their *magnum opus* on British post-war strategic requirements around the world.

---

134. U1266/36/70   135. U3922/36/70
136. *Ibid.* & COS(45)142nd Mtg (14)

6. 'The Security of the British Empire'

The first step towards the production of the world strategic survey had been taken by Warburton, who circulated his notion of an outline plan on 16 November 1944, the day after the revised paper on German dismemberment was completed. His note set out a structure for the paper and drew together the main points of the regional surveys, which were all, by then, at various stages of preparation. He held that British grand strategy would have to be a compromise between ideals and realities. It had been argued that a war with the United States need not be considered, but the Soviet Union had to be regarded as 'somewhat of an enigma'—and an enigma with a vast war potential at that.

> At one extreme it would be logical to say that if all nations of the world were pledged to the maintenance of peace there should be no need for armed forces other than some form of *gendarmerie*. At the other extreme with so powerful an enemy as Russia we should, to be logical, set about the provision of the necessary armed forces to enable us to preserve our interests should she at any time threaten them. It is clear, however, that neither of these ideals is practicable.

For a world organisation to be effective, it would have to be backed by armed strength; for complete insurance against a hostile Russia vast armies, navies and air forces beyond the manpower, wealth or inclination of the British Empire would be required. The task of the P.H.P.S. was, therefore,

> to find the compromise which will enable us to support wholeheartedly the principles of the maintenance of peace and at the same time to give us the necessary degree of insurance.[137]

The staff meeting which considered Warburton's note on 17 November agreed upon the basic approach to be adopted and the attitude to be taken to post-war international security arrangements:

> In the most favourable circumstances the World Organisation would be no more than a concert of nations, in which problems as they arose would be resolved by a bargaining process; this bargaining would inevitably be conditioned by a calculation of interests and armed strength.

---

137.   Note by D.P.H.P., Air Ministry—copy in CAB 21/1799

The global survey would correlate and sum up the principal conclusions of the regional papers on broad lines. The strategic sub-section of the P.H.P.S. was to begin working out a skeleton framework, and Jebb was invited to prepare a note describing the political background against which military commitments in 1955–60 should be planned.[138] This he provided by 18 December, remarking good-naturedly, in spite of his recent loss of the P.H.P.S. chairmanship, that

> this is in a way a labour of love, but I feel under an obligation to produce something. . . . At any rate, if the passage on the political background is inserted on anything like the present lines, it may do something to scotch the 'Russian bogey' thesis.

Jebb's draft predicted a 'troublous and difficult' post-war period in Europe, where there would be continuing civil disorder and where ' "Left Wing" administrations' would be the rule rather than the exception. Such unsettled circumstances might favour the spread of communism, but might equally play into the hands of populist dictators. The three Great Powers would remain responsible, in the first instance, for the maintenance of order in Europe, though the United States would have divested herself of most of her physical commitments on the Continent. It seemed unlikely that Russia would attempt to extend her controlling influence beyond a certain line; but this would

> almost undoubtedly be paramount in Poland, Czechoslovakia, Romania, Hungary, Bulgaria and probably in Yugoslavia,

and it was likely to be paramount in Austria as well. What this meant was that the countries concerned, though not necessarily under Soviet governments, would look to the Russians for armaments and would not take any very different line from theirs in international affairs. Concessions might well be made to Soviet demands concerning the Black Sea Straits, but penetration of Persia and Afghanistan would have to be resisted. There was a danger of Soviet intervention in the Levant if the British were unable to deal successfully with Arab unrest. Anarchy in China might also tempt the Russians to seek control over Manchuria and even Korea, leading quite probably to a clash with the

---

138.   Minutes of P.H.P.S. meeting of 17 November 1944—missing, but obtainable in CAB 21/1799

United States and consequent British involvement. As for Anglo-American relations, these would remain completely interlocked, with the United Kingdom unable to contemplate any serious war without wholehearted American support and with the United States unable to abandon the British for fear of a situation developing in which American interests could be menaced by a hostile united Europe. [139]

This contribution was incorporated in a preliminary draft of the world survey circulated by Davison on 5 February 1945. The author of this first attempt on the problem was Colonel Denis Capel-Dunn of the C.O.S. secretariat, who had agreed to help the Post-Hostilities Planners to tackle it. It was succeeded by another outline paper in March, written by Brigadier Curtis, who also intended to incorporate the Foreign Office forecast. [140] Ward—in charge of the Economic and Reconstruction Department while Jebb attended conferences at Yalta and San Francisco—decided to continue furnishing advice on this aspect of the survey, provided that it was clearly understood that

> F.O. are in no way responsible for its views even if we have helped in drafting. [141]

His attitude towards the P.H.P.S. was still considerably more hostile than Jebb's, but he realised that the world survey, when completed, might have a more lasting influence than its pigeon-holed predecessors:

> Distasteful and interrupting as these laborious and often futile papers are to hard-worked F.O. officials, we cannot overlook . . . that this *may* be adopted by the C.O.S. as the 'bible' for future Service planning. [142]

However, in the last of three full-scale drafts drawn up in April and May, the 'Political Forecast' was relegated to an appendix; [143] and when the Post-Hostilities Planners met with the Joint Intelligence Sub-Committee on 11 June, they revealed that they had decided to leave it out altogether. Instead, they would revert to the line enunciated by the

---

139. U8523/748/70 (1944)
140. U1080, U2274/36/70, & Hollis minute to Jacob of 5 December 1944 in CAB 21/1799 Capel-Dunn was head of the Joint Staff secretariat and secretary to the J.I.C. At the beginning of July, he was killed returning from the conference at San Francisco which established the United Nations Organisation.
141. U2885/36/70   142. U3390/36/70
143. PHP(45)29(0)(3rd Draft)—missing, but obtainable in U4024/36/70

Chiefs of Staff during the Dismemberment debate: of the only two countries capable of endangering British post-war security, the United States could be ruled out as a possible enemy and the potential danger of a hostile Russia should be examined 'whilst stressing the hope that there will never be any reason to believe that the U.S.S.R. will become a hostile Power'.

Cavendish-Bentinck regarded this as a change for the better, given the impossibility of prophesying what the political situation would be in 1955–60: 'even Old Moore's almanac will not go further than one year ahead!' His colleagues nevertheless requested the insertion of a disclaimer to the effect that the survey

> is from the purely strategical point of view and that it is based upon hypotheses the probability of which is in no way endorsed by the Foreign Office.[144]

Not surprisingly, its authors declined to insert anything of the kind. One newcomer to these matters—Paul Falla of the Economic and Reconstruction Department—was to suggest, on receipt of the final version of 29 June, that

> perhaps P.H.P.S. w[oul]d argue that the whole study is expressly based on hypothetical considerations & does not attempt to assess their probability.[145]

In reality, this had been the essential basis of all significant post-war military planning ever since the Chiefs of Staff had ordered the *possibility* of Soviet hostility to be taken into account almost twelve months previously. But it was an approach which few of Falla's colleagues had felt able or willing to accept.

Ward had been right to suppose that the world strategic survey would be regarded differently from the earlier 'exploratory' papers. It had long been intended to pave the way for:

(i) The first approach—which must necessarily be on very broad lines—by the Chiefs of Staff to Ministers.

(ii) The inevitable but much more difficult sequel in which the Joint Staffs must attempt—still on very broad lines—to indicate the general types and size of forces proposed.[146]

---

144. U4024/36/70   145.   U4969/36/70
146. Davison note of 19 March 1945, covering skeleton draft by Curtis, in U2274/36/70

The paper was therefore produced in the form of a draft report by the Chiefs of Staff for presentation to the government and for circulation to the Foreign Office and Service Departments as the strategic background for long-term planning.

An introductory section set the scene for the consideration of individual problems. It explained the choice of the period 1955–60 as intended to prevent perceptions of long-term interests from being distorted as a result of the pressing requirements of short-term commitments after the defeat of the Axis Powers. Security was defined in terms of the maintenance of the integrity of the British Empire against external and internal threats, and the protection of the sea and air communications upon which its cohesion and resources depended. Of six potential enemies capable of presenting—alone or in combination—a major threat, Germany and Japan might have achieved a considerable degree of post-occupation rearmament by playing off one Great Power against another; France and China would lack the strength to pose serious strategic problems; and, 'upon grounds of common heritage and common language', the United States could be disregarded as a menace. The Soviet Union, however, could not be ruled out in this way:

> It would be foolhardy to attempt to predict the relationship which will exist between ourselves and the U.S.S.R. ten years ahead, but the fact remains that the U.S.S.R. has proved herself to possess the war potential to constitute a serious threat to the British Empire.

In seeking to assess the requirements of imperial security, it was only 'common prudence' to take full account of Soviet potentialities. A determined policy of military preparedness might well prove the most effective deterrent, were the Russians to contemplate aggression.

The paper was therefore designed to consider the possibility of an Anglo-Soviet conflict, the need to insure against German or Japanese resurgence, possible clashes with minor Powers, the maintenance of internal security, and the obligation to contribute forces to the world organisation. With regard to the last-mentioned, it was perfectly clear that, as currently conceived, the United Nations Organisation would be unable to prevent conflicts between major Powers. It followed that its existence would not absolve the British Empire from the need to make provision for its own defence.

Some factors could not yet be fully evaluated—notably, scientific advances which would increase the speed and effectiveness with which calculated aggression could be carried out. The character of war itself might be radically altered by the development of 'an explosive . . . whose power may be many thousand times that of existing explosives'. The present survey could deal only with basic grand strategy for the maintenance of imperial security which was, essentially,

> a problem of preventing other Powers from imposing their will on us. This requires both political action and military strength. Diplomacy can prevent some threats and reduce others; it can secure allies, whose armed help or whose territory is important in war. Diplomacy by itself cannot, however, succeed unless it has, and is known to have, an adequate backing of military strength, sufficient to convince both our friends and our potential enemies of our ability and determination to fulfil our obligations.

Since the international situation could deteriorate far more quickly than armed forces could be built up, military preparedness was essential, no matter how reassuring the international situation might be. Military strength, of which conscription[147] would be notable evidence, was required both to enable diplomacy to succeed and to insure against its failure.

Just over half of the main body of the paper was devoted to the threat which a hostile Russia would present. The remainder was composed of short sections covering Germany and Japan; minor threats and internal security problems; the world organisation; and the question of collaboration with the Dominions. The best method of keeping the Germans under control would be for the three principal Powers and the French to guarantee to take timely and decisive action as circumstances required. This would depend upon the availability—despite the withdrawal of occupation forces—of military resources ready for

---

147. The retention of compulsory military service was favoured by the Foreign Office as essential to guarantee post-war European security. On the strength of its advice, and of that of all three Service Departments and the Ministry of Labour, the A.P.W. Committee had agreed on 22 March 1945 that 'in the foreseeable future we should be unable to provide sufficient forces to meet our inescapable commitments throughout the world without conscription'. Provisional endorsement of the A.P.W.'s conclusion had been given by the War Cabinet on 20 April, (APW(45)4, 8, 9, 20 & 22; APW(45)7th Mtg (1); WP(45)242 & WM(45)48th Concls (7)(Confidential Annex)). A hiatus of several months and a transitional call-up scheme were to follow the change of government in July and the unexpected end of the Japanese war in August, with no permanent scheme being enacted until the National Service Act received the Royal Assent in July 1947.

immediate action, on the basis of reliable intelligence of infringement by Germany of the simple and clear-cut restrictions which should be imposed upon her. Political willingness to act decisively would presuppose 'an educated public opinion' appreciating the need for firmness. Western European co-operation would lessen the strain on British resources and prevent too dominant a role being played by the Soviet Union, particularly if the Americans chose to disinterest themselves. It was unlikely that the Russians would connive at a revival of German militarism, but even without their assistance, or that of the United States, it should still be possible for the United Kingdom and her Continental allies to cope with a resurgent Germany—provided that the attempt to do so were to be made sufficiently promptly. In the Far East, it should be possible to rely on American and Soviet action, backed by the Chinese, to prevent Japanese military revival. Unlike in the case of Germany, economic controls in Japan after the end of occupation might be enough to limit her future war potential. If military action did become necessary, naval and air power might prove adequate unaided. Neither Germany nor Japan, it was felt, was likely to succeed in achieving a high level of rearmament without the acquiescence of the Soviet Union.

The main principle in coping both with fractious minor Powers and the demands of internal security would be to encourage the recruitment of loyal local forces to the greatest possible extent in the territories to be protected or rendered stable. Only thus could the British manpower burden be lightened. Aggression against British territory by small states might occur in East Africa from Abyssinia, in Aden from the Yemen, in India from Afghanistan, and in Burma and the Malay States from China or Siam. Commitments to Egypt, Iraq, Balkan and any new Levant States, and Portugal might also lead to British involvement should any of them clash with its neighbours. The use of coloured troops for internal security duties would seldom be politically practicable. Potential trouble-spots were numerous. In the Middle East, Arab nationalism (especially in Egypt), the Palestine question, and French policy in Syria and the Lebanon were all probable causes of disturbance—with only the third of these likely to have been resolved by 1955–60. British lives, property and strategic interests would be affected by unrest in the area more than those of any other major Power. Such unrest might also cause serious repercussions in India, where the risk of breakdown in the political and economic structure (requiring large-scale military intervention) could not be dismissed. Nationalism in Far Eastern territories formerly occupied by the Japanese could also be expected to cause internal security problems, though not to any significant level, except in Burma and Malaya. Other military commitments might include West and East Africa, Ceylon, the West Indies, Cyprus, Malta, Aden, Mauritius, and even a need to act in support of civil authorities in the Dominions or the British Isles themselves.

Only if strategic policy were to be backed by the resources of all its members, in a co-ordinated imperial plan agreed in peacetime, would the British Empire constitute a Great Power comparable with the United States and the Soviet Union. The reluctance of the Dominions to undertake firm commitments for fear of being drawn into war without an effective say in British foreign policy would have to be overcome by improved methods of imperial consultation. In an extension of the approach so deprecated by Ward, it was also suggested that 'all the peoples of the Empire should be educated to understand' that the security of the component parts of the British Empire could not be considered merely in the light of local interests, and that, conversely, a threat to any member of it locally constituted a threat to the Empire as a whole. All members should hold forces in readiness to serve in an imperial strategic reserve, and there should be much greater co-ordination of military training, equipment and organisation. The vulnerability of the United Kingdom to bombardment would put a premium upon industrial dispersal, and the experience recently gained from concerted exploitation of war potential should be built upon in the future.

The United Nations Organisation, as provisionally agreed at San Francisco, could best be viewed as an alliance of five major Powers designed to prevent aggression by smaller ones and to ensure the continued suppression of Germany and Japan once the Allied machinery of control had been superseded. To function successfully, it would need Great Power unanimity and the allocation of adequate forces to its Security Council. The latter requirement would involve a substantial British commitment, which could, however, probably be met largely by the forces which would have to be maintained in any case. The world organisation would make little difference to the actual measures needed to deal with Germany and Japan. Nor was it likely to have fostered international confidence to such an extent by 1955–60 that Great Power acceptance of general disarmament would have been achieved. British public opinion would have to be brought to appreciate that

> the existence of a World Organisation constitutes no permanent guarantee against aggression on the part of a Great Power. Misconception as to its efficacy in preventing a major threat to our security, might lead to demands for the reduction of our armed forces. If such views were to prevail, the existence of the World Organisation would become a menace to our security.

Its real strategic value would lie in its potential effect upon the relationships between the three Great Powers. It would be of the greatest importance if it promoted the desired closer collaboration of the United States and helped to prevent any clash with the Soviet Union. In particular, it was most unlikely that the Americans would overcome their aversion to 'entangling alliances' for any other reason in peacetime.

So far as the Russians were concerned, political infiltration and the sowing of inter-Allied discord could be expected in advance of any open aggression. Even if armed force were to be employed, this might take the form of a lightning campaign to seize limited—though important—objectives. Were the Soviet fleet to be expanded, it could pose a threat to imperial communications which would require a defensive effort out of all proportion to the cost to the Russians of mounting it. Their interests were most likely to clash with those of the British in the Middle East, control of which area would give them additional oilfields as well as adding defensive depth to their existing ones. Whether or not political manoeuvres would lead to military action would depend on Soviet estimation of the risk of a general conflict resulting; but even if desire to gain control of the region were not a primary objective, its seizure would be attempted by the Russians as a major feature of any world-wide campaign because of the importance to the Western war effort of Persian, Iraqi and Arabian oil. The Suez Canal area and the Mediterranean route would also be jeopardised by a Soviet attack on the Middle East—which would have the advantage of being able to draw on much greater resources near the theatre than would be available to the defending forces at the outbreak of hostilities. Three factors would determine the degree to which a serious reverse in the Middle East would affect an overall capability to resist the Russians elsewhere: success in reducing dependence upon the threatened oil-producing areas, possession of sufficient shipping resources to cater for the results of falling back upon the Cape sea route, and the development of alternative air routes across the African continent.

In Western Europe and the North Atlantic, the attitude of Germany would be crucial. Her full support for the Soviet Union after achieving any degree of rearmament would create a most formidable combination. In this theatre, Russia's large land forces could be deployed to best advantage. A successful campaign on their part would deprive the United Kingdom of depth to her defences and supply the Soviet Union with bases from which to attack key British communications and military or population centres. The position in the Western Mediterranean and in the Atlantic would be greatly influenced by the fate of France and the stance adopted by Spain and Italy. India's role would be vital for the security of imperial communications and also in relation to the defence of the Middle East and the Far East. Air attack on Indian cities and submarine attack on Indian Ocean routes would have severe consequences, quite apart from the danger of overland attack from the north-west on the sub-continent itself. Further to the east, there was only a remote chance of a clash with the Russians, and this would depend largely upon a prior extension of their influence over South China.

The overall situation was considered to be potentially 'extremely grave':

> The U.S.S.R. might commence hostilities with the limited objective of rapidly seizing some area of strategic importance, *e.g.*, the Middle East oilfields, calculating that we should accept the situation rather than precipitate a world-wide war.
>
> In a full-scale conflict, however, the U.S.S.R. could hope for the most decisive results in Western Europe, by attack on the United Kingdom and our vital Atlantic communications. The possibility of an airborne assault on Great Britain in the early stages of a war, will require reassessment from time to time.
>
> An attack on the Middle East, where our oil supplies and Mediterranean sea and air routes are within comparatively easy reach, would almost certainly be a feature of Soviet strategy. In India and the Indian Ocean, the U.S.S.R. could contain large British forces without a great expenditure of effort.

Only in South-East Asia and the Pacific was there little cause for immediate concern in the event of Soviet hostility.

Nor was there any prospect of effective offensive action to offset the situation. The Soviet Union would not be susceptible tó blockade. Her industries and raw materials would be safe from land attack and for the most part immune from effective aerial bombardment. There would be little likelihood of disrupting her internal communications. Her defeat could therefore be obtained only as the result of a long war. What defensive measures would have to be taken initially?

In Europe, a Western group should be set up, consisting of France, Norway, Denmark, Belgium, the Netherlands and the United Kingdom. It would be likely to retain its cohesion only if assured of the support of the United States and if all prospects of France falling under Soviet influence were eliminated. Germany must be prevented from making common cause with the Russians, but no effort should be made to build her up against them until Anglo-Soviet relations had deteriorated beyond repair. The fact that it would then be too late to make German help fully effective had to be accepted. It was most unlikely that a Soviet attack through a disarmed Germany could be withstood without the most prompt assistance from the United States. Facilities for the reception and deployment of American forces would have to be available immediately upon the outbreak of war. The vulnerability of the United Kingdom would necessitate stronger air defences than in the German war and a greater emphasis on dispersal. Naval bases would be needed in Europe, Eire, Iceland, the Atlantic Islands and North-West Africa. Spanish and Portuguese friendship would also be important in connection with the protection of sea communications. Only France could provide facilities essential for the defence of North Africa, and in the Central Mediterranean Italian co-operation would be of particular value.

Defence in depth, early American aid, and the presence of highly mobile reserve forces in the Middle East were all required to improve the security of British interests in that region. The need not to precipitate a crisis and sheer lack of manpower would, however, be limiting factors. The initiative would lie with the aggressor and it would probably result in the loss of the oilfields at an early stage. There was some likelihood of Egypt having to be evacuated, as well as Persia and Iraq, with attempts to contain the Soviet threat having to be made from bases to the west—and perhaps also to the south—of the evacuated area. Despite the inherent weakness of the British position there in war, sufficient forces should be kept in the Middle East in peacetime to preserve internal security, maintain British prestige and forestall Soviet encroachment.

Air and civil defence systems and considerable forces to meet a possible airborne invasion would be needed in North-West India. Afghanistan, like Persia, should be maintained as a friendly, independent buffer state, but a full-scale overland attack through these countries could probably not be repulsed. Indian and Burmese forces would also be required to assist in defending Indo-China, Siam and Malaya against threats from the direction of Southern China. The importance of naval bases, such as those in Ceylon, would increase with any loss of control in the Persian Gulf and the Suez Canal areas. Overland links between Central India and her north-western border should be developed, but the improvement of communications through neighbouring states should be discouraged. A prosperous India and Burma would offer the best prospect for internal security and would be the best answer to Soviet propaganda. The maximum possible development of Indian war potential would also be of great strategic importance—India was already one of the ten greatest industrial Powers in the world, and should be capable both of defending herself and of contributing to the overall imperial defence effort.

In South-East Asia and the Pacific, the main tasks would be to arrange the provision of air and naval base networks and to seek to deny offensive bases to the Russians. Much would depend on two factors: American involvement and the availability to the Western Powers rather than to the Soviet Union of Chinese manpower and raw materials. France, the Netherlands and Siam should be encouraged to participate in regional security arrangements, and a chain of key bases should run from Formosa (or, if made necessary by Sino-Soviet collaboration, from Indo-China) in semicircular sequence, first south, then east to Midway Island. It was hoped that measures taken as insurance against Soviet aggression in this theatre would not endanger Anglo-Soviet relations, as they 'would be equally applicable' against a rearmed Japan.

The question of priorities between all these regions was tackled for the first time in the world strategic survey. First had to come the defence of Western Europe and the security of Atlantic communications:

> The concentration of white man-power and industrial potential in the
> United Kingdom, and its importance as an operational base make it

essential to hold the British Isles if the Empire is to maintain its cohesion.

The second priority was the security of the Indian Ocean area—a vital link in imperial communications, whether or not the Mediterranean route remained open, and of great importance as a source of manpower and industrial resources and as a base. Moreover, its defence was at least practicable to a degree which that of the Middle East was not. The protection of Iraq, Persia, the Suez Canal and Egypt had, for that reason, to be regarded only as the third priority—a decision reinforced by consideration of the greater importance of Indian Ocean than of Mediterranean communications. Finally came Far Eastern interests, which would be subjected only to a comparatively small threat, and that in an area in which an immediate American response to Soviet expansionism could in any case be expected.

Apart from a résumé of the regional requirements and priorities, the conclusions of this final paper produced by the P.H.P.S. were that the avoidance of a clash with the Soviet Union must be a primary object of policy; that the possession of military strength would further this aim; that imperial unity and co-ordination would be essential for the maintenance of Great Power status; and that the full and early support in war of United States forces would be essential for survival. Further, a successful world organisation would aid tripartite collaboration and improve security, though without replacing the need for independent safeguards. The inherent quantitative disadvantages of British military potential were going to have to be offset by technical and organisational superiority, high standards of training and mobility, and the use of reserves and local forces. Matters requiring immediate consideration were: future storage capacities, civil defence planning and provision for dispersal, methods for developing British war potential, future availability of shipping and air-transport facilities, and the development and retention of efficient organisations for intelligence gathering, propaganda dissemination and clandestine operations.[148]

That this *tour de force* would definitely be the swan-song of the Post-Hostilities Planners was soon to become a certainty. On 4 April, the Chiefs of Staff had agreed in principle that the Joint Planning Staff should take over P.H.P.S. responsibilities once the world survey was completed.[149] This decision they confirmed on 29 June when the paper was circulated. The German war was at an end, and, although that

---

148. PHP(45)29(0)(Final)   149. COS(45)87th Mtg (8)

against Japan might continue for a year or more, the J.P.S. should not, in future, find difficulty in coping with the full range of strategic planning. Not only was it a question of a reduced J.P.S. workload, it was also the case that the problems with which the P.H.P.S. had been dealing would be increasingly of current concern. It was therefore decided that the Directors of Plans should be present when the world survey was considered by the Service chiefs and that the Post-Hostilities Planning Staff should be dissolved immediately afterwards, except for such of its sections as would be transferred to the J.P.S. for the sake of continuity.[150]

Before the paper was taken by the C.O.S. Committee, however, it was examined by the Directors of Plans, and on 9 July Michael Cresswell of the Foreign Office Services Liaison Department minuted that they had condemned it 'root and branch' and regarded it as 'unacceptable'.[151] This appears to have been an exaggeration. The J.P.S. attitude was spelt out in a brief prepared for the C.I.G.S. in the light of comments by Brigadier Geoffrey Thompson, the War Office Director of Plans. The survey fulfilled the aim of establishing the nature and extent of British military commitments throughout the world. It was, however, deficient as a guide for the detailed planning of the structure of the post-war forces:

> the Service Ministries cannot base any calculation on such a broad outline as this paper provides, . . . the next step is clearly to narrow down the broad strategical principles set out in the paper so as to provide a basis on which the post-war requirements of the three Services can be worked out in detail.

This was a task for the Joint Planning Staff, which should 'take the Russian threat into account as a potent factor influencing the nature and locations of our forces', though naturally recognising that to maintain the potential in peacetime to meet such a threat in full would be far beyond the post-war capacity of the British Empire. It was true that Cabinet guidance would eventually be needed on the place of Russia in strategic planning and on the allocation of volunteer and conscript manpower between the three Services; but the incoming government would first have to settle down, and no decisions from ministers could

---

150. COS(45)164th Mtg (6)
151. U4969/36/70 (No minutes of J.P.S. meetings after 1943 have been preserved.)

be expected anyway until the Chiefs of Staff could present more detailed information. The best policy would be to approve the world survey so far as it went, and to give copies to the Foreign Office and the various inter-Service committees concerned; to approach the Dominions Office on the question of machinery for military co-ordination; and to set the Joint Planners to work on a paper showing the basis upon which the post-war requirements of the Services should be calculated in the light of the strategic background supplied by the survey.[152]

In presenting their paper to the Chiefs of Staff on 12 July, the P.H.P.S. Directors explained that they had felt unable to consider more than questions of grand strategy because of instructions to them not to become embroiled in controversial inter-Service problems.[153] They added that 'opinions as to the political situation 10–15 years ahead had proved so varied' that it had been decided to base the report upon an assessment of the capabilities of potential enemies rather than of their intentions—which meant, after exclusion of the United States, 'that Russia was the only serious potential enemy'.

Brooke thought that the survey was most useful; he

congratulated the Directors of Post-Hostilities Planning on the report and thanked them for the energy they had displayed in writing this most difficult paper and in handling the many and diverse questions which had been referred to them in the past.

Portal, however, was less enthusiastic. The need for alliances should, he felt, have been given greater prominence. He asked why a higher priority had been accorded to the Indian Ocean area than to the Middle East, and doubted the ability of the Russians to overcome their present dependence on oil supplies from the Caucasus. The P.H.P.S. response was that as Middle Eastern oil resources appeared, after detailed study, to be indefensible, strategy would have to be based upon an assumption of their non-availability in war. As for Soviet vulnerability, there were numerous reports of industrial dispersal being carried out by the Russians and their future independence of the Baku oilfields was assumed on the basis of 'intelligent anticipation of events'.

As Ward had previously hoped, the Chiefs of Staff decided to 'take note' of the world survey as a staff study rather than formally to approve it. It was agreed that the paper set out the needs of imperial security, but

---

152. W.O. brief for C.I.G.S. of 11 July 1945, in WO 193/303
153. See p. 108 above

that it could serve only as a strategic background against which the Joint Planners would have to produce a further report showing how specific Service requirements should be formulated. This they were instructed to do. In the meantime, the world survey was not to be circulated outside the Service Departments.[154]

The members of the P.H.P.S. were well aware that there had also been another limiting factor upon the value of their final enterprise. This was the need to consider in what way warfare itself might have developed by 1955. As has been seen,[155] on 6 October 1944 the Chiefs of Staff had refused to endorse several P.H.P.S. recommendations for the adoption of a procedure for assessing the size of the post-war forces. These had included the notion of establishing a high-level body to examine future trends in warfare. Yet, while the Post-Hostilities Planners were proceeding with their global appreciation between November 1944 and June 1945, a parallel study of that very topic was being carried out by a specialised body in exactly the way they had vainly recommended. Though ostensibly the result of an initiative from outside the C.O.S. machine, the seeds of the idea to commission a study of this sort had almost certainly been sown by Allen, Curtis and Warburton.

154.   COS(45)175th Mtg (5)   155.   See pp. 125–7 above

5

THE JOINT TECHNICAL WARFARE COMMITTEE AND THE FUTURE NATURE OF WARFARE 1945–46

1. The Tizard Report

The decision to have prepared a comprehensive assessment of future changes in weapons and methods of warfare was taken almost as an afterthought on 1 November 1944. In his diary, Brooke noted laconically that there had been 'Nothing of special importance at C.O.S.' that day,[1] which was certainly true by wartime standards. The main item on the agenda had been an enquiry by Oliver Lyttelton—the Minister of Production—about general principles for future industrial location. Lyttelton was chairman of the Joint War Production Staff,[2] a War Cabinet body charged with ensuring 'that sufficient weapons of the right kind are available at the right time . . . [by providing] a link between strategy and production'.[3] He had suggested that

> It would clearly be of value if a full and careful appreciation of the nature and scale of possible future attacks upon this country could be prepared by the Chiefs of Staff to form a background for use by those who have to plan the location of vital industries and other essential components of our war potential,

but had realised that any such study would be a difficult and protracted undertaking in present circumstances. Instead, to furnish some immediate guidance if approved by the Service chiefs, Lyttelton advanced four basic propositions: that, despite the development of

---

1. Brooke, *Diary* (Alanbrooke Papers), 5/9, p. 125
2. Set up in March 1942, it comprised: the Ministers of Production, Supply, and Aircraft Production; officials from each of their departments and from the Ministry of War Transport; and representatives of the three Services.
3. JWPS(42)1

modern weapons, it would still be of advantage to site vital industries in the north and west of the United Kingdom; that the best security lay in duplication and dispersal; that, in the event of a clash of possibilities, such dispersal should override the preference for northerly and westerly locations; and that security would be increased if new industrial developments were to be kept away from the major centres of population.[4] This all seemed unexceptionable to the C.I.G.S. and the First Sea Lord, the latter merely remarking that no part of the British Isles would probably be beyond the range of attack as weapons development continued. The Chief of the Air Staff also agreed, but then moved on to the larger issue. Citing a twenty-fold increase in the weight/distance ratio of bomber aircraft since 1918, Portal suggested that a forecast be made of 'technical advance in the science of military weapons' over the coming twenty-five years, and instructions were given for suitable terms of reference to be drawn up for the Joint Technical Warfare Committee.[5]

The J.T.W.C. was a specialised sub-committee of the Chiefs of Staff, established in November 1943 to 'co-ordinate and direct the technical study of . . . operational projects and problems'.[6] It had been designed to replace the previous practice of considering such matters either on an isolated departmental basis, or by the creation of *ad hoc* inter-Service committees. Apart from the principal Scientific Advisers to the Services, its membership consisted of three Assistant Chiefs of Staff concerned with weapons and equipment, and the Chief of Combined Operations.[7] However, when the committee met to consider its latest task on 14 November, it took the unusual step of deciding that the investigation should be carried out 'in the first place' solely by the scientists, under the chairmanship of an individual who was not a member of the J.T.W.C. This was Sir Henry Tizard, currently President of Magdalen College, Oxford, and formerly head of the Department of Scientific and Industrial Research and of the Aeronautical Research Committee. From 1941 until 1943, Tizard had also served as an Additional Member of the Air Council, but he was a prickly

---

4. JWPS(44)34 (also COS(44)220)   5. COS(44)356th Mtg (0)(1)
6. TWC(43)1 TWC minutes from 1943 to 1945 and TWC papers for 1945 are closed to inspection for fifty years from date of origin; all subsequent material has been retained in the Cabinet Office indefinitely. Henceforth, the suffix '(Cl. 50)' or '(Retained—Cabt. Off./MoD.)' indicates a document discovered by the author though not intended for current release by the authorities.
7. Since March 1942, the holder of this post had served as a member of the C.O.S. Committee when relevant matters were under consideration.

character with a penchant for resignation,[8] and there could be no guarantee that his services would be forthcoming. Consequently, the committee agreed that

> the invitation to Sir Henry Tizard should come if possible from the Chiefs of Staff, in order that the importance which the Chiefs of Staff attached to the investigation might be made clear.

It was also decided that the scientific sub-committee would include four principal advisers to the Services—Professors P.M.S. Blackett (Admiralty), Charles Ellis (War Office), Sir George Thomson (Air Ministry), and Desmond Bernal (Combined Operations Head-quarters)—who 'would be free to consult such technical experts as they found necessary and would report to the J.T.W.C.'[9]

The process of investigation did not get under way until the beginning of 1945, when the Service Departments were notified of Tizard's acceptance of the chairmanship of the *ad hoc* committee and were requested to provide their

> separate views . . . on what appear to be, from the staff standpoint, the dangers to be provided against to secure the defence of the United Kingdom, and to maintain industrial war making capacity of the country against aggression during the next ten years.[10]

That no political aspects were to be considered was made perfectly clear to the scientists at a meeting between Tizard and the J.T.W.C. on 23 January. Ellis suggested that the Tizard Committee 'should ask for some indication of the forces likely to be ranged on either side in the next war and the theatre in which it might perhaps be fought', but was advised that 'it would be best to avoid any mention of specific countries. The assumption should be a war between highly industrialised countries'.[11] This advice was in keeping with the terms of reference by the Chiefs of Staff for the task to which Tizard and his colleagues were now to address themselves, namely:

> to review the position and to forecast to the best of their ability developments in weapons and methods in each important field of warfare

---

8. See, for example, R.V. Jones, *Most Secret War* (London, Coronet, 1979), p. 155
9. TWC(44)24th Mtg (1)(Cl. 50)   10. WW(45)2
11. TWC(45)1st Mtg (1)(Cl. 50)

during the next 10 years, having regard both to theoretical possibilities and also to the practical limitations at present foreseeable.[12]

Over a six-month period, they held some thirty formal meetings, interviewed about a hundred witnesses, and examined approximately three hundred documents;[13] but the final product of their labours was severely limited in value, for they were refused permission to question British physicists about the progress being made in Anglo-American atomic energy research. In view of Tizard's marked scepticism in the early days of speculation on the subject,[14] there was some irony in this refusal, which stemmed from a decision by the Prime Minister in person. On 19 April, Churchill minuted to Ismay:

> Sir Henry Tizard . . . surely has lots of things to get on with without plunging into this exceptionally secret matter. It may be that in a few years or even months this secret can no longer be kept. One must always realise that for every one of these scientists who is informed there is a little group around him who also hears the news.[15]

In spite of this rebuff, the Tizard Committee did make some attempt to assess the implications of atomic energy, but the greater part of its report—produced on 16 June—had perforce to consider less dramatic possibilities. It began with a general survey of probable developments in weapons and equipment. Amongst the most important would be the advent of supersonic jet fighter aircraft, upon which the future defence of British cities and convoys would principally depend. Radar and its variants would offer great scope for further refinement—as would the art of radio communications, with counter-measures and attempts to

---

12. COS(44)360th Mtg (0)(8) & Annex II
13. Apart from the final report, included in the C.O.S. series, Tizard Committee material does not seem to have been preserved. A copy of a note by the secretary (WW/51/45) of 19 February 1945, covering the report's third draft version, is available in CAB 120/770.
14. In May 1940, Tizard had forecast that 'uranium disintegration is not in the least likely to be of military importance in this war' (CAB 21/1263); but he had also been sufficiently broadminded to approve the foundation of an investigative body—later termed the 'MAUD Committee'—under Professor Thomson. The draft report it produced in June 1941 duly 'revealed to the Americans the true possibilities of using uranium for a bomb', and in so doing decisively intensified the effort to produce one. (M. Gowing, *Britain and Atomic Energy, 1939–1945* (London, Macmillan, 1964), pp. 76, 116–7; Jones, *Most Secret War*, p. 270)
15. Quoted in: R.W. Clark, *Tizard* (London, Methuen, 1965), p. 365

neutralise them resembling 'a game of chess, in which success goes to the side which is most skilful in divining the intentions of its opponent and countering them in advance'. Rockets and missiles might render the strategic bomber obsolete—or, at any rate, drastically reduce its future importance—and might revolutionise the size and armament of warships. The latter would also have to contend with a great increase in the underwater performance of submarines. Maintaining the sea communications of the United Kingdom would be crucial, as there seemed no possibility of conveying essential imports other than by merchant shipping. The scientists believed that these threats could be overcome, 'but only through unremitting and exhaustive study and experiment in peace-time'. It was, for example, essential to remain 'in the forefront of submarine design, so as to be able to have targets on which to develop and practise our counter-measures'. As 'a double-edged weapon only valuable to the side which has much less to lose than to gain by starting it', chemical or bacteriological warfare might well be deterred by an enemy's awareness of one's own ability to wage it and to administer prophylactic measures against it. Moreover, any such developments would be insignificant in comparison with the impact of atomic energy—'whatever the facts', concluded the committee a trifle huffily, 'which it is considered unwise for us to know'. Within ten years, its controlled release by means of atomic 'furnaces' could be expected to create an industrial revolution of 'immense and incalculable' consequences. Thus it might be expected that coal would decline in importance as fuel, that submarines of unprecedented endurance would be designed, and that very high-speed merchant vessels would also become practicable. As for the possibility of an explosive release of atomic energy,

> Even allowing for low efficiency, and for the probable need of elaborate and heavy gear to release the energy . . . a single bomber could do an amount of damage equal to that of a thousand bombers using normal bombs.

Before beginning its separate examination of each of the Services, the Tizard Committee laid particular emphasis upon the immense importance of a country's technical superiority during the opening stages of a war—especially if it was not the aggressor and was obliged to concentrate on immediate survival prior to an eventual build-up to offensive action. For the British to achieve this superiority, a reduction was required in the lapse of time between the design and the production of new weapons, which compared most unfavourably with that in the United States. Much work also remained to be done in making quantitative analyses of past operations as guides for the future. Again, if it could be assumed that there would be no major war in the immediate post-hostilities period, it would be

> necessary to concentrate much of the scientific effort available for defence on to basic research into the physical principles underlying the design of weapons of war, and not on improvements in detail for which there is naturally always a persistent demand from the Service departments . . . in the effort to provide for the immediate needs of everyone we run a risk of grasping at the shadow of things of the past and losing the substance of things to come.

All this led to the conclusion that the intimate co-operation between scientists and the Services begun in wartime should be continued and developed thereafter, by means of a specialist body tendering advice on the correct scientific strategy for a given military strategy.

The report then went on to consider the nature of a future war at sea. The 'supreme necessity' would remain the defence of sea communications to ensure the supply of vital imports. It would have to be achieved by strengthening the Royal Navy and reinforcing it with the judicious application of air power. Formidable improvements in aerial reconnaissance, in guided weapons, in submarines (with or without atomic propulsion), and in the range and performance of homing torpedoes, might well be effected within twenty years. It could be assumed that undetected passage across the Atlantic by merchantmen—either singly or in convoy—would become impossible, and that combined aircraft and submarine attacks upon Transatlantic convoys would greatly exceed in ferocity those so recently overcome. Air cover from land would be uneconomic, as well as inadequate at distances in excess of five hundred miles. Carrier-based supersonic fighters and extremely strong escort forces would be needed to deal with the aerial and undersea threats respectively. Fighter and shipborne anti-aircraft defences should be viewed as complementary, the presence of the former forcing hostile aircraft to fly in formation, thus increasing their vulnerability to the latter. High-performance submarines would be required, *inter alia*, for blockading enemy bases, detecting and destroying their counterparts in the opposing fleet, and also—perhaps—for direct participation in convoy defence. The employment of air-dropped sono-buoys could also assist in the detection of enemy submarines for subsequent destruction by such devices as the homing torpedo. If the prospect of atomic-powered merchant ships was excluded, there could be no question of convoys outdistancing submarines as in the past. Minelaying of increasingly sophisticated unsweepable types would require the provision of 'expendable ships for their successful removal'. It would also be important to develop sufficiently precise navigational aids to guide vessels through the narrow channels which were successfully cleared. A radio war of competing measures and counter-measures was anticipated, with steps being taken, for example, to prevent anti-ship weapons from homing in on radar transmissions. Where heavy enemy air activity was expected, the aircraft carrier would be indispensable. Its size should be reduced to the minimum compatible with the landing of supersonic fighters upon it. The size of the 'capital ship' of the future should also be limited to that required to mount its main armament— guided missiles; though of questionable value in comparison with rapid anti-aircraft weapons, these would undoubtedly supersede long-range guns in surface-to-surface encounters. Speed and manoeuvrability were more likely to offer a prospect of survival at sea than attempts at armoured protection:

> Numbers count, particularly by multiplying the targets for the enemy's fire, and so it is surely better, for instance, to have 4 capital ships of 10,000 tons in place of one of 40,000 tons, assuming the total number of weapons to be the same.

Without committing itself categorically, the committee felt that victory would go in future to the fleet that carried its weapons in a large number of units, that had the most refined electronic equipment, and that caused the maximum of confusion to the enemy's radar by tactical handling and the use of scientific devices. Whilst it was not anticipated that the supreme importance of the Navy would give way to that of the Air Force 'in our life-time', it had to be recognised that

> The Navy alone is no longer our sure defence and the scientific development that we foresee forces us to the conclusion that the air and sea war are indivisible.

Turning to the future of aerial warfare *per se*, the committee predicted no fundamental change undermining the general principle of success in fighter confrontations: the side which achieved and maintained technical superiority of performance would gradually wear down opposing forces in battle. Greater attention was paid to the future of strategic bombing, which would clearly continue to be 'a menace to our own densely populated and highly industrialised country'. It 'would certainly remain a subject of some controversy' whether or not the manpower absorbed by the British strategic air offensive against Germany could have been more effectively employed in other ways, but it was more important to consider if a similar effort was likely to be justified by results in future. The competition between fighters and bombers was expected to pass through two stages to a final stage. Within five years, the development of jet fighters with a top speed of 600 m.p.h. would make continuous large-scale bombardment of a strongly defended country too costly to maintain. The balance would then be redressed by the advent of jet bombers with a cruising speed of 500 m.p.h. and a range of 1,000 miles. However, before ten years had passed, fighters with similar cruising speeds but capable of reaching supersonic speeds up to 1,000 m.p.h. would regain 'a substantial advantage in performance' over any contemporary bomber. Anti-aircraft guided missiles and projectiles with proximity fuses, facilities for underground storage and manufacture, and the construction of stronger buildings, would increase defensive capability still further. Once again, it would become

> no longer practicable to achieve worthwhile results against a highly organised country by sustained strategic bombing.

The low-flying short-range bomber would probably be the most difficult to counter, apart from all-weather rocket attacks at ranges up to 200 miles once standards of accuracy were sufficiently improved. As for the precision-bombing of individual land targets, prospects of achieving this were unlikely to be significantly better under operational conditions in twenty years' time than they had proved to be in the present conflict.

The fourth section of the report, dealing with the future of land warfare, was also its shortest:

> Success will depend in future as in the past upon a knowledge of the enemy's disposition and on the power to disrupt his communications and protect our own, and on rapid concentration of force.

There was no indication that any improvement in static defences could bring about another stalemate on the model of the Western Front in the First World War. Indeed, the main problems likely to be lessened were those of speed and scale of movement overland. The limiting factor of the dead weight of equipment to be transported could be expected to diminish with increases in firepower, support from the air, and the use of light alloys. For cross-country performance, vehicles should be fitted with engines designed for the purpose—not merely adapted from commercial types. In tank warfare, as at sea, the advantages of larger numbers and higher mobility would be greater than those which improved armoured protection could confer. In the air, special low-performance aircraft of high carrying capacity would be required in support of army operations, but the deployment of medium-range rockets might often be a preferable substitute. Apart from pressing ahead with reconnaissance, radar and communications techniques, the overall trend would be towards 'combining the mobility of the less encumbered forces of the past with the tremendous firepower of the present'.

The committee then went on to consider the very topic which had been the cause of its own foundation—the home defence of the United Kingdom. On what was deemed a 'fairly safe' analogy with previous conflicts, it was assumed that in a future war there would once again be

an early phase in which our war potential would not be developed to the utmost, and in which an enemy possessing an initial superiority in numbers and weapons would have to be held off until our own forces were built up and support from allies secured.

The greatest attention would have to be given to peacetime preparations to cope with this opening phase. Experience in the present war had shown that a carefully prepared combined operation invariably led to a successful major coastal landing. For this, air and sea superiority were the essential ingredients; against it, prompt detection and highly mobile defensive land forces would be paramount. An inquiry into the possibility of storing several years' stocks in peacetime should be undertaken—petrol and oil being prime candidates for this treatment. Methods of passive air defence against bombardment could also be effected 'without radically altering the civilian life of the country in peace-time'. These would include provision of shelters, strengthened house-building, and dispersal of factories. Any reduction in dependence upon the capital would be especially worthwhile, and strenuous measures to protect internal communications from disruption would be essential.

This fifth and final section of the report ended on the same two topics as had the first: the need for continuous study of technical developments by means of the greatest possible integration of military and scientific thought, and the revolutionary impact of the coming atomic era. Upon the findings of the former, a firm decision about the value of industrial dispersal about the countryside would have to depend. Upon the dawning of the latter, it seemed clear that no defence would be possible without such major innovations as the underground location of key factories and the provision of 'deep dwellings' for much of the urban population. The effect of these measures, carried to their limits, would be to produce a 'troglodyte existence' which only the refinements of modern technology might perhaps make tolerable. Indeed, the members of the committee confessed themselves unable to be sure that there would be 'any defence on which a country could rely' against atomic weapons, even with the adoption of such drastic preparations. Their most telling observation on the subject had actually been included in the section on aerial warfare:

> the only answer that we can see to the atomic bomb is to be prepared to use it ourselves in retaliation. A knowledge that we were prepared, in the last resort, to do this might well deter an aggressive nation. Duelling was a recognised method of settling quarrels between men of high social standing so long as the duellists stood twenty paces apart and fired at each other with pistols of a primitive type. If the rule had been that they should stand a yard apart with pistols at each other's hearts, we doubt whether it would long have remained a recognised method of settling affairs of honour.[16]

Although the Tizard Committee had gathered its evidence from the Service Departments, it kept firm control of the fruits of its labours. Its findings were not presented to the Joint Technical Warfare Committee—nor, indeed, to any other inter-Service body—before being printed. According to the secretary of the J.T.W.C.,

> Sir Henry Tizard's Committee had originally been set up by the Joint Technical Warfare Committee but it had been agreed that it should

---

16.   COS(45)402(0)

report, not through the Joint Technical Warfare Committee, but direct to the Chiefs of Staff.

In fact, this bypassing of the main committee had certainly not been intended at the outset,[17] and the secretary felt bound to remind it, in slightly defensive terms, that draft extracts had been sent to its Service members so that their comments could be included in the report 'at a later stage'.[18]

On 21 June, the Chiefs of Staff agreed to hold a preliminary discussion with Tizard, and—probably because of its extensive reference to atomic matters—his paper was withdrawn from circulation within days of being issued.[19] This effectively ruled out any further departmental contributions before it came up for consideration by the Service chiefs on 3 July. Tizard took the opportunity to deploy his latest arguments for a central committee to direct post-war defence research. It was generally accepted that some such body would be required and agreed that his remarks should be 'borne in mind'; but the main decision was to obtain Service reaction to the report, whilst keeping the number of copies distributed to the 'minimum necessary'.[20]

In the month which intervened before the Tizard report was overtaken by events, it came under particularly detailed scrutiny in the department most responsible for its having been commissioned. After a meeting on 17 July between its Service representatives on the J.T.W.C., its scientific adviser, and a further five senior figures, the Air Staff prepared a point-by-point critique of the entire document. This implied that, in seeking to predict not only likely developments in weapons and methods of warfare, but also their 'effect on the tactics and strategy of warfare', the members of the Tizard Committee had overstepped their terms of reference. Attempts to modify strategy and tactics in the light of technical changes had to make allowance for other factors which the scientists were not competent to judge. The danger of considering technical changes in isolation was that

we may underestimate the part which superior strategy, tactics or morale may play against an enemy better equipped with the latest devices or that

---

17. See p. 180 above   18.   TW.C(45)5th Mtg (5)(Cl. 50)
19. The relevant secretary's minute suggesting this, COS 936/5, does not appear to have survived. However, it is known that Tizard had received advice via Ismay to tell Churchill that he did 'not intend to make any allusion to the topic' of atomic energy in his final report, when appealing for permission to examine it. (Clark, *Tizard*, pp. 364–5)   20.   COS(45)166th Mtg (13)

we may be led inadvisedly to abandon certain weapons or certain lines of development. The conclusion drawn by the Committee as to the future role of strategic bombing is an example of this . . . .

Though largely concerned with asserting the continued importance of land-based aircraft at sea, of transport aircraft for short-term supply, and of manned strategic bombers in addition to guided missiles, the commentary was particularly scathing about Tizard's cursory glance at biological warfare:

> The conclusions of the Committee on the subject of biological warfare as at present phrased may well induce a dangerous state of complacency about the possibility of enemy use of this method of warfare.

Neither the British nor the American authorities concerned shared the view that prophylactic measures against it could be discovered and made practicable. The findings of the committee in respect of B.W. research should therefore be amended to make out a stronger case.[21]

Atomic bombs were detonated over Hiroshima and Nagasaki on 6 and 9 August before any Service memoranda on the completed Tizard report had been submitted to the Chiefs of Staff. On 10 August, Ismay suggested that the Prime Minister be approached to ask Tizard to revise his paper in the light of the arrival of the new weapon. His draft letter to Attlee pointed out that

> Such secrecy has veiled the development of the bomb, that our knowledge of what is likely to be involved in future in its production, of its potentialities, and of possible counter-measures, is almost completely lacking . . . . Sir Henry Tizard . . . was not permitted to obtain official information on the release of atomic energy. His review is therefore largely nullified.

Amongst the questions to which he should now turn his attention were the prospects of an antidote to such bombs, the likely scale of their production, and the possibilities of simplifying their manufacture and of harnessing atomic energy as a source of power.[22] However, when this came before the Chiefs of Staff three days later, the C.A.S. opposed its

---

21. Minutes of Air Staff Mtg of 17 July & copy of Revised Brief (circulated on 31 July 1945) in AIR 20/4658

22. Ismay draft for Prime Minister of 10 August 1945, in AIR 20/4658

immediate despatch and urged that, this time, the Joint Technical Warfare Committee should be associated with Tizard in his endeavours.[23] The Air Staff's strictures on the shortcomings of the report had not been lost on Portal. When—after inadvertent leakage of its existence—the question of supplying the Americans with a copy arose towards the end of August, it was he who insisted upon their being told that it had not received C.O.S. approval, would have to be re-written, and had been prepared 'entirely by scientists and technicians' and not by members of the Services.[24]

It seemed at first that the Americans would have to be requested for access to the necessary atomic information by means of an approach at the highest political level; but with the C.I.G.S.'s appointment to Sir John Anderson's new Advisory Committee on Atomic Energy, the alternative of approaching its chairman[25] suggested itself to the Chiefs of Staff.[26] The A.C.A.E. was to make

> the recommendations which led to the first decisions on the shape of Britain's atomic programme and the attitude to international control.[27]

Brooke duly raised the question of access at its first meeting, and was pleased to be told that it would furnish or obtain all the information that might be needed for the revision of the Tizard report.[28] When the Service chiefs' secretary indicated that the way was now clear for Tizard to be invited to proceed, however, his Air Staff critics returned to the charge. In a strongly worded brief to Portal on 4 September, the Assistant Chief of the Air Staff (Policy)—Air Vice-Marshal William Dickson—reiterated their objections:

> We do not think that this course of action is sufficient. We have in mind that Sir Henry Tizard's previous report, although a thought-provoking document, suffered from the defect that it was written by scientists who ventured to apply their scientific thought to strategic and tactical problems . . . we found, on careful analysis within the Air Staff, that it did not satisfactorily cover certain important military factors. It would have

---

23.   COS(45)197th Mtg (21)   24.   COS(45)556(0) & COS(45)212th Mtg (9)
25.   An Independent M.P. and former P.U.S. at the Home Office, Anderson had had charge of atomic energy matters whilst serving successively as Churchill's Lord President of the Council and Chancellor of the Exchequer. During the war, Churchill had recommended him as replacement Prime Minister in the event of his own death and that of the Foreign Secretary.
26.   COS(45)200th Mtg (8) & COS(45)201st Mtg (14)
27.   M. Gowing, *Independence and Deterrence, Britain and Atomic Energy, 1945–1952* (London, Macmillan, 1974), i. p. 25   28.   See: COS(45)562(0)

been a very much more useful document had these factors been properly discussed with appropriate Service representatives before it was presented.[29]

To avoid the risk of his taking offence, the C.A.S. accordingly put it to his colleagues that Tizard be invited to serve temporarily as chairman of the J.T.W.C.: it included most of the scientists with whom he had worked, but was also 'the responsible authority for advising the Chiefs of Staff on these matters'. The issuing of this invitation was approved on 5 September, and the terms of reference of the original study were slightly widened to provide an excuse for involving the Service members of the J.T.W.C. in its revision.[30]

Several factors appear to have influenced Tizard's refusal, a fortnight later, to take on the task—his initial exclusion from membership of the A.C.A.E., the original rejection of his request to examine atomic developments, and the 'great personal difficulties and intrigue' he felt he had had to contend with in government service, being among the most significant.[31] His meeting with the Chiefs of Staff was, however, a cordial one, with Brooke expressing full support for the notion of establishing a central body to direct scientific research for the Services.[32] Tizard was invited to circulate a paper on the subject, which he did on 12 October. Nine months later, the Defence Committee of the Cabinet was to approve proposals for a Defence Research Policy Committee to advise on 'matters connected with the formulation of scientific policy in the defence field', and the Chiefs of Staff were to nominate Tizard as its first chairman.[33] In the meantime, however, the task of assessing the impact of atomic energy upon the future nature of warfare would have to proceed without him.

2. The First Phase of Revision—Atomic Facts and Theories

Tizard's refusal to do more than comment upon the process of revision simplified the adjustments deemed necessary to normal J.T.W.C.

---

29. Brief for C.A.S. of 4 September 1945 in AIR 20/4658
30. COS(45)215th Mtg (8)   31.   Clark, *Tizard*, pp. 365–6, 374
32. The record of this meeting was contained in a confidential annex to COS(45)229th Mtg(1), which has not survived; but Brooke's diary entry for 20 September covers this discussion. (See: Bryant, *Triumph in the West*, pp. 487–8)
33. See: COS(45)611(0), DO(46)82, DO(46)21st Mtg(1) & COS(46)106th Mtg (6)

arrangements. Professors Thomson and Blackett (who had both left government service by late September 1945) accepted an invitation from the Chiefs of Staff to participate, as did one newcomer—Sir Geoffrey Taylor.[34] A leading theoretician on atomic fission, Taylor could bring to bear his experience as a key British consultant at the wartime Los Alamos research centre. The chairmanship of the committee was retained by the A.C.I.G.S. (Weapons), Major-General Gordon MacMillan, with his naval counterpart, Rear-Admiral Robert Oliver, deputising when necessary. By 16 October, when most of the principals met to consider their approach, a first instalment of the privileged information formerly denied to Tizard had already been received.

Brooke had presented Anderson's Advisory Committee with a list of questions on atomic energy when he had broached the subject of access two months previously. Whilst definitive answers could be supplied only by the head of the British scientific team in America, Sir James Chadwick, a preliminary paper by the Director of Tube Alloys,[35] Wallace Akers, had been completed on 31 August. This drew together, for the benefit of the Chiefs of Staff, such limited information as was already available in the United Kingdom. Amongst its main revelations was a prediction that what had cost some £500 million to pioneer in the United States could in future be repeated elsewhere for one tenth—or less—of the expenditure. There seemed no reason why Russia, France, Belgium, the Netherlands, Switzerland, Sweden and Czechoslovakia, in addition to the United States, United Kingdom and Canada, should not be able to construct the necessary plant over a five- to ten-year period. The same would apply to Germany, Italy and Japan on restoration even to pre-war levels of scientific and industrial activity. The development of atomic energy as a source of power would either imply possession of the technology required to separate the U.235 content from uranium ore, or alternatively involve the production of plutonium as a by-product. In either case, a bomb-making potential would be conferred. Although it was not expected that present bomb types could be enlarged, the present efficiency of utilisation of fissile material was thought to be of the order of 10 per cent or less. This could give great scope to increase the power or reduce the size of atomic

34. TWC(45)32(Cl. 50)
35. This was the deliberately misleading title given, shortly after its inception late in
     1941, to the organisation originally set up within the Department of Scientific
     and Industrial Research to develop an atomic bomb.

devices, and there seemed no cause to doubt that rockets could be employed as a method of delivery. Nor did present types represent

the limit of explosive effect obtainable by the use of nuclear energy, as it might be possible, at some future time, to make use of the enormous temperature, produced in the uranium fission bomb, to set off some other nuclear reaction, with an enormously increased explosive effect.

The extraordinary speed of the development of the atom bomb clearly indicated that this rather distant prospect would become a reality before many years had elapsed. As for defensive measures, it already seemed

as if the only protection against an atomic weapon is to prevent it arriving or to live and carry on all industry in bomb-proof shelters burrowed some hundreds (or perhaps thousands) of feet in the earth.[36]

---

36. TWC(45)33(Cl. 50)—but see also DCOS(AWC)(45)3, to which this paper is appended as Annex I. Although the J.T.W.C. material concerned with the revision of the Tizard report remains either closed for fifty years or retained in the Cabinet Office indefinitely, a few papers have been declassified in the parallel DCOS(AWC) series (CAB 82/26). This Atomic Weapons Sub-Committee had been set up early in October 1945 under the Deputy Chiefs of Staff Committee—a C.O.S. body charged principally with the allocation of priorities for defence research and development, before Tizard's Defence Research Policy Committee was created to assume responsibilities of this kind. The A.W.C. was to report to the A.C.A.E. as well as to the D.C.O.S. Committee on atomic matters, but became dormant within a month of its foundation, pending the outcome of the revision of the Tizard report. However, both the C.O.S. and D.C.O.S. Committees had specifically considered at the outset whether or not its functions should be discharged by the J.T.W.C. instead. Its chairman, Professor Ellis, two of its senior Service members and one of its secretaries already served on the J.T.W.C. All its material consisted of papers furnished first to the J.T.W.C. for the purpose of revising the Tizard report. It is therefore quite misleading of the official historian to state that the A.W.C. 'began by enthusiastically collecting information about atomic energy and bombs, but then it found that another Chiefs of Staff Committee, the Joint Technical Warfare Committee, was charged with revising the Tizard report on future weapons. So it turned over all its "matters of fact relating to atomic energy" to this committee, went into suspension and never returned', (Gowing, *Independence and Deterrence*, i. p. 33). Though insistence on D.C.O.S. responsibility had proven to be misplaced, as the degree of overlap between the two bodies had proven to be excessive, there was no question whatever of the one part of the C.O.S. machine not having been aware of what the other was doing, where such vital matters were concerned. (See: DCOS(AWC)(45)1, COS(45)594(0), COS(45)238th Mtg (16), DCOS(45)14th Mtg & DCOS (AWC)(45)5)

At the J.T.W.C. meeting of 16 October, Taylor endorsed the main lines of Akers's report and confirmed Blackett's opinion that no comprehensive collection of the relevant data had yet been assembled in the United Kingdom. It was important to collate not only what was officially available in the Tube Alloys Directorate, but also 'what was in private hands, such as his own, and indeed, what was to some extent hearsay'. MacMillan suggested that the task of revision should concentrate upon new developments in biological warfare, crop destruction and rocketry, in addition to atomic energy. He circulated a list of further queries, which, though making no specific allusion to the P.H.P.S. world survey or its conclusions, included items making it plain that the new report would not be prepared in the same strategic vacuum as its predecessor:

> What scale of effort would be required *on the target* to knock out all cities of (a) over 100,000 or (b) over 50,000 in, for example, the U.S.S.R. assuming that there were no other targets worthy of attack? What then would be the total number of atomic weapons we should have to produce? Similarly, what number would the U.S.S.R. have to possess for a corresponding attack:—
> (a) Against the United Kingdom only.
> (b) All the major cities in the Dominions.
> (c) All major cities in the United States.

Accordingly, an extensive programme was agreed for the drafting of further questionnaires by departments, the circulating of opinions, and the collecting of further information.[37]

One cautionary note had been struck at that meeting by Dr Henry Hulme, Blackett's successor at the Admiralty as Director of Naval Operational Research. He warned that it was

> undesirable for the Committee to become too much obsessed by the changes which had undoubtedly taken place in the conception of weapons and methods of warfare as a result of the atomic bombs dropped on Japan; and that, nevertheless, many of the principal conclusions and recommendations of Sir Henry Tizard's report remained valid.[38]

This was no short-sighted nautical attempt to belittle the significance of the atomic revolution, but the product of what was almost certainly the

---

37.   TWC(45)9th Mtg (Cl. 50)   38.   *Ibid*.

earliest systematic departmental attempt to assess its significance. On the day after the Japanese surrender of 14 August, Rear-Admiral Oliver, in his capacity as A.C.N.S. (Weapons), had requested the various Admiralty Staff Divisions to contribute studies of their particular aspects of the problem. Although the responses had proven too diverse for inclusion in a comprehensive interim report as intended, a number of imaginative and perceptive contributions had been made. One, by the Director of Plans, envisaged that:

> On a fine Sunday morning or in the middle of a Sunday night, and with no warning whatever, it would be possible for 50 aircraft carrying 50 atomic bombs . . . to arrive simultaneously over England and drop these bombs roughly as follows:—
>
> > 10 over London
> > 3 over the Clyde
> > 3 over the Mersey
> > 2 on Belfast
>
> the remainder being evenly distributed round the naval bases and other ports and productive centres of England. . . . Thus, overnight, the main base of the British Empire could be rendered ineffective from the war-making point of view and the survival of the 'British Empire idea' would then hang upon the ability of the Dominions (and the United States of America) to bring forth a greater counter-blow with rapidity.

It concluded that dispersal was likely to be impracticable in the absence of absolutist State control, that 'going underground' and other counter-measures should be examined, but that the best hope for future generations would lie 'in the enlightenment of man's nature and an appreciation of the issues involved rather than in developing the material means of mutual destruction'. Conversely, the Director of the Gunnery Division argued that mutual possession of such devices might turn out to be most effective in impressing the issues at stake:

> Whatever its capabilities, . . . and whatever its progress is likely to be in the future, it is apparent that atomic power may become a stalemate weapon such as gas, due either to attempts at banning its use or from fear of the consequences. It will be essential therefore to proceed with the present development of present methods of warfare and of those future methods which do not include atomic power.

To some degree, this reflected Oliver's own view—though he had greater faith in the value of dispersal should the threat of retaliation fail to deter. Hulme himself was reluctant to press the gas-warfare analogy too far, but also came down in favour of retaliation as probably the most effective counter-measure. He had not the slightest doubt of the immense increase in destructive power wrought by atomic weapons. Calculating that the bombing of Germany had killed about one person per five tons of bombs, and that it had cost the United Kingdom four man-years to drop each ton of bombs, he observed that

> it therefore cost 20 man-years or 4 men working throughout the war to kill one German. This is clearly not a very decisive way to kill the enemy.

By Hulme's reckoning, the use of three atomic bombs against Japan would have been expected to kill the same number of people as the entire Anglo-American effort over Germany—a casualty rate no European nation could possibly stand. Under these circumstances, it appeared

> very doubtful whether surface craft can hope to survive against an attack by land-based aircraft carrying atomic bombs. The traditional function of sea-power, the defence of our lines of communication, may need a radical revision, if these lines of communication are most easily attacked at their end points.

The advent of the atomic bomb had greatly increased the price worth paying for peace. Hulme concluded that the main function of the Services should henceforth be the prevention of a major war rather than provision of the ability to fight one militarily after its outcome had already been decided either by the collapse of civilian morale or by the destruction of ports and industry. However, his study also recognised that

> there is always the possibility that two nations may start a war on the ordinary pre-atomic bomb lines because they are afraid of using atomic bombs. A strong nation might attack the U.K. by ordinary methods, if they felt fairly sure that we would suffer more from atomic bombs than they would, as in this case they might reasonably assume that we should not be the initiators of the use of this weapon.

This line of reasoning did not preclude its limited introduction against purely 'military' targets and the gradual widening of the definition of such targets as the conflict intensified; but it underlay, from the outset, an inclination on the part of the J.T.W.C. not to believe that the revolution in methods of mass warfare necessarily rendered more conventional considerations of no account in future.[39]

Akers's memorandum was supplemented by one from Chadwick, circulated to the committee members on 19 October. He also put a figure of the order of £50 million on plant development costs (though for a daily output of one kilogramme of fissile material—only two-thirds of the quantity cited by Akers), but was less convinced of the ability of a small country to develop an atomic project over a ten-year period without seriously dislocating its industrial economy. He confirmed that the Hiroshima uranium bomb had yielded energy at a rate of only 1½ per cent efficiency, though the Nagasaki plutonium bomb—with its much smaller content of active material and its superior implosion method of detonation—had been 26 per cent efficient. Little effort had yet been made to obtain power in a form useful to industry, and progress in this field should not be expected for another ten years or so. Akers had been correct about the almost inextricable link between the military and industrial applications of atomic energy, and also, in Chadwick's opinion, about the sole antidotes to attack of preventing delivery or sheltering below ground. Whilst the heavy bomber 'should not long remain a reliable method of attack', given intensive anti-aircraft research and the vulnerability of airfields, the space rocket would very soon constitute 'the ideal vehicle for the delivery of the atomic bomb'. There was even

> a further possibility of delivery, which should not be ignored, delivery by the cloak-and-dagger boys. It would be a very simple matter to bring into a country the active material necessary for a bomb, since its bulk is so small . . . . I think it would be possible for an unscrupulous power, by making use of its consulates and trading organisations, to assemble a number of atomic bombs at important points in a country which it wished to threaten or to destroy.

The position was clear—the advantage for the next few years would lie overwhelmingly on the side of the attack, especially of the surprise

---

39. D. of P., D.G.D., A.C.N.S.(W.) & D.N.O.R. memoranda in ADM 1/17259

attack. Bombs with powers of penetration could be constructed, to cause total destruction to depths of 400–500 feet below ground or sea level. And, within two or three years, a 'super-bomb' would probably be developed, using different nuclear reactions to explode larger quantities of active material.[40]

Chadwick's paper largely anticipated the detailed questionnaire which the J.T.W.C. produced at almost the same time. There remained, nevertheless, considerable gaps in the committee's knowledge, notably—in the absence, as yet, of a full report from Japan—concerning the heat, blast and radiation effects produced in the devastated cities and in the New Mexico desert trial. Could bombs be made of radioactive material, and, if so, what would be their comparative lethality against cities, crops, ships and tanks? Would radioactive 'minefields' be feasible, and could focused rays be produced? Would an atomic weapon dropped into the sea off an enemy-held coast cause a tidal wave able to swamp its defences? Or could atomic mines be laid offshore as a defence against invasion?[41]

Even without such detailed information, the views of more members of the committee about the overall significance of the atomic bomb were rapidly crystallising. On 24 October, Sir George Thomson submitted a six-point memorandum encapsulating in as many paragraphs its main implications for a war in the next few years to come. In the first place, as a conflict in which atomic bombs were used would probably be of short duration, wartime production levels would be negligible and the dominant factor would be the initial stock already accumulated. An arsenal of 100 to 200 bombs,

> if well distributed over centres of communication, manufacture and organisation, should reduce any nation to a level at which it could at best only wage a war of 19th century type,

though none would remain for minor targets. Secondly, rockets and fast manned bombers would constitute reliable methods of delivery, though factors of accuracy and fuel consumption would limit their range to a maximum of some 400 miles. However, slower manned bombers would be capable of attacking at distances up to at least 1,000 miles from their bases, and at a rate of losses deemed acceptable because

---

40.   TWC(45)35(Cl. 50)—also circulated as DCOS(AWC)(45)3 Annex II
41.   TWC(45)37(Cl. 50)

The bomb is so much more valuable than bomber or crew that they will be regarded as expendable.

Thirdly, counter-measures against atomic weapons were unlikely to prove more than partially successful: rocket attack, aircraft dispersal, a proliferation of airfields, assisted take-off from short runways, concealment underground, and the masking of the real attacker in a gaggle of conventionally armed bombers would all have to be forestalled or overcome. The main possibilities would lie in seizure on the ground brought about by a rapid overland advance (in a small country), or by airborne assault against key enemy sites. Fourthly, sea power would lack the time to take effect in a short atomic war; the first requirement on land would be defence against airborne troops; and the main effort would be in the air—bombing, escorting and masking the bombers, intercepting incoming aircraft, and delivering first-line assault troops. Fifthly, the advantages of dispersal enjoyed by the Soviet Union should not be exaggerated, and they would tend to diminish anyway with improvements in aerial navigation techniques:

Even in Russia the towns are, and are likely to remain, essential to waging modern war, and if they can be reached and found it matters little whether they are closely grouped or widely spread. The only advantage of large size, as such, is that towns in the centre can only be reached after a long flight over hostile territory. It is probably more important to be able to start from advanced bases close to the enemy centres while he has to go the whole way from his home country. At present Russia has the advantage over us in this respect also, but may not always do so.

Finally, Thomson developed a theory of warfare without atomic bombs but nevertheless contingent upon the possession of an independent atomic deterrent:

If either side has marked advantage in bombs or in strategic position the war will probably be settled by bombing, but there are two other possibilities to consider which might influence our armament policy:

(a) the war may persist after all the atomic bombs have been used; or
(b) fear of reprisals may prevent use of the bombs at all.

As regards (a), it would almost certainly pay to put the main effort available for defence into atomic bombs in time of peace, so as to win quickly rather than to hope to win a long-drawn war, which would certainly mean the destruction of everything worthwhile in the country.

As regards (b), the tendency in the recent past has been to wage war more and more unrestrictedly, and to press it more and more to complete conquest. It is just possible that the atomic bomb may reverse this trend. A nation may be prepared to use force, but not to the extent of accepting the almost certain destruction of most of its towns . . . . It is not inherent in the nature of things that a nation must always fight to the last limit of endurance rather than admit defeat; for most of recorded history it has not been the rule. Perhaps the atomic bomb will bring a return to sanity, and nations will be content to wage wars for limited objectives, which the weaker nation will be prepared to concede rather than bring destruction of itself as well as its enemy by calling in atomic energy. But no nation can hope for such a chance unless it has power of retaliation against probable rivals, otherwise it will either have to surrender at discretion or accept destruction without even the satisfaction of damaging its enemy in return.

Not only could Powers fight to a finish without initiating an atomic exchange, there might also develop

> an extension of what happened in Spain, where the intervening countries used force to gain their ends without committing themselves to actual war. If major powers had atomic bombs and minor ones not, there would be a temptation for a major power to push a small one forward and help it in a war against the protégé of its rival, hoping that the point at issue might be gained in this way without exposing itself to atomic bombs.

Thomson concluded that, as it was

> not certain that atomic bombs will actually be used in all wars between nations possessing them, but no nation will escape unless it has enough bombs to make retaliation serious,

it would be necessary to retain 'pre-atomic' defence forces in addition to the new devices and the means of their delivery.[42]

The Thomson memorandum was prepared shortly after the Chiefs of Staff had been obliged to formulate preliminary views on atomic matters, irrespective of the progress of the J.T.W.C. study. As early as

---

42. TWC(45)38(Cl. 50)

1 October, before the revision process had even begun, they had been alerted by their secretary to certain draft proposals[43] on the international control of atomic energy, for which Anderson was seeking governmental approval. Brooke stated at once that

> in view of the failure of previous international agreements . . . he thought that there would be little chance of a satisfactory agreement being reached,

and leave was requested to comment upon the A.C.A.E. paper prior to its approval.[44] In their submission to the Prime Minister on 10 October, the Chiefs of Staff warned of the 'obvious danger' of Russia secretly producing atomic weapons in some remote area after British and American agreement to renounce them. The right of inspection would provide no security unless it was completely comprehensive, and the crux of the problem was how this could be achieved under the existing Soviet system. In the absence of a treaty insisting upon this right, it was clear that

> possession of atomic weapons of our own would be vital to our security. The best method of defence against the new weapon is likely to be the deterrent effect that the possession of the means of retaliation would have on a potential aggressor . . . it is essential that British production of atomic weapons should start as soon as possible.

To delay commencement of production, they concluded, pending the outcome of negotiations about international control, might well prove fatal to Commonwealth security.[45]

This was not the view of Professor Blackett, despite the emphasis upon deterrence in the Tizard report to which he had put his signature in June. Though he seems not to have raised objection to the Thomson memorandum in his capacity as a temporary member of the J.T.W.C., he prepared a lengthy paper in November in his capacity as a member of the Anderson Advisory Committee. Entitled 'Atomic Energy: An Immediate Policy for Great Britain', this assumed *inter alia* that

43. See: COS(45)601(0) Annex III Retention of A.C.A.E. minutes by the Cabinet Office precludes confirmation of the absence of the C.I.G.S. from the Advisory Committee meeting which presumably considered the draft proposals.
44. COS(45)238th Mtg (17)
45. COS Sec Min 1449/5, annexed to COS(45)246th Mtg (1)

the U.S.S.R. must consider the war to have been an unmitigated disaster to the Soviet Union, having cost them a very large fall in living standards and a loss in killed of 5% of their population, and a reconstruction problem which will absorb all their industrial effort for many years,

and that, consequently, the Russians would 'inevitably take every possible step to avoid another major war'. It observed that

> The argument is sometimes used, that the possession of a few bombs, which could be used for retaliation against a much stronger power, would make this country safer. It can as plausibly be argued that the knowledge that a few bombs were being produced would be just as likely to stimulate attack to prevent more being made, as to ward it off.

It predicted that, as British possession of the atomic bomb could only be interpreted as a defence against Russia and a threat to her cities, this was 'very likely to stimulate the U.S.S.R. to an aggressive military reaction, not directly against the United Kingdom but elsewhere in Europe', leaving the British 'more vulnerable than before'. Blackett claimed it not to be possible to await the detailed report of the Chiefs of Staff on the role of the new devices before considering the general problem and adopting an interim policy. In his view—failing the conclusion of an international agreement—that policy should consist of a British renunciation of atomic weapons for a five- or ten-year period and a unilateral offer of full inspection facilities to United Nations observers. It was

> highly probable that nearly all countries other than the United States and the U.S.S.R. with its satellites, would immediately follow suit, as it is difficult to see any possible advantage, and many grave disadvantages, to any small country participating in an atomic bomb armament race.

With a system of inspection and international control thereby created over a considerable part of the world,

> the groups within the United States which are in favour of a similar policy would be greatly strengthened, while the groups which wish to use the bomb for coercive purposes would be correspondingly weakened.[46]

---

46.   See: COS(45)651(0) Annex

That such arguments and recommendations were at variance with the views of the Chiefs of Staff and with the trends of thought on the J.T.W.C. must have been fully appreciated by their author—if not by their recipient. No copy of Blackett's paper was apparently submitted to either body[47] before Anderson forwarded one to the Prime Minister. Attlee, unimpressed, promptly turned to the Service chiefs for their comments and concurred with their outright rejection, both of its assumptions and conclusions, when they considered the scheme on 12 November.[48] In the meantime, the members of the J.T.W.C. had been steadily receiving the information they required to assess the other developments in warfare identified by MacMillan as worthy of their attention.

3. Rockets, Crop Destruction and Biological Warfare

The department with the simplest task in advising the committee about its particular speciality was the Ministry of Supply. This was because,

---

47. Continued closure of the 1945 material precludes full confirmation of this point in respect of the J.T.W.C., but examination of accidentally declassified records indicates that the statement is correct.

48. Gowing, *Independence and Deterrence*, i. pp. 171–2. Blackett's memorandum, written in his non-Service role as a member of the A.C.A.E., is relevant to the present study only in so far as it elicited the views of the Chiefs of Staff or their subordinates. It is known to have been the subject of a 'short discussion' at the 12 November meeting (COS(45)270th Mtg (9)); what transpired was deemed of sufficient sensitivity, however, to be recorded solely in the Secretary's Standard File for 1945. Nearly all of its contents, according to the Cabinet Office, have been lost and are presumed to have been accidentally destroyed. The record of the discussion could not, therefore, have been seen by the Atomic Energy Authority's official historian, the value of whose narrative is impaired in this volume by a continual interweaving of fact and opinion not found in the Cabinet Office series. In this case, her complaint that Blackett's paper 'merited an answer on the same [intellectual] plane, but did not get it' is apparently based upon the terse comments of complete rejection ultimately tendered and upon the contents of a later memorandum quite unconnected with his. It was standard C.O.S. practice not to expatiate unnecessarily on sensitive matters in inter-departmental correspondence, irrespective of the profundity or otherwise of the reasoning underlying their decisions. In the absence of the missing material, the implicit charge of inadequate appreciation of the issues involved on the part of the Service chiefs cannot be sustained. Nor would it have been reasonable to expect of them a detailed commentary upon—let alone a preparedness to adopt—such irrevocable 'interim' measures as Blackett advocated, in advance of their consideration of the revised Tizard report. Indeed, his apparent failure to air these views within the C.O.S. organisation, taken in conjunction with one first-hand account of his general method of tackling problems (Jones, *Most Secret War*, Ch. 50, esp. p. 619), suggests that it might have been his intention deliberately to circumvent the Chiefs of Staff and the J.T.W.C.

in April 1945, its Controller of Projectile Development, Sir Alwyn Crow, had provided the Tizard Committee with two very detailed technical reports on future potentialities of rocket weapons. These he seems to have expected to constitute a separate section of the Tizard report, but, in the event, the topic had been covered at various points in the main body of the text. Now, with the problem of delivering the means of mass destruction becoming paramount, the data had to be examined again.

The original documents were re-circulated on 26 October, for the benefit in particular of the Service members of the J.T.W.C. They related how wartime pressures had restricted the development of rocketry as a result of the many competing demands for new equipment, though significant advances has been made. Ground- and sea-launched 'crash' barrages could be laid down by means of multiple projectors; the fire-power of a rocket-carrying fighter aircraft had been raised 'to the equivalent of a salvo from a small cruiser'; and a variety of devices for anti-aircraft, minefield clearance and assisted take-off purposes had been brought into use. Degrees of accuracy had been doubled or trebled between late 1943 and the advance into Germany, and the expected development of spinning rockets over the decade to come should lead to comparably substantial further improvements. Similarly, the substitution of light alloys for steel in rocket motors and the use of better propellants should increase ultimate velocities by a factor of about 2½, reversing currently unfavourable comparisons with those of orthodox shells. These two developments, plus its advantages of mobility, meant that the rocket was likely to become 'a more effective weapon than the gun for all purposes except the engagement of pin-point targets'. In its long-range variants, it would be of great strategic importance:

> This country, the insularity of which breaks down under such conditions of warfare, and which is faced on the continent with near neighbours incapable of defending themselves, must be in the forefront of technical advances likely both to enable her to reach out to attack from these shores and to counter such enemy weapons.

In the race to acquire this potential, there was no reason to doubt British prospects of success—given adequate facilities. Hitler's V.2 missile could carry a one-ton payload up to 200 miles already, though techniques were still in their infancy. Within ten years, accurate bombardment up to twice this distance could be anticipated, and the process would not end there. Ultimately, the range might be extended to 'several thousands of miles':

> The whole of Western Europe might be brought within range of bomb-proof home based installations. Similar installations at strategic points in the British Empire would cover a vast area of the world. The importance of the islands of the British Empire as firing bases may be paramount in future wars. [49]

Tizard and his colleagues had stressed in their report the 'great significance' of rocket development in all its forms: up to 200 miles, the long-range rocket would probably be more formidable than manned bomber aircraft, and there seemed no reason why its accuracy against stationary targets should not come to equal theirs at distances up to 400 miles. About the value of 2,000-mile rockets, however, the scientists had been much more doubtful, concluding that:

> The military advantages of very long-range bombardment by rocket are liable, in our view, to be grossly exaggerated. It has been calculated that ranges of 2,000 miles are possible—but only if the warhead is less than 1 per cent. of the starting weight of the rocket. We can imagine no method by which a sufficient accuracy could be obtained at these ranges to justify the effort; indeed, a great deal of successful experimental work will have to be carried out before we are convinced that rocket bombardment at such ranges will act as a poison rather than a tonic to an enemy. [50]

It was hardly necessary for Crow to point out the extent to which mass-destruction weapons would undermine this assessment and vindicate his original strategic claims. On 9 November, he informed the J.T.W.C. that, whilst it had been possible only to 'skim the surface' of all the relevant German material collected since April, the broad picture of the various devices was perfectly clear. There was little that could alter the fundamental conclusions of his original papers and nothing to suggest that their forecasts of future performance were not of the right order. Apart from minor amendments mainly to do with American progress, and a prediction that

> A two-stage liquid fuel rocket of the V.2 type weighing about 100 tons and carrying the same 1-ton warhead might achieve ranges of the order of

---

49.   TWC(45)39 Annex (Cl. 50)—also circulated as DCOS(AWC)(45)4 Annex
50.   COS(45)402(0)

1,500–3,000 miles, by using wings in the later stages of flight to give a horizontal or gliding path,

the reports were allowed to stand.[51]

MacMillan had fastened upon only one aspect of chemical warfare research as requiring review, and that was the prospect of crop destruction. This had by no means been the main concern of the responsible C.O.S. body—the Inter-Service Committee on Chemical Warfare[52]— which had devoted most of its attention during the war years to the dangers of poison gases. It had, in fact, reported the discovery of German 'nerve' gas stocks to the Chiefs of Staff on the very day of issue of the Tizard report; but it was not then suggested that the development of 'Tabun', 'Sarin' and 'Soman' would have a decisive influence on warfare.[53] In its periodic wartime assessments of the strategic situation, the Joint Planning Staff had consistently opposed the employment of gas weapons other than in reply to enemy attack. The inevitable retaliation had been viewed as potentially catastrophic in unprepared theatres and as likely to handicap offensive operations when these were eventually mounted.[54] The lack of interest of the J.T.W.C., however, almost certainly stemmed from the fact that toxic gases—given their delivery problems—had not been regarded as weapons of mass warfare. The mounting of a sustained attack would require a bombing effort of the order of that employed in conventional raiding. Weight for weight, the effects would not be greatly dissimilar from those of high explosives, except that lack of tactical surprise and efficiency in civil defence would tend to reduce them disproportionately. The single armed bomber in a gaggle of 'spoofs' or the single long-range rocket on target in a salvo might comfortably suffice for atomic warfare, but for most chemical weapons no such economical means of delivery would be possible. Only by developing crop-destruction

---

51. Reference TWC(45)39—Addendum (Cl. 50)
52. Currently chaired by Air Marshal Sir Norman Bottomley, Deputy Chief of the Air Staff, the I.S.C.C.W. had come into existence in September 1940. It was charged principally with the supervision of gas research, production and operational requirements, and the making of 'recommendations to the Chiefs of Staff as to the best method of employing the available resources for offensive purposes, the study of the defensive aspects, however, not being precluded'. (COS(40)645, COS(40)278th Mtg (1) & CCW(40)1 (Special Access))
53. CCW(45)31 (Final) (Cl. 50) & CCW(45)32(Final) (Cl. 50)—declassified as COS(45)400(0) & COS(45)401(0) respectively
54. See: JP(42)382, JP(43)96(Final), JP(44)177(Final) & COS(44)661(0)

Until 1944, Foreign Office influence on post-war military planning was predominant. Under Secretary Nigel Ronald (*above, left*) co-ordinated the setting-up of the first military post-war planning body, the Military Sub-Committee; Sir Alexander Cadogan (*above, right*), head of the Foreign Office, and his deputy, Sir Orme Sargent (*below, left*), were directly involved from the outset; and Christopher Warner (*below, right*) dealt with policy towards Russia from before the Anglo-Soviet Treaty until after the start of open confrontation.

The first post-war planning enquiries from the Foreign Office were reluctantly handled by the Future Operational Planning Section of the Joint Planning Staff, headed by Colonel Oliver Stanley (*above, left*). The Military Sub-Committee was then established with terms of reference drawn up on lines suggested by the War Office Director of Plans, Brigadier Guy Stewart (*above, right*). When the M.S.C. was re-formed as the Post-Hostilities Planning Sub-Committee in 1943, H. M. Gladwyn Jebb (*below, left*) became its Foreign Office chairman, following the precedent of William Cavendish-Bentinck (*below, right*) on the Joint Intelligence Sub-Committee of the Chiefs of Staff.

The replacement of the P.H.P. Sub-Committee by the P.H.P. Staff in May 1944 eventually led to the full integration of the post-war planning machine with the Service Departments. Included in this V.E.-Day photograph (*above*) of the War Office General Staff are: Brigadier Francis Curtis (*back row, 2nd from left*), Director of Post-Hostilities Plans; Professor Charles Ellis (*back row, 2nd from right*), Scientific Adviser to the Army Council and member of the Tizard Committee on the future nature of warfare; Brigadier Geoffrey Thompson (*back row, right*), Director of Plans; Acting Major-General Cecil Sugden (*middle row, centre*), Director of Military Operations and a former Director of Plans; Major-General Frank Simpson (*front row, 2nd from left*), A.C.I.G.S. (Operations) and later V.C.I.G.S.; Lieutenant-General Sir Archibald Nye (*front row, 3rd from left*), V.C.I.G.S.; and Field-Marshal Sir Alan Brooke (*front row, centre*), C.I.G.S.

Colonel (later, Brigadier) Arthur Cornwall-Jones (*left*), served as secretary of the Post-Hostilities Planning Staff during the opening phase of its argument with the Foreign Office over anti-Soviet contingency planning. He then became secretary of the British Joint Staff Mission in Washington, which liaised with the British Embassy on Top Secret post-war planning via the Soviet spy, Donald Maclean. In 1946, Cornwall-Jones was appointed head of the C.O.S. secretariat as Senior Assistant Secretary (Military) of the Cabinet.

Between November 1944 and June 1945, an *ad hoc* committee of defence scientists examined 'Future Developments in Weapons and Methods of Warfare'. Chaired by Sir Henry Tizard *(above, left)*, the committee included: Professor Sir George Thomson *(above, right)*, a pioneer of nuclear deterrence theory; Professor Patrick Blackett *(below, left)*, an opponent of British acquisition of atomic weapons; and Professor Desmond Bernal *(below, right)*, who became a leading post-war Communist propagandist.

The use of atomic weapons against Japan led the Chiefs of Staff to order their Joint Technical Warfare Committee to revise the Tizard Report. Major-General Gordon MacMillan (*above, left*) and Rear-Admiral Robert Oliver (*above, right*) both chaired sessions of the J.T.W.C. during the revision process. Hypothetical studies of atomic attacks on Britain by the Soviet Union and *vice versa* were drawn up by Dr Henry Hulme (*below, left*), and a report on the British biological warfare programme was submitted by Dr Paul Fildes (*below, right*). Fildes's report was to be seriously misused in a 1981 BBC Television feature about Churchill and germ warfare—see Appendix 8.

Churchill and the Chiefs of Staff were pictured in the garden of 10 Downing Street on V.E.-Day, 8 May 1945 (*front row, left to right, above*): Marshal of the R.A.F. Sir Charles Portal, Chief of the Air Staff; Field-Marshal Sir Alan Brooke, Chief of the Imperial General Staff; the Prime Minister; Admiral of the Fleet Sir Andrew Cunningham, First Sea Lord and Chief of the Naval Staff. Standing at the rear are Major-General Leslie Hollis, head of the C.O.S. secretariat, and General Sir Hastings Ismay, Churchill's representative on the committee.

Admiral Sir John Cunningham (*below, left*) and Marshal of the R.A.F. Sir Arthur Tedder (*below, right*) became First Sea Lord and Chief of the Air Staff respectively in 1946.

The new C.I.G.S., Field-Marshal Viscount Montgomery (*above, left*), and the other Service chiefs strongly opposed moves to abandon Britain's position in the Middle East.

The post-war Vice-Chiefs of Staff predicted that the development of mass-destruction weapons would not solve all of Britain's military problems: the V.C.N.S., Vice-Admiral Sir Rhoderick McGrigor (*above, right*), stressed the threat from high-performance submarines; the V.C.A.S., Air Marshal Sir William Dickson (*below*), warned of gravely deficient British air defences.

In June 1946, the Chiefs of Staff decided to set up a special Future Planning Section of the Joint Planning Staff specifically to produce a comprehensive 'Review of Defence Problems'. The Service representatives were: Brigadier Charles Richardson (*above, left*), Acting Rear-Admiral Charles Lambe (*above, right*) and Group Captain (formerly, Acting Air Vice-Marshal) Edmund Hudleston—pictured (*below*) with Tedder in The Netherlands in 1945. Completed in March 1947, the F.P.S. review formed the background to the overall strategic plan finalised in May and adopted at a Prime Ministerial Staff Conference on 11 June 1947.

techniques seemed there to be any chance of wreaking large-scale damage by chemical methods for a limited outlay of effort.

It had been in the course of experiments upon weedkillers in 1940–41 that scientists working for Imperial Chemical Industries and the government's Agricultural Research Council had discovered synthetic substances similar to plant hormones but capable of severely restricting plant growth. Field trials were conducted near Watton in Norfolk under conditions of great secrecy, but limited British resources and the extension of the German war into the corn-growing areas of South-East Europe led to the discontinuation of active development until 1944. In that year, closely related substances came under intensive study in the United States with a view to employment against Japan. After a period of full Anglo-American collaboration, and with the operational use of crop destruction becoming feasible, Churchill vested its further development and control in the Chiefs of Staff. In its first report to them on the subject, the I.S.C.C.W. revealed, in September 1944, the existence of two 'outstandingly destructive' agents—then code-named '1313' and '1414', but subsequently re-designated[55] as 'LN 33' and 'LN 32' respectively. The first could attack cereals, the second sugar beet and other root crops. Of particular importance was the fact that

> The dosage required to produce destruction is very low. As little as 5 lbs. per acre will produce almost complete destruction, and a dosage of only 1 lb. per acre will have serious effects on the home economy.

There was no known neutralising agent for either of the substances, sufficient quantities of which, for operational purposes, would probably take about three years to produce in the United Kingdom or about two years in the United States. However, the advantage conferred by the smallness of the dosages necessary was largely counteracted by the need for admixture with some such 'vehicle' as china clay for even aerial distribution. Effective operations would therefore

> probably entail the whole of the available bomber force being diverted to this purpose for some considerable time . . . [and] would presuppose a degree of air superiority which could probably be exploited to greater advantage by other forms of attack.[56]

---

55. CCW(45)33(Final)(Cl. 50)—also circulated as COS(45)417(0)
56. CCW(CD)(44)1(Final)(Cl. 50)—also circulated as COS(44)797(0)

By late February 1945, when the I.S.C.C.W. next reported to the Chiefs of Staff, it had become clear that great strides in research had been made in the United States. The Americans considered biological agents as likely to prove more effective than chemical ones; had produced three distinct pathogens inimical to rice and certain root crops; and regarded an attack by such means as 'a definite possibility within 12 months'. Contrary to expectations, their investigations had shown that '1414' could be used against rice—a discovery of particular significance given the failure of Australian and American attempts to set ablaze with oil the vital cultivated areas upon which isolated Japanese garrisons depended. All this suggested to the I.S.C.C.W. that

> crop destruction as a means of waging warfare is a more important and less problematical matter than we had previously supposed, so far as its particular application in the Japanese war is concerned.[57]

On 7 March, the Chiefs of Staff responded by requesting a report on possible defensive measures and endorsing the committee's offer to the Americans of field trials facilities at British research stations in India and Australia. The offer was, however, made subject to Portal's proviso that only chemical agents should be tested as, 'if field trials were carried out with biological agents, the effects might spread beyond control'.[58] It was reaffirmed in April that only prompt detection, ploughing and re-sowing could limit the impact of attacks on crops,[59] and confirmed in July that the legality of such attacks was dependent upon the substances employed being neither poisonous in themselves nor liable to render the affected plants poisonous to men or animals. Since it was estimated that, even with total plant retention of the agents, at planned levels of dissemination

> a fatal dose could only be taken by a human being if he consumed the vegetation growing on an area of 65 square yards, which would normally last him for about a year,

there was no legal obstacle to using those chemicals most likely to be brought into action against Japan. They now numbered three—'LN 8'

---

57. CCW(45)10(Final)(Cl. 50)—also circulated as COS(45)134(0)
58. COS(45)62nd Mtg (9)
59. CCW(45)17(Final)(Cl. 50)—also circulated as COS(45)300(0)

(formerly '1414A') having been developed by the Americans—all of which would be effective against rice.[60]

The Japanese surrender led to a reappraisal of the whole subject. The necessity for concentration on agents most suitable for speedy deployment no longer applied. It was considered that the technical feasibility of destroying field or garden crops without undue expenditure of effort had been established and that more economical methods of chemical dissemination could be developed. On 13 September, the I.S.C.C.W. pointed out that, although the atomic bomb and the prospect of biological warfare might make crop destruction appear superfluous,

> there may well be circumstances in which the use of the atomic bomb and of biological warfare would be held unethical.

The susceptibility of the United Kingdom to attacks on crops, the need for economic sanctions by a world security organisation against recalcitrant nations, the possible use of these agents to ensure the internal security of the Empire, and their agricultural value as selective weedkillers, all indicated that research and development should continue in peacetime: a proposition to which the Vice-Chiefs of Staff assented on 20 September.[61]

The report which the I.S.C.C.W. tendered to the J.T.W.C. at the end of October charted the latest advances in techniques. It was now possible

> to destroy or greatly reduce the yield of agricultural produce by the distribution of the order of 1 lb. per acre of a relatively easily manufactured chemical and without undue aircraft effort.

The Americans had been planning to devastate some 30 per cent of the Japanese rice crop in an attack upon the main islands in early 1946. A fourth compound, 'LN 14', had been perfected for the destruction of potatoes, and a composite assault could be envisaged using '5 lbs. per acre of LN 8 against rice, 5 lbs. per acre of LN 33 against corn and 1½ lbs. per acre of LN 8 or LN 32 against root crops'. It would require the application of some 31,000 tons of chemicals for full coverage of the

---

60. CCW(45)45(Final)(Cl. 50)—also circulated as COS(45)488(0)
61. CCW(45)48(Final)(Cl. 50)—also circulated as COS(45)575(0)—& COS (45)230th Mtg (4)

relevant parts of Japan, for example, which could most economically be achieved by dissemination of the agents in solid form. With this method still in its infancy, however, dissemination via spray solution called for a very much heavier aerial effort. Though biological agents stood some chance of creating epidemic infection in crops, little in the way of realistic field trials was understood yet to have been carried out. The four varieties of fungi on which the Americans were chiefly concentrating would, between them, attack rice, potatoes, sugar beet, soya beans, cotton and tobacco. All in all, the I.S.C.C.W. concluded, existing chemical agents constituted 'an offensive weapon of some value' and the use of biological ones—currently of 'uncertain effectiveness'—could not be discounted.[62]

The modesty of this assessment was reinforced at the meeting of the J.T.W.C. on 28 November, when the report was considered. Specialists from the Ministry of Agriculture and the War Office stressed the respective limitations of biological and chemical methods of crop destruction. Whilst the effects of the former might continue to spread after application, this would depend upon favourable climatic conditions, which could seldom reliably be predicted. The vagaries of the weather also ruled out the repetition of field tests under identical relevant circumstances, making it hard to judge the pattern of results. Those the Amercians had just attempted on fungus diseases did not seem to have met with great success. Most biological agents were non-persistent, seldom outliving the season of their application. They would not be able to withstand such temperatures as could be expected inside uninsulated rockets, but they could be released in solid form from about 3,000 feet or loose from between 200 and 300 feet. Chemical agents, it was made clear, could be mixed so as to attack all plants with which they came in contact regardless of their selectivity. They offered a guaranteed diminution of yield once applied, and no known antidote existed. Nevertheless, although potentially significant if used on a large enough scale,

> crop destruction would not change the face of war although it was a useful ancillary. It was, in fact, only a way of accelerating a blockade.[63]

Despite their considerable military value, the I.S.C.C.W. had come to appreciate that, after the war, selective weedkillers were going to be a

---

62. TWC(45)40(Cl. 50)   63. TWC(45)12th Mtg (1)(Cl. 50)

predominantly commercial and economic concern. It was consequently to seek, and obtain, V.C.O.S. approval for the surreptitious nomination of a chemical defence research scientist to a new 'Committee on the Control of Weeds by Chemical Means', which would shortly begin to oversee those aspects of the subject. Ostensibly an ordinary member of the Ministry of Supply, this individual would keep a watching brief on any new developments that might be applied to warfare, without alerting his committee colleagues to the interest and involvement of the Services in their work.[64] Thus was an increasingly important but essentially secondary dimension of military activity to be kept up to date in peacetime.

There remained the question of biological warfare, in which British interest had first been aroused by reports of German preparations, received in the Air Ministry in 1934. A sub-committee of the Committee of Imperial Defence had been established two years later and reconstituted on the outbreak of war as the Bacteriological Warfare Committee of the War Cabinet. It was cumbersome and ineffective, and consisted of a large number of civil servants dependent upon 'two bacteriologists who had never done any experiments and were unable to give authoritative advice' to it. Real progress began only with an initiative by Dr Paul Fildes[65]—a former President of the Pathological Section of the Royal Society of Medicine, who had been on the scientific staff of the government's Medical Research Council since 1934. In 1939, he warned that the exploitation of bacteria in war was a possibility which had not been taken sufficiently seriously. He was referred to Lord Hankey, then Minister without Portfolio and chairman of the Bacteriological Warfare Committee, who established him at the head of a small directorate at Porton near Salisbury in August 1940. For the remainder of the war, his efforts were to be devoted to the development of anthrax—usually referred to as 'N'—in increasingly virulent forms, though he made a point of issuing unpublished pre-war papers on two occasions to camouflage the nature of his wartime activities. In December 1941, Hankey wrote to Churchill about the risk of biological attack and the possibility Fildes now felt able to offer of preparing the means of retaliation. Regardless of having reaffirmed

---

64. CCW(46)1(Retained—Cabt. Off.)—also circulated as COS(46)46(Retained—Cabt. Off.)—& COS(46)25th Mtg (4)(Retained—Cabt. Off.)
65. The background to Fildes's involvement, but not the details of his work, is given in: G.P. Gladstone, *et al.*, *Paul Gordon Fildes*, in *Biographical Memoirs of Fellows of the Royal Society* (London, The Royal Society, 1973), xix. pp. 335–8.

their intention to abide by the 1925 Geneva Protocol outlawing gas and germ warfare, 'if driven to desperation' the Germans might still resort to such methods. Hankey therefore considered it to be

> a prudent disposition to provide some stocks of any material of this kind which our scientists may evolve on exactly the same principle as we provide stocks of gas,

and on 2 January 1942 Fildes's first project in fulfilment of this aim received governmental sanction. Incautiously entitled 'Operation ALADDIN', it was stated to involve the manufacture of two million pieces of 'cattle cake', each containing a dosage of 'N' fatal to cows.[66] In the event, five million pieces were produced and stored before the year was out, while work continued on the possible use of anthrax against human beings. Problems of airborne infection were investigated and resolved; a trip to the United States proved instrumental in establishing Camp (later, Fort) Detrick as a counterpart to the Porton group; and field trials rendering the Scottish island of Gruinard utterly uninhabitable were successfully carried out. During March 1944, an order was placed with the Americans for 500,000 charged 'N'-bombs designed to be dropped in 106-bomb clusters dispersing airborne clouds of anthrax. It was thought that half of this total would become available by the end of the year, but it soon became clear that delays in the production schedule would rule out the mounting of a sustained offensive before the middle of 1945 at the earliest.[67]

As in the case of crop destruction, Churchill waited until the new technique was passing out of the developmental stage before assigning responsibility for it to the Chiefs of Staff. At their meeting on 15 June 1944, they approved the setting up of a small Inter-Service Sub-Committee on Biological Warfare charged with keeping all aspects of the subject under constant review. Its chairman was Air Marshal Sir Norman Bottomley, who also headed the I.S.C.C.W. which the new body was intended to parallel, and the remainder of its membership consisted of representatives of the three Service ministries, plus the

---

66. DO(42)1st Mtg (3)(Confidential Annex) At least this sobriquet was an improvement, from the security point of view, upon its predecessor—'Operation VEGETARIAN'! The allocation of codenames indicative of the subjects they were supposed to conceal was practised by both sides during the war, and is discussed in Jones, *Most Secret War*, pp. 168–71 and D. Wheatley, *The Deception Planners* (London, Hutchinson, 1980), pp. 37–8.
67. COS(44)661(0) Annex II

Whitehall official of the Ministry of Supply responsible for the Porton Chemical Defence Station.[68] Fildes, however, insisted upon remaining formally on the staff of the Medical Research Council and was able to ensure the continuing near-autonomy of his unit.

In October 1944, the new sub-committee reported a number of setbacks. The initial order for 500,000 bombs, 'based on an appreciation that the number would be sufficient for retaliatory attack on six large enemy cities', might have to be increased by a factor of eight to achieve the results originally envisaged. Nor would it be possible to risk charging the weapons long before use, given 'considerable doubt about the stability of the filling' arising from 'the difficulty inherent in turning from production of culture on a laboratory to a factory scale'. Whilst it could be argued that biological warfare had still to be proven to be practicable, the I.S.S.B.W. was opposed to cancellation of the project, either at the present or after the war. It suggested that the existing order for bombs should stand, as it would be sufficient to produce a considerable effect if the operational need arose, and it pointed out that the production of deadly bacteria might well occur in the normal course of medical development without any *ad hoc* work. It therefore asked for authorisation

> to explore with the Medical Research Council the proposal that the latter should co-operate on post-war biological warfare research of a fundamental nature in order that work done by all research workers should be available equally for medical and offensive purposes.[69]

This line of approach, which the Chiefs of Staff endorsed[70] without demur, was to be pressed consistently by the I.S.S.B.W. until governmental approval could be obtained twelve months later. On 9 March 1945, Bottomley set out the findings of a mission to Canada and the United States by members of his sub-committee. Although the Americans had begun their efforts some thirty months later than the British, they had no fewer than 300 officers and 1,800 subordinates working on the research aspect of biological warfare alone. About forty million dollars had so far been spent. By contrast,

---

68. COS(44)514(0) & COS(44)194th Mtg (0)(10) Just over a year later, in his capacity as D.C.A.S., it was to be Bottomley who chaired the meeting of the Air Staff which attacked Tizard's complacency about the dangers of biological warfare. (See pp. 188–9 above)
69. BW(44)21(Cl. 50)—also circulated as COS(44)892(0)
70. COS(44)338th Mtg (0)(7)

Our small research team consisted of twelve workers at the peak of our efforts and now amounts to six workers only, although they have enjoyed the co-operation and help of the much larger Chemical Defence Experimental Station. The comparison between the present scale of effort in this country and the United States of America is most disproportionate. The Canadian programme also is on a greater scale than our own.

Both countries seemed keen to continue co-ordinating their activities with those of the United Kingdom, and both were experimenting with other agents in addition to 'N'. As regards the latter, it remained true that the material being obtained had 'only about 1/9th of the specified virulence', but it was hoped to modify production to raise the potency to at least the original specification. Bottomley concluded that, if biological warfare did indeed prove feasible, it would have to be regarded as a very serious menace, particularly to the United Kingdom:

We have considered medical methods of defence against specific agents and the use of anti-gas equipment, but have concluded that any one form of defence may prove impracticable. We feel therefore that we should ensure that we are ready to counter this form of warfare by retaliation on a heavy scale at short notice.

Without laying down binding programmes for future co-operation, it was necessary to take steps as speedily as possible to maintain tripartite liaison.[71] Once again, the Chiefs of Staff concurred,[72] and on 7 August they were duly informed of a major American breakthrough. A new agent, termed 'US', had been assessed as 'many hundred times' more potent than the projected 'N'-bomb—a clear indication that biological weapons might be found to have a revolutionary impact on the nature of warfare. It would therefore be 'most unwise' to allow research and development to lapse, urged the members of the I.S.S.B.W., adding that

We do not consider such research to be in any way ethically wrong. . . . The research will in effect be a study of the means by which the parasite 'wages war' on the host. The corollary is the need for an enlightened approach to the problem of defence against such attack.[73]

---

71.   BW(45)3(Final)(Cl. 50)—also circulated as COS(45)160(0)
72.   COS(45)68th Mtg (11)
73.   BW(45)17(Final)(Cl. 50)—also circulated as COS(45)518(0)

With the war now brought to its end, the Chiefs of Staff felt able to seek the political approval that was required. They prepared a memorandum describing the development of anthrax-based weapons in the United Kingdom and abroad and predicting that biological devices might yield results 'almost as sweeping as [those of] the atomic bomb'—with the advantage that these might be non-lethal and therefore 'more humane'. Without naming 'US', it repeated the claim about the expected magnitude of its potency, sought approval for the continuation of biological warfare research in peacetime, and recommended that urgent steps be taken to retain the services of the specialists required.[74] On 5 October, the C.O.S. paper was endorsed by the Defence Committee, which, with the winding up of the Armistice and Post-War Committee and the dissolution of the War Cabinet, was establishing itself as the political body most closely concerned with military matters.[75] Thus, by the time that the J.T.W.C. came to assess the significance of biological weapons, it had already been decided that the United Kingdom would remain involved in their development.

Fildes's detailed report on the situation was circulated to the

---

74. DO(45)15 According to Attlee's brief on this paper, the post-war team would consist of a nucleus of five scientists, three of whom would be fully acquainted with the latest American developments. (See: PREM 8/140)

75. DO(45)7th Mtg(5) Upon taking office in May 1940, Churchill had replaced a Ministerial Committee on Military Co-ordination founded by his predecessor soon after the outbreak of war with a War Cabinet Defence Committee (Operations) under his chairmanship. During 1940–1941, this was his main point of contact with the Service chiefs; but it declined in importance thereafter on account of the growing efficiency of the C.O.S. machine, and of his increasingly frequent attendance at C.O.S. meetings (which were then termed 'Staff Conferences'). Shortly after the ending of the wartime coalition in 1945, Churchill re-styled the Defence Committee (Operations) as the Defence Committee of the Cabinet, its 'hard core' membership then consisting of the Prime Minister, Foreign Secretary, Minister of Production, and the three Service Ministers, with the Chiefs of Staff in attendance. Its tasks were 'to keep under review, on behalf of the Cabinet, the main factors in the strategic situation, ... and to carry out preliminary examination of matters specially referred to it'. Effectively, it took over the role of the A.C.A./A.P.W. Committees as the body of ministers to whom post-war military plans should be presented, now that such plans had become current. In the 1946 White Paper on Central Organisation for Defence (Cmnd. 6923), it was to be designated as formal successor to the defunct Committee of Imperial Defence which had set up the 'Chiefs of Staff Sub-Committee' in 1924 to assist it in keeping the overall military situation under review—only to be displaced by it as the government's source of military advice as soon as hostilities began. (DO(45)1; Wilson, *The Cabinet Office to 1945*, pp. 101–2; Ismay, *Memoirs*, pp. 45–6, 51–2, 108–14, 159, 405)

members of the Joint Technical Warfare Committee on 12 November. The 'N'-bomb was described as having reached the initial stages of production and 'US' as being at an advanced stage of development. With regard to the former, it had been calculated from field trials and experiments upon monkeys that it would take as many as sixty of the 500-lb. bomb clusters to saturate each square mile of a built-up area, though only one-fifth of this quantity would be needed to have the same effect in open country. In each case, unprotected inhabitants would be subjected to a 50 per cent risk of death. The cities of Aachen, Wilhelmshafen, Stuttgart, Frankfurt, Hamburg and Berlin between them covered 538 square miles. Allowing a 25 per cent surplus for ineffective bombs, this meant that 40,350 bomb clusters, containing over 4¼ million 4-lb. 'N'-bombs, would be required for all six targets— roughly 8½ times the total originally expected to suffice. Nevertheless, a simultaneous attack could be envisaged, involving 2,690 Lincoln bombers carrying fifteen clusters apiece. Not only would about half the unprotected population be killed by inhalation, there would be many more casualties amongst the initial survivors—with or without respirators—as a result of contamination of the skin and subsequent infection. Despite the virulence of the agent, there was no danger of an epidemic spread which could recoil upon the attacker. The terrain would remain contaminated 'for years', and the risk of skin infection should be great enough to enforce evacuation of all affected areas:

> There is no satisfactory method of decontamination. There is no preventive inoculation at the moment, but at least the skin infection can be cured by penicillin under good hospital conditions. This would, however, be impracticable in the field.

Although great technical difficulties and dangers in the large-scale production of anthrax spores had yet to be fully overcome, it was estimated that the American plant at Vigo, near Terre Haute, Indiana, would be capable of charging the bombs required for an attack on the six German cities in an 8½-month period. Since bulk storage of the weapons without deterioration was unlikely to exceed nine months without further advances in research, this scale of operations marked the maximum possible in the absence of additional production capacity.

Turning to 'US', Fildes expressed himself in more detail and with more caution than had the I.S.S.B.W. to the Chiefs of Staff, or the latter to the Defence Committee. 'US' was brucella, an organism believed to be capable of production using the same plant as anthrax, but in much greater quantities and by much simpler processes. It would cause months of incapacitation and be harder to cure than anthrax, though it would probably contaminate the terrain for days rather than years, rendering the evacuation of cities unnecessary. Its principal advantage lay in the likely reduction in the weight of attack which would be required. According to Fildes, this might be one-tenth of that needed to cover a given area using 'N'-bombs—a much more modest estimate than the earlier ones for 'US', but evidence of a formidable potential nevertheless. He concluded with a warning that, since both weapons had never been used and were so contrary to normal types, attempted evaluation of their properties might be liable to great error.

> In particular, though it is known that humans are susceptible, quantitative data necessary for assessments are obtained from animals, and conclusions based on animal experiment are often wrong.[76]

The J.T.W.C. was to receive two further instalments of information putting the significance of biological warfare practically beyond question, despite Dr Fildes's professional reticence. On 21 November, he attended the meeting which considered his paper. He brushed aside the optimism of the Tizard report, which had largely derived from the prompt recovery after treatment of accidentally infected experimental workers, remarking that

> Little importance should be attached to statements that the use of penicillin would nullify the effects of bacteriological warfare. It was well-nigh impracticable to inject a population to maintain a sufficiently high concentration of penicillin in the blood.

It was true that some three years' research had almost certainly now led to the discovery of one defence against anthrax, though no tests on humans were possible. This treatment might give two or three years' protection, and it should be practicable—though laborious—to immunise a population. Yet, to immunise one's people like this might

---

76.   TWC(45)42(Cl. 50) This paper was to be central to an unfounded BBC Television allegation in May 1981 that Winston Churchill had intended to mount an attack with anthrax bombs on German cities in mid-1944 which would have left them contaminated indefinitely (see Appendix 8, esp. pp. 391 & 403 below.) It was similarly mistreated in an article in the *Guardian* newspaper on 9 January 1987.

well disclose to a potential enemy what weapons had been developed for offensive use. In any case, as more varieties of agent became available, the difficulty of taking such preparatory steps would be greatly increased.

Fildes explained that there would be no problem in insulating bacteria for use in ground-burst rockets, the employment of which would produce intense contamination of limited areas. The development of anti-personnel mines releasing coated pellets had been considered, and, although little work had been done, it was worth continuing research. Whatever the method of application, however, biological weapons would have a delayed effect, not causing casualties until two or three days had elapsed. Experts in chemical warfare had judged germ warfare already 'to be of a much higher order of potency in producing lethal effects', despite the fact that the latter had been much less thoroughly explored. The weight of attack using anthrax was currently little different from that required for ordinary bombing, though the 'N'-bomb would drive out the survivors indefinitely, which fire-raids would not; but there was great scope for improvements in efficiency. Only 4 per cent of the weight of the charging, for example, was actually that of the bacteria, the remainder being that of the water in which they were suspended; and, indeed, within a short time of his appearance before the committee, the microbiologist was able to report that the Americans had succeeded in stepping up the potency of 'N' by a factor of ten. 'In Dr Fildes's judgment,' the J.T.W.C. secretary noted, 'this confirms his statement that continued research by good men may produce important improvements.'[77]

The strongest advocacy of the case for major efforts in the field was yet to come. Brigadier Owen Wansbrough-Jones, a Fellow of Trinity Hall, Cambridge, was Deputy Director of Special Weapons and Vehicles at the War Office and was soon to take over as Scientific Adviser to the Army Council. Called in for the meetings on crop destruction and biological warfare, he felt apprehensive that the J.T.W.C. might fail to appreciate the full potential of Fildes's achievements. On 3 December, he sent a supplementary paper to MacMillan, who circulated it approvingly three days later. It stressed the pioneering nature of the work done at Porton and subsequently overseas, and warned the committee against the possibility of making

---

77.   TWC(45)11th Mtg (4)(As amended)(Cl. 50)

a comparison between Atomic Energy and B.W., which is substantially a comparison between Atomic Energy as it will probably be in ten years' time, and B.W. as it is now.

Fundamental research had been begun by Fildes only in 1940. The corresponding first phase of atomic research had started some twenty years earlier. Already there were good grounds for supposing that, in terms of bomb-load, biological warfare might become a hundred times as efficient by 1955. In the first place, though 'N', for example, was about 300,000 times more toxic than phosgene gas, it was only some 25 times more efficient in causing death when dispersed from existing weapons—16.7 tons of anthrax bombs as against 415 tons of phosgene bombs being required to cover each square mile. This meant that phosgene could currently be distributed 12,000 times more efficiently than anthrax. The disparity was largely the result of low ratios between the weight of the charging and the weight of the 'N'-bomb cluster, between the weight of the bacteria and the weight of their aqueous suspension, and between the proportion of material (about 2 per cent) released into an effective cloud and the remainder fruitlessly dispersed. Despite the difficulty of disseminating droplets of a critical size in the air, it seemed reasonable to expect the efficiency of dispersion to undergo a ten-fold improvement in the decade ahead. In the second place, a comparable increase in the potency of the agents themselves could also be anticipated and was already deemed practicable in the case of anthrax. Other key factors to be noted were the ease of production of biological weapons—in comparison with atomic bombs— and their relative cheapness and likely non-lethality, where agents like 'US' were concerned. There might be a special role for this form of warfare

> in minor wars on which it was not worth using atom bombs; or major ones in which they were being barred . . . . To some extent, the atom and the B.W. bomb may be complementary.[78]

These features of comparability and complementarity, made manifest by the development of brucella and the up-grading of anthrax, were to ensure that the final product of the J.T.W.C.'s labours would concentrate on the impact of biological as well as atomic warfare, although the committee's terms of reference had been merely

---

78. TWC(45)45(Cl. 50)

to revise the Tizard Report in the light of further information available on atomic energy and with the additional object of examining scientific aspects relating to future development and use of weapons.[79]

4. Practical Planning and the Revised Report

Throughout November 1945, while the other main developments in weapons were under consideration, there was considerable doubt how far the prime issue of atomic warfare would be capable of being studied. This arose because of a ruling by the A.C.A.E. chairman about information acquired personally by British members of combined atomic energy research teams in the United States. Anderson took the view that the J.T.W.C. could not properly be allowed to draw upon such information unless it had been made available officially by the Americans to Akers's organisation in London. Though still able to proceed for the time being, the members of the committee felt that this ruling would effectively prevent them from completing their task since the Tube Alloys Directorate had been apprised of 'only a fraction of United States knowledge on this subject', and they appealed to the Chiefs of Staff.[80] The latter agreed that advantage should be taken of imminent Washington talks on atomic energy to have the matter raised with President Truman by the Prime Minister;[81] but it was not until 28 November that the J.T.W.C. learnt that, as a result of this initiative, Anderson

> had now ruled that all information, however acquired, may now be made available to those needing it in the course of their duties.[82]

The value of personal testimony, in the non-scientific sphere, had already been well illustrated by this time. On 7 November, Group Captain Leonard Cheshire, V.C., the Royal Air Force observer at Nagasaki and a specialist in low-level marking for precision-bombing, gave evidence to the committee. Though Cheshire and Dr William Penney had been sent to Tinian in the Marianas specifically to represent the United Kingdom when the atomic attacks on Japan were

---

79.   COS(45)229th Mtg (1)(Confidential Annex)—believed destroyed, but quoted
        in TWC(45)43(Cl. 50)
80.   TWC(45)10th Mtg (2)(Cl. 50) & TWC(45)41(Final)(Cl. 50)
81.   COS(45)269th Mtg (10)   82.   TWC(45)12th Mtg (2)(Cl. 50)

carried out, the Americans had excluded them from the first raid and, initially, from the second one as well.[83] Then, with the latter restriction finally overcome, they found that the aircraft taking them to Nagasaki had missed its rendezvous, with the result that they were still some eighty miles from the target when the bomb exploded. Nevertheless, Cheshire reported, they witnessed an intense flash, a growing ball of fire visible for about fifteen seconds, and then a huge cloud shooting skywards at approximately 30,000 feet per minute. This was completely symmetrical, very turbulent and apparently luminous. Despite the distance of the observers from the stricken city, the upward suction on the ground could plainly be seen. After describing the physical characteristics of the two bombs, Cheshire stated that, although these had been the only ones in the theatre at the time of the raids, it had been said that 'about 25 might be available by the end of the year'. Turning to the future, he laid stress less upon the atomic bomb's potential as a producer of blast than as a source of radioactivity—the only protection against which was a 'considerable thickness of lead' and the effects of which would endure 'perhaps for a fortnight'. He argued that the choice of means of delivery would be crucial. Maximum height, range and speed should be combined with inconspicuous and dispersed bases:

All these facts pointed to the rocket as the best vehicle for attack, and he urged the development of this weapon. If such weapons were controlled from their point of launching, the greater the range the greater would be their inaccuracy. If control, however, was exercised from the point of impact, range would prove no bar to accuracy.

Cheshire's idea was a refinement of the technique in which he had specialised during the war—removing responsibility of control from the delivery vehicle by effective prior marking of the target. Some form of homing device should be developed to be 'dropped over the target by a very fast aircraft for the control of the weight-carrying rocket'.[84]

As a result of Cheshire's testimony, Hulme was invited to consider

---

83. The official history states this ban to have been imposed by the 'local Commander', but Cheshire's biographer quotes the C.-in-C. of the Pacific air forces, General Carl Spaatz, as claiming it to have been 'a Washington ruling' which required 'the personal authorisation of President Truman himself' in order to be countermanded. (*Cf.* Gowing, *Britain and Atomic Energy, 1939–1945*, p. 380 & A. Boyle, *No Passing Glory* (London, Reprint Society, 1957), pp. 255–8)   84. TWC(45)10th Mtg (1)(Cl. 50)

the potential of radioactive contamination in up-dating the committee's information on atomic energy, and MacMillan took up the question of delivery prospects in a review of progress and future procedure on 17 November. After listing the topics considered thus far, the J.T.W.C. chairman observed:

> The salient feature of the new facts produced for us appears to be that with atomic weapons and biological agents mankind has much more powerful means than hitherto to destroy life and the possibility of life in large centres of population, provided these means can be delivered on the targets.

An aggressor would employ them primarily against cities and probably without warning. He would have the triple objective of inflicting casualties, stopping all forms of production, and making unendurable the strain of continuing to fight. In estimating the necessary weight of attack on a population to have a decisive effect, and in assessing the practicability of mounting such an attack, it had to be borne in mind that only the three main wartime Allies would be capable of using all the new methods of warfare for several years to come. Taking cities of over 100,000 inhabitants as targets in each country, it seemed that major centres in North America and the Soviet Union were probably too far distant to be vulnerable from the territory of their respective governments during the next decade. MacMillan therefore suggested that:

> The general problem may conveniently be reduced for the immediate purposes of examination to the particular case of a war between the U.K. and the U.S.S.R. not because such a war is likely, but because it presents a suitable example of different vulnerability in each country.

He recommended the compilation of reports on the weight of attack required 'to knock out for practical purposes' target cities in the United Kingdom and Soviet Union, and on the likely losses involved in delivering such attacks, given the use of the most suitable vehicles. In the latter connection, feeling that more information about long-range rockets was needed, he invited the chairman of the central Co-ordinating Committee on Guided and Propelled Missiles and Projectiles,[85] Sir Frank Smith, to the next meeting of the J.T.W.C.[86] Since Smith's committee had yet to examine technical matters, however, the only opinions which could be given were the chairman's own. These amounted to an expectation that future ranges of at least 1,000 miles would be the main consideration; that a precision of 0.1 per cent of the range should be obtainable within ten years; and that use might eventually be made of atomic energy for propulsion—though, as Thomson remarked, hardly by 1955. In the end, it was the J.T.W.C. which agreed to give Smith guidelines about future staff requirements, rather than receiving much advice from him about probable developments. The most important point was that made by Ben Lockspeiser, Director-General of Scientific Research at the Ministry of Aircraft Production:

> In view of the limitations of the fuels at present available, he considered that aircraft would have to be used for loads of the order of five tons for at least some years to come.[87]

It is by reference to the record of this J.T.W.C. meeting of 21 November, which went on to endorse MacMillan's proposals for further reports, to interview Fildes about biological warfare, and to examine a note drawn up in conjunction with the J.P.S. and dealing with potential Soviet target cities, that a puzzling question concerned with the security of planning is seen to arise. On the one hand, there were to be severe repercussions at C.O.S. level when two J.T.W.C. papers produced in the course of revising the Tizard report were given 'a dangerously wide circulation', despite containing 'data affecting a particular Power' and ' "Top Secret" material vital to the security of this country'.[88] On the other, the C.O.H.Q. scientific member of the Joint Technical Warfare Committee, Professor Bernal, who attended the 21 November meeting and was to be closely involved in the

---

85. The establishment of the C.C.G.P., which had wide general powers to co-ordinate research and development of guided missiles, had been approved by the Chiefs of Staff in May 1945. Although Tizard had refused the proffered chairmanship, he was to assume its main responsibilities—as head of the Defence Research Policy Committee—on the dissolution of the C.C.G.P. exactly two years later. (COS(45)356(0); COS(45)139th Mtg (4); Clark, *Tizard*, p. 374; COS(47)60; COS(47)65th Mtg (5))
86. TWC(45)43(Cl. 50)   87. TWC(45)11th Mtg (1)(Cl. 50)
88. COS(45)286th Mtg (13) & COS(46)66th Mtg (2)

preparation or consideration of all these reports, was himself a long-standing supporter of Soviet communism in general and of Stalin in particular. Unlike others similarly committed, Bernal had never sought to conceal his views in the past; nor was he subsequently to renounce them.[89] Although warned of his political outlook in 1939, Sir John Anderson had been determined to bring him into government service 'as an additional adviser on civil defence "even if he were as red as the flames of hell" '—so impressive were the scientist's ideas on that subject.[90] By mid-1941, Bernal was acknowledged to be one of the two leading British experts on bombing effects, but he continued to be regarded in some quarters as a bad security risk.[91] Whether the Chiefs of Staff were ever made aware of this, or whether they would then have acquiesced in his continued membership of the J.T.W.C. after the end of the war, is very much open to doubt. Whilst it is true that Bernal's wartime reputation was substantial, the Service chiefs had consistently shown themselves to be cautious where hypothetical anti-Soviet planning was concerned. They had decreed that when it was necessary to commit the results of such investigations to paper, the utmost care should be taken to safeguard the documents in question and strictly limit their circulation. The involvement of Bernal in the revision of the Tizard report, notwithstanding his co-authorship of the original version, would appear to have been an early instance of the implications of the change in potential enemies not being fully thought through in terms of governmental personnel recruited during the war.[92]

By the end of January 1946, the J.T.W.C. had assembled the greater part of the information which MacMillan had deemed necessary. With J.P.S. assistance, detailed lists of potential Soviet and British targets had been prepared. The ranges of Russian cities were calculated as

89. See, for example: M. Goldsmith, *Sage: A Life of J.D. Bernal* (London, Hutchinson, 1980), pp. 98–9, 122. Throughout the 1950s, Bernal was to be heavily involved in the activities of the World Peace Council (W.P.C.) and the World Federation of Scientific Workers (W.F.S.W.)—both of which were, and remain, Soviet-controlled propaganda front organisations. He became Chairman of the W.P.C.'s Presidential Committee after the death of the W.P.C.'s first President, Frédéric Joliot-Curie, in 1958.

90. S. Zuckerman, *From Apes to Warlords, 1904–46* (London, Hamish Hamilton, 1978), p. 103

91. *Ibid.* & Lord Zuckerman to the author, 14 February 1981

92. In his study of *The Russia Complex: The British Labour Party and the Soviet Union* (Manchester University Press, Manchester, 1977), pp. 14–15, Dr Bill Jones lists both Bernal and Blackett as amongst the 'distinguished scientists [who] became communists in all but name' in the 1930s.

from three British-controlled bases—Norwich, Nicosia and Peshawar—from one or another of which the 'best minimum range coverage' would be obtainable. Of the 84 Soviet cities believed to contain over 100,000 inhabitants apiece, all but five were within 1,850 miles of the nearest British-controlled base. Though Norwich was the closest of the three in only 16 of these cases, it could still cover a further 33 cities at ranges up to this distance. Assuming no additional areas to be occupied by Soviet forces, the first 400, 600 and 300 miles travelled in flights from Norwich, Nicosia and Peshawar respectively would be over undefended territory.[93] Of the United Kingdom's 49 cities of over 100,000 inhabitants, London was 500 miles from the Magdeburg area in Soviet-occupied Germany and 970 miles from Libau in Latvia, the nearest base in Soviet territory. The remaining British cities were between 560 and 770 miles from Magdeburg and between 920 and 1,060 miles from Libau.[94]

On 22 January, the committee reaffirmed its instructions to Hulme and Bernal to proceed with estimating the scale of attack required on different countries,[95] and considered Thomson's memorandum[96] on the likely effect of atomic bombs on warfare. Thomson saw no reason to change his view that war might still continue without atomic weapons or after the initial stock had been used, and argued that

> it was easy to exaggerate the strength of the defences of a large country against deep penetration bombing

when, in fact, aircraft were likely to be less vulnerable in future than they had been in the past. It was agreed to take his points into account in the final report, subject to further information.[97] This was not to be long in coming.

On 30 January, a lengthy paper was circulated, filling out the introductory reports of Akers and Chadwick. This gave full details of existing types of bomb assembly and confirmed that

> It would be quite possible for enemy agents to smuggle in Plutonium and, provided they could acquire the necessary fuses, explosive, etc., an atomic bomb could be built in secret inside a country and exploded.

---

93. TWC(45)44(Revise)(Cl. 50) (Full text of Annex I in Appendix 4, pp. 354–6 below)
94. TWC(45)47(Cl. 50)
95. TWC(46)1st Mtg (2)(Retained—Cabt. Off.)
96. See pp. 198–200 above
97. TWC(46) 1st Mtg (6)(Retained—Cabt. Off.)

Under such circumstances the area of damage would be at least half as great as for a bomb exploding at optimum height. It would be extremely difficult to prevent attacks such as this, or, for that matter, the shipping-in of delayed-action bombs or atomic attack by commercial aircraft. The use of radioactive fission products *per se* seemed 'an unprofitable proceeding', whether in the form of gamma-rays or of radioactive gas, given the degree of protection afforded by buildings in the one case and tendencies to disperse in the other. The controlled use of atomic energy still appeared to be 'a long way off', and it was proposed that, so far as propulsion was concerned,

> at this stage the use of energy in weapons of the rocket or aircraft type should not be allowed to complicate the issue, since we shall have a long period where atomic war is possible with bombs before weapons driven with atomic energy make their appearance.

The preliminary findings of the British investigative team in Japan, led by Professor William Thomas and Dr Jacob Bronowski, had become available on 21 January.[98] These estimated *inter alia* that an atomic bomb similar to those already exploded would produce 50,000 fatalities if used in a surprise attack against London. The J.T.W.C. paper accordingly included a selection of the principal statistics for use in the revised Tizard report.

As to the cost of producing atomic weapons, the limiting factor was ore, not money—especially after the initial outlay on plant:

> Taking the time of building as 5 years, in 15 years' time £140 million would have been spent in producing about 600 Atomic Bombs. This is small compared with a total sum of the order of £3,000 million necessary to keep up the conventional armed forces over the same period.

Since the essence of the atomic bomb was its great concentration of explosive power for very little weight, it followed that

> A small number of aircraft can now deliver the equivalent of a very large amount of ordinary explosive per sortie. One must therefore count the bombs that get through rather than the aircraft shot down.

With war being waged on a virtually fixed capital of bombs possessed, only important targets would be 'worth a bomb' (unless a very long

---

98.   COS(46)22(0)

period of peace enabled a large stockpile to be prepared). The bulk of these would be large towns, the potential destruction of which—within a few weeks or days—introduced a new psychological problem:

> The future of war with atomic bombs will depend on how decisive the shock to morale turns out to be. Here lies the real uncertainty . . . .[99]

Matters had now reached a stage where the drafting of an overall report could be begun. On 26 March, the committee considered a first attempt which had been carried out by three staff officers specially attached from the J.P.S. Once again, the main contribution was made by Thomson. He criticised the paper for laying insufficient emphasis upon the effect that just a few atomic bombs would have on cities:

> In his view, the landing of, or even the threat of, a relatively small number of atomic bombs, perhaps only five or ten, would cause the evacuation of cities and it was a matter of vital importance to appreciate how far the life of a country and its war-making capacity could be sustained in these circumstances.

Though it was agreed in discussion that this should be stressed, the committee felt unable, as constituted, to deal comprehensively—or adequately—with broad strategic issues of this nature. The drafting staff officers were instructed to reduce their report to more modest proportions, reissuing it in the form of a covering paper to the original Tizard report, showing which of its conclusions needed modifying.[100]

At the next meeting, on 9 April, discussion centred on the question of conventional forces. Blackett argued that these would be required after an atomic attack. If the country attacked was large and strong, the aggressor would be 'very chary' of using up his initial stock of bombs at the outbreak of war, for fear of being unable to exploit the resultant disorganisation by means of military occupation. Thus, in a future war,

> there might be a period before atomic weapons were used, while contestants were competing for allies and preparing normal armed forces,

99. TWC(46)3(Revise) Annex (Retained—Cabt. Off.)—also circulated as DCOS(AWC)(46)1 Annex
100. TWC(46)4th Mtg (2)(Retained—Cabt. Off.)

and this situation might develop to such an extent that the armed forces of the enemy country actually became the most worthwhile target. Rear-Admiral Oliver, now serving his term as J.T.W.C. chairman, agreed that these comments accorded with a growing tendency by members of the committee not to regard the new weapons as wholly decisive; but doubts were expressed as to whether forces assembled for occupational duties as Blackett envisaged would be on a scale bearing any comparison with those needed normally for conventional operations. Tizard also took the view that

> war was not decided on the destruction of cities only and that forces were necessary for following up,

when commenting at this meeting on the process of revision as he had originally undertaken to do. He also pressed for more facts and figures about atomic and biological weapons to be included in the new report.[101]

One more major paper was to appear before the J.T.W.C. completed its assignment. This comprised the first attempt to describe, in quantitative terms, what would actually be involved in the mounting of atomic attacks against the United Kingdom and the Soviet Union, and it was circulated on 13 April. Described as a 'Preliminary Note' on air effort and loss in atomic warfare, it consisted of over twenty pages of calculations and projections collated for the committee by Dr Hulme. By this time, Hulme had taken over as Scientific Adviser to the Air Ministry. Together with Bernal, he had been made responsible for co-ordinating the work carried out by the operational research sections of the Services for the J.T.W.C. The report he now presented set out, for practical purposes, a 'suitable simple model' intended 'to provide a very tentative estimate of the situation ten years hence'.

It assumed equal technical proficiency on both sides; 500 m.p.h. high-level manned bombers, with no defensive armament and a radius of action of 2,000 miles; 600 m.p.h. fighters, each with four guided missiles and a radius of action of 750 miles; totals of 180 British and 540 Soviet defensive night-fighters; effective early warning from 200 miles; no fighters or warning equipment based in occupied territory; and reliable means of air-to-air and ground-to-air identification under conditions of mass raiding. And mass raiding it would have to be:

---

101.   TWC(46)5th Mtg (Retained—Cabt. Off.)

In an attack on Russia the major characteristic is the depth of penetration into defended territory, and the experience of the last war against deep targets with a strong radar-controlled fighter defence is sufficient to show that the chance of a *single* bomber getting through is negligible by day or night.

Each atomic bomb-carrying aircraft would have to be accompanied by a large covering force to maximise its prospects of success. The main tactical consequence of this would be that planning should proceed on the basis of groups of enemy target cities:

> Although the actual striking force for one target may be relatively small, the necessity for a large overall force can be made use of by attacking a fairly close group of targets in one raid, keeping the total force together as long as possible, peeling each target force off and routeing them [*sic*] back in as close proximity as possible.

Each group of targets therefore represented one raid. In Hulme's hypothetical plan, there were fifteen Soviet groups to be considered, and a further eleven cities which would have to be dealt with separately.[102] In order to attack 67 main Soviet centres containing 88 per cent of the urban population, 26 raids would therefore be required. Only one was worth launching from Peshawar on the grounds of minimising the time spent over hostile territory:

> Of the others, 12 [targets] would be attacked from England and 13 from Cyprus and 4 of the latter could in fact be attacked from England without much increase in the time spent over enemy territory.

Amongst the targets best attacked from the United Kingdom, in any event, would be both Moscow and Leningrad, containing between them 28 per cent of the urban population. To ensure delivery of the 242 bombs required on target, some 370 would have to be despatched. In all, 7,500 sorties would be flown and some 2,500 aircraft would be lost in mounting the full series of raids. However, if just the nine principal target groups plus a further eight individual cities were attacked, these 17 raids would still encompass 71 per cent of Russian town-dwellers. The number of bombs required on target would be reduced to 194—out

---

102. See frontispiece and Appendix 5, pp. 357–8 below, for details of these groups and individual targets

of 265 despatched—and only 5,500 sorties would have to be flown. A total of 47 cities would be attacked at a cost of some 1,200 bombers destroyed. The aircraft loss rate would thus fall from 33 per cent to 22 per cent, and no more than 700 bombers would be needed on any one raid.

Hulme pointed out that the latter set of figures compared reasonably with the number of bombs (159 on target out of 225 despatched) and sorties (4,600) required by the Soviet Union in an attack on the 42 main British centres of population. Although it would be possible to cover the entire urban population of the United Kingdom in only seven large raids and with fewer than 570 Russian aircraft lost (12 per cent), the much higher British loss rate, due to the much longer period of exposure to enemy defences, could be made psychologically acceptable to aircrew by adjusting

> the length of the 'operational tour' . . . to make the chance of survival equivalent to that of the last war.

It was stressed that a number of important factors favouring the attack had been ignored. Prominent amongst these were the extent to which surprise tactics might enable raiding operations to be mounted for a short period with relatively low losses; the possible development of effective bomber armament capable of beating off hostile fighters; and the use of radio counter-measures and diversionary attacks. The numbers of bombs required on target to produce at least 'B-damage'— partial demolition, beyond repair—of half the area of the target cities, might also have been over-estimated. If, for example, the lethality of fighter and ground-to-air defences turned out to be only one-third of the value calculated, the necessary numbers of bombs could then be delivered in only 900 sorties over the United Kingdom (135 losses), 1,100 sorties over 47 Soviet cities (330 losses), and 2,000 sorties over 67 Soviet cities (750 losses). In this case, the largest single raid on either country would involve only about 150 aircraft in comparison with the possible maximum of 700 on existing assumptions. Furthermore, since a cover force of some size would be required whatever assumptions were adopted, it was likely that

> the aircraft forming it would be able to carry considerable quantities of R.C.M. equipment and could be employed in distributing various forms of bacteriological warfare.[103]

---

103.   TWC(46)14(Retained—Cabt. Off.)

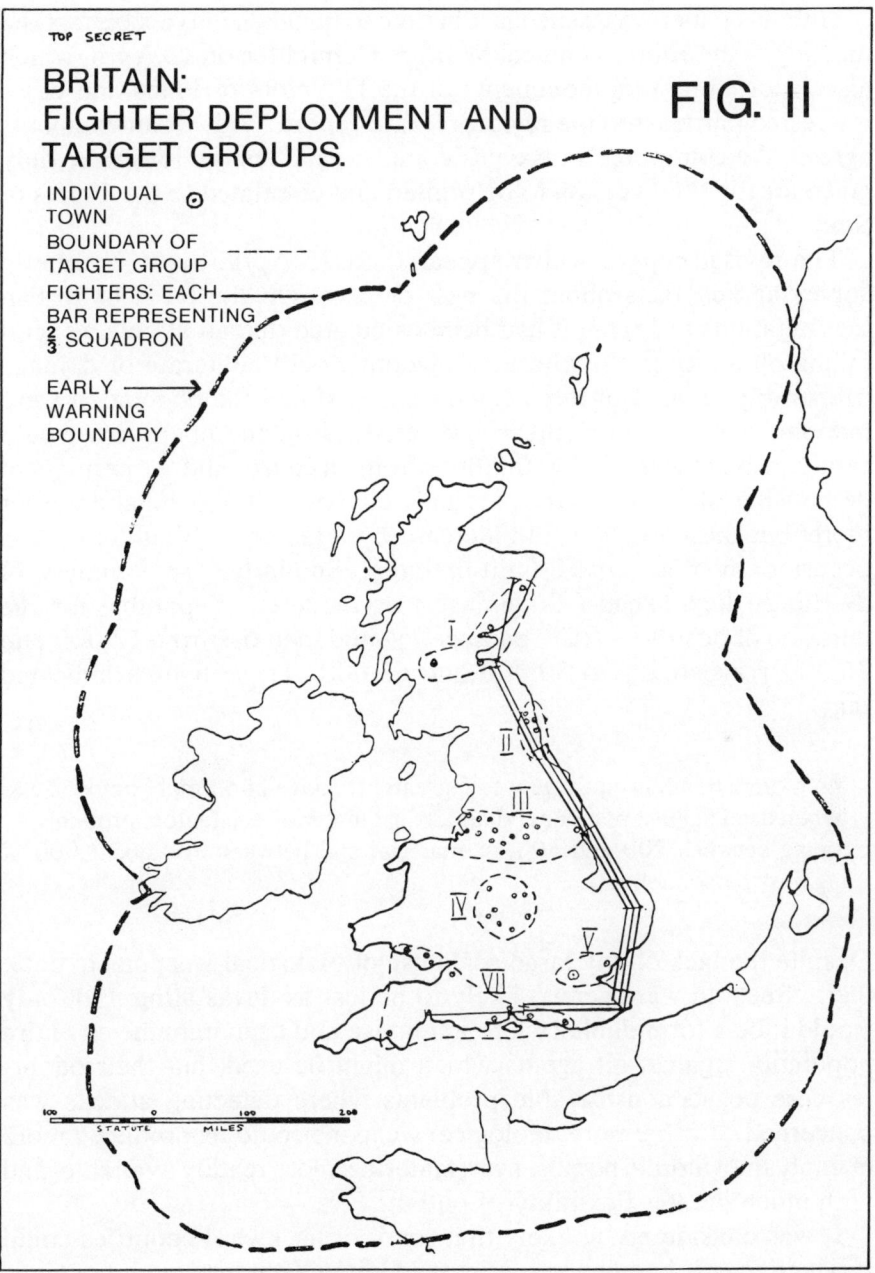

BRITAIN: FIGHTER DEPLOYMENT AND TARGET GROUPS.

FIG. II

INDIVIDUAL ⊙
TOWN

BOUNDARY OF ‒ ‒ ‒ ‒ ‒
TARGET GROUP

FIGHTERS: EACH ——————
BAR REPRESENTING
$\frac{2}{3}$ SQUADRON

EARLY ——————➤
WARNING
BOUNDARY

STATUTE   MILES

Targets for a hypothetical Soviet atomic attack on the United Kingdom, April 1946 (TWC(46)14 (Retained—Cabt. Off.), 13 April 1946) See pp. 228–30 and frontispiece

Hulme's paper was issued just in time to be taken into account at the meeting of the Joint Technical Warfare Committee on 16 April, which also incorporated the comments of the Directors of Plans and other interested parties into the revised Tizard report. With all amendments agreed, the committee's task was complete and instructions were duly given for the final version to be printed and circulated to the Chiefs of Staff.[104]

The revised report, which appeared on 25 April, began by briefly surveying key facts about the new devices. On the basis of British investigations in Japan, it had been calculated that an atomic weapon falling on a city in the United Kingdom would obliterate or damage irreparably an area of three square miles. If half the population were indoors, one-third in shelters and one-sixth in the open, this would result on average in 10,000 fatalities from all causes and the permanent de-housing of 70,000 survivors in a city of 100,000 inhabitants or more; but these totals would increase by a factor of 2½ if detonation occurred over a central built-up area. Similarly, the numbers of dwellings demolished ('B–damage') or rendered irreparable for the duration of hostilities ('Cb–damage') would then rise from 12,000 and 26,000 respectively to 30,000 and 65,000. These figures indicated that

an atomic bomb is equivalent to a greater tonnage of normal bombs . . . when used against personnel than against material, the factors probably being between 200 and 500 for material and between 500 and 1,000 against personnel.

Despite the lack of any large-scale use of biological weapons to date, their effects in war seemed likely to be just as devastating. Not only would it be a formidable task to immunise and keep immune an entire population against all agents which might be used, but their odour-lessness posed considerable problems where detecting attacks was concerned. Furthermore, biological weapons could be produced more cheaply than atomic bombs, from materials more readily available, and with much greater flexibility of output.

It was considered 'unlikely that small or backward countries could produce atomic bombs', but, from the United Kingdom's point of view, the £140 million required to produce 600 of them over fifteen years

---

104.   TWC(46)6th Mtg (1) & (2)(Retained—Cabt. Off.)

would be but a small proportion of total defence expenditure during that period. Peacetime stocks of the new weapons would be all-important:

In the last war, it would have been impossible both in terms of bombs and aircraft to have available at the outbreak of war sufficient quantities in store to cause decisive or even devastating attacks on the enemy's centres of population.

The preparation in advance of stocks of atomic bombs would, by contrast, be much more important than their rate of production in wartime, and the same would apply to biological devices, despite the deterioration of their contents over a period of months:

should the expected improvements in biological agents mature, production could be relatively rapidly initiated during a period of warning and, even if the storage problem is not solved, very dangerous quantities maintained.

Turning to the targets against which the weapons would be employed, the committee identified centres of population, distribution and communications as the most profitable objects of attack, though not ruling out main fleets and bases, convoys and military concentrations in exceptional circumstances. Of the three 'Great Powers', the United Kingdom was in by far the weakest position, with all her targets within 800 miles of the Soviet zone of Germany and with 42 per cent of her population confined to cities of 100,000 or more. From North-West India, Cyprus and the eastern counties of the United Kingdom, three-quarters of comparable Soviet cities lay within 1,500 miles, but only 14 per cent of the Russian population were concentrated in such targets. The relative position would be even worse 'should the U.S.S.R. advance on the Channel coast'. Existing Lancaster and Lincoln bombers could meet the range and payload requirements for atomic warfare, but only at the price of unacceptable losses in practice. Within five years, suitable high-level, high-speed replacements should be available, and, as it was not expected that rockets or pilotless aircraft with sufficient capacity, range or accuracy could be developed within ten years, manned aircraft would remain 'the only practical means of delivering atomic or biological weapons to ranges of over 400 miles' during this period.

It was in assessing the net requirements of bombs to produce collapse in each of the three main Powers that the report gave most consideration to political factors. Vulnerability would be maximised in countries of high urban concentration and dependence on delicate systems of transport and distribution. It would be minimised in states

> which have great military power in being, with which to follow up or fight back, or which have either a very high sense of National discipline, or a severe form of disciplinary control . . . .

From the estimates submitted to it—and with Thomson's remarks clearly in mind—the committee had concluded that

> a relatively small number of atomic bombs, such as five or ten, landed on urban targets in this country or the United States would cause the population to evacuate such centres, whether the Government of the day had ordered evacuation and made suitable preparations for it, or not. . . . [It was] doubtful if the expenditure of so few bombs would produce a similar result in an authoritarian country, where the spread of terror can be controlled.

The crucial question was whether it would be possible to win a war by dropping a sufficient number of bombs on the civilian population without defeating the enemy's armed forces. Not only would the former have to be brought to the point of desiring capitulation, it would also have to be able to enforce that desire upon the latter. Both these objectives could more easily be achieved in a highly urbanised, democratic United Kingdom than in a less concentrated, authoritarian Soviet Union:

> Taking these factors into account it appears that the number of bombs required on target to produce collapse in this country might be less than 100, or within limits, between 30 and 120, with the prospect of more to follow.

The number required to deal with the Americans would be 'about the same as for this country—if anything rather more', but the position of the Soviet Union was in no way comparable. To the Russians, the prospect of ultimate victory might well seem high, so that

> collapse if it occurred, would require the rapid delivery of several hundred bombs on target. If these bombs could not be delivered rapidly,

that is before the large towns had been evacuated, it might not be possible to cause collapse by any reasonable number of bombs, particularly if the army were in the meantime to have marched into Western Europe.

However, the overall ability to wage 'conventional war' might be so reduced that the Soviet Union could then be defeated by well-equipped and adequately supplied armed forces. On an assumption of 50 per cent as the highest rate of aircraft loss acceptable from the morale point of view, and given that at least half of the casualties would be incurred on the return journey, it could be expected that at least 75 per cent of the bombs carried would be released in the course of an attack. Allowing a substantial margin for inaccurate deliveries and other complications, it followed that a country's gross requirement for atomic bombs would certainly be no more than double its net requirement. Still, according to anticipated rates of production,[105] the United States would fail to be 'in a position to wage successful war against the U.S.S.R. with atomic bombs alone' for another five to ten years, and the addition of British stocks to those of the Americans would make no significant difference to this estimate. Even after this lapse of time, it would probably be necessary to supplement the use of the weapons by defeating the Soviet armed forces directly. On the other hand, the Russians could be expected to have acquired the necessary stock of bombs to cause the collapse of the United Kingdom by 1952–56, with biological weapons serving to reduce this time-scale in proportion to their effectiveness as substitutes for atomic bombs.

Having dealt with the nature, targets and requisite quantities of the new devices, the J.T.W.C. prefaced its evaluation of their impact upon future military planning by pointing out how much would have to be based on sheer speculation and how little on known facts:

There have been but few instances in history where an aggressor's plans have run out according to his expectations. It will thus be even more difficult in future for a potential aggressor to calculate that the prize will be worth the price. This uncertainty as to the degree of retaliation will be a deterrent to an aggressor, and much might be done by first-class high-

---

105. See: JIC(45)320(0)(Revise)—annexed to COS(45)286th Mtg(2)—covering a report prepared for the J.T.W.C. by a newly formed 'Joint Scientific Intelligence Sub-Committee', then under the chairmanship of Dr R.V. Jones of the Air Ministry. It was expected that the United States would have some 300 atomic bombs at the end of 1950, by which date the United Kingdom and Canada could between them be producing 60 bombs annually.

level deception about the character, numbers and effects of new technical developments in weapons.

In due course, the new weapons would make practicable 'devastating attacks' on urban population centres. If rapidly delivered, these would prove decisive 'in a period of weeks rather than years' in countries with a high proportion of the population living in large or medium-sized towns. To deter an attack by means of ground-to-air missiles or supersonic fighters was unlikely to be possible: not even these advanced systems could be expected to destroy the necessary 80 or 90 per cent of enemy bombers to make atomic attacks unprofitable. Whilst it had been suggested that conventional warfare might be resumed after approximately equivalent devastation of both sides by the new weapons, this would depend upon the number of the latter initially employed. If large quantities were employed, it was more likely that crucially dissimilar results would follow. In the past, it had always been necessary for the armed forces of one combatant to defeat those of the other, but in future

> air action against civilian morale may be decisive without a major clash between the armed forces of the nations involved.

All that might then be needed would be relatively modest occupational contingents, and a great deal of emphasis would, in any case, have to be laid upon a system of civil defence, industrial dispersal and storage of supplies far more ambitious than anything previously attempted.

As to individual Armed Services, the Royal Navy's traditional function of controlling sea communications would remain essential in any lengthy war. Yet the need to scatter convoys in preparation for atomic attack would render vessels even more vulnerable to the high-performance submarines which had so perturbed the Tizard Committee. Apart from referring to this development and to the need for protective measures to be taken in future warship design, the J.T.W.C. was content just to reiterate the need for an advanced anti-submarine and anti-aircraft capacity. If atomic weapons were to become so plentiful as to be decisive at sea, they would *a fortiori* become sufficiently numerous to pose a more important threat to the very existence of the population at home:

> it follows that a greater proportion of the national effort may have to be spent on the defence of the civil population than upon the defence of their seaborne supplies.

As in the case of convoys, land forces would also have to ensure that they did not present sufficiently compact targets to make the use of mass-destruction weapons worthwhile. Ports, base areas, troops massing for an attack, and overland lines of communication would be particularly susceptible in this respect. It would be a primary responsibility of the Army to provide anti-aircraft forces for the protection of cities, bases and ports against the new devices and to assist the civil defence organisation in controlling the 'civil population both in this country and overseas'. Since these tasks would leave comparatively few troops available for conventional land operations, imperial policing or U.N.O. action, it would be essential to compensate for numerical deficiencies by means of the highest standards of training and equipment. Where air warfare was concerned, the principal change would lie in the much greater level of losses which would have to be inflicted in order to defeat a strategic bombing attack. Until the distant prospect of long-range rockets materialised, the main burden of offence would rest upon the manned bomber or the pilotless aeroplane, whilst that of defence would rest upon interceptor fighters and guided projectiles. Indeed, it was only the development of the latter which seemed to hold out any prospect at all of defeating attacks by aircraft using such powerful weapons as were presently to become available.

It was concluded that there were now three factors undermining the United Kingdom's former reliance upon a period of 'strategic defence' in which to build up strength and assemble allies. First, the country was now as open to sudden attack as were its Continental neighbours; secondly, the next war would be a total conflict, encompassing the whole life of the country from the outset; and thirdly, the primary objectives in that war would probably be the centres of population and the destruction of morale. With a relatively small effort against the civil population, a decisive result might be obtained

> without a clash between the main military forces and too rapidly to permit either the building up of military forces or the exercise of sea power.

In an unprepared country, urban evacuation might seriously sap the means of waging war by conventional methods. On the other hand,

> some hundreds of atomic weapons might fail to cause the collapse of a country suitably organised physically and psychologically, and morally reinforced by adequate military power in being.

Most of the Tizard Committee's conclusions were endorsed—in the context of their limitations—by the J.T.W.C. They still included the controversial claim that future conventional strategic bombing was likely to become too costly to sustain for long, but this no longer generated great concern in the Air Ministry. This was because, as a brief later prepared for the C.A.S. was to observe, the revised report gave such an impression of the preponderance which the other tasks of the Air Force would have over those of the remaining two Services, that

> some of the paragraphs dealing with them could almost be read as an apologia for their existence.[106]

The report also listed the main problems which would confront future civil defence and military research. The former comprised town planning, civil and industrial dispersal, shelter accommodation, medical services and storage of concentrated foodstuffs. Apart from developing the new means of mass destruction, the latter included methods of delivering them, countering them, or reducing their effects by introducing, for example, an airborne early-warning system. Major tasks in the conventional sphere, such as improving submarine detection and maintaining superiority in electronic warfare, were also set out. All these matters should be considered by the appropriate Home Office and scientific Service authorities, and the entire question of future changes in warfare kept under continuous review.

Singled out for retention—to exploit the uncertainties of the new strategic outlook—was the wartime deception organisation which had so strikingly 'induced the Germans to make disastrously false dispositions in France'[107] prior to the Allied invasion of Europe in June 1944. This had originated as a section of the F.O.P.S. under Stanley at the end of 1941, and been established as a separate entity under Colonel John Bevan the following June.[108] Though the members of the J.T.W.C. were almost certainly unaware of the fact, their ideas in this direction were by no means original. As long before as December 1944, the outgoing Air Staff representative on the 'London Controlling Section', as Bevan's organisation was misleadingly entitled, had pointed out that,

---

106. Draft brief for C.A.S. of 17 May 1946 in AIR 20/4658
107. See: C. Cruickshank, *Deception in World War II* (Oxford, O.U.P., 1979), pp. 170–89, 220
108. Wheatley, *The Deception Planners*, pp. 20–2, 57

in peace-time, after the great reduction of our forces, military deception would be almost valueless in persuading our potential enemies (the Russians) that Britain was to be feared. But that it could be done by *scientific* deception

intended to suggest the possession by the United Kingdom of non-existent capabilities. However, nothing had apparently come of this suggestion at the time.[109]

Tizard's own concurrent campaign for a central inter-Service scientific staff was also supported in the revised version of his report, and his previous emphasis on encouraging the further integration of scientific and military thought at all levels, and on promoting technical education throughout the Services, was also reiterated. Finally, it was recommended that, if the Chiefs of Staff saw fit to endorse the J.T.W.C. paper, its findings should be taken into account in any future planning based on the strategic appreciations of the P.H.P.S. or the J.P.S.[110]

Although the Service chiefs were informed of the completion of the report on 3 May, they did not formally approve it until 26 June. On two occasions, Viscount Alanbrooke—as he had now become—suggested postponements: once in order to give the Service Departments enough time to examine it, and once to enable him to consider it more fully himself.[111] The unintended consequence of this delay, however, was that he attended his last meeting as C.I.G.S. two days before it was eventually taken. The C.N.S. had retired a fortnight earlier—to be succeeded by his namesake, Admiral Sir John Cunningham—and the then Sir Arthur Tedder, formerly Deputy Supreme Allied Commander in Europe, had taken over as C.A.S. at the beginning of January. Two of the Vice-Chiefs had also relinquished their posts, Nye to become Governor of Madras and Syfret to command the Home Fleet; and it fell to their successors to defend the interests of their Services in the face of the new developments.

---

109. *Ibid.*, pp. 227–8 The question of whether or not to continue the L.C.S. after the war is known to have been discussed by the Chiefs of Staff on two occasions in September 1945. Although the results of their deliberations have been closed for a fifty-year period, it is clear from close scrutiny of successive editions of the Army List that the L.C.S. was still in being as late as April 1947. (Refs.: COS(45)564(0), COS(45)220th Mtg (6) & COS(45)233rd Mtg (7)—all unobtainable before 1996)
110. TWC(46)15(Retained—Cabt. Off.) The Joint Planning Staff had completed a survey of 'The Strategic Position of the British Commonwealth' a month before the completion of the revised Tizard report. (See pp. 252–9 below)
111. COS(46)70th Mtg (8) & COS(46)86th Mtg (15)

The new V.C.N.S., Vice-Admiral Sir Rhoderick McGrigor, put his case succinctly by stating that

> he would like to underline the fact that irrespective of atomic bombs and biological warfare, if no antidote to the latest types of fast submarine was found before any future war, our ability to continue the struggle would be seriously impaired in a very short time.

It was thus as important to find such an antidote as to prepare for defence against weapons of mass destruction. His War Office counterpart, Lieutenant-General Frank Simpson, was equally forthright. Parts of the report implied that the task of land forces would be reduced primarily to 'mopping-up' and occupational duties in territory already pulverised by atomic bombs:

> He felt that a revolutionary conclusion of this nature could not be accepted unless the evidence to support it was incontestable. No such evidence was likely to be available in advance of a future major war and the War Office considered that they must be prepared, as in the past, for normal 'land warfare'.

Simpson argued that to accept the conclusion that there was little chance of preventing the accurate delivery of at least half of the total number of weapons launched would be to adopt a 'dangerous attitude in that it implied that the United Kingdom would be untenable in any future war'. If the country were to survive, the highest priority must be accorded to the finding of methods of nullifying a large proportion of any attacking forces armed with the new devices. In this connection, anti-aircraft defences had become vitally important—to such an extent that their manpower and equipment requirements might completely upset the balance of the post-war British Army as at present being planned.

Ironically, the main justification for the continuing role of the other two fighting Services was to come from the Chief of the Air Staff. Despite the persistence of Thomson on the subject, the J.T.W.C. had felt unable to go further into the questions of if or when mass-destruction weapons would actually be used. The report merely mentioned that this would probably occur only in a conflict involving the Great Powers (though whether this meant on both sides, or simply on one, was not completely clear). It was Tedder who took up the Thomson line, remarking that while he agreed that anti-aircraft defence would become increasingly important if these new weapons were to be employed, he felt that it was not certain whether they would, in fact, be employed in any future war.

There might be a danger, therefore, of overloading the anti-aircraft defence aspect at the expense of other requirements. Like some Admiralty commentators eight months before, the C.A.S. drew a comparison between uncertainty as to the use of the new devices and wartime reluctance to initiate chemical warfare.

For the time being, however, it was decided that detailed or contentious points arising from the revised report could be left aside and that the Defence Committee should be told that the Chiefs of Staff had given the document their general approval.[112] On 22 July, the members of the Defence Committee agreed to do likewise.[113]

There was, apparently, to be only one significant challenge to the findings of the J.T.W.C.—when the Home Office drew attention to the disparity between the committee's estimate of 25,000 fatalities in a central built-up area and the 50,000 predicted in the report of the British Mission to Japan. In the event, it was quickly realised that this could be accounted for by the degree of sheltering allowed for in Hulme's calculations, but not in Bronowski's, and that no alterations to the former would therefore be necessary.[114] Nevertheless, a full year had been lost between the presentation of the Tizard report and C.O.S. approval of its successor. As will be seen, strategic planning had not been brought to a complete halt in the meantime; but it was probably no coincidence that instructions for British defence problems to be comprehensively examined in depth were not to be issued until June 1946.[115]

---

112. COS(46)99th Mtg (9)(Retained—Cabt. Off.)
113. The final version of the revised report is briefly discussed by Gowing (*Independence and Deterrence*, i. pp. 174-5), whose account confirms that ministerial endorsement was given. The date of the Defence Committee discussion—which had to be postponed—has been confirmed for the author by the Cabinet Office. (Refs.: DO(46)89 & DO(46)23rd Mtg (3)—both unobtainable before 1997)
114. TWC/59/46 & TWC(46)7th Mtg (Retained—Cabt. Off.)
115. See p. 268 below

6

THE JOINT PLANNING STAFF AND AN APPROVED DEFENCE STRATEGY 1945–47

1. The Directors of Plans Take Over

Had it not been for the need to have the Tizard report revised almost as soon as it was completed, the Joint Planning Staff would have been quite well placed to carry long-term strategic planning forward swiftly on supplanting the Post-Hostilities Planners in July 1945. It was not as, if the Directors of Plans were unfamiliar with the type of work involved. They had often been consulted by the P.H.P.S., and the Chiefs of Staff had occasionally turned to them for advice when more immediate post-war topics arose rather than to Allen, Curtis and Warburton. It was they, for example, who had been handling the question of Service man-power requirements in 'Stage II'—the expected lengthy period between the defeat of Germany and that of Japan. More significantly, perhaps, they had been called upon to produce assessments of future British and Soviet strategic interests in the Far East and of the military aspects of post-war Anglo-Spanish relations;[1] and they had even been responsible for preparing a paper on British prospects in a Continental war with the Soviet Union, though the writing of this report was never officially recorded.[2]

It was on 24 May, just over a fortnight after the German surrender, that the C.I.G.S. noted in his diary that his evening had been spent going 'carefully through the Planners' report on the possibility of taking on Russia should trouble arise in our future discussions with her'. He went on:

---

1. See Chapter 4, Section 5, pp. 143–4 & 154 above
2. Having examined all the 1945 C.O.S. and J.P.S. material held by his department, the Departmental Record Officer of the Cabinet Office has confirmed there to be no trace of any such paper. Alanbrooke's subsequent remarks about its reception give support to his view that 'this might have been one of those occasions when certain matters were raised at a meeting but not recorded, and papers looked at, possibly in draft, and have gone no further'. (J. Robertson to the author, 3 December 1980)

We were instructed to carry out this investigation. The idea is, of course, fantastic and the chances of success quite impossible. There is no doubt that from now onwards Russia is all-powerful in Europe.[3]

Brooke was to refer to this paper again on two further occasions. The first was on 31 May, when he recorded that he and his colleagues had discussed 'the "unthinkable war" against Russia' at that morning's Chiefs of Staff meeting, and had become 'more convinced than ever that it is "unthinkable" '.[4] The second was when he commented upon these entries a decade after they had been made. After a slightly inaccurate account of the Dismemberment clash, when the Service chiefs had had to fight for the right to consider possible Soviet aggression as a factor in their plans, he recalled:

Now, only a few weeks [*sic*] later, Winston had come to us expressing his anxiety at seeing 'that Russian bear sprawled over Europe' and instructing us to examine from the military point of view the possibility of driving him back to Russia before the Americans and ourselves demobilized our forces!

To cover his position, Brooke asked the Prime Minister if he 'took charge of all the political aspects of launching a war on our ally!' Churchill's reply was the same as that so often vainly pressed upon the Foreign Office—the political dimension should be disregarded whilst a purely military examination was carried out. However, the upshot of this enquiry, according to Brooke, was a conclusion that

the best we could hope for was to drive the Russians back to about the same line the Germans had reached. And then what? Were we to remain mobilized indefinitely to hold them there?[5]

There is no indication of this matter being taken further. It clearly served to confirm the apprehension with which the Chiefs of Staff viewed any prospect of open conflict with the Soviet Union, despite their insistence that the preparation of defensive plans against that country dare not be shirked. Presumably Churchill was informed of the outcome, but he ceased to be Prime Minister, in any case, on 26 July.

---

3. Bryant, *Triumph in the West*, pp. 469–70
4. Brooke, *Diary* (Alanbrooke Papers), 5/11, p. 11 There is no mention of this discussion in the minutes of the meeting concerned. (COS(45)141st Mtg)
5. Viscount Alanbrooke, *Notes on My Life* (Alanbrooke Papers), 3/B/xv. pp. 84–5

By this time, the J.P.S. had assumed the functions of the Post-Hostilities Planners. As well as Tizard's findings concerning the nature of future warfare, its members had at their disposal the series of broad strategic surveys of likely British requirements around the world in 1955–60. It was true that, of those of the latter still in circulation, only the Far Eastern paper had been reprinted over the signatures of the Chiefs of Staff; but the designation of the remainder as 'useful Staff Studies' to be merely 'noted' was very largely a cosmetic exercise in deference to the sensitive nature of their contents. For all practical purposes, the P.H.P.S. surveys were considered to have been provisionally approved, and towards the end of 1945—when the Foreign Office was beginning to take a more robust view of Anglo-Soviet relations—the Service chiefs were to have no hesitation in saying so.[6]

The first task facing the Directors of Plans in their new role was to carry out the 12 July instruction of the Chiefs of Staff to turn the broad provisions of the global survey into concrete proposals on future Service requirements. Within twenty-four hours, terms of reference had been issued[7] to the members of the Strategical Planning Section, who duly produced a draft paper intended to take the P.H.P.S. report a stage further. Thus it, too, focused on the years 1955–60 in expectation that the size and composition of the forces to be maintained after the defeat of Japan would be geared to conform to the needs of that period. It was also assumed that war with America was inconceivable, that ex-enemy states would be held down efficiently, and that only the possibility of a Soviet threat to the British Commonwealth would then remain.

The STRATS took the view that, since aggression by the Russians would threaten the Commonwealth as a whole, its members could be relied upon to rally to the support of the United Kingdom immediately. After an unpredictable interval, the United States would also enter such a conflict, once her interests were deemed to have been sufficiently endangered. In peacetime, apart from standing commitments for internal security and international policing for the United Nations, the function of the armed forces would be to form the nucleus from which full national mobilisation could be promptly carried out in a crisis. Though its size would be subject to financial as well as manpower constraints, this nucleus should be designed to be capable of expansion to a level limited by only the second of these factors. If war ever came, economic welfare would once again have to be disregarded. The first step should therefore be to estimate the total manpower likely

6.   See, for example: COS(45)699(0) of 28 December 1945
7.   JP(45)174(S)(T.R.)

to be available for the Services, for civil defence and for war production, in the event of hostilities in from ten to fifteen years' time. Next, on the basis of the Tizard report—then still current—and of the lessons learned from the present war, a specific strategy should be evolved for the defence of each region considered in the world survey. This would require the resolution of complex and controversial questions: notably, the extent to which the security of the United Kingdom would be threatened by long-range bombardment; how far sea communications should be defended by surface craft, or by shore-based or carrier-borne aircraft; the degree of reduction in army manpower which air-power and air-transport capacity would make practicable; and the prospects for new methods to be used for the defence of military bases. After the technical questions had been settled and the regional strategies had been combined into an overall scheme taking account of potential wartime manpower resources, it would be possible to determine the shape and size of the forces which would have to be mobilised. The ideal structure of the nucleus to produce those forces could then be calculated and, finally, made subject to the peacetime constraints which would have to be applied.[8]

The sudden end to the Japanese war immediately transformed the situation: the Strategic Planners' ambitious programme was stillborn before it could even be presented to the full J.P.S. for approval. In a note to the Directors of Plans on 7 October, they pointed out that

> As a result of the successful use of the atomic bomb, our long-term requirements of the Services cannot be assessed until the Tizard Committee report has been reviewed. This will take some months.

The further development of the work begun by the Post-Hostilities Planners would have to be shelved for the present, but it would be necessary in the meantime to prepare fresh plans for the *immediate* post-war structure of the forces. The STRATS therefore recommended that the time-scale for strategic planning should be foreshortened. Even when the results of revising the Tizard report became available, they would relate only to a long-term strategy which might be quite different from that required before the new weapons could be produced in quantity. The P.H.P.S. had always avoided dealing with the short to medium term in the strategic surveys, so as not to be sidetracked by temporary post-war problems which might distort the ultimate picture. The intention had been to cope with these largely on an *ad hoc* basis, whilst tailoring the measures adopted into conformity with whatever

---

8. STRATS draft for JP(45)174—undated. Obtainable in CAB 119/97 (Special Access)

coherent strategy for 1955–60 it had been possible to envisage. This would now clearly be impracticable if the nature of warfare was likely to be transformed between the two phases, and if the character of that transformation was going to take months to assess. Already, on 2 September, the J.P.S. had produced a report on the size and deployment of the armed forces to be achieved by the middle of the following year.[9] The STRATS therefore suggested that the next step should be

> to examine our post-war requirements to cover the interim period between 30th June, 1946 and the time when atomic power has been sufficiently developed to change the weapons of war and therefore the shape and size of the armed forces. We propose to assume that atomic energy will not be available to potential enemies before it is available to us and by this time our long-term strategic appreciation will be completed. We propose further to assume that this interim period will continue to at least 1950.[10]

The Directors of Plans agreed, and on 13 October they requested authority from the Chiefs of Staff to initiate an inter-Service study along these lines.[11]

The Strategic Planners had argued that, although the only conceivable potential enemy in the interim period would be Russia, to determine the size of the nucleus armed forces by reference to possible Soviet ambitions

> must tend to be unrealistic in the light of the present state of war-weariness of the world and the possession by the Americans of atomic bombs.

They had also felt such an approach unlikely to prove acceptable to the Cabinet, and had suggested the alternative procedure of

> taking the total manpower likely to be available to the armed services under conditions of national mobilisation and thence estimating the minimum peacetime forces required to mobilise within a given period.[12]

It was the adoption of this procedure that the Directors, in turn, recommended to the Chiefs of Staff. To Portal, however, the

---

9. JP(45)205(Final), approved as amended at COS(45)215th Mtg (5) & COS(45)216th Mtg (7) The relevance of such plans to the present study lies solely in the extent to which the need to prepare them led to the formulation and/ or adjustment of strategic policy.

10. Note by STRATS of 7 October 1945 in CAB 119/97 (Special Access)

11. JP(45)275(Final)   12.   Note by STRATS of 7 October 1945, *loc. cit.*

preparation of any assessment of this sort in a political vacuum seemed quite unsatisfactory. He secured C.O.S. agreement that some political assumptions must be given as the basis for the study[13] and advised his colleagues on 16 October that the criterion governing the proportion of effort to be devoted to each of the Services should be 'the possibility of having to meet Russian aggression'.[14] Effectively, though, the Joint Planners retained the freedom to tackle the problem as they wished, but—as the Chiefs of Staff were later to tell the Defence Committee— permission for the J.P.S. to attempt the five-year forecast of commitments in the interim period was given only with considerable misgivings:

> It is sufficiently difficult even to come to firm conclusions about next year, until we have seen how things develop this winter.

Factors of immediate uncertainty included the occupational situation in Germany, the attempt to restore stable government in Greece, the possibility of serious unrest in Palestine, and quite unexpected problems in Java over restoring Dutch sovereignty to the Netherlands East Indies. Looking beyond 1946, the situation was 'still more nebulous'. It might well be that the results of the J.P.S. study would be too speculative to be of any value, even as an approximate guide to the medium-term structure of the Services.[15]

In facing up to the task, the Directors of Plans continued to favour the original STRATS notion of calculating nucleus forces by reference to standing commitments and likely overall manpower resources available on mobilisation for war. This meant that the strategic problems of a major East-West conflict would not have to be considered, as no particular breakdown in relations with the Russians during the next five years was posited. Nevertheless, some estimate of likely trends in Europe and the Middle East was felt to be necessary, if only as a guide to occupational and internal security commitments. This was duly supplied by the Joint Intelligence Sub-Committee on 4 December. It pointed out that American anxiety to carry out a rapid rundown of occupational forces, and an equally rapid (and probably premature) transfer of administrative authority to the Germans, would increase the burden on the British and French. Conversely, assistance from other Western European countries in future would to some extent lighten the load. There was no clear evidence of Soviet policy towards Germany;

13. Minute by C.A.S. of 15 October 1945 in AIR 8/861
14. COS(45)252nd Mtg (1) 15. DO(45)29

Russian troop withdrawals would probably depend upon reductions in the other three zones. If agreement could be reached over Austria, significant manpower economies should become possible within a few months. By the middle of 1946, too, the only British liability in Italy would be in respect of the disputed province of Venezia Giulia. Without the maintenance of occupational troops in Greece, however, the situation there was 'likely to lead to a rapid return to anarchy', with incalculable effects in the Balkans generally. As for the Middle East, growing Russian influence in Persia and pressure on the Turks over two frontier provinces and the Black Sea Straits might well heighten the general level of unrest. Moreover, any decision on the future of Palestine would

> almost inevitably disappoint the Jews or the Arabs, or more probably both Jews and Arabs, and . . . lead to disturbances for a considerable period of time.[16]

The five-year plan was not completed until 7 January 1946—about a month later than anticipated. On account of this delay, the period covered was advanced by a year to 1947-51, but there was little of strategic interest in the paper because of the decision that the armed forces should not be 'designed to meet any particular hypothetical contingency'. Particular attention was paid to the unique availability, in the years in question, of large trained reserves of wartime personnel who could quickly be reabsorbed into the Services in an emergency. Reconstruction would remain the prime national need, and the guiding principle would have to be that of avoiding over-insurance. Various dispositions to meet internal security commitments were suggested, and it was expected that occupational requirements would fall to a stable minimum by the spring of 1949. In a national crisis, full expansion in the production of munitions and equipment would be achieved over a three-year period, if allowance were made for wartime residues. It would be essential for Service mobilisation to be able to keep pace with this, and a similar time-scale was therefore laid down for the expansion of the nucleus forces to a level incorporating all available manpower. The ultimate targets should be an army of 2,220,000, a navy of 645,000 and an air force of 870,000; but, as the J.P.S. readily conceded, the balance between the three Services set out in these

---

16. JIC(45)307(Final)(Retained—Cabt. Off.)—available in CAB 119/97 (Special Access)

figures was based on nothing more than the fact that it had broadly applied at the end of 1944, 'when all . . . were engaged in major operations in a world war'. At present it was impossible to foresee what course a future conflict might follow. It was therefore impossible to give

> guidance, based on a strategical forecast of such a war, on the types and numbers of units and formations to which each Service should expand within its final total of manpower.

The best that could be done was to lay down various assumptions as a common basis upon which the War Office, Admiralty and Air Ministry should calculate future nucleus strengths. These included similar wastage rates, as in the recent war; a gradual reduction in the National Service term to two years; eighteen months' expansion before the outbreak of war; assistance from the Dominions, India and the Colonies on a scale similar to that in the Second World War; and the need to have available, as soon as hostilities began, all forces necessary for the security of the British Isles themselves and their sea communications.[17]

As the Chiefs of Staff had feared, however, the entire project proved to be a waste of effort. On 29 October, the Foreign Secretary, Ernest Bevin, had recommended that

> there should be a new approach to the problem of the size of the armed forces. He considered that a global sum of money to cover the requirements of all three Services should first be decided upon in relation to the national income. This sum having been fixed, it would then be for the Chiefs of Staff to work out balanced defence forces within this figure . . . . We were faced with a very serious economic problem over the next two years, during which every effort should be made to release men and materials for the expansion of our export trade. Our defence plans for these two years ought not, however, to determine our future policy, and decisions should not be made now on the size of the armed forces which might prejudice the future security of the Empire. The United Nations Organisation had not yet come into being or proved itself, and we were living in a world dominated by power politics. We could not afford to take too many risks.

---

17. JP(45)277(Final)

Despite opposition from the First Lord of the Admiralty, A.V. Alexander, Attlee had endorsed the idea of a global figure in principle, though not calling for action to adopt one for the time being.[18] As a result of this discussion in the Defence Committee, though agreeing to let the five-year paper proceed, the Chiefs of Staff had instructed the Joint Planners to make reductions in their September estimate of forces required in mid-1946 and to prepare a further paper giving target figures for the end of March 1947.[19] These tasks were completed on 19 December.[20] On 21 January, the Defence Committee considered the new estimates of Service manpower put forward by the Chiefs of Staff: 2,068,000 by 30 June 1946 and 1,440,000 by 31 March 1947.[21] The Prime Minister stated bluntly that

> there was no doubt that the nation could not afford either the manpower or the money for forces of the size suggested . . . . A cut in the size of the forces was unavoidable.

He had examined the matter and felt that to try to consider in detail the various commitments listed in the reports would be 'an ineffective proceeding'. Reverting to Bevin's idea, he proposed to set ceiling strengths of 1,900,000 at 30 June and 1,100,000 at 31 December 1946. More important than the figures themselves, from the strategic point of view, was the basic decision that economic needs would have to take priority over defence requirements. In the absence of an immediate threat, the preparation of plans for the post-war structure of the forces would proceed largely independently of whatever strategy was chosen to deal with a hypothetical major conflict. This was spelt out in Attlee's reply to renewed objections by Alexander:

> it was not necessary in present circumstances to have a large fleet ready for instant action, as there was no one to fight. We had to face actualities in our present situation and a certain amount of inefficiency might have to be accepted.[22]

---

18. DO(45)11th Mtg (2)
19. COS(45)264th Mtg (2) & COS(45)265th Mtg (6)
20. JP(45)289(Final) & JP(45)307(Final)
21. COS(46)5(0) & COS(46)9(0)(Revise) The total strength of the U.K. armed forces had risen from 681,000 at the outbreak of war to 4,683,000 at June 1945. (*Strength and Casualties of the Armed Forces and Auxiliary Services of the United Kingdom, 1939 to 1945* (Cmd. 6832 of June 1946))
22. DO(46)3rd Mtg (1)

A C.O.S. report on the proposed reductions in manpower estimates was taken by the Defence Committee on 15 February. It concluded that the cuts would mean liquidating some commitments entirely—notably in Greece and Venezia Giulia—and also incurring a general loss of efficiency which would make it impossible for the Services to cope with a major crisis for two years to come. Only if ministers were satisfied that no such crisis would have to be faced for the next two or three years, should the Prime Minister's figures be confirmed.[23] Despite the misgivings of the Service chiefs, it was decided that this would have to be done. Current defence policy should be founded on three assumptions: that the United Kingdom would not have to fight a major war for two or three years; that, in any future conflict, the Americans would probably side with the British and would certainly not combine with their enemies; and that no fleet capable of endangering the security of the United Kingdom would exist for the next few years.[24] Three days later, the Cabinet endorsed this line of approach and approved a draft White Paper incorporating the Attlee ceilings.[25]

One effect of the imposition of the reduced figures was to ensure that the Joint Planners' five-year plan never came before the Chiefs of Staff Committee. From time to time, efforts were made to re-draft it in line with revised force totals, but as the J.P.S. secretariat later recorded, the real object of the paper—as the link translating broad strategic needs into medium-term manpower requirements—had been overtaken by events. Portal's scepticism about the wisdom of issuing a report of this kind anyway was also recalled, and the whole project was eventually put into cold storage in May.[26] Its passing was no loss from the strategic planning aspect, since, as the STRATS had observed in attempting to up-date it in March, there was still

in any case insufficient evidence to be able to forecast where or in what form a major war, should it occur, might be fought nor who our Allies might be. We do not, therefore, consider that in the period to 1951 our forces should be designed to meet any particular hypothetical contingency.[27]

23. DO(46)20   24. DO(46)5th Mtg (1)
25. CM(46)16th Concls (6) & CP(46)65
26. Gleadell minute to Hollis of 7 May 1946 & Hollis reply of 16 May 1946 in CAB 119/97 (Special Access)
27. JP(45)277(Revised)(2nd Draft)—missing, but obtainable in CAB 119/97 (Special Access)

Had it come to fruition, the medium-term plan would have led to essentially technical arguments about the share of available resources to be allocated to each Service if balanced nucleus forces were to be provided. Instead of being a plan relating eventual strategic requirements to the post-war structure of the forces, it had first linked the latter primarily to more imminent commitments in a period during which a major war was not expected. Then even these had had to be restricted by the introduction of arbitrary manpower ceilings, before the project lapsed.

Effectively, strategic planning had become divorced from pressing post-war questions to do with the future of the forces. This meant, in practice, that the Services could argue amongst themselves how limited resources should be allocated between the different arms of essentially inadequate nucleus forces—as, indeed, they were to do—whilst continuing to co-operate fully in the evolution of a long-term strategy. After all, if it ever had to be implemented, such a strategy would imply the existence of a situation in which economic constraints would give way to military necessities, so that sufficient forces to carry it out would *have* to be made available.[28]

2. The Convergence of Military and Diplomatic Thinking

The decision in February 1946 that the level of Service manpower should, for the present, be based on a two- to three-year no-war rule coincided with pressure from the Prime Minister for the Chiefs of Staff to consider the overall strategic interests of the British Commonwealth. This issue developed from differences of opinion about how to dispose of Italy's former overseas possessions.

As early as 1 January 1945, the P.H.P.S. had reported that

> It is strategically important that none of the Italian overseas possessions should come under the control of any state which might become a potential enemy since they flank our sea and air communications

---

28. The C.O.S. attitude to short-term strategic planning during the unexpectedly brief period of American atomic monopoly was to be summed up early in 1949, whilst it still endured: 'We have always maintained that Russia is unlikely to embark on a premeditated war before 1957 .... Should it come unexpectedly we shall have to fight with what we have got; but we shall have a monopoly of the atomic bomb .... We believe, therefore, that having taken precautionary measures, we must turn our attention to longer term plans.' (DO(49)3)

through the Mediterranean and the Red Sea. They also provide bases from which Egypt, the Sudan and Kenya could be attacked.[29]

The following September, the Joint Planners had strongly deprecated a Soviet proposal to be given the trusteeship of Tripolitania as incompatible with

our military object ... to maintain our predominant position in the Middle East and Eastern Mediterranean.[30]

The question was still current five months later, when the Chiefs of Staff reiterated their endorsement of these views and declared themselves in general agreement with the South African Prime Minister's

mistrust of Russian intentions which have, during the past few months, become more openly directed towards strategic and political influence in the Mediterranean and Middle East.

Under no circumstances would sole Soviet trusteeship of any of the Italian colonies be militarily acceptable, and combined trusteeship should be agreed to only as a last resort—and then only on condition that the Principal Administrator in any particular colony should never be Russian. Militarily, it would be better to return Tripolitania to the Italians.[31]

Attlee was unhappy with the whole basis of this approach, and he attacked it as outdated and impractical in a paper circulated to the Chiefs of Staff on 22 February 1946. He remained to be convinced that Mediterranean communications were a vital British interest, or that they could be safeguarded under modern conditions of warfare. The United Kingdom could not, in his opinion, afford the very great expenditure required to secure what was, at best, merely a chance of being able to use this route in wartime. With India by no means certain to stay within the Commonwealth, and in any case becoming increasingly dependent upon her own army for defence, it was

doubtful if the time saved by the use of the Mediterranean route for the purpose presumably of reinforcing India is worth the cost.

---

29. PHP(44)30(0)(Final) 30. JP(45)251(Final)
31. COS(46)43(0)—based upon JP(46)26(Revised Final)(Special Access)

Nor could it be justified by reference to Persian and Iraqi oil supplies, as the area seemed indefensible against a determined attack from the north. In the changed conditions of the world, and under modern conditions of warfare, long-standing strategic conceptions had to be re-examined:

> In the present era we must consider very carefully how to make the most of our limited resources. We must not, for sentimental reasons based on the past, give hostages to fortune. It may be we shall have to consider the British Isles as an easterly extension of a strategic era [*sic*], the centre of which is the American Continent, rather than as a power looking through the Mediterranean to India and the East.

What was needed was a review of the strategic position of the British Commonwealth in the light of existing technical and economic conditions.[32]

The Chiefs of Staff considered all this on 25 February. Alanbrooke suggested that the Joint Planning Staff should certainly prepare a report of the type requested, but that, in the meantime, the Prime Minister should be told that Service views on the strategic importance of the former Italian colonies remained unaltered.[33] Although the findings of the Joint Technical Warfare Committee were still awaited, preliminary guidance now had to be given to the J.P.S. on the significance of the atomic bomb, and its members were advised that the new device

> had not altered the principles of war on which our strategy had always been based. It had intensified certain factors affecting these principles.

Scientific developments would be an asset to the United Kingdom in offsetting the advantages of an opponent with greater resources of manpower. As for the issue worrying Attlee, it would be difficult for an aggressive Russia to support large forces capable of disrupting British communications in the Mediterranean and Middle East.[34]

It took until 27 March for the report to be completed, but, when it came before the Chiefs of Staff two days later, Tedder and Alanbrooke felt that an increase in emphasis on the need for defensive depth was required. The V.C.N.S. concurred, and added, with respect to Attlee's argument, that

---

32.   COS(46)54(0)   33.   COS(46)31st Mtg (16)
34.   JP(46)45(T.R.)(Special Access)

whereas the Russians were developing a policy of surrounding their country with a belt of satellite states, thus gaining depth in defence, by withdrawing our influence from the Middle East we should be doing exactly the opposite.

Tedder remarked that the security of the alternative route via the Cape depended entirely upon South Africa being a belligerent—a state of affairs on which it might be unsound to rely—and it was also agreed that a paragraph should be included on the importance of the oil factor, despite the fact that 'the oil bearing areas were "in the outpost line" in any war with Russia'.[35]

After making the necessary alterations, the Directors of Plans re-circulated the paper on 31 March, and the following day it was approved virtually as it stood for submission to the Defence Committee.[36] Entitled 'Strategic Position of the British Commonwealth', it was intended to establish where British vital interests lay as a prelude to the development of plans to protect them. They were examined in the context of a war between the Soviet Union and 'her satellites' on the one hand and the Commonwealth and United States on the other. The first step was to identify what were termed 'main support areas'—those regions containing such concentrations of manpower, industrial potential or sources of food or raw materials as to render them essential to the British war effort. The situation of one of these, the United Kingdom, was peculiar in that it contained 63 per cent of the white manpower of the Commonwealth, and an even greater proportion of its industrial potential, but was at the same time in a highly vulnerable position geographically. Failing impracticable mass transfers of population and industry, it would have to remain classified as a main support area regardless of this handicap. The other three such regions were the American continents; Africa, south of the Sahara but including East Africa; and Australia and New Zealand. India was not included for the present on account of her uncertain political future, though it was hoped that eventual stability and development would enable her to take her place as a main support area at the earliest possible opportunity. Not only were there vast resources of men and industrial potential in the sub-continent, but—as preliminary J.T.W.C.

---

35.   JP(46)45(Final)(Retained—Cabt. Off.) & COS(46)51st Mtg (3)(Retained—Cabt. Off.)

36.   JP(46)45(Revised Final)(Retained—Cabt. Off.) & COS(46)52nd Mtg (16) (Retained—Cabt. Off.)

researches had confirmed, and a map attached to the paper illustrated—
the airfields of North-West India had great offensive possibilities
against the Soviet Union. Atlantic, Pacific and Indian Ocean sea
communications between the main support areas were of vital
importance, the first of these especially so if the United Kingdom were
to survive.

Turning to the Attlee thesis, the report observed that a policy of
concentrating on the protection only of main support areas and their
communications in peacetime might, on the face of it, serve to reduce
the level of Commonwealth commitments and to create substantial
buffer zones between Western forces and those of the Soviet Union. It
was, however,

> a fallacy to suppose that, where territories of strategic importance are
> concerned, hiatus areas would exist for long between zones of Russian
> interest and those of our interest. If we cut our commitments and thereby
> lose our predominant position in such areas, these areas with the war-
> making potential they contain will, sooner or later, be dominated by
> Russia.

If the British moved out in peacetime, the Soviet Union would move in,
pursuing her policy of extending her influence to further strategic areas
by all means short of open war. Concentration solely on main support
areas would result in Soviet domination of all of Europe less the United
Kingdom, of North-West Africa, and of the Middle East and North-
East Africa. This would present a grave threat to British sea communications, arising from hostile control of the entire Atlantic coastline
from the North Cape to French Morocco. Mediterranean communications would be cut, and reinforcement by air would be severely restricted because of the much greater distances now involved. Under the
circumstances, it was doubtful if the industrial potential of the United
Kingdom could then be sustained:

> The threat to its sea communications, coupled with the direct threat by
> air attack and long-range bombardment from the mainland of Europe,
> would introduce a grave risk that the United Kingdom would be reduced
> to a Malta-type existence, contributing little to the main war
> potential.

Soviet control of Western Europe, Northern Africa and the Middle
East would also exacerbate the threat to India and South Africa, and

would add considerably (if not decisively) to Soviet resources of manpower and industry. It would greatly reduce the prospect of offensive operations against the Russians; it would increase the depth of Soviet defences; and it would correspondingly diminish the depth of defence available to the Western Powers, thus depriving them of the time needed to organise their forces. Although the West would very probably have to give ground in some of these areas were a conflict to begin, there was no justification whatsoever for surrendering British influence in them in advance of the outbreak of war.

Only the maintenance of a scientific and technical lead and of air and naval superiority might counterbalance the very great manpower advantage of the Soviet Union. It seemed, indeed, that

the threat of attack by air or long-range weapons will be our one effective military deterrent to Russian aggression.

Yet, of the main support areas currently certain to be available, only the United Kingdom could constitute a base from which to mount such attacks; and such were the ranges involved—a 2,000-mile arc falling significantly short of the Urals—that the United Kingdom would not be sufficient for the purpose alone. Five further regions were therefore considered, not just as possible counter-offensive bases, though, but also as territory essential to the security of the main support areas because of the time they could buy them and the resources they contained, which should, at least, be denied to the 'probable enemy' in peacetime.

In the first place, the loss of Western Europe and Scandinavia would pose a direct threat to the British Isles and add appreciably to Soviet war potential. It might not be possible 'entirely to prevent this' after the outbreak of hostilities, but sufficient support at least to prevent Soviet domination there in peacetime should certainly be provided. Secondly, apart from denying access to the Western and Central Mediterranean, Soviet control in North-West Africa and the Iberian peninsula would also adversely affect the British position in peace and would directly threaten Atlantic communications in war. India's role was re-emphasised as a supplementary region fulfilling three functions: as a source of war potential, an air-striking base, and a shield for Western influence in South-East Asia—a fourth area of considerable import-ance, in this case in relation to the defence of both India and Australia.

However, in view of Attlee's preoccupations, the greatest attention was paid to the value of the Middle East, despite the temptation to believe that withdrawal might lead to Soviet over-extension and despite the difficulties of trying to defend the region in wartime. The Middle East offered the easiest route for a European-Asiatic Power to advance into Africa. Pre-existing military facilities in Egypt and Palestine would give the Russians a ready-made jumping-off base from which to expand westwards and southwards and to exert influence in the Indian Ocean. British control of the Middle East would buy time to organise the defence of South Africa and India. The region could also make an important contribution to the deterrence of Soviet aggression. Its air-force bases were closer to South Russian industrial and oil centres than any in other areas which might perhaps be retained in peacetime. Furthermore, the importance of the Middle Eastern oilfields was such as to justify holding on to them for as long as was physically possible.

It was not suggested that, in all five additional areas, a display of military force would be needed to prevent the spread of Soviet influence:

> Our influence can be established in varying ways, by political action and
> by our economic policy as well as by the presence of armed forces.

It was perfectly clear that the country could not afford to maintain in peace all the forces that would be required if political action alone would not suffice in some cases. Since it was expected to do so, and since Foreign Office views indicated that political and economic interests were tending to coincide with strategic ones, the fulfilment of the requirements outlined might well prove practicable. The Chiefs of Staff were pleased to see that the diplomats were opposed to any abandonment of the Mediterranean role, and the paper fully endorsed claims that this would destroy British influence in Spain, France, Italy, Yugoslavia, Greece and Turkey; that it would mean the forfeiting of interests in Iraq and Egypt; that the 'principles of Western civilisation' would be lost to the area; that trade would suffer; and that the formation of what was now termed a 'Western Zone' under the aegis of the United Nations would become impossible. Finally, the report stated that new developments in weapons and methods of warfare would probably not radically alter the nature of the Commonwealth's main strategic needs, since these were based principally upon unchanging facts of geography and the distribution of manpower and natural resources.[37]

At the Defence Committee meeting of 5 April which considered the C.O.S. appreciation, Alanbrooke recapitulated all the basic points and enlarged on the atomic dimension:

> although it was too early to estimate precisely the effect of the tactical use of atomic bombs, our attacks on the depots and bases from which any enemy advance was maintained, might well cripple such an advance for a long period.

In response to Prime Ministerial doubts whether the Commonwealth could provide the forces necessary to support a 'forward' policy in the Mediterranean and Middle East, the C.I.G.S. argued that, as the Chiefs of Staff were proposing just a small garrisoning force in the area, this was

> militarily a small premium to pay for ensuring that we obtained the time necessary to mobilise our resources at the start of a major war. If there was no opposition to an enemy advance into the Middle East, we should be faced at the outset with an immediate threat to the security of our support areas and communications, and the prospect of losing the whole Middle East oil supply.

No sooner had Alanbrooke finished than Bevin intervened. He backed the Chiefs of Staff completely. Diplomatic strength could not be maintained if military support were to be withdrawn. The Russians only respected nations with the power to command respect, and, in any case,

> our presence in the Mediterranean served a purpose other than military, which was very important to our position as a Great Power. Through this area we brought influence on Southern Europe, Italy, Yugoslavia, Greece and Turkey. Undoubtedly, if we left the Mediterranean, Russia would move in, and the Mediterranean countries together with their commerce and trade, and their importance to our economy, would be lost to us.

In the face of this combined onslaught, Attlee retreated. He still insisted that the 'general approval' which the meeting gave to the paper

---

37. DO(46)47

as a basis for discussions with the leaders of the Dominions should be only provisional; and he stressed that it should be subject to the results of a special examination of the vulnerability of the United Kingdom, about which he was particularly concerned.[38] Nevertheless, there could be no doubt that his radical approach had been severely undermined by the identity of outlook between his Foreign Secretary[39] and his military advisers.

This development could hardly have taken him by surprise. Bevin had set out his own ideas at length in a paper circulated on 13 March in opposition to the Prime Minister's memorandum. This deplored any move to allow France, Italy, Yugoslavia, Greece and Turkey to 'fall, like Eastern Europe, under the totalitarian yoke', and it described the United Kingdom as

> the last bastion of social democracy. It may be said that this now represents our way of life as against the red tooth and claw of American capitalism and the Communist dictatorship of Soviet Russia.[40]

Nor did Attlee himself challenge the basic assumption of possible Soviet hostility, when fighting his rearguard action at the Defence Committee meeting. The fact was that the political climate had drastically changed, and Service hypotheses which had aroused diplomatic anger not many months previously were now no longer objects of contention. It was not that the prospect of open conflict had drawn nearer: despite a J.I.C. estimate that war was unlikely during the coming five years, the Chiefs of Staff had reaffirmed their view on 18 March that it was still too early to make an assumption of any sort for planning purposes as the situation remained too uncertain.[41] Neither were changes in Foreign Office personnel responsible for all the old controversies about tripartite harmony and international order passing into history. Sargent had succeeded Cadogan as Permanent Under-Secretary in February 1946, but as early as the previous November, his former chief had realised that the embryo United Nations Organisation was apparently

---

38.   DO(46)10th Mtg (2)
39.   Alanbrooke's contemporary assessment of Bevin was as 'a most wonderful help-
       ful individual always full of ideas . . . . It is astonishing the ease with which he
       absorbs international situations and the soundness of his judgement.' (Quoted in:
       Bryant, *Triumph in the West*, p. 531)   40.   DO(46)40
41.   COS Sec Min 295/6—missing, but obtainable as Annex VI to COS(46)38th
       Mtg—& COS(46)42nd Mtg (1)

a moderate parody of the League [of Nations], with *all* the failings and no advantages, that I can see.[42]

Soviet insistence on the Great Power veto had ruled out any possibility of it preventing a breakdown in international security in the event of those states strong enough to endanger it actually deciding to aggress. In July 1945, Sargent himself had still anticipated basing post-war foreign policy upon the principle of Three Power co-operation, and had still been emphasising Soviet desires for security.[43] Even in September, John Ward was writing minutes to the effect that

Whereas the Foreign Office have had primarily in mind reinsurance against a renewal of German aggression ... the Chiefs of Staff have made it plain that their main interest in the Western Group is their fear of Russia entering on a Napoleonic phase.[44]

Yet, by January 1946, Sir Nigel Ronald—one of the foremost proponents of the 'Four Power' thesis in its day—was remarking that

We must not blink the obvious fact that the real struggle is fundamentally an ideological one: social democracy versus communism.[45]

The key to this hardening of attitudes was Soviet behaviour in Eastern Europe, notably—according to Jebb[46]—the cynical mockery it made of the Yalta 'Declaration on Liberated Europe' of February 1945. This had proclaimed the 'right of all peoples to choose the form of government under which they will live', and had anticipated 'the earliest possible establishment through free elections of governments responsible to the will of the people'.[47] Commenting on the communisation of the Soviet zone of Germany, Bevin observed in March 1946 that

The aim of these manoeuvres seems to be to include the eastern half of Germany in a solid block of Soviet-controlled territories stretching from Lübeck to Trieste. Finland, Poland, Hungary, Romania, Yugoslavia,

42.   Quoted in: D. Dilks (ed.), *The Diaries of Sir Alexander Cadogan, 1938–1945* (London, Cassell, 1971), p. 786   43.   U5471/5471/70
44.   U7851/445/70   45.   Z2410/120/72
46.   Interview with Lord Gladwyn, 12 November 1980
47.   Quoted in: Dilks, *op. cit.*, p. 716

> Bulgaria and Albania are either in the bag already or very nearly so. The prospect of Czechoslovakia holding out is not too hopeful.

The fate of Austria was in the balance, as was that of Greece, where the leftist 'E.A.M.' (Popular Front) was fighting for control. Turkey was being subjected to a 'war of nerves' designed to force her, also, into 'the Soviet orbit'.[48]

Even more vehement was a memorandum circulated in the Foreign Office on 2 April, and entitled 'The Soviet Campaign against this Country and Our Response to It', which declared that the Russian leaders

> both in their recent pronouncements and in their actions have made it clear that they have decided upon an aggressive policy based upon militant Communism and Russian chauvinism . . . . The interests of this country and the true democratic principles for which we stand are directly threatened.

The Soviet Union had returned to the pure doctrine of Marx-Lenin-Stalinism and had announced to the world that it proposed to play an aggressive political role while making an intensive drive to increase its own military and industrial strength. It would be as unwise to refuse to take the Russians at their word as it had been not to take *Mein Kampf* at its face value, concluded the author of this document—the head of the Northern Department and long-time antagonist of the Chiefs of Staff on this very issue, Christopher Warner. Nor was he the sole apostate by any means. His paper had, in fact, been produced in connection with the first meeting of a formal Foreign Office 'Committee on Policy towards the Soviet Union', the minutes of which recorded the view that

> we should not be mesmerised by the Soviet talk of the need for security. It was a catchword which was being used to support something very like aggression.

This was the antithesis of Sargent's outlook the previous July, but in the weeks ahead the Permanent Under-Secretary was to circulate the memorandum with the full authority of his department.[49]

It was thus apparent, by the time that serious strategic planning was

---

48.　GEN 121/1—annexed to COS(46)93(0)
49.　N5169/5169/38 & N6344/605/38 For extracts from the Warner memorandum, see Appendix 6(i), pp. 359–363 below

resumed in the spring of 1946, that Foreign Office apprehension about post-war Soviet intentions had come into line with C.O.S. apprehension about post-war Soviet capabilities. Probably the most striking illustration of the fact was the fate of a paper on the future of Germany, which the Chiefs of Staff finalised on 5 April.[50] This defined British strategic aims in Western Europe as preventing its being dominated by a potentially hostile Power, and as maintaining an effective strategic frontier as far to the east as possible at the outbreak of hostilities. Consequently, the utmost effort should be made to retain the friendship of France and the Low Countries, and the overall British position would be greatly strengthened if a 'western democratic Germany' were to be established. The magnitude of a combined Russo-German military potential meant that Soviet domination of Germany had to be avoided at all costs. If Germany were regarded as the greater threat, then her war-making capacity should be kept to a minimum; but,

> if Russia is considered the more serious danger, our policy towards Germany should be such as would not prevent us from building her up again if this becomes necessary.

Though high-level political issues which could not yet be finally settled were involved in this matter, if a policy had to be chosen for the immediate future, there could be no doubt that, from the military point of view, the Soviet Union was the more likely potential enemy. Should a conflict with the Russians occur, German resistance might gain the time required for the British effort to be developed and for American resources to be brought into play:

> It would clearly be politically unacceptable, nor is it militarily necessary, to adopt a policy of rebuilding Germany in the immediate future. We consider, however, that our policy should be shaped to give us maximum freedom to do this later in case it should prove to be necessary.

Whatever measures were selected, long-term policy could not be determined solely with a view to preventing a renewed German threat.[51]

---

50. COS(46)54th Mtg (6)
51. COS(46)105(0)—based upon JP(46)65(Final)(Special Access) of 4 April 1946
   Both versions refer to 'keeping at least Western Germany outside the "iron curtain" ', Churchill's speech immortalising the metaphor having been delivered early the previous month.

The recapitulation of this argument, which had caused such a stir when first set out in July 1944, now produced not the slightest Foreign Office objection. Not only did Bevin circulate the C.O.S. paper to the Cabinet as an annex to one of his own, but he summarised its arguments and incorporated them *en bloc* into the body of his text.[52] The military-diplomatic conflict was over.

3. Components of Commonwealth Defence

The imminence of a conference of Dominions Prime Ministers, due in April-May 1946, largely shaped the direction of strategic planning immediately after the report on the Commonwealth's strategic position was given provisional approval. In their regional surveys from July 1944 onwards, the Post-Hostilities Planners had regularly stressed the value of imperial defence co-operation after the war, but the most substantial study of the subject had already been carried out towards the end of March of that year by the members of the Joint Planning Staff. They had regarded it as of

> great importance that the British Commonwealth should be in a position to throw its whole weight into the scale when vital issues are at stake. . . . its representatives in any one region must be able to call upon the whole resources of the Commonwealth when required.

If it were to take its place alongside the United States and Russia in the settlement of post-war problems, its constituent states would have to forge much closer links.[53] Accordingly, a number of J.P.S. proposals to this end had been endorsed by the Vice-Chiefs of Staff and put to a meeting of Dominions leaders in May 1944. The South Africans had been absent and the Canadians non-committal, but Australia and New Zealand had been generally enthusiastic. However, no further action was taken until October 1945, when the Chiefs of Staff agreed to recommend that another approach should be made to the four governments with a view to co-ordinating national defence policies at periodic imperial conferences.[54]

It was with this in mind that, on 1 March 1946, the Service chiefs adopted a suggestion of Alanbrooke's that the Joint Planners be

---

52. CP(46)139 considered at CM(46)36th Concls (3)
53. JP(44)87(Final)—circulated by the Vice-Chiefs as COS(44)58 & DPM(44)18
54. COS(45)625(0) & COS(45)252nd Mtg (8)

instructed to draft a report for the Defence Committee on the organisation of 'zones of defence' in the Middle East, India, South-East Asia and Australasia.[55] This was completed on 27 March[56] and formed the basis of a C.O.S. paper presented to the same ministerial meeting which considered the one on the strategic position of the Commonwealth. A map attached to this report set out three vertical zonal boundaries and one horizontal one. The Middle East Zone would cover the Mediterranean and Middle East, including Persia, Arabia and East Africa. The central Indian Zone would consist of the sub-continent itself, Burma, Ceylon and the Indian Ocean area. However, the Far Eastern theatre would be subdivided into a northerly South-East Asia Zone and a southerly Australia/New Zealand Zone (or Zones), as those two Dominions would probably not agree to participate in a unified Far East Zone under British control, yet lacked the resources to take overall responsibility for such an extensive area themselves. In each zone, there would be an inter-Service headquarters and a 'Defence Committee' to co-ordinate civil and military require-ments; but

> The planning of . . . overall strategy and policy for the defence of the Commonwealth must . . . be carried out in . . . London and the Dominion capitals, since the overall picture in regard to resources, political information, intelligence and scientific developments will not be available to individual zones.

The defence organisations within the zones would be complementary to the higher defence machinery in London and the other capitals— providing information and advice upon which overall policy could be based, and co-ordinating the measures necessary to implement it.[57]

Alanbrooke explained to the ministers that Canada had been excluded from consideration in view of her reluctance to undertake Commonwealth commitments which might jeopardise her position *vis-à-vis* the United States. Apart from being requested to contribute to security arrangements in the Caribbean and West Indies, Canada should mainly be looked to as a potential partner in plans to standardise British and American arms and equipment. The Defence Committee duly approved the report for discussion at the forthcoming Prime Ministers' meeting.[58] Twelve days later, on 17 April, the J.P.S. brought

---

55.   COS(46)33rd Mtg (5) & JP(46)49(0)(T.R.)(Special Access)
56.   JP(46)49(Final)(Special Access)
57.   DO(46)46   58.   DO(46)10th Mtg (4)

out a somewhat revised version, incorporating a limited Canadian
Zone after all and carving out a separate South African Zone from that
formerly covering the Middle East;[59] but the Chiefs of Staff agreed with
Vice-Admiral McGrigor on 18 April that the paper

> raised questions of some controversy and appeared to reach definite
> conclusions on them before the Dominions had been consulted.

It was therefore decided to use it as an *aide-mémoire* rather than to give
copies to Dominions leaders, at least until the progress of talks on this
subject could be discerned.[60]

Other C.O.S. papers received less qualified endorsement for the
impending conference, however. One was a re-draft of the report on the
Commonwealth's strategic position, which had initially been devised
largely to rebut Attlee's doubts about the Mediterranean and Middle
East. The new version was essentially an abridgement. The whole
question of not withdrawing to the main support areas was dealt with
summarily, the detailed case against withdrawal being cut out
completely. Yet there were some substantive alterations—notably in
the emphasis placed on India *as* a main support area, which it would be
'of the utmost importance' to retain, rather than as a future candidate
for this status. Some topical elements were also introduced, including a
comment that, in Western Europe and the Middle East,

> Russian pressure is already evident and we must anticipate that this will
> be extended to India and possibly South-East Asia also.[61]

At Alanbrooke's insistence, it had been pointed out that the distinction
drawn between regions which were and were not main support areas

---

59.   JP(46)74(Final)(Special Access)
60.   COS(46)62nd Mtg (4) The zonal scheme was to be reconsidered in May 1947,
       in view of the impending loss of India. The then C.I.G.S., Viscount
       Montgomery, produced a paper allocating enlarged zones to all four
       Dominions, but with notable gaps in the system where the formerly interlinked
       Indian and Middle Eastern Zones were concerned. On this occasion, though,
       the Chiefs of Staff declined to endorse the readjustment, though agreeing that
       'any move on the part of the Dominions to extend their responsibility towards
       Empire defence, and in particular to the extension of responsibility for their own
       zones of defence, would be cordially welcomed'. (COS(47)99(0)(Retained—
       MoD) & COS (47)64th Mtg (4)(Retained—MoD))
61.   COS(46)119(0)(Retained—Cabt. Off.)—based upon JP(46)82(Revised Final)
       (Retained—Cabt. Off.)

should not be obscured by the need to maintain influence in both. Military preparations would have to be concentrated on the former, with only limited commitments being made in respect of the latter:

> Naturally, it was our policy to keep our frontiers as far from the main support areas as possible, but the method of doing this in peacetime would depend largely on political action.[62]

Another report prepared for the conference sought definite undertakings from the Dominions in respect of future contributions towards Commonwealth defence. According to this, each Dominion should accept responsibility for the development and defence of its respective main support area and surrounding strategic zone, and should acknowledge the importance of helping to maintain the Commonwealth position wherever its own military security might otherwise be adversely affected. The principle of joint responsibility for the protection of lines of communications between main support areas by those Commonwealth nations concerned in each case should also be endorsed. Specific commitments were not set out in that part of the report destined for the Dominions leaders themselves, but the Chiefs of Staff had a very clear idea of what they wanted 'as a first step': South African assistance in the Middle East; an Australian and New Zealand contribution in Malaya and South-East Asia generally, as well as in Japan as at present; reversal of the Canadian intention to withdraw occupational forces from the British Zone in Germany; and the provision, if required, of Canadian garrisons in the West Indies.[63]

As the senior C.O.S. secretary was later to note, however, the meeting of Prime Ministers led to 'no concrete offers of assistance' on the part of the Dominions. It showed there to be no prospect of concluding definite political agreements with members of the Commonwealth which would bind them to act together when its security was endangered.[64] Apart from general agreement upon the fundamental strategic propositions put forward as a basis for future discussions, the only practical progress made was the adoption of a scheme outlined in a fourth C.O.S. paper, which recommended that

---

62.   COS(46)61st Mtg (4)(Retained—Cabt. Off.)
63.   COS(46)117(0)—based upon JP(46)71(Final)(Special Access)
64.   Cornwall-Jones minute to Home of 9 October 1946, in CAB 21/1800

the United Kingdom should maintain a mission in each Dominion while the Dominions should maintain similar missions in London.[65]

It was approved in principle by the conference on 2 May,[66] and, just over twelve months later, a system of 'Service Liaison Staffs' came into operation. This was comparable to that used successfully with the Americans through the Joint Staff Mission in Washington, though modified in certain respects to cater for differences in the structure of military organisations in the Dominions.[67]

With the distraction of the conference behind them, and the revised report on future warfare about to be approved, the Chiefs of Staff were able by mid-1946 to consider once again how to take overall strategic planning a stage further forward. As in the case of the setting up of the Tizard Committee nearly two years before, however, the particular stimulus to action came from outside the military machine. On 21 June, the Service chiefs endorsed a suggestion by the Foreign Secretary that an 'Oil Planning Staff' should be created to prepare plans for oil development and the location of oil refineries.[68] In the course of their discussion of this proposal,

> it was suggested that a Special Future Operational Planning Section should be established to prepare an appreciation of the general military situation that might arise in approximately 5–7 years.

This new F.P.S. should draw upon the expertise of the Joint Planners, but would have to be separate from them in view of their almost total commitment to the study of current problems. Though the production of a major appreciation would naturally take some time, the new section would be confined solely to that task. In recognition of the importance of their role in furnishing a 'reasoned background' against which present-day problems could be assessed, its members should be of a rank 'equivalent to or perhaps above Director level'.[69]

This last point caused some concern amongst the Directors of Plans. On 25 June, a draft paper was prepared strongly pressing for

> any planners exclusively engaged on the study referred to ... to be responsible to the Directors of Plans.

65.   DO(46)54—based upon JP(46)78(Final)(Special Access) and approved at
       DO(46)13th Mtg (1)   66.   PMM(46)20 & PMM(46)10th Mtg (1)
67.   COS(47)63   68.   COS(46)96th Mtg (7)   69.   COS(46)96th Mtg (8)

There would be

> grave disadvantages in creating two parallel but independent bodies with responsibility for the formulation of strategic and operational plans.

The abolition of the post of wartime F.O.P.S. Director and the bringing of his organisation fully within the J.P.S.; the failure of the Future Operations (Enemy) Section as a body distinct from the J.I.C.; and the growing tendency towards calling in the Joint Planners to comment upon the work of the Post-Hostilities Planning Staff, were all cited in support of the thesis that 'strategy is indivisible'. What was needed was an additional team working alongside the rest of the J.P.S. in the Cabinet Offices and making periodic reference to it. The rank of the new planners should be at least that of Colonel or its equivalent, but it would create difficulties were it to be senior to that of the Directors themselves.[70]

Although this J.P.S. draft was never finalised, the arguments it contained would appear to have been put to the Chiefs of Staff informally by 3 July, when they decided that the new section should indeed be 'constituted under the Directors of Plans' as soon as the Army and Royal Air Force representatives were posted to it.[71] However, questions of rank were not allowed to interfere unduly with the choice of nominees. Brigadier Charles Richardson, formerly a planner with Montgomery's 1944 invasion force, would be the War Office representative. He could begin preliminary work as a member of the J.P.S. with effect from 1 August.[72] A temporary R.A.F. representative would work with him until Group Captain Edmund Hudleston became available in January 1947. Despite his formal listing, Hudleston had held the wartime substantive rank of Air Commodore and had even been designated Acting Air Vice-Marshal, for a period, late in 1944. Most senior of all would be the Admiralty member—Acting Rear-Admiral Charles Lambe, a successful wartime Director of Plans who had been appointed A.C.N.S. (Air) in 1945. His release to the new section would not be possible before December 1946.

On 11 July it was agreed by the Vice-Chiefs of Staff that the bulk of the collating and drafting work should be carried out by a special team of junior staff officers,[73] and on 20 August the Future Planning Section

70. JP(46)126(Draft)(Special Access)
72. JP(46)134(Final)(Special Access)
71. COS(46)102nd Mtg (3)
73. COS(46)107th Mtg (1)

was issued with formal terms of reference. The object of its study would be

> to provide a reasoned background against which H.M. Government can formulate Commonwealth Defence Policy in its widest aspects, with particular reference to the critical period when we are likely to be in the transitional stage between accepted conventional methods of war and the radical changes foreshadowed.

It should evaluate long-term strategic requirements on the supposition of a conflict within the decade ahead and in the light of the developments examined in the report of the Joint Technical Warfare Committee. Finally, it should make recommendations about the shape and size of the armed forces to be maintained, the priorities governing their expansion in a crisis, and the scale of such expansion at which to aim.[74]

Whilst the Future Planners began to get this review under way, the rest of the C.O.S. machine continued to tackle more limited strategic topics. The two examined in most depth were those about which the Prime Minister had expressed serious concern[75]—the British role in the Middle East and the vulnerability of the United Kingdom to bombardment.

The Joint Planners' first attempt to re-examine Middle Eastern strategic requirements after the 5 April Defence Committee meeting had been prompted by more than the reservations made by the Prime Minister in the course of it. By 23 May, when their next paper on the subject was finalised, requests had already been received from three separate sources for advice on the military significance of Palestine, Cyrenaica and the Anglo-Egyptian Treaty. To deal with such matters in piecemeal fashion would have gone very much against C.O.S. orthodoxy, and the J.P.S. report therefore took the form of a draft paper for presentation to ministers on the overall situation in the theatre.[76] This was circulated to the members of the Defence Committee on 25 May, and was considered when they met two days later. It painted a grim picture of uncertainty regarding post-war facilities in Egypt, Palestine, the Levant and the former Italian colonies in Africa, and argued that

---

74.   JP(46)164(T.R.)(Special Access)   75.   See pp. 253–4 & 259–60 above
76.   JP(46)100(Final)(Special Access)

from the military point of view, there is a certain basic minimum below which we cannot go if we are to maintain our position in the Middle East at all.

This position would have to be maintained for the reasons of defensive depth, counter-offensive potential, and oil richness which had been set out in the survey of the Commonwealth's strategic position. The key to the whole area lay in Egypt and Palestine. The former was the political and industrial centre of the Middle East and the nodal point of its communications; the latter comprised the core of the natural defences of Egypt against attack from the north. The forces which would be needed to protect the area and to mount offensive counter-action could be maintained only from Egypt in war, though, for political reasons, they could not be stationed there in peacetime. If the Mediterranean route were to remain open, British air bases in Cyrenaica would be essential and there must be no hostile Power in control of Tripolitania. What further measures would be required to safeguard the oil areas had yet to be determined, but—given the constraints of current treaty negotiations—it could be seen that the bare strategic minima would be Egyptian development of facilities for the British to use in a crisis, retention of full military rights in Palestine to enable Egypt to be defended, and possession of fairly substantial ones in Cyrenaica for the protection of the Eastern Mediterranean.[77]

At the Defence Committee meeting on 27 May, Attlee frankly doubted the possibility of meeting these requirements. He did not revert to attacking the actual notion of holding the Middle East and was thus able to command general agreement that the report should not be approved. The Chiefs of Staff should re-examine the whole question once again, this time 'with particular reference to what in the Middle East would it be essential . . . to defend in a possible future war'.[78] They therefore decided that the oil factor and the wider strategic dimension should be fully covered and the importance of the Suez Canal also brought·out:

> Its loss through its effect on communications would not mean the loss of the Middle East area, but its full use was a *sine qua non* to the successful outcome of a war in that area.[79]

---

77. DO(46)67(Revised)   78. DO(46)17th Mtg (1)
79. COS(46)83rd Mtg (22) & COS(46)84th Mtg (4)

The J.P.S. was set to work on 30 May, and on 7 June the Chiefs of Staff approved a paper on Soviet interests and intentions in the Middle East by the J.I.C. which concluded that Russia was resuming her traditional policy of southward expansion in the region.[80] High priority was accorded to the Joint Planners' task, and on 11 June a lengthy draft report to the Defence Committee was finalised for the Chiefs of Staff to consider.[81] This was approved[82] in essence after two C.O.S. meetings, at the first of which it was agreed that measures to defend the oil-producing areas should not be stressed at the expense of encouraging the development of safer, more southerly parts, and that

> in the event of war during the next ten years we should have some forces in Germany for occupational reasons, otherwise we should avoid sending forces to the Continent to fight rearguard action at the expense of maintaining forces in countries overseas where air bases could be established from which to strike at the enemy.[83]

The concept of a counter-offensive of this sort was prominent in the paper circulated for the Defence Committee on 18 June. If British strategy were restricted to the local defence of the United Kingdom, this would enable an enemy

> to concentrate unimpeded his entire effort against us, and would expose us to gradual reduction by the proportion of long-range weapons and aircraft that would penetrate our defences.

If Russia were that enemy, her manpower advantage would have to be offset by making the maximum use of technical and scientific superiority. In particular, this would involve employing air power to strike back at vital centres, war potential, and communications. Abandonment of the Middle East would seriously prejudice British security. Irreplaceable air bases would be lost; Russia would be able to secure her most vulnerable flank; the world's greatest potential source of oil would be denied to the United Kingdom; and a formidable base from which to attack British main support areas would be conceded to the Soviet Union. The forces needed to guard against the resultant

---

80.   JP(46)108(S)(T.R.)(Special Access) & COS(46)90th Mtg (3)(Retained—Cabt. Off.) The conclusion of the J.I.C. report—JIC(46)38(0)(Final)—is recorded in the J.P.S. appreciation.
81.   JP(46)108(Final)(Retained—Cabt. Off.)
82.   COS(46)93rd Mtg (2)   83.   COS(46)92nd Mtg (1)(Retained—Cabt. Off.)

threat from a Sovietised Middle East would be no smaller—though a good deal less favourably placed—than those needed for the defence of the Middle East itself. The vital importance of Egypt and Palestine and the considerable value of Cyrenaica were emphasised once again, and the basic requirements for facilities and/or the right to station forces in those countries were reiterated.[84]

Just over a month was to elapse before the Defence Committee faced up to the issue again, but on 12 July—a week before it did so—Attlee chaired a Staff Conference with the Chiefs of Staff to consider British strategy, with particular reference to this report. He argued that it gave inadequate consideration to the fundamentals of British strategic policy:

> It had been previously accepted that it was vital for the security of the United Kingdom that adjoining coasts should not be in enemy hands. If the problem were considered against the background of war with Russia, there were, between Russia and the United Kingdom, a number of ill-prepared states . . . . He asked whether it was right to assume, therefore, that Russian forces, in the event of a war with Russia, would be in possession of the coasts immediately threatening the United Kingdom.

Tedder, for one, was not prepared to tackle this sort of question on the basis of a regional appreciation; but, in justifying the weight which had been placed upon the Middle East as an offensive air base, the C.N.S. conceded that, at least for the time being, Western Europe could not be considered defensible from the Russians. In which case, retorted Attlee, the United Kingdom would be extremely vulnerable to bombardment by modern projectiles, which were expected to be effective at ranges of up to 400 miles. Although dispersal within the British Isles might be of only limited practicability, 'would not drastic steps have to be taken for the safety of the civilian population?' The new C.I.G.S., Viscount Montgomery, agreed that opportunities for dispersal would be meagre, but he took the view that

> an immediate attack on vital Russian points from the Middle East was the best defence.

Tedder added that Soviet raids on bases in Egypt would also reduce the weight of attack brought to bear against the United Kingdom; but

---

84. DO(46)80

neither point seemed convincing to the Prime Minister, who recalled that

> in spite of German preoccupation elsewhere during the recent war, this country had been subjected to enemy air attack. It was reasonable to assume that if Russia went to war, she would predominate over States in Eastern Europe and have a call on the manpower of those States. Would not any counter-attack we could launch from the Middle East be so limited as to have no appreciable effect on the Russian effort against this country?

Not if directed against essential products such as oil, replied the C.A.S., without which Russia could not fight, and against which attacks could not be ignored. Cunningham also felt that if the United Kingdom could survive the first blow, attacks on vital Soviet resources would then prevail. He agreed that the Middle East was not an ideal base for offensive operations against the Russians, but it remained the best available and its defence was an essential complement to that of the British Isles.

It took Ismay, who normally seldom intervened on purely strategic matters, to make the point that the crucial time-factor had hitherto been ignored:

> If we were right in supposing that there would not be a war for at least five years, the position at the beginning of a war might have considerably changed. For instance, France might have built up her armed forces and the position in Western Europe might be considerably stronger.

On this all could agree, but it in no way weakened the arguments marshalled for a Middle Eastern strategy: a Western bloc would be complementary to it. As for the United States, if she was to give assistance, the first way she would be able to do so would be by participating in the aerial counter-attack from the Middle Eastern bases. The harm caused to her interests in the area by a British withdrawal might damage the prospects for American aid to the United Kingdom in a future war.

Attlee was informed about the F.P.S. review, on which the development of a detailed future strategy would have to depend. He accepted that the United Kingdom could no longer be regarded as the sole base for Commonwealth operations, and pressed for investigations to be made into fuels other than oil and into methods of defending the

British Isles from bombardment.[85] However, if the Chiefs of Staff thought that their paper would now proceed more smoothly through the Defence Committee, they were soon to be disappointed. After lengthy discussion on 19 July, it was generally deemed premature to do more than take note of the report, pending the outcome of the forthcoming Peace Conference—which would enable the future status of European and Middle Eastern countries to be foreseen. Attlee considered that

At the present stage of international negotiations, it would be most dangerous to create suspicion in the mind of the Russians that we were threatening her [*sic*] security in the Middle East.

He also used the compiling of the F.P.S. review against its initiators by arguing that definite decisions on Middle Eastern policy ought not to be taken until the impact of new developments in warfare upon overall strategic conceptions had been fully examined.[86]

Nevertheless, the debate at the 12 July Staff Conference did affect strategic planning in a number of other respects. According to the minutes, the least forthcoming of the three Service chiefs had been the new C.I.G.S. If his own account is to be relied upon,[87] however, Montgomery was rapidly coming to the conclusion that

there was in ministerial and military circles in Whitehall no clear conception about how we would fight a major war . . . . I told my two colleagues that the Chiefs of Staff should write a paper on western strategy in a major war, and submit it to the Prime Minister. They did not agree, pleading lack of sufficient evidence of the power of future weapons and lack of time for their staffs; I then said I would produce the paper in the War Office within a week.

This paper was apparently produced towards the end of July, but agreement could be reached upon only two of its three basic contentions—that sea communications must be secured, and that the Middle East should be fought for and utilised for the launching of a 'tremendous air offensive' against an Eastern aggressor. The third contention was that support be given to the formation of a strong Western bloc, with the undertaking of a commitment

---

85. COS(46)108th Mtg (Retained—Cabt. Off.)   86. DO(46)22nd Mtg (1)
87. There are inaccuracies—such as a description of the Middle East as a 'main support area'.

to fight on the mainland of Europe, alongside our Allies, with all that that entailed.

This the other two Service chiefs were not prepared to countenance in mid-1946, and, as a newcomer to Whitehall, the C.I.G.S. felt unable to force the issue for the time being.[88] It seems that the relevant documents were withdrawn from circulation before any serious confrontation could develop at C.O.S. Committee level.[89]

It was also in the aftermath of the conference with Attlee that attention became focused more closely upon the air defence problem which was causing him such concern. A.D.G.B. planning had continued steadily since the basic policy paper by the Post-Hostilities Planning Sub-Committee had been provisionally approved in May 1944.[90] Most of it was undertaken by a C.O.S. 'Sub-Committee on the Allocation of Active Air Defences', which had been established under the Deputy Chiefs of Staff in November 1939, to 'consider all applications for active air defence', and to make recommendations where necessary.[91] On 25 August 1944, a report had been produced, tentatively suggesting that a nucleus force of some 37,000 R.A.F. and 34,000 Anti-Aircraft Command personnel would suffice as the post-war basis for full-scale expansion over a two-year period. The importance of intelligence, research and technical superiority was emphasised, and apprehension expressed at 'the appalling vulnerability of London' to bombardment.[92] This report was revised in the light of departmental comments, and was re-circulated on 15 June 1945. Its central conception now was the division of the United Kingdom into 'Defended' and 'Shadow' areas. The former would extend clockwise around the country from North-East Scotland to the coast of South Wales, and would be manned by a nucleus force which could be

---

88. Viscount Montgomery, *The Memoirs of Field-Marshal Montgomery* (London, Collins, 1958), pp. 435–6; 498
89. Two papers—COS(46)201(0) & COS(46)202(0)—are recorded as having been withdrawn in late July 1946, but their contents cannot now be ascertained. A Cabinet Office search has confirmed there to be no retained material referring to this episode. (J. Robertson to author, 24 March 1981)
90. See pp. 85–6 above
91. DCOS(39)13th Mtg (3) & DCOS(AA)1 From October 1940, this sub-committee usually reported to the Vice-Chiefs of Staff, (DCOS(AA)195). In January 1947, it was to be amalgamated with a C.O.S. 'Defence of Bases Committee' to form a 'Sub-Committee for Air, Coast and Seaward Defences', (COS(46)275 & COS(47)10th Mtg (3)).
92. COS(AA)(44)30(Final)—also circulated as COS(44)766(0)

expanded 'to provide a reasonable active defence at short notice'. The latter, covering the remainder of the British Isles, would be served only by an 'air defence framework' capable of expansion to full efficiency within two years, but of very limited value in the short run.[93] When this was put to the Prime Minister in July,[94] however, Churchill remarked that it was impracticable to consider A.D.G.B. in isolation from 'the whole post-war lay-out' and declined to approve the paper.[95] Yet it still remained the basis for planning, subject to specific steps needing immediate sanction being put to the appropriate departmental or ministerial committees as they arose.[96]

Attlee's first direct involvement with the issue as Prime Minister had been in connection with one of these steps—a proposal made to the Defence Committee on 8 March 1946 that the Royal Observer Corps, stood down the previous May, should be revived on an unpaid voluntary basis. By its visual reporting of aircraft movements in detail, it could provide a service which modern radar alone still could not match.[97] Attlee felt that the Chiefs of Staff should review existing air defence arrangements before any decision on the corps was taken.[98] This they were in any case bound to do on receiving a report dated 10 April from Air Marshal Sir James Robb, the Commander-in-Chief of Fighter Command. So far as short-term protection was concerned, Robb declared the present set-up to be totally inadequate. Only a greatly increased manpower commitment, coupled with greatly improved radar coverage and provisions for rapid reinforcement and the retention of many more installations than those currently earmarked, could prevent the outflanking of the Defended Area and the defeat of the A.D.G.B. system.[99] On 17 June, the Chiefs of Staff accepted the view of their Active Air Defences Allocation Sub-Committee that

> our present defences, as well as being ineffective through lack of resources, are obsolescent, having been built up by hasty wartime improvisation,[100]

---

93. COS(AA)(45)8(Final)—also circulated as COS(45)390(0)
94. COS(45)436(0)
95. Prime Minister's Personal Min No D.(Ter.)1/5 of 17 July 1945, annexed to COS(45)478(0)   96. COS(45)182nd Mtg (4)   97. DO(46)33
98. DO(46)7th Mtg (6)
99. COS(AA)(46)18(Final)(Retained—Cabt. Off.)—also circulated as COS (46)157(0)   100. *Ibid.* & COS(46)94th Mtg (19)

and by 12 July a draft report, spelling out the situation for the Defence Committee, had been prepared.[101] Consequently, the Prime Minister's remarks on the subject at the Middle Eastern strategy Staff Conference added urgency and emphasis to the review. The new V.C.A.S., Air Marshal Sir William Dickson, felt that the Defence Committee

> should not be deluded that any more than a very small measure of air defence could be provided in an emergency during the next two years.[102]

The finalised review was circulated on 2 August and considered by the Defence Committee five days later. It revealed that, over the preceding twelve months, manpower restrictions had forced the Air Ministry temporarily to reduce Fighter Command to a minimum of just nine day-fighter and three night-fighter squadrons. Though just sufficient to 'maintain the technique' of fighter defence, this force afforded cover to only about half of the originally designated Defended Area. A slow build-up was planned, but if an emergency occurred within the next two years, very little protection for the rest of the country would be available in the early stages. For the long term, emphasis would have to be placed on research, development, preparation of reserves, and the establishment of an effective raid-reporting organisation; but the fact ought to be accepted that

> during the next two years our fighter defence organisation immediately available will be restricted to the area in south-eastern England between Flamborough Head and Portland Bill.[103]

This time-scale was, of course, in line with the 'no-war' planning assumption which had been adopted in February. The Defence Committee thus approved the adoption of those measures requiring immediate implementation, according to the review, if a satisfactory air defence system were to become operational in 1948.[104]

Anticipatory planning continued with a report ·produced by the C.O.S.(A.A.) Sub-Committee on 29 August. This took the revised Tizard report into account, showed that effective fighter operations

---

101. COS(AA)(46)23(Revise)(Retained—Cabt. Off.)—also circulated as COS (46)176(0)(Revise)
102. COS(46)116th Mtg (10) & COS(46)120th Mtg (4)   103. DO(46)98
104. DO(46)24th Mtg (2)

Vulnerability of the United Kingdom to air attack, 1946 (CAB 80/101: COS(46)157(0)
—also COS (AA)(46)18(Final)—Annex III)

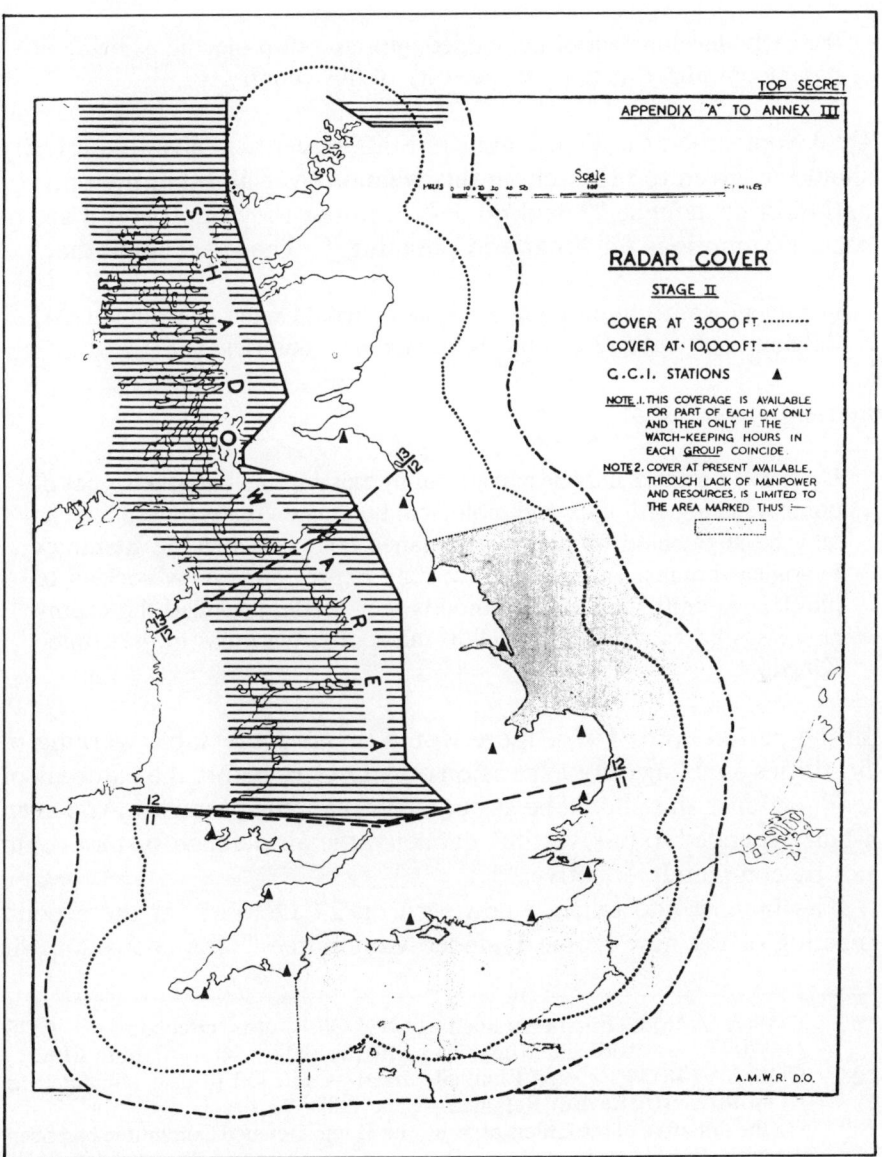

'The Raid Reporting and Control System in the Shadow Area cannot be manned. Not only, therefore, is the cover in the Defended Area sparse and inadequate, but the defences could be outflanked and the country could thus be attacked without warning.'—*Chiefs of Staff Sub-Committee on the Allocation of Active Air Defences, 6 June 1946*

over the sea would largely depend upon early warning from the Continent, and recognised

> the early development of the guided anti-aircraft projectile as being of paramount importance to the security of this country.[105]

On 3 September, the Vice-Chiefs of Staff agreed that absolute priority should be given to research on this weapon over all other methods of anti-aircraft defence,[106] and on 1 November they approved a set of basic assumptions for long-term planning.[107] These accepted that

> in a major war to come a potential enemy would again overrun France, Belgium and Holland and the Scandinavian countries,

and anticipated that

> Up to 1951 attacks may be carried out by existing and improved types of bombers using orthodox and biological bombs; thereafter these attacks may be augmented by high performance bombers carrying atomic or biological bombs. In addition, we may expect attacks by rockets or pilotless aircraft fitted with orthodox war-heads, provided the enemy possesses bases within 600 to 800 miles of target areas in the United Kingdom.

In the period up to 1956, there would be no appreciable warning of hostilities enabling prior expansion of A.D.G.B. before the outbreak of war—at least, this should be assumed for planning purposes. And even when expanded to full wartime capacity, the air defence system could not be completely effective.[108]

The inquiry had taken a new turn on 24 October, at the second meeting of the new Home Defence Committee.[109] Its chairman, Sir

---

105. COS(AA)(46)32(Final)(Retained—Cabt. Off.)—also circulated as COS (46)207   106. COS(46)135th Mtg (4)   107. COS(46)160th Mtg (1)

108. COS(AA)(46)39(Revised Final)(Retained—Cabt. Off.)—also circulated as COS(46)251(0)(Revise)(Retained—Cabt. Off.)

109. On the initiative of the Chiefs of Staff, the Home Defence Committee had been set up in June 1946 to assist the Defence Committee 'on all matters of major policy relating to Home Defence against air attack (other than active defence measures) . . .' Its permanent members belonged to the Home Office, the V.C.O.S. Committee, the Board of Trade, and the Scottish Office. (COS(46)45th Mtg (4); COS(46)60th Mtg (15); COS(46)80th Mtg (16) & Annex; CP(46)227)

Findlater Stewart, had asked the Vice-Chiefs for an estimate of the likely weight of attack which might be expected to penetrate the active air defences of the United Kingdom and fall upon the country in a future war. On the basis of such an estimate, Stewart hoped that a working-party would be able to assess

> the degree of destruction and disorganisation that would be brought about in the flow of imports into the country and their handling at the ports, in the inland transportation and distribution system, in production, and on the morale of the civilian population.[110]

The first step would be to estimate the scale and nature of the attack which might be mounted. This task was assigned to the Joint Intelligence Sub-Committee, now chaired by William Hayter of the Foreign Office. Its members were advised to bear in mind the possibility of biological attack by the Russians at an earlier date, even if no Soviet atomic threat were to materialise for a decade. It should be assumed that Western Europe would be overrun, and that the main bombardment effort would be directed against the United Kingdom, with minor diversions in other theatres, including the Middle East but excluding the Far East.[111] On 12 November, the J.I.C. reported that attacks by up to 600–650 Soviet heavy bombers could be possible at the outbreak of a war in 1951 or 1956. After sixty days, a further 1,300 medium bombers would be able to be deployed from captured Continental bases, the report continued, and detailed estimates of potential conventional payloads were set out. So far as atomic bombs were concerned, if Russia had any at all by the end of 1951, they would be unlikely to number more than 5—though a total of 25 was conceivable in the worst case. By 1956, she might possess 40–60 of these weapons:

> It has been estimated that it would require 30–120 bombs *accurately* delivered to knock out this country, and since it is unlikely that this could be achieved with a total stock of 60 bombs, we consider that in 1956 this weapon would only be used in conjunction with others.

Amongst these other weapons might be high-explosive rockets, pilotless aircraft, and chemical and biological warfare agents. Of the

---

110. COS(46)157th Mtg (5)(Retained—Cabt. Off.)
111. COS(46)158th Mtg (5)(Confidential Annex)(Retained—Cabt. Off.)

nerve gases, Russia could be producing only Tabun in quantity by 1951, and that was expected to cause 10 per cent fewer casualties than would an equal conventional payload; but by 1956 Sarin and Soman would also have become available, and they were expected to cause about 3 times as many casualties as ordinary high-explosive. Attacks using both main biological warfare agents would be possible by 1951, but a ten-fold increase in the potency of each over the following five years was believed likely. Thus, by 1956, anthrax might cause 40 times as many casualties as conventional bombing, whilst the equivalent factor for brucella—non-lethal though it was—could rise from 3,000 to no less than 30,000 times the conventional casualty rate.[112]

After detailed consideration and computation of the extent to which defensive action might reduce the weight of attack, a long report was produced by the Joint Planning Staff on 28 November. It stressed the uncertainties of the whole examination, assumed Russia to be the potential enemy and America to be allied with the United Kingdom from the outbreak of war, and duly set out estimates of the net weights of attack which might be expected on target despite the efforts of the active defences. The Vice-Chiefs, however, still felt that 'any reference to a particular potential enemy should be omitted throughout the report', which would probably be fairly widely circulated.[113] The version for the Home Defence Committee was therefore to be shorn of such references. More significantly, an 'arbitrary cut' of 50 per cent in the probable weight of flying-bomb and rocket attacks was to be imposed and the detailed calculations were to be confined to a brief for use by the Vice-Chiefs on the Home Defence Committee. Although the estimate of 40–60 Soviet atomic bombs by 1956 remained, the worst case possibility of 5–25 by 1951 was omitted—no European Power was likely to have atomic weapons ready for use by then, 'though there can be no absolute guarantee of this'. Both versions nevertheless included a key passage on the question of *using* atomic weapons when they became available:

> It has been pointed out above that the estimated scale of attack may include a limited number of atomic bombs. In the event of failure to obtain international agreement on the limitations [*sic*] of weapons of mass destruction, a time will come when the number will be far less

112. JIC(46)95(0)(Final)(Retained—Cabt. Off.)
113. JP(46)201(Final)(Retained—Cabt. Off.) & COS(46)175th Mtg (1)(Retained—Cabt. Off.)

limited. Moreover, it must be remembered that the effects of even one atomic bomb which gets through the defences will be equivalent to several raids at maximum intensity using the normal weapons. An enemy who has embarked upon atomic warfare will, therefore, be prepared to accept an extremely high loss rate if under cover of a normal raid he is enabled to drop even one or two atomic bombs. As the number of atomic bombs available increases, this tendency will become accentuated. A comparatively limited number of atomic bombs might decisively affect the war-making capacity of this country, and it is possible to envisage a situation in which it might be virtually impossible to prevent this number being dropped. Nevertheless, the possibility of a war in which both sides refrained from the use of atomic bombs cannot be excluded. The view, that, because of the existence of atomic bombs, it is useless to prepare against other forms of attack, cannot, therefore, be justified.[114]

At the V.C.O.S. meeting of 9 December, the Home Defence Committee chairman was informed of the arbitrary adjustment which had been made to the figures concerning rockets and flying bombs. He was advised, by the V.C.A.S. in particular, to concentrate his working-party's attention upon 1956, as the 'temptation to aggression would probably not be completely formed' by 1951. Dickson also suggested that

a possible aggressor might not, owing to certain definite tactical disadvantages, wish to commence bombing until bases near to the Channel had been obtained.

If so, a period of three or four months might elapse from the outbreak of war, enabling civil defence to be put in order. This ought not, however, to be assumed for planning purposes. Stewart wondered whether it would not be wise to plan for the contingency of up to half-a-dozen Soviet atomic bombs having become available by 1951. He was told that there was 'no positive knowledge on this point either in London or Washington', and that though the use of such weapons by that date was thought unlikely, the possibility could not be ruled out. The report was approved, as amended in the discussion, for forwarding to the Home Defence Committee.[115]

---

114.   JP(46)201(Final)(Retained—Cabt. Off.); JP(46)218(Final)(Special Access); JP(46)220(Final)(Retained—Cabt. Off.)
115.   COS(46)180th Mtg (1)(Retained—Cabt. Off.)

Whilst the military planners had been exploring the two aspects of future strategy of most concern to the Prime Minister, the ground was also being prepared for a major change in the organisation for defence. On 17 September, the Cabinet had approved a draft White Paper incorporating *inter alia* C.O.S. suggestions for the formal supersession of the defunct Committee of Imperial Defence by the Defence Committee and for the appointment of a Minister of Defence, who should serve as its deputy chairman. The Chiefs of Staff organisation would be transferred from the Cabinet Offices to a separate Ministry of Defence which would begin to function on 1 January 1947. At its head would be the new minister, whose primary responsibilities were to be for administrative matters affecting all three Services and for the apportionment of resources between them. As the draft White Paper made clear, however, although the Service chiefs would remain responsible for the preparation of strategic plans, before any of the main ones were submitted to the Defence Committee, the Minister of Defence would usually discuss them with the Chiefs of Staff—'though not with a view to acting as their mouthpiece in the Defence Committee'.[116]

By December 1946, A.V. Alexander had been designated as the first incumbent of the new post. Currently Minister without Portfolio, he had previously served as First Lord of the Admiralty under three different Prime Ministers—before, during and after the war. On 17 December, he wrote to the Chiefs of Staff suggesting a meeting

at the earliest possible date . . . [to] reach some conclusions in general terms about future British Defence Policy as distinct from man-power and fiscal problems in 1947.

This proposal they warmly welcomed,[117] and—despite the short notice—the J.P.S. managed to produce a fairly full brief for this meeting almost at once. The reason that it was able to do so was that preliminary studies had been undertaken intermittently since the end of August with a view to preparing an interim report to the Defence Committee on the main principles which should govern imperial defence in the foreseeable future.[118] Production of this report had apparently been held up by fears that its findings would be largely nullified by those of

116. CM(46)82nd Concls (4); COS(46)33(0); CP(46)345
117. COS(46)184th Mtg (5) & Annex I
118. COS(46)133rd Mtg (1) & JP(46)174(S)(T.R.)(Special Access)

the Future Planners when they became available. After strong pressure from Tedder for the project to proceed, however, fresh terms of reference had been issued on 13 September.[119] Though no paper had resulted by the time of Alexander's initiative, the scheme had already borne fruit by calling forth from the Foreign Office a comprehensive examination of the 'Strategic Aspect of British Foreign Policy'.

This survey, forwarded by Sargent on 1 October, was particularly trenchant and outspoken. Though assuming that the United States would continue her present active intervention in international questions, it recognised that

> The Americans are a mercurial people, unduly swayed by sentiment and prejudice rather than by reason or even by consideration of their own long-term interests. Their Government is handicapped by an archaic constitution, sometimes to the point of impotence, and their policy is to an exceptional degree at the mercy both of electoral changes and of violent economic fluctuations, such as might at any moment bring about a neutralisation of their influence in the world.

If this were to happen, the whole position would need to be reconsidered, owing to the inability of the Commonwealth to sustain a full-scale war without American help.

Although the Russians apparently wished to avoid war in the short term, there was, unfortunately,

> every evidence, in spite of occasional tactical disavowals, that the leaders of the Soviet Union are convinced of the inevitability of a clash between the Communist State and the capitalist world . . . . As long as this delusion persists we can hope for no change in the present Soviet policy of building up Soviet industrial and military potential to the maximum in preparation for the supposedly inevitable struggle.

Attempts could be expected, by all means short of war, to consolidate control where it had already been acquired and to seek it in other areas—such as Persia and France—which it was considered necessary to dominate. The present policy of discrediting the United Nations Organisation, 'by raising frivolous charges and by irresponsible use of the veto', was also likely to continue. Even on the hypothesis that it was dictated primarily by considerations of security, current Soviet policy was

---

119.   COS(46)138th Mtg (5) & JP(46)180(S)(T.R.)(Special Access)

directed to undermine British and American influence in all parts of the world and, where possible, to supplant it.

Unless checked politically, it would eventually result in British helplessness to offer effective resistance to the Russians in a future war with modern weapons despite American assistance. Nor could the possibility be ruled out in the shorter term of war by miscalculation. Thus,

> in certain circumstances an extra bit of clumsiness and an outburst of mass emotion in America, coinciding with a sudden spasm of suspicion or display of truculence in Russia, might produce results which might get beyond control and lead to disaster.

In this dangerous international situation, the United Kingdom should aim, with the United States, to find a *modus vivendi* with the Soviet Union. If this objective were to prove unattainable, the British should be in a position to mount an effective resistance based upon a strong economy. Territory of strategic importance should not voluntarily be evacuated:

> There is always in such cases the danger that Russia will move in and that the areas will become lost to us militarily, politically and economically. Even if Russia is not in a position to exercise direct control, she would no doubt in such cases do her best to obtain remote control through local communist parties.

In her external propaganda, the United Kingdom should constantly emphasise the values of freedom and tolerance, as against the 'differing merits' of the Soviet system; should encourage less-developed countries to modernise along Western lines; and should discourage the use of the methods of the police state, 'except as a very last resort'. It also seemed necessary

> so to dispose our military forces in peacetime as to give the maximum impression of our strength and of the efficiency of our modern armaments in those areas where we appreciate that the Soviet Union is actively extending her influence, and thus underpin our threatened political position.

Such deployments might not coincide with those most appropriate from the point of view of defence in a major war.

A direct military clash with the Russians was most likely to occur in those regions to the south which were needed to complement the western belt of subservient states already acquired by the Soviet Union. Russian requirements would therefore be the domination of Turkey and of North Persia, the establishment of a leftist government in Greece, and an eventual increase in influence over the Afghans. Further mischief would be fomented elsewhere in the Middle East, with the Soviet Union representing herself as the champion of Arab nationalism on the one hand, whilst continuing to assist illegal Jewish immigration into Palestine, so as to heighten unrest, on the other. In Western Europe, she would be especially interested in Scandinavia because of its control of the Baltic entrances, and she would also

> seek to establish Communist Governments or at least powerful 'fifth columns' in France, the Low Countries and Italy; to bring about a Communist revolution and civil war in Spain, and ultimately to establish thereby a firm hold on the whole Iberian peninsula.

Despite probable political ambitions in Germany and Austria, the fact that Russia was directly faced with Western forces might reduce the chances of open conflict, assuming that the Soviet leadership did indeed wish to avoid it for the present. The Far East seemed destined to be the principal scene for a clash of interests between the Soviet Union and the United States:

> The Soviet Union is, however, likely to leave this until a later phase, meanwhile consolidating her position there and seeking to set up a system of satellite states, including if possible a Communist China or, at least, a separate Communist state in North China from which she will seek to expel British and American influence. In Korea, Soviet and American forces are now contiguous, and a direct clash between the two policies is to be expected. The United States Government is committed to a policy of unification of Korea under trusteeship, while the Soviet Government are clearly aiming at the undermining of American influence in South Korea and the establishment of a satellite Communist government over the whole peninsula.

There was as yet no evidence of Russian designs upon India or South-East Asia, but the Soviet Union was unlikely to neglect opportunities to stir up trouble there as well and spread her influence by exploiting and intensifying nationalist feelings.

British policy in Europe was directed towards the establishment of 'a stable system of democratic states under British leadership', and the prevention in particular of the industrial resources of the Continent coming under Soviet control in peacetime. In Germany, the objectives were to prevent any revival of militarism and aggressiveness; to rebuild the country as a decentralised federal state on Western democratic lines; and to resist the 'centralising and authoritarian pressure of the Soviet-inspired Communist and Socialist Unity parties'. It was no part of government policy permanently to divide the country into two: that course would be fallen back upon—reluctantly—only if Soviet action in the Eastern Zone made a united Germany impossible. Little could be done for the states of East and South-East Europe already under Soviet domination, except

> to support and encourage as far as we can our friends in those countries, and so to keep alive in them the connexion with Western democratic ideas which our policy towards them represents. The best hope of this is in Poland, since the Poles are born conspirators.

The more complete became Russia's political ascendancy in the area, the greater would become the danger of it extending further afield.

As for the British interest in other regions, the importance of Greece and Turkey to the security of the Mediterranean was stressed, and that of Afghanistan to the security of India and Persia. In the rest of the Middle East, every available means of maintaining the British position should be employed. The Arab States must be encouraged to resist Soviet penetration and to pursue enlightened social policies which would 'take the wind out of the sails of Communist subversive propaganda'. The way in which the Palestine problem was settled would probably be of crucial importance in this respect. Little more than encouragement could be offered to the Americans in their struggle with the Russians for 'control of the body and soul' of China. Non-involvement rather than intervention was, indeed, in the general interest of the Commonwealth so far as most of the Far East was concerned, though American prevention of Japanese resurgence and of Soviet domination of Korea was directly relevant to British interests further to the south.

The Foreign Office survey concluded that a purely passive attitude towards Soviet penetration must not be adopted. Though abjuring totalitarian methods, the United Kingdom would occasionally have to use offensive tactics for the prosecution of what was, after all, a defensive political purpose:

It is in no sense an aim of British policy to force other countries to subscribe to Western democratic ideas, and, unlike the Soviet Union, the British Commonwealth has no ideological purpose of propagating a political idea with something resembling a religious fanaticism. It is the purpose of British policy, on the other hand, to emphasise constantly the values of freedom and tolerance, as against the advantages claimed by the Soviet Union for the Leninist totalitarian system, and to maintain, particularly in the countries of Western Europe, that European culture which has spread itself over the 'Western' world, and has resisted, three times in the last 75 years, armed assault from the Eastward.[120]

The Joint Planners' brief for the C.O.S. Staff Conference with Alexander on 23 December also held to the view that premeditated war by the Soviet Union was unlikely before 1956. Should this prove incorrect, British involvement could be envisaged only in conjunction with active American aid from the outset. Without this, even mere survival might be very difficult. The Soviet strategy would probably consist of simultaneous efforts against Europe and the Middle East, designed to eliminate the United Kingdom as a factor promptly—by bombardment of the British Isles, severance of their sea communications, and denial of the oil resources and counter-offensive bases of the Middle East.

Top priority must be accorded to the security of the home base and its sea links with North America. Next in order of importance would be the development of a strategic air base in the United Kingdom, followed by that of others in the Middle East and (possibly) in North-West India, and also the security of the sea communications linking them. Fourth in importance would be the protection of areas outside the United Kingdom and North America from which Commonwealth war potential was derived. For Australasia, South Africa and India (if participating), a naval commitment would probably suffice; but in the Middle East a full-scale land attack would probably succeed in cutting off oil supplies. Therefore, stockpiling and the development of more defensible sources should be maximised in peacetime. Finally, an offensive capability other than just by air would have to be maintained as the basis for the 'eventual assumption of a land offensive' when British and Allied strength had been built up. It had to be borne in mind that, though these war requirements probably related to a period not less than a decade ahead, cuts imposed upon the forces in the immediate future would

---

120. COS(46)239(0)(Retained—Cabt. Off.) See Appendix 6 (ii), pp. 363–9 below

need to be tailored so as to allow them to be met if and when the crisis ever came.[121]

Amongst the assumptions which Alexander, for his part, put to the Chiefs of Staff were that even the most ardent support of the United Nations Organisation could not fully guarantee its success in averting a war involving the United Kingdom, and that 'there was only one enemy which was likely to attack us in the foreseeable future'. Tedder explained that studies were in hand—and that Tizard's D.R.P. Committee was being set up—to monitor the effects of scientific developments upon warfare, and he mentioned that some preliminary talks about future planning had just been held with American military representatives.[122] He identified the Balkans, Persia and Korea as the three main danger areas, and he cited the recent transfer of an Indian brigade to Iraq when trouble had loomed over the Persian oilfields as a successful example of how to forestall danger:

> in peacetime it was clearly necessary to retain small and highly mobile forces which by deployment to the appropriate places, would demon- strate the earnest of our intentions, and act as a deterrent to those who wished to press up to the point of a world war, but no further.

Future forces would have to serve in this role as well as constituting a basis for full wartime mobilisation. They would also, added Cunningham, have to take the strain alone for a period, unless allied help was immediately forthcoming on the outbreak of hostilities. As for the Western bloc idea, to which Alexander had made reference, the C.N.S. thought that

> for the immediate future, . . . this concept could not be depended on as a material factor, since he regarded it as idealistic rather than a realistic influence on our future policy.

With this, Montgomery concurred:

> As he saw it, only a small regular army force could be maintained. He would suggest that in the Middle East, a field force of perhaps two

---

121.   JP(46)229(Final)(Special Access)
122.   With the Prime Minister's authority, members of the J.P.S. had attended staff talks with American and Canadian representatives in Washington. The subject of discussion was not strategic policy, however, but standardisation—of weapons, equipment, research, training and tactical doctrine. (COS(46)159th Mtg (3); JP(46)224(Final)(Special Access); DO(47)6)

divisions would provide the nucleus to which could be added in war the forces from our Allies, and at the same time prove sufficient to hold our position in that area. The balance of the Army, other than the small garrisons required throughout the world, would be in the United Kingdom. This meant that the United Kingdom force would be too small for operations on the Continent in the early stages of war, and the extension of the Army to meet the needs of a major war could only be based upon the Territorial Army Organisation.

The old concept of operations involving the sending of forces to the Continent was virtually useless against an enemy who possessed almost unlimited man-power.

He pressed for the recognition of three fundamentals of British defence policy: the defence and safety of the United Kingdom base; the maintenance of its sea communications; and, for counter-offensive purposes, the retention of a firm hold on the Middle East. All had been mentioned in the J.P.S. brief for the conference, which had particularly advocated the earliest possible launching, from British, Middle Eastern and—if available—Indian bases, of

a strategic air bombardment ... with the object of paralysing and destroying the enemy's war effort and his will to fight.

Tedder also felt that opposition to an enemy with effectively unlimited manpower would have to depend upon technical superiority, and it was left to Ismay to point out the *politico*-strategic significance of a Continental commitment:

If it was decided that our forces should never again be sent to the aid of a Power on the Continent, France might turn to an Eastern alliance for her future security .... The military implications of our relationship with France were, therefore, either to accept that we would in the future have to send forces to her aid, or to run the risk that the whole of the European Continent was available to a potential aggressor, and of the latter's ability to attack this country to the point of destruction with air weapons, and to attack our sea lines of communication.[123]

Although it may be just that Montgomery's memory played him false when recalling the consistency of his support for a Western European strategy,[124] it is possible that concern once and for all to secure

---

123.   COS(46)187th Mtg (1)   124.   See pp. 275–6 above

acceptance of the need to defend the Middle East had deterred him from fighting on two issues at once. According to his account, the Prime Minister chose this time to revive his argument with the Chiefs of Staff on the question of the Middle East, and in January 1947 the C.I.G.S.

> asked . . . [my colleagues] if they were prepared, with me, to resign rather than give way over that area. I added that I would do so, with or without them. They both agreed whole-heartedly and this information was conveyed privately to Attlee. We heard no more about it.[125]

A private initiative of this sort would certainly explain the fact that despite

> a full and detailed discussion about the factors governing the position of the Middle East in relation to the defence of the Commonwealth,

a Staff Conference chaired by Attlee on 7 January arrived at no conclusions on the subject;[126] yet, at a second one six days later, the Prime Minister said that he agreed with the necessity of basing future defence policy on all three fundamentals outlined by the C.I.G.S. at the conference with Alexander on 23 December. These were now described by Tedder as 'the tripod on which our security rested', and by Montgomery as 'pillars'—the collapse of any one of which would bring down the whole structure of Commonwealth defence. In response to Attlee and Bevin, he agreed that, the stronger France could be made, the more secure the United Kingdom would become, and the conference endorsed an *aide-mémoire* setting out the basic factors and principles of defence upon which the Services were in full agreement.[127]

The list of basic factors began by recognising that the ability and readiness of the Great Powers to keep the peace was essential, if the United Nations aim of world security was to be achieved. As a first-class Power, the Commonwealth should make a contribution in proportion to her world-wide responsibilities. This would depend upon possession of a strong economic base on which to expand industrially

---

125. Montgomery, *Memoirs*, p. 436   126. COS(47)6th Mtg
127. COS(47)9th Mtg (2) Since these factors and principles did not depend upon the nomination of Russia as the potential enemy, and Attlee considered it dangerous to base their importance on that assumption, a paragraph containing it was cut out.

and militarily with the onset of war. Owing to the United Kingdom's vulnerability to modern weapons, the supreme object of British policy must be to prevent a war occurring. If a global conflict erupted within the next few years, the results would be economically disastrous; but the only effective deterrent to a potential aggressor would be tangible evidence of an intention to withstand attack and retaliate immediately. Commonwealth and American forces would probably become engaged at some stage, but the availability of Indian manpower seemed unlikely. The development of a Western defence region should be encouraged, but the level of military support to be given to it could not be decided without further study. Finally, only technical superiority could redress the insufficiency of manpower to which the armed forces would be subject in the years ahead.

As for the basic defensive concept, this should be to keep the war-making potential of the Commonwealth intact until—with allies—a counter-offensive could be mounted, and to retain control of such bases as would be needed to launch it at the earliest possible moment. After stressing that unaided resistance must be for as short a period as possible, the *aide-mémoire* set out once again the three fundamental strategic tasks canvassed at the Staff Conferences and finally accepted by the Prime Minister.[128] What their fulfilment might entail in conditions of modern warfare was soon to become much clearer.

4. The Report of the Future Planning Section

On 31 March 1947, Rear-Admiral Lambe and his colleagues completed their report. Its magnitude justified the open-endedness of its title: 'Review of Defence Problems'. Over a hundred pages of text were supplemented by sixteen detailed annexes, three maps and an index. The whole area of strategic concern was surveyed—from political projections and an estimate of probable Soviet strategy, to problems of war economics and the future nature of warfare. The ground covered by the P.H.P.S. strategic surveys was fully re-examined for the first time since the revision of the Tizard report. Nor did the F.P.S. call a halt on arriving at its conclusions about Commonwealth strategy. On the basis of these findings, statistical projections were made for the shape and size of the armed forces required at the outbreak of a war in 1956. In

---

128. COS(47)5(0)(Final)

their introduction dealing with the scope of their undertaking, the authors remarked that

> The technical, political and economic developments which now influence our future security have so changed that they demand a reconsideration not only of the form that our Commonwealth Defence Policy should take, but, more fundamentally, what the aims of such a Defence Policy should be.

It was, however, too early to say if the price to be paid for preparedness in peace or for victory in war was already too great to be paid. A decision on this would depend on further assessment of the threat of mass-destruction weapons, and on world political developments, the beginnings of which were, as yet, only dimly discernible:

> Our task we conceive to be to put forward concrete proposals for a Commonwealth Defence Policy which shall place us in a position, with our Allies, to resist aggression by force with reasonable prospects of success.

These proposals would be based upon separate examinations of the political, technical and economic factors likely to affect strategy in 1956, followed by a tentative forecast of future Soviet military policy, an examination of the British and Commonwealth strategic situation, and an estimate of the forces likely to be needed.

The section dealing with the first of these topics contained the most forthright and explicit political statements yet made by any of the planning staffs dealing with post-war matters. Clearly influenced by the October 1946 Foreign Office survey, the F.P.S. assessed the significance of Russia's emergence as the only first-class Power in Europe to lie less in the disappearance or temporary eclipse of all the other Continental Powers than in the fact that

> the U.S.S.R. is a totalitarian State of great military power activated by an ideology foreign to the British and American way of life.

This new world force might develop either into a militant and imperialistic Power seeking ultimate world domination, or, perhaps, with the improvement of internal conditions, into a more democratic and less totalitarian society. Communism as a theory currently possessed an appeal possibly greater than that of any world movement since the birth of Christianity. Those dissatisfied with traditional forms of government and seeking improved living-standards tended to look to the Soviet Union as the embodiment of this theory in practice. They were apt to forget that

> Russia to-day is a police State with little, if any, personal freedom and moreover, a State which shows every sign of exploiting the foreign Communist Party [*sic*] as a means of furthering its own purely nationalist ends.

It was vital to dispel the illusion that Communism was the only system offering fair shares for all. Social democracy was the 'only comparable alternative' to the Soviet approach, and the fact that it was gradually satisfying the precepts of genuine Communism had led the Russians to regard it as the greatest potential rival to their totalitarian ideology. If the former, with its relatively mundane background, was to demonstrate its inherent superiority over the natural appeal of dynamic communism, it would have to do so quickly for any such demonstration to be effective. This could be done only by the speedy return of the British Commonwealth to economic prosperity, and by an attempt, with American help, to bring about similar progress throughout the non-Soviet world.

The growth of nationalism and the decolonisation of the British, French, Belgian and Dutch Empires would magnify the problems of long-term defence planning and provide opportunities for further Soviet penetration. Other new factors were the American monopoly of the atomic bomb,[129] effective banning of which could not of itself ensure the elimination of war, and the setting up of the United Nations Organisation, where the sincerity of Soviet support was open to considerable doubt. That was hardly surprising, since

> Soviet policy ... is founded on the principle that communism is incompatible with any other ideology, and that an ultimate clash between the U.S.S.R. and the Western Democracies is inevitable.

---

129. The decision to manufacture British atomic weapons had, in fact, already been taken early in January 1947 by 'GEN 163'—an *ad hoc* meeting of six senior ministers: Attlee, Bevin, Herbert Morrison (Lord President), Alexander, Viscount Addison (Dominions), and John Wilmot (Supply). The decision to construct a 'graphite pile' for the production of plutonium had been taken in December 1945, but a C.O.S. recommendation that building two of these units would be disproportionately valuable had not been endorsed. (JP(45) 317(S)(T.R.) & JP(45)317(Final); COS(45)291st Mtg (13); Gowing, *Independence and Deterrence*, i. pp. 167–70; 182–3)

Russian actions and propaganda constantly belied periodic declarations
to the contrary, and as long as this attitude was maintained, the Soviet
and Western worlds would remain

> at the minimum in a state of political belligerency, a situation in which
> force is being used and will continue to be used, although open and
> declared war may never develop.

The Soviet leadership wished to achieve a position of strength and
greatness internationally commensurate with Russia's vast size and
resources. Coupled with this was a desire for the limitless expansion of
Communism and the achievement of territorial gains—whether for
security or self-aggrandisement—whenever this seemed practicable.
Yet there appeared to be no urgency for such expansionism. On the
contrary, at least a decade would be needed for recovery, consolidation
at home and in the new satellite states, the rectification of the
technological disparity between East and West, and the building-up of
Communism as a 'fifth column' inside countries against which future
wars might be fought. However, the shunning of open warfare in the
short and possibly medium terms did not imply any period of inactivity
in Russia's external policy:

> While we expect the U.S.S.R. to avoid planned war within the next ten
> years, throughout this period we foresee the vigorous pursuit of her
> external objectives—the spreading of communism and, where possible,
> the acquisition of additional satellite buffer States.

There was thus the risk of accidental war caused by Soviet
miscalculation in some such disputed area as Greece or the Dardanelles,
though the Politburo's relative freedom of action in foreign-policy
matters constituted something of a safety-valve—it made a speedy
about-turn practicable by the Soviet leadership, in the event of a
provocative move getting unexpectedly out of hand.

As international relations stabilised, the probability of war by
accident would diminish; but that of a planned conflict would increase
as Soviet deficiencies were made good or as Soviet expansion by means
short of war became gradually more difficult. Any future Soviet
decision to resort to war would largely be determined by the success or
failure of Anglo-American policy in the meantime. Part of this policy
would be a demonstration of the economic well-being of the Western

Democracies; but the degree of success of efforts to 'bolster up' countries threatened by Soviet pressure would greatly depend upon American steadfastness in support of indigenous populations anxious to resist the spread of Communism. So far, the continued interest and active participation of the United States in foreign affairs had been the principal post-war feature of democratic politics. The physical and economic exhaustion of the United Kingdom brought about by two world wars, a vast increase in her vulnerability, and the extent of her dependence upon the United States, meant that the British government

> does not now possess and may well never again possess, the ability to pursue a selected course of action regardless of world reaction.

The advantages of trying to steer a middle course between Russia and America were nevertheless more apparent than real. If war broke out between those two countries, it was unlikely that British neutrality would be able to last for very long:

> Allied to the U.S.S.R. in a war with the United States we might survive as an island, but we should cease to exist as an Empire. Allied with the United States, the security of the Empire would be assured and we might still survive as an island.

Nor did economic factors permit of any other alignment, at least until the Soviet Union began to trade on a global basis, quite apart from the political, military and ethnic factors in favour of ever-closer Anglo-American linkage.

As for other sources of support, the Second World War had shown the extent to which British guarantees of Dominions security had been undermined, whilst British dependence upon help from the Dominions had increased. At recent conferences, they had refused to accept more clearly defined defence commitments, and a reorientation towards the United States was already evident in Canada, Australia and—to a lesser extent—New Zealand. Furthermore, there was a grave danger of central government breaking down in India and a bloody transitional period ensuing. By 1956, some measure of stability would probably have been achieved, but the best that could be hoped for in the coming ten to fifteen years was that the country would be friendly towards the United Kingdom and neutral in any war.

In Europe, French recovery might be the key to short-term stability, but German revival would be at least as important later on. The formation of a Western bloc was most desirable, but, for the decade ahead, its significance would be political rather than military. As decolonisation proceeded—a process perhaps ultimately proving to be a source of strength—it would be particularly important to remain on friendly terms with the Arab world. The French North African colonies should not be antagonised; nor should the Russians be allowed to gain footholds in Libya or Somalia when their fate was decided. In Greece, the British attempt to uphold a democratic regime had become a public test of strength between East and West. Failure would have grave consequences for British influence throughout Europe and the Middle East.

The effective warning time for a future war could be anything from two years down to a few months, if the Soviet Union were allowed to make steady progress before Western opposition began to stiffen. However, once the Russians were being held in check, the likelihood of war being sudden if it happened at all would increase. The period of warning might then be reduced merely to a few weeks. On the other hand, evidence of major Western weakness—including any Soviet success in inducing the Americans to renounce their atomic-bomb capacity—could encourage the Russians to believe that they could overrun parts of Western Europe or the Middle East without bringing about a general conflagration. They might then go to war at any time, with a view to seizing so great an immediate advantage as to be able to negotiate a settlement on terms entirely favourable to themselves.

The F.P.S. concluded that a *modus vivendi* might be achieved between Russia and the West, but the prospects were delicately balanced. Any trend generally favouring one side or the other by 1956 would probably continue with accelerated force thereafter; and if, in fact, the trend was in favour of the West,

> there should come at some time soon afterwards a particularly critical period in international relations. This will be the point at which the Soviets, with particular regard to the availability of mass-destruction weapons, calculate they must gain their ends by means of communist revolutions and war, or accept the necessity for sharply curtailing their expansionist objectives.

Which decision they made would largely be determined by the military preparedness of the West when the time came.

If, indeed, the greatest danger of deliberate war would arise in the period from 1956, what form might a conflict then take technologically? The Future Planners thought that all three main Powers might have stocks of atomic weapons, but noted that the J.I.C. did not expect Soviet totals to exceed 5–25 by 1952 or 30–60 by 1957. Preliminary findings by the Home Defence Committee indicated that fewer than 20 atomic bombs, accurately delivered against key targets,

> might cause the collapse of the United Kingdom without invasion, *under present conditions of dispersion and passive defence*,

whereas several hundred bombs might be needed to have a similar effect upon the Soviet Union. On the reasonable assumption that half of the Russian bomb-carrying force successfully completed its mission, 40 of the devices would be required for use against the British Isles. Whilst decisive results could not, therefore, be achieved against the United Kingdom by the Soviet Union before 1957, it was expected that the Americans might be able to destroy a high proportion of Soviet priority targets from 1953 onwards. The Soviet leadership was probably quite well aware of this, in view of a recent leakage[130] of information on atomic-energy matters.

Biological weapons had yet to be perfected. The weight of anthrax attack was still only 20 per cent smaller than that of the nerve gas Tabun needed to produce the same number of casualties. In the foreseeable future, however, up to a hundred-fold increase in the effectiveness of the former could be anticipated, quite apart from the development of other agents:

> This plainly brings biological warfare into the same category as the atomic bomb as a weapon against personnel. Moreover, by incapacitating people without destroying installations, it has certain advantages.

From what little was known of Soviet research in the subject, it was felt unsafe to assume that Soviet production of biological weapons could not equal that of the other main Powers by 1951. The slower their

---

130. For an account of the career of Dr Alan Nunn May, a left-wing Cambridge graduate recruited into the Tube Alloys Directorate in 1942 and convicted of espionage in May 1946, see: R. W. Reid, *Tongues of Conscience: War and the Scientist's Dilemma* (London, Constable, 1969), pp. 223–33

atomic progress, the more impetus the Russians might give to an easier and cheaper B.W. programme. If the British accorded high priority to the task, they might well be producing greatly improved devices by 1951–52 on a scale in proportion to the level of investment in production plant. Immunisation could be expected greatly to mitigate casualties as research continued; perhaps within the coming two decades, the general expectation that defence would eventually outstrip offence in this field would be fulfilled. Yet, it was very doubtful if complete protection would ever be a practical possibility. As for the new German gases, the Soviet Union should be well equipped to build up stocks of Tabun[131] after 1948, and of the more toxic Sarin and Soman after 1951—the latter period coinciding with that of the United Kingdom's own production of the means of delivering nerve agents.

By 1956, it was likely that the manned bomber would still be required for the delivery of mass-destruction weapons at ranges of over 400 miles. The Soviet Union might have 1,000–1,500 heavy bombers with a range of 1,000–2,000 nautical miles. The United Kingdom and United States would nevertheless probably maintain a marked lead in efficiency, performance and technique. American bombers with an operational radius of 2,000–2,500 nautical miles would already be available by 1956, and it seemed technically feasible to develop improved types by 1960–65 capable of striking up to 3,000 or 4,000 nautical miles from their bases. It was 'most improbable' that any power would have acquired rockets with atomic warheads by 1965, but, by that date, the Russians might be able to mount a sustained attack up to ranges of 300–600 miles with weapons based upon the German V.1 and V.2. Up to 400 miles, reasonable accuracy might be possible, and Soviet use of rockets for the delivery of biological agents could not be ruled out. Nor should the possibility be overlooked of atomic weapons being delivered to their targets by covert means in advance of hostilities.

Defensive measures against aerial attack would most probably fail to keep pace with the development of offensive weapons. Fighter performance, though much improved, would no longer yield as great a measure of superiority over strategic bomber performance as in the past. This would remain the case at least until the attainment of supersonic speeds. High-performance bombers would reduce raid warning times, but, in this respect, the Soviet advantage of greater

---

131.   Although the Western Allies had captured most of the German stocks of Tabun, the Russians had overrun the production plant. (*Ibid.*, p. 310)

defensive depth would be more than offset by British superiority in defensive techniques. By 1956, all three Powers would have supersonic guided anti-aircraft projectiles in various stages of development or production. These might inflict losses of between 10 and 20 per cent on massed bomber formations. With the benefit of captured wartime equipment, the Russians would also be able by then to provide an adequate radar coverage for all towns of over 40,000 inhabitants. Whether such a system would be able to stand up to Western radio counter-measures, however, was quite uncertain.

All in all, it was clear that, by the period under consideration, some Soviet atomic bombs—possibly even a critical number—would be capable of reaching their mark in the United Kingdom. The prospect of a heavy scale of high-explosive and perhaps biological attack upon the British Isles would have to be faced. On the other hand,

> the Soviet's [sic] difficulties in maintaining an adequate air defence of such a vast area will be enormous and we see no reason to doubt that the strategic bomber forces of the Western Powers would be able in 1956 to deliver their loads on target.

If mass-destruction weapons were employed, high rates of bomber losses would become acceptable; but the effects of using these devices would vary greatly according to the degree of sheltering and dispersal achieved by the attacked country. Of the conventional arms, a large Soviet fleet of 'true' submarines, capable of high speed and great endurance underwater, would pose a very grave threat until the perfection of counter-measures.

The main impact of the new weapons in a war in 1956 would be four-fold: they would give possibilities of rapid and decisive results; they would raise what would be acceptable standards of defence to levels unlikely to be reached during the decade ahead; they would radically improve prospects of achieving offensive surprise; and they would increase the threat to British sea communications to a degree unknown even in the recent war.

As in the past, three methods of waging war would be available: (1) destruction of the enemy's armed forces, (2) direct attack upon his war-making capacity, and (3) breaking his will to resist. If it appeared that the first of these might suffice by itself, the other two might well remain unused. It would be necessary to be prepared for the employment of all three methods simultaneously or consecutively in any order, even though a country with overwhelmingly preponderant armed forces might well hesitate before commencing attacks on its victim's war-making capacity and will to resist. Nevertheless, the need for comprehensive preparations should not obscure the fact that some types of warfare were more likely to be waged than others:

> Should substantial stocks of atomic bombs be available to both sides and should the means of defence against them be as ineffective as they are now, we can foresee circumstances in which there might be great reluctance to initiate atomic warfare . . . . In the event of a war in 1956 between the U.S.S.R. and the Western Powers, we think it possible that the U.S.S.R. might delay the initiation of either atomic or biological warfare. Should she have been able to soften the Western European Powers by communist infiltration and should world opinion (and particularly American opinion) be strongly mobilised against the use of mass destruction weapons, the U.S.S.R. might, as a first and ostensibly 'last' step occupy the Low Countries and France at the 'invitation' of communist groups in these countries, thus exploiting her vast superiority in land forces while there was a chance that the technical superiority of the Allies would not be brought into play against her. The Allied Governments would then be faced with a difficult choice. A 'conventional' offensive against Russia would be slow, costly and uncertain; the powerful factors of vast space and teeming man-power, which have so often saved her in the past might well do so again. Yet, to seek a quicker decision by initiating the use of the new weapons might entail for the United Kingdom the loss of a large part of her population and the destruction of her economy for generations.

If no agreement were reached on an effective system of general disarmament, it had to be accepted that all three methods of belligerency (including the use of mass-destruction weapons) *might* be employed by the Russians from the outset. This was therefore the contingency to meet which planning should proceed, even if it was not the one considered most probable. No longer might the British propensity for winning the 'last battle' prove sufficient, for—under such circumstances—the first battle might be the last. Greater preparedness, more rapid mobilisation and improved flexibility would all be essential to cope with the danger of a powerful onslaught delivered with little or no warning. The ability to retaliate with mass-destruction weapons would be a powerful deterrent. Forces would have to be maintained at a high state of readiness in peacetime, and the fact of their availability must be made known to all potential aggressors. Self-sufficiency by stockpiling should be promoted, and the vulnerability of ports should be compensated for by the development of amphibious supply vehicles which would not be dependent upon them:

> The present conception of a fixed line of communication working between concentrated terminals will require drastic modification to achieve greater dispersion and flexibility. Reduced capacities may have to be accepted.

Stockpiling should also be attempted at base areas abroad, and greater Commonwealth manpower contributions should be sought to offset the increased numbers tied down in efforts to reduce the new vulnerability of the United Kingdom.

To obtain anything approaching an acceptable degree of security, unremitting research into methods of air defence, C.B.W. detection, and the protection of shipping would be indispensable. Retaliatory forces should be ready for instant and effective use—though inevitably limited in size—and should be based as far forward as possible. Whilst Western European allies should be encouraged to deny to the Russians for as long as they could short-range bases for use against the United Kingdom, such encouragement would

> have to be limited to political and economic backing in peace, and, in war, the support of naval and air forces based in the United Kingdom. We cannot afford to commit forces to the Continent in the early stages of a war.

The British Army would be greatly involved in air defence measures and in aiding the civil authorities if mass casualties were actually inflicted. Vital elements of war potential should be protected underground, where possible, or moved overseas—as should 'useless mouths'. Ideally, the whole balance of industrial potential should be shifted away from the United Kingdom and towards the other parts of the Commonwealth. The whole question of imports would have to be examined, with particular attention being paid to supply by air. Peacetime planning with the Americans should include schemes to compensate for reduced British productivity and imports in war, and an overall strategy should be worked out to redress manpower deficiencies by the effective exploitation of technical superiority.

Having considered the nature of a future war, the F.P.S. had proceeded to examine the likely war potential of the Commonwealth if it became involved in one. In the first place, years of strenuous effort would be required to make good the ravages of the 1939–45 conflict. Without a restoration of national economic strength there could be no war economy firmly based—as it would have to be—upon the coal, electricity, iron and steel, shipbuilding, and general light and heavy industries. Even a return to full 1939 manufacturing output levels would fail to be adequate in various fields. Yet the Dominions, by contrast, were significantly stronger in terms of war potential than they had been in 1939. This indicated that the

> long-term solution of many of the problems arising from the geographical position of the United Kingdom in relation to the effect of new weapons of war,

would lie in drawing an increasing proportion of the resources needed from parts of the Commonwealth other than the United Kingdom. The corollary of this would be a corresponding shift of skilled manpower—a problem requiring examination by experts.

Since a future war would reach its climax relatively quickly, there would be less time than ever before in which to mobilise the munitions industry. That would have to be done with great rapidity in whatever period of warning was available. Other vital factors would be the extent to which both economic self-sufficiency and co-ordination with the Americans could be achieved. Oil and shipping resources were deemed important enough to warrant separate scrutiny in detail. With regard to the former, it was conceded that, although minor oilfields might be retained in the Egypt-Palestine-Transjordan area, control of those in Iraq, Persia and the Gulf would inevitably be lost. Production in the Americas and the Far East would then become the main source of supply, and an annual deficiency of some 17 million tons could be expected in respect of a Commonwealth attempt to meet its own needs after sustaining such losses in the Middle East. With stockpiling and a sufficient tanker fleet, however, it should be able to sustain a war for from 12 to 18 months. As for shipping, British dependence upon a large merchant fleet in wartime would be absolute; but if one were to be maintained in peacetime it would have to be profitable, and the possibility of this would depend upon the level of trade. Given the vulnerability of ports to atomic attack, the use of small harbours and beaches would have to be considered—daunting though this prospect would be. Once again, United States and Dominions assistance would be required, for shipbuilding in the United Kingdom would be impossible if atomic weapons were being employed.

What, then, might the Russians actually do in the context of the situation outlined thus far? Of the two main obstacles to Soviet world domination, the greater one—the United States—would not be able to defeat the Russians from her own distant continent. Elimination of the lesser obstacle—the United Kingdom—and expansion into Europe, Asia and Africa, would prevent the Americans from coming to grips with them. An advantageous peace might therefore be negotiated, 'with a view to the ultimate reduction of the United States at a later stage'.

Many factors favoured the Soviet aim of spreading Communism throughout the world. Unlike in the West, domestic opinion could be manipulated and controlled. A fifth column could be built up by the Russians to undermine each potential victim from within. Soviet intelligence-gathering would probably outclass similar Western activity. Economic self-sufficiency would enable the maintenance of all forces needed by 1955–60 for a major conflict and tremendous reserves of manpower could be marshalled. However, not enough mass-destruction weapons to eliminate even just the United Kingdom would be available before 1956–57, and the Russians would also face problems in developing internal communications and keeping them intact. Whatever the outcome of international negotiations for the abolition of atomic bombs, the Russians might still manufacture stocks of them in secret. Arguments favouring Soviet use of such weapons, if available, would be the possibility of breaking Western will to resist and the advantage to be derived from delivering the first blow. Contrary factors would be the limited stocks available (though this need not apply to biological weapons); the prospect of rapid success by using conventional forces alone; the possibility of dividing the Western Powers—with the British urging restraint upon the Americans, for fear of being first in line for Soviet retaliation if the United States began atomic warfare; and the effects on public opinion on both sides if the first bomb to be dropped was American. It was therefore considered that

> so long as the reduction of the United Kingdom by orthodox means appears possible in the time available, the Soviet [*sic*] will be inclined to avoid initiating the use of weapons of mass destruction. If, however, programmed campaigns are behindhand, or if American intervention is more quickly effective than anticipated, the Soviet will not hesitate to initiate their use.

In all probability, the Soviet strategic concept would aim to reduce American deployment options against Soviet forces to just two alternative courses: either merely the mounting of very long-range air attacks, or the undertaking of overseas operations on an unprecedented scale. Facing only these possibilities, the United States government might well feel obliged to agree, instead, upon terms very favourable to the Russians. If the United Kingdom were defeated, any avenue of attack via the British Isles would be blocked. Similarly, the occupation of Spitzbergen and Northern Norway, of Western Europe and the North African Atlantic seaboard, of Egypt and the Persian Gulf, and of Northern China would eliminate most other potential Western offensive bases—though measures against Iceland, India and Japan might also be necessary. From such a commanding position, the Soviet Union would be well placed for the final campaign against the United States:

> The industrial potential and the high-grade man-power of the whole of Europe, including the United Kingdom and Germany, are at her disposal, the Mediterranean Sea and its outlets as well as the complete oil-bearing areas of the Middle East come under Russian control, and India lies open for exploitation.

The United States would thus be forced into a position of trying to hold the southern half of Africa, perhaps up to Kenya and the Gold Coast, and of trying—with Australian and New Zealand help—to block further Soviet expansion in Burma, Malaya and Southern China.

Since the key to Russia's success would lie in seizing her advantage before effective American intervention, the time-factor would be crucial. There would probably be a warning period while a political offensive was being mounted. This offensive would be designed to gain as much ground as possible in advance of military conflict. It would also serve to confuse Western public opinion and aim to cause dispersal of Anglo-American forces over a wide area. Its main impact would probably be in Western Germany, France, Spain, Italy, Greece, Persia, Afghanistan and probably Turkey. In these countries, Communist fifth columns would move into action and 'invitations to enter and restore order' would be manufactured for the Russians. No overt military attack would be launched, pending evidence of Western determination to resist by force if necessary. It was possible, though by no means certain, that bombardment of the United Kingdom would not precede the seizure of forward bases, so as to maximise its impact when it did begin. If a political offensive had, indeed, been in operation, an airborne assault upon the British Isles would not be possible as a surprise attack. Yet, to succeed under any other circumstances, such an assault would require 'the winning of another Battle of Britain'. According to a detailed annex on the subject, British air superiority, aided by land and naval operations, should suffice to thwart an attempted invasion of the United Kingdom. As for attacks upon the United States, it was true that early long-range bombardment might provoke an outcry for improved air defences and thus delay the despatch of forces to Europe; but it was just as likely that, since

> the cumbrous governmental machinery in Washington may, by itself, prevent quick and effective military action . . . the stimulus of a bomb on Pittsburgh might react to the Soviet disadvantage.

Given British vulnerability to mass-destruction weapons, the possibility of reducing the weight of an attack by denying parts of the Continent to the Russians was examined. The conclusions of the F.P.S. were pessimistic:

> The conception of a Western Association, at present, does not envisage any more than defensive alliances between the countries concerned. But, since independently each country would be of little value, some far more complete military co-ordination will be required. This implies that the following will be necessary:–
> (a) An overall defence plan of the whole area with a supreme head-quarters to control operations.
> (b) Inter-supply of military equipment, which would involve a measure of standardisation.
> (c) A measure of co-ordination of training, staff and administrative arrangements.

A loose system of alliances would be inadequate. Something approaching 'a "United States of Europe" ' would be needed, for—despite the considerable potential of their combined resources—individually the Continental Powers could contribute hardly anything of value. The obstacles to creating such integration in the decade ahead seemed well-nigh insurmountable. Consequently, whilst fostering to the maximum moves to set up a Western Association, the United Kingdom should confine its help in war to that which could be provided without committing forces to the Continent. In the event of a Soviet attack in 1956, it could be assumed that, after about 40 days, all of France would have been overrun.

On the assumption that the Russians would then be free to bombard the United Kingdom from the far side of the English Channel, an estimate was needed for the length of time for which this could be withstood. If 'absolute weapons' were not used, it was suggested that

> a period of about nine months must elapse from the start of a war in 1956 until either the position of the United Kingdom must improve or the internal situation will break down.

Nor, it was later remarked, could the possibility be excluded of a future war lasting up to eighteen months or even longer. The F.P.S. noted that a detailed examination of atomic potentialities had been carried out by the Home Defence Committee. Its members had tentatively estimated that if, in addition to rocket and high-explosive conventional attack, about 17 atomic bombs were accurately placed on any one of five principal target systems—ports, electricity, oil, steel and transport— then the United Kingdom would lose her power to fight. A similar number would probably also produce a critical situation if accurately used against housing and population. In view of likely delivery problems, however, the Future Planners were not willing to concede that the country could be brought to its knees in less than two months from the dropping of the first atomic bomb—unless Soviet stocks of these weapons turned out to be greatly in excess of the 30–60 currently anticipated:

> If the war should open with the use of such weapons, it must be accepted, however, that these two months represent the total period of endurance of the United Kingdom. If we are to survive, it becomes necessary for us to win the war before this climax is reached.

Furthermore, even if not using them initially, it would always remain in the Russians' power to bring the war to a sudden and rapid conclusion by resorting to atomic bombs at a later stage.

Generally speaking, the same arguments applied to biological weapons, though with a lesser degree of assurance. They had never been tested on men experimentally, but the danger they posed might be more insidious, widespread and persistent. It was felt that their threat would largely be countered in the end by advances in immunisation techniques. If the difficulty of detecting nerve gases could be overcome, that danger could likewise be diminished; but the Future Planners were not prepared to quantify either their potential effects or those of crop-destruction agents.

Three main steps would have to be taken to reduce the vulnerability of the United Kingdom: to organise the strongest possible air defence system; to develop a means of impeding rocket attack; and to prepare stocks of essential resources. Stockpiling, in fact, was the one foreseeable answer to weapons of mass destruction, provided that the attacker's supply of them was limited and that the defender concentrated all his industrial output on vital defence requirements.

Clearly, the principal factor shaping British strategy in a future war would be time. Whether or not absolute weapons were used, ideas of marshalling strength over a period of years for a final counter-offensive, as in previous wars, could no longer be sustained:

> The balance of our resources available after allocating the necessary quota for the most efficient defence of the United Kingdom must be applied with the object of bringing the war to an end within the limit set by the endurance of the United Kingdom. To do this we must provide for a counter offensive force as well as a strong defence; and this force must be available immediately . . . . Our whole strategy must be shaped with this urgency in view.

Nor did just vulnerability to bombardment dictate this emphasis on speed. An examination of the prospects of defending the Middle Eastern oil areas indicated that neither those in Persia and Iraq nor even those in the Persian Gulf could be held indefinitely, even were it possible to make sufficient forces available for the attempt. This factor would reduce the time for which the Commonwealth could fight a war alone to the order of from nine to twelve months, and might also restrict the duration of joint Anglo-American resistance.

By 1956 or 1957 at the latest, the United States would have the 400–500 atomic bombs believed to be necessary for decisive results against the Soviet Union. By 1957, too, the Russians would have enough to eliminate the United Kingdom only, and from 1963 all three countries might have decisive quantities. If discussions at the United Nations led to the imposition of controls, however, the Western Powers would be 'deprived of the only weapons which might enable us to obtain a quick victory over the U.S.S.R.' If bomber forces were restricted as well, the only means of developing an effective counter-offensive would also be lost. On the other hand, if conventionally-armed long-range rockets and projectiles were to be included in disarmament provisions, British vulnerability would be so reduced as to enable Western strength to be built up over a period for a counter-attack. Thus,

> To achieve its purpose, a disarmament agreement must aim at a progressive reduction so devised as to give parity to each party at each stage.

This would involve taking account of the geographical, ethnological, industrial and economic circumstances of each country concerned, and finding a formula to compensate for these factors. In the view of the F.P.S.,

> to obtain a stage of equilibrium in armaments we should have to go right back to the 1910 level; at no intervening stage can anything approaching security for all powers be obtained.

Great difficulties would confront the adoption of any such comprehensive agreement.

Even if atomic weapons were abolished, this did not mean that they would fail to be used in a war between East and West. Provided that the necessary fissile material was available (as it would be—from peaceful use of atomic energy), and that the necessary research and design work had already been completed, atom-bomb production could recommence after a delay of only about six months. In such a situation, there would be a great temptation to use the weapons the moment they became available, so as to forestall the enemy's own revived production programme. For the United Kingdom, however, this temptation would probably apply anyway:

> If absolute weapons are initially available, we consider our attacks should be directed to breaking the enemy's will to continue the fight by combined attacks against his war production, his local administration and the morale of his civil population. Our targets should therefore be the large towns, and more particularly those which accommodate large numbers of his industrial population, and we estimate that a stock of about 400 to 500 atom bombs would be required.

It could not be proven that, by this method, the Soviet Union would be forced to abandon the war before the United Kingdom had been 'knocked out', but the Future Planners believed it to offer the best prospect of success.

They therefore concluded that, in order to obtain a decisive result before the limit of British endurance had been reached, weapons of mass destruction should be employed as soon as possible. A comparatively modest bomber force would be required to mount such a strategic offensive; but that could serve only as the nucleus of the much larger one needed to mount conventional attacks on the alternative targets of oil and transportation if atomic weapons were not immediately available.

Since Western Europe would be indefensible, the necessary offensive air bases could be sited in one or more of only four locations: the United Kingdom, French North Africa, the Middle East and India. Political uncertainties militated against developing the second and fourth of these. Offensive air bases in Egypt could be recommended only for a transitional period while the Russians lacked the means of eliminating the United Kingdom quickly. This was because of the time it would take to move in the British forces in war which it seemed unlikely could be based there in peace. If the maximum use were made of Cyprus, Malta and—especially—Cyrenaica as advanced staging-posts, it was conceivable that a base in Egypt could be held, given six months in which to prepare its defences. Egypt's role as an offensive base should therefore be continued until 1956–57, when the Russian stock of atomic weapons would suffice to cause the collapse of the United Kingdom before any Middle Eastern counter-offensive mounted from Egypt could possibly take effect. Thereafter Aden, Malta, perhaps Cyrenaica, and (for a limited period) Cyprus would have to be used in combination—pending the development of 3,500-mile-range bombers which could operate from a fully developed base in Kenya. This change in strategy would enable a saving to be made of approximately 100,000 soldiers and sailors formerly required for the defence of Egypt.

There would be other vital areas to be protected besides the United Kingdom herself and the bases for her counter-offensive. As well as that of the American continent and of the Dominions, the security of India would have to be preserved—if she were allied with the West—for, as well as contributing massive resources, India was of great potential value as an offensive air base. Japan would be important not only, as in the case of Malaya and the East Indies, for her war potential, but also as an additional potential air base and as a stepping-stone for

Western assistance to the Chinese. It would be possible to allocate forces for internal security duties only in vital areas. A major effort to protect sea communications would also be unavoidable.

The Future Planners therefore proceeded to review in depth the commitments involved and forces possibly required in the United Kingdom, Middle East and Mediterranean, Indian and Far Eastern theatres, before summarising their strategic conclusions. These drew attention to the key distinction between transitional and long-term strategy. From about 1957, the one would have to be radically transformed into the other. Until then, it was possible to envisage a war of relatively long duration, because the Russians would have insufficient atomic bombs to cause collapse in the United Kingdom unaided. Biological weapons would be available at an earlier date, but their potentialities remained uncertain.

In the transitional period, American intervention would have to be forthcoming within a few weeks, at most, of the outbreak of war. British priorities should reflect the need for quick results from efforts to avoid defeat before American aid became effective. Even if absolute weapons were not used at the outset, the members of the F.P.S. could discern

> no method of achieving victory except by the use of them at a later appropriate time. The further development of the war would indeed be largely governed by the possibilities of accumulating effective stocks of these weapons before the enemy, and of using them more effectively than he could.

Strategy would be based upon the virtual abandonment of Western Europe:

> To avoid being committed to a continental campaign by political considerations, any forces provided for the occupation of Germany must be small and must not form part of the strategic reserve. In emergency they would have to be withdrawn.

The use of the Middle East in war would be an operational necessity, and its defence would be greatly prejudiced if forces could not be stationed in Egypt and Palestine in peace. These countries would certainly have to be reoccupied at the start of hostilities, and their bases supplemented by facilities in Cyprus, Malta, Aden, Cyrenaica and Kenya. Oil supplies would be severely restricted. Indian neutrality should be assumed for the decade ahead, but Japan should be cast in the role of a useful additional air base. For the first two months of a war in the transitional period, the Mediterranean sea route would be essential for a rapid build-up in the Middle East; but its closure thereafter would have to be accepted as a result of the loss of Western Europe. The aim should be to hold Malta and Cyprus for at least five months. As the security of Iceland, Ireland and the Azores would be essential for the protection of Atlantic communications, their occupation by the United States might be necessary at an early stage. There would be sufficient time to reinforce French North Africa, but uncertainties regarding India might result in the air deployment route via the Indian Ocean having to be re-routed to the south. Any threat to British positions further east would probably take some time to develop. The eventual outcome of a war in the transitional period would depend upon what happened with regard to the use of mass-destruction weapons; the effects of bombardment upon the United Kingdom; the impact of the Western strategic air offensive; the relative oil resources retained by each side; and the logistical limitations of the Western campaign in the Middle East.

The whole picture would change once Russia was able to use absolute weapons or to prepare effective quantities of them soon after a war began. The climax would have to be brought about before the British two-month survival period had elapsed. Immediate American participation would be indispensible, and the means of mass destruction would have to be employed at once. Offensive bases outside the United Kingdom would be of value only if they were available from the outset. Unless the political situation altered sufficiently over the next ten years for peacetime preparations to be possible in Egypt and Palestine, a time might therefore come when the concept of an air base in the Middle East ought to be abandoned. Kenya, Malta, Cyprus, Aden and—if possible—Cyrenaica would then be required as substitutes for Egypt.

As for the armed forces which would be needed at the outbreak of a war in 1956, the speed at which its climax might come demanded a higher level of preparedness than ever before. The necessary peacetime minima were estimated to be 185,250 personnel for the Royal Navy, 431,000 for the Army and 400,000 for the Royal Air Force. This inter-Service pattern reflected the changed balance of responsibilities likely in the long term, and the total of 1,016,250 personnel, and the annual expenditure of some £845 million involved, though well in excess of what could currently be contemplated, would not necessarily be beyond British capabilities once economic recovery was assured. However, the Future Planners readily acknowledged that

> economic recovery must be a first step in the formulation of our Policy for the years to come. Whether we like it or not, therefore, Defence Policy in common with many other aspects of our national life, must be subordinated to economic recovery for the next few years, at least.

The only aspect of military preparedness which dare not be subordinated in this way would be scientific research and development aimed at reducing the adverse balance of geography and resources. Fortunately, there seemed no likelihood of planned war before 1956 at the earliest—in other words, not until the closing stage of the 'transitional' period; but the prospects for holding the required offensive base in the Middle East, even then, would remain very uncertain.

If, despite the anticipated increase in danger once Russia acquired an effective atomic capability, the risk of war in 1956–60 could be discounted, then many difficulties might be overcome. A more even distribution of Commonwealth resources might be achieved, reducing their concentration in the British Isles and hence the temptation to attack the United Kingdom as the linchpin of the system. Again, if the operational range of bomber aircraft increased sufficiently during this period, the outstanding military importance of the United Kingdom and the Middle East as offensive bases would drastically decline. An extensive ring of American and British-owned bases, from Alaska and the Far East to Ceylon, Kenya and Newfoundland, would become available from which to launch the counter-offensive.

Nevertheless, the disadvantages of planning on this time-scale might be very great. The abandonment of the transitional strategy would preclude any chance of holding the Middle East if war were to break out before 1960, so counter-offensive potential would be severely restricted. Adoption of the peripheral bases plan would also reduce strategic flexibility, as it was totally dependent on the use of absolute weapons. Furthermore, manifest British unreadiness for war in the period until very long-range bombing became possible, would so weaken British influence upon world affairs that it would probably rob us of any firm and independent foreign policy and have consequential repercussions on the economic field. It would also force us, during the intervening years, to achieve a *modus vivendi* with the Soviet [Union], which owing to our weakness, would be largely dictated by her.

There thus appeared to be two broad policies for Commonwealth defence between which to choose: to plan on an assumption of the need to be prepared for a war with Russia in about 1956–60, or to assume that no war was likely for the next twenty years. Half-measures between the two could not be entertained, as they would reduce the degree of security afforded by the first course without reaping the economic advantages of the second. Beyond setting out the implications of each possibility, the Future Planners were not prepared to go.[132]

5. The Formulation of the Overall Strategic Plan

Whilst the F.P.S. was putting the finishing touches to its review, political developments had been of more immediate concern to the C.I.G.S. On 22 February, Montgomery wrote from abroad, instructing the War Office to draw up a paper on the effects of recent governmental action:

> we have chucked our hand in regarding Palestine; we have announced our withdrawal from India. Previously we lost our position in Egypt, and had taken a grave chance over Cyrenaica.
>
> When the Government take these matters *one by one* they may seem to be of small account individually.
>
> But *collectively* they are terrific.

All the Chiefs of Staff were doing was to comment upon each '*individual monstrosity*' as it occurred. They had failed to protest at the collectively immense repercussions of what was happening:

> The Government would be entitled to take our silence as acquiescence. They must never be able to get away with it like that.

If, as the politicians had now agreed, the Middle East were to be held, a reorientation of strategy would be essential. A short, sharp memor-

---

132.   JP(46)164(Final)(Retained—MoD)

andum should immediately be prepared for the Service chiefs'
consideration.[133] This it received on 5 March, when Montgomery
enlarged upon his theme and pointed out that the government's
statement of the transfer of power in India had been approved without
the Chiefs of Staff even being consulted. It was agreed that a paper
based upon the War Office memorandum should be sent to the Minister
of Defence, regardless of the risk that this might prejudice the main
report on which the F.P.S. was still working. The need to place military
opinion on record could not be delayed.[134] This was done in the form of
a memorandum for the Defence Committee, circulated two days later
and entitled 'The Defence of the Commonwealth'.

Referring to the basic principles endorsed by Attlee at the 13 January
Staff Conference, the paper listed all the recent international setbacks:
the referral of the Palestine question to the United Nations; the decision
to give no further aid to Greece after June 1947—which would
probably consign her to Communist control unless the Americans
stepped in; the lack of progress over Cyrenaica; and the decision to
hand over power in India in June 1948. Taken as a whole, all this would
rule out prospects of fighting in and for the Middle East in war. Yet the
air bases of the region were essential for mounting the counter-offensive
which alone could reduce the weight of air attack on the United
Kingdom. Nor would those in India be available to the Commonwealth,
and that country's role as a source of manpower and industrial
resources, and as a major link in communications with Australia and
the Far East, would no longer be fulfilled.

The loss of these great areas meant that the Commonwealth might be
forced to fight from peripheral bases—North America, South Africa,
Australia and New Zealand—with only the United Kingdom from
which to launch aerial attacks:

> Such a withdrawal to the 'outer ring' would entail long, arduous and
> costly operations before we could even start hitting back at the enemy; in
> fact the United Kingdom would begin the war by fighting in the last ditch,
> and it is open to serious doubt whether she could survive so long . . . . If
> the present trend of events continues, it must eventually lead the
> Commonwealth to disaster.

---

133.   Montgomery to Simpson, 22 February 1947, in WO 216/204 The War Office
       paper was circulated under cover of COS Sec Min 256/7. As with all military
       secretariat minutes, this series has not been preserved.
134.   COS(47)35th Mtg (2)(Confidential Annex)

It was national policy to prevent war. To this end, everything which could be done to improve relations with the Russians should be done. However, aggression could be deterred—or survival in war assured—only if the agreed minimum strategic objectives of securing the United Kingdom base, its sea communications and the Middle East, were pursued to the utmost in international dealings. In particular, treaties should be negotiated with Egypt and India, military rights should be preserved in Palestine and Cyprus, the closest possible links should be forged with the United States and the Dominions, facilities should be obtained in Cyrenaica, and improved relations sought with the Arab States.[135]

Despite the speed with which the Chiefs of Staff had agreed upon the contents of this paper, its further progress flagged. Alexander chaired a Staff Conference on 19 March and agreed to recommend to the Prime Minister that it should be laid before the Defence Committee;[136] but, on 3 April, Bevin, who was in Moscow attending a meeting of Foreign Ministers, successfully pressed for consideration of the memorandum to await his return.[137] By now, however, the F.P.S. had completed its review and the Chiefs of Staff were therefore in possession of the raw material needed for a much more comprehensive report to be compiled.

There was never any question of the Future Planners' findings being adopted *en bloc*.[138] As soon as they were known to be available, the C.N.S. sought to tie them in with the January *aide-mémoire*. According to Cunningham, what the Prime Minister had so far approved was

little more than a skeleton of what would have to be submitted in due course to the Cabinet. The Chiefs of Staff had yet to indicate their agreed supporting arguments to these principles of defence, and much of this would need to be drawn from the agreed portions of the Joint Planning Staff report.

Anticipating what was soon to become a source of great friction with his colleagues, Montgomery criticised the breadth of the terms of reference

---

135.   DO(47)23
136.   COS(47)41st Mtg   137.   Prime Minister's Personal Min No M.173/47
138.   The F.P.S. review was to remain in circulation as a 'Staff Study', though its conclusions were never adopted by the Chiefs of Staff. Its contents were still being referred to several months later, in connection with further work by the J.P.S. (See: JP(48)2(S)(T.R.) of 2 January 1948)

which the Future Planning Section of the J.P.S. had originally been given.[139] He circulated a list of half-a-dozen specific questions arising from the review for the Chiefs of Staff to resolve, and these were supplemented by a further list drawn up in the Admiralty.[140] Provisional answers to all the points raised were formulated on 14 April, discussed with the Minister of Defence and the chairman of the Defence Research Policy Committee[141] at a Staff Conference three days later,[142] and finally adjusted on 23 April at a meeting chaired by the V.C.A.S., Air Marshal Sir William Dickson.

Dickson took the opportunity to suggest that

> in the event of a potential enemy not employing weapons of mass destruction at the outset of a war, the political objections against our initiating their use might be so great that we should be prevented from taking the initiative by being the first to use them.

In his view, it would be necessary to plan for the use of conventional weapons as well, and he was in any case not convinced that the only hope of survival lay in using atomic bombs as soon as a conflict began.[143] This point was urged upon the Directors of Plans, for whom draft terms of reference to prepare a report on 'Future Defence Policy' were confirmed.[144] They were to assume a state of preparedness to use mass-destruction weapons immediately to be a cardinal principle of defence planning; but in the course of their report they were to examine the advisability of actually doing so in advance of an enemy. They should include the views of the Chiefs of Staff on essential objects of foreign policy, as stated in the 7 March memorandum which had still not been taken by the Defence Committee. As for potential enemies, whilst the main strategic arguments would not be affected were German resurgence to occur, the Russians should preferably be cast in this role

---

139. COS(47)48th Mtg (2) For the argument over the use of the J.P.S. system, see: COS(47)115th Mtg(1) & Annex; COS Sec 'Notes on the Work of the Chiefs of Staff Committee', 21 April 1948, in AIR 8/1354; and Montgomery, *Memoirs*, pp. 436–7   140. COS(47)72(0) & COS(47)78(0)

141. Terms of reference for the new D.R.P. Committee under Tizard, as recommended by the Service chiefs on 15 January 1947, were: 'To advise the Minister of Defence and the Chiefs of Staff on matters connected with the formulation of scientific policy.' (COS(47)11th Mtg (1); see also p. 191 above)

142. COS(47)52nd Mtg (1); COS(47)54th Mtg; COS(47)79(0)(Revise)

143. COS(47)57th Mtg (5)   144. COS(47)84(0) & COS(47)57th Mtg (4)

since their great strength and capabilities would be bound to influence the measures recommended.[145]

In carrying out their task, the Joint Planners had available a summary of C.O.S. opinions on the issues culled from the F.P.S. review by Montgomery and Cunningham. This began with confirmation of the fundamental principles agreed in January: defence of Commonwealth war resources pending the development of an all-out Allied counter-offensive, and retention of bases from which to launch it at the earliest possible moment. The 'three pillars' upon which the achievement of these aims would depend were also re-stated: defence of the United Kingdom, defence of sea communications, and defence of the Middle East. This time, however, equal priority was accorded to two more. One was expansion of organisation for scientific research and development—to ensure the maintenance of technical superiority and to enable future decisions on re-equipment to be made wisely. The other was development of the actual counter-offensive force—for the ability to strike back would

represent both a very strong deterrent to aggression and one of our principal means of defence . . . .

Next were listed basic factors which would underlie future military policy. The objects of the United Nations Organisation could be attained only if the Great Powers were ready and able to keep the peace. To the limit of its economic ability, therefore, the Commonwealth must be strong and prepared at all times to contribute a share corresponding to its world-wide responsibilities as a first-class Power. A sound economy would be essential if industry and the armed forces were to be capable of immediate expansion as the need arose. Since the greater part of Commonwealth war-making resources was concentrated in the British Isles, which were particularly vulnerable to atomic, biological and rocket attack,

A third major war within the next few years would be economically disastrous. The supreme object, therefore, of British policy must be to prevent war.

United Kingdom forces should thus aim to deter aggression which

---

145.   COS(47)57th Mtg (6)(Confidential Annex)

might lead to war, as well as to provide the means of safeguarding Commonwealth and U.N.O. interests in the event of an attack:

> The only effective deterrent to a potential aggressor is tangible evidence of our intention and ability to withstand attack and to retaliate immediately. Our aim must be to refashion our forces and our war potential to meet the needs of the future, but in the process, we must remain strong enough to demonstrate our ability to withstand and our intention to counter aggression at any time.

Support from other members of the Commonwealth could be counted upon, and American aid was also likely; but some time might elapse before help was received from either source. It was very doubtful if active Indian assistance would be forthcoming. Further study was needed concerning what help should be given to a West European defence system and what the reciprocal benefits might be. Still, the creation of such a system—with France as its keystone—should certainly be fostered. To redress the inevitable unfavourable balance of manpower at the outbreak of a war, it would be essential that the Services should be equipped with the most modern weapons and the most efficient technical skills.

As for the detailed points raised by the C.N.S. and the C.I.G.S., it was generally agreed that the Future Planners' prediction of 1956–60 as a critical period was sound. Planning should proceed on the assumption that there was little likelihood of a war in the coming five years, but that the danger would increase gradually to the mid-1950s, and more sharply thereafter. However, the risk at any stage would be lessened in proportion to the demonstrable strength of the United Kingdom and her allies. The two-month and nine-month crisis deadlines for atomic and conventional war respectively were not endorsed, though, since so much would depend upon future developments in methods of offence and defence. Intelligence of 'sound facts' on which conclusions could be based would have to be gathered; but it should be assumed that the time available after the outbreak of war in which defensive preparations could be made would be shorter than ever before.

Although stressing *preparedness* to use mass-destruction weapons at once as 'the best deterrent for war in peacetime', the brief for the J.P.S. did not confirm the Future Planners' conclusion that British survival during the initial defensive phase could be secured only by actually using them. Nor was it accepted that the Soviet Union would be bound to resort to them sooner or later, regardless of what the United Kingdom decided to do:

> The argument that the preparedness by both sides to use Chemical Warfare in the last war stopped its use during the war, is relevant.

The only circumstances under which Russia would show restraint in this matter would be when the use of absolute weapons would react to her disadvantage. A situation might arise in which the United Kingdom found herself initially alone and at war with the Soviet Union. To meet this eventuality, British policy in peacetime should aim to secure promises of material aid from the United States at the earliest possible opportunity and an immediate supply of atomic bombs. If these were to be used, however,

> No plan must be based on the assumption that Russian morale will break. Mass destruction weapons must be directed against the means to make war, and not the will to make war, although by attacking the former the latter may well be affected.

It was agreed that no reliance could be placed on substantial help from West European allies within the foreseeable future, despite the intention to build up a strong regional association. The possible loss of Middle Eastern oil supplies was also conceded, and the main threats to sea communications were acknowledged to be fast submarines, shore-based aircraft and minelaying. On the other hand, F.P.S. predictions of the rapid reduction of the United Kingdom by conventionally-armed rocket or aerial attack were not accepted. Neither was the recommendation for 'qualitative disarmament', which—by turning back the clock—would mean abandonment of the very technical superiority which alone could compensate for manpower deficiencies. The whole question of industrial dispersal throughout the Commonwealth would have to undergo thorough examination before its economic feasibility could be assessed. Finally, planning should not assume that the trusteeship of Cyrenaica would be obtained—desirable though this would be—and the possibility of trading Gibraltar for more secure alternative facilities should be considered, although this was unlikely to be practicable in peacetime.[146]

On 24 April, the STRATS was set to work on drafting the report.

---

146. COS(47)87(0)

The Joint Planners had been instructed to have it ready by 8 May, and this was achieved with a day to spare.[147] When the terms of reference were being finalised, Tizard had suggested that his own D.R.P. Staff should be involved in the drafting process.[148] The views its members tendered can be gauged from a short statement prepared for the Chiefs of Staff by the D.R.P. Committee chairman and approved, as amended, for forwarding to them on 29 April.[149] This set out the principal scientific factors expected to affect defence policy during the next few years. It stressed that, unless present policy changed, the United Kingdom was unlikely to possess enough atomic bombs to have a decisive effect in war within the next ten years. It recommended that research into chemical and biological weapons should be given effectively equal priority to that into atomic energy, and wrote an epitaph—in passing—upon the Second World War policy of conventional area bombing:

> It should be accepted that in a major war against a highly industrialised country, mass attacks, as opposed to precision bombing, against centres of population and industry with bombs of the type used in the last war will be ineffective and wasteful in manpower.

For a decade at least, long-range aircraft capable of 600 m.p.h. at 40,000 feet or above would be the best means of delivery. It would be hard to mount an adequate defence against them, and their development, though difficult in detail, would be basically straightforward. Unlike pilotless aircraft or rockets, manned bombers could easily be transported to bases overseas, and they were also cheaper to operate in terms of overall manpower. The long-range rocket was, in any case, unlikely to mature within ten years. It would also probably take a decade before supersonic fighters and guided anti-aircraft projectiles offered effective protection against high-flying bombers attacking the United Kingdom. Nor was there any better prospect of thwarting a V.2-type rocket, once launched, than of stopping a long-range shell. Only against low-flying aircraft might techniques soon improve: eventually unacceptably high losses might be inflicted upon them. As for sea communications, the ships to protect them would have to be repaired in new, less-vulnerable overseas bases. Over the next five years, top priority should be given to developing high-performance submarines

---

147.   JP(47)55(S)(T.R.) & JP(47)55(Final)(Retained—MoD)
148.   COS(47)57th Mtg (4)   149.   DRP(47)8th Mtg (2)(Retained—MoD)

and experimental escort vessels, if methods of dealing with underwater and aerial attack were to be evolved. As its overall recommendation, the D.R.P. paper advised that the experimental establishments should be allowed to concentrate upon the development of radically new weapons and equipment, and that, to facilitate this,

> all necessary re-equipment of the Forces during the next five years should be based on the best that was available in 1946 unless there are strong reasons to the contrary.[150]

By the time that the Chiefs of Staff came to take note of Tizard's paper on 14 May,[151] however, the Directors of Plans had already submitted the major draft on future strategic policy. Both the C.A.S. and the C.I.G.S. felt it to be a creditable piece of work. The former's amendments concerned greater emphasis upon the steadily growing risk of war in the period 1952–57, its more dramatic likely rise thereafter, and the value of *immediate* offensive and defensive counter-action on the outbreak of hostilities. The latter considered it 'basically sound' and appears to have refrained from reopening the question of committing land forces to the Continent in wartime. Though doubting the military potential of a Western European group, the paper did at least give strong backing to the idea of establishing one.[152] Only Cunningham offered substantive criticism, complaining that

> the report was colourless, lacked conviction, and did not place sufficient emphasis on some essential points of our defence policy.

Not only the lack of time to organise defence measures once the fighting had begun, but also the likely loss of Middle Eastern oil and the vital need to stockpile such essential commodities, had been insufficiently stressed. It was agreed that the Minister of Defence should be present when the re-draft was considered. Thereafter, the Future Planning Section would be dissolved, the J.P.S. would prepare a further paper on the forces needed at the outbreak of war to implement the approved strategy, and the Service Departments would assess the forces needed

---

150. DRP(47)53(Retained—MoD)   151. COS(47)64th Mtg (2)
152. *Cf.* pp. 275–6 & 290–1 above. In March 1948, the long-envisaged Western bloc was to be set up under the terms of the Brussels Treaty. According to his own account, however, it was to take Montgomery until the following May to obtain C.O.S. agreement upon the need to fight a campaign on the Continent in the event of Soviet aggression. (Montgomery, *Memoirs*, pp. 498–502)

in peacetime as the basis upon which to expand in an emergency.[153]

At the meeting with Alexander on 21 May, it was agreed that references to the importance of Middle Eastern communications should be strengthened, as should those dealing with peacetime preparations to maintain reserves of resources and efficient Intelligence services able to give timely warning of aggression. The minister mentioned that the Defence Committee would want an idea of the forces required to carry out the suggested policy, but he appreciated that estimates would have to await decisions yet to be made on future defence research policy.[154]

The following day, the finalised report was produced over the signatures of Cunningham, Montgomery and Dickson. It was designed with two aims in view: to enunciate and justify the fundamental principles of future defence policy, and to set out clearly the basic requirements of a strategy for the defence of the Commonwealth in accordance with those principles.

The first of the paper's two main sections began by dismissing the United Nations Organisation as irrelevant to the prevention of war between the Great Powers. Its operations depended for success upon their willingness and ability to keep the peace, as aggression on their part could be shielded by the use of the veto:

> In this situation, we believe that the only effective deterrent to a potential aggressor is tangible evidence of our intention and ability to withstand attack and to hit back immediately.

Disarmament measures would have to be coupled with adequate guarantees of security before they could be accepted. British policy of preventing war whilst safeguarding vital interests would depend, for fulfilment, upon a restored economy and the provision of sufficient forces and resources to deter and defend. Commonwealth strength lay in the presentation of a united front to the world, but this was a two-way process. Although herself relying upon the contribution of the Dominions, the United Kingdom was just as vital to them for the preservation of their security. A British defeat would bring about the disintegration of the Commonwealth, since its other members were too

---

153. COS(47)64th Mtg (1) Subsequent inter-Service wrangling over the shape and size of the nucleus forces required to implement agreed strategy in the context of economic constraints, does not fall within the scope of this study.
154. COS(47)66th Mtg (4)

weak to stand alone. A future war was not inevitable, but the possibility of a conflict with the Russians could not be ruled out in the prevailing political atmosphere—whether caused by deliberate aggression or by sheer miscalculation of the extent to which expansionism would be tolerated by the West. Germany could not pose a major threat by herself for many years, and even should she eventually do so, it would be possible to cope with the situation by adjusting a strategy designed to deal with a greater danger. A strong alliance which was clearly ready to act would reduce the risk of war. That risk, small at present, would gradually increase until the second half of the 1950s. From then onwards, the growing momentum of Russia's rehabilitation would intensify the danger more dramatically.

Only a combination of increased technical superiority and the securing of allied help could offset this threat. No European bloc could, as of old, be relied upon to resist aggression effectively; but a regional association 'would at least delay the enemy's advance across Europe'. It was active and early American support which was really indispensable. American manpower, industrial resources and supplies of mass-destruction weapons alone could turn the scale against what was by no means just a threat to the Continent:

> The Russian policy of territorial and ideological expansion by the absorption of satellite States and by the spread of Communism in peace constantly threatens various countries whose continued integrity and independence profoundly affect Commonwealth security. Our interests are challenged, not only throughout Europe but also in the Middle East and throughout the world.

In keeping with the stand they had taken against Attlee, the Chiefs of Staff had strengthened the original passage of the J.P.S. draft concerning the Middle East. This was now stated to be the 'area in which Russian expansion would be easiest and at the same time would hurt us most'; there was no doubt that any vacuum created by withdrawal in peacetime would speedily be filled. Not only would Russia deprive the Western Powers of vital oil resources and base facilities, she would also acquire a position of such dominating strategic and economic strength as to be fatal to Commonwealth security.

New weapons of mass destruction had raised acceptable standards of defence to levels unlikely to be reached within the decade. This opened up the prospect of rapid and decisive results being obtained by attacks on key industrial targets and cities. The relatively light payloads required meant that effective surprise attacks could be mounted as never before, thus putting a premium upon adequate warning by a highly developed Intelligence organisation. Sea communications also would be endangered to an unprecedented extent, and, even in a purely conventional conflict, the vulnerability of the United Kingdom would be such as to preclude the possibility of a lengthy campaign. Neither technical superiority nor American help would, in any event, be able to halt a Soviet advance to the Channel coast. Having achieved this objective, the Russians would be able to bombard the British Isles with high-explosive rockets and missiles, causing irreparable damage and perhaps eliminating the country from the conflict completely:

> It is essential that before such destruction—from which we might never recover—could be achieved we ourselves should assume the initiative and destroy the enemy's means of making war . . . . This initiative must be assumed from the outset.

If a build-up on the Continent were to be impeded and the war-making potential of the Soviet Union attacked, a decisive aerial campaign with weapons of mass destruction might have to be initiated. It was true that only a small operational effort of the same sort by the Russians would be required to knock out the United Kingdom. Yet, although the margin between victory and defeat in an atomic exhange would therefore be a very narrow one, this was no argument for mutual disarmament in this field—for within a few months of the outbreak of war new atomic bombs could be in production. The Russians could see the vulnerability of the British position as clearly as anyone else. Soviet use of absolute weapons could be forestalled only by the threat of retaliation. It was impossible to decide at this stage under what circumstances the United Kingdom should or should not resort to them:

> The one certain point is that it must be a cardinal principle of our policy to be prepared, equipped and able to use them immediately.

Whether the British counter-offensive was atomic, biological or conventional, however, bases would be needed from which it could be launched. Whilst those within the United Kingdom would be the most vital, large areas of Russia would remain beyond their reach for many years and they would all be liable to heavy bombardment. If Soviet war potential were to be attacked with any prospect of significantly limiting the weight of attack on the British Isles, Middle Eastern and North-West Indian air bases would also be essential.

From all this, the fundamentals of future defence policy could be deduced. The 'supreme object of British policy' was to prevent war, provided that this could be done without prejudicing British vital interests. Possible Soviet aggression, especially from 1956 onwards, was the main threat requiring precautionary measures to be taken. Tangible evidence of an ability and intention to respond with immediate offensive action would be the best deterrent to aggression. Essential peacetime measures were listed as: the preparation of balanced forces and reserves at a high state of readiness; the maintenance of Commonwealth unity; assurance of American and Western European support; exploitation and development of techno-logical superiority; active opposition to Soviet ideological and territorial expansionism, especially in areas of strategic value; an arresting of the decline in British power and prestige in the Middle East, and a continuation of encouragement to Greece and Turkey to maintain their independence; retention of British Intelligence organisations at a high standard of efficiency; readiness to take immediate offensive air action from the United Kingdom, from the Middle East, and—if possible—from North-West India; and, finally, being equipped, ready and able to use mass-destruction weapons as a part of this offensive action.

The second main section of the paper set out a strategy in conformity with the agreed fundamentals. It had been given a strengthened preamble by the Chiefs of Staff during the amending of the J.P.S. draft. In this passage, they stressed—as had the Future Planners originally—the crucial importance of the time-factor in any future war:

The days when we could afford to remain on the defensive, while gathering our great strength for the knock-out blow, ended with the advent of the cross-channel pilotless missile and with the dropping of the first atom bomb. A far higher degree of preparedness in peace is now imperative if we are to survive the opening phases of another war—a preparedness which must enable us to hit back hard at the outset to defend our very existence. Moreover, in view of the speed with which we could be knocked out, it is vital that we possess the ability by ourselves to withstand and counter the initial onslaught. This entails stockpiling of reserves in peace-time.

The weight and tempo of this onslaught may, however, be beyond our power to bear alone for more than a short period. This places a new value on Dominion and Allied support, and calls for much more rapid assistance than of old, even if it is thereby limited.

The 'three pillars' of Commonwealth strategy enunciated in January were re-stated. With regard to the role of the United Kingdom base, its capacity to develop an air offensive would be crucial as a counter to atomic, biological or the build-up of rocket attack. Air superiority would also be needed, as in the past, to defeat normal methods of air attack, including the prospect of airborne invasion. To defend the British Isles, four elements were necessary: strong air defences, both active and passive; an effective bomber force; army formations able to deal with raids or attempts at invasion; and naval and air control of the sea approaches.

The last of these elements overlapped with the second strategic 'pillar'—control of essential sea communications generally. The danger to those in North Atlantic and Home waters would be immensely increased by enemy occupation of the Channel and Western European Atlantic ports. The utility of the Mediterranean route for defence of the Middle East was particularly emphasised, and the principal threats to shipping were identified as fast submarines, aircraft and minelayers.

In dealing, thirdly, with the Middle East, the Chiefs of Staff had strengthened the references to oil resources as Cunningham had suggested. The J.P.S. draft[155] had stated that

> We cannot be certain of being able to extend our defences to cover the existing main sources of our oil supply,

and had gone on merely to recommend the development of less vulnerable alternative supplies. The final version now insisted that, although the defence of Middle Eastern oil could not be undertaken with certainty of success, 'every effort' must be made to do this. Pipelines and other oil communications should be 'as well placed strategically as possible', and the resources of safer oilfields should be supplemented by the creation of stockpiles in the main base areas of the Commonwealth. The defence of Egypt against land attack from the north would require a campaign to be fought in Southern Syria/

---

155. JP(47)55(Final)(Retained—MoD)

Northern Palestine, where the Russians would be operating at the end
of difficult lines of communications. It was believed that

> Provided we are established in the Middle East area before the Russian
> advance and provided early reinforcements can be obtained from the
> Dominions and the United States it should be possible to defend our
> interests in the Middle East.

Were the area once to be lost, however, its recapture would require an
expenditure of resources out of all proportion to that entailed in
defending the Middle East if firmly established there at the outset.
Once again, an effective defence would depend upon four main
features: the right to re-enter Egypt when war threatened; peacetime
strategic rights in Palestine; continued sovereignty over Cyprus; and
resistance by the Turks to Soviet encroachment in peace or war. East
Africa would have value as a location for reserves. Greek independence
and British trusteeship in Cyrenaica would also improve prospects of
mounting an effective defence.

The only other area considered relevant to the overall strategy was
North-West India. The sub-continent could not at present be included
as an integral part of the general defence plan, given the impending
transfer of power; but an agreement to obtain India's active co-
operation in a future war should vigorously be sought. The same would
apply to any new state emerging separately in the important north-
western region.

A general indication could now be given of the future tasks of the
armed forces and of the principles which should govern their post-war
structure. The first requirement was to foster British organisation for
scientific research and development, enabling the maintenance of
technical superiority and ensuring the provision of information in good
time on which to base re-equipment policy. Secondly, as the ability
to strike would serve both as a deterrent and as a main element in
defence, the development of an air offensive had to be given high
priority. Next came the 'three pillars'. The defence of the United
Kingdom would involve the Royal Navy and Royal Air Force in
securing control of the sea approaches, and the Army and Royal Air
Force both in active and passive A.D.G.B. and in defence against
invasion. The protection of world-wide sea communications with the
United States, with other sources of supply, with the Dominions, and
with the Middle East—and the denial of their control to the enemy—

would fall to the Navy with Air Force assistance. Defence of the Middle East would be the Army's primary task, apart from its duties of A.D.G.B. and aid to the civil authorities in the United Kingdom. Even preparations against airborne invasion of the Home Islands should not be accorded as high a priority as this. Air power, too, would be needed in the Middle East and (if possible) in India; and the Navy would also be engaged in any Middle Eastern campaign.

As well as requesting Defence Committee approval of the fundamentals of defence policy and of the basic strategy and tasks of the armed forces thus outlined, the report recommended that ministers should note C.O.S. views on the relationship between defence policy and national policy. These clearly recognised that the impact of long-term foreign and economic policy upon security would be as important as any adjustments made to the structure of the post-war forces. It was conceded that the government was already committed to particular courses of action concerning Palestine and India, but, on the model of the 7 March paper on Commonwealth Defence, a list of militarily desirable foreign policy objectives was set out. All the original requirements were reiterated: the closest possible link with the Americans; agreements for facilities in Egypt, Palestine and India; rights in Cyrenaica; sovereignty over Cyprus; and a determination to let nothing impede Anglo-Arab relations. To these were added: support for the United Nations, but no disarmament without security; resistance to the spread of Communism in peace; closer links with the Commonwealth, the creation of a Western regional defence association, and the prevention of Soviet domination in Germany; a satisfactory political solution in Spain, and avoidance of measures prejudicing access to Spanish or French North African colonies in war; exclusion of Soviet influence in Libya and Somalia, when their fate was decided; independence and security for Greece, Turkey, Persia and Afghanistan; the development of oil-producing areas in less vulnerable parts of the Middle East and elsewhere; and the stockpiling of reserves of resources essential to Commonwealth war-making capacity.

It was fully acknowledged that

> The outstanding consideration from a strategical point of view is that the economy of the United Kingdom should be thoroughly sound and able to support a powerful war potential and adequate armed forces.

Dispersal within the United Kingdom was already an accepted factor in industrial planning, and the report concluded by recommending that, in view of the increased vulnerability of the British Isles, the practicability of a limited dispersal overseas of strategic industries should be thoroughly examined by experts.[156]

Although the Chiefs of Staff had intended the paper to be submitted to the Defence Committee, the Minister of Defence arranged for it to be considered at a much smaller Staff Conference initially. This was held on 11 June, and, in the event, its selectivity was justified by the reaction to the report of its most senior participants. Both Attlee and Bevin were reluctant to permit a document 'largely oriented to meet a Russian threat' to be generally disseminated. The former feared that to pursue this line

> would probably lead us to take steps which would be obvious to Russia as being directed against her and which might well inevitably precipitate a war.

Bevin also felt it to be dangerous if a report which specified Russia as the potential enemy were given

> anything but the most restricted circulation, since to do so would tend to bias our whole outlook in international affairs, and might thereby lead to a war with Russia,

and he argued that the fundamental principles of defence would apply equally, whether Russia or Germany were the more probable enemy. Yet, as the Chiefs of Staff pointed out, this did not apply to the section on basic strategic requirements—notably with regard to the development of North-West India as an offensive base. Though the Foreign Secretary's opinion that

> Germany in time might well regain her previous position as the chief threat to the peace of the world

was possibly correct, they had to present the military facts as they saw them—and these did not support the view that Germany alone could threaten world peace in the period covered by the report. They were, however, quite content to give no further circulation to the report, *provided that its recommendations were approved*. It mattered little to the Chiefs of Staff whether that approval were accorded by the full

---

156.   DO(47)44—also COS(47)102(0)(Not circulated)—(Retained—Cabt. Off.) Full text in Appendix 7, pp. 370–87 below

Defence Committee or just by Prime Ministerial Staff Conference, as long as they received the permission they needed to continue planning in conformity with the provisions of their paper. They therefore offered to omit any mention of Russia as the potential enemy in subsequent reports on the shape and size of the forces required to implement their strategy, once that strategy had the governmental sanction it needed.[157]

Attlee was still reluctant to approve the report. He reverted to his former scepticism that the Middle East would be defensible and that the weight of attack on the United Kingdom would be significantly reduced by the launching of a counter-offensive from that region. He was particularly reluctant to become embroiled in furnishing support to Middle Eastern regimes, which 'through their decadent social structures were peculiarly vulnerable to Russian propaganda methods'; but Bevin once again re-stated the lack of any alternative to the maintenance of British influence in the area. He was convinced that the Soviet Union was so concerned at her vulnerability on this flank that

> our presence in the Middle East would act as a definite check on Russian aspirations and would make her hesitate before embarking on a major war.

Furthermore, this presence was essential in view of British dependence upon local oil resources both in peace and war; and the Foreign Office was at present engaged,

> with the object of lessening the chances of unrest caused by the infiltration of Communist propaganda,

---

157. After citing Attlee's and Bevin's objections to the naming of Russia as the Commonwealth's potential enemy, Professor Gowing comments that 'The Chiefs of Staff report was circulated no further', and omits to mention that its recommendations were adopted. In a later footnote, she remarks that it 'had been discussed by, but not confirmed by, Ministers'. Neither the restrictions imposed upon its subsequent circulation, nor the record of the meeting which considered and approved it, justify this interpretation. (*Cf.* Gowing, *Independence and Deterrence*, i. pp. 186–7; 215 fn.) In point of fact, the report was sent to the Chancellor of the Exchequer very soon after the Staff Conference, and also—after representations by the C.N.S.—to the Service Ministers as well in July. (COS Sec Mins 621/12/6/7 & 720/3/7/7; Prime Minister's Personal Min No D.2/47; COS Sec Min 735/7/7/7; Prime Minister's Personal Mins Nos M.274/47, 275/47 & 276/47)

in persuading the oil companies to develop the amenities available to their employees in the oilfield areas. A far-reaching scheme to develop Iraq was under discussion with the Americans, and it still appeared possible that United Nations action over the Palestine Mandate, Anglo-Egyptian Treaty and Cyrenaican Trusteeship might yet result in British strategic needs in those countries being met. Bevin reiterated his belief that Russia would fill the vacuum created by withdrawal. He also supported the Chiefs of Staff on the importance of maintaining technical superiority, and suggested *inter alia* the construction of atomic energy plants in South Africa:

> In general he supported the recommendations of the Chiefs of Staff. He recommended in particular that the Conference should adhere to their previous view,[158] whether Germany or Russia was regarded as the most likely enemy, that to retain our strategic position in the Middle East was one of the three pillars vital to the security of the British Empire.

The Minister of Defence concurred, arguing that there would be little need for capital expenditure in the Middle East. Although the risk of war during the next five years was considered small, an agreed long-term defence policy was needed now. Like Bevin, Alexander believed that 'Russia faced by a strong front tended to withdraw from her position', as had already occurred over Persia:

> On the other hand, however, evident weakness on our part might well lead to war and might have a detrimental effect on America's determination to stand up against Russia.

For their part, the Chiefs of Staff claimed the Middle East to be the one area in which successful British resistance could be mounted with relatively smaller forces. They pointed out that the further eastwards Russia moved her oilfield areas, the more necessary became the need for bases from which to launch attacks against dispersed components of her war potential. Finally, they emphasised that

> the best deterrent against a future war would be our known preparedness to defend ourselves and to hit back. To this end we should increase and exploit our present scientific and technical lead, especially in the development of weapons of mass destruction.

---

158.   COS(47)9th Mtg (2)

One other voice was raised in support of the overall strategic plan. Sir Henry Tizard, who attended as chairman of the Defence Research Policy Committee, stated that such developments as could currently be foreseen favoured the offensive rather than the defensive in warfare, and that the trend was towards greater dependence upon oil than ever before. These were points in favour of a continued presence in the Middle East, at least for the time being. Whilst it was true that the British Isles were particularly vulnerable to the atomic bomb, the Americans and the Russians both seemed just as apprehensive at the prospect of its use against them:

> He suggested that if atomic bombs had not been developed, war in the near future might have been more likely and the United Kingdom might have been comparatively more vulnerable.

Consequently, no rights over British use of these weapons should be surrendered whilst the possibility existed of their employment by other Powers.

In the face of this unanimity, Attlee suggested that the recommendations of the report—including endorsement of the fundamental principles of defence and of Commonwealth strategy—should be accepted, though its circulation should be strictly limited and no reference should be made to a specific enemy in follow-up papers for wider distribution. This was agreed.[159] The United Kingdom had an approved anti-Soviet defence strategy. Despite the impossibility of reconciling it with more immediate economic constraints,[160] it was to remain the basis of long-term British military planning until after the onset of open confrontation with the Soviet bloc and the start of concerted Western opposition to it.[161]

---

159. COS(47)74th Mtg (1)(Retained—MoD)
160. For example, after examining a proposal to impose a financial ceiling on military expenditure of £600 million per annum, the J.P.S. reported on 11 November 1947 that the government 'would have to accept responsibility for ordering reductions which are incompatible with security, and for the decision on the means by which the financial limit was to be reached'. (JP(47)129 (Final)(Retained—MoD))
161. Thus, in May 1948, with the Brussels Treaty having been concluded on 17 March, the Joint Planners were still being required to refer to the 1947 report when drawing up strategic plans (JP(48)59(S)(T.R.)). Similarly, in June 1949, with N.A.T.O. an established fact since 4 April and agreement on the future shape and size of the Services as far off as ever, the Chiefs of Staff were still defining long-term strategy in terms of the 'three pillars' and the mounting of an air offensive from the United Kingdom and the Middle East. The only addition was their intention to supply 'Such assistance as we can afford, as a measure of self-preservation, to the forces of the Western Union'. (DO(49)50)

CONCLUSIONS

1. Foreign Policy and the Selection of a Potential Enemy

Until the successful invasion of Europe made the outcome of the war seem only a matter of time, long-term British defence planning was largely dominated by the Foreign Office. There is no evidence that post-war considerations figured to any significant extent in the wartime strategy of the Chiefs of Staff. On the contrary, they devoted considerable efforts to ensuring that the two strands remained separate—condemning the Military Sub-Committee to operating in an administrative limbo, and eventually setting up Jebb's P.H.P. Sub-Committee (under Foreign Office pressure), largely with non-strategic activities in view.

Whereas the Service chiefs were overwhelmingly preoccupied with the prosecution of the war, the demands on the diplomats were significantly less pressing. They could look forward to a time when the fruits of their labours would again count for something; and they gladly assumed the unwanted burden which their original approach to Ismay had briefly threatened to impose on the J.P.S. Schemes could be drawn up on a grand scale in the fairly sure knowledge that the people who really mattered had neither the time nor the inclination to give them their attention. Not only did this apply to the military authorities, it also largely applied to the Prime Minister himself where such issues as the Four Power Plan, the Western bloc and dismemberment of Germany were concerned. Typically, referring to the first of these late in 1942, he had commented to Eden's chagrin:

> I hope that these speculative studies will be entrusted mainly to those on whose hands time hangs heavy, and that we shall not overlook Mrs Glass's Cookery Book recipe for Jugged Hare—'First catch your hare.'[1]

---

1. Prime Minister's Personal Min No M.461/2 of 18 October 1942 in PREM 4/100/7

This hunting metaphor was a good one; for, having raised their har
the diplomats were disconcerted to find it speeding off in the wror
direction. Despite the low priority they accorded to their post-w;
planning apparatus, the Chiefs of Staff were not prepared to let
continue to be used in furtherance of what seemed to them to k
political pipe-dreams. When they saw what was happening, i
February 1944, they enlisted unsuspecting Foreign Office approval fc
a move to cut away Jebb's support amongst the Post-Hostilitie
Planners. At the first sign of persistent trouble in July, they finished th
job by cancelling his chairmanship. Thereafter, the diplomats could dc
little but grumble, until in due course developments in Europe anc
elsewhere made them somersault into line.

C.O.S. concern about Russia did not derive from bellicosity. Far
from it: for they, better than anyone, knew the limitations of British
military power. Their anxiety stemmed from pure appreciation of the
massive imbalance of power which would exist after the war. Though
there were political factors in their calculations, these were only of the
broadest significance—that, whereas war with America was politically
inconceivable, the same could not be said about relations with the
Russians. Planning should therefore proceed on alternative assumptions
of concord or hostility in the latter case, though not in the former.

This the Foreign Office would not tolerate. It became essentially
antipathetic towards the whole conception of *contingency* planning—
that is, the preparation of schemes to have in hand *if* certain
circumstances arise, without prejudice to whether they are considered
likely to arise or just not so unlikely as to rule them out as serious
possibilities. (It should be remembered, indeed, that throughout the
period considered, and even after the start of open confrontation, it
remained the military view that Russia would probably *not* want full-
scale war to occur for at least several years to come.)

The Foreign Office wanted Three Power co-operation to continue;
therefore, in its opinion, planning had to proceed only on the basis that
it would continue. Of course, it was argued that if the Russians got wind
of the existence of plans including an assumption of Soviet hostility—
which, thanks to Maclean, they certainly did in 1944—then this
discovery would change their hypothetical hostility into the genuine
article. Yet there is no good reason why this should have been so. As
Portal had stated, without rebuttal, during the Dismemberment debate,
nations are perfectly entitled to take reasonable precautions against
possible misbehaviour by their neighbours. Had the United Kingdom

learned of Soviet contingency planning for the possibility of Western hostility, this would not have caused the abandonment of any British policy of co-operation if that were the present objective. Only if co-operation ceased to be the objective would there be any cause to fear the implementation of such plans.

In April 1942, six months before the formulation of the Four Power Plan, it had seemed perfectly normal for the Foreign Office to ask the Joint Planners to consider Russia as a potential enemy.[2] In September 1943, Warner had voiced his opinion that the Russians had probably yet to make up their minds about Western intentions and would probably have in readiness alternative plans corresponding to different possible eventualities.[3] There should have been nothing to prevent the Chiefs of Staff doing likewise. Indeed, as at least the Service planners realised, Foreign Office plans for a Western bloc were far more likely to arouse Soviet suspicions than was strategic contingency planning. Here, again, the diplomats' view was that if only Russia could be persuaded that the United Kingdom was 'sincere' in her aim to use this just against the Germans, then all would be well. In the event, all was not well, and Churchill had to intervene in an attempt to mollify Stalin by assuring him that he himself had not yet considered the matter. 'I do not know how these ideas of what is called a "Western bloc" got around in Foreign Office and other influential circles,' he admonished Eden in November 1944.[4]

Throughout the war, a great deal of effort had been devoted to laying the 'myth of the Russian bogey' so strongly exploited by the Nazis. It would appear that, to some extent, the Foreign Office gradually became a victim of its own propaganda and a dupe of its own wishful thinking, quite apart from the pressures upon it to mirror American enthusiasm for the United Nations ideal. Cut off from the realities of power, the diplomats mistook the shadow for the substance of international relations. Their disillusionment was to be all the greater when by 1946, they found the whole basis of their policy to have been misconceived.

For the Chiefs of Staff, however, the transition was to be far less traumatic. This was not because they had wanted confrontation to occur, nor even because they had felt it bound to occur. It was simply that they were concerned with contingencies rather than predictions,

---

2.   See pp. 7–8 above   3.   See p. 59 above
4.   Prime Minister's Personal Telegram No T.2183/4 & Prime Minister's Personal
     Min No M.1144/4 in CAB 21/1614

and contingencies are concerned with tangible weights in the balance of power rather than nebulous indications of political goodwill. On their own criterion, therefore, confrontation with the Soviet Union was bound to seem an obvious danger to the Chiefs of Staff from the moment when they reluctantly took the trouble to consider the post-war situation.

2. The Organisational Aspect and Strategic Problems

Refined and developed under the stress of war, the C.O.S. machine worked well in systematically examining the new military situation. When the atomic bomb made its appearance, the Joint Technical Warfare Committee was ready to hand for its importance to be assessed on an inter-Service basis. A relatively compact body itself, it could call on key witnesses from all parts of the military establishment and then present their testimony in digestible form. In some cases, such as Thomson's, this was of the highest intellectual calibre—anticipating, within months of Hiroshima, theoretical considerations which academic strategists thought themselves to have originated some considerable time later. When broad strategic guidelines were needed, standard C.O.S.–J.P.S. exchanges could thrash them out in principle, and an *ad hoc* team like the F.P.S. could be set up to explore them. In the end, it was always clear to see either what agreed inter-Service policy was at any given time; or, if there was disagreement, to know exactly where it lay.

The success of the Joint Staff system in providing straight answers to straight questions within a reasonable space of time owed much to the standardised format of its procedures and to the common link provided by members of the C.O.S. secretariat. This was in stark contrast to Foreign Office procedures, which were relatively unstructured—with 'policy' emerging almost haphazardly according to which individual bestirred himself on a given question at a given moment. In particular, it was not to be until April 1946, with the foundation of the 'Russia Committee',[5] that policy towards that country began to be systematically co-ordinated by the diplomats. As one man with considerable experience in exploiting organisational lacunae was later to note,

> It was facile then [1940], as it is now, to speak of a Foreign Office view. There are a lot of people in the Foreign Office and quite a few views.[6]

---

5. See p. 262 above
6. Kim Philby, *My Silent War* (London, MacGibbon & Kee, 1968), p. 18

The personalised approach to policy-making may conceivably have served purposes of diplomatic flexibility—a doubtful benefit—but the military planners certainly showed no signs of suffering from its absence. By the end of the war, they had been furnished with a general catalogue of strategic requirements in a series of studies by the Post-Hostilities Planners. By the middle of 1946, they had received detailed information on mass-destruction weapons from the J.T.W.C. By mid-January 1947, the Prime Minister had been induced to approve the basis of C.O.S. strategy; and by mid-June of that year, the overall plan had been endorsed. One step had followed another in steady sequence until the job was done with a thoroughness not soon to require reversal.

There was, nevertheless, little cause for complacency about the issues themselves. It had been recognised at a very early stage that loss of insular invulnerability and an urgent need for allies would be major problems in post-war defence preparations. The United Kingdom might, perhaps, remain a Great Power, but she would be incapable of standing alone. From the start of planning until the end of the German war, there had seemed little prospect of a capacity being available to strike back hard against Soviet aggression, or of a definite American commitment being made to rally to the defence of the United Kingdom. Both prospects looked markedly more probable by the time that the overall plan was adopted. The question of a British commitment to send troops to the Continent had still to be resolved, their deployment being a symbol of political determination in a cold war rather than a strategic requirement for an open one; but then an open conflict was not currently anticipated in any case, and an independent long-term strategy had been worked out. There remained, however, two more major problems threatening to prevent the implementation of that strategy if ever the need arose: the political impossibility of retaining the non-British bases needed for a counter-offensive against the Soviet Union, and the economic necessity of imposing on the Service budgets arbitrary financial ceilings lower than those needed for the maintenance of adequate nucleus forces.

The first of these problems was to be solved by technical developments enabling deterrence to function on an inter-continental basis. The second remains almost as intractable today as it was in 1947.

APPENDIX 1

Principal Figures in British Military Planning, 1942–47

(i) MEMBERS OF THE CHIEFS OF STAFF COMMITTEE

C.N.S.

Admiral of the Fleet Sir Dudley Pound	(until October 1943)
Admiral of the Fleet Sir Andrew Cunningham†	(until June 1946)

   [*later:* Admiral of the Fleet Viscount
   Cunningham]
Admiral Sir John Cunningham†

C.I.G.S.

General Sir Alan Brooke†	(until June 1946)

   [*later:* Field-Marshal Viscount Alanbrooke]
Field-Marshal Viscount Montgomery†

C.A.S.

Air Chief Marshal Sir Charles Portal†	(until December 1945)

   [*later:* Marshal of the R.A.F. Viscount Portal]
Marshal of the R.A.F. Sir Arthur Tedder†
   [*later:* Marshal of the R.A.F. Lord Tedder]

Chief Staff Officer to the Minister of Defence

Lieutenant-General Sir Hastings Ismay†	(until December 1946)

   [*later:* General Sir Hastings Ismay]
Lieutenant-General Sir Leslie Hollis†

C.C.O.

Vice-Admiral Lord Louis Mountbatten	(until October 1943)
Major-General R. E. Laycock	(until June 1947)

Major-General G. E. Wildman-Lushington
   [Chief of Combined Operations Staff]

(ii)   MEMBERS OF THE VICE-CHIEFS OF STAFF COMMITTEE

V. C. N. S.

Vice-Admiral H. R. Moore	(until June 1943)
[*later:* Vice-Admiral Sir Henry Moore]	
Rear-Admiral Sir Neville Syfret	(until October 1945)
[*later:* Vice-Admiral Sir Neville Syfret]	
Vice-Admiral Sir Rhoderick McGrigor†	(until October 1947)
Vice-Admiral Sir John Edelsten	

V. C. I. G. S.

Lieutenant-General A. E. Nye†	(until February 1946)
[*later:* Lieutenant-General Sir Archibald Nye]	
Lieutenant-General F. E. W. Simpson†	
[*later:* Lieutenant-General Sir Frank Simpson]	

V. C. A. S.

Air Chief Marshal Sir Wilfrid Freeman	(until October 1942)
Air Vice-Marshal C. E. H. Medhurst—	
Acting V.C.A.S.	(until March 1943)
Air Marshal Sir Douglas Evill	(until May 1946)
[*later:* Air Chief Marshal Sir Douglas Evill]	
Air Marshal Sir William Dickson†	

(iii)   MEMBERS OF THE JOINT PLANNING STAFF

Director of Future (Operational) Planning Section

Colonel the Rt. Hon. O. F. G. Stanley†	(until July 1942)

Directors of Plans, Admiralty

Captain E. G. H. Bellars	(until March 1942)
Captain C. E. Lambe†	(until April 1944)
Captain G. Grantham	(until January 1946)
Captain J. F. Stevens	

Director of Plans, War Office

Brigadier G. M. Stewart†	(killed, 29 January 1943)
Brigadier W. Porter	(until October 1943)
Brigadier C. S. Sugden†	(until February 1945)
Brigadier G. S. Thompson†	(until April 1946)
Brigadier J. H. N. Poett	

Director of Plans, Air Ministry
Air Commodore W. F. Dickson†   (until April 1942)
Air Commodore W. Elliot   (until June 1943)
Air Commodore W. L. Dawson   (until June 1946)
Air Commodore G. H. Mills

(iv) MEMBERS OF POST-WAR PLANNING BODIES

Military Sub-Committee, 1942–43
Rear-Admiral R. M. Bellairs
Brigadier W. E. van Cutsem
Dr J. M. Spaight

Post-Hostilities Planning Sub-Committee, 1943–44
H. M. G. Jebb†
Rear-Admiral R. M. Bellairs
Major-General M. F. Grove-White
Air Vice-Marshal Sir Arthur Longmore
C. H. M. Waldock
Brigadier W. E. van Cutsem
Dr J. M. Spaight

Post-Hostilities Planning Staff, 1944–45
H.M.G. Jebb [Full Member to August 1944, only]†
Captain C. C. A. Allen
Brigadier F. C. Curtis†
Air Commodore P. Warburton
[Brigadier F. G. French — Civil Affairs]

(v) MEMBERS OF THE TIZARD COMMITTEE, 1944–45

Sir Henry Tizard†
Professor P. M. S. Blackett [D.N.O.R. Admiralty]†
Professor C. D. Ellis [Scientific Adviser, Army Council]†
Professor Sir George Thomson [Scientific Adviser, Air Ministry]†
Professor J. D. Bernal [Scientific Adviser, C.O.H.Q.]†

(vi) MEMBERS OF THE JOINT TECHNICAL WARFARE COMMITTEE DURING THE REVISION OF THE TIZARD REPORT, 1945–46

Service Representatives
Rear-Admiral R. D. Oliver [A.C.N.S.(W.)]†
Major-General G. H. A. MacMillan [A.C.I.G.S.(W.)]†

Air Vice-Marshal J. N. Boothman [A.C.A.S.(T.R.)]
Major-General R. E. Laycock [C.C.O.]

Scientific Representatives
Admiralty
Dr H. R. Hulme†/
E. M. Gollin

War Office
Professor C. D. Ellis†/
Brigadier C. G. Leitch/
Brigadier N. M. Balchin

Air Ministry
Dr B. G. Dickins/
Dr H. R. Hulme†

Combined Operations Headquarters
Professor J. D. Bernal†/
Captain T. A. Hussey

'Ad Hoc' Members
Professor P. M. S. Blackett†
Professor Sir Geoffrey Taylor
Professor Sir George Thomson†

(vii) MEMBERS OF THE FUTURE PLANNING SECTION
OF THE JOINT PLANNING STAFF, 1946–47

Acting Rear-Admiral C. E. Lambe†
Brigadier C. L. Richardson†
Group Captain E. C. Hudleston†

Annex

PRINCIPAL FOREIGN OFFICE PERSONNEL INVOLVED IN POST-
WAR MILITARY PLANNING, February 1942–August 1944*

Permanent Under-Secretary: Sir Alexander Cadogan†
Deputy Under-Secretary: Sir Orme Sargent†

---

*(*i.e.*, from the commencement of post-war planning until the loss of the chairmanship of the
P.H.P.S.)

Under Secretary:	N. B. Ronald†
Services Liaison Department:	V. F. W. Cavendish-Bentinck†
	C. Norton
	O. A. Scott
Economic and Reconstruction Department:	H. M. G. Jebb†
	J. G. Ward
	Viscount Hood
Eastern Department:	C. W. Baxter
	The Hon. R. M. A. Hankey
Central Department:	F. K. Roberts
Northern Department:	C. F. A. Warner†
	G. M. Wilson
	J. S. Somers Cocks

† Photographs of these individuals are to be found in the section of illustrations.

APPENDIX 2

Directives to Specialised Post-War Planning Bodies, 1942–44

(i) DIRECTIVE TO THE MILITARY SUB-COMMITTEE OF THE MINISTERIAL COMMITTEE ON RECONSTRUCTION PROBLEMS—Established, August 1942

1. The Sub-Committee has been formed to assist the Ministerial Committee on Reconstruction Problems and to ensure that the military issues which will affect our policy when hostilities cease receive due consideration in the deliberations of the committee.

2. The Sub-Committee will be under the general direction of the Chiefs of Staff Committee through the Directors of Plans, and will be on permanent loan to the Paymaster-General, being accommodated in his office.

3. The Sub-Committee will first undertake a study of the military aspects of lessons that may be drawn from previous attempts to secure lasting peace. Previous armistice conventions, policies and methods of disarmament and peace treaties are to be studied to this end. Consideration is also to be given to (a) past methods of enforcing armistice terms and disarmament agreements both in occupied and unoccupied areas, and (b) methods used to control, directly or indirectly, the administration of occupied areas.

4. In the light of these lessons, the Sub-Committee is then to turn its attention to the problems of military interest with which we are likely to be faced when hostilities cease. This latter study should include, for example, requirements in armistice terms; main principles of Allied Occupation in Europe and of the administration and government of occupied areas, the problems connected with such occupation and the manner in which they might be solved.

5. In advising the Ministerial Committee about these and related problems, the Sub-Committee will be collectively responsible for representing the joint Service viewpoint in regard to strategic questions and matters of interest to the Services generally. Individual members will be responsible for representing the interests of their respective Service Ministries. The Sub-Committee will

refer matters on which they require strategic guidance to the strategic section of the Joint Planning Staff, and will refer to the Departments concerned in Ministries in connection with subjects affecting them.

Close touch is also to be maintained with the existing interdepartmental committees dealing with specialised post-war problems, *e.g.*, the Demobilisation Committee.

(ii) DIRECTIVE TO THE POST-HOSTILITIES PLANNING SUB-COMMITTEE OF THE CHIEFS OF STAFF COMMITTEE— Established, August 1943

1.   You are appointed a Sub-Committee of the Chiefs of Staff Committee for the purpose of insuring that military issues which will affect the policy of His Majesty's Government in the United Kingdom when hostilities cease are given due consideration. You will be collectively responsible for representing the Joint Service viewpoint in regard to post-hostilities strategic questions, and you will also act as a channel through which the Service Departments can exchange views with the Foreign Office and with other interested Departments of State.

2.   Your primary task will be to prepare drafts of such instruments as may be deemed suitable for the formal suspension of hostilities with Enemy Powers, and to submit plans for the enforcement of such instruments by armistice and disarmament commissions, inspecting officers, and the like. There will be excluded from the sphere of the Sub-Committee those measures regarding the control of enemy territory which properly fall within the responsibility of a Commander-in-Chief in the field.

3.   In preparing these draft documents you will have regard to the equivalent documents used in former wars and, in particular, during the war of 1914–18, and to the lessons which can be drawn from our experience of the working of these documents.

4.   In addition to the preparation of the draft documents referred to above, you will be responsible for replying to such enquiries on military questions relating to the 'post-hostilities' period as may from time to time be put to you by the Foreign Office or other Departments of State, by the Chiefs of Staff Committee, or by the Joint Planning Staff. You should also consider such post-war strategic problems as you deem to be of major importance, and consult with Departments concerned with a view to ensuring that these problems are taken under examination in the manner which seems most appropriate. You will also be responsible for advising the Ministerial Committee on Reconstruction Problems on any military questions arising in the course of their work with a view to ensuring that those military considerations which will affect British policy when hostilities cease, receive due consideration in the deliberations of that Committee.

5.   In carrying out your duties under this directive, you will maintain close touch with the three Service Departments and with the Foreign Office as well as other Government Departments so as to ensure that your work is co-ordinated with strategic requirements and with the policy of His Majesty's Government. In particular, you will keep in touch with the A.T.(E) Committee* and the Directorate of Civil Affairs in the War Office. You should also keep in view the importance of seeking, through the appropriate Departments, the views of the Dominions and Colonies on matters likely to affect their interests, and similarly, though subject to the direction of the Chiefs of Staff Committee, taking into consultation American and other Allied bodies working on these problems. In this connection you will keep yourselves informed as far as possible of the work of the Combined Civil Affairs Committee and General Strong's Committee in Washington, of AMGOT at Algiers and of the A.T.(B) Committee.

6.   You will be assisted by a small staff of officers drawn from the three Services and by a small secretariat.

Your reports will normally be made to the Chiefs of Staff Committee or to the Ministerial Committee on Armistice Terms and Civil Administration.

(iii)   DIRECTIVE TO THE POST-HOSTILITIES PLANNING STAFF— Established, May 1944

1.   You are appointed a Staff of the Chiefs of Staff Committee.

2.   Your tasks will be:—

   (a)   To prepare, normally under the instructions of Ministers or the Chiefs of Staff Committee, drafts of such instruments as may be necessary for the formal suspension of hostilities with enemy powers, and to submit outline plans for the enforcement of such instruments by Armistice and Disarmament Commissions, Inspecting Officers and the like. Measures regarding the control of enemy territory which properly fall within the responsibility of a Commander-in-Chief in the field will be excluded from the sphere of your responsibility.

   (b)   To prepare, normally on the instructions of the Chiefs of Staff, appreciations on post-war military problems. In preparing these appreciations you will consult the Joint Planning Staff and ensure that the views you put forward to the Chiefs of Staff are in line with current military policy. If you wish yourselves to initiate the study of a problem in this category you will first obtain the approval of the Chiefs of Staff.

---

*[Neither this 'Administration of Territories (Europe) Committee' nor the other bodies cited in this paragraph were involved in the strategic planning role of the P.H.P.]

3. Your reports will normally be made to the Chiefs of Staff Committee, but you will also be prepared to report to the Ministerial Committee on Armistice Terms and Civil Administration in cases where that Committee asks for your advice. In the latter case, when the matters are of sufficient importance you will submit your reports through the Chiefs of Staff.

4. The Minister of Reconstruction, the European Advisory Commission,* and possibly other bodies and Departments, may require military advice on post-war problems. Requests for such advice will normally be addressed to the Chiefs of Staff Committee, but it is possible that that Committee will refer such problems to you. You should, accordingly, be prepared to advise on them as occasion arises.

5. You will keep in touch with the Economic and Industrial Planning Staff.† You should also keep in mind the importance of seeking from the appropriate Departments the views of the Dominions and the Colonies on matters likely to affect their interests and, similarly, though subject to the direction of the Chiefs of Staff Committee, take into consultation American and other Allied bodies working on these problems.

6. You will be assisted by small departmental and inter-Service staffs of officers drawn from the three Services and by a secretariat furnished by the Offices of the War Cabinet.

---

*[Dealing with armistice and control matters on an international basis.]
†[Dealing with economic and industrial problems connected with the occupation and control of Germany.]

APPENDIX 3

C.O.S. Attitudes to the Soviet Union in 1944

(i) C.O.S.(44)248th Mtg. (0) Minute 14, (Confidential Annex)—26 July 1944
SECURITY IN WESTERN EUROPE AND THE NORTH ATLANTIC (P.H.P.(44)17(0)(Final))

The Committee had before them a Report by the Post-Hostilities Planning Staff considering the policy which should be adopted to safeguard British strategic interests in Western Europe and the North Atlantic when the forces of occupation had been withdrawn from Germany. It was explained that the Report had been prepared as one of a series of regional studies being undertaken by the P.H.P. Staff. It was presented in reply to a request* from the Foreign Secretary for the views of the Chiefs of Staff on the idea that we should try and create some system of regional defence in Western Europe.

The Committee were in full agreement with the general thesis of the Report that for the future security of the United Kingdom we must obtain greater depth to our defence and enlist the assistance of all the Western European states. The Committee felt, however, that the Post-Hostilities Planning Staff had failed to face up to the hard military facts of the problem. Their main criticisms were as follows:—

  (a) It was quite true to say that our efforts must be first put into ensuring the success of the proposed world organisation, and that our primary object will be to see that Germany does not rise again. On the other hand, the real military problem that had to be faced was the fact that the world organisation might break down, and this had not received nearly sufficient emphasis in the Report.

  (b) It was perfectly true to say that we should require the assistance of France and the Western European states, and the closer we were

---

*COS(44)113

349

bound together the better. It would be a great mistake, however, to convey the impression, as the Report inclined to do, that this would provide the solution to the future defence of the United Kingdom; on the contrary, the creation of a Western European Group would only be a first step towards a system which, if the security of these Islands were to be secured, must include a part, if not the whole, of Germany.

(c) In fact, Germany would be the key to the security of these Islands in the future and, however unpalatable the fact might be, there might well come a time when we should have to rely on her assistance against a hostile Russia. This fact again had not been made sufficiently clear in the Report.

(d) The policy we adopt in dealing with Germany at the end of the war is thus fundamental to the problem of the future defence of the United Kingdom, as on it may well depend the extent to which we could hope for German assistance. The case for and against dismemberment of Germany must be argued with this in mind.

To sum up, the Committee were impressed with the far-reaching importance of the problem discussed in the Report, and took the view that a much more detailed examination of the problem was required before a firm view could be formed regarding our future policy for the defence of the United Kingdom. Meanwhile, however, there would be every advantage in proceeding with the proposal to form an association of the Western European states, provided it was clearly understood that such an association would only be the first step towards the development of a wider system which, if Russia ever becomes hostile, must be extended to include the whole or at least part of Germany.

The Committee:—

(a) Instructed the Secretary to draft for their approval a letter to the Foreign Office in reply to the query raised in C.O.S.(44)113.

(b) Instructed the Post-Hostilities Planning Staff to revise their Report in the light of the discussion, taking a purely military view of the situation with which we should be confronted in the event of a breakdown of the world organisation.

(ii) Note by the Chiefs of Staff for the Foreign Office—2 October 1944

THE STUDY OF POST-WAR PROBLEMS

1. The Secretary of State for Foreign Affairs has circulated to the A.P.W. Committee a memorandum on the Dismemberment of Germany (A.P.W. (44)90). It consists of his covering note, and of a paper written by the Foreign Office after studying the Chiefs' of Staff report (C.O.S.(44)822(0)), and a

report by the Economic and Industrial Planning Staff. The Foreign Office paper, with which the Foreign Secretary expresses his agreement, concludes 'that dismemberment would fail to advance the main object we all have at heart, namely security from the German menace'.

2. The arguments used in the Foreign Office paper seem to us unconvincing, and reveal a number of misconceptions of the views of the Chiefs of Staff. But before we can discuss the merits of the arguments, there is a point of fundamental importance which we must immediately take up. This is the attitude towards the study of post-war problems which is revealed in the Foreign Office paper.

3. This attitude can best be exemplified by the following quotations from the covering note by the Foreign Secretary and from the Foreign Office paper. In paragraph 5 he writes:—

> 'Finally, I would draw my colleagues' special attention to the conclusions in the Chiefs' of Staff report that dismemberment is to be recommended on the ground that it would offer a measure of reinsurance against possible Soviet aggression. It seems to me essential that any such conception should be avoided like the plague in our consideration of German problems. If we prepare our post-war plans with the idea at the back of our minds that the Germans may serve as part of an anti-Soviet bloc, we shall quickly destroy any hope of preserving the Anglo-Soviet Alliance and soon find ourselves advocating relaxations of the disarmament and other measures which we regard as essential guarantees against future German aggression.'

Paragraph 40(e) says:—

> 'It is therefore essential that the problem should be considered solely from the angle of security against Germany.'

4. As we understand it, the Foreign Office argument runs as follows:—

It is the accepted policy of His Majesty's Government to maintain friendly relations with Russia, with whom we have a 20 years' Treaty of Alliance. We intend to set up a world security organisation, the main object of which is to keep down Germany and Japan. To write papers on the basis of Russia as a possible enemy is thus to fly in the face of our accepted policy. We must not even have at the back of our minds the thought that we should take precautions against possible Soviet aggression. Provided we eliminate the German menace, and pursue a policy of friendship towards Russia, all is bound to be well.

5. No-one will dispute for a moment the value of friendship with Russia or of a successful world security organisation. No-one would be better pleased than the Chiefs of Staff if a permanent solution to our military problems could be achieved by this means. We should be very foolish if we advocated measures which would hinder the perpetuation of the present close relations between the three great powers. But it is the duty of the Chiefs of Staff to examine all

serious eventualities. We cannot be debarred from taking into account the possibility that for some reason or other the world security organisation may break down, and that Russia may start forth on the path to world domination, as other continental nations have done before her.

6.   When the Chiefs of Staff consider any important post-war problem, we start with the security of the British Empire as the cardinal objective, and try to examine the world situation with an open mind. In studying long-term strategical questions, we are bound to adopt two alternative hypotheses:—

(a) That unanimity of view prevails among the three great powers, and that a successful world security organisation results.
(b) That the world security organisation either fails to materialise, or later breaks down.

7.   The first hypothesis presents no serious military problem. It is the second that cannot with safety be neglected. After the last war we made just that mistake; we assumed that the League of Nations would ensure the security of the British Empire, and we based all our post-war arrangements on that assumption. The results were disastrous. We found ourselves caught in a vicious circle. Our weakness led us to seek to appease our potential enemies. The more we appeased, the weaker we became.

8.   If one looks at the situation which will exist in the world when Germany and Japan have been thoroughly beaten and demilitarised, one finds only two possible menaces to the security of the British Empire, namely the United States and Russia. We eliminate the United States, and are left with Russia, a country of enormous power and resources which has been cut off for 25 years from contact with the outside world and the trend of whose policy no-one can foretell. Taking a long view, we cannot possibly afford to eliminate from our mind the conception of an expansionist and perhaps eventually aggressive Russia, and this applies whether we are considering the German problem or any other problem which affects our security.

9.   The examination of an unpleasant situation which may perhaps arise is in no way incompatible with the pursuit of a policy designed to prevent that situation arising. Yet the Foreign Office seems to recoil from the precaution of considering how to insure against the failure of our policy. They seem in effect to presume that the policy we intend to pursue is bound to be successful provided no thought is taken to meet the possibility of failure. It is this attitude that we feel bound to challenge.

10.   We ask that this fundamental question should be resolved before the Dismemberment Paper is taken by the A.P.W. Committee. We regard it as

our duty as the military advisers of His Majesty's Government to examine quite freely those problems which affect the security of the British Empire, and we must be free to put forward the military view without being debarred from taking into account any consideration which we regard as relevant.

(Signed) A. F. BROOKE
C. PORTAL
ANDREW CUNNINGHAM

APPENDIX 4

**Revision of the Tizard Report, January 1946
(Annex I to TWC(45)44(Revise)(Cl. 50))**

SIZE AND RANGE OF TARGET CITIES IN U.S.S.R.

TOWN	POPULATION (thousands) —in 1939	RANGES IN STATUTE MILES (least range underlined)		
		Norwich	Nicosia	Peshawar
Moscow	4137	1520	_1500_	2230
Leningrad	3191	_1310_	1780	–
Kiev	846	1250	_1080_	–
Kharkov	833	1510	_1050_	–
Baku	809	2400	_970_	1260
Gorki	644	1740	_1600_	2050
Odessa	604	1380	_800_	2300
Tashkent	585	–	1970	_540_
Tiflis	519	2150	_750_	1560
Rostov	510	1700	_910_	1900
Dniepropetrovsk	501	1500	_940_	2150
Stalino	462	1610	_920_	2000
Stalingrad	445	1970	_1110_	1730
Sverdlovsk	426	2400	2020	_1680_
Kazan	402	1960	_1570_	1840
Riga	393	_1000_	1630	–
Kuibishev	390	2050	_1550_	1700
Saratov	376	1850	_1320_	1760
Koenigsberg	368	_800_	1520	–
Voronezh	327	_1600_	1210	2030
Lwow	318	_1000_	1110	–
Yaroslavl	298	_1620_	1660	2220

Zaporozhe	289	1530	<u>890</u>	2110
Ivanovo	285	1660	<u>1620</u>	2180
Archangel	281	<u>1770</u>	<u>2180</u>	–
Omsk	281	–	2400	<u>1470</u>
Novosibirsk	275	–	2700	<u>1570</u>
Cheliabinsk	273	2450	1980	<u>1550</u>
Tula	272	1520	<u>1500</u>	2230
Perm (Molotov)	255	2250	<u>1950</u>	<u>1790</u>
Astrakhan	254	2140	<u>1100</u>	<u>1500</u>
Ufa	246	2250	<u>1770</u>	1640
Irkutsk*	243	–	–	<u>2080</u>
Makeyevka	240	1630	980	<u>1990</u>
Minsk	239	<u>1100</u>	<u>1360</u>	–
Alma-Ata	231	–	2350	<u>700</u>
Maripol	222	1640	<u>880</u>	<u>2000</u>
Kalinin	216	<u>1450</u>	1590	2200
Voroshilovgrad	213	1670	<u>990</u>	1930
Vilna	208	<u>1000</u>	1450	–
Vladivostock*	206	–	–	–
Krasnodar	204	1740	<u>760</u>	1880
Erivan	200	2210	<u>680</u>	1560
Khabarovsk*	199	–	–	–
Krivoi Rog	198	1450	<u>900</u>	2250
Krasnoyarsk	190	–	–	<u>1790</u>
Taganrog	189	1690	<u>880</u>	<u>1920</u>
Izhevsk	176	2170	<u>1800</u>	<u>1790</u>
Chkalov	173	2320	1620	<u>1490</u>
Grozny	172	2100	<u>880</u>	<u>1530</u>
Stalinsk	170	–	–	<u>1575</u>
Vitebsk	167	1200	1400	–
Nikolayev	167	<u>1400</u>	<u>830</u>	2300
Karaganda	166	–	<u>2300</u>	<u>1100</u>
Nizhni Tagil	160	2400	2050	<u>1750</u>
Penza	157	1800	1400	<u>1860</u>
Smolensk	157	1290	<u>1380</u>	–
Shakhty	155	<u>1720</u>	960	1860
Kaunas	152	<u>950</u>	<u>1480</u>	–
Barnaul	148	–	–	<u>1480</u>
Dnieprodzerzhinsk	148	1450	960	<u>2200</u>
Magnitogorsk	146	2380	<u>1800</u>	<u>1470</u>
Gomel	144	1240	<u>1230</u>	–
Kirov	143	1980	<u>1830</u>	1990
Simferopol	143	1570	<u>690</u>	2180

Tomsk	141	–	–	1680
Rybinsk	139	1590	1680	2270
Tallinn	138	1090	1780	–
Samarkand	134	–	1840	490
Poltava	130	1450	1000	2200
Ulan-Ude*	129	–	–	2200
Ordzhonikidze	127	2090	810	1580
Ashkhabad	127	–	1400	800
Tambov	121	1680	1310	1980
Kostroma	121	1660	1680	2270
Kursk	120	1480	1300	–
Murmansk	117	1800	2480	–
Chishinov	113	1280	900	–
Sevastopol	112	1560	650	2200
Semipalatinsk	110	–	–	1210
Cernauti	110	1120	980	–
Kerch	104	1640	720	2020
Chita*	103	–	–	2400
Ulyanovsk	102	1940	1570	1790
Kirovograd	100	1380	940	2300
Total	28,622			

*These cities are more than 1850 miles from all three bases.
– These ranges exceed 2500 miles.

APPENDIX 5

Revision of the Tizard Report, April 1946
(TWC(46)14(Retained—Cabt. Off.) Tables I & III)

Table I — GROUPING OF RUSSIAN TARGETS (see also frontispiece)

GROUP	TOWNS	AGGREGATE POPULATION (100,000s)	BOMBS ON TARGET
*Leningrad	Leningrad	31.8	30
I	Koenigsberg, Kaunas, Vilna, Minsk	9.7	10
II	Chishinov, Odessa, Nikolayev	8.8	9
III	Moscow, Kalinin, Tula	46.3	43
*Fringe	Tabruin, Murmansk, Cernauti, Baku, Tashkent, Riga, Lwow	24.8	23
IV	Stalino, Voroshilovgrad, Makeyevka, Taganrog, Rostov, Shakhty, Maripol	19.9	19
V	Tiflis, Erivan, Grozny, Ordzhonikidze	10.2	10
VI	Kirovograd, Krivoi Rog, Poltava, Kharkov, Dnieprodzerzhinsk, Dniepropetrovsk, Zaporozhe	22.0	21
VII	Sevastopol, Simferopol, Kerch, Krasnodar	5.5	5
VIII	Rybinsk, Yaroslavl, Gorki, Kostroma, Ivanovo	14.9	14
IX	Kiev, Gomel	9.9	10
	Sub-Total	203.8 (71%)	194

X	Kazan, Ulyanovsk, Kuibishev	8.9	9
XI	Sverdlovsk, Cheliabinsk, Magnitogorsk, Ufa	11.0	10
XII	Kirov, Izhevsk, Perm	5.8	6
XIII	Kursk, Voronezh, Tambov	5.7	6
XIV	Penza, Saratov	5.4	5
*Medium	Stalingrad, Archangel, Astrakhan	9.8	9
XV	Vitebsk, Smolensk	3.3	3

Sub-Total 253.7 (88%)   242

18 towns not included   31.9   —

Total 285.6   242

*[Cities marked thus would be attacked in separate raids.]

Table III — GROUPING OF BRITISH TARGETS (see also p. 231)

GROUP	TOWNS	AGGREGATE POPULATION (100,000s)	BOMBS ON TARGET
I	Glasgow, Edinburgh, Aberdeen, Dundee	18.7	18
II	Newcastle, Gateshead, South Shields, Sunderland	8.4	8
III	Huddersfield, St. Helen's, Blackpool, Liverpool, Salford, Bolton, Oldham, Sheffield, Bradford, Preston, Stockport, Hull, Birkenhead, Blackburn, Leeds [2 raids]	46.1	43
IV	Nottingham, Leicester, Stoke, Derby, Birmingham, Wolverhampton, Coventry, Walsall	23.3	22
V	London, Southend	56.3	52
VI	Plymouth, Swansea, Cardiff, Portsmouth, Rhondda, Bournemouth, Brighton, Bristol, Southampton	18.3	16

Total 171.1   159

APPENDIX 6

Foreign Office Views on the World Situation, 1946

(i) FO 371/56832: N6344/605/38, The Warner Memorandum, 2 April 1946

THE SOVIET CAMPAIGN AGAINST THIS COUNTRY AND OUR RESPONSE TO IT

1. The reports from the Embassy in Moscow on recent Soviet pronouncements, in particular the election speeches made by Stalin, Molotov and other members of the Politburo and the publicity campaign in connexion with the elections to the Supreme Soviet, bring out the following points in the Soviet Government's declared policy:—

(a) The return to the pure doctrine of Marx-Lenin-Stalinism.
(b) The intense concentration upon building up the industrial and military strength of the Soviet Union.
(c) The revival of the bogey of external danger to the Soviet Union.

2. The return to Marx-Lenin-Stalinism includes of course the glorification of Communism as the inevitable religion of the future, the natural antagonism between Communism on the one hand and imperialism and capitalism on the other (both Russia's major allies being regarded as imperialistic and capitalistic); the natural antagonism between Communism and Social Democracy; the Soviet Union's duty to propagate Communism; and all the rest of the doctrine. In other words, the Soviet Union has announced to the world that it proposes to play an aggressive political role, while making an intensive drive to increase its own military and industrial strength. We should be very unwise not to take the Russians at their word, just as we should have been wise to take *Mein Kampf* at its face value.

3. All Russia's activities in the past few months confirm this picture. In Eastern Europe, in the Balkans, in Persia, in Manchuria, in Korea, in her zone

in Germany, and in the Security Council; in her support of Communist parties in foreign countries and Communist efforts to infiltrate Socialist parties and to combine left-wing parties under Communist leadership; in the Soviet Union's foreign economic policy (her refusal to co-operate in international efforts at reconstruction and rehabilitation, while despoiling foreign countries in her sphere, harnessing them to the Soviet system, and at the same time posing as their only benefactors); in every word on foreign affairs that appears in the Soviet press and broadcasts; and most of all in the tremendous reaction which Mr Winston Churchill's Fulton speech brought from Stalin, the Soviet Union's acts bear out the declarations of policy referred to above.

4. The Soviet Union is no doubt war-weary, and, as the Soviet leaders have proclaimed, wants a prolonged peace to build up her strength. But she is practising the most vicious power politics in the political, economic, and propaganda spheres and seems determined to stick at nothing, short of war, to obtain her objectives. Having regard to the declarations of policy referred to above, it would be very rash to assume that her present political strategy and tactics are short-term only.

5. Soviet spokesmen and apologists, from M. Maisky during the war onwards, have been at pains to explain that Russia's acquisitive policy everywhere is due to not unnatural suspicion. But the Soviet authorities in their press and broadcasts seem now to be at pains to intensify this suspicion among their own people. Can it be, in reality, a convenient excuse for an aggressive policy; after all, at the end of the war, the only two countries that could threaten Russia were her allies, Great Britain and America, and these, as any good Soviet observers must have reported, were only too anxious to relax and demobilise? Or again, are anxiety about the internal situation in Russia and the need to apply the spur to their own people the principal motives? Whichever of these explanations be correct, the fact remains that Russian aggressiveness threatens British interests all over the world. The Soviet Government are carrying on an intensive campaign to weaken, depreciate and harry this country in every possible way. There is no guarantee that this is not going on indefinitely. The tempo and the pressure may vary for tactical reasons. But the revival of the Marx-Lenin ideology, and the fact that this country is under the present Government the leader of Social Democracy in Europe and is at the same time the less formidable of the two great 'imperialist and capitalist' powers, suggest on the contrary that the attack on this country will continue indefinitely. If this be so, concessions and appeasement will merely serve to weaken our position while the Soviet Union builds up her industrial and economic strength; therefore we must defend ourselves.

6. Russia's policy is normally coordinated over the whole field and she will no doubt direct her attack equally against our strategic, political and economic

interest, using military, economic, propaganda and political weapons and also the driving force generated by Communism. And Communism in this connexion must be viewed not merely as a political creed but as a religious dogma and faith which can inspire such fanaticism and self-sacrifice as we associate with the early Christians and the rise of Islam and which in the minds of the believers transcends all lesser loyalties towards family, class or even country. We must therefore study this Russian aggressive policy as a whole in all its different manifestations, and not only make up our minds what measures we should take to defend ourselves against the Soviet Union's present manoeuvres, but also to try to foresee the future development of her campaign against us and how we can meet it. We should also consider whether, in some directions at least, we should not adopt a defensive-offensive policy.

7. As regards Russia's use of the military weapon, the Chiefs of Staff have endorsed the opinion expressed in the J.I.C's recent paper (J.I.C.(46)1(0) of 1st March) that the Russians do not wish to get involved in another war for at least the next five years and the Chiefs of Staff are considering their plans on this assumption. We understand that they will be making their recommendations shortly. It is relevant however to the political problems which concern the Foreign Office to remark that in their use of military pressure, in areas affecting our vital interests or those of the Americans, the Russians will, of course, have to rely on their own appreciation to judge how far they can go without making war inevitable. In their anxiety to justify themselves to the British people and the world His Majesty's Government may have misled Hitler. We should always keep this in mind in dealing with the Russian problem now.

8. In the economic sphere, the broad lines of Russian policy are clear. It is entirely selfish. It is at the same time ideological. They are ruthlessly despoiling the countries occupied by the Red Army, in the guise of booty, restitution and reparation. Simultaneously, they are using their puppets to gear the economies of those countries to the Soviet machine. They are contributing nothing to United Nations international efforts to restore economic stability and the free flow of trade and transport. They are making exclusive commercial treaties and securing a predominant share in the control of basic industries from Germany and the Adriatic right across to Manchuria. By this means they hope to control the whole economic life of this vast area for the benefit of the Soviet Union, in order to speed up the achievement of their own long-term industrial development. In doing so they are reducing the standard of living throughout this area to the Soviet level, partly presumably in the process of coordinating the economic life of the whole area, partly because it is not good for their own internal propaganda that the many Soviet citizens who are likely to move about in that area should see that Russia's satellites have a higher standard of living than the Soviet Union.

9. Russia's foreign economic policy thus serves political, economic and ideological ends simultaneously. It will speed up the achievement of her own vast plan of industrial and military development. It will make an enormous area economically, and therefore, politically, dependent upon herself. It will serve the spread of Communism and it will give the Kremlin a tremendous economic weapon to use in the Marx-Leninist struggle against capitalism and for Russian imperialistic political ends.

10. To the extent that it is successful it will destroy the hopes of world prosperity based upon a free economy.

11. It will be necessary to carry on a constant study of the Soviet use of the economic weapon against this country and the rest of the world, to try to foresee its manifestations, to work out a coherent policy ourselves and to keep counter-measures under constant review. Since our opponent always coordinates policy and economics, our own trade, financial and economic policy must take account of the security and foreign policy aspects and the Foreign Office must claim a voice in these matters, which before the war was often denied to it. How this coordination of policy can best be secured is being considered separately.

12. The economic and political aspects of the Soviet campaign against us are so interlocked that they must be considered together.

13. Wherever they have an opportunity the Soviet Government seeks to stir up trouble for His Majesty's Government or to weaken their influence. Everywhere they are accused of being imperialistic, 'anti-democratic' (for a month now the Secretary of State's policy has consistently been so described in Soviet propaganda), reactionary, effete, lax in rooting out fascism. And now, in Stalin's retort to Winston Churchill this country is pilloried as aggressive and war-mongering.

14. Added to such straightforward propaganda the Soviet Government will mobilise in every way possible the driving force generated by the Communist 'religion' in foreign countries and in international bodies such as the World Federation of Trade Unions, the World Youth Organisation, the Women's Federation and others which the Soviet Government will no doubt seek to found and to bring under Communist control. At the same time in the purely diplomatic sphere the Soviet Government will use the United Nations Organisation wherever possible to put Great Britain on the defensive and to make mischief by championing 'colonial' peoples and nationalist movements and they will of course also as occasion offers use direct diplomatic pressure upon and wage wars of nerves against our friends and allies.

15. In all this we have apparently been selected as the weaker of the two protagonists of the liberal, democratic and Western conceptions which have been proclaimed by the Soviet leaders as the rivals of Marx-Leninism. The

Soviet ideological war against these conceptions has therefore been opened with an attack upon us and we are called upon to defend those conceptions in defending ourselves.

[. . . Paragraphs 16–27 . . .]

28. To sum up, the Soviet Government, both in their recent pronouncements and in their actions have made it clear that they have decided upon an aggressive policy, based upon militant Communism and Russian chauvinism. They have launched an offensive against Social Democracy and against this country. They must have realised already that their clumsiness is alarming the whole non-Communist world and in particular American public opinion, and is thus consolidating opposition to them and support for His Majesty's Government. They will very probably adopt henceforth more subtle tactics and lay themselves out to allay these suspicions. But it would be in the highest degree rash to suppose that they will drop their policy of challenging this country, which they must regard as the leader of Social Democracy and the more vulnerable of the two great Western powers. The interests of this country and the true democratic principles for which we stand are directly threatened. The Soviet Government makes coordinated use of military, economic, propaganda and political weapons and also of the Communist 'religion'. It is submitted, therefore, that we must at once organise and coordinate our defences against all these and that we should not stop short of a defensive-offensive policy. If general approval is given to these propositions, further study should be given as a matter of urgency to the various suggestions outlined in this memorandum.

C. F. A. Warner
2nd April, 1946

(ii) Retained Document: COS(46)239(0) Annex I, The Foreign Office Strategy Paper, 5 October 1946

THE STRATEGIC ASPECT OF BRITISH FOREIGN POLICY
I. GENERAL POLICY

Present Political Alignment

1. The post-war alignment of the Allied Powers has resulted in the co-existence of—

(a) two political systems, the Soviet Union and its satellites on the one hand, and the United States of America and the British Commonwealth, and a number of States less rigidly attached, on the other; (this division is not exclusive, as there remain countries not yet committed to either group);

and

(b) a world-wide system of international consultation and a forum for the discussion and peaceful settlement of political disputes, in the shape of the United Nations, which the Member States are pledged by the Charter to support; equipped with the machinery of the Security Council, Economic and Social Council and Military Staff Committee.

2. The possibility of solving the conflicts arising out of the co-existence of these two systems depends to a great extent on the development of the policy of the United States and the Soviet Union, the two most powerful forces in the modern world.

United States Policy

3. In drawing up this paper it is throughout assumed that the United States will continue its present policy of active intervention in all international questions and of the exertion of its influence in directions which coincide by and large with British interests. But it must be recognised that this assumption is not necessarily valid. The Americans are a mercurial people, unduly swayed by sentiment and prejudice rather than by reason or even by consideration of their own long-term interests. Their Government is handicapped by an archaic constitution, sometimes to the point of impotence, and their policy is to an exceptional degree at the mercy both of electoral changes and of violent economic fluctuations, such as might at any moment bring about a neutralisation of their influence in the world. If this were to occur, the outlook for the British Commonwealth would be very serious, for it must be assumed that without United States assistance the Commonwealth would be unable to maintain a full-scale war with modern weapons. It is obvious that if this contingency were to arise the whole position would need to be reviewed.

Soviet Policy

4. We accept as accurate the conclusion that the short-term aim of the Soviet Union is to avoid any course of action which in the opinion of the Soviet leaders may lead to war with the British Commonwealth or the United States. Indeed we think that the Soviet Government are unlikely at any stage deliberately to take the initiative in provoking a major war. But unfortunately there is every evidence, in spite of occasional tactical disavowals, that the leaders of the Soviet Union are convinced of the inevitability of a clash between the Communist State and the capitalist world. This is undoubtedly a fact which they have been inculcating on the Soviet people by every means of

propaganda and publicity available to them. It is, of course, necessary for the British and American Governments to do everything in their power to dispossess the Soviet Government and people of this dangerous idea. But it will be difficult to do so, because it is clearly a sincerely held belief and an essential part of Soviet political philosophy. As long as this delusion persists we can hope for no change in the present Soviet policy of building up Soviet industrial and military potential to the maximum in preparation for the supposedly inevitable struggle. The Soviet Government will also seek by all means short of war to prevent the political position of the Soviet Union being undermined in those countries already under predominant Soviet influence and to include among them further areas which they consider it necessary to dominate either strategically, such as Persia, or politically, such as France. For this purpose the Soviet Government can, in practically all countries, use the local Communist Party as an effective fifth column.

5.   While the Soviet Government are in this frame of mind, it is hopeless to expect from them any sincere collaboration in the United Nations Organisation. On the contrary, they may be expected to continue their present policy of discrediting it by raising frivolous charges and by irresponsible use of the veto. We consider further that present Soviet policy (even on the hypothesis that it is dictated primarily by considerations of security) is directed to undermine British and American influence in all parts of the world and, where possible, to supplant it. If unchecked by political means, this policy will ultimately lead to the British Commonwealth being placed in such a position that, in spite of the assistance of the United States of America, a combination of military, economic and political factors would render it incapable of affording effective resistance to the Soviet Union in a large-scale war using the weapons which will be available in a few years' time.

6.   Lastly, there remains the persistent danger that the Soviet Government may misjudge what measures can be safely taken without producing a serious crisis, and may involve themselves in war with the Western Powers through miscalculation. For instance, in certain circumstances an extra bit of clumsiness and an outburst of mass emotion in America, coinciding with a sudden spasm of suspicion or display of truculence in Russia, might produce results which might get beyond control and lead to disaster. For both of these Powers are in large measure bluffing. The Soviet Government display their armed strength in the shape of about 1,500,000 men spread out across Eastern Europe, and hide the internal weaknesses—certainly economic and possibly also political—with which they are at grips in Russia itself. The United States, for their part, point to the vast industrial and economic wealth of America and forget the military impotence to which the United States Government have been reduced in Europe by over-hasty demobilisation.

British Policy

7.   The principal objects of British policy must be—
   (a) to find with the United States Government a basis on which the Soviet world and the Anglo-Saxon world can live together, if not in friendship, at any rate without open conflict;
   (b) to ensure that, should all efforts to avoid such conflict ultimately prove unsuccessful, the British Commonwealth should not, at the outbreak of war, be in such a strategic position that it is unable to afford effective resistance;
   (c) to secure and extend our external sources of raw materials and our export markets, in order to strengthen the peacetime economy of the United Kingdom and the countries of the British Commonwealth, and to maintain the standard of living of its peoples.

8.   In the pursuit of this policy we may require the use of military forces, either as our contribution to the United Nations or for the protection of the national interests of the United Kingdom or the Commonwealth, for five categories of cases—
   (a) the maintenance of order in British territory or in support of our policy there;
   (b) intervention to prevent local disturbances and to protect British lives and property in the event of the outbreak of disorders in areas where we have important strategic or economic interests;
   (c) the maintenance of our commitments in respect of the occupation of Germany, especially the Ruhr, and the control of German disarmament under the United States draft Treaty;
   (d) intervention following a decision by the Security Council, to prevent the spread of a local conflict involving minor Powers;
   (e) a major conflict with the Soviet Union, whether arising from a local conflict involving a Soviet satellite or from a direct clash with the Soviet Union herself.

9.   Part II of the present memorandum contains a consideration of the above five categories by areas. Theoretically there is a sixth category, namely, action in execution of one of our treaty commitments (other than that under the United Nations Charter which is covered by sub-paragraph (d) above). These treaty commitments are set out in the Appendix to this paper. It will be seen, however, that in point of fact they are all really covered under one or other of the above five categories and they are more conveniently considered under those headings.

10.   Before proceeding to consider the separate areas, there are certain general considerations affecting British policy. In the first place there is the factor of confidence. The majority of the countries not now in the Soviet group still believe in the United Nations idea and look to the United States and

ourselves for leadership in upholding it. This situation might be fatally prejudiced by a situation such as that arising over Manchuria in 1931, or that arising in Europe after the accession of the Nazis to power in Germany, if one Great Power—in this case the Soviet Union—were able successfully to defy the United Nations and to impose her will on another State not already under Soviet influence by the threat or the use of force, without the armed intervention of the British Commonwealth and the United States of America. Such a situation would undermine the confidence of the smaller countries, particularly in Europe and the Near East, and might result in our losing the sympathies and assistance of Allies who would be of the greatest value in war.

11.   If in peacetime we move out of areas at present under our influence, they are unlikely to remain a vacuum, particularly if they are contiguous to areas under Soviet control. There is always in such cases the danger that Russia will move in and that the areas will become lost to us militarily, politically and economically. Even if Russia is not in a position to exercise direct control, she would no doubt in such cases do her best to obtain remote control through local Communist parties. We cannot, therefore, afford to weaken our strategic position in peacetime by surrendering our influence in areas of major strategic importance.

12.   Then there is the economic factor. Account must be taken of the possible loss to the British Commonwealth, by the expansion of Soviet influence or from other causes, of areas which, as markets for our exports or as sources of raw materials, are essential to our peacetime economy or as main support areas for our war effort. The exclusive control which the Soviet Union has established over the countries under her political influence is sufficient evidence of the extent to which our economy would suffer by the expansion of that political influence.

13.   The analysis of Soviet policy in paragraphs 4 – 6 shows the necessity of our pursuing an active policy, by continuing to play a leading political role at U.N.O. and elsewhere, and by using to the full both our economic resources (in conjunction with the United States) and a positive publicity to make known the advantages of the Western way of life among those still backward populations which the Soviet Union is seeking to influence in another direction. In such propaganda our policy must be to emphasise constantly the values of freedom and tolerance as against the differing merits of the Soviet system. Our line should be to encourage the countries concerned to go ahead with social and economic reforms and bring themselves up to date along Western lines, and we should discourage the use of the methods of the police State except as a very last resort.

14.   It also seems necessary so to dispose our military forces in peacetime as to give the maximum impression of our strength and of the efficiency of our

modern armaments in those areas where we appreciate that the Soviet Union is actively extending her influence, and thus underpin our threatened political position.

15.   This purpose may call for an expenditure of economic resources in directions where this would not appear justified on the sole criterion of short-run commercial advantage, and the stationing of military forces in peacetime in areas different from those of an ideal disposition judged solely from the point of view of readiness for a future war.

II. BRITISH POLICY AND STRATEGIC INTERESTS BY AREAS

[. . . . Paragraphs 16–52 . . . .]

Conclusion

53.   It is in no sense an aim of British policy to force other countries to subscribe to Western democratic ideas, and, unlike the Soviet Union, the British Commonwealth has no ideological purpose of propagating a political idea with something resembling a religious fanaticism. It is the purpose of British policy, on the other hand, to emphasise constantly the values of freedom and tolerance, as against the advantages claimed by the Soviet Union for the Leninist totalitarian system, and to maintain, particularly in the countries of Western Europe, that European culture which has spread itself over the 'Western' world, and has resisted, three times in the last 75 years, armed assault from the Eastward.

54.   While, however, it can be no part of our policy or of that of our allies to use the methods of the totalitarian police State, we cannot afford to adopt a purely negative attitude towards Soviet penetration. While our main political purpose is defensive, we must on occasion use offensive tactics to achieve it, and we must throughout use a positive line to encourage those countries where we maintain our influence, to go ahead with social reform and economic progress.

APPENDIX [to Foreign Office Paper]—TREATIES OF ALLIANCE, GUARANTEE ETC., OR INSTRUMENTS CONTAINING PROVISIONS WHICH MIGHT POSSIBLY INVOLVE THE UNITED KINGDOM IN HOSTILITIES

Charter of the United Nations, 1945.
Portugal: Treaties of Alliance, 1373–1904.
        Agreement respecting the Azores of 1943.
Iraq: Treaty of Alliance of 1930.

Egypt: Treaty of Alliance of 1936.

Transjordan: Treaty of Alliance of 1946.

Turkey: Straits Convention of 1936.

Treaty of Mutual Assistance, 1939.

Persia: Treaty of Alliance of 1942.

Soviet Union: Treaty of Alliance of 1942.

Poland: Agreement and Protocol of 1939 regarding Mutual Assistance.

Czechoslovakia: Treaty of Alliance of 1942.

Greece: United Kingdom Assurance of 13th April, 1939.

Agreement of 9th March, 1942 respecting Armed Forces.

Belgium: Exchange of Notes of 24th April, 1937.

United States: Bases Agreement and Protocol regarding Defence of Newfoundland. [1940]

Ethiopia: Agreement of 1944 replacing Agreement and Military Convention of 1942.

APPENDIX 7

The Overall Strategic Plan, May 1947
(DO(47)44 (Also COS(47)102(0)) (Retained—Cabt. Off.))

FUTURE DEFENCE POLICY

Report by the Chiefs of Staff

OBJECT

The object of this paper is to set out the fundamental principles which should govern our Future Defence Policy and to arrive at a clear statement of the basic requirements of our Strategy, on which the shape and size of our armed forces can subsequently be planned.

We have accordingly arranged the paper in two parts:—

PART I. — Commonwealth Defence Policy. This Part concludes with a definition of the fundamentals of our Defence Policy.

PART II. — The Strategy of Commonwealth Defence. This Part begins with a statement of the basic requirements of our Strategy and concludes with a statement in general terms of the basic tasks of our armed forces and the principles which should govern their shape and size in order to fulfil this Strategy.

Any examination of Future Defence Policy inevitably gives rise to some consideration of long-term political and economic developments, since these affect our security quite as much as the shape and size of the armed forces. We have therefore attached at Annex our views on the political and economic objects which should be pursued in support of Commonwealth Defence Policy.

PART I. — COMMONWEALTH DEFENCE POLICY

International Relations

2.   The fulfilment of the main object of the United Nations, the maintenance of world peace, depends on the ability and readiness of the Great Powers to keep the peace.

The supreme object of British policy is to prevent war, provided that this can be done without prejudicing our vital interests.

3.   The United Kingdom, as the senior member of the British Commonwealth and a Great Power, must be prepared at all times to fulfil her responsibilities not only to the United Nations but also to herself as a Great Power. To fulfil her obligations, she must achieve a strong and sound economy which will give her the ability to expand industry and the armed forces immediately on to a war basis.

4.   Because of the Veto, the United Nations Organisation provides no security against war between the Great Powers. In this situation, we believe that the only effective deterrent to a potential aggressor is tangible evidence of our intention and ability to withstand attack and to hit back immediately. No measure of disarmament should be accepted without adequate guarantees of security. Our aim must be to refashion our forces and our war potential to meet the needs of the future. We must remain strong enough to demonstrate our ability to withstand and our intention to counter aggression at any time.

5.   Whether, therefore, we are acting in pursuit of national policy or in support of the United Nations, it is necessary to maintain British forces in peacetime to deter aggression which might lead to a major war and to defend our own interests. In support of these forces there must be reserves of essential resources.

Importance of Commonwealth Unity

6.   The security of the United Kingdom is the keystone of Commonwealth defence. The United Kingdom contains 60 per cent. of the white man-power and industrial capacity of the Commonwealth and the bulk of her scientific development. The Commonwealth gains its strength through the united front that it presents to the world. If the United Kingdom were to succumb, disintegration of the Commonwealth would inevitably follow, because the Dominions would not be strong enough to stand alone. Thus the defence of the United Kingdom is the vital concern, not only of the people of this country, but also of each separate member of the Commonwealth. Equally, the United Kingdom alone without the support of the Commonwealth would lose much of its effective influence and flexibility of power. It is, therefore, essential that the machinery for close and continuous co-operation in Defence matters between the Dominions and the United Kingdom should be constantly reviewed and brought to the highest efficiency.

Possible Threats to World Peace

7.   Although we do not regard a future war as inevitable, we cannot yet be sure that all the Great Powers are determined to keep the peace. Until the

general political atmosphere improves, we cannot, therefore, rule out the possibility of war with Russia, either by actual aggression on her part or by a miscalculation of the extent to which she can pursue a policy of ideological and territorial expansion short of war with the Democratic Powers.

8. The issue which cannot be avoided is that our Defence Policy must at present be based on the possibility of war with Russia. We do not consider that Germany by herself will constitute a danger for many years, but should a resurgent Germany again become a menace, it would be possible to adjust our Defence Policy, if we have meanwhile prepared against a presently greater threat.

9. We are convinced that we can reduce the risk of war if from now onwards we and our potential allies show strength and a preparedness to use this strength if necessary. Subject to this, we believe that the likelihood of war in the next five years is small; that the risk will increase gradually in the following five years, and will increase more steeply thereafter as the rehabilitation of Russia gathers momentum.

Characteristics of Russia as a Potential Enemy

10. The power of Russia as a potential enemy rests on the following factors:—

(a) Her very great superiority in man-power.

(b) She has vast territory and great resources, is practically self-contained economically, and has the benefit of wide dispersion of industries and centres of population, all under strict Government control.

(c) Her present political organisation and the degree of control exercised over the people by the Government would effectively stifle any public clamour against war. In addition, the high standard of security achieved renders our collection of intelligence difficult and makes it the more likely that Russia will have the advantage of surprise at the outset.

(d) She makes full use of Communist Parties in other countries, both to achieve an advantageous position for herself before the outbreak of war and to undermine the effort of her enemies when war has broken out.

On the other hand, Russia suffers from the following elements of weakness:—

(e) Large parts of Russia have been completely devastated.

(f) The population is ignorant and ill-educated and the standard of living is low. She is at present inferior to the Western Powers both industrially and technically and though her industrial potential and technical ability are growing, she has still a long way to go.

(g) Her transportation system is vulnerable and comparatively un-developed.

(h) Her oil production is barely sufficient for her needs and her main sources are badly placed strategically.

11. Against Russia as a potential enemy we must redress the balance in favour of the Commonwealth by:—

    (a) Increasing and exploiting our present scientific lead. This applies particularly to the development of mass destruction weapons.

    (b) Seeking to unite with us all powers which are determined to resist aggression.

European Allies

12. In the past we have relied on building up an alliance of European countries to unite with us from the very beginning in resisting aggression. There is now, however, no combination of European Powers capable of standing up to Russia on land, nor do we think that the probable military capabilities of an association of European States at present justify us in relying upon such an association for our defence.

Nevertheless, any time which we can gain to improve our defences would be of such value that every effort should be made to organise an association of Western European Powers, which would at least delay the enemy's advance across Europe.

Support from the United States

13. We must have the active and very early support of the United States. The United States alone, because of her man-power, industrial resources and her lead in the development of weapons of mass destruction, can turn the balance in favour of the Democracies. Apart from other considerations the United States will for some years at any rate, be the sole source from which we can draw a supply of atomic bombs.

Threat of Russian Expansion

14. The Russian policy of territorial and ideological expansion by the absorption of satellite States and by the spread of Communism in peace constantly threatens various countries whose continued integrity and independence profoundly affect Commonwealth security. Our interests are challenged, not only throughout Europe but also in the Middle East and throughout the world.

Middle East

15.   The area in which Russian expansion would be easiest and at the same time would hurt us most would be the Middle East. We may be sure that if we abandon our position there in peace Russia will fill the vacuum.

16.   Our experience in other areas such as Eastern Europe has shown that when Russia gains control our economic interests are forfeited and our communications are cut. The first impact of Russian expansion into the Middle East would therefore be upon our oil supplies and upon Commonwealth sea and air communications. The importance to us of present and potential oil supplies in the area is as great, if not greater, than ever, particularly in peace. The importance of the Middle East as a centre of Commonwealth communications remains, and will remain, beyond question.

If the use of the Middle East communications was denied to us it would be necessary to divert our supplies round the Cape or across Central Africa, which would increase immeasurably the burden on our resources. Moreover, our strategic signal communications would be disrupted.

17.   The powerful position which Russia would acquire by linking the Middle East countries to her influence and economy would prepare the way for further infiltration into both Asia and Africa. If Russia were to establish herself in the Middle East in peace or war, her power and influence would dominate the Moslem world and would be likely to spread eastwards through India, Burma and Malaya; southwards through the Sudan; and westwards in North Africa.

18.   In all these areas cells of communism exist, but so far in isolation. Once Russia is established in the Middle East she will create from these isolated cells a comprehensive and unified organisation. This would seriously undermine our strategy and economic interests in all these areas. Her eastward expansion would threaten the security of India, our control of sea communications in the Indian Ocean and our resources of oil, tin and rubber. Her westward expansion would create a new threat to our Atlantic sea communications already likely to be gravely endangered.

19.   Moreover, by ejecting the influence of the Western Powers from the Middle East, Russia would be securing her most vulnerable flank. It is from the Middle East area that her own vital oil industry and new industrial centres can most effectively be threatened. At the same time we should be placed in the position of having to be prepared to meet direct attacks on our own territories and interests in Africa, Aden, the Mediterranean and India and on our communications in the Indian Ocean.

20.   *To sum up, if Russia secured control of this area not only would we lose very important resources and facilities but she would acquire a position of such dominating strategic and economic power that it would be fatal to our security. It is therefore vital that we must retain a firm hold on the Middle*

East. This can only be achieved by our physical presence there in peace and by tangible evidence of our intention to remain.

An important contribution to the security of our position will be the continued independence of Greece and Turkey.

21. The need to retain our strategic and economic position in the Middle East is of equal importance if we should be engaged in war with a power other than Russia. This is demonstrated by the fact that in two world wars we have had to defeat Germany in the Middle East.

Implications of New Weapons

22. The main implications of the new weapons likely to be available by the critical period about 1956 may be summarised as follows:—

   (a) The possibility exists of achieving rapid and decisive results by the use of mass destruction weapons against economic key targets and the civil population.

   (b) Owing to the vastly greater destructive power of atomic and biological weapons, acceptable standards of defence have gone up immeasurably. Within the next ten years there is little possibility that these higher standards of defence can be reached.

   (c) There are greater possibilities than before of surprise attack, since the preparations required to deliver decisive attacks with the new weapons could be on a smaller scale than with conventional weapons. Militarily we must be prepared to exploit any such opportunity, although politically we are always likely to be severely handicapped.

   (d) The potential threat to our sea communications will be greater than at any time in the last war.

Russian Technical Development

23. All our intelligence sources indicate that Russia is striving, with German help, to improve her military potential; and to catch up technically and scientifically.

We must expect that from 1956–57 Russia will probably be in a position to use some atomic bombs and biological warfare; that she may have developed, probably with German advice and technical assistance, rockets, pilotless aircraft, a strategic bomber force and a submarine force; and that she will continue to maintain very large land forces, a considerable proportion of which may be equipped and trained up to Western standards.

United Kingdom Intelligence Organisation

24. It is of the greatest importance that our Intelligence Organisation should be able to provide us with adequate and timely warning. The smaller the armed

forces the greater is the need for developing our Intelligence Services in peace to enable them to fulfil this responsibility.

Vulnerability of the United Kingdom

25.   The advent of mass destruction weapons and other new means of offence has greatly increased the vulnerability of the United Kingdom with her dense and concentrated population and industries. We do not think that it will be possible by purely defensive action to prevent the delivery of all weapons of mass destruction, and the effect of even a small number will be proportionately greater in the United Kingdom than in a larger country with a widely dispersed industry.

26.   In spite of our industrial and technical lead and in spite of the assistance of allies, including America, we should be unable to prevent the vastly superior land forces of Russia overrunning North-West Europe. From this position rockets and other long-range missiles might, if the build-up cannot be impeded, cause irreparable damage or even the elimination of the United Kingdom, even without recourse to atom attack. It is essential that before such destruction—from which we might never recover—could be achieved, we ourselves should assume the initiative and destroy the enemy's means of making war. The vulnerability of this country to modern weapons would bring the war to its climax much earlier than in the past. This initiative must be assumed from the outset. This entails not only the readiness of offensive forces, but the presence in this country of the essential resources to maintain them at intensive rates immediately on the outbreak of war.

Offensive Action

27.   If we are to impede the enemy build-up in Western Europe and to strike at the enemy's means of making war we must possess Air Forces capable of penetrating into enemy territory. The time required to achieve decisive results with conventional weapons is open to doubt. It may be, therefore, that weapons of mass destruction will have to be used to achieve decisive results before irreparable damage to our industries has been caused. It is only by early offensive action that the weight of attack on the United Kingdom can be materially decreased.

Use of Mass Destruction Weapons

28.   Thus to achieve victory or avoid defeat, it may be essential for us to use weapons of mass destruction.
    On the other hand, in view of the small number of atom bombs and possibly of biological warfare and chemical warfare weapons required to knock out the

United Kingdom, and the relatively small operational effort involved, the margin between victory and defeat, if once they are used, will be an extremely narrow one.

29.   It may, therefore, be argued that, in view of the vulnerability of the United Kingdom, it would be to our advantage if they were not used by either side, and that for that reason we should favour their abolition in peace and not initiate their use in war. Nevertheless, their abolition by international convention would give us no guarantee of immunity, since their production in war, as a result of the development of atomic energy for other purposes, would be possible in a matter of months.

30.   Furthermore, we are convinced that Russia's attitude towards the use of these weapons will be determined solely be self-interest. She will no doubt appreciate that a comparatively small number of bombs will knock us out, and that it will be impossible for us, by action taken solely against the aircraft delivering the weapons, to prevent this small number being delivered.

The only means whereby we can prevent her using them, therefore, is by facing her with the threat of large-scale damage from similar weapons if she should employ them. This threat can only be achieved by evidence of our ability to use weapons of mass destruction on a considerable scale from the outset.

In addition we believe that the knowledge that we possessed weapons of mass destruction and were prepared to use them would be a most effective deterrent to war itself.

31.   The decision whether or not to use these weapons obviously cannot be taken now. The one certain point is that it must be a cardinal principle of our policy to be prepared, equipped and able to use them immediately.

Bases for Offensive Action

32.   Irrespective of weapons used, bases for launching the air offensive are essential. There are three possible main areas from which effective offensive action can be launched against the U.S.S.R.
  These are:—
  (a) *The United Kingdom.*—The United Kingdom provides the best base for mounting an air offensive because of the airfields and resources that exist there. In this country, moreover, we can make full preparations in peace for the development of an immediate offensive in war and for the subsequent build-up for our allies.
    The United Kingdom is, however, likely to be subject to a heavy scale of air attack and its capacity to sustain large offensive forces may therefore be limited; moreover, there are important areas of Russia which, for many years at any rate, will remain out of range of aircraft based in the United Kingdom.

We cannot, therefore, rely upon the United Kingdom as our sole offensive base. Moreover, without the use of overseas bases for offensive action it would not be possible to limit to any extent the weight of Russian effort against the United Kingdom.

(b) *The Middle East.*—From the Middle East it is possible to reach many vital areas of Russia which cannot effectively be dealt with by forces based in the United Kingdom. In particular, it is by far the best base for attack on Russia's oil producton, one of the weak points in Russia's war potential.

(c) *North-West India.*—From bases in North-West India large areas of Russia can be covered, including the Siberian industrial areas which cannot effectively be dealt with from any other bases likely to be available to us.

FUNDAMENTALS OF OUR DEFENCE POLICY

33. From all the above factors we can now deduce the fundamentals of our Defence Policy:—

(a) The supreme object of British policy is to prevent war, provided that this can be done without prejudicing our vital interests. This entails support of the United Nations and ability to defend our own interests.

(b) The most likely and most formidable threat to our interests comes from Russia, especially from 1956 onwards, and it is against this worst case that we must be prepared, at the same time taking every possible step to prevent it.

(c) The most effective step towards preventing war is tangible evidence that we possess adequate forces and resources, that we are fully prepared and that we have the intention and ability to take immediate offensive action.

(d) Essential measures required in peace to give us a chance of survival and victory in the event of war are:—

(i) Retaining at a high state of readiness properly balanced armed forces for immediate use on the outbreak of war, with the necessary reserves of resources to support them.

(ii) Maintaining the united front of the British Commonwealth and doing everything possible to ensure that in the event of war we have the immediate and active support of all its members.

(iii) Ensuring that we have the active and early support of the United States of America and of the Western European States.

(iv) Increasing and exploiting our present scientific and technical lead, especially in the development of weapons of mass destruction.

(v) Actively opposing the spread of Russian influence by adopting a

firm attitude to further Russian territorial and ideological expansion, particularly in all areas of strategic value to the defence of the British Commonwealth.

(vi) Arresting by all possible means the deterioration that has already begun in our own position and prestige in the Middle East, and encouraging the continued independence of Greece and Turkey.

(vii) Maintaining our Intelligence Organisations at a high standard of efficiency.

(viii)Being prepared to take offensive air action from the outset since the war will rapidly reach a climax and the endurance of the United Kingdom cannot be guaranteed for any considerable period against attacks by modern weapons, still less by weapons of mass destruction. The best bases for this offensive action are United Kingdom, Middle East and if possible North-West India.

(ix) Being ourselves prepared, equipped and able to use weapons of mass destruction as a part of this offensive action.

PART II. — THE STRATEGY OF COMMONWEALTH DEFENCE

34. Having arrived at conclusions on the fundamental principles which should govern our future Defence Policy, we proceed to examine further the strategy which would be required to implement that policy in war.

Our examination shows that in a future war, time will be an all-important factor. The days when we could afford to remain on the defensive, while gathering our great strength for the knock-out blow, ended with the advent of the first atom bomb. A far higher degree of preparedness in peace is now imperative if we are to survive the opening phases of another war—a preparedness which must enable us to hit back hard at the outset to defend our very existence. Moreover, in view of the speed with which we could be knocked out, it is vital that we possess the ability by ourselves to withstand and counter the initial onslaught. This entails stockpiling of reserves in peace-time.

The weight and tempo of this onslaught may, however, be beyond our power to bear alone for more than a short period. This places a new value on Dominion and Allied support, and calls for much more rapid assistance than of old, even if it is thereby limited.

35. If war should be forced upon us, it is obvious that our first consideration must be the defence of the United Kingdom, which is both the focus of Commonwealth strength and also its most vulnerable point. Besides the actual defence of these islands, we must also defend the resources on which the Commonwealth must draw to prosecute a major war, and preserve the means by which the Dominions and our allies can come to our aid, so that with our

united strength we can develop an eventual all-out offensive. The control of sea communications is essential to the achivement of these aims.

BASIC REQUIREMENTS OF OUR STRATEGY

36.   It is now apparent that in pursuance of our Defence Policy the following are the basic requirements of our strategy:—

(a) *The defence of the United Kingdom and its development as an offensive base.*

(b) *The control of essential sea communications.*

(c) *A firm hold in the Middle East and its development as an offensive base.*

These three pillars of our strategy must stand together. The collapse of any one of them will bring down the whole structure of Commonwealth Strategy.

To them we would add a fourth, which though not essential would give a most desirable addition of strength:—

(d) *The co-operation of India: the provision of the necessary assistance to ensure her security; and the development of an offensive base in North-West India.*

We discuss below methods of attaining these strategic aims.

Defence of the United Kingdom

37.   We must be prepared for a situation in which the Russians attempt to build-up rocket and air forces within easy striking range of the whole of the United Kingdom. The reduction of attack by enemy aircraft to acceptable proportions, if weapons of mass destruction are not used, is not a novel problem but we can see no way of combating the rocket once it has been launched. As we have shown, the capacity to develop an air offensive is an essential defence against attack by absolute weapons and against the build-up of rocket attack. The forces required for this would also be required in the battle for air supremacy to defeat normal methods of air attack. The possibility of attempts at invasion, particularly by air, cannot be ruled out. Finally, it must not be forgotten that the whole conduct of our defence will depend on the continued flow of our supplies, which must be transported by sea.

38.   We must have, therefore:—

(a) Strong air defences, including strong and up-to-date anti-aircraft and civil defences.

(b) An effective bomber force.

(c) Naval control and air superiority over, on and under the waters surrounding these islands, and along our sea communications.

(d) Sufficient land forces for defence against invasion on a limited scale and against raids.

Control of Sea Communications

39.   We have already pointed out that the security of the sea communications of the United Kingdom is an essential part of the defence of the United Kingdom both against invasion and to sustain the whole war effort of the country. This security must be extended world wide to cover communications with the Dominions, with the United States and with sources of raw materials and essential supplies throughout the world.

The threat in Home waters and the North Atlantic would be immensely magnified by an enemy advance to the Channel ports and the Atlantic seaboard. Our powers of resistance to this threat would be much increased if we had the use of Irish bases.

40.   We must also exercise control of sea communications to gain flexibility and mobility of deployment of all the Armed Forces wherever they may be required and to deny those advantages to the enemy. By control of the sea communications through the Mediterranean we could most quickly deploy our forces for the defence of the Middle East and obtain rapid assistance in that theatre from the United States and the Dominions, while at the same time by denying the use of that sea to the enemy, we confine him to difficult land communications and prevent him from obtaining a foothold in North Africa from which he might advance to outflank our defence of Egypt or to establish bases from which to threaten our Atlantic communications.

41.   To enable us to exercise control of sea communications through the Mediterranean, we must retain our existing strategic possessions there and obtain additional base facilities on the North African coast. To these ends we must ensure that Spain does not fall under Russian domination, is prepared to resist aggression, and that the French North African dependencies are friendly to our cause.

42.   To attain security and control of sea communications, naval and air forces, adequate and suitably organised to meet any threat or challenge, and bases for their effective operation will be required. At present it appears that the chief threats to our sea communications will be from fast submarine attack, air attack and minelaying. But the threat of surface attacks on our shipping must still be guarded against and the capacity of the potential enemy to challenge our control of sea communications must be constantly watched and provided against.

Defence of the Middle East

43.   The main problem of the defence of this area is the time factor and the effect of present political changes upon our position at the outbreak of war.

The vital strategic area of the Middle East is Egypt, since it possesses the essential air bases, ports, communications and man-power. Our defensive preparations therefore must be directed primarily to the retention of that area.

We cannot be certain of being able to defend our oil resources in the Middle East but we must make every effort to do so. It should be our aim to ensure that oil pipelines and other oil communications are as well placed strategically as possible. We should also endeavour, by all the means in our power, to develop sources of supply in less vulnerable areas in the Middle East and elsewhere and to build up our oil reserves, particularly by stockpiling in the United Kingdom and our other main base areas.

44.   The defence of Egypt against a land attack from the north must be conducted in the area Southern Syria–Northern Palestine. The land forces which the Russians can deploy in this area would be operating at the end of long and difficult lines of communications, and would be reduced by maintenance difficulties. They would be further hampered if we were able to take early air action against their communications, from bases in the Middle East. A further advantage our Land Forces would enjoy would be the support of Naval Forces operating to their seaward flank. Provided we are established in the Middle East area before a Russian advance and provided early reinforcements can be obtained from the Dominions and from the United States it should be possible to defend our interests in the Middle East. The expenditure of resources required to recapture our position in the Middle East, if it is lost through our inability to concentrate there in time, will be out of all proportion to the expenditure needed to defend it if we are firmly established at the outbreak.

45.   The problem is primarily one of time, *i.e.*, whether we can get the necessary forces into position before the Russians can attack in strength. If the necessary arrangements are made for rapid assistance from the United States and the Dominions, we consider that an effective defence is well within our capacity provided that:—

    (a) We have the right to re-enter Egypt on threat of war and develop the base facilities we shall require there.

    (b) We have strategic rights in Palestine in peace.

    (c) We retain the sovereignty of Cyprus.

    (d) Turkey refuses Russian demands for strategic facilities in peace and opposes Russian invasion of her territory. This will modify the time factor to our advantage.

Continued independence of Greece will greatly encourage the Turks to stiffen their attitude.

Our position in the Middle East would be given greater depth if we obtain the Trusteeship of Cyrenaica.

East Africa has been suggested as a possible alternative to the retention of Middle East administrative facilities in peace. The time factor rules it out, however, as the cost in air and sea transport to meet the necessary speed of movement would be prohibitive. On the other hand East Africa would be a useful location for reserves.

Co-operation of India and her Defence

46.   The importance of North-West India as an offensive base, together with the man-power and resources which India can provide, requires that every effort should be made to obtain an agreement with India whereby she will co-operate actively with us in war. We cannot, however, count upon this at present.

Except in the case of air defence, India should be able herself to undertake the main burden of defence. Should she agree to co-operate with us, we would have to provide the necessary assistance to ensure her security.

The same considerations would apply, in the case of a divided India, should a viable State emerge covering the north-west part of the country.

CONCLUSION—TASKS OF THE ARMED FORCES AND PRINCIPLES AFFECTING THEIR BUILD-UP

47.   *Our strategic needs lead to conclusions on the tasks of our armed forces which can now be stated in general terms. It is also possible to indicate certain general principles which should govern the nature and size of our future forces:—*

   (a)   *Research and Development*

      Our first requirement is to build up our organisation for scientific research and development to a level which will ensure that we can maintain our technical superiority on the one hand, and on the other provide the necessary information to enable us to decide in good time on our re-equipment policy.

   (b)   *Offensive Force*

      As our ability to strike will represent both a very strong deterrent to aggression and one of our principal means of defence, the development of an air offensive force must be given high priority.

   (c)   *Defence of the United Kingdom*

      The security of the United Kingdom is of vital importance. While the possession of a powerful offensive force is essential to our security, the development of our active and passive air defence organisations, in all their aspects, must be complementary to the build-up of our air striking force.

      The Army must provide for the manning of the anti-aircraft defences; readiness to aid the Civil Power; and defence against invasion, primarily by air.

The Navy and the R.A.F. must ensure control over the waters surrounding these islands.

(d) Control of Sea Communications

While our ability to hit back and the knowledge that we possess a sound defence will be a very strong deterrent to a potential aggressor, once war starts the security of our sea communications will rapidly assume vital importance.

The task of the Navy, assisted by the R.A.F., will be to secure to our own use sea communications, not only in the approaches to the United Kingdom but world-wide with the Dominions, the United States and sources of supply, and also through the Mediterranean to the Middle East; at the same time denying them to the enemy.

The maintenance and development in peace of the necessary naval and air forces to ensure security and control against any threat or challenge will therefore continue to be of high importance.

At present it appears that the chief threats to our sea communications will be from fast submarine attack, air attack and minelaying. But the threat of surface attacks on our shipping must still be guarded against and the capacity of the potential enemy to challenge our control of sea communications must be constantly watched and provided against.

(e) Defence of the Middle East and India

The primary task of the Army, apart from the manning of anti-aircraft defences and readiness to aid civil power in the United Kingdom, will be to ensure the security of our Middle East base. Despite the possible risk of invasion of the United Kingdom by air we consider the provision of forces to meet our requirements in the Middle East must be given priority over the anti-invasion role in the United Kingdom.

Air forces will be required for the defence of the Middle East base and in support of the Army there. They will also be required in India if she is co-operating with us.

Naval forces capable of giving all necessary support to the Army's land battle will be required.

(f) Combined Operations

We do not foresee a necessity for major combined operations, in the form of assault landings by sea or air, in the early stages of a war. Nor would our military strength at the outset permit of their being undertaken. But it is impossible to forecast how the war would develop. Minor landings in furtherance of a land campaign already undertaken might be required. When the full strength of the Commonwealth and the Allies is built up, and an overseas operation is necessary, combined operations on a large scale may be required.

It will, therefore, be necessary in peace to provide for keeping the art of Combined Operations and Airborne Assault alive in all the Armed Forces, and for research, experiment and development in the technique required.

RECOMMENDATIONS

48.   We recommend that the Defence Committee should:—

(a) Approve the fundamentals of our defence policy as given in paragraph 33 and accept the basic requirements of our strategy as given in paragraph 36 above.

(b) Approve the tasks of our armed forces as set out in paragraph 47 above as a basis for planning the shape and size of our future armed forces.

(c) Take note of our views on the relations between our Defence policy and National policy, as set out in the Annex.

(d) Direct that an examination be made of the desirability of increased dispersal of industry throughout the Commonwealth, as suggested in the Annex.

(Signed)

J. H. D. CUNNINGHAM
MONTGOMERY of ALAMEIN
W. F. DICKSON (V.C.A.S.)

Ministry of Defence, S.W.1,
    22nd May, 1947.

ANNEX

National Policy

1.   Our examination of Future Defence Policy has led us to the conclusion that long-term political and economic developments are factors as vital to our future security as any adjustments in the shape and size of the Armed Forces. We, therefore, give below our views on the relations between Defence Policy and both Foreign [and] Economic Policies.

2.   We recognise that His Majesty's Government are committed to certain policies which may profoundly affect our Commonwealth strategic position, *e.g.*, the reference of the Palestine question to the United Nations and the transfer of power in India. Nevertheless, we feel strongly that we should strive with all the means at our disposal, in consultation, as appropriate, with the

Dominions and the United States, to achieve certain definite objects of policy.

3.   Our examination shows that in support of Commonwealth defence policy the following objects should be pursued:—

(a) We must support and strengthen the United Nations organisation, and seek to make it effective as a means of preventing war.

(b) We should insist upon adequate guarantees of security before any measures of disarmament are undertaken.

(c) We should continue to do everything possible to combat the spread of communism so as to prevent our position being prejudiced before the outbreak of war.

(d) We should strengthen the links with the Dominions, including Eire, and all parts of the Colonial Empire.

(e) We should have the closest possible tie-up with the United States.

(f) We should strive for an agreement with India, or any part of India, which allows us all essential military facilities.

(g) We must encourage the building up of a strong Western Region of Defence, with France as its key-stone, and ensure that Germany does not become a Russian Satellite.

(h) We must strive to ensure that the solution of the Spanish problem is favourable to the democracies.

(i) We should not adopt any policy in peace which might lead to difficulties in our obtaining in war our strategic requirements in the French or Spanish North African dependencies.

(j) We must retain our essential strategic requirements in Palestine in peace.

(k) We should negotiate a treaty with Egypt which will:—

(i)   Safeguard our right of re-entry into that country on the threat of war;

(ii)   Ensure the maintenance in peace of the minimum base facilities which we shall require on the outbreak of war.

(l) Our position in the Middle East would be given greater depth if we obtained military rights in Cyrenaica.

(m) We should not relinquish our sovereignty over Cyprus.

(n) We must not allow Russia to establish her influence in Libya or Somalia when the final disposition of these countries is determined.

(o) Nothing should be allowed to interfere with the improvement of our relations with the Arab States.

(p) We must ensure the integrity and independence of Greece and Turkey in peacetime and their capacity and willingness to resist aggression in war.

(q) We must support the continued independence of Persia and Afghanistan.

(r) We must encourage and assist the development of oil production in the less vulnerable areas of the Middle East and elsewhere.

(s) We must build up by stockpiling reserves of resources essential for our war-making capacity, particularly in the United Kingdom.

Economic Policy

The outstanding consideration from a strategical point of view is that the economy of the United Kingdom should be thoroughly sound and able to support a powerful war potential and adequate armed forces.

The greatly increased vulnerability of the United Kingdom suggests that dispersion of industry, not only within the United Kingdom, but also to less vulnerable Dominions, is of importance. Dispersion within the United Kingdom is already accepted as one of the considerations in our industrial planning. The practicability of a limited dispersion overseas of those industries vital to the prosecution of a war will depend on economic considerations. It is urgent that a thorough examination of this subject should be carried out by experts.

APPENDIX 8

Churchill and Biological Warfare, 1944

The following article by the author originally appeared in the February 1982 edition of Encounter *magazine and is reproduced by permission of the Editors. Despite the absence of any subsequent attempt to refute its findings, no apology has ever been offered to the Churchill family by the British Broadcasting Corporation for propagating a myth which was reported around the world and which still occasionally resurfaces. It was not repeated, however, in the book by its originator Robert Harris — A Higher Form of Killing, The Secret Story of Gas and Germ Warfare (Chatto & Windus, 1982) — which was published shortly after this article.*

THE PLAN THAT NEVER WAS—CHURCHILL AND THE 'ANTHRAX BOMB'

In the summer of 1981, a sensational allegation was widely reported by the British press (and then echoed internationally, not least in the German newspapers): CHURCHILL GERM RAID PLAN DISCLOSED (*Guardian*); HORROR BID TO END WAR (*Sun*); BLITZ OF POISON—CHURCHILL PLANNED TO BOMB GERMAN CITIES WITH ANTHRAX (*Daily Express*); CHURCHILL PLANNED ANTHRAX BOMB RAID ON GERMANY (*Daily Telegraph*). All these headlines derived from a BBC Television feature programme (*Newsnight*, transmitted on 1 May 1981), and all of them were wrong.

The following passage from the broadcast, and I take it from the BBC transcript, shows how its tone was demagogically set from the beginning:

> PETER SNOW: ... I suppose it's only natural that the British like to think that whatever the Nazis stooped to during the Second World War at least we tried to maintain standards of conduct which set us apart from the tyranny we were

388

fighting. But *Newsnight* has uncovered evidence of a terrible weapon invented, developed and tested by British scientists during those dark days of the early 1940s, and even today, forty years on, if you venture too close to the test site you too could still fall victim to a deadly disease.

Apparently, then, wartime Britain had done something to place herself on a par with Nazi Germany. But what could this possibly be? In the report by Robert Harris which followed, the answer took a long time in coming.

Most of the *Newsnight* feature simply related how the British germ warfare programme developed, rightly indicating as its motivating force the fear of a German biological attack. The deadly effects of anthrax were spelt out—this being the disease on which research was concentrated by scientists at Porton, near Salisbury, from August 1940. A detailed account was also given of the testing of an anthrax device on a small Scottish island nearly two years later, and of the continuing contamination of that island up to the present day. Yet there was nothing fundamentally new, or scandalous, in these revelations. As the obituarists of Paul Fildes, the principal bacteriologist involved, had noted in a memoir published in 1973:

> That much of the war work at Porton has now become declassified is evident from the publicity given in television programmes to the experiments on Gruinard Island. Tourist trips from Ullapool round the 'forbidden island' are advertised as a holiday attraction.[1]

One such programme had been broadcast by the BBC itself in April 1967. An account based upon it had appeared in print in 1969, naming anthrax as the agent used on Gruinard and quoting the then Director of the Porton centre as predicting no reduction in the level of contamination for a further hundred years.[2]

It was only in the closing stages of the *Newsnight* report that the screw began to tighten. Robert Harris's emphasis shifted from eyewitness accounts of the nature and development of biological weapons to what was claimed to be documentary evidence of an intention to initiate their use. The viewers were told how America developed the British discoveries as a result of inter-Allied co-operation. It was also revealed that in 1944 Churchill approved a proposal to order 500,000 anthrax bombs from the United States government. However, the purely defensive rationale for this step was not referred to, though clearly set out by the Prime Minister when he took it on 8 March:

---

1. G. P. Gladstone, *et al.*, 'Paul Gordon Fildes' in *Biographical Memoirs of Fellows of the Royal Society* (1973), Vol. XIX, p. 337
2. R. W. Reid, *Tongues of Conscience: War and the Scientist's Dilemma* (1969), pp. 307–8

.... I have had most secret consultations with my Military Advisers. They consider, and I entirely agree, that if our enemies should indulge in this form of warfare, the only deterrent would be our power to retaliate.[3]

Nor had his thinking changed by 21 May, when he directed his military advisers—the Chiefs of Staff—to take over responsibility in this field from the Chancellor of the Duchy of Lancaster. To his personal representative on the C.O.S. Committee, Lieutenant-General Sir Hastings Ismay, he wrote:

As you know, great progress has been made in bacteriological warfare and we have ordered a half million bombs from America for use should this mode of warfare be employed against us. ....[4]

As I later managed to confirm, Mr. Harris was familiar with both these minutes. But the inclusion of such remarks would hardly have been helpful to what was to follow.

Since this is an article about bowdlerisation and selective misquotation, the following paragraphs are reproduced in full from pp. 5–6 of the BBC transcript:

"HARRIS: In 1944 the secret weapon which Hitler had warned the Allies about at Danzig finally appeared. It was not a germ weapon. It was the flying bomb. Soon it was causing such damage in London that the British began to consider using anthrax as a reprisal against German cities. We have discovered a previously unpublished memorandum written by the Prime Minister, Winston Churchill, to the Chiefs of Staff. From the very beginning he had taken a close interest in the development of poison gas and germ weapons. Now, he argued, was perhaps the moment to use them:

[CHURCHILL:] 'If the bombardment of London really became a serious nuisance [. . .], I should be prepared to do *anything* that would hit the enemy in a murderous place. [. . .] I do not see why we should always have all the disadvantages of being the gentleman while they have all the advantages of being the cad. [. . .] It may be several weeks, or even months, before I shall ask you to drench Germany with poison gas and, if we do it, let us do it one hundred percent. In the meantime I want the matter studied in cold blood by sensible people and not by that particular set of psalm-singing, uniformed defeatists which one runs across now, here and there. Pray address yourself to this.'

---

3. P.M.'s Personal Min No M.246/4, Churchill to Brown, 8 March 1944, in PREM 3/65
4. P.M.'s Personal Min No D.162/4, Churchill to Ismay, 21 May 1944, in CAB 120/782

HARRIS [holding open file of documents]: This was the report that Churchill's military advisers produced. It's a chilling assessment of what using chemical and biological weapons would have meant in the Second World War. They advised against using poison gas on the grounds that the bombs we were dropping on German cities were already doing enough damage, but they put biological weapons in a different category.

[QUOTE FROM REPORT:] 'Biological warfare would cause heavy casualities, panic and confusion in the areas affected. It might lead to a breakdown in administration with a consequent decisive influence on the outcome of the war.'

HARRIS: Everything had been worked out to the last detail. [FRONT COVER OF DOCUMENT SHOWN] This top secret report shows how scientists reduced the mass destructive power of anthrax into a neat mathematical formula. The Allies code-named the anthrax weapon N. Each bomb weighed about four pounds. They were loaded into large aircraft cluster bombs 106 at a time. N was not designed for use on the battlefield but specifically for strategic bombing against enemy cities. A few hundred feet above the target the large mother bomb would burst open and scatter the anthrax bomblets over a wide area.

Six German cities were provisionally selected as targets: Aachen, Wilhelmshaven, Stuttgart, Frankfurt, Hamburg and Berlin. They were all to be attacked in a single day by a force of 2,700 heavy bombers carrying over 40,000 cluster bombs. Twelve cluster bombs to the square mile; 1,272 anthrax bomblets in that square mile. An almost total saturation of bacteria.

The cities would have become a wasteland. According to the scientists' report 50% of the inhabitants might be killed by inhalation, many more might die through contamination of the skin. This would have meant a death toll of around three million people.

[QUOTE FROM REPORT:] 'The terrain will be contaminated for years, and danger from skin infection should be great enough to enforce evacuation. [. . .] There is no satisfactory method of decontamination. There is no preventive inoculation [. . .].'

[HARRIS:] What stopped Churchill using anthrax against Germany was not moral scruples but time. His military advisers told him that the American factories were not yet producing N bombs in sufficient quantities to enable a full-scale attack to be launched.

[QUOTE FROM REPORT:] '[. . .] There is no likelihood of a sustained attack being possible much before the middle of 1945.'

[HARRIS:] Germany was saved from biological attack by her own defeat.

All this took place little more than two years after Dr Fildes and his team first rode out to Gruinard with their prototype anthrax bomb. If a handful of bombs could make this island uninhabitable for forty years, what might have happened if the Allies had gone ahead with their plans to drop four and a quarter million bombs on Germany?"

With the obvious answer secured from the Director of Porton that cities like Berlin would still be contaminated had anthrax been used against the Germans, and after adding that 'there does now seem to be little doubt that at one time it was contemplated', Mr Harris concluded that biological warfare 'is arguably the last great Allied secret of the war'. A closing studio reference to 'Robert Harris's disturbing report' rounded off *Newsnight*'s contribution to British military historiography. The newspaper headlines followed.

The Planning Machinery

Although it had little to do with Churchill *per se*, the academic research I was completing when the story broke included a long section on the British biological warfare programme and was based on some three years' study of the documents of Churchill's (and Clement Attlee's) military advisers. These were the Chiefs of Staff, and some grasp of the nature of their organisation is essential for an understanding of what really happened in 1944.

The C.O.S. Committee was made up of the heads of the three Services, the Chief of Combined Operations (when such matters were under consideration), and the Chief Staff Officer to the Minister of Defence—General Ismay. Ismay was Churchill's channel of communication with his military advisers who sat at the head of a pyramid of inter-Service sub-committees and staffs. There was also a Vice-Chiefs of Staff Committee, set up in 1940 to lighten the decision-making burden of the main body. Of the specialist sub-committees, only the Joint Planning Staff was charged with the preparation of strategic plans for the consideration of the Service Chiefs or Vice-Chiefs. The Joint Intelligence Sub-Committee collated information on which plans might be based. The Joint Technical Warfare Committee co-ordinated the technical study of operational projects and problems. The Inter-Service Committee on Chemical Warfare and the Inter-Service Sub-Committee on Biological Warfare respectively supervised all developments appertaining to poison gas and germs. But the J.T.W.C., the I.S.C.C.W., and the I.S.S.B.W. had *no strategic planning role* at all. They were purely technical and/or administrative bodies, and the papers they produced were designed to show the strategic planners what was technically feasible and what simply could not be done. Their adoption of a particular strategic hypothesis in the course of a given feasibility study in no way implied that the implementation of that hypothesis had ever been considered as a matter of policy by the responsible military authorities.

Nor did the strategic views of the Joint Planning Staff itself count for anything in advance of endorsement by the parent C.O.S. Committee. As Brigadier A. T. Cornwall-Jones, a former secretary to the C.O.S. organisation, had warned me in a letter of 18 May 1976 (near the start of my research):

> ... it needs to be understood that the views of these bodies were never authoritative. They were groups of men who operated under the Chiefs of Staff but it was the Chiefs of Staff whose views mattered, it being accepted that the signature of the Vice-Chiefs was just as good as the Chiefs' on any but the terribly big issues. . . . Very often the planners' views would be accepted. Just as often perhaps they would be changed and sometimes 'chucked out'.

In the summer of 1981, for example, it was a failure to clarify the precise status and purposes of certain Joint Technical Warfare Committee papers drawn up soon after the war which led to a press report headed 'GERM ATTACK IN 1946 CONSIDERED' and to a mischievous Parliamentary Question in the House of Lords from Fenner Brockway.[5] In fact, these 'plans for an attack on Russian cities by Britain using atomic bombs and germ warfare weapons' were nothing more than hypothetical studies compiled to help the J.T.W.C. assess the likely future nature of warfare. They were not even 'contingency plans' against the Russians. Not only had Britain no atomic weapons in 1946, but—as will be seen—she had no effective biological weapons either.

Gas, Not Germs: The Misquoted Minute

Shortly after the programme was screened, I got in touch with Professor R. V. Jones of Aberdeen University. As Churchill's Assistant Director of Intelligence (Science) at the Air Ministry during the war, he had been a key figure in the fight against Hitler's flying bombs and rockets. He confirmed what my reading of such C.O.S. documents on the subject as I had already seen suggested: that the Prime Minister had advocated the use of gas, not germs, in response to the V–weapon threat. Indeed, he had mentioned this incident himself in a biographical memoir of Churchill published by the Royal Society in 1966, and in connection with a television series which gave rise to a BBC publication in 1978. His own book on British scientific intelligence in the Second World War had stressed how greatly the 'experts' had erred in overestimating the size of the V.2 rocket (*not* the V.1 flying bomb referred to by Harris on the BBC), with each being thought capable by some of inflicting

---

5. *The Times*, 15 June 1981; Lord Brockway, House of Lords Debate, *Hansard* (Vol. 422, No. 107, Col. 188), 30 June 1981

up to 4,000 casualties (according to the Ministry of Home Security in 1943), and with the size of the warhead still being thought—at the time of the Churchill initiative of July 1944 dramatised by *Newsnight*—to be between three and seven times as great as it really was.[6] In any case, as Professor Jones wrote on 5 May to George Carey, the programme's editor:

> There was no mention, so far as I know, of biological, as opposed to chemical, warfare in what Churchill had said, and I think that the anthrax story is really quite distinct.

In this belief he was absolutely correct; but the BBC *Newsnight* team remained resolutely unimpressed.

The charges levelled against the BBC during the press controversy that followed the broadcast concentrated on its misrepresentation of comments about the use of poison gas (a crude, and rather ineffective weapon) as relating also to germ warfare, and its interleaving and distortion of C.O.S. material in such a way as to confuse hypothetical contingency planning with serious consideration of germ warfare as a policy for implementation.[7] These charges were perfectly well-founded. Yet there was an even more basic flaw in the *Newsnight* case which only systematic research could uncover: (1) that Churchill never asked for the use of anthrax to be considered in any way whatever, and (2) that the document in which it was claimed that he did never even existed.

Let me examine first the Prime Minister's outspoken 6 July 1944 minute[8]— *Newsnight*'s prized discovery purportedly showing that 'the British' began to consider using anthrax in response to 'the flying bomb', and in which Churchill was originally claimed to have 'argued' that the moment to use 'gas *and germs*' had perhaps arrived. It was addressed to General Ismay for the Chiefs of Staff Committee, and its serial number was *D.217/4*. This number is important. We shall be meeting it again, so it is as well to understand that every such minute had its own serial number, the last figure of which was simply the last figure of the year in which it was written—in this case, 1944. The subject of the minute was spelt out in its opening paragraph. It was not anthrax:

6. R. V. Jones, 'Winston Leonard Spencer Churchill', in *Biographical Memoirs of Fellows of the Royal Society* (1966), Vol. XII, pp. 82–3; Brian Johnson, *The Secret War* (BBC, 1978; Arrow, 1979), p. 199; R. V. Jones, *Most Secret War* (Hamish Hamilton, 1978; Coronet, 1979), pp. 437, 547–8, 562–8

7. *Guardian*, 7, 9, 13, 20, 30 May 1981, 2 June 1981; *The Times*, 11, 20 May 1981; *Daily Telegraph*, 18, 21, 25, 29 May 1981, 2, 11 June 1981; *Listener*, 4, 25 June 1981, 2 July 1981, 17 August 1981

8. P.M.'s Personal Min No D.217/4, 6 July 1944, in PREM 3/89 (also in CAB 120/775)

1. I want you to think very seriously over this question of poison gas. I would not use it unless it could be shown either that (a) it was life or death for us, or (b) that it would shorten the war by a year.

2. It is absurd to consider morality on this topic when everybody used it in the last war without a word of complaint from the moralists or the Church. On the other hand, in the last war the bombing of open cities was regarded as forbidden. Now everybody does it as a matter of course. It is simply a question of fashion changing as she does between long and short skirts for women.

3. I want a cold-blooded calculation made as to how it would pay us to use poison gas, by which I mean principally mustard. We will want to gain more ground in Normandy so as not to be cooped up in a small area. We could probably deliver 20 tons to their 1 and for the sake of the 1 they would bring their bomber aircraft into the area against our superiority, thus paying a heavy toll.

4. Why have the Germans not used it? Not certainly out of moral scruples or affection for us. They have not used it because it does not pay them. The greatest temptation ever offered to them was the beaches of Normandy. This they could have drenched with gas greatly to the hindrance of our troops. That they thought about it is certain and that they prepared against our use of gas is also certain. But the only reason they have not used it against us is that they fear the retaliation. What is to their detriment is to our advantage.

5. Although one sees how unpleasant it is to receive poison gas attacks, from which nearly everyone recovers, it is useless to protest that an equal amount of H.E. [high explosive] will not inflict greater cruelties and sufferings on troops or civilians. One really must not be bound within silly conventions of the mind whether they be those that ruled in the last war or those in reverse which rule in this.

6. If the bombardment of London really became a serious nuisance and great rockets with far-reaching and devastating effect fell on many centres of Government and labour, I should be prepared to do *anything* that would hit the enemy in a murderous place. I may certainly have to ask you to support me in using poison gas. We could drench the cities of the Ruhr and many other cities in Germany in such a way that most of the population would be requiring constant medical attention. We could stop all work at the flying bomb starting points. I do not see why we should always have all the disadvantages of being the gentleman while they have all the advantages of being the cad. There are times when this may be so but not now.

7. I quite agree that it may be several weeks or even months before I shall ask you to drench Germany with poison gas, and if we do it, let us do it one hundred per cent. In the meanwhile, I want the matter studied in cold blood by sensible people and not by that particular set of psalm-singing uniformed defeatists which one runs across now here now there. Pray address yourself to this. It is a big thing and can only be discarded for a big reason. I shall of course have to square Uncle Joe [Stalin] and the President; but you need not bring this into your calculations at the present time. Just try to find out what it is like on its merits.

W.S.C.

A comparison of this minute with the first two of the *Newsnight* paragraphs quoted on p. 390 shows how seriously it was mistreated. If its opening passage had to be suppressed, it should at least have been accurately paraphrased. Nothing could justify the assertion that Churchill was recommending the use of biological as well as chemical warfare. As Peter Hennessy (whose accurate summaries of the relevant documents were written for *The Times* without the benefit of a viewing of the *Newsnight* report) told me on 18 August:

> It appeared to me from the moment I read the documents that the two things— mustard and anthrax—were entirely separate; and I didn't actually make a great point of saying to myself 'Ah, these are separate and we must be careful', because it was obvious to me that they were.

Nor were the Chiefs of Staff in any doubt about what Churchill was discussing. Two of them kept unofficial diaries on a daily basis during their period of office, and those of the Chief of the Naval Staff, Admiral of the Fleet Sir Andrew Cunningham, are now available in the British Library archives. This is what Cunningham wrote on Saturday, 8 July 1944:

> C.O.S. meeting at 1100. Discussion on P.M.'s rather immoderate minutes (a) on the use of gas (b) on General Alexander's plans in Italy. In the first he talks of 'uniformed psalm-singers' presumably referring to the Directors of Plans [on the Joint Planning Staff]. . . . He obviously had a bad day after his statement [of 6 July, on flying bombs] in H[ouse] of C[ommons].[9]

It was certainly true that the Joint Planning Staff had recently deprecated using gas, which was felt unlikely to stop the V-weapon campaign and more likely to prove a net disadvantage to advancing Allied troops.[10] Churchill's 6 July outburst had been largely in response to this J.P.S. report, but the Chiefs of Staff agreed with the views of their own strategic planners. As Cunningham noted, the question was considered just two days later. The Chief of the Air Staff, Air Chief Marshal Sir Charles Portal, launched the main attack on what the official record described as 'a minute (Serial No. *D.217/4*) from the Prime Minister directing that a comprehensive examination be made of *the question of employing gas* against Germany' (italics added). In his view, gas would not produce the effects Churchill anticipated. It would be very difficult to achieve a heavy concentration of gas over a wide area, and Portal simply did not believe that concentrated attacks on flying-bomb sites would prove effective either. The J.P.S. planners had already made one attempt on the problem, and in the ensuing discussion it was suggested that the task should be undertaken under the supervision of the Vice-Chiefs of Staff this time, and that both the Chemical *and* Biological Warfare sub-committees should also be consulted.

---

9.   Cunningham Papers, Vol. XXI, *Diary*, 1944 (British Library, Add. MS. 52577)
10.   JP(44)177(Final), 5 July 1944, in CAB 84/64

In other words, the Chiefs of Staff took it upon themselves to widen the terms of reference for the proposed report to bring in germ warfare as well as gas. This broadening of the task was specified in the formal instruction to the Vice-Chiefs to 'carry out a comprehensive examination of the points raised in the Prime Minister's minute, and to include in their examination consideration of the possibilities of biological warfare and of the form which enemy reprisals might take'.[11] As Churchill had not asked for biological warfare also to be covered, the C.O.S. secretary who reported back to him immediately after the meeting did not even bother to mention that it had also been decided to take a look at germs as well as gas in the feasibility study:

> Prime Minister, Reference your minute at Flag 'A' (*D.217/4*) about the use of gas, the Chiefs of Staff this morning directed the Vice-Chiefs of Staff to go into this matter with the greatest care and thoroughness, bringing into consideration all interested authorities.
> 2. A report will be submitted to you as soon as possible.[12]

The Non-Existent Paper

On 4 June 1981, an article appeared in the *Listener*, in which Robert Harris significantly modified what had been broadcast by *Newsnight*. The *Listener* is a weekly BBC journal normally publishing items based on broadcasts within days of their transmission. When I suggested that a month's hiatus—as in this case—was rather unusual, one of the *Listener* editorial staff agreed. It seemed to me that efforts were being made to rectify in print what had been irresponsibly put out over the air but subsequently challenged by Professor R. V. Jones, Winston Churchill, MP, and myself.

In particular, the 6 July minute was no longer claimed to be about anthrax. The crucial opening paragraph was belatedly restored; and the expostulation about being prepared to do '*anything*' was described merely as a 'hint' by Churchill that 'he might go even further than using poison gas'. The phrase about 'great rockets with far-reaching and devastating effect' falling on London was still cut out, however; and the point that the massive overestimation of their potential had been rectified by mid-August—before the V.2 attack had even begun—was never made at all.

What Robert Harris really now relied upon ('Churchill and the Germ Bomb', the *Listener*, 4 June 1981) was his belief that

> a week later, in an individual minute circulated to each of the Vice-Chiefs of Staff, Churchill significantly extended the terms of reference of the report he wanted on poison gas: now he called for an evaluation of the implications of

---

11.   COS(44)227th Mtg (0)(14), 8 July 1944, in CAB 79/77
12.   COS Sec Min 1140/4, Hollis to Churchill, 8 July 1944, in CAB 120/775

using gas '*or any other method of warfare* [Harris's italics] which we have hitherto refrained from using against the Germans'. This was a carefully veiled but unmistakable reference to anthrax.

Carefully veiled? Unmistakable? If indeed it was a reference to anthrax, it had certainly not been made by the Prime Minister. . . .

As the controversy progressed, I had been becoming increasingly doubtful about this so-called 13 July minute by Churchill. It was true that I had seen a C.O.S. document indicating that the Prime Minister had asked for other methods in addition to gas also to be considered. I had mentioned this in my first critique of the *Newsnight* report, published in the *Guardian* on 7 May. And I had presumed that Mr Harris must have seen some such further minute from Churchill (as his replies in the press implied) since he seemed able to assign a precise date to it. In this I was very much mistaken. All my subsequent efforts to track down this document proved fruitless. It was certainly not to be found in the Prime Minister's file cited by Robert Harris in a letter to the *Daily Telegraph* published on 21 May 1981. Eventually, on 25 June, I wrote to Professor Jones, who had referred to it in one of his own criticisms of the *Newsnight* presentation. In his reply (29 June), he drew my attention to page 726 of Anthony Cave Brown's *Bodyguard of Lies*.

This book had aired some contentious hypotheses when it appeared in 1976. One of its most notorious charges had been that, in November 1940, Churchill deliberately failed to take the maximum possible level of measures to protect the city of Coventry from impending aerial attack—a decision which was praised as essential for the security of the '*Ultra*' code-breaking technique. But in fact it was a melodramatic myth. The Official History of wartime Intelligence later showed that the identity of the target city simply had not been known in time for extra preparations to be made.

As it turned out, Anthony Cave Brown's propensity for documentary imprecision had reasserted itself in his coverage of biological warfare, and Mr Harris had drawn on Cave Brown without checking the 'sources' for himself. For there was no '13 July minute'. Churchill had never expanded his request for a report on gas to include anthrax at all. After his initial approach, he did not again raise the subject with the C.O.S. organisation until 25 July 1944, when he rather testily reminded Ismay that:

> On July 6 I asked for a dispassionate report on the military aspects of threatening to use lethal and corrosive gases on the enemy if they did not stop the use of indiscriminate weapons.
> I now request this report within three days.
>
> W.S.C.[13]

---

13. P.M.'s Personal Min No D.234/4, Churchill to Ismay, 25 July 1944, in PREM 3/89 (also in CAB 120/775)

This minute referred neither to anthrax nor, as a matter of fact, to any intervening instruction to widen the scope of the report. And a copy of it was included in the principal file cited by Robert Harris in his *Daily Telegraph* correspondence.

What had happened between 6 and 25 July? It is not hard to find this out from a close reading of the Chiefs of Staff papers. Unlike those of the Prime Minister's Office (on which *Newsnight* had mainly relied), C.O.S. documents nearly always cited the serial numbers of minutes to which cross-reference might be made. The record of the meeting of the Vice-Chiefs of Staff, *held on 13 July* with a view to discharging the task laid upon them by their Chiefs five days earlier, was no exception in this respect.

Certainly the Vice-Chiefs considered the contents of a minute by Churchill—but, as the serial number cited in the record of the meeting shows, *it was the very same minute he had written on 6 July*—which Mr. Harris's *Listener* article belatedly conceded to have been a minute about poison gas. What the Vice-Chiefs had before them was

> a minute (*COS.1150/4*) by the Secretary, circulated personally to each Vice-Chief of Staff, referring to a minute (Serial No. *D.217/4*) by the Prime Minister directing that a comprehensive examination be made of the question of employing gas against Germany.

It was agreed that the examination would have to be carried out by the Joint Planning Staff as the (technical) Inter-Service Committee on Chemical Warfare 'was not a suitable body to carry out an investigation of this nature'. Clear terms of reference would have to be given to the J.P.S. and these should exclude ethical and political factors. The only specific reference to germ warfare came right at the end of the V.C.O.S. discussion, and even that was of a rather indirect nature:

> With reference to the decision that the investigation should cover all forms of chemical and biological warfare [*i.e.* the decision of the Chiefs of Staff on 8 July], it was suggested that the Germans might react to the initiation of gas warfare by the employment of bacteriological warfare. The investigation should, therefore, include consideration of German readiness to undertake bacteriological warfare.

The C.O.S. secretariat was set to work to draft appropriate terms of reference for the Joint Planning Staff, which would receive technical advice from the other (non-strategic) sub-committees of the Chiefs of Staff.[14]

On 16 July 1944, Colonel Denis Capel-Dunn, head of the Joint Staffs secretariat, drew up the document which ultimately misled Robert Harris, Anthony Cave Brown, an earlier historian—Roger Parkinson, on whose book,

---

14. COS(44)234th Mtg (0)(1)(Confidential Annex), 13 July 1944, in CAB 79/89

A Day's March Nearer Home (1974), both drew heavily—and also myself, until I went into the matter a little more systematically. For in issuing these terms of reference to the J.P.S., Colonel Capel-Dunn failed to differentiate between what the Prime Minister had asked for on 6 July and the decision by the Chiefs of Staff, on considering Churchill's minute two days later, that biological warfare should also be looked into. It was irrelevant to the task in hand to make such a distinction, so Colonel Capel-Dunn conflated the two strands in the following way:

> The Prime Minister has directed that a comprehensive examination should be undertaken of the military implications of our deciding on an all-out use of gas, principally mustard gas, or any other method of warfare which we have hitherto refrained from using against the Germans, in the following circumstances:—
>
> > (*a*) As a counter-offensive in the event of the use by the enemy of flying bombs and/or giant rockets developing into a serious threat to our ability to prosecute the war;
> >
> > or, alternatively,
> >
> > (*b*) as a means of shortening the war or of bringing to an end a situation in which there was a danger of a stalemate.[15]

That was the passage which had suggested to me that a further Churchill minute must have been written between 6 and 16 July. It had been more seriously misread by Harris, Cave Brown and Parkinson, who took it to be the *text* of another Churchill minute and presumed it to be what the Vice-Chiefs had seen at their 13 July meeting. But, as we now know, it was merely a gloss on what Churchill had written about gas (6 July), what the Chiefs of Staff had added about germs without telling him (8 July), and what the Vice-Chiefs had decided about how to tackle the job (13 July). The C.O.S. and V.C.O.S. contributions were implied more strongly in the second paragraph of Capel-Dunn's directive to the Joint Planning Staff:

> 2. The Chiefs of Staff have instructed the Joint Planning Staff [another gloss—the C.O.S. actually instructed the V.C.O.S., who in turn instructed the J.P.S.] to carry out this examination, which should cover the possibilities of the use of biological warfare by us or by the enemy. It should take the form of a thorough and practical examination of the military factors involved and should ignore ethical and political considerations. . . .

I do not doubt that Robert Harris genuinely, though erroneously, believed that the Prime Minister had followed up his 6 July minute about gas with a further one asking for any other unused methods of warfare also to be considered. Yet, had he troubled to look behind his secondary sources (Cave

---

15. JP(44)190(0)(T.R.), 16 July 1944, in CAB 84/64

Brown and Parkinson), both of which dealt with this topic only as a side issue, he would have found—as I did—that Churchill never expanded his request for a report about gas in any way whatsoever. With that, any vestige of an excuse for quoting the 6 July minute as if its comments about gas also applied to anthrax would have finally disappeared.

The 'Chilling' Assessment and the Interleaved Report

More blameworthy by far than the mistreatment of the 6 July minute, however, was *Newsnight*'s presentation of the report that the Joint Planning Staff eventually produced in response to it. At least four separate copies of this paper were openly declassified at the Public Record Office in 1972 when most of the wartime material was released,[16] so it can hardly be described as having accidentally slipped out.

The record of the Chiefs of Staff meeting of 26 July 1944 notes that they considered Churchill's 25 July minute as the sixth item on their agenda that day. As the C.O.S. secretary put it, this requested that the Prime Minister 'should be provided, within three days, with the report on the military aspects of the initiation of gas warfare for which he had asked (*D.217/4*) on July 6th'.[17] The report was completed late that night. It was overwhelmingly concerned with poison gas (eight and a half pages). Not only was anthrax covered in much less detail (one and a half pages), but there was also no conceptual comparison between the two. Whereas gas warfare was distinctly possible and was argued against at length, germ warfare was simply out of the question. And, as the short section on anthrax showed, an anthrax attack was a non-starter because Britain simply did not have the bombs which would be needed. So it was pointless to go into the question of what targets to attack or what even the military effects of long-term contamination would be. Neither was considered. Both sections of the report were prefaced by a summary of the whole. It had this to say about biological warfare:

> 19. [*Paras. 2–18 were all about gas*] If the claims of *N* [anthrax] are substantiated, its use could probably make a material change in the war situation, but there is no likelihood of a sustained attack being possible before the middle of 1945.
> 20. There is no known prophylactic against *N*. If it can be used in practice, the effect on morale will be profound.
> 21. It is improbable that the Germans will initiate biological warfare. There is no evidence to show whether they are in a position to retaliate in kind, were we to initiate it.[18]

---

16. See: PREM 3/89; CAB 80/85; CAB 84/64; CAB 120/775
17. COS(44)248th Mtg (0)(6), 26 July 1944, in CAB 79/78
18. COS(44)661(0), 26 July 1944, in CAB 80/85

Robert Harris's version in a letter to the *Listener* given pride of place on 2 July 1981 was rather different:

> The one and a half pages on anthrax were sufficiently detailed to show that an anthrax attack was feasible [he wrote], given the bombs.

In the words of Norris McWhirter (who replied on 17 August), this was 'like claiming that a man can be described as a millionaire "given enough wealth" while omitting to mention that he is, in fact, an undischarged bankrupt! . . .' Mr Harris's problem was that, if anthrax really was out of the question, any rejection by Churchill of the report's conclusions could only apply to gas. This was something I had always maintained to be obvious—even without knowing that Churchill's interest in 'any other method of warfare' was just a secretary's gloss.

The fact of the matter was that, while the Joint Planning Staff report claimed chemical (*i.e.* gas) warfare to be feasible but undesirable, it showed effective biological warfare not to be feasible at all.

The Chiefs of Staff discussed the report at their 28 July 1944 meeting. The records show their deliberations to have been limited to the case against using gas.[19] In view of his impatience to obtain a response to his 6 July minute, Churchill had been given a copy the night before. Ismay now wrote to tell him of the amendments made, and the endorsement given to it by the Service chiefs. His letter to the Prime Minister again referred only to the chemical warfare aspect. Churchill's last words on the subject were in reply to that communication from Ismay:

> I am not at all convinced by this negative report. But clearly I cannot make head against the parsons and the warriors at the same time.
>   The matter should be kept under review and brought up again when things get worse.
>
> W.S.C.[20]

Given the sheer impossibility of a germ attack (not to mention the fact that he had asked only about gas anyway, as we now know), it was clearly nonsensical to claim that these remarks applied to anthrax. At an early stage in the controversy, Robert Harris said that he knew of 'no evidence whatever' for my assertion that this 29 July minute was a minute about gas. Though I failed to see the need for 'evidence' of what was fairly obvious, I was able to point out that, on 31 July, the Chiefs of Staff had taken note of Churchill's remarks as comments on their report on initiating 'chemical' warfare, and that the relevant

---

19.   COS(44)251st Mtg (0)(7), 28 July 1944, in CAB 79/78
20.   Ismay to Churchill, 28 July 1944 & P.M.'s Personal Min No D.238/4, Churchill to Ismay, 29 July 1944, both in PREM 3/89 (also in CAB 120/775)

record was actually included in a file used for the programme.[21] This drew the response (*Daily Telegraph*, 2 June 1981) that I had alighted on 'merely a routine acknowledgement' and loaded it 'with enormous significance' to suit my own case. Considering the weight placed on the vaguest phrases by Mr Harris himself, I referred to Admiral Cunningham's diary,[22] which was not subject to the considerations of brevity or security suggested by Mr Harris as grounds for C.O.S. coyness in official minutes. This is what it said:

> *Monday, July 31st, 1944*
> C.O.S. meeting at 1100. Nothing much of importance, P.M.'s minute on the study of retaliation by gas was to the effect that he could do nothing if the warriors as well as the parsons were against him.

And what, now, about the BBC's description of the J.P.S. report as 'a chilling assessment of what using chemical *and biological* weapons would have meant in the Second World War'; what now of all those delightful predictions of three million deaths, specific target cities, and near-permanent contamination, culminating in a reversion to the J.P.S. conclusion that insufficient bombs would be available for a sustained attack as the reason that this never came to pass? Curiously enough, Anthony Cave Brown had also described the report as 'a chilling assessment'—of the advantages and disadvantages of poison gas.

Any assessment of the use of anthrax in warfare—however cursory—can by definition be regarded as chilling. But the fact remains that most of the horrifying details quoted in *Newsnight* were simply not in the report which Churchill was given. They came from a completely different document prepared (by the Inter-Service Sub-Committee on Biological Warfare for the Joint Technical Warfare Committee) in November 1945, months after the end of hostilities, and even longer after Churchill had left office. *That* was the 'scientists' report' in which 'Everything had been worked out to the last detail.' It had nothing at all to do with the July 1944 V-weapon crisis. Indeed, the notion of having enough anthrax bombs to attack six German cities, should retaliation against German biological aggression prove to be necessary, had been worked out long before that crisis. The 500,000 bombs ordered from the Americans in March 1944 had been thought sufficient for this. However, in October 1944, the Biological Warfare sub-committee told the Chiefs of Staff that

> it may be necessary to arrange provision of 8 times this number of bombs in order to achieve results on the scale originally intended.[23]

21. COS(44)253rd Mtg (0)(3), 31 July 1944, in PREM 3/89
22. Cunningham Papers, Vol. XXI, *Diary*, 1944 (British Library, Add. MS. 52577)
23. Closed (50 years) Document: BW(44)21, 10 October 1944—also circulated as COS(44)892(0), 10 October 1944, in CAB 80/88

The empty bomb cases were being manufactured satisfactorily, but preparation of their contents was fraught with difficulties which had not been overcome by the end of the war. The hypothetical figure of bombs required to 'saturate' six cities thus went up—in theory—from 500,000 to the 4¼ million cited in the 1945 'scientists' report' used by *Newsnight* to step up the horror of the very limited coverage of anthrax in the 1944 report which Churchill received.

The Allies never had a plan to drop this quantity of bombs on Germany as the BBC claimed. Nor did Britain. Nor did the Chiefs of Staff, who decided on 13 October 1944 to let what was termed 'the present token order for 500,000 bombs' stand.[24] There was never any question of ordering another 3¾ million of them. What Robert Harris did was to take an essentially academic study prepared by one technical C.O.S. sub-committee to help another in its post-war calculations of the future potentialities of mass-destruction weapons, and to intertwine its contents with those of the July 1944 Joint Planning Staff feasibility study.

Not a word was said in the TV programme to make it clear that two reports, not one, were being quoted. As the camera zoomed in portentously to focus on the words 'TOP SECRET' on the 1945 report—in reality, a very common Chiefs of Staff classification—its date could admittedly be seen for a few seconds. But I doubt if even one viewer in a hundred appreciated its significance. Apart from Peter Hennessy's *Times* reports (written before he had seen the programme), all the newspaper accounts erroneously conflated the two documents—as if Churchill had wanted the six German cities (cited by Dr Fildes, the Porton bacteriologist, merely as 'typical') actually to be attacked with anthrax. These accounts were based on a Press Association release by Robert Hutchinson which completely failed to distinguish between the separate C.O.S. papers quoted (exactly as one might expect). Publicly, it was maintained that the BBC had at no stage even implied that Churchill saw the 1945 document, but privately Mr. Harris was more forthcoming. As he told me on 6 July 1981:

> What I think is fair comment and attack is the fact that the film could have so misled at least one journalist [Hutchinson]. I accept what you say—that it could have led people to have said: 'Churchill planned the death of three million civilians', and that I think is fair criticism of the programme . . .

He also dissociated himself from the introductory comparison with the Nazis. Apparently, he had not seen this before it went out over the air. Even on his interpretation of Churchill's actions he felt, he says, that the Prime Minister behaved perfectly justifiably under the prevailing circumstances. And so far as the categorical claim that 'Germany was saved from biological attack by her

---

24. COS(44)338th Mtg (0)(7), 13 October 1944, in CAB 79/81

own defeat' was concerned, it was good to hear him concede: 'I think that, given my time again, I wouldn't have said that . . .'

Regrettably, the fact remains that it *was* said, and Churchill's reputation was gravely damaged as a result of the programme, notwithstanding the good intentions which possibly underlay it.

The most that can be said of the 1944 events is that on one brief occasion the feasibility of using anthrax was investigated by the Chiefs of Staff organisation, only to be immediately dismissed as impracticable. The first Churchill knew of this investigation was when he saw it tacked on to the end of a report on gas warfare as an unavailable extra option about which he had never inquired. Nor would it have made any difference even if the war had lasted longer, as Harris, Cave Brown and Parkinson all suggested, for the production difficulties proved far too great to be fully overcome even by November 1945 and a further eight months at least would have been required to produce enough charged bombs to attack 'six German cities'. By this time, a far more effective agent had been discovered in the United States—brucella, seldom fatal, simpler to produce, unlikely to cause contamination for more than a period of days rather than years, and requiring perhaps only a tenth of the weight of bombs necessary to deliver an equivalent attack with anthrax . . .

As for the British programme of biological warfare research, the chairman of the Defence Research Policy Committee noted as late as March 1949: 'Although there is no practical weapon of biological warfare yet in sight, it may be fairly said that the possibilities of producing one are at least as high as the possibilities of producing atomic weapons were in 1940 . . .'[25] And that had been five years before the atom bomb finally appeared.

War history is too important to be left to television sensationalism, eager to ferret out 'secrets' whether they exist or not. More than that, the wartime record of the Western democracies should not be left undefended against those who, in distorting the historical evidence (the bombing of Coventry, the 'murder' of General Sikorski, the anthrax bomb), suggest that there was nothing to choose between Churchill and Hitler, between one side and the other in the Second World War.

---

25. Retained Document: Note by Defence Research Policy Committee, 23 March 1949

SOURCES

I Government Archives

(a) Public Record Office

ADM 1   Admiralty and Secretariat: Papers
ADM 116   Admiralty and Secretariat: Files
ADM 205   First Sea Lord: Papers

AIR 8   Chief of the Air Staff: Papers
AIR 9   Director of Plans: Papers
AIR 20   Air Ministry: Unregistered Files

CAB 21   Cabinet Office: Registered Files
CAB 65   War Cabinet: Meetings
CAB 66   War Cabinet: Memoranda
CAB 69   Defence Committee (Operations): Meetings and Memoranda
CAB 79   Chiefs of Staff Committee: Meetings [to 1946]
CAB 80   Chiefs of Staff Committee: Memoranda [to 1946]
CAB 81   Chiefs of Staff Sub-Committees: Meetings and Memoranda
CAB 82   Deputy Chiefs of Staff Committee and Sub-Committees:
               Meetings and Memoranda
CAB 84   Joint Planning Staff: Meetings [to 1943] and Memoranda
               [to 1945]
CAB 87   Reconstruction Committees: Meetings and Memoranda
CAB 92   Committees on Supply, *etc.*: Meetings and Memoranda
CAB 119   Joint Planning Staff: Secretariat Files
CAB 120   Minister of Defence: Secretariat Files
CAB 122   British Joint Staff Mission: Washington Office Files
CAB 131   Defence Committee: Meetings and Memoranda

DEFE 4   Chiefs of Staff Committee: Meetings [from 1947]
DEFE 5   Chiefs of Staff Committee: Memoranda [from 1947]
DEFE 6   Joint Planning Staff: Memoranda [from 1947]

FO 371   Foreign Office: General Correspondence after 1906, Political—Central, Eastern, Economic and Reconstruction, General, and Northern Departments

PREM 4   Prime Minister's Office: Confidential Papers [to 1945]
PREM 8   Prime Minister's Office: Correspondence and Papers [from 1945]

WO 32   War Office: Registered Papers, General Series
WO 106   Directorate of Military Operations: Papers

(b) Cabinet Office (Special Access)

CAB 21   As above: Selected Files
CAB 84   Joint Planning Staff: Memoranda for 1946—later released to the Public Record Office

II Official Histories

(a) Cabinet Office—History of the Second World War

F. S. V. Donnison: *Civil Affairs and Military Government: Central Organisation and Planning* (London, H.M.S.O., 1966).
Sir Llewellyn Woodward: *British Foreign Policy in the Second World War*, Volume V (London, H.M.S.O., 1976).

(b) U.K.A.E.A. Series

Margaret Gowing: *Britain and Atomic Energy, 1939–1945* (London, Macmillan, 1964).
Margaret Gowing: *Independence and Deterrence: Britain and Atomic Energy, 1945–1952* (London, Macmillan, 1974).

III Interviews

(a) Duke of Portland [*formerly:* V. F. W. Cavendish-Bentinck]
     Chairman, Joint Intelligence Sub-Committee, to 1945;
     Foreign Office Adviser to Directors of Plans, 1942–45;
     Assistant Under-Secretary, Foreign Office, 1944;
     Ambassador to Poland, 1945–47.

(b) Lord Gladwyn [*formerly:* H. M. G. Jebb]
     Head of Economic and Reconstruction Department, Foreign Office, 1942–45;
     Chairman, Post-Hostilities Planning Sub-Committee, 1943–44;

Chairman, Post-Hostilities Planning Staff, 1944;
Acting Secretary-General, United Nations, 1946;
Assistant Under-Secretary and U.N. Adviser, Foreign Office,
1946–47.

(c) Brigadier A. T. Cornwall-Jones
Secretary, Middle East Defence Committee, to 1943;
Assistant Secretary, Offices of the War Cabinet and Minister of
Defence, 1943–44;
Secretary, Post-Hostilities Planning Sub-Committee, 1944;
Secretary, Post-Hostilities Planning Staff, 1944;
Secretary, British Joint Staff Mission, Washington, 1944–46;
Senior Assistant Secretary (Military) of the Cabinet, 1946–50.

IV Contemporary Articles

Viscount Alanbrooke: 'Empire Defence' [1946], *Journal of the Royal United Service Institution* (May 1947).
P. M. S. Blackett: 'The Military Consequences of Atomic Energy' [1948], in P. M. S. Blackett: *Studies of War* (Edinburgh, Oliver & Boyd, 1962).
Sir Arthur Tedder: 'Air, Land and Sea Warfare' [1946], *Journal of the Royal United Service Institution* (February 1946).
Sir Henry Tizard: 'Science and the Services' [1946], *Journal of the Royal United Service Institution* (August 1946).

V Biographies and Memoirs*

Viscount Alanbrooke: *Diary* and *Notes on My Life* (Alanbrooke Papers, King's College, University of London).
Andrew Boyle: *No Passing Glory* (London, Collins, 1955; Reprint Society, 1957).
Sir Arthur Bryant: *The Alanbrooke Diaries: Triumph in the West, 1943–1946* (London, Collins, 1959).
Ronald W. Clark: *Tizard* (London, Methuen, 1965).
David Dilks (ed.): *The Diaries of Sir Alexander Cadogan, 1938–1945* (London, Cassell, 1971).
G. P. Gladstone, *et al.*: 'Paul Gordon Fildes', in *Biographical Memoirs of Fellows of the Royal Society*, Volume XIX (London, The Royal Society, 1973).

---

*Biographies or memoirs of Viscounts Cunningham and Portal, Lord Tedder, and Generals Kennedy and Hollis are available, but shed no further light on the subjects here considered.

Lord Gladwyn: *The Memoirs of Lord Gladwyn* (London, Weidenfeld & Nicolson, 1972).

Maurice Goldsmith: *Sage: A Life of J. D. Bernal* (London, Hutchinson, 1980).

Lord Ismay: *The Memoirs of Lord Ismay* (London, Heinemann, 1960).

R. V. Jones: *Most Secret War* (London, Hamish Hamilton, 1978; Coronet, 1979).

George Mallaby: *From My Level* (London, Hutchinson, 1965).

Viscount Montgomery: *The Memoirs of Field-Marshal Montgomery* (London, Collins, 1958).

Dennis Wheatley: *The Deception Planners* (London, Hutchinson, 1980).

Dennis Wheatley: *Stranger Than Fiction* (London, Hutchinson, 1959).

Dennis Wheatley: *The Time Has Come*, Volume III (London, Hutchinson, 1979).

Solly Zuckerman: *From Apes to Warlords, 1904–46* (London, Hamish Hamilton, 1978).

VI Publications based upon Government Archives

L. Bell and M. Roper: *The Second World War: A Guide to Documents in the Public Record Office* (London, H.M.S.O., 1972).

Charles Cruickshank: *Deception in World War II* (Oxford, O.U.P., 1979).

Tony Sharp: *The Wartime Alliance and the Zonal Division of Germany* (Oxford, O.U.P., 1975).

S. S. Wilson: *The Cabinet Office to 1945* (London, H.M.S.O., 1975).

VII Private Papers

(1) *British Library:*
  A. B. Cunningham Papers—*Diaries*, 1944–1946 (Add. MSS. 52577–9), useful as a daily record of events.

(2) *Christ Church, Oxford:*
  C. F. A. Portal Papers—No diaries, but copies of contemporary official documents.

(3) *King's College, London:*
  A. F. Brooke Papers—*Diaries* and *Notes on My Life*.
  F. H. N. Davidson Papers—Insights on the J.I.C. and F.O.E.S. by a former Director of Military Intelligence.
  H. L. Ismay Papers—No diaries, nor official papers relevant to this subject.

VIII Public Record Office Files from which the History of the Military Sub-Committee was Reconstructed

P.R.O. Class	*Piece Nos.*
ADM 1	12072; 12853
AIR 20	3739
CAB 21	2294
CAB 65	26; 28
CAB 66	24; 30; 38; 40
CAB 79	21; 22; 27
CAB 80	36; 37; 40
CAB 84	4; 5; 6; 46; 47; 51
CAB 119	64; 65
FO 371	30868; 30930; 30931; 31337; 31338; 31500; 31520; 31525; 31529; 32482; 32832; 32853; 35259; 35261; 35396; 35397; 35407; 35412; 35446; 35449
WO 106	2759

NOTE ON SOURCES

The subject of post-war strategic planning by the military does not feature centrally, for the years under examination, in any of the published material listed. This has been drawn upon solely to cover individual points as indicated in the text, or to acquire background knowledge and atmosphere. Apart from the contemporary diarists, only the official historians had full access to post-war strategic defence plans at the time of writing; but their works are not primarily concerned with the Service planners in this field. A small number of C.O.S. papers relevant to atomic energy questions are briefly summarised by Gowing, and, since these were for the most part scheduled for continued closure or retention, they could not in any case have been dealt with more fully. On the foreign policy side, Woodward covers the Four Power Plan and the debate about Dismemberment in great detail and with admirable objectivity. Victor Rothwell's *Britain and the Cold War* (London, Jonathan Cape, 1982) gives a comprehensive and lucid account of its subject based on the Foreign Office records, though making only limited reference to the role of the Chiefs of Staff. Nor is C.O.S. strategic planning featured in Hugh Thomas's major historical survey, *Armed Truce: The Beginnings of the Cold War, 1945–46* (London, Hamish Hamilton, 1986). However, Nigel Hamilton's *Monty: the Field-Marshal, 1944–1976* (London, Hamish Hamilton, 1986) sheds new light on Montgomery's troubled period as C.I.G.S.

REFERENCES

(These references give the full British Public Record Office key to official documents cited in the footnotes to the text, and contain a small amount of additional information on individual points. It should be noted that most files to which 'Special Access' had to be sought when the research for this study was undertaken have since become freely available in the Public Record Office.)

CHAPTER 1: The Foreign Office Origins of Post-War Strategic Planning, 1942

1. CAB 119/64:   Ismay to Howkins, 20 February 1942.
2. FO 371/24828:   N7471/213/30, Dormer to Halifax, 16 December 1940.
3. FO 371/29421:   N214/87/30, Dormer minute, 11 January 1941.
4. FO 371/29421:   N693/87/30, Phillips to Scott, 19 February 1941.
5. FO 371/29421:   N693/87/30, Butler minute, 12 March 1941;
   CAB 87/1:   RP(41)1, 24 February 1941.
6. FO 371/29422:   N6510/87/30, Sargent minute, 14 November 1941; Cadogan minute, 14 November 1941.
7. FO 371/29422:   N7205/87/30, Eden to Collier, 2 December 1941.
8. FO 371/32832:   N518/463/30, Undated memorandum (January 1942).
9. FO 371/32832:   N463/463/30, Somers Cocks minute, 26 January 1942.
10. FO 371/32832:   N518/463/30, Undated memorandum (January 1942); Cadogan minutes, 22 January & 16 February 1942; Eden minute, 17 February 1942; Cadogan minute, 18 February 1942.

11. —
12. FO 371/32832:   N978/463/30, Norton to Cadogan,
                         13 February 1942.
13. CAB 119/64 &   N978/463/30 (formerly N978/978/G),
    FO 371/32832:   Cadogan to Ismay, 19 February 1942.
14. CAB 79/18:   COS(42)65th Mtg (8), 26 February 1942.
15. FO 371/32832:   N1150/463/30, Hollis to Cadogan,
                         27 February 1942.
16. AIR 8/1354:   COS Sec 'Notes on the Work of the Chiefs of
                         Staff Committee—Appendix: History of the
                         Joint Planning Organisation', 21 April 1948;
                         see also CAB 120/50: Prime Minister's
                         Personal Mins Nos D.21, M.52, D.149 &
                         D.160 of 24 August 1940, 31 August 1940,
                         22 December 1940 & 27 December 1940,
                         respectively.
17. CAB 84/41:   JP(42)94, 3 February 1942.
18. CAB 79/18:   COS(42)45th Mtg (10), 10 February 1942.
19. CAB 84/43:   JP(42)279(0)(T.R.), 14 March 1942.
20. FO 371/32832:   N1150/463/30, Makins minute, 5 March
                         1942; Warner minute, 7 March 1942;
                         Cadogan minute, 8 March 1942.
21. FO 371/32832:   N518/463/30, Eden minute, 17 February
                         1942; Cadogan minute, 18 February 1942.
22. FO 371/32832:   N1150/463/30, Warner to Howkins, 13 March
                         1942.
23. CAB 84/43:   JP(42)279(0)(T.R.), 14 March 1942;
    CAB 119/65:   JPS Sec Min 42/282, 14 March 1942.
24. FO 371/32832:   N1441/463/30, Warner minute, 19 March
                         1942; Norton minute, 22 March 1942.
25. CAB 84/4:   JP(42)63rd Mtg (7), 3 April 1942.
26. CAB 84/44:   JP(42)354, 4 April 1942.
27. FO 371/32832:   N1806/463/30, Somers Cocks minute, 7 April
                         1942; Warner minute, 10 April 1942.
28. CAB 84/44:   JP(42)401(0)(T.R.), 14 April 1942.
29. CAB 84/44:   JP(42)432(0)(Draft), 22 April 1942.
30. CAB 84/45:   JP(42)497, 13 May 1942.
31. FO 371/32832:   N2550/463/30, Scott minutes, 12 & 13 May
                         1942; Somers Cocks minute, 15 May 1942;
                         Coote minute, 15 May 1942; Butler minute,
                         28 May 1942; Warner minute, 7 June 1942;
                         Makins minute, 21 June 1942.
32. FO 371/32832:   N2551/463/30, Warner minute, 23 May 1942.

33. FO 371/30868: C3562/685/62, Ronald minute & draft note, 5 March 1942; Ronald minute, 13 March 1942; Law minute, 20 March 1942.

34. FO 371/32481: W343/81/49, Note of informal F.O. meeting held on 6 January 1942.

35. FO 371/29145: W1375/1375/50, Report on the F.R.P.S., 10 January 1941;

    FO 371/31499: U1898/26/72, Viscount Astor to Eden (Open & Confidential Letters), 9 December 1942; Eden to Viscount Astor (Open & Confidential Replies), 24 December 1942;

    FO 371/35264: U2587/2278/750, Terms of F.O./R.I.I.A. Agreement, 1 April 1943; U2725/2278/750, Ronald circular despatch, 18 June 1943.

36. CAB 119/64: Provisional Scheme for F.O. Handbooks, revised 23 December 1941.

37. FO 371/32481: W343/81/49, Note of informal F.O. meeting held on 6 January 1942.

38. FO 371/32481: W343/81/49, Ronald to Stowell, Slade & Medhurst, 8 January 1942; Medhurst to Ronald, 24 January 1942; W821/81/49, Stowell to Ronald, 10 January 1942.

39. FO 371/32481: W821/81/49, Norton to Howkins, 21 March 1942.

40. CAB 84/44: JP(42)427, 21 April 1942.

41. CAB 84/44: JP(42)362(0)(T.R.), 4 April 1942.

42. CAB 84/44: JP(42)309(0)(T.R.), covering C2943/685/62, 21 March 1942.

43. CAB 84/44: JP(42)427, 21 April 1942.

44. FO 371/32482: W5996/81/49, Ronald minute, 23 April 1942.

45. *Ibid.*

46. —

47. CAB 84/44: JP(42)432(0)(Draft), 22 April 1942;
    CAB 84/4: JP(42)87th Mtg (6), 1 May 1942.

48. FO 371/31337: E2583/49/65, Baxter to Howkins, 26 April 1942.

49. CAB 84/45: JP(42)461(0)(T.R.), covering N2081/463/30 (formerly N2081/978/G) of 29 April 1942;
    FO 371/30868: C4681/685/62, Eden to Bland, 6 May 1942.

50. CAB 119/64: JPS Sec Min 42/483, covering Stanley note of 4 May 1942.

51. CAB 119/64: JPS Sec Min 42/497, covering F.O. draft memorandum, 7 May 1942.

52. CAB 84/4:   JP(42)90th Mtg (7), 8 May 1942.
53. CAB 119/64:   JPS Sec Min 42/504, covering Scott minute of 8 May 1942.
54. CAB 119/64:   JPS Sec Min 42/540, 17 May 1942.
55. CAB 84/4:   JP(42)99th Mtg (Revise)(3), 21 May 1942.
56. CAB 84/4:   JP(42)101st Mtg (3), 22 May 1942.
57. FO 371/32482: W5996/81/49, Ronald to Carver, 15 May 1942;

    CAB 119/64:   JPS Sec Min 42/545, 18 May 1942.
58. CAB 119/64:   JPS Sec Min 42/553, covering Scott note of 20 May 1942.
59. CAB 84/4:   JP(42)99th Mtg (Revise)(3), 21 May 1942;
    CAB 84/4:   JP(42)101st Mtg (3), 22 May 1942;
    CAB 84/4:   JP(42)102nd Mtg (3), 24 May 1942;
    CAB 84/4:   JP(42)103rd Mtg (Revise)(1), 26 May 1942.
60. CAB 119/64:   JPS Sec Min 42/558, 24 May 1942.
61. CAB 119/64:   JPS Sec Min 42/653, 17 June 1942.

CHAPTER 2: The Military Sub-Committee, 1942–43

1. CAB 66/24:   WP(42)205(Revise), 14 May 1942.
2. CAB 84/4:   JP(42)90th Mtg (7), 8 May 1942.
3. CAB 119/64:   JPS Sec Min 42/553, covering Scott note of 20 May 1942.
4. CAB 66/24:   WP(42)205(Revise), 14 May 1942.
5. CAB 65/26:   WM(42)70th Concls (5), 1 June 1942.
6. —
7. —
8. FO 371/30931: C4173/241/18, M.O.11 draft Secretary of State for War memorandum, covered by French to Malkin, 22 March 1942;

    FO 371/30931: C4174/241/18, French memorandum, covered by French to Malkin, 17 April 1942.
9. FO 371/30868: C3562/685/62, Kennedy to Ronald, 10 March 1942.
10. CAB 119/64:   JPS Sec Min 42/1116, le Mesurier to Davison, 3 October 1942.
11. FO 371/32482: W3465/81/49, van Cutsem to Ronald, 2 March 1942;
    FO 371/30930: C2657/241/18, van Cutsem to Ronald, 6 March 1942;
    FO 371/30930: C3740/241/18, van Cutsem to Ronald, 3 April 1942;

FO 371/30930:   C3778/241/18, van Cutsem to Ronald, 7 April 1942;

FO 371/30930:   C3967/241/18, van Cutsem to Ronald, 11 April 1942;

FO 371/30930:   C4167/241/18, van Cutsem to Ronald, 16 April 1942.

12. FO 371/30930:   C2657/241/18, van Cutsem to Ronald, 6 March 1942.

13. FO 371/30930:   C2926/241/18, Ronald minute, 8 April 1942.

14. FO 371/30931:   C4450/241/18, Ronald minute, 3 May 1942.

15. CAB 119/64:   JPS Sec Min 42/558, 24 May 1942.

16. CAB 21/2294:   Bridges to Hollis, 15 May 1942; Price to Bridges, 18 May 1942.

17. CAB 80/36:   COS(42)297, 8 June 1942.

18. CAB 79/21:   COS(42)175th Mtg (8), 10 June 1942.

19. AIR 20/3739:   ACAS(P)/CR/209, Slessor minute, 2 July 1942.

20. —

21. ADM 1/12072:   CS 125/42, 'J.S.B.' minute, 1 August 1942.

22. CAB 84/46:   JP(42)595(S)(T.R.), 12 June 1942.

23. CAB 119/64:   JPS Sec Min 42/634, covering Stewart note, 12 June 1942.

24. CAB 119/64:   JP(42)597(S)(Preliminary Draft), 13 June 1942.

25. CAB 119/64:   JP(42)597(S)(Draft), 15 June 1942.

26. CAB 119/64:   van Cutsem to Howkins, 18 June 1942.

27. CAB 84/46:   JP(42)637, 24 June 1942.

28. ADM 1/12072:   A/POL/ALLIES/13, 13 July 1942.

29. CAB 79/22:   COS(42)247th Mtg (3), 25 August 1942.

30. CAB 80/37:   COS(42)380, 21 August 1942.

31. ADM 1/12072:   Admiralty minute to Hollis, 9 June 1942.

32. FO 371/32832:   N3121/463/30, Ronald minute, 9 July 1942.

33. CAB 84/4:   JP(42)145th Mtg (2), 16 August 1942;

CAB 79/22:   COS(42)247th Mtg (3), 25 August 1942.

34. FO 371/31520:   U120/120/70, Draft of decisions at meeting of 9 July 1942.

35. FO 371/31500:   U396/61/72, Record of meeting of 29 July 1942;

CAB 119/64:   JPS Sec Min 42/653, 17 June 1942.

36. CAB 119/64:   JPS Sec Min 42/545, 18 May 1942.

37. FO 371/31500:   U606/61/72, MSC/30/2, 21 August 1942.

38. FO 371/32832:   N3121/463/30 (formerly N3121/978/G), Jebb to Bellairs, 30 July 1942;

	CAB 119/65:	Bellairs to Howkins, 5 August 1942.
39.	CAB 84/47:	JP(42)727(S)(T.R.), 6 August 1942.
40.	*Ibid.:*	Annex II.
41.	FO 371/32853:	N4245/3271/30, Jebb minute, 10 August 1942; Roberts minute, 12 August 1942; Sargent minute, 13 August 1942.
42.	FO 371/32832:	N4586/463/30, Jebb minute, 17 August 1942.
43.	CAB 119/65:	MSC/51, Bellairs to le Mesurier, 11 August 1942.
44.	CAB 119/65:	PWP(42)1, circulated under cover of JPS Sec Min 42/885, 15 August 1942.
45.	CAB 119/65:	JPS Sec Min 42/870, 13 August 1942.
46.	FO 371/32832:	N4586/463/30, Jebb minute, 21 August 1942.
47.	FO 371/32832:	N4586/463/30, JPS Sec Min 42/885, 15 August 1942.
48.	FO 371/32832:	N4594/463/30, MSC/51, Bellairs to Jebb, 25 August 1942;
	Ibid.:	Law minute, 30 September 1942.
49.	FO 371/32832:	N5554/463/30, Eden minute, 17 October 1942.
50.	CAB 66/30:	WP(42)480, 22 October 1942.
51.	CAB 65/28:	WM(42)149th Concls (3), 3 November 1942.
52.	FO 371/31525:	U742/742/70, Jebb minute, 9 September 1942.
53.	FO 371/32832:	N5716/463/30, Jebb minute, 29 January 1943.
54.	FO 371/36868:	N7700/219/63, Warner minute, 21 December 1943.
55.	FO 371/43209:	N4239/196/63, Warner minute, 20 July 1944; Jebb minute, 24 July 1944; Warner minute, 27 July 1944; Jebb minute, 31 July 1944.
56.	CAB 84/44:	JP(42)309(0)(T.R.), covering C2943/685/62, 21 March 1942;
	CAB 84/45:	JP(42)456(0)(T.R.), covering E2583/49/65, Baxter to Howkins, 26 April 1942.
57.	CAB 119/65:	MSC/55, Bellairs to le Mesurier, 9 September 1943.
58.	CAB 119/65:	PHJP/MSC/3, 12 September 1942.
59.	CAB 119/65:	JPS Sec Min 42/1059, 21 September 1942.
60.	FO 371/31338:	E7171/49/65, MSC/55, van Cutsem to Baxter, 8 December 1942.
61.	CAB 84/51:	JP(42)986(S)(T.R.), 2 December 1942, covering MSC(42)3(3rd Revise) of 9 November 1942.

62. CAB 119/65:   JP(42)991(S), 4 December 1942.
63. FO 371/31337:   E2583/49/65, Baxter to van Cutsem,
                     4 December 1942.
64. FO 371/31338:   E7171/49/65, MSC/55, van Cutsem to
                     Baxter, 8 December 1942.
65. CAB 119/65:   JPS Sec Min 42/1383, 8 December 1942.
66. —
67. CAB 84/5:   JP(42)197th Mtg, 10 December 1942.
68. FO 371/31529:   U1821/1179/70, Bellairs to Jebb,
                     14 December 1942;
    CAB 84/51:   JP(42)1025, 20 December 1942.
69. CAB 119/64:   JPS Sec Min 42/1116, le Mesurier to Davison,
                     3 October 1942.
70. FO 371/31529:   U1179/1179/70, MSC/50/1, Bellairs to Jebb
                     & MSC(42)5(Third Draft), 27 October
                     1942; Hood minute, 26 November 1942.
71. FO 371/30930:   C2167/241/18, 20 February 1942;
    FO 371/31500:   U420/61/72, Mabbott to Jebb, 8 September
                     1942.
72. FO 371/31525:   U742/742/70, Jebb memorandum (revised
                     version), 20 October 1942.
73. FO 371/31525:   U1797/742/70, Bellairs to Ronald,
                     3 December 1942.
74. CAB 84/5:   JP(42)197th Mtg, 10 December 1942.
75. CAB 65/28:   WM(42)161st Concls (2), 27 November 1942.
76. CAB 66/30:   WP(42)516, 8 November 1942.
77. CAB 66/33:   WP(43)31, 16 January 1943.
78. FO 371/35396:   U1158/402/70, MSC draft memorandum,
                     10 March 1943.
79. CAB 66/38:   WP(43)300, 7 July 1943.
80. FO 371/35397:   U2889/402/70, Jebb minute, 30 June 1943.
81. FO 371/31500:   U1047/61/72, F.R.P.S. memorandum,
                     12 October 1942.
82. FO 371/35261:   U641/58/72, MSC/48, Bellairs to Jebb,
                     6 February 1943.
83. CAB 119/65:   MSC/53(4th Draft), 20 January 1943; MSC/
                     53(Final), 25 June 1943.
84. FO 371/35407:   U516/516/70, Record of 28 January 1943
                     F.O. meeting, 2 February 1943.
85. FO 371/31529:   U1821/1179/70, Hood minute, 22 December
                     1942.
86. CAB 119/65:   JPS Sec Min 43/530, 28 April 1943.
87. FO 371/35407:   U2937/516/70, Record of 23 June 1943 F.O.
                     meeting, 29 June 1943.

88. CAB 119/65: Vintras minute, 30 April 1943.
89. CAB 119/64: Bridges confidential note, 31 May 1943. (Copy also in CAB 21/2294)

90. —
91. CAB 84/6: JP(43)20th Mtg (4), 19 March 1943.
92. WO 106/2759: MSC/14/4, June 1943; MSC/14/4/1, 21 June 1943; MSC/40/4, 20 July 1943.
93. CAB 21/2294: MSC(43)6/6—Progress Report No 10, 7 June 1943.
94. ADM 116/5118: MSC/54, 28 June 1943.
95. CAB 119/64: MSC/9, Bellairs to Hollis, 4 February 1943.
96. CAB 119/64: Ismay to Bellairs, 3 March 1943;
      JPS Sec Min 43/318, 10 March 1943

97. —
98. CAB 84/6: JP(43)20th Mtg (4), 19 March 1943.
99. FO 371/35449: U2231/2231/70, Cavendish-Bentinck minute, 3 April 1943; Ronald minute, 4 April 1943.
100. FO 371/35449: U2232/2231/70, Cavendish-Bentinck minute, 9 April 1943.
101. CAB 119/64: JP(43)30th Mtg (Confidential Annex), 9 April 1943.
102. FO 371/35449: U2232/2231/70, Cavendish-Bentinck minute, 9 April 1943; Jebb minute, 11 April 1943.
103. CAB 119/64: JPS Sec Min 43/501, Howkins to Hollis, 21 April 1943.
104. FO 371/35449: U2234/2231/70, Cavendish-Bentinck minute, 6 May 1943;
      FO 371/35449: U2235/2231/70, Jebb minute, 11 May 1943; Jebb to Cadogan, 12 May 1943; Cadogan annotation, 12 May 1943; Eden annotation, 13 May 1943.
105. CAB 21/2294: COS Sec Min 329/3, 12 May 1943.
106. CAB 21/2294: Bridges confidential note, 31 May 1943. (Copy also in CAB 119/64)
107. ADM 1/12853: 'H.V.M.' minute, 29 May 1943.
108. CAB 21/2294: Bridges to Markham, 21 June 1943; Alexander to Bridges, 22 June 1943.
109. FO 371/35449: U2235/2231/70, Cavendish-Bentinck minute, 12 May 1943; Jebb to Cadogan, 12 May 1943;
      FO 371/35449: U2471/2231/70, Jebb minute, 4 June 1943; Cavendish-Bentinck minutes, 7 & 9 June 1943.

110.	FO 371/35449:	U3033/2231/70, Jebb minute, 23 June 1943.
111.	FO 371/35449:	U3498/2231/70, Ronald minute, 1 July 1943; Cavendish-Bentinck minute, 3 July 1943.
112.	CAB 21/2294:	Bridges minutes, 6 & 8 July 1943.
113.	CAB 66/24:	WP(42)205(Revise), 14 May 1942.
114.	CAB 80/40:	COS(43)193, 9 July 1943.
115.	CAB 80/40:	COS(43)198, 14 July 1943.
116.	CAB 79/27:	COS(43)114th Mtg (2), 15 July 1943.
117.	CAB 21/2294:	Hollis to Bridges, 16 July 1943.
118.	CAB 79/27:	COS(43)117th Mtg (1), 22 July 1943.
119.	CAB 80/40:	COS(43)199(Final), 25 July 1943.
120.	CAB 66/39:	WP(43)350, 4 August 1943;
	CAB 87/83:	ACA(43)1, 5 August 1943;
	CAB 87/83:	ACA(43)19, 26 November 1943.
121.	CAB 21/2294:	Departmental letters to Bridges, 29, 30 & 31 July 1943.
122.	CAB 66/40:	WP(43)351, covering COS(43)199(Final), 31 July 1943.
123.	FO 371/35449:	U2471/2231/70, Jebb minute, 4 June 1943.
124.	*Ibid.:*	Cavendish-Bentinck minute, 7 June 1943.

CHAPTER 3: The Post-Hostilities Planning Sub-Committee, 1943–44

1.	CAB 119/65:	JPS Sec Mins 43/78 & 43/79, covering Scott note of 9 January 1943 to Northern and Southern Departments, 17 January 1943.
2.	CAB 84/55:	JP(43)294(Final) Annex, 20 September 1943.
3.	CAB 119/65:	JPS Sec Min 43/137, covering F.O. reply to Scott, 28 January 1943.
4.	CAB 80/71:	COS(43)364(0), 5 July 1943.
5.	FO 371/35449:	U3765/2231/70, Lambert minute, 25 August 1943.
6.	CAB 84/54:	JP(43)240(Final), 20 July 1943;
	CAB 79/62:	COS(43)170th Mtg (0)(8), 23 July 1943.
7.	FO 371/35407:	U3763/516/70, PHP(43)5(T.R.), 11 August 1943.
8.	CAB 81/40:	PHP(43)4th Mtg (1), 16 August 1943.
9.	CAB 81/41:	PHP(43)5(Final), 16 August 1943.
10.	CAB 84/55:	JP(43)283(Final), 24 August 1943.
11.	CAB 79/63:	COS(43)197th Mtg (0)(9), 26 August 1943.
12.	CAB 84/55:	JP(43)294(Final), 20 September 1943.
13.	CAB 79/64:	COS(43)223rd Mtg (0)(1), 22 September 1943.

14. CAB 79/64:   COS(43)224th Mtg (0)(1) & Annex I,
                    23 September 1943.
15. FO 371/26992:   N6007/499/38, Warner minute, 24 September
                    1943.
16. CAB 81/40:   PHP(43)18th Mtg (Agendum), 11 October
                    1943.
17. CAB 81/44:   PHP(43)1st Mtg (0)(1), 12 October 1943.
18. CAB 81/41:   PHP(43)6(Final), 26 August 1943.
19. CAB 80/42:   COS(43)299, 13 November 1943.
20. CAB 81/41:   PHP(43)41(Final), 13 December 1943.
21. —
22. CAB 79/68:   COS(43)306th Mtg (0)(6), 16 December
                    1943.
23. CAB 79/68:   COS(43)312th Mtg (0)(7), 22 December
                    1943.
24. CAB 81/45:   PHP(43)3(0)(Final), 1 January 1944.
25. CAB 79/69:   COS(44)3rd Mtg (0)(12), 5 January 1944.
26. CAB 79/69:   COS(44)15th Mtg (0)(11), 19 January 1944.
27. —
28. CAB 80/41:   COS(43)237, 22 August 1943;
    CAB 79/27:   COS(43)134th Mtg (4), 24 August 1943.
29. CAB 81/40:   PHP(43)10th Mtg (2), 8 September 1943.
30. —
31. CAB 81/40:   PHP(43)13th Mtg (1), 24 September 1943;
    CAB 81/41:   PHP(43)17(Final), 25 September 1943.
32. CAB 79/64:   COS(43)219th Mtg (0)(13), 17 September
                    1943;
    CAB 81/41:   PHP(43)7(a)(Final), 6 September 1943.
33. CAB 79/65:   COS(43)230th Mtg (0)(11), 29 September
                    1943.
34. CAB 81/40:   PHP(43)33rd Mtg (2), 20 December 1943.
35. CAB 81/44:   PHP(43)1st Mtg (0)(2), 12 October 1943.
36. CAB 81/40:   PHP(43)19th Mtg (1), 18 October 1943.
37. CAB 81/40:   PHP(43)25th Mtg (2), 16 November 1943;
    CAB 81/41:   PHP(43)24(Final), 16 November 1943.
38. CAB 81/40:   PHP(44)3rd Mtg (1), 27 January 1944.
39. —
40. CAB 81/41:   PHP(43)24a(Final), 3 February 1944.
41. CAB 79/70:   COS(44)50th Mtg (0)(3), 17 February 1944.
42. —
43. —
44. FO 371/40740:   U1751/748/70, Jebb minute, 19 February
                    1944.

45. CAB 79/70: COS(44)50th Mtg (0)(4), 17 February 1944.
46. FO 371/40740: U1751/748/70, Jebb minute & draft Eden letter, 19 February 1944; Cadogan minute, 21 February 1944.
47. CAB 79/27: COS(43)147th Mtg (9), 21 October 1943.
48. FO 371/40740: U1751/748/70, Jebb minute, 7 March 1944.
49. CAB 79/71: COS(44)88th Mtg (0)(1), 16 March 1944.
50. CAB 79/72: COS(44)98th Mtg (0)(1) & (2), 23 March 1944;

    CAB 81/42: PHP(44)8(Final), 20 March 1944.
51. CAB 79/89: COS(44)98th Mtg (0)(7)(Confidential Annex—Secretary's Standard File), 23 March 1944.
52. AIR 20/2681: Ismay memorandum, circulated to VCOS on 2 March 1944.
53. *Ibid.:* Kennedy memorandum, circulated to VCOS on 23 March 1944.
54. CAB 79/89: COS(44)98th Mtg (0)(7)(Confidential Annex—Secretary's Standard File), 23 March 1944.
55. CAB 79/72: COS(44)105th Mtg (0)(1), 30 March 1944.
56. CAB 80/43: COS(44)59, 1 April 1944.
57. See CAB 81/41: PHP(43)31(Final), 8 November 1943.
58. WO 32/10358: Grove-White to ACIGS(O)(*i.e.* Kennedy), 18 January 1944.
59. CAB 81/42: PHP(44)27(Draft), 17 April 1944.
60. CAB 79/73: COS(44)130th Mtg (0)(2), 20 April 1944.
61. FO 371/40736: U3498/573/70, Jebb minute, 2 May 1944.
62. CAB 79/63: COS(43)197th Mtg (0)(3), 26 August 1943.
63. CAB 81/41: PHP(43)25(Final), 15 December 1943.
64. CAB 79/69: COS(44)3rd Mtg (0)(14), 5 January 1944.
65. WO 106/5184: Kennedy minute, 6 January 1944.
66. Closed (50 years): JP(43)338, 27 September 1943. (Removed from CAB 84/56)
67. CAB 119/65: JPS Sec Min 43/734, 22 June 1943.
68. FO 371/40740: U1762/748/70, PHP(43)45(Preliminary Draft), 25 February 1944.
69. CAB 81/42: PHP(44)8(Final), 20 March 1944.
70. FO 371/40736: U1950/573/70, PHP(44)23rd (Private) Mtg, 2 March 1944.
71. FO 371/40740: U2268/748/70, PHP(43)45(Second Draft), 10 April 1944.
72. FO 371/40740: U2079/748/70, Hood minute, 15 March 1944.

73. FO 371/40740: U2268/748/70, Hood minute, 15 April 1944; Roberts minute, 16 April 1944.
74. CAB 81/40: PHP(44)19th Mtg, 17 April 1944.
75. CAB 81/41: PHP(43)45(Final), 26 April 1944. (Erroneously dated 24 April 1944 on front cover)
76. FO 371/40740: U3554/748/70, Roberts minute, 27 April 1944.
77. FO 371/40740: U3707/748/70, PHP(44)36th (Private) Mtg (1), 26 April 1944.
78. CAB 79/75: COS(44)172nd Mtg (0)(3), 25 May 1944.
79. CAB 80/84: COS(44)477(0), Jebb to COS Secretary, 27 May 1944;
    CAB 79/75: COS(44)179th Mtg (0)(4), 1 June 1944.
80. FO 371/40740: U1383/748/70, PHP(44)3(T.R.), 7 February 1944.
81. CAB 81/42: PHP(44)38(Final), 18 May 1944.
82. FO 371/40740: U1383/748/70, PHP(44)3(T.R.), 7 February 1944.
83. FO 371/40740: U4150/748/70, PHP(44)3(Preliminary Draft), redesignated as PHP(44)6(0)(Preliminary Draft), 28 April 1944.
84. *Ibid.:* PHP(44)6(0)(2nd Preliminary Draft), 24 May 1944.
85. CAB 81/41: PHP(43)32(Final), 2 February 1944.
86. CAB 81/45: PHP(44)3(0)(Final), 3 April 1944.
87. CAB 84/62: JP(44)95(Final), 4 April 1944.
88. CAB 80/82: COS(44)322(0), 5 April 1944.
89. CAB 81/45: PHP(44)4(0)(Final), 26 April 1944;
    CAB 79/74: COS(44)142nd Mtg (0)(8), 2 May 1944.
90. —
91. CAB 80/43: COS(44)25, 14 February 1944;
    CAB 79/70: COS(44)51st Mtg (0)(3), 17 February 1944.
92. FO 371/40791: U3978/3978/70, PHP(44)20(Preliminary Draft), 29 April 1944.
93. CAB 81/40: PHP(44)26th Mtg, 12 May 1944.
94. CAB 81/42: PHP(44)20(Final), 19 May 1944.
95. AIR 20/2738: ACAS(P) brief for VCAS, 24 May 1944.
96. CAB 79/75: COS(44)172nd Mtg (0)(2), 25 May 1944;
    CAB 80/84: COS(44)484(0)(PHP), 25 May 1944;
    FO 371/40791: U4584/3978/70, Jebb minute, 26 May 1944.
97. CAB 81/45: PHP(44)2(0)(Final), 22 January 1944.
98. CAB 66/47: WP(44)111 Annex II(= PHP(44)2(0)(Final)), 16 February 1944;

	CAB 65/41:	WM(44)25th Concls (4), 24 February 1944.
99.	CAB 81/42:	PHP(44)32(Final), 19 May 1944.
100.	CAB 81/40:	PHP(44)29th Mtg (1), (2) & (4), 19 May 1944.
101.	FO 371/40803:	U5780/4404/70, Jebb minute, 23 May 1944.
102.	CAB 66/49:	WP(44)222, 19 April 1944;
	CAB 87/67:	APW(44)1, 19 April 1944.
103.	CAB 80/84:	COS(44)485(0)(PHP), 25 May 1944;
	CAB 79/75:	COS(44)179th Mtg (0)(3), 1 June 1944.
104.	FO 371/40803:	U4582/4404/70, Jebb to Hollis, 7 June 1944;
	FO 371/40740:	U5911/748/70, Jebb minute, 14 June 1944.
105.	FO 371/43335:	N2832/183/38, Eden annotation, 6 May 1944.
106.	FO 371/43335:	N1008/183/38, Warner minute, 4 January 1944; F.O. memorandum, printed version, 29 April 1944;
	ADM 116/5118:	F.O. memorandum, original version, 10 February 1944.
107.	ADM 116/5118:	PHP(43)1(0)(Second Preliminary Draft), 8 March 1944.
108.	—	
109.	CAB 81/45:	PHP(43)1(0)(Final), 1 May 1944.
110.	ADM 116/5118:	Grantham brief for VCNS, 25 May 1944.
111.	—	
112.	CAB 79/75:	COS(44)172nd Mtg (0)(4), 25 May 1944.
113.	CAB 81/45:	PHP(44)13(0)(Final), 6 June 1944.
114.	CAB 79/76:	COS(44)195th Mtg (0)(1), 15 June 1944;
	CAB 80/84:	COS(44)527(0)(PHP), 15 June 1944.

CHAPTER 4: The Post-Hostilities Planning Staff, 1944–45

1.	CAB 79/75:	COS(44)172nd Mtg (0)(1), 25 May 1944.
2.	CAB 80/83:	COS(44)470(0), 27 May 1944.
3.	CAB 79/75:	COS(44)172nd Mtg (0)(5), 25 May 1944.
4.	—	
5.	FO 371/40740:	U4379/748/70, Willoughby draft memorandum, 14 May 1944; Butler & Warner minutes, 23 May 1944; Roberts minute, 26 May 1944; Hankey minute, 27 May 1944; Cavendish-Bentinck annotation (undated).
6.	FO 371/40740:	U4978/748/70, PHP(44)12(0)(Draft), 26 May 1944.
7.	CAB 81/45:	PHP(44)12(0)(2nd Revised Draft), 7 June 1944.

8. FO 371/40740:   U6253/748/70, Jebb minute, 7 June 1944; Ronald minute, 8 June 1944; Sargent & Cadogan minutes, 9 June 1944.

9. CAB 79/76:   COS(44)195th Mtg (0), 15 June 1944;
    AIR 20/2681:   COS Sec Min 1011/4, 13 June 1944; Warburton & Colyer minutes, 14 June 1944.

10. FO 371/40741A: U6254/748/70, Jebb minute, 15 June 1944; Cavendish-Bentinck minute, 16 June 1944; Sargent minutes, 18 & 28 June 1944; Cadogan minute, 28 June 1944.

11. CAB 81/45:   PHP(44)11(0)(Final), 13 June 1944.

12. CAB 79/76:   COS(44)195th Mtg (0)(2), 15 June 1944.

13. —

14. CAB 81/45:   PHP(44)8(0)(T.R.), 2 May 1944.

15. FO 371/40740:   U4424/748/70, PHP(44)14th (0) Mtg (1), 16 May 1944.

16. CAB 122/1566:   CJ/44/163, 14 June 1944.

17. FO 371/40740:   U5910/748/70, CJ/44/172, 17 June 1944.

18. CAB 21/1614 &   U5909/748/70, PHP(44)17(0)(T.R.), 19 June
    FO 371/40740:   1944.

19. CAB 122/1566:   CJ/44/215, 18 July 1944.

20. CAB 80/81:   COS(44)282(0), 29 March 1944. Based upon
    CAB 81/41:   PHP(43)24a(Final), 3 February 1944.

21. CAB 87/66:   APW(44)1st Mtg (1), 22 April 1944;
    CAB 87/67:   APW(44)4, 19 April 1944.

22. WO 193/303:   CJ/44/74, 11 May 1944.

23. FO 371/40740:   U5909/748/70, PHP(44)17(0)(T.R.), 19 June 1944.

24. CAB 21/1614:   CJ/44/132, 31 May 1944.

25. —

26. CAB 80/44:   COS(44)113, 23 June 1944.

27. FO 371/40741A: U6283/748/70, PHP(44)17(0)(Draft), 7 July 1944.

28. FO 371/40741A: U6283/748/70, Roberts minute, 10 July 1944; Warner minute, 12 July 1944.

29. FO 371/40741A: U6791/748/70, Warner minute, 17 July 1944; Cavendish-Bentinck minute, 18 July 1944; Jebb minute, 18 July 1944; Cadogan minute, 18 July 1944.

30. FO 371/40741A: U6691 & U6792/748/70, PHP(44)17(0) (Final), 20 July 1944. (Copy also obtainable in CAB 79/78, attached to COS(44)248th Mtg (0) minutes.)

31. FO 371/40741A: U6792/748/70, Warner minute, 24 July 1944;
Cavendish-Bentinck minute, 24 July 1944;
Jebb minute, 25 July 1944.

32. —

33. CAB 122/1566: Davison to Redman, 27 July 1944.

34. CAB 79/78: COS(44)248th Mtg (0)(14), 26 July 1944.

35. CAB 21/1614 & U6793/748/70, COS(44)248th Mtg (0)(14)
FO 371/40741A: (Confidential Annex), 26 July 1944.

36. CAB 79/78: COS(44)249th Mtg (0)(7), 27 July 1944;
FO 371/40741A: U6793/748/70, COS Sec Min 1289/4,
27 July 1944.

37. FO 371/40741A: U6793/748/70, Jebb minute, 28 July 1944.

38. FO 371/36991: N499/499/38, Preston memorandum,
13 January 1943; Wilson minute,
26 January 1943.

39. CAB 66/53: WP(44)409, Cooper to Eden, No 295,
30 May 1944.

40. *Ibid.:* Eden to Cooper, No 311, 25 July 1944.

41. —

42. FO 371/40741A: U6793/748/70, Jebb minute, 28 July 1944;
Warner minute, 29 July 1944; Roberts
minute, 31 July 1944; Cavendish-Bentinck
minute, 31 July 1944; Ward minute,
2 August 1944.

43. FO 371/40741A: U6793/748/70, PHP(44)17(0)(Revised T.R.),
29 July 1944.

44. CAB 79/78: COS(44)249th Mtg (0)(2), 27 July 1944.

45. FO 371/40736: U6770/573/70, Ismay to Cadogan, 2 August
1944.
(Also CAB 80/44: COS(44)143 Annex I, 2 August 1944.)

46. *Ibid.:* Cadogan to Ismay, 5 August 1944.
(Also CAB 80/44: COS(44)143 Annex II, 5 August 1944.)

47. CAB 81/42: PHP(44)66, 7 September 1944;
CAB 79/80: COS(44)306th Mtg (0)(7), 13 September
1944.

48. FO 371/40736: U6770/573/70, Ward minute, 18 August
1944.

49. FO 371/40741A: U7619/748/70, Cavendish-Bentinck minute,
18 September 1944; Ward minute,
25 September 1944.

50. CAB 80/87: COS(44)819(0), 7 September 1944;
CAB 79/80: COS(44)304th Mtg (0)(14), 11 September
1944.

51. FO 371/40741A: U7619/748/70, PHP(44)23(0)(Draft),
                     16 September 1944.
52. CAB 122/1566:   Davison to Cornwall-Jones, 21 September
                     1944; see also F. H. N. Davidson Papers,
                     King's College, London, for notes on this
                     subject by a wartime Director of Military
                     Intelligence.
53. FO 371/40741A: U7619/748/70, Cavendish-Bentinck minute,
                     18 September 1944.
54. *Ibid.:*   PHP(44)23(0)(Draft), 16 September 1944.
55. FO 371/40741A: U7703/748/70, Hood minute, 8 October 1944.
56. CAB 81/45:   PHP(44)23(0)(Final), 3 October 1944;
    CAB 79/81:   COS(44)330th Mtg (0)(4), 6 October 1944.
57. —
58. CAB 122/1566:   Davison to Cornwall-Jones, 17 October 1944.
59. FO 371/40741A: U7703/748/70, Hood minute, 8 October 1944.
60. —
61. —
62. CAB 80/84:   COS(44)508(0), 13 June 1944.
63. FO 371/39080:   C11955/146/18, PHP(44)15(0)(Final),
                     25 August 1944.
64. FO 371/39080:   C11955/146/18, Ward minute, 28 August
                     1944.
65. CAB 79/80:   COS(44)303rd Mtg (0)(5), 9 September 1944;
    CAB 80/87:   COS(44)822(0), 9 September 1944.
66. FO 371/39080:   C13517/146/18, APW(44)90, 20 September
                     1944.
67. —
68. CAB 79/81:   COS(44)323rd Mtg (0)(6), 2 October 1944.
69. FO 371/39080:   C13518/146/18, COS Sec Min 1659/4,
                     2 October 1944.
70. FO 371/39080:   C13518/146/18, Sargent (?) minute, 4 October
                     1944; 'C.R.' (?) minute, 10 October 1944.
71. FO 371/43336:   N6177/183/38, Minutes of 4 October 1944
                     meeting, 6 October 1944.
72. *Ibid.* &
    CAB 122/1566:   Davison to Cornwall-Jones, 17 October 1944.
73. CAB 79/81:   COS(44)330th Mtg (0)(3), 6 October 1944.
74. CAB 79/81:   COS(44)336th Mtg (0)(5), 12 October 1944.
75. CAB 81/45:   PHP(44)15(0)(Revised Final), 15 November
                     1944;
    CAB 80/89:   COS(44)1012(0)(PHP), 7 December 1944.
76. CAB 81/45:   PHP(44)22(0)(Final), 3 January 1945;

	CAB 87/69:	APW(45)40, 19 March 1945;
	CAB 81/46:	PHP(45)14(0)(T.R.), 7 April 1945;
	CAB 87/69:	APW(45)10th Mtg (2), 13 April 1945.
77.	CAB 79/83:	COS(44)390th Mtg (0)(11), 5 December 1944.
78.	—	
79.	CAB 79/82:	COS(44)346th Mtg (0)(13)(Confidential Annex), 24 October 1944.
80.	CAB 122/1566:	West to Cornwall-Jones, 8 & 29 August 1944; Davison to Cornwall-Jones, 10, 22 & 30 August 1944; Cornwall-Jones circulation note: 'The only paper that need go outside this building is PHP(44)15(0) which should go to Mr Maclean', 5 September 1944; Davison to Cornwall-Jones, 17 & 30 October, 14 & 25 November 1944.
81.	FO 371/40741A:	U6793/748/70, Warburton note, 31 July 1944.
82.	—	
83.	CAB 81/45:	PHP(44)20(0)(Final), 11 August 1944.
84.	FO 371/40741A:	U6875/748/70, Noble ('A.N.N.') minute, 18 September 1944;
	CAB 122/1566:	Davison to Cornwall-Jones, 30 August 1944.
85.	—	
86.	FO 371/47860:	N678/20/38, Cavendish-Bentinck annotation, 19 December 1944; Warner minute, 15 January 1945.
87.	*Ibid.:*	JIC(44)467(0)(Final), 18 December 1944.
	(Also CAB 80/89:	COS(44)1053(0)(PHP) Annex, 29 December 1944.)
	CAB 79/84:	COS(44)411th Mtg (0)(3), 27 December 1944;
	FO 371/47860:	N678/20/38, Cavendish-Bentinck minute, 4 January 1945; Cadogan minute, 15 January 1945; Sargent to Hollis, 22 January 1945;
	CAB 79/29:	COS(45)29th Mtg (3) & Annex I, 26 January 1945.
88.	CAB 80/44:	COS(44)108, 11 June 1944.
89.	CAB 81/45:	PHP(44)18(0)(Final), 25 August 1944.
90.	CAB 79/80:	COS(44)294th Mtg (0)(7), 31 August 1944.
91.	CAB 80/88:	COS(44)934(0), 30 October 1944.
92.	CAB 81/45:	PHP(44)26(0)(Final), 6 November 1944;
	CAB 79/82:	COS(44)361st Mtg (0)(3), 7 November 1944;

	CAB 80/89:	COS(44)955(0), 8 November 1944.
93.	CAB 21/1614:	CJ/44/132, 31 May 1944; Prime Minister's Personal Min No M.1144/4, 25 November 1944.
94.	FO 371/40741A:	U7618/748/70, Warner minute, 20 September 1944; Eden minute, 28 September 1944.
95.	—	
96.	FO 371/40741A:	U7841/748/70, PHP(44)16(0)(Preliminary Draft), 10 September 1944; PHP(44)16(0)(Draft), 17 September 1944.
97.	FO 371/43336:	N5598/183/38, Clerk-Kerr to Eden, No 531, 31 August 1944; Wilson minute, 23 September 1944.
98.	FO 371/43336:	N7629/183/38, Preston memorandum, 12 November 1944; Wilson minute, 8 December 1944.
99.	FO 371/40741B:	U7975/748/70, Jebb minute & re-draft, 24 October 1944.
100.	FO 371/40741B:	U8181/748/70, Jebb minute, 21 November 1944.
101.	—	
102.	CAB 81/45:	PHP(44)27(0)(Final), 9 November 1944.
103.	CAB 79/83:	COS(44)374th Mtg (0)(13), 20 November 1944.
104.	FO 371/40741B:	U8181/748/70, Jebb minute, 21 November 1944;
	CAB 79/84:	COS(44)405th Mtg (0)(11), 19 December 1944.
105.	FO 371/40741A:	U7658/748/70, PHP(44)6(0)(Draft), 1 October 1944;
	FO 371/40741A:	U7841/748/70, PHP(44)16(0)(Draft), 17 September 1944.
106.	CAB 84/67:	JP(44)278(0)(T.R.), 27 October 1944.
107.	CAB 79/82:	COS(44)349th Mtg (0)(1), 26 October 1944.
108.	—	
109.	CAB 84/67:	JP(44)278(Final), 1 January 1945.
110.	CAB 79/28:	COS(45)6th Mtg (1), 4 January 1945;
	CAB 79/28:	COS(45)7th Mtg (8), 5 January 1945.
111.	—	
112.	CAB 81/45:	PHP(44)6(0)(Final), 31 January 1945.
113.	FO 371/50774:	U890/36/70, Sterndale Bennett minute, 20 February 1945; Jebb minute, 24 February 1945; Allen minute, 28 February 1945; Cavendish-Bentinck

minute, 3 March 1945; Wilson minute, 5 March 1945; Ronald minute, 26 March 1945.

114. CAB 79/29: COS(45)48th Mtg (7), 21 February 1945;
    CAB 80/92: COS(45)120(0)(PHP), 21 February 1945.
115. CAB 80/89: COS(44)1053(0)(PHP), 29 December 1944.
116. CAB 81/46: PHP(45)10(0)(Final), 27 March 1945.
117. FO 371/50774: U2273/36/70, Hankey minute, 31 March 1945.
118. CAB 79/31: COS(45)90th Mtg (14), 6 April 1945.
119. CAB 80/98: COS(45)644(0), 3 November 1945.
120. CAB 79/41: COS(45)269th Mtg (14), 9 November 1945.
121. —
122. CAB 80/88: COS(44)890(0), 9 October 1944.
123. CAB 79/82: COS(44)369th Mtg (0)(6), 14 November 1944.
124. CAB 84/67: JP(44)288(Final), 7 December 1944.
125. CAB 79/84: COS(44)401st Mtg (0)(2), 14 December 1944.
126. CAB 81/45: PHP(44)24(0)(Revise)(Final), 8 January 1945.
127. CAB 79/28: COS(45)11th Mtg (13), 10 January 1945;
    CAB 80/90: COS(45)30(0), 12 January 1945.
128. CAB 81/46: PHP(45)6(0)(Final), 19 May 1945.
129. CAB 79/34: COS(45)142nd Mtg (13), 1 June 1945.
130. FO 371/50775: U3923/36/70, Desultory minutes, May 1945.
131. CAB 81/46: PHP(45)3(0)(Revised Final), 30 March 1945;
    CAB 79/31: COS(45)87th Mtg (15), 4 April 1945.
132. —
133. CAB 81/46: PHP(45)15(0)(Final), 19 May 1945.
134. FO 371/50774: U1266/36/70, Hood minute, 22 February 1945; Wilson minute, 22 February 1945.
135. FO 371/50775: U3922/36/70, Hood to Davison, 8 June 1945.
136. *Ibid.:* Davison to Hood, 11 June 1945;
    CAB 79/34: COS(45)142nd Mtg (14), 1 June 1945.
137. CAB 21/1799: Warburton note, 16 November 1944.
138. CAB 21/1799: Minutes of 17 November 1944 P.H.P.S. meeting, 18 November 1944.
139. FO 371/40741B: U8523/748/70, Jebb minute & draft, 18 December 1944.
140. FO 371/50774: U1080/36/70, Draft survey, 5 February 1945;
    FO 371/50774: U2274/36/70, Curtis outline, 17 March 1945;
    CAB 21/1799: Hollis to Jacob, 5 December 1944.
141. FO 371/50775: U2885/36/70, Ward minutes, 23 & 29 April 1945.
142. FO 371/50775: U3390/36/70, Ward minute, 23 May 1945.

143. FO 371/50775: U4024/36/70, PHP(45)29(0)(3rd Draft), 25 May 1945.
144. FO 371/50775: U4024/36/70, Cavendish-Bentinck minute, 11 June 1945; Cresswell to Davidson [*sic*], 13 June 1945.
145. FO 371/50775: U4969/36/70, Falla minute, 6 July 1945.
146. FO 371/50774: U2274/36/70, Davison note, 19 March 1945.
147. CAB 87/69: APW(45)4, 5 January 1945; APW(45)8, 21 January 1945; APW(45)9, 23 January 1945; APW(45)20, 19 February 1945; APW(45)22, 2 March 1945; APW(45)7th Mtg (1), 22 March 1945;
      CAB 66/64: WP(45)242, 12 April 1945;
      CAB 65/52: WM(45)48th Concls (7)(Confidential Annex), 20 April 1945.
148. CAB 81/46: PHP(45)29(0)(Final), 29 June 1945.
149. CAB 79/31: COS(45)87th Mtg (8), 4 April 1945.
150. CAB 79/35: COS(45)164th Mtg (6), 29 June 1945.
151. FO 371/50775: U4969/36/70, Cresswell minute, 9 July 1945.
152. WO 193/303: Brief for CIGS, 11 July 1945.
153. —
154. CAB 79/36: COS(45)175th Mtg (5), 12 July 1945.
155. —

CHAPTER 5: The Joint Technical Warfare Committee and the Future Nature of Warfare, 1945–46

1. —
2. —
3. CAB 92/39: JWPS(42)1, 30 March 1942.
4. CAB 92/41: JWPS(44)34, 25 October 1944.
    (Also CAB 80/46: COS(44)220, 25 October 1944.)
5. CAB 79/82: COS(44)356th Mtg (0)(1), 1 November 1944.
6. CAB 81/24: TWC(43)1, 16 November 1943.
7. —
8. —
9. Closed (50 years): TWC(44)24th Mtg (1), 14 November 1944.
10. Retained: WW(45)2, 13 January 1945.
11. Closed (50 years): TWC(45)1st Mtg (1), 23 January 1945.
12. CAB 79/82: COS(44)360th Mtg (0)(8) & Annex II, 7 November 1945.
13. CAB 120/770: WW/51/45, 19 February 1945.
14. CAB 21/1263: Tizard to Elliot, 4 May 1940.

15. See also   Tizard to Churchill, 8 April 1945; Prime
    CAB 120/842:   Minister's Personal Min No D.116/5,
                    19 April 1945.
16. CAB 80/94:   COS(45)402(0), 16 June 1945.
17. —
18. Closed (50 years): TWC(45)5th Mtg (5), 19 June 1945.
19. —
20. CAB 79/35:   COS(45)166th Mtg (13), 3 July 1945.
21. AIR 20/4658:   Minutes of Air Staff meeting of 17 July 1945
                    & revised brief for VCAS of 29 July 1945.
                    (Both circulated on 31 July 1945.)
22. AIR 20/4658:   Ismay draft for Prime Minister, 10 August
                    1945. (Copy also in CAB 120/842.)
23. CAB 79/37:   COS(45)197th Mtg (21), 13 August 1945.
24. CAB 80/97:   COS(45)556(0), 30 August 1945;
    CAB 79/38:   COS(45)212th Mtg (9), 31 August 1945.
25. —
26. CAB 79/37:   COS(45)200th Mtg (8), 17 August 1945;
    CAB 79/37:   COS(45)201st Mtg (14), 20 August 1945.
27. —
28. CAB 80/97:   COS(45)562(0), 3 September 1945.
29. AIR 20/4658:   ACAS(P) brief for CAS, 4 September 1945.
30. CAB 79/38:   COS(45)215th Mtg (8), 5 September 1945.
31. —
32. —
33. CAB 80/97:   COS(45)611(0), 12 October 1945;
    CAB 131/3:   DO(46)82, 2 July 1946;
    CAB 131/1:   DO(46)21st Mtg (1), 5 July 1946;
    CAB 79/50:   COS(46)106th Mtg (6), 10 July 1946.
34. Closed (50 years): TWC(45)32, 5 October 1945.
35. —
36. Closed (50 years): TWC(45)33, 10 October 1945.
    (Also CAB 82/26: DCOS(AWC)(45)3 Annex I, 19 October
                    1945.)
    CAB 82/26:   DCOS(AWC)(45)1, 13 October 1945;
    CAB 80/97:   COS(45)594(0), 28 September 1945;
    CAB 79/39:   COS(45)238th Mtg (16), 1 October 1945;
    CAB 82/3:   DCOS(45)14th Mtg, 2 October 1945;
    CAB 82/26:   DCOS(AWC)(45)5, 27 October 1945.
37. Closed (50 years): TWC(45)9th Mtg, 16 October 1945.
38. *Ibid.*
39. ADM 1/17259:   ACNS(W) note & memorandum, 15 August
                    1945; D of P memorandum, 2 September

1945; DGD memorandum (undated);
DNOR memorandum, 4 September 1945.

40. Closed (50 years): TWC(45)35, 19 October 1945.
(Also CAB 82/26: DCOS(AWC)(45)3 Annex II, 19 October
1945.)

41. Closed (50 years): TWC(45)37, 20 October 1945.

42. Closed (50 years): TWC(45)38, 24 October 1945.

43. CAB 80/97: COS(45)601(0) Annex III, 6 October 1945.

44. CAB 79/39: COS(45)238th Mtg (17), 1 October 1945.

45. CAB 79/40: COS(45)246th Mtg (1), COS Sec Min 1449/
5, 10 October 1945. (Copy also in CAB
120/842.)

46. CAB 80/98: COS(45)651(0) Annex, 10 November 1945.

47. —

48. CAB 79/41: COS(45)270th Mtg (9), 12 November 1945;
See also
CAB 120/842: Ismay Telegram to Jacob (HORIZON 4),
12 November 1945; Jacob to Attlee,
12 November 1945.

49. Closed (50 years): TWC(45)39 Annex, 26 October 1945.
(Also CAB 82/26: DCOS(AWC)(45)4 Annex, 26 October 1945.)

50. CAB 80/94: COS(45)402(0), 16 June 1945.

51. Closed (50 years): Addendum to TWC(45)39, 9 November 1945.

52. CAB 80/16: COS(40)645, 19 August 1940;
CAB 79/6: COS(40)278th Mtg (1), 23 August 1940;
Special Access: CCW(40)1, 9 September 1940.

53. Closed (50 years): CCW(45)31(Final), 16 June 1945.
(Also CAB 80/94: COS(45)400(0), 16 June 1945.)
Closed (50 years): CCW(45)32(Final), 16 June 1945.
(Also CAB 80/94: COS(45)401(0), 16 June 1945.)

54. CAB 84/44: JP(42)382, 10 April 1942;
CAB 84/53: JP(43)96(Final), 31 March 1943;
CAB 84/64: JP(44)177(Final), 5 July 1944;
CAB 80/85: COS(44)661(0), 26 July 1944.

55. Closed (50 years): CCW(45)33(Final), 26 June 1945.
(Also CAB 80/95: COS(45)417(0), 26 June 1945.)

56. Closed (50 years): CCW(CD)(44)1(Final), 4 September 1944.
(Also CAB 80/87: COS(44)797(0), 4 September 1944.)

57. Closed (50 years): CCW(45)10(Final), 27 February 1945.
(Also CAB 80/92: COS(45)134(0), 27 February 1945.)

58. CAB 79/30: COS(45)62nd Mtg (9), 7 March 1945.

59. Closed (50 years): CCW(45)17(Final), 30 April 1945.
(Also CAB 80/94: COS(45)300(0), 30 April 1945.)

60. Closed (50 years): CCW(45)45(Final), 23 July 1945.
    (Also CAB 80/96: COS(45)488(0), 23 July 1945.)
61. Closed (50 years): CCW(45)48(Final), 13 September 1945.
    (Also CAB 80/97: COS(45)575(0), 13 September 1945.)
    CAB 79/39: COS(45)230th Mtg (4), 20 September 1945.
62. Closed (50 years): TWC(45)40, 31 October 1945.
63. Closed (50 years): TWC(45)12th Mtg (1), 28 November 1945.
64. Retained: CCW(46)1(Final), 12 February 1946.
    (Also Retained: COS(46)46, 12 February 1946.)
    Retained: COS(46)25th Mtg (4), 14 February 1946.
65. —
66. CAB 69/8: DO(42)1st Mtg (3)(Confidential Annex),
    2 January 1942, covering Hankey to
    Churchill, 6 December 1941.
67. CAB 80/85: COS(44)661(0) Annex II, 26 July 1944.
    (*Note:* Although CAB 80/88: COS(44)892(0)
    of 10 October 1944 states the order for 'N'-
    bombs to have been placed with the
    Americans in February 1944, Churchill did
    not actually approve this step until early the
    following month. See CAB 120/782: Prime
    Minister's Personal Min No M.246/4,
    8 March 1944.)
68. CAB 80/84: COS(44)514(0), 12 June 1944;
    CAB 79/76: COS(44)194th Mtg (0)(10), 15 June 1944.
69. Closed (50 years): BW(44)21, 10 October 1944.
    (Also CAB 80/88: COS(44)892(0), 10 October 1944.)
70. CAB 79/81: COS(44)338th Mtg (0)(7), 13 October 1944.
71. Closed (50 years): BW(45)3(Final), 9 March 1945.
    (Also CAB 80/92: COS(45)160(0), 9 March 1945.)
72. CAB 79/30: COS(45)68th Mtg (11), 14 March 1945.
73. Closed (50 years): BW(45)17(Final), 7 August 1945.
    (Also CAB 80/96: COS(45)518(0), 7 August 1945.)
74. CAB 69/7: DO(45)15, 13 September 1945;
    PREM 8/140: Brief on above for 5 October 1945 Defence
    Committee meeting (undated).
75. CAB 69/7: DO(45)7th Mtg (5), 5 October 1945;
    CAB 69/7: DO(45)1, 5 July 1945.
76. Closed (50 years): TWC(45)42, 12 November 1945.
77. Closed (50 years): TWC(45)11th Mtg (4)(As amended),
    21 November 1945.
78. Closed (50 years): TWC(45)45, 6 December 1945.
79. Closed (50 years): TWC(45)43, 17 November 1945.

80. Closed (50 years): TWC(45)10th Mtg (2), 7 November 1945;
    Closed (50 years): TWC(45)41(Final), 6 November 1945.
81. CAB 79/41: COS(45)269th Mtg (10), 9 November 1945.
82. Closed (50 years): TWC(45)12th Mtg (2), 28 November 1945.
83. —
84. Closed (50 years): TWC(45)10th Mtg (1), 7 November 1945.
85. CAB 80/94: COS(45)356(0), 25 May 1945;
    CAB 79/34: COS(45)139th Mtg (4), 29 May 1945;
    DEFE 5/1: COS(47)60, 6 May 1947;
    DEFE 4/4: COS(47)65th Mtg (5), 16 May 1947.
86. Closed (50 years): TWC(45)43, 17 November 1945.
87. Closed (50 years): TWC(45)11th Mtg (1), 21 November 1945.
88. CAB 79/42: COS(45)286th Mtg (13), 19 December 1945;
    CAB 79/47: COS(46)66th Mtg (2), 25 April 1946.
89. —
90. —
91. —
92. —
93. Closed (50 years): TWC(45)44(Revise), 5 January 1946.
94. Closed (50 years): TWC(45)47, 22 December 1945.
95. Retained: TWC(46)1st Mtg (2), 22 January 1946.
96. —
97. Retained: TWC(46)1st Mtg (6), 22 January 1946.
98. CAB 80/99: COS(46)22(0), 21 January 1946.
99. Retained: TWC(46)3(Revise) Annex, 30 January 1946.
    (Also CAB 82/26: DCOS(AWC)(46)1 Annex, 30 January 1946.)
100. Retained: TWC(46)4th Mtg (2), 26 March 1946.
101. Retained: TWC(46)5th Mtg, 9 April 1946. (Circulated on 10 April 1946.)
102. —
103. Retained: TWC(46)14, 13 April 1946.
104. Retained: TWC(46)6th Mtg (1) & (2), 16 April 1946.
105. CAB 79/42: COS(45)286th Mtg (2) of 19 December 1945, covering JIC(45)320(0)(Revise), 17 December 1945.
106. AIR 20/4658: ACAS(P) draft brief for CAS, 17 May 1946.
107. —
108. —
109. Closed (50 years): COS(45)564(0), 8 September 1945;
     Closed (50 years): COS(45)220th Mtg (6), 11 September 1945;
     Closed (50 years): COS(45)233rd Mtg (7), 25 September 1945.
110. Retained: TWC(46)15, 25 April 1946.
111. CAB 79/47: COS(46)70th Mtg (8), 3 May 1946;
     CAB 79/49: COS(46)86th Mtg (15), 3 June 1946.

112. Retained: COS(46)99th Mtg (9), 26 June 1946.
113. Closed (50 years): DO(46)89, 8 July 1946;
      Closed (50 years): DO(46)23rd Mtg (3), 22 July 1946.
114. Retained: TWC/59/46, 16 September 1946;
      Retained: TWC(46)7th Mtg, 27 September 1946.
115. —

CHAPTER 6: The Joint Planning Staff and an Approved Defence Strategy, 1945–47

1. —
2. —
3. —
4. CAB 79/34:   COS(45)141st Mtg, 31 May 1945.
5. —
6. CAB 80/98:   COS(45)699(0), 28 December 1945.
7. CAB 84/73:   JP(45)174(S)(T.R.), 13 July 1945.
8. Special Access: STRATS draft for JP(45)174 (undated). (Item 2 in CAB 119/97.)
9. CAB 84/74:   JP(45)205(Final), 2 September 1945;
    CAB 79/38:   COS(45)215th Mtg (5), 5 September 1945;
    CAB 79/38:   COS(45)216th Mtg (7), 6 September 1945.
10. Special Access: STRATS note, 7 October 1945. (Item 5 in CAB 119/97.)
11. CAB 84/76:   JP(45)275(Final), 13 October 1945.
12. Special Access: STRATS note, 7 October 1945. (Item 5 in CAB 119/97.)
13. AIR 8/861:   CAS minute, 15 October 1945.
14. CAB 79/40:   COS(45)252nd Mtg (1), 16 October 1945.
15. CAB 69/7:   DO(45)29, 5 November 1945.
16. Special Access: JIC(45)307(Final), 4 December 1945. (Item 16 in CAB 119/97.)
17. CAB 84/76:   JP(45)277(Final), 7 January 1946.
18. CAB 69/7:   DO(45)11th Mtg (2), 29 October 1945.
19. CAB 79/41:   COS(45)264th Mtg (2), 1 November 1945;
    CAB 79/41:   COS(45)265th Mtg (6), 2 November 1945.
20. CAB 84/76:   JP(45)289(Final), 19 December 1945;
    CAB 84/77:   JP(45)307(Final), 19 December 1945.
21. CAB 80/99:   COS(46)5(0), 8 January 1946;
    CAB 80/99:   COS(46)9(0)(Revise), 15 January 1946.
22. CAB 131/1:   DO(46)3rd Mtg (1), 21 January 1946.
23. CAB 131/2:   DO(46)20, 13 February 1946.
24. CAB 131/1:   DO(46)5th Mtg (1), 15 February 1946.

25. CAB 128/5:   CM(46)16th Concls (6), 18 February 1946;
     CAB 129/7:   CP(46)65, 15 February 1946.
26. Special Access: JPS Sec Min 46/70, Gleadell to Hollis, 7 May
                       1946 & Hollis to Gleadell, 16 May 1946.
                       (Both = item 22B in CAB 119/97.)
27. Special Access: JP(45)277(Revised)(2nd Draft), 18 March
                       1946. (Item 22A in CAB 119/97.)
28. CAB 131/7:   DO(49)3, 7 January 1949.
29. CAB 81/45:   PHP(44)30(0)(Final), 1 January 1945.
30. CAB 84/75:   JP(45)251(Final), 14 September 1945.
31. CAB 80/99:   COS(46)43(0), 13 February 1946;
     Special Access: JP(46)26(Revised Final), 12 February 1946.
                       (In CAB 84/78.)
32. CAB 80/100:   COS(46)54(0), 22 February 1946.
33. CAB 79/45:   COS(46)31st Mtg (16), 25 February 1946.
34. Special Access: JP(46)45(T.R.), 25 February 1946. (In CAB
                       84/79.)
35. Retained: JP(46)45(Final), 27 March 1946;
     Retained: COS(46)51st Mtg (3), 29 March 1946.
36. Retained: JP(46)45(Revised Final), 31 March 1946;
     Retained: COS(46)52nd Mtg (16), 1 April 1946.
37. CAB 131/2:   DO(46)47, 2 April 1946.
38. CAB 131/1:   DO(46)10th Mtg (2), 5 April 1946.
39. —
40. CAB 131/2:   DO(46)40, 13 March 1946.
41. CAB 79/45:   COS(46)38th Mtg Annex VI, COS Sec Min
                       295/6, 11 March 1946;
     CAB 79/46:   COS(46)42nd Mtg (1), 18 March 1946.
42. —
43. FO 371/50912:   U5471/5471/70, Sargent memorandum,
                       11 July 1945.
44. FO 371/50826:   U7851/445/70, Ward minute, 1 September
                       1945.
45. FO 371/59911:   Z2410/120/72, Ronald memorandum,
                       4 January 1946.
46. —
47. —
48. CAB 80/100:   COS(46)93(0) Annex I, GEN 121/1,
                       11 March 1946.
49. FO 371/56885:   N5169/5169/38, Russia Committee, minutes
                       of 1st Mtg, 2 April 1946;
     FO 371/56832:   N6344/605/38, Warner memorandum, 2 April
                       1946; Sargent to Street, 14 May 1946.

50. CAB 79/47:   COS(46)54th Mtg (6), 5 April 1946.
51. CAB 80/101:   COS(46)105(0), 5 April 1946;
     Special Access: JP(46)65(Final), 4 April 1946. (In CAB 84/
                       80.)
52. CAB 129/8:   CP(46)139, 15 April 1946;
     CAB 128/5:   CM(46)36th Concls (3), 17 April 1946.
53. CAB 84/62:   JP(44)87(Final), 28 March 1944;
     CAB 80/43:   COS(44)58, 31 March 1944;
     CAB 99/27:   DPM(44)18, 7 April 1944.
54. CAB 80/97:   COS(45)625(0), 17 October 1945;
     CAB 79/40:   COS(45)252nd Mtg (8), 16 October 1945.
55. CAB 79/45:   COS(46)33rd Mtg (5), 1 March 1946;
     Special Access: JP(46)49(0)(T.R.), 2 March 1946. (In CAB
                       84/79.)
56. Special Access: JP(46)49(Final), 27 March 1946. (In CAB
                       84/79.)
57. CAB 131/2:   DO(46)46, 30 March 1946.
58. CAB 131/1:   DO(46)10th Mtg (4), 5 April 1946.
59. Special Access: JP(46)74(Final), 17 April 1946. (In CAB 84/
                       80.)
60. CAB 79/47:   COS(46)62nd Mtg (4), 18 April 1946;
     Retained: COS(47)99(0), 7 May 1947;
     Retained: COS(47)64th Mtg (4), 14 May 1947.
61. Retained: COS(46)119(0), 18 April 1946;
     Retained: JP(46)82(Revised Final), 17 April 1946.
62. Retained: COS(46)61st Mtg (4), 17 April 1946.
63. CAB 80/101:   COS(46)117(0), 17 April 1946;
     Special Access: JP(46)71(Final), 15 April 1946. (In CAB 84/
                       80.)
64. CAB 21/1800:   Cornwall-Jones to Home, 9 October 1946.
65. CAB 131/2:   DO(46)54, 15 April 1946;
     Special Access: JP(46)78(Final), 12 April 1946. (In CAB 84/
                       80.)
     CAB 131/1:   DO(46)13th Mtg (1), 17 April 1946.
66. AIR 8/998:   PMM(46)20, 1 May 1946;
     AIR 8/998:   PMM(46)10th Mtg (1), 2 May 1946.
67. DEFE 5/1:   COS(47)63, 14 May 1947.
68. CAB 79/49:   COS(46)96th Mtg (7), 21 June 1946.
69. CAB 79/49:   COS(46)96th Mtg (8), 21 June 1946.
70. Special Access: JP(46)126(Draft), 25 June 1946. (In CAB 84/
                       82.)
71. CAB 79/50:   COS(46)102nd Mtg (3), 3 July 1946.
72. Special Access: JP(46)134(Final), 5 July 1946. (In CAB 84/83.)

73. CAB 79/50:   COS(46)107th Mtg (1), 11 July 1946.
74. Special Access: JP(46)164(T.R.), 20 August 1946. (In CAB 84/84.)
75. —
76. Special Access: JP(46)100(Final), 23 May 1946. (In CAB 84/81.)
77. CAB 131/2:   DO(46)67(Revised), 25 May 1946.
78. CAB 131/1:   DO(46)17th Mtg (1), 27 May 1946.
79. CAB 79/48:   COS(46)83rd Mtg (22), 28 May 1946;
    CAB 79/48:   COS(46)84th Mtg (4), 29 May 1946.
80. Special Access: JP(46)108(S)(T.R.), 30 May 1946. (In CAB 84/82.)
    Retained: COS(46)90th Mtg (3), 7 June 1946.
81. Retained: JP(46)108(Final), 11 June 1946.
82. CAB 79/49:   COS(46)93rd Mtg (2), 14 June 1946.
83. Retained: COS(46)92nd Mtg (1), 12 June 1946.
84. CAB 131/3:   DO(46)80, 18 June 1946.
85. Retained: COS(46)108th Mtg, 12 July 1946.
86. CAB 131/1:   DO(46)22nd Mtg (1), 19 July 1946.
87. —
88. —
89. —
90. —
91. CAB 82/1:   DCOS(39)13th Mtg (3), 7 November 1939;
    CAB 82/14:   DCOS(AA)1, 21 November 1939;
    CAB 82/14:   DCOS(AA)195, 23 October 1940;
    CAB 80/55:   COS(46)275, 27 December 1946;
    DEFE 4/1:   COS(47)10th Mtg (3), 13 January 1947.
92. CAB 82/19:   COS(AA)(44)30(Final), 25 August 1944.
    (Also CAB 80/86:   COS(44)766(0), 25 August 1944.)
93. CAB 82/19:   COS(AA)(45)8(Final), 15 June 1945.
    (Also CAB 80/94:   COS(45)390(0), 15 June 1945.)
94. CAB 80/95:   COS(45)436(0), 7 July 1945.
95. CAB 80/96:   COS(45)478(0) Annex I, Prime Minister's Personal Min No D.(Ter.)1/5, 17 July 1945.
96. CAB 79/37:   COS(45)182nd Mtg (4), 24 July 1945.
97. CAB 131/2:   DO(46)33, 2 March 1946.
98. CAB 131/1:   DO(46)7th Mtg (6), 8 March 1946.
99. Retained: COS(AA)(46)18(Final), 6 June 1946.
    (Also CAB 80/101:   COS(46)157(0), 6 June 1946.)
100. *Ibid*. &
    CAB 79/49:   COS(46)94th Mtg (19), 17 June 1946.
101. Retained: COS(AA)(46)23(Revise), 12 July 1946.
    (Also CAB 80/102:   COS(46)176(0)(Revise), 12 July 1946.)

102.	CAB 79/50:	COS(46)116th Mtg (10), 25 July 1946;
	CAB 79/50:	COS(46)120th Mtg (4), 1 August 1946.
103.	CAB 131/3:	DO(46)98, 2 August 1946.
104.	CAB 131/1:	DO(46)24th Mtg (2), 7 August 1946.
105.	Retained:	COS(AA)(46)32(Final), 29 August 1946.
	(Also CAB 80/55:	COS(46)207, 29 August 1946.)
106.	CAB 79/51:	COS(46)135th Mtg (4), 3 September 1946.
107.	CAB 79/52:	COS(46)160th Mtg (1), 1 November 1946.
108.	Retained:	COS(AA)(46)39(Revised Final), 23 October 1946.
	(Also Retained:	COS(46)251(0)(Revise), 23 October 1946).
109.	CAB 79/46:	COS(46)45th Mtg (4), 22 March 1946;
	CAB 79/47:	COS(46)60th Mtg (15), 15 April 1946;
	CAB 79/48:	COS(46)80th Mtg (16) & Annex, 20 May 1946;
	CAB 129/10:	CP(46)227, 25 June 1946.
110.	Retained:	COS(46)157th Mtg (5), 25 October 1946.
111.	Retained:	COS(46)158th Mtg (5)(Confidential Annex), 28 October 1946.
112.	Retained:	JIC(46)95(0)(Final), 12 November 1946.
113.	Retained:	JP(46)201(Final), 28 November 1946;
	Retained:	COS(46)175th Mtg (1), 2 December 1946.
114.	Retained:	JP(46)201(Final), 28 November 1946;
	Special Access:	JP(46)218(Final), 5 December 1946;
	Retained:	JP(46)220(Final), 7 December 1946.
115.	Retained:	COS(46)180th Mtg (1), 9 December 1946.
116.	CAB 128/6:	CM(46)82nd Concls (4), 17 September 1946;
	CAB 80/99:	COS(46)33(0), 12 February 1946;
	CAB 129/12:	CP(46)345, 11 September 1946.
117.	CAB 79/54:	COS(46)184th Mtg (5) & Annex I, 18 December 1946.
118.	CAB 79/51:	COS(46)133rd Mtg (1), 30 August 1946;
	Special Access:	JP(46)174(S)(T.R.), 30 August 1946. (In CAB 84/84.)
119.	CAB 79/51:	COS(46)138th Mtg (5), 13 September 1946;
	Special Access:	JP(46)180(S)(T.R.), 13 September 1946. (In CAB 84/84.)
120.	Retained:	COS(46)239(0), 5 October 1946.
121.	Special Access:	JP(46)229(Final), 19 December 1946. (In CAB 84/86.)
122.	CAB 79/52:	COS(46)159th Mtg (3), 30 October 1946;
	Special Access:	JP(46)224(Final), 13 December 1946. (In CAB 84/86.)

	CAB 131/4:	DO(47)6, 8 January 1947.
123.	CAB 79/54:	COS(46)187th Mtg (1), 23 December 1946.
124.	—	
125.	—	
126.	DEFE 4/1:	COS(47)6th Mtg, 7 January 1947.
127.	DEFE 4/1:	COS(47)9th Mtg (2), 13 January 1947.
128.	DEFE 5/3:	COS(47)5(0)(Final), 23 January 1947.
129.	CAB 84/77:	JP(45)317(S)(T.R.), 18 December 1945;
	CAB 84/77:	JP(45)317(Final), 27 December 1945;
	CAB 79/42:	COS(45)291st Mtg (13), 31 December 1945. (See also CAB 120/842: COS Sec Min 3/6, 1 January 1946.)
130.	—	
131.	—	
132.	Retained:	JP(46)164(Final), 31 March 1947.
133.	WO 216/204:	Montgomery to Simpson, 22 February 1947.
134.	DEFE 4/2:	COS(47)35th Mtg (2)(Confidential Annex), 5 March 1947.
135.	CAB 131/4:	DO(47)23, 7 March 1947.
136.	DEFE 4/3:	COS(47)41st Mtg, 19 March 1947.
137.	CAB 21/2278:	Prime Minister's Personal Min No M.173/47, 5 April 1947.
138.	DEFE 6/5:	JP(48)2(S)(T.R.), 2 January 1948.
139.	DEFE 4/3:	COS(47)48th Mtg (2), 2 April 1947;
	DEFE 4/7:	COS(47)115th Mtg (1) & Annex, 3 September 1947;
	AIR 8/1354:	COS Sec 'Notes on the Work of the Chiefs of Staff Committee', 21 April 1948.
140.	DEFE 5/4:	COS(47)72(0), 3 April 1947;
	DEFE 5/4:	COS(47)78(0), 14 April 1947.
141.	DEFE 4/1:	COS(47)11th Mtg (1), 15 January 1947.
142.	DEFE 4/3:	COS(47)52nd Mtg (1), 14 April 1947;
	DEFE 4/3:	COS(47)54th Mtg, 17 April 1947;
	DEFE 5/4:	COS(47)79(0)(Revise), 21 April 1947.
143.	DEFE 4/3:	COS(47)57th Mtg (5), 23 April 1947.
144.	DEFE 5/4:	COS(47)84(0), 21 April 1947;
	DEFE 4/3:	COS(47)57th Mtg (4), 23 April 1947.
145.	DEFE 4/3:	COS(47)57th Mtg (6)(Confidential Annex), 23 April 1947.
146.	DEFE 5/4:	COS(47)87(0), 23 April 1947.
147.	DEFE 6/2:	JP(47)55(S)(T.R.), 24 April 1947;
	Retained:	JP(47)55(Final), 7 May 1947.
148.	DEFE 4/3:	COS(47)57th Mtg (4), 23 April 1947.

149. Retained: DRP(47)8th Mtg (2), 29 April 1947.
150. Retained: DRP(47)53, 1 May 1947.
151. DEFE 4/4:   COS(47)64th Mtg (2), 14 May 1947.
152. —
153. DEFE 4/4:   COS(47)64th Mtg (1), 14 May 1947.
154. DEFE 4/4:   COS(47)66th Mtg (4), 21 May 1947.
155. Retained: JP(47)55(Final), 7 May 1947.
156. Retained: DO(47)44, 22 May 1947. (Also COS(47)
                        102(0)(Not circulated).)
157. Retained: COS Sec Min 621/12/6/7, 12 June 1947;
     Retained: COS Sec Min 720/3/7/7, 3 July 1947;
     Retained: Prime Minister's Personal Min No D.2/47,
                        4 July 1947;
     Retained: COS Sec Min 735/7/7/7, 7 July 1947;
     CAB 21/2278:   Prime Minister's Personal Mins Nos 274/47,
                        275/47 & 276/47, 8 July 1947.
158. DEFE 4/1:   COS(47)9th Mtg (2), 13 January 1947.
159. Retained: COS(47)74th Mtg (1), 11 June 1947.
160. Retained: JP(47)129(Final), 11 November 1947.
161. DEFE 6/6:   JP(48)59(S)(T.R.), 20 May 1948;
     CAB 131/7:   DO(49)50, 22 June 1949.

CONCLUSIONS

1. PREM 4/100/7:   Prime Minister's Personal Min No M.461/2,
                     18 October 1942.

2. —
3. —
4. CAB 21/1614:   Prime Minister's Personal Telegram No
                     T.2183/4, 25 November 1944; Prime
                     Minister's Personal Min No M.1144/4,
                     25 November 1944.

5. —
6. —

APPENDICES

Appendix 1:
—

Appendix 2:
(i)   CAB 80/37:   COS(42)380, 21 August 1942.
(ii) CAB 80/40:   COS(43)199(Final), 25 July 1943.
(iii) CAB 80/43:   COS(44)59, 1 April 1944.

Appendix 3:

(i)	CAB 21/1614 & FO 371/40741A:	U6793/748/70, COS(44)248th Mtg (0)(14) (Confidential Annex), 26 July 1944.
(ii)	FO 371/39080:	C13518/146/18, COS Sec Min 1659/4, 2 October 1944.

Appendix 4:

Closed (50 years): TWC(45)44(Revise) Annex I, 5 January 1946.

Appendix 5:

Retained: TWC(46)14 Tables I & III, 13 April 1946.

Appendix 6:

(i) FO 371/56832: N6344/605/38, 2 April 1946.

(ii) Retained: COS(46)239(0) Annex I, 5 October 1946.

Appendix 7:

Retained: DO(47)44, 22 May 1947. (Also COS(47) 102(0)(Not circulated).)

Appendix 8: Full P.R.O. references in footnotes.

INDEX